# 1st Marine Division

*Legacy of the Old Breed*
*2019*

Acclaim Press
MORLEY, MISSOURI

Acclaim Press™
— Your Next Great Book —

P.O. Box 238
Morley, MO 63767
(573) 472-9800
www.acclaimpress.com

Book Committee: Jerry Johs, President, 1MDA; Dennis J. Coady; June Cormier
Publishing Consultant: Duane A. Sikes
Book Design: Rodney Atchley
Cover Design: Frene Melton



ISBN: 978-1-948901-21-5 / 1-948901-21-8
Library of Congress Control Number: 2019900636



First Printing: 2019
Printed in the United States of America
10 9 8 7 6 5 4 3 2 1

# Contents

*Marine motor detachment at Marine Corps Air Station New River, Jacksonville, NC, May 1942. Photo by Alfred T. Palmer courtesy Library of Congress.*

# INTRODUCTION

Marines and FMF Corpsmen:

I would like to thank you for participating in the project of making the legacy book for the First Marine Division Association. Your stories and experiences of your time in the Marine Corps with the First Marine Division tell the story of why it's the most decorated division in the Marine Corps.

I hope you find this book to be useful and a way to share the stories with family and friends.

Thanks to all for your service to our country.

Best wishes to all of you.

Semper Fidelis,

Jerry Johs
FMDA President

***United States Marine Corps Mascot***

*PFC Chesty the XIV, official mascot of the United States Marine Corps, May 15, 2013. Chesty XIV retired in August 2018 and a new English bulldog, Chesty XV, now holds the honor. Department of Defense photo by Adrian R. Rowan*

*The Marine Corps War Memorial in Arlington, Virginia, June 4, 2013.*
*U.S. Department of Defense photo*

*This commemorative book is dedicated to the nearly 39,000 United States Marines who unselfishly sacrificed their lives in the name of freedom, and to the families and friends who keep their memories alive.*

# USMC Insignia & Effects

## The USMC Emblem

The **Eagle**, **Globe**, and **Anchor** is an emblem used to represent the Marine Corps. Whether it appears on a uniform, printed page, or a flag, the Eagle, Globe and Anchor is an icon of greatness.

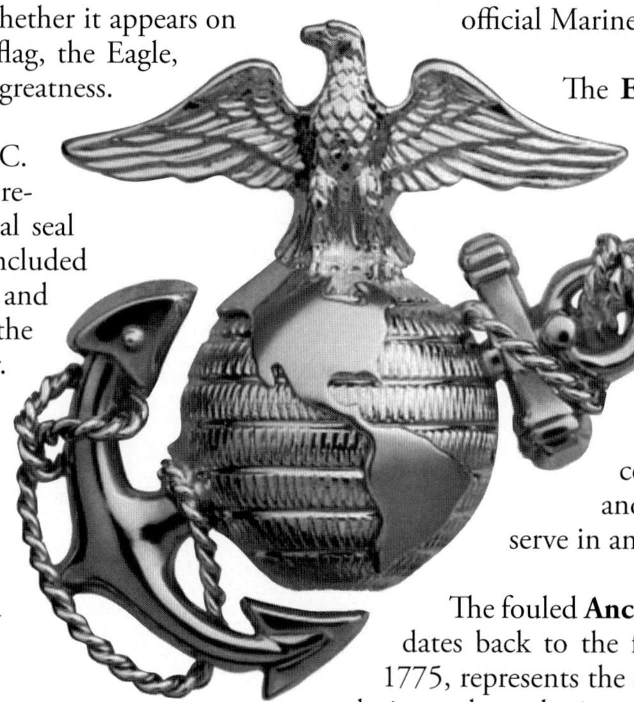

In 1954, General Lemuel C. Shepherd Jr., Commandant, requested the design of an official seal for the Corps. The new seal included the traditional Eagle, Globe, and Anchor emblem in gold, with the Globe and anchor rope in silver. The emblem is displayed on a scarlet background encircled with a blue band bearing the phrases "Department of the Navy" above and "United States Marine Corps" below in white letters, the whole edged in a gold rope.

U.S. President Eisenhower approved the design on 22 June 1954. The emblem as shown on the seal was adopted in 1955 as the official Marine Corps emblem.

The **Eagle** is the symbol of the United States, and it is the one part of the emblem that readily associates the Marine Corps with the United States. The eagle proudly carries a streamer in its beak that bears the motto of the Corps: **Semper Fidelis** (Always Faithful).

The **Globe** signifies the worldwide commitment of the Marine Corps and its areas of responsibility. Marines serve in any clime or place.

The fouled **Anchor** (tangled in rope), whose origin dates back to the founding of the Marine Corps in 1775, represents the amphibious nature of the Marines' duties and emphasizes the close ties between the Marine Corps and the U.S. Navy.

*We stole the Eagle from the Air Force,*
*The Anchor from the Navy,*
*The Rope from the Army,*
*And on the seventh day when God rested,*
*We overran His perimeter and stole the Globe*
*And have been running the show ever since.*
*—United States Marines*

## 1st Marine Division Insignia

The 1st Marine Division shoulder patch originally was authorized for wear by members of units who served with or were attached to the Division in the Pacific in World War II. It was the first patch to be approved in that war and specifically commemorated the Division's sacrifices and victory in the Battle for Guadalcanal. It features the National colors — red, white, and blue — in its diamond-shaped blue background with a red number "1" inscribed with white lettering, "GUADALCANAL". The white stars featured on the night-sky blue background are in the arrangement of the Southern Cross constellation, under which the Guadalcanal fighting took place.

# U.S. MARINE CORPS VALUES

**Honor** This is the bedrock of our character. It is the quality that empowers Marines to exemplify the ultimate in ethical and moral behavior: to never lie, cheat, or steal; to abide by an uncompromising code of integrity; to respect human dignity; and to have respect and concern for each other. It represents the maturity, dedication, trust, and dependability that commit Marines to act responsibly, be accountable for their actions, fulfill their obligations, and hold others accountable for their actions.

**Courage** The heart of our Core Values, courage is the mental, moral, and physical strength ingrained in Marines that sees them through the challenges of combat and the mastery of fear, and to do what is right, to adhere to a higher standard of personal conduct, to lead by example, and to make tough decisions under stress and pressure. It is the inner strength that enables a Marine to take that extra step.

**Commitment** This is the spirit of determination and dedication within members of a force of arms that leads to professionalism and mastery of the art of war. It promotes the highest order of discipline for unit and self and is the ingredient that instills dedication to Corps and country 24 hours a day, pride, concern for others, and an unrelenting determination to achieve a standard of excellence in every endeavor. Commitment is the value that establishes the Marine as the warrior and citizen others strive to emulate.

# THE MARINES' HYMN

*Members of "The President's Own", the official United States Marine Band, perform during the 60th anniversary of the Battle of Iwo Jima commemoration ceremony at the Marine Corps War Memorial, 2005. Founded in 1798 by an Act of Congress, the Marine Band is the Nation's oldest continuously active professional musical organization.*

The Marines' Hymn is one of the most readily recognized songs in the world today and is the oldest of the service songs of our country. The history of the hymn has been clouded by the passing of time and confused by oral tradition. But there is no confusion on the part of the hearer when The Marines' Hymn is heard. It is as easily identified with the Marine Corps as "The Star-Spangled Banner" is with our nation. To all Marines it has become a sacred symbol of the pride and professionalism of a Marine and you will find them standing straight and tall at the position of attention when it is performed.

The music to the hymn is believed to have originated in the comic opera Geneviéve de Brabant composed by the French composer Jacques Offenbach. Originally written as a two-act opera in 1859, Offenbach revised the work, expanding it to three acts in 1867. This revised version included the song "Couplets des Deux Hommes d'Armes" and is the musical source of The Marines' Hymn.

The author of the words to the hymn is unknown. One tradition suggested that an unknown Marine wrote the words in 1847. This would have been 20 years before the music was written by Offenbach and is not likely. The first two lines of the first verse were taken from words inscribed on the Colors of the Corps.

After the war with the Barbary pirates in 1805 the Colors were inscribed with the words "To the Shores of Tripoli." After Marines participated in the capture of Mexico City and the Castle of Chapultepec (also known as the Halls of Montezuma) in 1847, the words on the Colors were changed to read "From the shores of Tripoli to the Halls of Montezuma." The unknown author of the first verse of the hymn reversed this order to read "From the halls of Montezuma to the shores of Tripoli."

In 1929 the Commandant of the Marine Corps authorized the following verses of The Marines' Hymn as the official version:

"From the Halls of Montezuma
To the shores of Tripoli;
We fight our country's battles
On the land as on the sea;
First to fight for right and freedom
And to keep our honor clean;
We are proud to claim the title
Of United States Marine.

Our flag's unfurled to every breeze
From dawn to setting sun;
We have fought in ev'ry clime and place
Where we could take a gun;
In the snow of far-off Northern lands
And in sunny tropic scenes;
You will find us always on the job
The United States Marines

Here's health to you and to our Corps
Which we are proud to serve;
In many a strife we've fought for life
And never lost our nerve;
If the Army and the Navy
Ever look on Heaven's scenes;
They will find the streets are guarded
By United States Marines."

Nov. 21, 1942, the Commandant of the Marine Corps approved a change in the words of the fourth line of the first verse to read, "In the air, on land, and sea."

*Source: The official website of the United States Marine Corps*

# MARINE CORPS COMMANDANTS

*The Commandant of the Marine Corps is the highest-ranking officer in the United States Marine Corps and a member of the Joint Chiefs of Staff.*

Not Pictured: Anthony Gale, *1819-1820*

Samuel Nicholas
*1775-1781*

William W. Burrows
*1798-1804*

Franklin Wharton
*1804-1818*

Archibald Henderson
*1820-1859*

John Harris
*1859-1864*

Jacob Zeilin
*1864-1876*

Charles G. McCawley
*1876-1891*

Charles Heywood
*1891-1903*

George F. Elliott
*1903-1910*

William P. Biddle
*1911-1914*

George Barnett
*1914-1920*

John A. Lejeune
*1920-1929*

Wendell C. Neville
*1929-1930*

Ben H. Fuller
*1930-1934*

John H. Russell, Jr.
*1934-1936*

Thomas Holcomb
*1936-1943*

Alexander A. Vandegrift
*1944-1947*

Clifton B. Cates
*1948-1951*

Lemuel C. Shepherd, Jr.
*1952-1955*

Randolph M. Pate
*1956-1959*

David M. Shoup
*1960-1963*

Wallace M. Greene, Jr.
*1964-1967*

Leonard F. Chapman, Jr.
*1968-1971*

Robert E. Cushman, Jr.
*1972-1975*

Louis H. Wilson, Jr.
*1975-1979*

Robert H. Barrow
*1979-1983*

Paul X. "PX" Kelley
*1983-1987*

Alfred M. Gray, Jr.
*1987-1991*

Carl E. Mundy, Jr.
*1991-1995*

Charles C. Krulak
*1995-1999*

James L. Jones, Jr.
*1999-2003*

Michael W. Hagee
*2003-2006*

James T. Conway
*2006-2010*

James F Amos
*2010-2014*

Joseph F Dunford, Jr.
*2014-2015*

Robert B Neller
*2015-current*

# LINEAGE & HONORS

### *1913-1914*

Activated 23 December 1913 at Philadelphia, Pennsylvania, as the 1st Advance Base Brigade
Deployed during January 1914 to Culebra, Puerto Rico
Relocated during February 1914 to New Orleans, Louisiana
Redesignated 1 April 1914 as the 1st Brigade
Deployed during April 1914 to Vera Cruz, Mexico
Participated in the Landings and Occupation of Vera Cruz, Mexico, April - November 1914
Relocated during December 1914 to Philadelphia, Pennsylvania

### *1915-1935*

Deployed during August 1915 to Port Au Prince, Haiti
Participated in the Occupation of Haiti, August 1915 - August 1934
Participated in the Occupation of The Dominican Republic, June - December 1916
Deactivated 15 August 1934 at Port Au Prince, Haiti
Reactivated 1 September 1935 at Quantico, Virginia, as the 1st Brigade and assigned to the Fleet Marine Force
Redesignated 16 September 1935 as the 1st Marine Brigade

### *1940-1949*

Deployed during October 1940 to Guantanamo Bay, Cuba
Redesignated 1 February 1941 as the 1st Marine Division
Relocated during May 1941 to Quantico, Virginia, and Parris Island, South Carolina
Deployed during April - July 1942 to Samoa and Wellington, New Zealand
Participated in the following World War II campaigns:
Guadalcanal
Eastern New Guinea
New Britain
Peleliu
Okinawa
Participated in the Occupation of North China, September 1945 - June 1947
Relocated during June 1947 to Camp Pendleton, California

### *1950-1964*

Deployed during July - September 1950 to the Republic of Korea
Participated in the Korean War, September 1950 - July 1953, operating from:
Inchon-Seoul
Chosin Reservoir
East-Central Front
Western Front

Participated in the Defense of the Korean Demilitarized Zone, July 1953 - March 1955
Relocated during February - April 1955 to Camp Pendleton, California
Elements participated in the Cuban Missile Crisis, October - December 1962

### *1965-1971*

Deployed during July 1965 - May 1966 to the Republic of Vietnam
Participated in the war in Vietnam from July 1965 - April 1971, operating from
Chu Lai
Da Nang
Dong Ha
Qui Nhon
Hue
Phu Bai
Quang Tri
Relocated during April 1971 to Camp Pendleton, California

### *1972-1998*

Elements participated in Operation New Arrival, the Relocation of Refugees from Indochina, April-May And June-December 1975
Participated in Operations Desert Shield and Desert

Storm, Southwest Asia, September 1990 - February 1991
Elements participated in Operation Sea Angel, Bangladesh, May - June 1991
Elements participated in Operation Restore Hope, Somalia, December 1992 - April 1993
Elements participated in Fire-Fighting Efforts, Western United States, July - September 1994
Elements participated in support of Hunter Warrior Advanced Warfighting
Laboratory experiment, Camp Pendleton, California, September 1996 - March 1997

## HONORS

***Presidential Unit Citation Streamer with one Silver and two Bronze Stars***

***World War II***
Guadalcanal-1942
Peleliu, Ngesebus-1944
Okinawa-1945

***Korea***
1950
1950
1951

***Vietnam***
1966-1967
1967-1968

***Navy Unit Commendation Streamer with one Bronze Star***

***Korea***
1952-1953

***Southwest Asia***
1990-1991

Mexican Service Streamer
Dominican Campaign Streamer
Haitian Campaign Streamer with one Bronze Star
Marine Corps Expeditionary Streamer
World War I Victory Streamer with one Bronze Star
American Defense Service Streamer with one Bronze Star
Asiatic-Pacific Campaign Streamer with one Silver and one Bronze Star
World War II Victory Streamer
Navy Occupation Service Streamer with 'Asia'
China Service Streamer
National Defense Service Streamer with two Bronze Stars
Korean Service Streamer with two Silver Stars
Armed Forces Expeditionary Streamer
Vietnam Service Streamer with two Silver and three Bronze Stars
Southwest Asia Service Streamer with two Bronze Stars
Korean Presidential Unit Citation Streamer
Vietnam Cross of Gallantry with Palm Streamer
Vietnam Meritorious Unit Citation Civil Actions Streamer

# COMMANDING GENERALS OF THE 1ST MARINE DIVISION

MajGen Holland Smith
*1 Feb 1941 - 13 Jun 1941*

MajGen Philip H. Torrey
*14 Jun 1941 - 22 Mar 1942*

MajGen Alexander Vandegrift
*23 Mar 1942 - 7 Jul 1943*

MajGen William H. Rupertus
*8 Jul 1943 - 1 Nov 1944*

MajGen Pedro del Valle
*2 Nov 1944 - 8 Aug 1945*

MajGen Dewitt Peck
*9 Aug 1945 - 9 Jun 1946*

MajGen Keller E. Rockey
*10 Jun 1946 - 17 Sep 1946*

MajGen Samuel L. Howard
*18 Sep 1946 - 17 Jun 1947*

Col Alva B. Lasswell (Acting)
*18 Jun 1947 - 6 Jul 1947*

MajGen Graves B. Erskine
*7 Jul 1947 - 25 Jul 1950*

MajGen Oliver P. Smith
*26 Jul 1950 - 23 Feb 1951*

BGen Lewis B. Puller (Acting)
*24 Feb 1951 - 4 Mar 1951*

MajGen Oliver P. Smith
*5 Mar 1951 - 26 Apr 1951*

MajGen Gerald C. Thomas
*27 Apr 1951 - 10 Jan 1952*

MajGen John T. Selden
*11 Jan 1952 - 28 Aug 1952*

MajGen Edwin A. Pollock
*29 Aug 1952 - 15 Jun 1953*

MajGen Randolph M. Pate
*16 Jun 1953 - 11 May 1954*

MajGen Robert H. Pepper
*12 May 1954 - 23 Jul 1954*

MajGen Robert E. Hogaboom
*24 Jul 1954 - 18 Jan 1955*

MajGen Merrill B. Twining
*19 Jan 1955 - 17 Aug 1956*

MajGen Robert O. Bare
*18 Aug 1956 - 30 Jun 1957*

MajGen David M. Shoup
*1 Jul 1957 - 2 Jan 1958*

BGen Harvey C. Tschirgi (Acting)
*3 Jan 1958 - 4 Feb 1958*

MajGen Edward W. Snedeker
*5 Feb 1958 - 7 Oct 1959*

BGen Thomas F. Riley (Acting)
*8 Oct 1959 - 13 Nov 1959*

MajGen Henry R. Paige
*14 Nov 1959 - 6 Jun 1961*

BGen Frederick E. Leek
*7 Jun 1961 - 30 Jul 1961*

MajGen James M. Masters, Sr.
*31 Jul 1961 - 14 Jun 1962*

MajGen Herman Nickerson Jr.
*15 Jun 1962 - 9 Apr 1963*

MajGen William T. Fairbourn
*10 Apr 1963 - 9 Jul 1965*

BGen Edward H. Hurst (Acting)
*10 Jul 1965 - 10 Aug 1965*

MajGen Lewis J. Fields
*11 Aug 1965 - 30 Sep 1966*

MajGen Herman Nickerson Jr.
*1 Oct 1966 - 31 May 1967*

MajGen Donn J. Robertson
*1 Jun 1967 - 26 Jun 1968*

MajGen Carl A. Youngdale
*27 Jun 1968 - 20 Dec 1968*

MajGen Ormond R. Simpson
*21 Dec 1968 - 14 Dec 1969*

MajGen Edwin B. Wheeler
*15 Dec 1969 - 26 Apr 1970*

MajGen Charles F. Widdecke
*27 Apr 1970 - 29 Apr 1971*

MajGen Ross T. Dwyer
*30 Apr 1971 - 10 Aug 1972*

BGen Adolph G. Schwenk
*11 Aug 1972 - 30 Apr 1973*

MajGen Kenneth J. Houghton
*1 May 1973 - 12 Aug 1974*

BGen William L. McCulloch
*13 Aug 1974 - 1 Jun 1975*

MajGen Charles D. Mize
*2 Jun 1975 - 29 Jul 1976*

MajGen Edward A. Wilcox
*30 Jul 1976 - 5 Jul 1977*

BGen Marc A. Moore (Acting)
*6 Jul 1977 - 7 Aug 1977*

MajGen Charles G. Cooper
*8 Aug 1977 - 8 Aug 1979*

MajGen Francis X. Quinn
*9 Aug 1979 - 31 Jul 1980*

MajGen James L. Day
*1 Aug 1980 - 12 Aug 1982*

MajGen Ernest C. Cheatham Jr.
*13 Aug 1982 - 13 Jun 1985*

MajGen Clyde D. Dean
*14 Jun 1985 - 23 Apr 1986*

BGen Matthew T. Cooper
*24 Apr 1986 - 13 Aug 1986*

MajGen James J. McMonagle
*14 Aug 1986 - 19 Jul 1988*

MajGen John P. Monahan
*20 Jul 1988 - 7 Aug 1990*

MajGen James M. Myatt
*8 Aug 1990 - 8 Jul 1992*

MajGen Charles E. Wilhelm
*9 Jul 1992 - 8 Dec 1992*

BGen Jerry C. McAbee (Acting)
*9 Dec 1992 - 23 Mar 1993*

MajGen Charles E. Wilhelm
*24 Mar 1993 - 22 Jun 1994*

MajGen Frank Libutti
*23 Jun 1994 - 6 Jun 1996*

MajGen John H. Admire
*7 Jun 1996 - 24 Jul 1998*

MajGen Michael Hagee
*25 Jul 1998 - 24 Jul 1999*

MajGen Gregory S. Newbold
*24 Jul 1999 - 11 Jul 2000*

MajGen James T. Conway
*11 Jul 2000 - 8 Aug 2002*

MajGen James N. Mattis
*9 Aug 2002 - 1 Aug 2004*

MajGen Richard F. Natonski
*2 Aug 2004 - 1 Jun 2006*

MajGen John M. Paxton Jr.
*2 Jun 2006 - 22 May 2007*

BGen Richard P. Mills
*22 May 2007 - 1 Sep 2007*

MajGen Thomas D. Waldhauser
*1 Sep 2007 - 1 Jul 2009*

MajGen Richard P. Mills
*1 Jul 2009 - 1 Aug 2010*

MajGen Michael R. Regner
*1 Aug 2010 - 30 Jun 2011*

MajGen Ronald L. Bailey
*30 Jun 2011 - 10 Jun 2013*

MajGen Lawrence D. Nicholson
*10 Jun 2013 - 30 Jul 2015*

BGen Daniel D. Yoo
*30 Jul 2015 - 10 Sep 2015*

MajGen Daniel J. O'Donohue
*10 Sep 2015 - 23 Jun 2017*

MajGen Eric M. Smith
*23 Jun 2017 - 6 Jul 2018*

MajGen Robert F. Castellvi
*6 Jul 2018 - present*

## 1941 - 2019

MajGen Holland Smith
*1 Feb 1941 - 13 Jun 1941*

MajGen Robert F. Castellvi
*6 Jul 2018 - present*

# LEGENDS OF THE 1ST MARINE DIVISION

*While the Old Breed historically has produced the proudest and bravest Marines in our great Nation, the following Legends are a few notable examples of the few and the proud.*

### *G/Sgt. John Basilone (4 November 1916 – 19 February 1945)*

Gunnery Sergeant John Basilone was killed in action during WWII and received the Medal of Honor for his heroism during the Battle for Henderson Field at Guadalcanal, and the Navy Cross for his efforts during the Battle of Iwo Jima. He was the only enlisted Marine to receive both decorations in WWII.

He was killed in February 1945 on the first day of the invasion of Iwo Jima, after he single-handedly destroyed an enemy blockhouse and led a Marine tank under fire safety through a minefield.

### *Lt. Gen. Lewis B. "Chesty" Puller (26 June 1898 – 11 October 1971)*

One of the most decorated Marines in American history, he is one of two United States servicemen to be awarded five Navy Crosses and one Army Distinguished Service Cross. In 1941, he was given command of 1st Battalion, 7th Marines of the 1st Marine Division, leading his Battalion in action at Guadalcanal. Promoted to Executive Officer of the 7th Mariner Regiment, he saw action at the Battle of Cape Gloucester and later, after being promoted to Colonel in February 1944 in charge of the 1st Marine Regiment at Peleliu. He would continue with the 1st Marine Regiment during the Korean War, leading at the Battle of Chosin Reservoir.

He retired from the US Marine Corps in 1955 after 37 years of service.

### *Master Gunnery Sgt. Leland Diamond (30 May 1890 – 20 September 1951)*

Master Gunnery Sergeant Leland Diamond enlisted in the U.S. Marine Corps in Detroit, MI on 25 July 1917 at the age of 27 and served in WWI with the famous 6th Marine Regiment. Following the war he returned to civilian life, but reenlisted on 23 September 1921, working his way up to Master Gunnery Sergeant by 10 July 1939.

Following the Japanese attack on Pearl Harbor, he shipped to Guadalcanal with Company H, 2nd Battalion, 5th Marines, 1st Marine Division, where he served as an expert with both 60- and 81-mm mortars, for which he was credited as the turning point of many battles on Guadalcanal.

Following a hospital stay in New Zealand, he bummed rides on planes, ships and trains to join his old outfit in Australia, later coming back to the States as an instructor at MCRD Parris Island, SC. He retired from service on 23 November 1945.

### *Cpl. Joseph Vittori (1 August 1929 – 16 September 1951)*

Cpl. Joseph Vittori of Beverly, MA, was killed during the Battle of the Punchbowl while defending against an assault on Hill 749 near Songnea-dong, Korea on the night of 15-16 September 1951.

Vittori earned his first Purple Heart after being wounded near Yanggu, and requested to return to his old infantry platoon following his recovery. On 16 September, he dashed into hand-to-hand combat to give the Marine company time to consolidate its position, then volunteered to defend an isolated heavy machine gun position on the flank of his company's sector, and made repeated trips through heavy shellfire to replenish his ammunition, keeping the enemy out of the breach in his company's lines until he was killed. The next morning Marines counted almost 200 enemy dead in the area.

Cpl. Vittori was awarded the Medal of Honor posthumously on 7 September 1952.

### *Sgt. Charles "Chuck" Mawhinney (1949 – still living)*

Charles Benjamin "Chuck" Mawhinney, son of a WWII Marine Corps veteran, grew up in Oregon and joined the

U.S. Marine Corps in 1967. Following enlistment, he attended Scout Sniper School at Camp Pendleton and graduated in April 1968.

*Photo courtesy of Mawhinney's website: https://www.chuckmawhinney.com*

Mawhinney spent 16 months in Vietnam with the 5th Marines and is credited with 103 confirmed People's Army of Vietnam (PAVN)/Viet Cong kills and 216 probables. Following his tour, he spent a brief time as a marksmanship instructor at Camp Pendleton before leaving the Corps in 1970.

### *G/Sgt. Carlos Hathcock (4 May 1942 – 23 February 1999)*

Gunnery Sergeant Carlos Hathcock enlisted in the U.S. Marine Corps on 20 May 1959 and won many shooting championships before his deployment to Vietnam in 1966. Because he won the Wimbledon Cup, the most prestigious prize for long-range shooting in 1965, he was recruited as a sniper soon after arriving in Southeast Asia.

During the war, he had 93 confirmed kills of PAVN and Viet Cong personnel, but by his estimates the actual number was between 300-400 enemy personnel. Due to his effectiveness, the PAVN placed a $30,000(US) bounty on his life, and killed every known Vietnamese marksman who tried to claim it. Known as "White Feather" or "White Feather Sniper" because of a feather he kept in a band on his bush hat, he returned to the States in 1967 after killing a PAVN General. He returned to Vietnam in 1969 to command a platoon of snipers.

Hathcock was awarded the Silver Star in 1996 not for sniping, but for saving the lives of seven fellow Marines after their AMTRAC struck a landmine. The Springfield M25 White Feather rifle was named in his honor.

### *MGen James Mattis (8 September 1950 – still living)*

MGen James Mattis commissioned in the Marine Corps through the Naval Reserve Officers' Training Corps after graduating form Central Washington University. A career Marine, he commanded the United States Joint Forces Command from 2007-2010, United States Central Command from 2010-2013, and the 26th United States Secretary of Defense from January 2017-December 2018.

Mattis commanded the 1st Battalion, 7th Marines during the Persian Gulf War, the 7th Marine Regiment during the War in Afghanistan, and the 1st Marine Division during the 2003 invasion of Iraq and the Iraq War.

### *Cpl. Jason Dunham (10 November 1981 – 22 April 2004)*

Jason Lee Dunham of Scio, NY, joined the U.S. Marine Corps in 2000. In early 2004, he was serving as a squad leader with 4th Platoon, Company K, 3rd Battalion, 7th Marine Regiment, 1st Marine Division, I Marine Expeditionary Force. His unit was based in Al-Karabilah.

On 14 April 2004, the battalion commander's convoy came under attack near Husaybah, Iraq and 4th Platoon was dispatched to investigate. When the squad approached a white Toyota Land Cruiser and discovered AK-47s, the driver exited and attacked the Marines in an attempt to flee, dropping an armed hand grenade.

To save the rest of his men, Dunham deliberately threw himself on the grenade using his helmet to shield himself from the explosion. Severely wounded by the grenade blast, he was immediately evacuated to National Navy Medical Center in Bethesda, MD, in a coma. After being diagnosed with brain damage and unlikely to recover, he was taken off life support on 22 April 2004.

He was posthumously awarded the Medal of Honor for his sacrifice.

*Marine training post, Marine Corps Recruit Depot San Diego, San Diego, CA, Dec. 1949. Photo by Lee Russell courtesy Library of Congress.*

# History of the Old Breed

# HISTORY OF THE OLD BREED

## THE BEGINNINGS

1st Marine Division was activated aboard the battleship USS *Texas* on February 1, 1941, the first Division to be formed in U.S. Marine Corps history. It is the oldest, largest and most decorated division in the United States Marine Corps. Nicknamed "The Old Breed" or the "Blue Diamond", the Division is comprised of Headquarters Battalion, 1st, 5th, 7th, and 11th Marine Regiments, 1st Reconnaissance Battalion, 1st and 3rd Light Armored Reconnaissance Battalions, 1st Tank Battalion, 1st and 3rd Combat Engineer Battalions and 3rd Assault Amphibian Battalion. These units represent a combat-ready force of more than 22,000 Marines and Sailors.

*Lewis machine gun captured from bandits at El Chufon by the 52d Co., 11th Regt on 19 Oct 1928 in Nicaragua. The Marine holding the gun is Cpl Martin F. O'Donnell. Marine Archives photo*

*Fifth Regiment Marines returning from the trenches passing through Sommedieue, France, during WWI, May 11, 1918. Bain News Service photo courtesy Library of Congress.*

*Recruting poster showing a Marine carving another notch in the stock of his rifle following the Battle of Chateau-Thierry, France, 1918. Artwork by Adolph Treidler, courtesy of Library of Congress.*

*Panorama showing the 1st, 2nd & 3rd Regiments, U.S. Marines, Deer Point Camp, Guantanamo Bay, Cuba, April 26, 1911. Photo by American Photo Company, courtesy Library of Congress.*

## Forming the Regiments

Division regiments were in existence as early as March 8, 1911, when the 1st Marine Regiment was formed at Guantanamo Bay, Cuba. The Marines saw action in Haiti in 1915, the Dominican Republic in 1916, and throughout the Caribbean during World War I. The 5th Marine Regiment was established on July 13, 1914, in Veracruz, Mexico. In 1925 they served in Santo Domingo, Dominican Republic, and participated in fifteen major engagements during World War I. These include Belleau Wood, Chateau-Thierry and St. Mihiel.

On August 11, 1917, 7th Marine Regiment was activated in Philadelphia. It spent the duration of World War I in Cuba and was disbanded after the war. It was reactivated in 1941. The 11th Marines was formed in January 1918 at Quantico, Virginia, as a light artillery regiment. The regiment went to France as an infantry unit, providing a machine gun company and a guard company. Decommissioned and reactivated twice between world wars, the regiment again served as infantry in Nicaragua. Reformed in 1940 as a full-fledged artillery unit, 11th Marines joined 1st Marine Division.

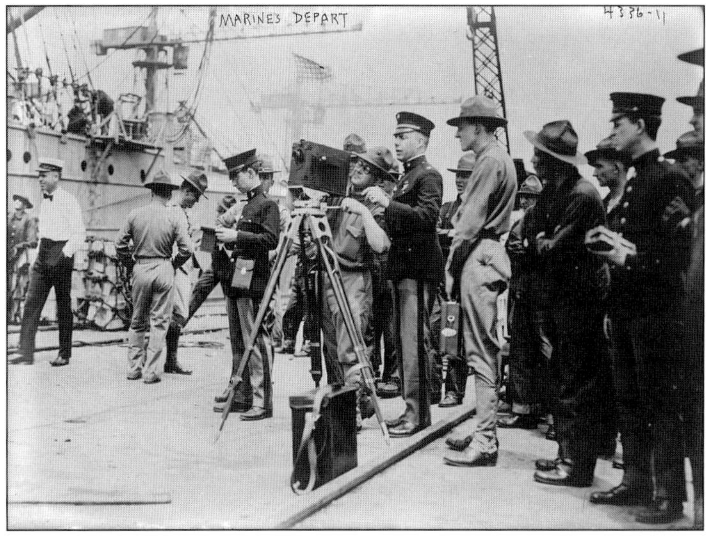


*Photographers are on hand to document U.S. Marines boarding a transport ship during WWII, June 28, 1917. Bain News Service, courtesy Library of Congress.*

*"American Marines in Belleau Wood", 1918, by Georges Scott (1873-1943), originally published in the French magazine "Illustrations". Courtesy of Wikimedia Commons*

## WORLD WAR II IN THE PACIFIC

Following the outbreak of World War II, the Division sailed to the Southwest Pacific. The initial assault against the Japanese occupied islands of Guadalcanal and Tulagi began on August 7, 1942, in the end lasting six months with over 3,000 1st Marine casualties.

Guadalcanal was the first major American Pacific campaign in World War II and the first time 1st Marine Division conducted combat operations as a division. The Division's actions during this operation won it the first of three Presidential Unit Citations during the war.

Following the Guadalcanal campaign, the Division moved to Australia for rest and reorganization before joining Operation Cartwheel against Japanese forces in Eastern New Guinea and New Britain, beginning with the Battle of Cape Gloucester on December 26, 1943 and continuing until February 1944.

Further action was found at the battle of Peleliu from September to November 1944, and Okinawa from March to June 1945, for which the Division received additional citations.

Three weeks after Japan surrendered, thereby ending World War II, the Division was dispatched to North China for occupation duty.

*Jim Goodin on Guadalcanal during WWII. Wikipedia photo*

### *Guadalcanal (7 August, 1942- 9 February, 1943)*

The Battle for Guadalcanal began at 0740 on 7 August, 1942 with the invasion of Tulagi, Gavutu and Tanambogo by the 1st Raider Battalion (Edson's Raiders), 2nd Battalion, 5th Marines and the 1st Parachute Battalion (Para Marines). At 0909, the

*Two Marines from the 2nd Battalion, 1st Marine Regiment during fighting at Wana Ridge during the Battle of Okinawa, May 1945. At left, Davis Hargraves provides covering fire with his M1 Thompson submachinegun, and Gabriel Chavarria prepares to break cover to move to a different position.*

*Communication Section, HQ, 3rd BN, 5th Marines at New River in 1942 just before departure for New Zealand. 1MDA photo*

*Joe Koester (D/1/5) and George Kohler (K/3/5), ca. 1940s. 1MDA photo*

*Col Frank B. Goettge with approximately $30,000 in Japanese currency, August 11, 1942. Col Goettge was killed the next day. 1MDA photo*

*Members of H&S-2-11 on a chow run at Ballarat, Australia, 1943. Pictured back row, l-r: Ellridge, Markovich, Keen, Rollins, ?, G. Hoffman. Front row: Lain, Vuckovich, Lynch, and Zant. 1MDA photo courtesy of Bill Lynch*

main force, made up of 1st and 3rd Battalions, 5th Marines and the 1st Marines, landed unopposed on the island of Guadalcanal.

The Japanese were taken by surprise by this invasion and, though the Tulagi and Gavutu landings were opposed, most of the defenders of the main island of Guadalcanal had scattered.

The objective of the invasion was to seize the airfield then under construction, secure the island, and use it as a base for further attacks against the Japanese forces in the Solomon Islands. The Marines quickly moved inland, seized the airfield, and began completing its construction for their own use. They named it Henderson Field after a Marine Aviator killed at the Battle of Midway.

On the night of 8 August, Japanese Naval forces engaged and defeated the Allied Naval screening force for the invasion at the Battle of Savo Island, leaving the transport ships unprotected. The following morning, the ships landed as much of their supplies as they could before leaving Guadalcanal. This left the Marines on the Island without much of their heavy equipment, supplies and the troops that were still aboard the transports.

Realizing the importance of the island and the threat posed by the 1st Marine Division, the Japanese began sending in reinforcements and organizing their attack plan. The first major battle, the Battle of the Tenaru (actually the Ilu River), took place on the night of 21 August and continued until late afternoon the following day. Intending to move quietly close to the airfield and launch a surprise attack against the Marine defenders, the Japanese instead stumbled into the 1st Marines dug in along the Tenaru River. The Japanese forces suffered approximately 800 men killed out of 900 who made the attack and the disgraced commander committed suicide. The 1st Marines recorded 34 men killed and 75 wounded.

As more Japanese forces landed on the island, the next major battle occurred at what became known as "Bloody Ridge", part of the perimeter around Henderson Field. The attack began at

*U.S. 5th Marines evacuate injured personnel during actions on Guadalcanal on November 1, 1942. USMC photo*

2100 on 12 September against the ridge manned by the Raiders and Para Marines, both now commanded by Col. Edson. These Marines withstood three separate attacks, some at the point of their bayonets. But by 0230 on the 13th, they had stopped the attackers for the night. That day the Marines consolidated their positions and were reinforced by the 2nd Battalion, 5th Marines. After dark that night, the Japanese attacked again, this time slipping behind the defenders. The resulting battle was fearfully intense and was, in many cases, hand-to-hand, and the 105mm Howitzers of the 11th Marines were firing point blank against the Japanese attackers. By morning, the Marines counted 600 Japanese dead and estimated another 600 had been wounded in the bloody battles. Their own losses were 59 killed, 194 wounded and 10 missing. Attacks against other parts of the perimeter had been defeated during this time as well with the Japanese losing over 200 more of their soldiers.

Morale on the island was boosted by the return of the US Navy, which brought the 7th Marines as well as food, ammunition, and medical supplies. Marines wounded in the previous battles were now able to be evacuated. Marine and Navy pilots, supported by the returned fleet, were able to engage in daily battles with the enemy planes flying in from Rabaul and inflict great losses on them.

The Japanese forces received further defeats at battles along the Matanikau River in early October, losing some 700 more men. On the 13th, the US Army's 164th Infantry Regiment of the Americal Division arrived to reinforce the Marines on the Island.

The enemy again attacked Bloody Ridge on the night of 24-25 October, this time defended by Chesty Puller's 1st Battalion, 7th Marines and 3rd Battalion, 164th US Infantry. The lines bent but did not break The Japanese attacked the perimeter the following night but were again defeated. All told in these attacks, the Japanese lost some 3,500 men against US losses of 300 killed and wounded. The rest of October and November were spent consolidating the US presence on the Island and wiping out small pockets of Japanese resistance.

In early December, the 1st Marine Division departed Guadalcanal for Australia, leaving the task of finishing off the last of the enemy forces to the Army Divisions now taking over. General Vandegrift said to the Division before leaving the island that their "unbelievable achievements had made Guadalcanal a synonym for death and disaster in the language of our enemy."

### *Australia (December, 1942 – December, 1943)*

After a three week stop at Espiritu Santo, the victorious Marines came ashore in Melbourne to the cheers of the citizens of Australia, grateful for the Marines halting the Japanese march toward their country. There followed nearly twelve months of rest, recuperation, resupply and reinforcement. Many Marines suffered from malaria and malnutrition from lack of supplies on Guadalcanal, but by December of 1943, the 1st Marine Division was ready to again enter the fray.

### *New Britain (26 December, 1943 – April, 1944)*

This was another battle focusing on airfields, as many of the Pacific Theater battles would be. It began on 26 December, 1943 with the 7th Marines coming ashore, unopposed, at Borgan Bay, east of Cape Gloucester. The Japanese commander believed the terrain inland of these beaches to be nearly impassable, but the Marines managed to struggle through the swamps onto dry ground and establish a perimeter. 1st and 3rd Battalions of the 1st Marines, moving from the beachhead toward the airfield at Cape Gloucester, soon ran into opposition, but used combined tank and infantry tactics to destroy the numerous bunkers blocking their way. 2nd Battalion, 1st Marines landed 12 miles away on the opposite side of the Cape to establish a blocking position to deny Japanese reinforcements access to the airfield. Upon landing, 2nd Battalion quickly severed the coastal road and dug in to protect the rest of the Division at the Cape.

The first Japanese attempt to disrupt the Marine invasion came on the night of 27-28 December with an attack against 2nd Battalion, 7th Marines, holding a sector of the main perimeter of the beachhead. This attack was repulsed with losses of approximately 200 Japanese soldiers killed.

*Combat loaded LST en route to Cape Gloucester where Marine pioneers of 2/17 will sort it for delivery to supply areas. 1MDA photo*

*Members of the 1st Marine Division led by the Division Band, march in Melbourne, Australia, February 1943. The drum major leading the band was LtCol Robert J. McArthur. Behind him saluting on the extreme right flank is Col Leon Brusiloff (then Major). 1MDA photo*

As the 1st Marines approached the airfield on the 28th, they encountered a strong point of roughly 250 Japanese soldiers with machine guns and mortars in well camouflaged bunkers. This battle, at what came to be called "Hell's Point," again saw the effective use of tanks and infantry to destroy the enemy positions. The Marines took the airfield on the 29th of December against minimal opposition, but the Japanese launched furious counter-attacks on the 30th against both the airfield and the blocking forces. On 1 January, 1944, after the Marines defeated these attacks, Gen. MacArthur announced to the American public that the airfield was secure.

The Japanese, however, still held high ground. From Hill 660, which overlooked the airfield, artillery was able to shell the Marine positions. Starting on 2 January, the Marines made slow progress toward Hill 660 through thick jungle and difficult terrain and encountered stiff resistance. After reaching the base of the hill, 660 was shelled by mortars and artillery and bombed by aircraft before the infantry advanced. The Japanese were well dug in and their strong bunkers were not greatly affected by the bombardment. 3rd Battalion, 7th Marines began the attack against the north-west slope of the hill on the 13th but were stopped by the determined defenders. A group of Marines with a bulldozer circled around to the south side of the hill to establish a blocking force. On the 14th, another attack drove the defenders from their positions and into the sights of the blocking force. Many Japanese soldiers were killed as they attempted to escape. On the 16th, the Japanese counter-attacked the hill and fierce fighting ensued, much of it at close quarters. Failing to retake the hill, the Japanese forces started to fall apart. The Marines consolidated their beachhead and advanced on the Willaumez Peninsula, reaching the base on 5 March. The next day the 5th Marines launched an amphibious assault to take the airfield at Talasea. The Japanese offered stiff resistance but were overcome and the airfield was reached on the 9th of March and secured the following day. Final mopping up operations ended the Japanese

*Colors and Guard at the Japanese surrender at Tientsin, China, 1945. Photo by Jesse C. Canale courtesy of 1MDA*

*Bgen Merrit A. Edson, CG, Service Command Fleet Marine Force Pacific, Mgen DeWitt Peck, CG, 1st Marine Division, and Louise E. Woods, CG, 1st Marine Aircraft Wing, at Tientsin, September 1945. USMC Signal Corps photo*

*Members of H&S-1-1 march through the streets of Tientsin, 1945. Photo by Jesse C. Canale courtesy of 1MDA*

*Members of H&S-1-1 getting off the train at Tientsin, China, 1945. Photo by Jesse C. Canale courtesy of 1MDA*

*Marine MajGen Rockney signs the surrender documents at Tientsin, China, 1945. Photo by Jesse C. Canale courtesy of 1MDA.*

resistance on the western half of New Britain and the Marines were relieved by the 40th Infantry Division of the US Army.

The 1st Marine Division spent 131 days on New Britain, suffering 310 Marines killed and 1,083 wounded. Japanese losses were reported as 3,868 killed. Securing western New Britain allowed US forces to isolate the large Japanese garrison at Rabaul at the eastern end of the island and let it whither on the vine, thus avoiding unnecessary casualties.

## Pavuvu (April, 1944 – August, 1944)

Anticipating their happy and triumphant return to Australia, the men of the 1st Marine Division were vastly disappointed and disgusted to find themselves landing on the island of Pavuvu, 65 miles northwest of Guadalcanal. This island was swamp infested, received frequent downpours of rain, had minimal facilities, and none of the creature comforts associated with Australia. To top it off, it and the surrounding island were unsuitable for amphibious training. Through work details, often comprised mostly of replacements, the Marines improved living conditions on the island as much as could be expected while recuperating from the wet and dismal living conditions and combat encountered on New Britain. On 26 August, 1944, the Division departed Pavuvu for Guadalcanal to undertake amphibious training in preparation for their next invasion: Peleliu.

## Peleliu (15 September – 27 November, 1944)

General Rupertus, commanding general of the 1st Marine Division, told his Marines that the battle for Peleliu would be "rough but fast." He got the first part right but it was anything but fast as the final resistance was not eliminated until 73 days later. The island was finally declared secure on 27 November.

*A squad of wary 1st Marine Division Leathernecks prepares for a Japanese counterattack on Peleliu. National Archives photo*

*1st Platoon, A-1-1, taken shortly after Peleliu on Pavuvu in the Russell Islands in 1944. Photo by Clifton Burton courtesy 1MDA.*

The plan for the invasion was for all three infantry regiments to land along a two mile stretch of beach at the southwest end of the island on 15 September with the 1st Marines on the left, the 5th Marines in the center, and the 7th Marines on the right. A planned three day naval and air bombardment began on 12 September but ended one day early as the task force commander, Admiral Oldendorf reported: "We have run out of targets."

The invasion began on the morning of the 15th with naval and air bombardment followed by rocket attacks from landing craft equipped with launchers. Amtracks carrying the first waves of Marines reached the beach at 0830 and came under heavy shelling from the nearly untouched and well protected enemy artillery batteries. In the first 90 minutes of the invasion, 60 amtracks were destroyed or severely damaged.

Peleliu was the 1st Marine Division's baptism to the new Japanese strategy of in depth defense using underground bunkers and tunnels. Artillery was dug into caves with retractable gun mounts and blast doors to protect them from US shells and bombs. The objective of the enemy commander was to delay the US invasion of the Philippines by holding the island as long as possible and by killing as many attackers as they could.

The 1st Marines fought a fierce three day engagement to take a section of the island jutting out from the left side of the beachhead the Marines called "the point." The 5th and 7th Marines advanced across the southern part of the island on D-Day, with 3rd Battalion, 5th Marines reaching the shore opposite the landing beach. During the afternoon, the Japanese launched a tank and infantry attack across the airfield against the 1st and 2nd Battalions, 5th Marines. All 15 tanks were destroyed and about 450 Japanese soldiers were killed. The Japanese never again attacked in the open and in daylight for the rest of the campaign. On day two, the 5th Marines attacked across the airfield and by the 19th they were in control. The 7th Marines continued to secure the southern part of the island.

With the southern half of the island cut off, the advance north was set to begin. The 1st Marines and 2nd Battalion, 7th Marines advanced on the Umurbrogol Ridges, the spine of the island, where the Japanese were securely dug in. The Marines suffered heavy casualties in these attacks and named this area of the island "Bloody Nose Ridge." By 21 September, the 1st Marines had taken so many casualties that Major General Roy Geiger, III Amphibious Corps commander, ordered (against Gen. Rupertus's objections) that they be relieved. The 81st Infantry Division's 321st Regimental Combat Team took up the 1st Marines positions on the 23rd. As costly as it was, the 1st Marines had taken 10 ridges, destroyed 3 major strongpoints and 22 pillboxes, cleared 144 caves and inflicted roughly 3500 Japanese casualties.

The 5th Marines moved up along the west road and secured the north end of the island to stop the Japanese from infiltrating replacements from the northern islands in the chain. 3rd Battalion attacked the small island of Ngesebus on the 28th securing it and the airfield on 29 September. On the 30th, Gen. Rupertus declared the north end of the island secure.

This left the Umurbrogol pocket, an area of roughly 400 by 900 yards that was held by 1,500 determined and well dug in defenders in the center of the island. Both the 5th Marines and the 7th Marines each had their turn at the cave complex in the mountains as did the soldiers of the 81st Division. During this time the Marines developed and perfected combined operations with their air wings in digging and burning out the determined defenders of the island. Because the airfield was secured early in the invasion, Marine fighter wings started operating on the island as early as day three. The Corsairs of VMF-114 were so close to the fighting that they never cranked up their landing gear during their support missions; Fifteen seconds after take-off, they were dropping their ordinance on the Japanese. Rockets

*US Marines embarking on LCTs at Peleliu, 1944. National Archives photo*

and napalm proved most effective against the hidden caves in the coral ridges.

The Marines were finally pulled off the line on 15 October, leaving the mopping up to the Army, which resorted to siege tactics to eventually subdue the last of the defenders. 6,500 Marines were killed, wounded or missing in taking the island that ultimately proved to be of questionable value in the overall strategy in the Pacific. General MacArthur had insisted that Peleliu must be taken to protect his right flank as he returned to the Philippines. But even before 15 September, it was apparent that the island was not much of a threat. It was never used as an operating base to support further invasions as were Guam, Saipan and Tinian nor was the airfield used as an emergency landing site for damaged Allied aircraft as Iwo Jima was later in the war. Adding insult to injury, MacArthur's celebrated return to the Philippines overshadowed this battle in the news, making the battle for Peleliu a nearly forgotten but very costly footnote in the history of WWII.

*MajGen Pedro A. del Valle (left), CG, 1st Marine Division, talks strategy with Bgen Louis R. Jones, his ADC, at an observation post near Kunishi Ridge. 1MDA photo*

## *Okinawa (1 April – 22 June, 1945)*

Following another period of rest and refitting on Pavuvu, the 1st Marine Division returned to combat on April Fool's Day, 1945. April 1st was also Easter Sunday and the Marines received a gift when the beach landing was essentially unopposed. After the horrors of Peleliu, it was hard for the veteran Marines to believe that this landing was coming off so easily. The Division was part of the U.S. Tenth Army, commanded by U.S. Army Lieutenant General Simon Buckner, and was comprised of the 1st, 2nd, and 6th Marine Divisions as well as the 7th, 27th, 77th, and 96th Infantry Divisions.

The 2nd Marine Division pulled off a demonstration landing on the Southeast shore of the island to mislead the Japanese defenders. Unfortunately for them, all of the U.S. air cover was focused on defending the real landing site and kamikaze attacks took their toll on this fleet. LST 844 and the troop transport Hinsdale took multiple hits. Most of the 2nd Division remained in reserve for the remainder of the campaign.

The initial job of the 1st Marine division was to secure the central region of the island while the 6th Marine Division moved north and the Army moved south. As the Army Divisions in the south came up against increasingly stiff resistance,

*Division Intelligence Section on Okinawa, June 1945. Front row, l-r: Walter Sterhan, Herbert Hinesly, Clifton T. Lambert, Vann D. Kline, John Loos, Donald W. Johnson. Second row: Charles B. Hansford, Frank G. Moreland, William P. Fleming, John G. McLean, Donald F. Fuhrmann, Oliver Plunkett, Edward M. Petronik, William W. Ebbert. Back row: Glen D. Sturges, Dean A. Hamilton, Milton J. Howe, James R. Merrifield, Gene R. Morgan, William S. Bostick, Charles Haynes, and Allen R. Cooter. 1MDA photo courtesy of John G. McLean*

*4th BN, 11th Marines, Okinawa, 1945, Fire Direction Center Tent, back row, l-r: LtCol Leonard F. Chapman Jr., Capt Chapin, 1stLt Crottinger (dec), 2ndLt Hochull, PFC Richard "Red" Mulholland, PFC Pete Peterson, Cpl Larry ?, PFC "Pappy" Thang. Front row: Cpl Johnson, PFC "Bud" Mory, Cpl Charles "Bud" Starbuck, Pvt West, PFC Herb Slanina, Cpl Thorman, and ? Martinez. Photo by Richard Mulholland courtesy of 1MDA*

they began requesting access to the Division's ammunition stocks, followed by a request for the 11th Marines Artillery and then the tank battalion. General Del Valle, now the commander of the 1st Marine Division, was against splitting his Division and requested that the whole Division be moved into place. Buckner agreed.

As soon as the Marines began to move into the line on May 1st, they were greeted with Japanese artillery barrages. The Division took the right of the line along the west coast of the island and once again faced a dug in enemy with mutually supporting positions similar to what they faced at Peleliu.

On the night of May 3rd, the Japanese attempted an amphibious counter attack against the 1st Marine Division's right rear flank at Oyama. The landing craft pilots became disoriented, however, and came ashore near Kuwan and the southern end of Machinato airfield. Marine mortar and machine gunners destroyed these forces and, by the morning of the 4th, the attack had utterly failed.

The Division's experience integrating tanks, artillery and infantry tactics paid dividends on Okinawa but it was still an extremely slow and costly advance through the defenses around Shuri. No sooner would the Marines take a part of a ridge and begin to consolidate their positions than the Japanese soldiers would lunge out of hidden cave entrances or attack from their positions on the reverse slopes. After weeks of fighting, the Marines took Wana Ridge, Wana Draw and Dakeshi Ridge overlooking the Shuri line of defenses. With the high ground in the hands of the Division, the Japanese positions became untenable and they had to pull back to the next line of defenses. This withdrawal was observed, however, and naval and aerial bombardments took a heavy toll on the retreating forces.

Despite maintaining heavy pressure on the retreating Japanese, prepared positions along Kunishi Ridge covered the withdrawal and stopped the Marines from finishing off the defenders of Shuri. Extreme-

*Machine gun section of the 2d Plt, F Company, 2d BN, First Marines, First Marine Division, who helped secure Okinawa in 1945. 1MDA photo Machine gun section of the 2d Plt, F Company, 2d BN, First Marines, First Marine Division, who helped secure Okinawa in 1945. 1MDA photo*

ly wet weather also hindered the Marines as supplies were unable to reach the front lines by vehicle. Most of the food and ammunition had to be manhandled forward through deep mud. Wounded Marines had to be evacuated the same way.

In the early morning of the 12th of June, the 7th Marines succeeded in fighting their way up to the top of Kunishi Ridge, one of the last major defensive positions on the Island. Daylight revealed that Japanese defenders still held the slopes, however, and the Marines found themselves cut off. Supplies had to be parachuted in or carried by tanks for four days before attacks by the 1st and then the 5th Marines pushed the defenders back. By the 16th of June, Kunishi ridge was firmly in our hands.

*4th JASCO, early 1945 before the battle for Okinawa. Standing l-r: 1stLt Hoppin, Sgt Beck, SSgt Moyle, Sgt Hutton, Sgt Hayden, Sgt Goings, RM2/c Golder, SSgt Francis, Sgt Kinney, and 1stLt Thompson. Kneeling: TSgt Auclair, SSgt Andersen, SM1/c Boudreaux, and SM2/c Durecki. Photo by Don Durecki courtesy of 1MDA.*

The last positions along Mezado and Makabe Ridges were taken by combined attacks of the 1st and 6th Marine Divisions as well as the 8th Marine Regiment of the 2nd Marine Division which was attached to the 1st Marine Division. It was at this time that 10th Army Commanding General Simon Buckner, who had gone forward to watch the attack by the 8th Marines, was killed during an artillery barrage on the 18th of June.

By June 21, it was apparent to the Japanese commander that the battle was lost and he announced his intentions to commit ritual suicide to his remaining officers. With his death, the effective resistance on Okinawa was over, leaving just isolated mopping up actions to completely secure the island.

*Marines hit three feet of rough water as they leave their LST to take the beach at Cape Gloucester, New Britain." Sgt. Robert M. Howard, December 26, 1943. 127-G-68998. National Archives Identifier: 532361*

During the 82 days of this campaign, the Japanese defenders suffered 141,058 casualties. This total includes roughly 30,000 civilian casualties. US casualties were high as well. The 10th Army reported 7,374 soldiers and Marines killed, 31,807 wounded and 230 missing. There were also 26,221 non-battle casualties. The Navy claimed 4 vessels had been sunk, 368 suffered damage, 4,907 navy personnel had been killed or were missing and 4,824 had been wounded.

Following the dropping of the atomic bombs on the cities of Hiroshima and Nagasaki, the Japanese government surrendered. The 1st Marine division was sent to China to disarm the Japanese garrisons there and to try and maintain order during the Chinese civil war between the Nationalist and Communist forces. In 1947, the Division returned to the United States and established Camp Pendleton as its home base, where it remains to this day.

## Conclusion

World War II saw the Division move from generally under strength and separate regiments to become a full size division that has remained in service until the present day, though at times reduced in size. The 1st Marine Division was there at the beginning of offensive land operations as well as at the end and saw some of the worst and bloody fighting of the war.

The United States Marines of WWII proved and improved the concept of amphibious warfare and learned many important lessons that benefitted later invasion planners. They devised and implemented the fire team concept that is still used today by all US armed forces as well as many other practices and concepts. Perhaps most notable of all, though, is the level of Esprit de Corps marines share. This spirit is usually only seen at the level of Special Forces, yet every Marine experiences it. Once one becomes a Marine, he or she is always a Marine.

*Marines of the 1st Division at Tientsin, China, 1946. Pictured l-r: Bell, Robert Backes, Ysidoro M. Balli, Chick, and Doc. Courtesy of Ysidoro M. Balli*

*PFC Gerald Churchby (left) and PFC Douglas Lightheart, who is cradling his 30-cal. machine gun, take a cigarette break while mopping up the enemy on Peleliu Island, September 14, 1944. Photo by Cpl. H.H. Clements courtesy 1MDA*

*F-2-1 Marines on Guadalcanal during a cleanup detail, December 1942. Pictured in front, l-r: George Schuster, Joseph Mussi, Hank Abbott. Back row: Freddy Bayre, ?, Coin, Joe Carr. Photo by Joseph Mussi courtesy of 1MDA.*

*Marines crossing a Cape Gloucester stream looking for Japanese snipers, January 1944. Library of Congress photo*

*A-1TK crew including Raymond Hayes, "Houston", "Punchie", "Keeter", and "Gillespie". 1MDA photo*

*The 3rd Battalion, 5th Marines landed on Wolmi-Do Island in Inchon Harbor and secured it prior to the main landing. The 1st Marine Division under the command of Major General Oliver P. Smith landed at Inchon and began the Inchon-Seoul campaign. (U.S. Marine Corps photo).*

*"U.S. Marine 'Raiders' and their dogs, which are used for scouting and running messages, starting off for the jungle front lines on Bougainville." T.Sgt. J. Sarno, ca. November/December 1943. 127-GR-84-68407. National Archives Identifier: 532371*

*Japanese flags are displayed by the weary Marines*

*The 1st Marine Division Cemetery at Okinawa, ca. 1940s. 1MDA photo*

*Company A, 1st Motor Transport Battalion in Melbourne, Australia, 1942. 1MDA photo*

*U.S. Marines on Guadalcanal, ca. 1942. Library of Congress photo*

LtGen Chesty Puller during WWII preparing to initiate "pollywogs" during a Shell Back ceremony. Photo by Maj Tom Barry courtesy of 1MDA

Retreating at first into the jungle of Cape Gloucester, Japanese soldiers finally gathered strength and counterattacked their Marine pursuers. These machine gunners pushed them back." Brenner, January 1944. 127-N-71981. National Archives Identifier: 532522

Rifle sights lined on the entrance to an Okinawan cave, Marines await the results of an explosive charge to pick off any Japs who attempt to escape. These bitterly contested cave positions formed the Japanese "Little Siegfried Line", defending the capital city of Naha. Library of Congress photo

U.S. troops go over the side of a Coast Guard manned combat transport to enter the landing barges at Empress Augusta Bay, Bougainville, as the invasion gets under way." November 1943. 26-G-3183. National Archives Identifier: 513194

Women Marines at the main gate at Camp Pendleton, California, 1944. 1MDA photo

Two Marines proudly show their captured Japanase flag, ca. 1944. 1MDA photo

The 1st Forward Observer Team, Fox Battery, 11th Marines, paused for a group photo on Hill 43 in Yongdong-do, Korea, September 23, 1940, prior to crossing the Han River to Seoul.

## Korean War

When war broke out in Korea in June 1950, 1st Marine Division provided support by initially sending the 5th Marine Regiment to help hold the Pusan Perimeter, while the rest of the Division prepared to be the lead amphibious assault known as the Inchon Landing on September 15, 1950, the largest amphibious operation conducted up to that time.

After landing, the Division moved north and secured the South Korean capital of Seoul after heavy fighting with North Korean Communist forces.

The Division, as part of the U.S. Army X Corps, subsequently pushed back enemy forces north into mountains around the Chosin Reservoir before being surrounded by Chinese forces, who suffered more than 40,000 casualties trying to stop the Marines' withdrawal from reservoir. This battle, including actions between April and September, earned the Division three Presidential Unit Citations.

The Old Breed remained a front-line unit for the remainder of the war, and after the fighting ended in July 1953, the Division remained in defensive positions for nearly two more years.

*Two battle-hardened Marines manage a smile during the Korean War. 1MDA photo*

*American Marines in Korea*

*Troops and armor of the 1st Marine Division during their successful breakout from the Chosin Reservoir in North Korea, 1950. USMC photo*

*SgtMaj Meyer with Company D, 2d Battalion, 5th Marines, in the Bean Patch, Masan, Korea. 1MDA photo*

*Marines watch a Marine Corsair after dropping napalm on an enemy position, 6 December 1950. USMC photo*

*Change of Command Ceremony in Korea as General Pollock succeeds General Selden, 1952. 1MDA photo*

*First Division Marines raise the flag in front of the Changdok Palace after the capture of Seoul, Korea, 1951. The Division earned its 4th Presidential Unit Citation that year. 1MDA photo*

*W-2-1 (Heavy Machine Gun Platoon) Korea, 1951-52. Pictured front row, l-r: Navy Corpsman, Charles Gastgaber, Northcutt, SSgt Rakus. Second row: Phillips, Charlie Foster, Henry "Guts" Gutierrez, Leo Hajjar, Charlie Dyer, Robert Moll. Third row: Richardson, Robles (or Rojas), Charles Allen, Joe Williams, and Robert Francis. 1MDA photo*

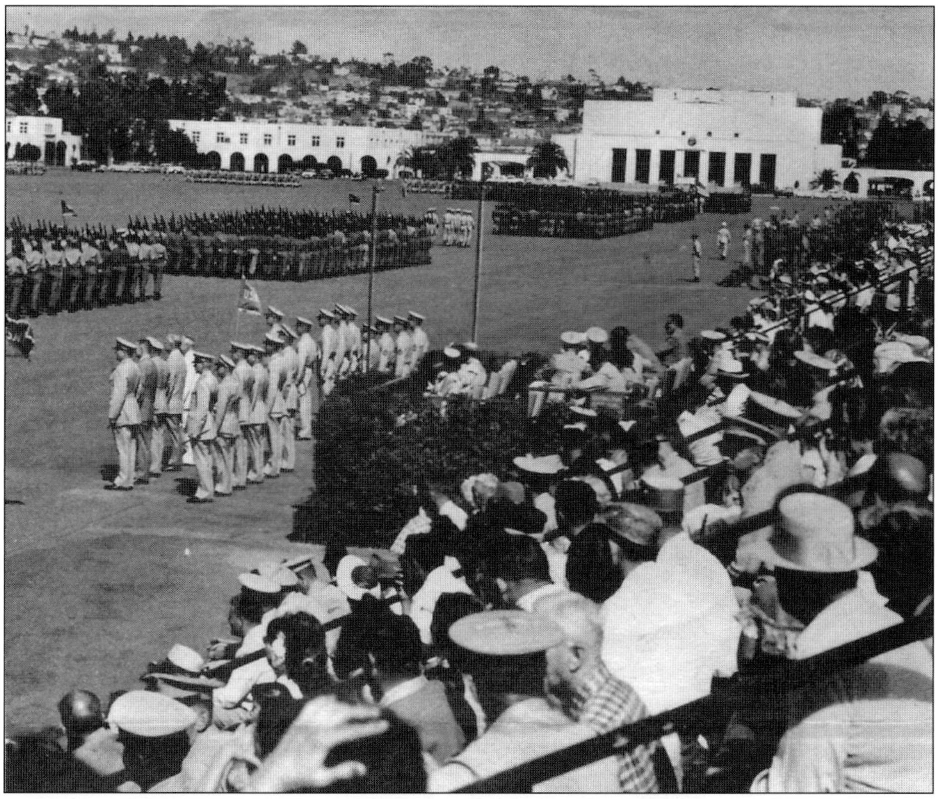

*First Marine Division Association members jam the stands at the San Diego Recruit Depot as 2,000 troops parade in their honor, October 1957. General Holland M. Smith, first commanding genreal of the Division, was the reviewing officer. 1MDA photo*

*Shin Pai Yung, Korean minister of defense, is shown placing a pennant on the regimental colors of the 5th Marines in recognition of the award of the Korean Presidential Unit Citation to the 1st Marine Division, 1954. 1MDA photo*

*Australia dedicates a memorial gate to the Fighting First Marine Division, ca. 1955. 1MDA photo*

*COL James S. Blais of the 1st Marine Division Association presents a check to CAPT Eric T. Pedersen for the purchase of PFC Reckless, the Mongolian mare famous for her exploits during the Korean War, December 1955. 1MDA photo*

## CUBAN MISSILE CRISIS

In 1962, 2nd Battalion, 1st Marine Regiment, deployed to Guantanamo Bay for two months during the Cuban Missile Crisis. More than 11,000 Marines of the 5th Marine Expeditionary Brigade participated in the naval blockade, which forced the withdrawal of the missiles from Cuba.

## VIETNAM

In 1965, 7th Marine Regiment participated in the first major engagements for American ground troops in South Vietnam. In March 1966, 1st Marine Division Headquarters was established at Chu Lai. By June, the entire Division was in South Vietnam. Its zone of operation included the southern two provinces of I Corps, Quang Tin and Quang Ngai. Between March 1966 and May 1967, the Division conducted 44 named and unnamed operations. Major engagements included Operations Hastings and Union I and II.

During the 1968 Tet Offensive, the Division was involved in fierce fighting with both Viet Cong and North Vietnamese Army elements. It successfully defended every enemy assault in its area of operations, pursuing the enemy back to their strongholds. It was during this period that the Division earned its seventh and eighth Presidential Unit Citations. After six years, 1st Marine Division returned to Camp Pendleton, California in 1971. In 1975, the Division supported the evacuation of Saigon by providing food and temporary shelter at Camp Pendleton for Vietnamese refugees as they arrived in the United States.

*LCpl C.D. Bradford, a radioman with Co G, 2d Bn, 5th Marines, patrols a city street in Vietnam in February 1968. 1MDA photo*

*The Marines launch Operation Starlite in the Van Tuong peninsula in Quang Ngai Province. In this, the first major U.S. ground battle of the Vietnam War where 5,500 Marines destroyed a Viet Cong stronghold, scoring a resounding victory.*

*Members of K/3/1 at Thon Tham Khe in April 2006. Several members featured in the February 1968 photo are present, along with a Viet Cong squad leader who participated in the battle. 1MDA photo*

*11th Marines OH-23 light observation helicopte*

*1st Reconnaissance Battalion Sign, ca. 1967*

*1th Marine 105mm in Vietnam*

*Gunnery Sergeant C.L. Waldrep proudly displays a letter declaring him the Republican nominee for Sheriff of Gastonia County, North Carolina, ca. 1970. He retired from active service in August that year. 1MDA photo*

*Kilo 3/1 leaders in Vietnam, February 1968. Photo by Cpl. Mal Wolfe courtesy 1MDA*

*A corpsman with G Co., 2nd Bn, 7th Marines, comforts a wounded Marine during a firefight in a search and clear operation 23 miles south of Da-Nang. 1MDA photo*

*Marines of Co. D, 1st Bn, 5th Marines, rush their wounded to waiting helicopters after a grenade explosion in their position near An Hoa, Vietnam, during Operation Taylor Common, January 1969. 1MDA photo*

*Pvt. L.L. Linegar of the 3d Bn, 7th Marines, diplays a prisoner "in his pocket" during Operation Citrus, south of Da Nang in Vietnam, December 1967. 1MDA photo*

*PFC Thomas C. Myers of H-2-5 stands shoulder deep in a river 17 miles southwest of DaNang, Vietnam, 1970. USMC photo by Cpl G.N. Zimmerman, courtesy 1MDA*

*The Massed Colors of the 1st Marine Division, 1965. 1MDA photo*

## OPERATIONS DESERT SHIELD AND DESERT STORM

On August 26 1990, 1st Marine Division formed the core of the force sent to Southwest Asia in response to Iraq's invasion of Kuwait. During Operation Desert Shield, the Division provided the ground combat element of I Marine Expeditionary Force in Saudi Arabia. In 1991, the Division fought alongside 2nd Marine Division and the rest of the coalition forces in Operation Desert Storm. In 100 hours of offensive ground combat, 1st Marine Division destroyed the enemy in its path as it led the breakthrough to Kuwait City.

*Marines from A/1/11 firing their M198 howitzer from Camp Fallujah, Iraq, during Operation Vigilant Resolve April 2004.*

## DISASTER RELIEF AND SOMALIA

Immediately following the Persian Gulf War, the Division sent units to assist in disaster relief efforts in Bangladesh through Operation Sea Angel and the Philippines through Operation Fiery Vigil. In 1992, 2nd Battalion, 9th Marine Regiment and the 15th Marine Expeditionary Unit brought relief to famine-stricken Somalia. The final phase of the operation involved the transition to a United Nations peacekeeping force. U.S. Marine involvement in Operation Restore Hope officially ended April 27, 1993, when the humanitarian relief sector of Mogadishu was handed over to Pakistani forces. Elements of the Division participated in the extraction of U.N. forces from Somalia.

## OPERATION IRAQI FREEDOM

In early 2003, the Division deployed by air and sea to link up with its advanced headquarters deployed to Kuwait under I Marine Expeditionary Force. In a high-speed attack, and in conjunction with 1st (UK) Armoured Division and the U.S. Army 3rd Infantry Division, 1st Marine Division conducted the longest ground march in Marine Corps history. The Division attacked to Baghdad alongside the U.S. Army and seized Saddam Hussein's hometown of Tikrit. Afterward, the Division conducted stability operations in Baghdad, Tikrit and south-central Iraq from May to October 2003. These actions earned the Division its ninth Presidential Unit Citation.

In March 2004, 1st Marine Division relieved the 82rd Airborne Division in Iraq's Sunni Triangle. During Operation Iraqi Freedom II, the Division conducted counter-insurgency operations throughout the Al Anbar Province, culminating in Operation Al Fajr, which liberated the insurgent stronghold of Fallujah and enabled the first legitimate elections to occur in Iraq. During February and March 2005, 1st and 2nd Marine Divisions successfully conducted the largest relief in place in the history of the Marine Corps. In 2006, 1st Marine Division once again deployed to Iraq as the ground combat element for I Marine Expeditionary Force.

## OPERATION ENDURING FREEDOM

Throughout the course of the war, 1st Marine Division personnel and units deployed to Afghanistan to provide both advisory support and maneuver elements. In 2010, 1st Marine Division (Forward) deployed to Helmand province, Afghanistan, as part of the surge of more than 30,000 troops into the country. While in Afghanistan, the Division served as the ground combat element for Task Force Leatherneck, leading a multinational coalition and working alongside Afghan National Security Forces. They conducted large-scale offensive operations throughout Helmand province, including Sangin and Musa Qal'eh districts.

In 2012, 1st Marine Division deployed to Afghanistan to serve as the headquarters for Task Force Leatherneck, the ground combat element for Regional Command (Southwest). During the year, the Division focused primarily on training and advising Afghans to take over security and stability operations. They assisted with the closure and transition of many posts throughout Helmand province. During spring and summer, coalition and Afghan forces cleared large areas of insurgent forces as part of Operation Jaws.

Currently, 1st Marine Division units are in Afghanistan supporting Operation Enduring Freedom.

*Memorial honoring Marines and sailors who served with 5th Marines or under Regimental Combat Team 5 who gave the ultimate sacrifice during combat operations in Afghanistan, 7 June 2013. USMC photo by Lance Cpl. James Gulliver*

*1st Recon Marines engage Taliban fighters, 31 July 2013. USMC photo*

*3rd LAR strikes a key insurgent border hub during Operation Raw Hide.*

*1st Recon Marines prepare for an upcoming deployment with the 11th Marine Expeditionary Unit at Camp Pendleton, CA, 15 July 2013. USMC photo*

*Marines of Third Light Armored Reconnaissance Battalion bow their heads in prayer during a memorial service for their fallen comrads, 26 August 2006. USMC photo*

*General James F. Amos visits the 1st Battalion, 5th Marine Regiment Memorial durign a tour of Marine Corps Air Station Camp Pendleton, CA, May 19, 2014. USMC photo*

*Marines of 1st Marine Regiment in Fallujah. Infantrymen from 1st Platoon, Company E, 2nd Battalion, 1st Marine Regiment, 1st Marine Division, look on from a rooftop as M-1A1 tanks from 1st Tank Battalion fire on buildings where enemy snipers took positions. The company entered Fallujah, Iraq, April 6, 2004, to combat enemy fighters who were attacking Coalition Forces from the city6 April 2004. U.S. Marine Corps photo by Sgt. Jose E. Guillen.*

*A 155 mm artillery shell hurtles out of the barrel of a 11th Marine Regiment M-198 howitzer during live fire and maneuver training on November 20, 2000, at the Al Hamra Training Area in the United Arab Emirates. DoD photo by Corporal Branden P. O'Brien, U.S. Marine Corps*

*Marines with 1st Reconnaissance Battalion, 1st Marine Division conduct free fall jump training from a C-130 Hercules with 3rd Marine Aircraft Wing aboard Marine Corps Base Camp Pendleton, California, October 16, 2015. 1MDA photo*

*LAV-25 armored vehicle*

*Marines assigned to the Camp Pendleton, Calif.-based 3rd Assault Amphibian Battalion patrol the dusty streets of Dulab, Iraq, July 17, 2006. USMC photo by Sgt. Roe F. Seigle*

*Petty Officer 3/c Dylan Morris, Delta Co, 3rd Light Armored Reconnaissance BN, gives candy to local children during a patrol in Afghanistan, ca. January 2011. 1MDA photo*

*3/5 machine gunners refresh their skills at Camp Pendleton, February 4, 2015. At left is LCpl Connor J. Schelabarger, machine gunner for Company K, 3rd Battalion, 5th Marines. 1MDA photo*

*LtCol Benjamin T. Watson, former battalion commander of 3rd Battalion, 1st Marine Regiment, relinquishes the battalion's colors to LtCol Fridrik Fridriksson, the battalion's new commander, during a change-of-command ceremony at Camp Pendleton's Camp Horno, Feb. 4, 2010. 1MDA photo*

*Gen. John R. Allen, International Security Assistance Force commander, speaks with troops gathered at Combat Outpost Jannat in southern Afghanistan on Christmas Day, 2012. 1MDA photo*

*MGen Michael Regner (left), CG, 1st Marine Division, stands beside Sgt. Maj. Michael Kufchak, the new sergeant major of 1st Marine Division during a post and relief ceremony, April 22, 2011. 1MDA photo*

*LCpl Benjamin Ferry (left) and his grandfather, Richard T. Ferry, as they appeared while serving to the same unit more than 60 years apart, 3rd Battalion, 5th Marines. Richard was with the 3/5 during the Korean War, fighting in Inchon and the Chosin Reservoir before being evacuated with two wounds suffered in combat. Benjamin served with the Battalion Landing Team 3/5, 31st Marine Expeditionary Unit when this photo was taken in 2018. 1MDA photo*

*Marines of 1st Explosive Ordnance Disposal Company, 1st Marine Logistics Group at Camp Pendleton, California, with James Gallant (center-front) who had recently been diagnosed with brain cancer, July 25, 2015. Thanks to the 1st MLG Marines and the Make-A-Wish Foundation, Gallant lived a day in the life of a U.S. Marine. Photo by Cpl. Carson Gramley courtesy 1MDA.*

*Marines of Company K, 3rd Battalion, 7th Marine Regiment conduct embassy reinforcement training at Joint Forces Training Base Los Alamitos, February 15, 2015. 1MDA photo*

*Ryan Forbes pulls a lanyard firing an M777 lightweight howitzer with Marines of Lima Battery, 3rd Battalion, 11th Marine Regiment at Marine Corps Air Ground Combat Center, Twentynine Palms, California, 2014. 1MDA photo*

*A U.S. Marine, 3rd Light Armored Reconnaissance Battalion, provides security near a CH-53E helicopter near Ar Rutbah, Iraq, 22 December 2004. U.S. Navy photo by Builder 2nd Class Michael W. Hollman*

*Members of the 1st Marine Division Association salute during the marching on of the colors during a morning colors ceremony in front of the 1st Marine Division's headquarters building, February 3, 2010. 1MDA photo*

*Plaque honoring the fallen Marines of 2-1, "The Professionals", dedicated in their honor at the Camp Horno Memorial Garden, Camp Pendleton, ca. 2017. USMC photo by Sgt. Paris Capers courtesy 1MDA*

*Marines fasten battle streamers to the colors during the battle colors rededication ceremony aboard Marine Corps Base Camp Pendleton, California, January 22, 2015. 1MDA President Cpl. Jerry Johs places a streamer and a junior Marine from the 1st Marine Division presented the battle streamers to MGen Lawrence D. Nicholson, CG of the 1st Marine Division. 1MDA photo*

*Members of G-1-1 (Korea) with members of the 3rd Battalion, 1st Marines at Camp Pendleton, October 18, 2011. The Korean War veterans, pictured in the center in suit and tie, presented the Battalion a plaque in rembrance of 149 Marines killed at "Bloody George" during the Korean War. 1MDA photo*

*The main gate of Camp Pendleton in November 1997, staffed by the Military Police since 9 November 2012. USMC photo*

*Hyun-myung Kim, ambassador from the Republic of South Korea, awards and thanks a Korean War veteran for his service in Korea aboard Marine Corps Base Camp Pendleton, January 22, 2015. 1MDA photo*

*Members of the 1st Marine Division Association gather at 1st Marine Division HQ, Camp Pendleton, to celebrate the Division's 69th Anniversary, 2010. 1MDA photo*

*USMCR rifle team fires a 21-gun salute at Kenner, Louisiana, 2014. Photo by LCpl Mackenzie Schlueter courtesy of 1MDA*

*Veteran and active duty Marines salute to "Waltzing Matilda", the 1st Marine Division's battle hymn aboard Marine Corps Base Camp Pendleton, January 22, 2015. The 1st Marine Division adopted this song as their battle hymn after the Battle of Guadalcanal. 1MDA photo*

# CURRENT UNITS OF THE 1ST MARINE DIVISION

## 1ST MARINE DIVISION HEADQUARTERS BATTALION

*Mission: Headquarters Battalion provides communications and information systems network, motor transportation, security, administration and personnel support to the 1st Marine Division in order to facilitate the Division's ability to command and control.*

Headquarters Battalion, 1st Marine Division consists of four companies: Communications Co., Headquarters Co., Truck Co., and Military Police Co. It was activated on 23 December 1913 at Philadelphia, Pennsylvania as Field Staff and Headquarters Detachment, 1st Advance Base Brigade. The next month, in January 1914, it deployed to Culebra, Puerto Rico, followed by New Orleans, Louisiana in February. It was redesignated as Field, Staff and Headquarters Detachment, 1st Brigade, on 1 April 1914, and deployed to Veracruz, Mexico in April 1914. The Detachment participated in the landings in occupation of Vera Cruz, Mexico from April-November 1914, then relocated back to Philadelphia in December that year.

In August 1915 the Detachment deployed to Port-Au-Prince, Haiti, where it remained until August 1934. The Detachment was redesignated several times throughout this period: Brigade Headquarters Detachment, 1st Provisional Brigade on 24 November 1916; Brigade Headquarters Detachment, 1st Brigade on 1 July 1921; Headquarters and 57th Company, 1st Brigade on 1 July 1924; and Brigade Headquarters and Headquarters Company, 1st Brigade on 1 July 1925.

Deactivated on 15 August 1934, it was reactivated on 1 September 1935 at Quantico, Virginia as Headquarters and Headquarters Company, 1st Marine Brigade, Fleet Marine Force, and redesignated as Headquarters Company, 1st Marine Brigade, Fleet Marine Force on 1 April 1936.

Following deployment in October 1940 to Guantanamo Bay, Cuba, it was redesignated as Headquarters Company, 1st Marine Division, Fleet Marine Force on 1 February 1941, then relocated to Quantico, Virginia in May 1941, then to New River, North Carolina in September 1941.

In June 1942 the Company deployed to Wellington, New Zealand and was redesignated as Headquarters Battalion, 1st Marine Division, Fleet Marine Force on 2 December 1942. HQ Battalion participated in the following World War II campaigns: Guadalcanal, Eastern New Guinea, New Britain, Pelielu, and Okinawa. Following the war, HQ Battalion deployed to Tientsin, China, where it remained until June 1947, at which time it relocated to Camp Pendleton, California.

In August 1950, HQ Battalion deployed to Kobe, Japan, then to the Republic of Korea in September 1950. It participated in the Korean War from September 1950-July 1953, operating from Inchon-Seoul, Chosin Reservoir, East Central Front, Western Front, then participated in the defense of the Korean Demilitarized Zone from August 1953-March 1955, at which time it relocated back to Camp Pendleton, California.

Elements of the Battalion participated in the Cuban Missile Crisis from October-December 1962. In March 1966, HQ Battalion deployed to the Republic of Vietnam, operating from Chu Lai and Da Nang until April 1971, at which time it relocated back to Camp Pendleton, California.

Throughout the 1970s and 1980s, it participated in numerous training exercises, then was part of Operations Desert Shield and Desert Storm, Southwest Asia, from September 1990-March 1991. The Battalion also participated in Operation Restore Hope, Somalia, from December 1992-May 1993.

## 1ST MARINE REGIMENT
### *"Inchon"*

*Mission: On order, 1st Marine Regiment deploys as the Ground Combat Element (GCE) for the 1st Marines Expeditionary Brigade (MEB) in support of crisis response operations and provides mission capable battalions in support of enduring and emerging operational requirements in order to meet operational commitments across the range of military operations.*

The 1st Marine Regiment was activated 27 November 1913 at Philadelphia, Pennsylvania as the 2nd Advance Base Regiment, and relocated to Pensacola, Florida in December 1913 before assignment to the 1st Advance Base Brigade in January 1914. The Regiment participated in the Vera Cruz Operation from March-November 1914, relocating to Philadelphia that December.

After participating in the Haitian Campaign from August 1915-May 1916, and the Occupation of Dominican Republic from May-December 1916, it was redesignated the 1st Regiment on 1 July 1916, then the 2nd Provisional Brigade in November 1916. After deactivation on 20 December 1916 at Santo Domingo, Dominican Republic, it was reactivated on 25 January 1917 at Philadelphia, Pennsylvania and assigned to the Fixed Defense Force.

In November 1918 the Regiment relocated to Guantanamo Bay, Cuba and was reassigned to the 6th Provisional Brigade in December, later relocating to Philadelphia, Pennsylvania in June 1919 and detaching from the 6th Provisional Brigade

In October 1920 it relocated to Quantico, Virginia and was assigned to the 3rd Brigade in December, later deactivating on 22 April 1922.

On 1 August 1922, it was reactivated at Santo Domingo, Dominican Republic, and assigned to the 2nd Brigade, participating in the occupation of the Dominican Republic through July 1924.

For the next several years the Regiment went through a series of activations and deactivations: deactivated 1 July 1924 at Santo Domingo, Dominican Republic; reactivated 15 March 1925 at Quantico, Virginia; redesignated 10 July 1930 as the 1st Marines; deactivated 1 November 1931.

1st Marine Regiment was reactivated on 1 March 1941 at Guantanamo Bay, Cuba and assigned to the 1st Marine Division, relocating to Parris Island, South Carolina in April 1941, then New River, North Carolina in February 1942, and deploying to Wellington, New Zealand in June-July 1942.

The Regiment participated in the following WWII Campaigns: Guadalcanal, Eastern New Guinea, New Britain, Peleliu, and Okinawa. Following the war, the Regiment was assigned to North China from September 1945-May 1947 and October 1947-February 1949 at which time it relocated to Camp Pendleton, California, before deactivation on 1 October 1949.

1st Marine Regiment was reactivated on 4 August 1950 at Camp Pendleton and assigned to 1st Marine Division, deploying to Kobe, Japan in September 1950. It participated in the Korea War from September 1950-July 1953 operating from: Inchon-Seoul, Chosin Reservoir, East Central Front, and Western Front. It later participated in the defense of the Korean Demilitarized Zone from July 1953 - April 1955, then relocated during April 1955 to Camp Pendleton, California. It participated in the Cuban Missile Crisis from October-December 1962.

The Regiment deployed during August 1965 - January 1966 to the Republic of Vietnam and participated in the war in Vietnam, August 1965 - June 1971 operating from: Da Nang, Chu Lai, Phu Bai, Quang Tri, Hue, Camp J.E. Muir, Camp D.M. Oerdue, Dong Ha, Cua Viet, Khe Sanh, and Duong Son.

In April 1971, it detached during from the 1st Marine Division and was reassigned to the 3rd Marine Amphibious Brigade, later relocating from May-June 1971 to Camp Pendleton, California, and reassigned to the 1st Marine Division.

Since 1972, the Regiment has participated in the following:

Operation New Arrival, the relocation of refuges from Indochina, April-May 1975; Operation Desert Shield and Desert Storm, Southwest Asia, August 1990-April 1991; element participated in Operation United Shield, Somalia, February-March 1995; element participated in Operation Enduring Freedom, Afghanistan, December 2001-February 2002; deployed during January 2003 to Kuwait in support of Operation Enduring Freedom; Operation Iraqi Freedom, Iraq, March - July 2003 and February 2004, April 2005, January 2008-January 2009; Operation Enduring Freedom, Afghanistan, September 2010-October 2011, February-August 2014; and an element participated in Operation Enduring Freedom, Afghanistan, December 2011-February 2012, June-December 2012.

*Source: The official 1st Marine Division Website*

## 5TH MARINE REGIMENT
### *"The Fighting Fifth"*

*Mission: The 5th Marine Regiment mans, trains and equips battalions, detachments, and individuals to deploy in support of our national security needs while maintaining a high state of readiness and professionally develops our Marines and Sailors to respond to crisis and/or contingencies when the nation calls.*

The activation of the Fifth Marines dates back to June 1917, just prior to the U.S. force deployment to France during World War I. The Regiment won its nickname, the "Fighting Fifth," on the battlefields of western Europe. So fierce were its efforts in the Battle of Belleau Wood and subsequent victories that the French government awarded the Regiment the Croix de Guerre with two palms and one gilt star. Today, each Marine serving in the Regiment also wears the Fourragere, a French unit award, on the left shoulder of his uniform to recognize the legacy and valor of his predecessors.

Briefly deactivated, the Regiment was reactivated in June 1920, to guard the delivery of the U.S. Mail against domestic bandits. While they were on the job, not one Marine was killed and not one piece of mail was lost to thieves. In March 1927, the Regiment deployed to South America and fought in support of the Nicaraguan government against rebel bands until April 1930. Shortly thereafter, the Regiment was again briefly deactivated. Troubled times and small conflicts in the Americas however, led to the Regiment's reactivation on 1 September 1934.

After further service in the U.S. and in Guantanamo Bay, Cuba, the Fifth Marines deployed to New Zealand in 1942 as part of the U.S. Pacific Campaign against Japan. During the course of World War II, the Regiment further distinguished itself in action at Guadalcanal, Eastern New Guinea, Peleliu and Okinawa. The post-war years found the Regiment on occupation duty in North China until May 1947, when it relocated to Guam. In August 1950, it moved to its current home, Camp Pendleton, California.

The country again called upon the Fifth Marines in August 1950, when the Regiment found itself in combat on the Pusan Perimeter in Korea. During the next three years the Regiment fought at Inchon and Seoul, the Chosin Reservoir, and on both the East Central and Western Fronts. The Fifth Marine Regiment returned to Camp Pendleton in March 1955, and remained there for the next eleven years.

In May 1966, the Fifth Marines arrived in the Republic of South Vietnam where it would remain until April 1971. Vietnam era Marines added the names Rung Sat, Chu Lai, Phu Bai, Hue, Khe Sahn, An Hoa, Tam Ky, and Da Nang to the Regiment's long list of distinguished battle actions.

In August 1990, the nation again called on the "Fighting Fifth" – this time in support of Operation Desert Shield. On 26 January 1991, while embarked with the largest amphibious task force since World War II, Regimental Landing Team (RLT) Five, in conjunction with RLT-2, conducted heliborne and surface assaults for Exercise Sea Soldier IV in Southern Oman. On 25 February 1991, the Regiment disembarked in direct support of Operation Desert Storm and the liberation of Kuwait. Less than three months later, Fifth Marines received an executive order to conduct humanitarian assistance and relief operations in Bangladesh. The Regiment returned to Camp Pendleton on 29 June 1991.

In the decade following Operation Desert Storm, the Regiment deployed to Yellowstone National Park, the Umatilla National Forest in Oregon and Clear Creek, Idaho to combat wild fires. Simultaneously it sourced the battalion landing teams for the 31st Marine Expeditionary Unit (Special Operations Capable), or MEU (SOC).

In January of 2003, the Fifth Marines deployed to Kuwait to take part in Operation Iraqi Freedom. On 21 March, the Regiment became the first unit to cross the line of departure into Iraq as it moved to seize the Rumayllah Oilfields. During the course of the next few weeks, the Regiment repeatedly distinguished itself in combat actions as it continued the offensive to liberate Baghdad and collapse the regime of Saddam Hussein. During much of the attack north, the Regiment led the 1st Marine Division in the deepest attack in Marine Corps history.

Today, the Regiment continues to participate in exercises and contingency deployments with the 1st Marine Division, and to prepare forces for deployment with the 31st MEU (SOC).

*Source: The official 1st Marine Division website*

## 7TH MARINE REGIMENT
### *"Magnificent Seventh" "Task Force Ripper"*

*Mission: On-order, 7th Marines conducts mechanized, combined-arms operations and other expeditionary operations in order to support theater engagement plans and contingency operations. The Regiment will be prepared to deploy within 48-hours of the receipt of an execute order as either the ground combat element for the 1st MEB or as a major subordinate element of the 1st Marine Division. As directed, the Regiment will prepare infantry battalions for deployment to the PACOM AOR in order to support III MEF operations and training.*

The 7th Marine Regiment was formed during World War I on 14 August 1917 at Philadelphia, PA and immediately deployed to participate in the occupation of Cuba from August 1917 to August 1919. They returned to Philadelphia in August 1919 and were deactivated on 6 September in the demobilization that followed the war. When the Marine Corps was called upon to provide peacekeepers in the Caribbean, elements of the Regiment were reactivated on 6 September 1933 at Quantico, VA and deployed on Naval ships off the Cuban coast. At the end of the crisis, 7th Marines was again deactivated on 17 January 1934.

With the cloud of World War II on the horizon, the nation expanded the size of the Corps and on 1 January 1941 the 7th Marine Regiment was reactivated in Guantanamo Bay, Cuba and assigned to the 1st Marine Brigade. The Regiment moved to Parris Island, SC before settling in New River, NC. On 2 April 1942, the Magnificent 7th embarked for the Pacific to reinforce units already there to stem the Japanese march towards Australia. On 18 September 1942, after training in jungle warfare in the Samoa Islands, the Regiment landed in the Solomon Islands on Guadalcanal. For four long months the Regiment relentlessly attacked the Japanese defenders and repulsed their Banzai charges and suicidal attacks. Over the course of a hundred fights, the Regiment earned a reputation for courage and daring. On Guadalcanal the heroism of Medal of Honor winners Manila John Basilone and Mitchell Paige, and Navy Cross winner "Chesty" Puller, represented the actions of the Marines of the 7th Marine Regiment.

Arriving in Australia in January 1943, the vast majority of the Regiment suffered from malaria, wounds, or just plain fatigue; but they had accomplished their mission. Though the Regiment went to Australia to train and refit for the coming battles and not for liberty, a grateful population gave them a tumultuous welcome. Again and again the Regiment was called upon to storm the Japanese-held islands in the Pacific. The 7th Marine Regiment fought in such places as Eastern New Guinea, New Britain, Peleliu, and the island fortress of Okinawa. From Guadalcanal to Okinawa, the Regiment had written a history of courage and ferocity in combat.

In the years after the war, 7th Marines continued to serve on far off shores, occupying North China from 1945-1947 and disarming the Japanese troops still stationed in that country and keeping the peace in a China torn by civil war. Upon returning to Camp Pendleton, CA from China in January 1947, the Regiment was deactivated yet again on 6 March only to be reactivated on 1 October. The reactivation was short lived, however, and 7th Marines was deactivated on 1 October 1949.

On 17 August 1950 the Regiment was reactivated, and on 21 September 1950 the Regiment landed as part of the 1st Marine Division in General MacArthur's brilliant stroke to stem the North Korean tide at Inchon, South Korea. The Marines of the Regiment fought in Korea with the same tenacity and bravery that their predecessors had shown on the battlefields of World War II. From Inchon to the Yalu River, at the "Frozen Chosin" Reservoir, and in the long defense of South Korea until the armistice in 1955, Marines of the Regiment wrote further glorious chapters in their unit's history. The Korean War, however, was only the prelude to the long Cold War period that would hold the world on the brink of nuclear confrontation for the next 40 years.

In November 1962, substantial parts of the Regiment embarked for the Caribbean and possible action in Cuba, aimed at forcing the removal of Soviet nuclear missiles pointed at the heart of America. As the crisis subsided, 7th Marines returned to Camp Pendleton, CA. The confrontation with Communism, however, was not finished with the removal of Soviet missiles from Cuba.

In July 1965, the Regiment went into action against the foes of freedom. This time the battleground was Vietnam. On thousands of squad sized patrols, in scores of Battalion and Regimental sized operations, and in fierce Division sized battles such as the TET Offensive, the Marines of the Magnificent 7th proved that they were worthy successors to those who had gone before them. Whether in armed action against the enemy in places like Chu Lai, Da Nang, and Duc Pho, or in civic action with the local populace, the Marines of the Regiment performed magnificently. Through the long course of the war in Vietnam, until they left as part of the American withdrawal, the Marines and Sailors of 7th Marines never wavered from their duty. As the Regiment sailed for the United States in September of 1970, the members of the Regiment were proud of their role fighting against Communist aggression.

During the 1970s and 1980s, the Leathernecks of 7th Marines trained in every clime and place preparing for the moment when they would once again be called to fight the Nation's battles. In August of 1990, shortly after shifting the home of the Regimental colors from Camp Pendleton, CA to Marine Corps Air Ground Combat Center Twentynine Palms, CA, the Marines and Sailors of the Regiment deployed to Saudi Arabia to halt Iraqi aggression against its neighbors in Operation DESERT STORM and Operation DESERT SHIELD. Manning the "Line in the Sand", the Regiment faced the Iraqi invaders. For the attack into Kuwait, the Regiment fought with skill and aggressiveness, overwhelming the enemy. After their victory, they returned to Twentynine Palms in March 1991 with the knowledge they were warriors shaped in the mold of those who had served their Country and Corps before them as members of this elite Regiment.

In August of 1991, 7th Marine Regiment became Regimental Combat Team Seven (RCT-7) due to unique organizational changes that occurred with the addition of 3rd Light Armored Infantry (LAI) Battalion, 1st Tank Battalion and Delta Company, 3rd Amphibious Assault (AA) Battalion. In December 1992, RCT-7 deployed on Operation RESTORE HOPE to relieve famine and return order to Somalia. Over a five month period the Marines and Sailors paid in blood as they worked tirelessly to alleviate the suffering of the Somalian people and to restore order to their ravaged nation. On 13 August 1993, on the eve of the Regiment's 76th anniversary, the Regiment formally marked the return to its original designation by changing from RCT-7 to 7th Marines (Reinforced).

On 8 October 1994 the action cycle began again for 7th Marines (Reinforced) when a crisis situation in Southwest Asia forced the decision to terminate a combined arms exercise in order to prepare for a Maritime Prepositioning Force (MPF) deployment. This high paced contingency operation was titled Operation VIGILANT WARRIOR. Although the National Command Authority did not give the order to deploy the entire Regiment, its advanced elements moved into the Arabian Gulf in response to Iraqi troop movements toward Kuwait. In Operation VIGILANT SENTINEL, from August to November 1995, this sequence was repeated.

In August of 1996, organizational changes designated 3rd Light Armored Reconnaissance Battalion (formerly LAI Bn) and 1st Tank Battalion as separate battalions in direct support of the 7th Marines' MPF mission along with Delta Company, 3rd AA Battalion, who returned to their parent unit.

In the intervening years of relative calm, the 7th Marine Regiment continued to maintain a high state of readiness by continual and rigorous training evolutions. The calm was shattered on 11 September 2001 by a terrorist attack on the World Trade Center, the Pentagon, and an unknown target that resulted in a plane crash in Pennsylvania. With the Nation suddenly involved in the Global War On Terrorism, 7th Marines prepared for its duty. In January 2003, the Regiment deployed to Kuwait in support of Operation IRAQI FREEDOM (OIF) and was instrumental in the "March to Baghdad" with 1st Marine Division in March 2003. Over the next six years, RCT-7 would deploy to OIF five additional times and fight in towns like Ramadi, Fallujah, Al Qiam and Hit in Al Anbar province. Through each deployment, the Marine of the Regiment could proudly display the earned nickname of the Magnificent 7th.

Concurrently, the United States was fighting battles in Afghanistan as part of Operation ENDURING FREEDOM (OEF). Though subordinate battalions of 7th Marines had a near continual presence in the Helmand River valley, the Regimental Headquarters deployed as RCT-7 three times starting in March 2008. Cities such as Marjeh, Sangin, and Lashkar Gah, where some of the heaviest fighting in the country took place, were all under the command of RCT-7. On 31 July 2013, RCT-7 furled its colors as the final RCT to serve in OEF.

As the 7th Marine Regiment nears its centennial, the Marines of the Magnificent 7th have a proud heritage to look upon. Though the uniforms and equipment have changed, the Honor, Courage and Commitment that resides within each Marine is steadfast and everlasting.

*Source: The official 1st Marine Division website*

## 11TH MARINE REGIMENT
### *"Cannon Cockers"*

*Mission: To provide effective artillery support to the various task forces comprising the 1st Marine Division.*

The present 11th Marine Regiment has been preceded by three other organizations having similar designations. The first was activated during World War I on 3 January 1918 as the 11th Marine Regiment. Originally planned as a light artillery regiment, it was converted to an infantry unit and went to France as part of the 5th Marine Brigade in the waning days of the war. It failed to see combat and returned home to be disbanded on 11 August 1919.

On 9 May 1927, another 11th Regiment was activated from troops in Haiti and at Quantico for service in Nicaragua of brief duration. The regimental headquarters was disbanded on 51 July 1927, and the two battalions in September. Renewed political problems in Nicaragua and the intensified guerrilla campaign of the bandit leader Augusto Sandino caused the activation of another 11th Regiment at Norfolk, Virginia, and San Diego, California, in January 1928. A third battalion was organized on the east coast on 21 March 1928. Again, service in Nicaragua was brief, with the third battalion being disbanded on 15 June 1929 and the remainder of the regiment on 31 August 1929.

With the approach of World War II and the consequent expansion of the Marine Corps, an 11th Marines (Artillery) was activated at Guantanamo Bay, Cuba, on 1 March 1941. Activation of the regiment's organic battalions already had been underway since 1 September 1940 when the 1st Battalion was created. After its return to the United States from Cuba, the regiment (less the 1st Battalion) shipped overseas with the 1st Marine Division to New Zealand in June-July 1942. The 1st Battalion went to Samoa with the 7th Marines in March 1942.

The 11th Marines landed on Guadalcanal in August with the 1st Marine Division and played an especially significant part in the Battle of the Tenaru and the Battle of Edson's Ridge. The 1st Battalion rejoined the regiment in September on Guadalcanal. On 15 December 1942, the 11th Marines left Guadalcanal for Australia, rested and reorganized, and then reentered combat on New Britain at Cape Gloucester on 26 December 1943. Here the regiment furnished support to the infantry in their capture of the Japanese airdrome. Following the New Britain campaign came a period of preparation for the Peleliu landing where the regiment was actively engaged.

For the first two weeks after the 15 September 1944 landing on Peleliu, artillery support was provided massed preparatory, harassing, and interdicting fire. Later, the artillery was used to fire directly into the mouths of enemy caves. In March 1945, the 11th Marines left for Okinawa, its final combat operation of World War II. There the regiment played an important defensive role with effective counter-battery fire, and steadily suppressed enemy attempts to counter-attack objectives already won by U.S. forces. With the war won, in the fall of 1945 the 11th Marines moved to Tientsin in North China where it was soon involved in trying to keep peace in the midst of the increasing conflict between rival Chinese factions. Early in 1947, the regiment returned to the United States to be reduced virtually to a battalion-sized unit.

Three years later the Communist North Koreans invaded South Korea, and the 1st Battalion was part of the 1st Provisional Marine Brigade deployed in August 1950 to the Pusan Perimeter to help stem their advance. Other battalions were organized in the United States and were available for service when the 1st Division made the Inchon landing. Shifted back to the east coast of Korea, the battalions were attached to regimental combat teams and participated in the Chosin Reservoir campaign of 1950. The 11th Marines participated in continued heavy action on the East Central Front throughout 1951, and in March 1952, moved to the Western Front. The 11th was finally able to sail from Korea for the United States and Camp Pendleton on 7 March 1955.

The years between 1955 and 1965 were spent in continued training to maintain a constant state of readiness. During the Cuban Missile Crisis of October 1962, the 11th Marines played a role in the task force ordered to impose a naval quarantine against arms shipments to Cuba.

A new era opened on 8 March 1965 when the Marines were committed to ground action in South Vietnam. Beginning on 16 August 1965, the regiment was gradually deployed to South Vietnam. The transfer was completed by the arrival of the 2d Battalion on 27 May 1966. The nature of the war required the artillerymen to defend their own positions against numerous enemy probes and brought about a vastly increased employment of artillery by helicopters, both for displacement and resupply.

The regimental history in Vietnam was characterized as fighting by detachments in dispersed areas. Hastings, Hue City, Napoleon-Saline II, Oklahoma Hills, Pipestone Canyon, and Imperial Lake were some of the more significant operations in which the regiment participated. Redeployment to the United States started in October 1970 when the 4th Battalion left for Twentynine Palms, California. The 1st Battalion was the last unit of the regiment to depart for the United States and Camp Pendleton in May 1971.

During the next decade, the 11th Marines experienced a high level of activity, participating in many training and support exercises. In 1975 the regiment provided support for Operation New Arrival and the Vietnamese refugees. The 11th Marines participated in numerous training exercises throughout the 1980s to maintain the regiment's high level of operational readiness.

The regiment's ability to respond quickly to a crisis was put to the test in August 1990, when Iraq invaded and occupied its neighbor, Kuwait. President George Bush immediately ordered American forces, including Marines, to the Persian Gulf, to deter a possible Iraqi assault into Saudi Arabia. Elements of the 11th Marines began departing Camp Pendleton on 25 August as part of the 7th Marine Expeditionary Brigade, enroute to Saudi Arabia and Operation Desert Shield. Early in September, 7th MEB was absorbed by I Marine Expeditionary Force. The mission of the 11th Marines was to provide effective artillery support to the various task forces comprising the 1st Marine Division. Upon arrival in Saudi Arabia, the regiment began an intensive training program, which included liaison with the famous British "Desert Rats," the 40th Field Regiment Royal Artillery

Iraq's refusal to remove its forces from occupied Kuwait soon changed the 11th Marines tactical posture from defense to offense. Close study of Iraqi defense arrangement began in earnest, as well as efforts to develop effective countermeasures. The 11th Marines enhanced its combat posture during November and December 1990 with live-fire artillery training exercises.

Operation Desert Storm began early on 17 January 1991, and the 11th Marines fired its first artillery mission against Iraqi forces, when elements of the regiment conducted an early morning surface artillery raid just south of Khafji. This was the first in a series of 11th Marines artillery raids conducted along the Saudi Arabian/Kuwaiti border, both on the Persian Gulf coast and along the south-west border area near several oil fields. As the major coalition ground offensive began on 24 February, the 11th Marine Regiment was already inside Kuwait providing vital fire support to Task Forces Grizzly and Taro. Throughout Operation Desert Storm, the 11th Marines provided close and continuous fire support to the 1st Marine Division.

Upon the 28 February 1991 ceasefire, which ended the fighting, the 11th Marines prepared to leave the Persian Gulf for home. The regiment's seven-month deployment and the Gulf War came to an end on 5 April with a much-deserved welcome at Camp Pendleton, California.

Throughout the remaining years of the decade, elements of the 11th Marines participated in Operation Sea Angel in Bangladesh and in Operation Restore Hope in Somalia. The regiment also assisted in fire-fighting efforts in the western United States during the summer of 1994 and again, four years later in the summer of 1998. In March of 1997, batteries participated in support of the Hunter Warrior Advanced Warfighting Experiment. The experiment took place on Camp Pendleton, California and brought back valuable information on maneuver warfare in conjunction with supporting arms.

The horrific terrorist attacks of 2001 marked the start of the global war on terror. The Cannon Cockers were ready when the order was given to deploy. Beginning in 2003, the 11th Marine Regiment actively participated in Operations Enduring Freedom and Iraqi Freedom. This included deploying as a regiment to Kuwait and Iraq in January-May of 2003. From 2004-2009, elements from the Regiment deployed in support of all major contingency operations in Iraq and Afghanistan. In 2009, the world's focus shifted towards the Afghanistan area of operations. From 2009-to present day, Cannon Cocker batteries have supported Operation Enduring Freedom without any lapse in coverage.

*Source: The official 1st Marine Division website*

## 1st Light Armored Reconnaissance Battalion
### *"The Highlanders"*

*Mission: Conduct reconnaissance, security, and economy of force operations and within its capabilities limited offensive or defensive operations that exploit the unit's mobility and firepower.*

First Light Armored Vehicle Battalion was activated in May 1985 and began receiving the first of its LAV-25 light armored vehicles in July 1985. On 9 October 1988 the battalion's name was changed to First Light Armored Infantry Battalion.

In August 1990, First Light Armored Infantry Battalion deployed to Southwest Asia in response to Iraq's invasion of Kuwait. During OPERATION DESERT SHIELD, First Light Armored Infantry Battalion was the forward unit of the First Marine Division, conducting screening and counter-reconnaissance operations along the Kuwaiti-Saudi Arabian border. During OPERATION DESERT STORM, after breaching the Iraqi defensive positions, First Light Armored Infantry Battalion attacked north to locate and destroy enemy forces. On the third day of the ground offensive, First Light Armored Infantry Battalion was the first of the Allied Forces to enter Kuwait City, capturing Kuwait International Airport on 28 February 1991. The battalion redeployed to the United States in April 1991. On 1 May 1992, First Light Armored Infantry Battalion deployed to Los Angeles on a four-hour notice and assisted the Long Beach Police Department in quelling civil disturbances and looting. After a successful deployment as part of the Special Purpose Marine Air Ground Task Force Los Angeles, the battalion returned once again to Camp Pendleton. On 12 June 1992, First Light Armored Infantry Battalion was redesignated as First Reconnaissance Battalion (Light Armored). Almost two years later, on 1 March 1994, First Reconnaissance Battalion (Light Armored) underwent another name change and was redesignated First Light Armored Reconnaissance Battalion.

In December 2001, Bravo Company, First Light Armored Reconnaissance Battalion deployed to Afghanistan as part of the 15th Marine Expeditionary Unit (Special Operations Capable) in support of OPERATION ENDURING FREEDOM. The performance of the company again demonstrated the value of Marine Corps light armored reconnaissance assets as it performed a variety of combat missions in the rugged terrain of Afghanistan.

First Light Armored Reconnaissance Battalion again answered the call to arms in January 2003 when it was deployed to Southwest Asia in support of OPERATION IRAQI FREEDOM. The Battalion, operating as part of Regimental Combat Team Five, was the first unit to cross the Iraqi-Kuwaiti Border on 20 March 2003. After a lightning attack northward through Iraq, First Light Armored Reconnaissance Battalion was instrumental in securing the capital of Baghdad. Due to its unique mobility and reconnaissance capabilities, the battalion left Regimental Combat Team Five and was assigned to Task Force Tripoli. As part of Task Force Tripoli, the battalion advanced further north, ultimately securing former Iraqi dictator Saddam Hussein's hometown of Tikrit. Following the cessation of major combat operations, First Light Armored Reconnaissance Battalion moved from the northern portion of Iraq to the country's extreme southern area along the Saudi-Arabian border to halt and deter illegal smuggling into Iraq. First Light Armored Reconnaissance Battalion redeployed to the United States at the end of May 2003. In February 2004 First Light Armored Reconnaissance Battalion again returned to Iraq, this time in support of OPERATION IRAQI FREEDOM II. The battalion conducted security and stability operations in the Al Anbar province of western Iraq as part of Regimental Combat Team Seven. First Light Armored Reconnaissance Battalion performed a wide range of critical missions, including key roles in regimental size operations, in order to capture or kill terrorist and insurgent forces. Additionally, the battalion was vital in patrolling the western borders of Iraq in order to prevent the infiltration of arms and insurgents. The battalion returned to the United States in October 2004. With its inherent mobility and lethality, coupled with high states of training and readiness, First Light Armored Reconnaissance Battalion is prepared to be the "tip of the spear" for any future contingency.

*Source: The Official 1st Marine Division website*

## 1st Tank Battalion
***"1st Tanks"***

*Mission: To close with and destroy the enemy using expeditionary armor-protected firepower, shock effect, and maneuver in support of the MAGTF across the range of military operations.*

The 1st Tank Battalion was activated on 1 November 1941 at Camp Lejeune, North Carolina and was attached to the 1st Marine Division. At this time, Headquarters and Service Company and Company B were organized. Company A had been in existence prior to this activation and then fell under the umbrella of 1st Tanks. Alpha was originally activated on 1 August 1940 as the 3d Tank Company. Its designation was changed to Company A, 1st Tank Battalion, on 1 May 1941. Other companies of the battalion were later activated in early 1942.

After the outbreak of World War II, the battalion embarked on an extensive training program to prepare itself for combat duty. The unit subsequently was ordered to the South Pacific and began movement to the area in the spring of 1942. Companies from the battalion were eventually deployed to Samoa and New Zealand. The first combat operation for units from the battalion was the Guadalcanal campaign. On 7 August 1942, Companies A and B took part in the 1st Marine Division's landings on the Japanese held island. Tanks from these two companies had their first major encounter with the enemy on 21 August. The next month saw tanks from the battalion supporting infantry units in the Battle of Bloody Ridge. The two companies continued to engage the enemy until the end of the year when the 1st Marine Division was relieved by the Army forces. The division was then moved to Australia in January 1943 where units of the 1st Tank Battalion were once again reunited.

That fall the battalion moved to New Guinea to begin preparations for the Cape Gloucester, New Britain operation. First Marine Division units including the 1st Tank Battalion, les Company B which remained in New Guinea, subsequently made an amphibious assault on Cape Gloucester on the day after Christmas. Battalion tanks were immediately committed to the drive to expand the beachhead; but progress was impeded, not only by the resistance of the Japanese but also by the torrential rains and the rough terrain. For the rest of the month and into early January, the Marines were in heavy contact with Japanese forces. Tanks from the battalion were continually used to support the infantry in their attacks on the enemy. As a result, numerous casualties were inflicted on the Japanese forces by 1st Tank Battalion.

Company B, which had been located on New Guinea, landed in the Arawe area of New Britain on 12 January 1944 to support Army forces there. Battalion units remained committed to the struggle for New Britain until spring. By the beginning of May, however, all elements of the 1st Tank Battalion had been withdrawn from both New Britain and New Guinea and relocated to Pavuvu Island in the Russell Islands.

The assault and capture of Peleliu in the Palau Group was the next combat mission for the battalion. On 15 September 1944, it participated in the initial landing on the island. During this campaign, 1st Tank Battalion rendered conspicuous service in defeating the enemy. On the first day of the battle, battalion tanks played an important role in beating back a determined Japanese counterattack. This time the enemy spearheaded their counterattack with enemy tanks. In the encounter, the 1st Tank Battalion destroyed over 20 Japanese armored vehicles. Bitter fighting for the battalion continued for another two weeks and on 2 October 1944, Tanks was able to successfully withdraw and redeploy to the Russell Islands.

The last campaign of World War II for 1st Tank Battalion was the assault on Okinawa. Beginning on 1 April 1945, the battalion was actively engaged in wresting control of the island fortress from the Japanese. The ferocity of the fighting during the battle was shown through the statistics of 28 tanks destroyed and 163 more damaged.

The cessation of hostilities was followed by the deployment of the battalion to North China in early October for occupation duty. While stationed in Tientsin, the battalion assisted and supported the program of repatriating enemy military and civilian personnel. It also helped protect American interests, lives, and property as part of its garrison duties. In January 1947, the battalion minus Company B was relieved of its responsibilities in China and ordered to Guam. Another transfer occurred four months later. This time the unit with the exception of Company A was returned to the United States. The battalion arrived at Camp Pendleton, California on 1 May 1947, where it remained for the following three years.

Shortly after the Communist invasion of South Korea in June 1950, the battalion was ordered to prepare for a deployment to the Far East. The first element of the battalion to sail for Korea was Company A which left San Diego in July, arriving in the war zone on 2 August 1950. Upon arrival, it disembarked at the port of Pusan and immediately commenced operations against the enemy. In the meantime, the rest of the battalion began moving to the beleaguered nation. The battalion, with Company A now reattached, participated in the amphibious landing at Inchon that began on 15 September. The 1st Tank Battalion remained locked in battle with both North Korea and Chinese Communist forces for three years. Following the signing of the armistice in July 1953, the battalion stayed in Korea and once again assumed the role of a garrison force. Redeployment occurred in 1955. Company C was the first unit of the battalion to depart from Korea for Camp Pendleton in late February. A few weeks later, the rest of the battalion began relocating to its old home base. This peacetime stint lasted ten years. While at Pendleton, it was primarily occupied in training exercises and maneuvers.

The expansion of the American involvement in the war in Vietnam in early 1965 was the determining factor in the next relocation of the battalion to the Far East. The 1st Tank Battalion did not move directly to Southeast Asia but was first ordered to Okinawa. The majority of the battalion remained on the island bastion from September 1965 to the following March. Late that month, most of its elements were deployed to the Republic of Vietnam. All of the battalion's components were reunited in Vietnam during May. Upon entry into the war-torn country, the battalion was directed to support 1st Marine Division units in operations against Viet Cong and North Vietnamese forces. The 1st Tank Battalion remained an active combat force in Vietnam until March 1970. Beginning in the previous summer, the United States had initiated a program of withdrawing from Indo-China while de-escalating its war effort. As part of this phased reduction in troop strength, the 1st Tank Battalion was redeployed to Camp Pendleton in early spring 1970. After its return to the United States, 1st Tank Battalion embarked upon a retaining program of maintaining its combat readiness so that it could effectively respond to any future emergency.

When Iraq invaded Kuwait in August 1990, 1st Tank Battalion deployed to Saudi Arabia as part of I Marine Expeditionary Force. On 7 September, the battalion was fully equipped with M60A1 tanks from Maritime Preposition Squadron 3 and was deployed from Al Jubail, Saudi Arabia as the armored backbone of the multinational force which established the Desert Shield. On 13 September, Company D arrived in Saudi Arabia by amphibious ships from Okinawa where it had been on unit deployment. During the next five months the battalion provided armor units to all of the task forces established by I Marine Expeditionary Force. Besides the continuing mission of maintaining the defense of Saudi Arabia, intensive training for the pending offensive to liberate Kuwait was conducted. On 24 February 1991, 1st Tank Battalion spearheaded the assault of Task Force Papa Bear into Kuwait. Meanwhile, Company A supported Task Force Ripper. By 27 February, 1st Tank Battalion had reached the Kuwait International Airport and all Iraqi forces were destroyed. The cease-fire was established on 28 February and by April 1991, the battalion returned home to Las Flores, Camp Pendleton.

On 2 June 1992, 1st Tank Battalion moved its guidon from Las Flores, Camp Pendleton to Marine Corps Air Ground Combat Center located at Twentynine Palms, California. From then until present day the battalion calls the High Desert home.

Following the events on September 11, 2001 the nation's armed forces mobilized to fight the Global War on Terror. Following the initial push to Baghdad in 2003, the Marine Corps began to transition to a different style of warfare. Individual companies and MEU platoons, vice the whole battalion, began to deploy in support of OIF. Throughout this Long War, 1st Tank Battalion continues to provide the armored combat power to Marine Expeditionary Units (MEU) and Regimental Combat Teams fighting in and rebuilding Iraq. Aside from entire line companies and platoons deploying, this battalion also supports the GWOT by sending Individual Augments to fulfill higher staffing requirements and Border, Police, and Military Transition Teams (BTT, PTT and MTT). Thus far, 1st Tanks has participated in operations such as the Battle of Fallujah, Steel Curtain, and Al Majie. Meanwhile this battalion's companies routinely conduct Counter Insurgency (COIN) operations in order to allow the Iraqi populace to live in peace.

1st Tank Bn conducted its final deployments to Iraq in 2008, and by the end of 2009 was called upon to support Operation Enduring Freedom (OEF) with company-size deployments to Afghanistan. Company C was the first to deploy to Afghanistan in early 2010 where the company conducted security operations for RCT-7. Company A followed shortly thereafter to conduct route clearance operations for I MEF as the presidential troop surge drew extra forces into the theatre of operations. Each company performed these alternative missions exceptionally well and demonstrated to OEF planners that 1st Tank Bn was an essential part of the Marine Corps' fight in Afghanistan. Concurrently, 1st Tank Bn continued to prove its capabilities when it participated in a newly constructed Marine Corps Security Cooperation MAGTF to Eastern Europe as the Ground Combat Element of the Black Sea Rotational Force (BSRF). This mobilized Marines from across the battalion to advise and assist partner nations in all facets of military operations.

Multiple deployments during 2010 further increased the battalion's push to get more of its Marines in the fight, which was realized when Company D deployed late in 2010 as the first tank company sent to Afghanistan by U.S. Forces. Companies B and C continued to conduct route clearance missions in 2011-2012, and Company A deployed again to Afghanistan in 2012 – this time on tanks, following in the tracks left by Company D. The battalion reached the height of its OEF deployment tempo in 2012 when it mobilized elements of H&S Company, including the command deck, and Company B for the NATO Training Mission – Afghanistan (NTMA), where they joined Companies A and C in theatre. The NTMA teams conducted Personal Security Detail (PSD) missions in and around Kabul supporting Regional Command – Capitol (RC(C)), and advised multiple levels of command within the Afghan National Security Forces (ANSF). This included O-6 level commands in RC(C) and Afghan National Civil Order of Police (ANCOP) brigades in volatile Helmand Province districts such as Gereshk and Nad Ali. Few units can claim at any point in their history to have so proficiently executed so many simultaneous and diverse missions in combat.

The combined exploits of our Marines throughout Afghanistan in Marjeh, Sangin, Musa Qal'eh, Now Zad, Nad Ali, Garmser and Kabul strengthened the battalion's reputation as adaptive and aggressive, and bolstered the combat power of Marine Forces in Afghanistan to secure broader successes in the continuing fight. As 2012 draws to a close, 1st Tank Bn continues to provide forces in support of Marine Expeditionary Unit deployments, and to support OEF in multiple roles including tank companies; Afghan National Army, Police, and Border Patrol Security Force Assistance and Advisory Teams (SFAAT); and skilled individual augments for RCT and MEB staff billets.

*Source: The official 1st Marine Division website*

## 3D LIGHT ARMORED RECONNAISSANCE BATTALION
### *"Wolfpack"*

*Mission: 3dLAR conducts light armored reconnaissance, security and offensive operations IOT provide mission capable task organized forces in support of enduring and emerging operational commitments across the Range of Military Operations.*

In 1980, the Marine Corps identified a requirement to enhance the mobility and firepower of the units tasked with rapid deployment responsibilities. A family of six Light Armored Vehicles was determined to be the means of meeting this requirement.

On 27 September 1982, a production contract for the LAV-25 and a companion development contract for five other LAV configurations (Maintenance/Recovery, Logistics, Mortar, Anti-Tank, and Command and Control) were awarded to General Motors of Canada. The LAV family of vehicles was highly mobile and able to move on land and water, therefore providing a fighting capability previously unrealized.

The 3d Light Armored Vehicle Battalion originally began as Company A (Reinforced), 1st Light Armored Vehicle Battalion in May 1983, and began receiving LAVs in April of 1984. Company A, 1st Light Armored Vehicle Battalion became Company A, 3d Light Armored Vehicle Battalion in late 1985. The 3d Light Armored Vehicle Battalion, 27th Marines, 7th Marine Amphibious Brigade was activated on 11 September 1986. The battalion was redesignated as the 3d Light Armored Infantry Battalion on 1 October 1988 and subsequently relocated to Okinawa, Japan in February 1989.

The battalion returned to Twentynine Palms on 18 July 1991 and was assigned to Regimental Combat Team (RCT) 7. A detachment from the battalion deployed to Saudi Arabia on 16 August 1990 in support of Operation DESERT SHIELD, as part of the 7th Marine Expeditionary Brigade, Task Force Lima. Later, the battalion conducted screening and deception operations as part of Task Force Shepherd, the forward unit of the First Marine Division. On 25 January 1991, Company B saw combat in the first ground offensive action of the war by participating in an artillery raid with 5th Battalion, 11th Marines. On the night of 29 January 1991, during the battle of Umm Hjul, Company D was the primary unit to turn back a major Iraqi attack. Once the ground war commenced, 3d Light Armored Infantry Battalion again found itself at the forefront of the action. While assigned to the First Marine Division Command Post on the second day of the ground war, Company B repelled an Iraqi counterattack on the Division's Command Post. Additionally, Company D provided a mobile screen for Task Force Ripper, the leading unit for the Division. On the third day of the ground offensive, Task Force Shepherd was the first coalition force to enter Kuwait City where it liberated the Kuwait International Airport from Iraqi occupation.

In March of 1991, the 3d Light Armored Infantry Battalion detachment returned to Twentynine Palms, California. While the rest of the battalion was deterring Iraqi aggression, Company A had been assigned to Marine Air Ground Task Force 4-90 in the Far East with a mission to conduct security patrols. When a large earthquake hit the Philippine Islands, Company A participated in relief efforts. In April of 1991, Mount Pinatubo erupted and once again, Company A was called upon to provide security against looters as well as to assist in the clean up efforts. During this deployment, Company A also participated in Exercise Cobra Gold in Thailand and Exercise Team Spirit in Korea. Company A returned to Twentynine Palms on 7 August 1991 after completing an arduous 15-month deployment.

From December 1992 to April 1993, 3d Light Armored Infantry Battalion deployed Company B and Company C along with the forward command group and forward logistics support for Operation RESTORE HOPE in Somalia. The mission consisted of convoy escorts, which delivered over 4,000 metric tons of grain to outlying areas. Additionally, during this relief operation, the battalion also conducted over 400 day and night security patrols and was involved in numerous combined patrols and security checkpoints with other United Nations units.

On 1 March 1994, 3d Light Armored Infantry Battalion was re-designated as 3d Light Armored Reconnaissance (LAR) Battalion. Throughout 1994, the battalion participated in counter-drug operations in support of Joint Task Force 6 in Arizona. In 1995, the battalion had one platoon from Company A participate in Operation UNITED SHIELD: the retrograde of United Nations forces from Somalia.

In late January through February 2003, the battalion, minus Company C who was in the UDP, deployed with the First Marine Division to Kuwait in support of Operation IRAQI FREEDOM. Upon arrival, the battalion attached Company B, 4th LAR Battalion, which was subsequently re-designated as Company E. On 21 March, 3d LAR Battalion and its attachments kicked off Operation IRAQI FREEDOM by attacking into the Rumaylah oil fields of southern Iraq. The battalion then cleared in zone, seized the Safwan Airfield, and secured artillery positions north of the battalion's battle space. The WOLFPACK, along with 1st LAR Battalion, led the Division's rapid attack north by passing through Task Force Tarawa just 56 hours after attacking into Iraq, then crossing the Euphrates River and continuing the attack north along Highway 1.

On 23 March 2003, while advancing hundreds of kilometers in front of the Division to seize a bridge over the Tigris River, the battalion uncovered a night ambush by dozens of Iraqi irregular forces known as the Fedeyeen. This was the first major and only battalion-level engagement of the war which resulted in several dozen enemy killed in action and the destruction of Iraqi armor forces attempting to maneuver south against the Division.

From the afternoon of 24 March until 1 April, the battalion was attached to RCT-5. On 25 March, the battalion's advance north was temporarily halted due to "The Mother of All Sandstorms'" which reduced visibility throughout Southern Iraq to less than a few feet during daylight and to nothing during hours of darkness. Once the sandstorm lifted on 26 March, the battalion continued its advance north on Highway 1 until the entire Division was temporarily halted west of Ad Diwaniyah in order to allow for supplies and logistics to catch up to the lead units.

From 24 through 31 March, all four companies continued to participate in company-level engagements, both while working directly for the battalion and while attached temporarily to other battalions.

On 31 March, the battalion attacked north as part of RCT-5 and secured the northern portion of the Hantush Airfield. As the battalion continued its advance north, Company D was attached to RCT-7 on 29 March. They remained attached until 6 April, where they led RCT-7's attack to seize the Salman Pak peninsula. As the Division continued its attack north, the battalion was assigned to conduct a moving flank screen north of Highway 6. As the Division attacked into Baghdad, the battalion screened the area east of the city to prevent enemy forces from reinforcing, as RCTs 1, 5, and 7 stormed across the Diyala River.

On 10 April, the battalion was tasked to provide a headquarters and two companies to Task Force Tripoli. This adhoc task force comprised of elements of 1st, 2nd and 3d LAR Battalions, as well as G/2/23 and the TOW Plt from 1st Tank Bn attacked north toward Tikrit. The remainder of Task Force WOLFPACK, Companies B, E, and one half of H&S Company, as well as the Rear Command Post element, remained outside Baghdad conducting stabilization operations while attached to 3d Assault Amphibian Battalion. In its advance north towards Tikrit, the elements of the battalion attached to Task Force Tripoli made national headlines in the town of Samarra. On 13 April 2003, Marines from Company D rescued 7 American servicemen and women who had been taken prisoner earlier in the conflict. The rescued prisoners included two Army helicopter pilots and Shoshanna Johnson, a soldier from the same unit as Jessica Lynch. An image from this moment is captured in the "Operation IRAQI FREEDOM" mural on a building in Twentynine Palms. After this rescue, the battalion continued north to Tikrit where it attacked into the city the same day, then blocked south of it and cleared several former palaces and residences of Saddam Hussein and other prominent Ba'ath party members.

On 21 April, the battalion reformed in Ad Diwaniyah, Iraq. Shortly thereafter, the battalion was again tasked to provide forces to Task Force Tripoli, this time moving south to the Saudi Arabian border as part of a reconnaissance in force mission in an area that had not seen US forces or witnessed combat operations since the war commenced. Within a week of returning to Ad Diwaniyah, the battalion again provided a show of force which demonstrated the speed and mobility of the LAV. This time the battalion moved north and east to the Iranian border and back south through several towns that had rarely seen a Coalition presence in order to develop an assessment of the area as the Division prepared to take control of an expanded area of operations. Shortly after completing this final mission, the battalion retrograded to Kuwait in preparation for redeployment to the United States. By mid-June 2003, the entire battalion had redeployed to Twentynine Palms, with the remainder of the Division following in September.

In November of 2003, the battalion was given a warning order to prepare to redeploy to Iraq in August 2004 in order to participate in the Division's resumption of support and stability operations in the Al Anbar province. In preparation for this deployment, the battalion executed platoon, company and battalion-level training which culminated with a two-week deployment to the US Army's National Training Center in Ft. Irwin, CA in conjunction with a US Army brigade training exercise. In early August of 2004, the battalion deployed the advance party to Kuwait with the remainder of the battalion arriving in Kuwait during September 2004. In September, 3d LAR conducted a relief in place (RIP) with 1st LAR Battalion. Upon arrival at Camp Korean Village, the battalion attached Battery S, 5/10 as a provisional infantry company as well as Company A, 1/23, a reserve infantry company out of Houston, TX. The battalion's higher headquarters was RCT-7. During the early part of the deployment, Company D operated out of Al Qaim, north of the Euphrates River and along the Syrian border, while the remainder of the battalion operated out of Camp Korean Village.

In late October 2004, the battalion was tasked to provide a headquarters element and one LAR company to RCT-1 in support of the Division's effort to retake the city of Fallujah. This mission forced the creation of two separate battalion task forces. Task Force WOLFPACK, comprised of the battalion command element, part of Headquarters and Service Company, and Company C (reinforced) moved to Habbiniyah and attached Company B/1/23, C/1-9 IN, Small Craft Company, 36 Commando/ISOF Brigade, the Scout Sniper Platoon from BLT1/4, and an Interim Iraqi Security Force Platoon. Task Force Naha, consisting of H&S Company (-), Company A (-)/ 3d LAR, A/1/23, and S/5/10 remained at Camp Korean Village and was later reinforced with a detachment of four CH-46s from Marine Medium Helicopter Squadron (HMM) 265. Task Force Naha continued to execute the same enduring tasks that Task Force WOLFPACK had executed prior to its departure.

Beginning on 7 November 2004, Task Force WOLFPACK participated in Operation AL FAJR (Phantom Fury), the Division's operation to retake Fallujah. Task Force WOLFPACK's mission was to attack to seize three key objectives on the Fallujah Peninsula—the North and South Bridges and the Fallujah Hospital. Both bridges spanned the Euphrates River and connected the peninsula to the city of Al Fallujah. Across these bridges, insurgents could either reinforce efforts in the city or withdraw onto the peninsula. Coalition forces suspected that the insurgents used the hospital as a strong point or received medical care at the facility. At 1900 on 7 November 2004, Task Force WOLFPACK attacked north onto the peninsula and seized all three battalion objectives. During this time, Company D was attached to 1st Battalion, 23d Marines and operated near the cities of Hit and Haditha securing the main supply routes and patrolling known insurgent areas. Task Force Naha continued securing the theater-level supply routes in its area of operations while conducting offensive operations against the insurgents in and around Ar Rutbah. They also maintained security and enforced customs regulations at two of the border crossing points located in Trebil and Waleed, Iraq.

In late November 2004, Task Force WOLFPACK departed the Fallujah peninsula and was attached to the US Army's 2nd Brigade Combat Team (2BCT), 1st Infantry Division. Task Force WOLFPACK quickly conducted a re-arm/re-fit operation in Ar Ramadi and then participated in several operations to capture Division and Brigade-level high value individuals. In December, Task Force WOLFPACK began conducting route security operations in the Fallujah-Ar Ramadi corridor. In early 2005, both Task Force Naha and Task Force WOLFPACK supported the 2005 Iraqi National and Provincial Elections. During this period, Task Force Naha was reinforced with Company C, 1/3, and significant Naval Mobile Construction Battalion (SeaBee) assets. Task

Force Naha utilized these new attachments to construct, secure, and operate four separate polling stations in conjunction with Iraqi security forces and the International Electoral Commission.

At the end of February 2005, Task Force WOLFPACK reattached to RCT-7 and conducted offensive operations along the Euphrates River in vicinity of the cities of Hit and Haditha as part of Operation RIVER BLITZ. When these operations were completed in early March, Task Force WOLFPACK returned to Camp Korean Village where the battalion reformed and subsequently conducted a RIP with 2d LAR Battalion. During April of 2005, the battalion redeployed to Twentynine Palms, CA.

In May 2005, 3d LAR was given a warning order to prepare two line companies and Headquarters and Service Company to deploy in support of OIF 05-07.1. Once again the battalion quickly re-organized, while still supporting the UDP rotation to Okinawa with Companies B and C. Pre-deployment training consisted of individual, crew, platoon and company-level training at the Army's NTC in Fort Irwin, CA during September and October 2005 and a battalion deployment to Stu Segall's Strategic Operations Studios near Miramar, CA in January of 2006.

In March of 2006, the battalion deployed in support of OIF 05-07.1 and subsequently became Task Force WOLFPACK by attaching C/1/10 as a provisional infantry company, one HET detachment and one CAG detachment. Immediately upon arrival, Task Force WOLFPACK detached Company D to RCT-5 in Fallujah to reinforce this AO in order to support decisive operations in and around Baghdad, Iraq. In June 2006, Task Force WOLFPACK received Company D back from RCT-5 and began conducting more aggressive Counter Insurgency (COIN) operations in and around Ar Rutbah, Iraq.

In July 2006, Task Force WOLFPACK was tasked with splitting the battalion by providing a headquarters and maneuver capability to operate near Rawah, Iraq. Task Force Rutbah, which consisted of Company A, 3d LAR, C/1/10 and one half of Headquarters and Service Company (-), 3d LAR continued to conduct counter-insurgency operations in and around Ar Rutbah, Iraq. Task Force Rawah, consisting of one half of Headquarters and Service Company (-) (REIN), 3d LAR and Company D, 3d LAR, conducted a RIP with 4-14 CAV and subsequently began COIN operations in and around Rawah and Anah, Iraq. In September of 2006, Task Force Rutbah and Task Force Rawah conducted a RIP with 2d LAR in both areas of operation. By early October 2006, the battalion had redeployed to Twentynine Palms, CA. The battalion deployed again to Iraq in November 2008, where it conduct COIN operations in AO Rutbah. The WOLFPACK redployed to Twentynine Palms, CA in May 2008.

Upon returning from Iraq, 3d LAR Bn began pre-deployment training for its fifth deployment to Iraq, including a month long alternate mission rehearsal exercise at the U.S. Army National Training Center (NTC) at Fort Irwin, CA, in January of 2009.

In March 2009, the battalion deployed in support of Operation IRAQI FREEDOM 09.1. While deployed to Iraq, Task Force WOLFPACK operated from the expeditionary air base Sahl Sinjar Airfield, conducting full-spectrum counterinsurgency operations throughout Iraq's restive and austere Ninewa Province. In partnership with U.S. Army Special Forces, U.S. State Department, and Iraqi Security Forces, the Wolfpack engaged with local political and military leaders from the Kurdish Regional Government and the Iraqi central government in order to facilitate a peaceful resolution of political disputes in an area with a long history of ethnic conflict. 3d LAR Battalion also interdicted smuggling efforts along the Iraq-Syrian border, with a presence that spanned more than 200 miles from the Jazirah Desert to the Tigris River and Iraq-Turkey border. The Wolfpack then conducted the light armored reconnaissance community's last military operation in Iraq, executing the responsible drawdown of the entire light armored reconnaissance equipment set and its return to the continental United States in September 2009.

Concurrent to the deployment in support of Operation IRAQI FREEDOM, Company A provided a platoon in support the 31st Marine Expeditionary Unit.

In January 2010, the WOLFPACK began pre-deployment training for its inaugural deployment to Afghanistan in support of Operation ENDURING FREEDOM. The training included squad, platoon, company, and the capstone battalion-sized training at Exercise ENHANCED MOJAVE VIPER in August 2010.

In November 2010 the battalion departed Twentynine Palms, CA and conducted a transfer of authority with 1st Light Armored Reconnaissance Battalion in the Southern Helmand River Valley of Afghanistan.

*Source: the official 1st Marine Division website*

## 1st Reconnaissance Battalion
### *"Black Diamonds"*

*Mission: To provide task organized forces in order to conduct amphibious reconnaissance, ground reconnaissance, battlespace shaping operations, raids, and specialized insertion and extraction.*

The 1st Reconnaissance Battalion deployed to Guantanamo Bay, Cuba in 1937, and fought there during WWII. From 1950-1964, the Battalion participated in the Korean

War from various points on the globe, relocating to Camp Pendleton in March 1955 and participating in the Cuban Missile Crisis from November-December 1962.

From 1965-1971, the Battalion deployed to Camp Schwab, Okinawa and to the Republic of South Vietnam in 1966. The participated in the Vietnam War until March 1971, when the Battalion returned to Camp Pendleton that Spring.

The 1st Recon Battalion has received numerous awards, including:

- Presidential Unit Citation Streamer with One Silver and Three Bronze Stars for WWII and Korea (1950)
- Korea (1951)
- Vietnam (1966-1967)
- Vietnam (1967-1968)

In 1990-1991, the 1st Reconnaissance Battalion participated in the Persian Gulf War, then was redesignated as 1st Reconnaissance Battalion (Light Armored) in June 1992, then redesignated 1st Recon Battalion again in 2000.

In January 2003, the Battalion deployed to Kuwait in support of Operation Enduring Freedom, participating in the invasion of Iraq from March-June 2003. The Battalion then redeployed to Iraq for Operation Iraqi Freedom from February-October 2004, where it took part in Operation Vigilant Resolve.

In 2010, 1st Recon Battalion deployed to Helmand Province, Afghanistan, where they produced 300-plus enemy KIA, did not lose a single man in their seventh-month deployment, and was regarded as "The deadliest battalion in Afghanistan right now" by LtGen James Mattis.

THE RECON CREED

Realizing it is my choice and my choice alone
to be a Reconnaissance Marine,
I accept all challenges involved with this profession.
Forever shall I strive to maintain the tremendous reputation
of those who went before me.
Exceeding beyond the limitations
set down by others shall be my goal.
Sacrificing personal comforts and dedicating myself
to the completion of the reconnaissance mission shall be my life.
Physical fitness, mental attitude, and high ethics --
The title of Recon Marine is my honor.
Conquering all obstacles, both large and small,
I shall never quit.
To quit, to surrender, to give up is to fail.
To be a Recon Marine is to surpass failure;
To overcome, to adapt and to do whatever it takes
to complete the mission.
On the battlefield, as in all areas of life,
I shall stand tall above the competition.
Through professional pride, integrity, and teamwork,
I shall be the example
for all Marines to emulate.
Never shall I forget the principles
I accepted to become a Recon Marine.
Honor, Perseverance, Spirit and Heart.
A Recon Marine can speak without saying a word
and achieve what others can only imagine.

## 1st Combat Engineer Battalion
### *"The Super Breed"*

*Mission: Provide mobility, counter mobility, survivability, and limited general engineering support to the 1st Marine Division.*

The 1st Combat Engineer Battalion was formed on February 24, 1941 at Guantanamo Bay, Cuba, as the 1st Pioneer Battalion, 1st Marine Division, to be a specialized unit used for shore party operations during amphibious assaults, and to provide close combat engineer support to the Marine infantry. The Battalion relocated to Marine Corps Recruit Depot, Parris Island, South Carolina in April 1941, then again to "Tent City One" at Marine Corps Air Station New River, North Carolina, in September 1941.

On June 14, 1942, the Battalion was reassigned to Wellington, New Zealand beginning with a cross-country train journey to San Francisco, California, to across the ocean on the USAT John Ericsson (NY-307). It was redesignated the 1st Battalion, 17th Marines on January 12, 1943, and later the First Engineer Battalion on June 30, 1944.

During World War II, 1st Combat Engineers participated in combat during the Battle of Guadalcanal, Eastern New Guinea, the Battle of New Britain, the Battle of Peleliu, and the Battle of Okinawa. After the war, the Battalion was assigned to Tientsin, China in September 1945, where it served as a peacekeeping force prior to its return to Camp Pendleton, California in June 1947.

In August 1950, the Battalion deployed to Kobe, Japan, where it joined the 1st Provisional Marine Brigade prior to joining the 1st Marine Division in Inchon, Korea in September 1950. During the Korean War they participated in the following battles: Battle of Pusan Perimeter, Battle of Inchon-Seoul, Battle of Chosin Reservoir, East-Central Front, and Western Front.

Following the Korean War, the Battalion remained in defense of the Korean Demilitarized Zone from August 1953-April 1955, when it returned to Camp Pendleton in April 1955. On May 1, 1957 it was redesignated as the 1st Pioneer Battalion.

On May 1, 1963, the Battalion was again redesignated the 1st Engineer Battalion and shipped with the 7th Marine Regimentto Camp Hensen, Okinawa on May 23, 1965. From Okinawa it deployed to Qui-Nhon, South Vietnam on July 6-7, 1965, then to Chu Lai, Republic of Vietnam on November 10, 1965.

During the Vietnam War the 1st Engineer Battalion supported the 1st, 2nd, and 3rd Battalions of the 1st, 5th, and 7th Marines in combat operations from July 1965-April 1971, operating from Qui-Nhon, Chu-Lai, and Da-Nang.

Two decades later, the Battalion participated in Operations Desert Shield and Desert Storm in Southwest Asia, from August 1990-March 1991. From December 1992-February 1993 the Battalion was assigned to Operation Restore Hope in Somalia, and elements of the Battalion helped in fire-fighting efforts in the western United States during August/September 1994.

The 1st Combat Engineer Battalion has participated in Operation Iraqi Freedom since March 2003, and Battalion HQ and three engineer companies deployed to Afghanistan in 2009 as part of NATO efforts in the Helmand Province, and to Musa Qal'eh in 2010, 2011 and 2013.

1st Combat Engineer Battalion has received the following Unit Awards:

Presidential Unit Citation one Silver and two Bronze Stars
Joint Meritorious Unit Award
Navy Unit Commendation with one Bronze Star
Meritorious Unit Commendation with one Bronze Stars
American Defense Service Medal
Asiatic-Pacific Campaign Medal with four Bronze Stars
World War II Victory Medal
Navy Occupation Service Medal with Asia clasp
National Defense Service Medal with two Bronze Stars
China Service Medal
Korean Service Medal with two Bronze Stars
Armed Forces Expeditionary Medal
Vietnam Service Medal with two Bronze Stars
Southwest Asia Service Medal with two Bronze Stars
Korean Presidential unit Citation
Vietnam Cross of Gallantry with Palm Streamer
Vietnam Meritorious Unit Citation Civil Action Medal
Iraq Campaign Medal
Global War on Terrorism Expeditionary Medal
Global War on Terrorism Service Medal

## 3D ASSAULT AMPHIBIAN BATTALION
### *"3rd Tracks"*

*Mission: To land the surface assault element of the landing force and their equipment in a single lift from assault shipping during amphibious operations to inland objectives; to conduct mechanized operations and related combat support in subsequent operations ashore.*

3D Assault Amphibian Battalion was originally activated 16 September 1942 at San Diego, California, as 3D Amphibian Tractor (Amtrac) Battalion and assigned to the 3d Marine Division. During December 1942, the battalion relocated from San Diego a short distance up the coast to Camp Pendleton. After training for a few months, the battalion then deployed in February-March 1943 to Auckland, New Zealand in preparation for combat in the Pacific theater.

During World War II, the battalion was primarily armed with Landing Vehicle Tracked (LVT), specifically the LVT-2 also known as "WATER BUFFALOS." The battalion fought in the following combat actions:

- Bougainville with 124 LVT-1s
- Guam with 193 LVT-2s and LVT-4s
- Iwo Jima with 90 LVT-2s

For its actions in World War II, 3d Amphibian Tractor Battalion was awarded the Presidential Unit Citation Streamer, Asiatic-Pacific Campaign Medal Streamer With Four Bronze Stars, and the World War II Victory Medal Streamer.

At the conclusion of World War II, the battalion redeployed in March 1945 to Maui, territory of Hawaii and then relocated during February 1946 back to Camp Pendleton, California. It was deactiviated several months later on 1 May 1946.

On 1 April 1952 at Camp Pendleton, California, 3d Amphibian Tractor Battalion was reactivated and assigned to Fleet Marine Force Pacific. It was subsequently reassigned during October 1955 to the 1st Marine Division Elements, where it participated in the Cuban Missile Crisis October-December 1962. During this period, the battalion was still armed with LVTs — transitioning primarily to the LVT-5 in the late 1950s.

3d Amphibian Tractor Battalion deployed during February 1966 to Camp Schwab, Okinawa and redeployed again in March 1966 to the Republic of Vietnam. There, the battalion fought in the Vietnam War from March 1966 - January 1970. During this conflict, the battalion distinguished itself at Chu Lai, Da Nang, An Hoa, and Hoi An. Throughout Vietnam, the battalion was armed with variants of the LVT-5.

For its actions in Vietnam, 3d Amtrac Battalion was awarded the Presidential Unit Citation Streamer, Navy Meritorious Unit Commendation Streamer, National Defense Service Medal Streamer, Vietnam Service Medal Streamer With Two Silver Stars, Vietnam Gallantry Cross with Palm Streamer, and the Vietnam Civil Actions Medal Unit Citation Streamer.

The battalion relocated during February 1970 to Camp Pendleton, California, and was reassigned to the 5th Marine Expeditionary Brigade. It was again reassigned in August 1970 to the 5th Marine Amphibious Brigade. Subsequently, in April 1971, the battalion was reassigned to the 1st Marine Division with whom it remains to this day. In the early 1970s the battalion transitioned from the LVT-5 to its replacement the LVT-7.

On 30 December 1976, the battalion was re-designated from 3d Amphibian Tractor Battalion to 3d Assault Amphibian Battalion (written as 3d AABn). The battalion participated in numerous training exercises throughout the remainder of the 1970s.

Throughout the 1980s, 3D Assault Amphibian Battalion deployed companies on its regular schedule of six-month deployments to the forward units in Hawaii and Okinawa, including units aboard amphibious troop ships for fast-reaction forces in the Pacific and Indian Oceans and into the Persian Gulf. It shared personnel and vehicles with the 1st Armored Assault Battalion as part of the Unit Deployment Program.

In the early 1980s the battalion's LVT-7s underwent a Service Life Extension Program (SLEP), which converted the LVT-7 vehicles to the improved Amphibious Assault Vehicle-7A1 (AAV-7A1) by adding an upgraded engine, transmission, and weapons system improving the overall maintainability of the vehicle.

Realizing the need to mechanize units participating in the Combined Arms Exercises (CAX), two platoons of AAVs were transferred to the Marine Corps Air Ground Combat Center Twentynine Palms (MCAGCC) in July of 1979. The two platoons were formed from Camp Pendleton — one went to Company A, 3D Tank Battalion, and the other platoon went to Company B, 3D Tank Battalion. The two platoons later merged and became Company D, 3D Tank Battalion, in September 1980. Two additional platoons from 3D Assault Amphibian Battalion in Hawaii arrived onboard the Marine Corps Air Ground Combat Center in December 1981. A redesignation ceremony was held on 18 January 1982 in which the colors of Company D, 3D Tank Battalion were formally retired and replaced with the new colors of Company D (Rein), 3D Assault Amphibian Battalion. The company was instrumental in training Marines in desert warfare as they rotated in and out of the live-fire desert training area, a key to the Marine Corp's success in the 1991 Gulf War.

For its superior performance from 1983 - 1985, the battalion was awarded a Navy Meritorious Unit Commendation.

In August 1990, 3D Assault Amphibian Battalion received orders to prepare for an overseas deployment to Southwest Asia as a response to the Iraqi invasion of Kuwait. In the following month the unit deployed to Saudi Arabia and received shipments of its Amphibious Assault Vehicles from Maritime Prepositioning ships to augment its current vehicle ranks.

During this time, the battalion began upgrading its P-7A1s to carry the UGWS (UpGunned Weapons Station), which mounts a .50 cal (12.7mm) M2HB machine gun and a Mk-19 40mm grenade launcher.

In preparation for the assault into Kuwait, the battalion divided into two main mechanized infantry task forces, along with 1st and 3D Tank Battalions, to form Task Force Ripper and Task Force Papa Bear respectively. The units trained and patrolled the Saudi frontier with Kuwait until the start of the ground war in February 1991. After five days of combat, the two task forces, along with other other Marine task forces, British and Pan-Arab units, captured Kuwait International Airport and a cease-fire was announced. During the march to Kuwait City, the mechanized infantry task forces were responsible for the defeat of numerous Iraqi regiments, the capture of tens of thousands of Iraqi prisoners, and the capture or destruction of thousands of enemy armored vehicles. 3D Assault Amphibian Battalion returned to Camp Pendleton in March 1991.

For its actions during the Gulf War, the Battalion was awarded a Navy Unit Commendation Streamer, National Defense Service Medal Streamer, and the Southwest Asia Service Medal Streamer With Two Bronze Stars.

On 9 December 1992, in support of Operation Restore Hope, elements of 3D Assault Amphibian Battalion attached to the 15th Marine Expeditionary Unit landed on the beach just outside the Mogadishu International Airport in Somalia. These initial forces were soon followed by Bravo, Delta, and Headquarters and Service Companies of 3D Assault Amphibian Battalion. These units' operations stretched from Mogadishu to Bardera, Baidoa, and Kismayo. The battalion served as a blocking force for the International Airport's reception of airlifted humanitarian supplies, then extended its services as road guards for supply convoys and foot patrols in and around Mogadishu.

Elements of 3D Assault Amphibian Battalion served in Somalia or off the coast aboard MEUs from 1992 until approximately 1995. For its actions during Operation Restore Hope, the battalion was awarded the Joint Meritorious Unit Award Streamer and the Armed Forces Expeditionary Medal Streamer.

In 2003, 3D Assault Amphibian Battalion participated in Operation Iraqi Freedom as part of the 1st Marine Division. They first deployed in February of 2003 to Kuwait and crossed the border into Iraq in March, attacking all the way to Baghdad. The battalion served as the primary mechanized assault support for the infantry and proved to be an invaluable asset in crossing the vast distances and urban areas of Iraq. The battalion continues to support operations throughout the world.

The battalion's actions in support of the Global War on Terror have earned it a Presidential Unit Citation Streamer, Navy Meritorious Unit Commendation Streamer, National Defense Service Medal Streamer, Global War on Terrorism Expeditionary Medal Streamer, and the Global War on Terrorism Service Medal Streamer.

*Source: The official 1st Marine Division website*

*Bootcamp, 1137th Platoon, USMC, San Diego, 1943. Courtesy of Anthony J. Procassini*

*Honor Platoon 270, Marine Corps Recruit Depot, San Diego, California, 1955. Courtesy of Delbert Greer*

# MEDAL OF HONOR AWARDS

The Congressional Medal of Honor is our Nation's highest medal for valor. It is a symbol of courage and sacrifice, commitment and integrity, citizenship and patriotism awarded for conspicuous gallantry and intrepidity at the risk of life above and beyond the call of duty.

The following Marines were awarded the Medal of Honor while serving their country while attached to the 1st Marine Division since World War II. The listing presents their name, rank, and home town.

### *World War II*

Maj Kenneth D. Bailey (1st Raider Bn, Guadalcanal) Pawnee, OK [1]
Sgt John Basilone (7th Mar, Guadalcanal) Buffalo, NY [3]
HA1/C Robert E. Bush, USN (5th Mar, Okinawa) Tacoma, WA [3]
Cpl Lewis K. Bausell (5th Mar, Peleliu) Pulaski, VA [1]
Cpl Anthony Casamento (5th Mar, Guadalcanal) Brooklyn, NY [3]
Col Merritt A. Edson (1st Raider Bn, Guadalcanal) Rutland, VT [3]
Cpl John P. Fardy (1st Mar, Okinawa) Chicago, IL [1]
PFC William A. Foster (1st Mar, Okinawa) Cleveland, OH [1]
PhM2 William D. Halyburton, Jr. USN (5th Mar, Okinawa) Canton, NC [1]
Pvt Dale M. Hanson (1st Mar, Okinawa) Wisner, NE [1]
Cpl Louis J. Hauge, Jr. (1st Mar, Okinawa) Ada, MN [1]
PFC Arthur J. Jackson (7th Mar, Peleliu) Cleveland, OH [3]
Sgt Elbert L. Kinser (1st Mar, Okinawa) Greeneville, TN [1]
PFG Richard E. Kraus (Amtrac, Peleliu) Chicago, IL [1,2]
PFC John D. New (7th Mar, Peleliu) Mobile, AL [1]
PltSgt Mitchell Paige (7th Mar, Guadalcanal) Charleroi, PA [3]
Pvt Wesley Phelps (7th Mar, Peleliu) Neafus, KY [1]
Capt Everett P. Pope (1st Mar, Peleliu) Milton, MA [3]
PFC Charles H. Roan (7th Mar, Peleliu) Claude, TX [1]
2dLt Carlton R. Rouh (5th Mar, Peleliu) Lindenwold, NJ [3]
PFC Albert E. Schwab (5th Mar, Okinawa) Washington, DC [1]
MajGen Alexander A. Vandegrift (Guadalcanal) Charlottesville, VA [3]

### *Korean War*

Cpl Charles G. Abrell (1st Mar) Terre Haute, IN [1]
Capt William E. Barber (7th Mar) DeHart, KY
PFC William B. Baugh (1st Mar) McKinney, KY [1]
HC3 Edward C. Benford, USN, Staten Island, NY [1]
Pvt Hector A. Cafferata, Jr. (7th Mar) New York, NY [3]
Cpl David B. Champagne (7th Mar) Wakefield, RI [1]
HC3 William R. Charette, USN, Ludington, MI [3]
PFC Stanley R. Christianson (1st Mar) Mindoro, WI [1]
lstLt Henry A. Commiskey, Sr. (1st Mar) Hattiesburg, MS [3]
Cpl Jack A. Davenport (5th Mar) Kansas City, MO [1]
LtCol Raymond G. Davis (7th Mar) Fitzgerald, GA [3]
HN Richard D. Dewert, USN, Taunton, MA [1]
Cpl Duane E. Dewey (5th Mar) Grand Rapids, MI
PFC Fernando Louis Garcia (5th Mar) Utuado, PR [1]
PFC Edward Gomez (1st Mar) Omaha, NE [1]
SSgt Ambrosio Guillen (7th Mar) LaJunta, CO [1]
HN Francis C. Hammond, USN, Alexandria, VA [1]
Sgt James E. Johnson (7th Mar) Pocatello, ID [1]
PFC John D. Kelly (7th Mar) Youngstown, OH [1]
PFC Jack W. Kelso (7th Mar) Madera, CA [1]
SSgt Robert S. Kennemore (7th Mar) Greenville, SC [3]
HN John E. Kilmer, USN, Highland Park, IL [1]
PFC Herbert A. Littleton (7th Mar) Mena, AR [1]
lstLt Baldomero Lopez (5th Mar) Tampa, FL [1]
Sgt Daniel P. Matthews (7th Mar) Van Nuys, CA [1]
Sgt Frederick W. Mausert III (7th Mar) Cambridge, NY [1]
PFC Alford L. McLaughlin (5th Mar) Leeds, AL [3]
lstLt Frank N. Mitchell (7th Mar) Indian Gap, TX [1]
PFC Walter C. Monegan, Jr. (1st Mar) Melrose, MA [1]
PFC Whitt L. Moreland (5th Mar) Waco, TX [1]
2dLt Raymond G. Murphy (5th Mar) Pueblo, CO [3]
Maj Reginald R. Myers (1st Mar) Boise, ID [3]
PFC Eugene A. Obregon (5th Mar) Los Angeles, CA [1]
2dLt George H. O'Brien (7th Mar) Fort Worth, TX [3]
Cpl Lee H. Phillips (7th Mar) Stockbridge, GA [3]
Sgt James 1. Poynter (7th Mar) Bloomington, IL [1]
lstLt George H. Ramer (7th Mar) Meyersdale, PA [1]
2dLt Robert D. Reem (7th Mar) Lancaster, PA [1]
SSgt William E. Shuck, Jr. (7th Mar) Cumberland, MD [1]
PFC Robert E. Simanek (5th Mar) Detroit, MI
Capt Carl L. Sitter (1st Mar) Syracuse, MO [3]
2dLt Sherrod E. Skinner (11th Mar) Hartford, CT [1]
SSgt Archie Van Winkle (7th Mar) Juneau, AK [3]
Cpl Joseph Vittari (1st Mar) Beverly, MA [1]
SSgt Lewis G. Watkins (7th Mar) Seneca, SC [1]

TSgt Harold E. Wilson (1st Mar) Birmingham, AL [3]
SSgt William G. Windrich (5th Mar) Chicago, IL [1]

### *Vietnam War*

PFC Oscar P. Austin (7th Mar) Nacogdoches, TX [1]
1stLt Harvey C. Barnum (H-2-9 Att: 7th Mar) Cheshire, CT
PFC David D. Bruce (5th Mar) Michigan City, IN [1]
PFC Robert C. Burke (27th Mar) Monticello, IL [1]
SgtMaj John L. Canley (A-1 1st Mar) Oxnard, CA
Lt Vincent R. Capodanno, ChC USN (5th Mar) Staten Island, NY [1]
HM3 Wayne R. Caron (7th Mar) Middleboro, MA [1]
SSgt Peter S. Connor (3rd Mar) Orange, NJ [1]
Sgt Rodney M. Davis (5th Mar) Macon, GA [1]
LCpl Emilio A. De La Garza, Jr. (1st Mar) East Chicago, IN [1]
PFC Ralph E. Dias (7th Mar) Shelocta, Indiana County, PA [1]
Sgt Alfredo Gonzales (1st Mar) Edinburg, TX [1]
Capt James A. Graham (5th Mar) Wilkinsburg, Allegheny County, PA [1]
SSgt Jimmie E. Howard (1st Recon Bn) Burlington, IA [3]
LCpl James D. Howe (7th Mar) Six Mile, Pickens, SC [1]
HM3 Robert R. Ingram (7th Mar) Coral Gables, FL
LCpl Jose F. Jiminez (7th Mar) Mexico City, MEX [1]
PFC Ralph H. Johnson (1st Recon Bn) Charleston, SC [1]
SSgt Alan J. Kellog, Jr. (5th Mar) Bethel, CT
PFC Gary W. Martini (1st Mar) Lexington, VA [1]
PFC Melvin E. Newlin (5th Mar) Wellsvile, OH [1]
Cpl William T. Perkins, Jr. (1 st Mar) San Francisco, CA [1]
Sgt Lawrence D. Peters (5th Mar) Johnson City, NY [1]
PFC Jimmy W. Phipps (1st Engr Bn) Santa Monica, CA [1]
LCpl Richard A. Pittman (5th Mar) French Camp, San Joaquin, CA [3]
HM3 David R. Ray (11th Mar) McMinnville, TN [1]
Cpl Larry F. Smedley (7th Mar) Front Royal, VA [1]
SSgt Karl G. Taylor Sr. (26th Mar) Laurel, MD [1]
LCpl Lester W. Weber (7th Mar) Aurora, IL [1]

LCpl Roy M. Wheat (7th Mar) Moselle, MS [1]
PFC Dewayne T. Williams (1st Mar) Brown City, MI [1]
LCpl Kenneth L. Worley (7th Mar) Farmington, NM [1]

### *Iraq War*

Cpl Jason Dunham (7th Mar) Scio, NY [1]

[1]Posthumous
[2]Attached
[3]Deceased

# THE LAST OF THE FIRST CLUB

Ralph McGill, editor and publisher of the *Atlanta Constitution* and a WWI Marine, donated a bottle of Joseph Etournaud & Company Extra Grand Fine Champagne, 1st Grand Cru Cognac to be opened by the last survivor among the Marines and sailors who survived in combat with the Division during WWII.

Reports from that time estimated the bottle to be over 100 years old, while in actuality the bottle was probably corked from 1920-25. The bottle was placed in the vault of the 1st National Bank of Atlanta for safekeeping between annual meetings, and wrapped in the August 9, 1942 edition of the *Constitution* that reported the landing on Guadalcanal.

In 1947, the 1st Marine Division Association assumed formal custody of the bottle, although the bottle remained in the same Atlanta bank vault and only appeared at the annual Association reunion. However, in 1965 the bottle was delivered with great fanfare, when Sgt. Bob Bowen, a reporter for *Leatherneck* magazine, was ordered to withdraw the bottle from the Atlanta bank and deliver it to the 1st Marine Division Association annual reunion at the Park Sheraton Hotel in Washington, D.C., then return it safely following the reunion. The bottle was insured for $25,000 against theft, loss or willful destruction, delivered to the airport via a Brinks armored car, with the bottle handcuffed to Bowen's ankle during the flight.

In 1988, the bottle was transferred to the Command Museum at Marine Corps Recruit Depot in San Diego. In 1999 the bottle went back across country with G/Sgt Luis O. Arce, a member of the 1st Marine Division Band, who delivered it to Association headquarters in Northern Virginia. Later, in 2003 when Association HQ transferred to the west coast at Oceanside, California, the bottle went cross-country again.

The bottle remained at the Association offices until 2006, when Col Len Hays, Executive Director, found it while conducting an inventory. Recognizing its historical value, he asked MajGen Mike Myatt, CEO of the Marines Memorial Club in San Francisco, California, if the club could better care for the bottle. Gen. Myatt agreed, and Col Jack Kelly delivered the bottle to the Club, where it now fittingly resides in a secure display case attached to a wall in the Leatherneck Steakhouse.

As of 2012, an estimated 1,000 WWII Marine veterans were still alive to lay claim to the honor of opening the bottle.

### *The Charter and Bylaws for "The Last of the First Club"*

Excerpts from *The Old Breed News*, November-December 2006

This club was organized on 7 August 1944 in the City of Atlanta, Georgia.

The purpose of this club is to commemorate the First Marine Division (Reinforced), which performed the first successful American amphibious landing against an organized enemy in World War II, and to do such acts of charity and benefit to the members, widows and dependents of members of the First Marine Division (Reinforced), Fleet Marine Force, U.S. Marine Corps, as shall be decided by the majority vote of members in attendance of the annual meeting.

### *ByLaws*

I: The organization shall consist only of Marines and Navy members of the First Marine Division (Reinforced), Fleet Marine Force, United States Marine Corps, who have actually participated in active combat during World War II and who are on active duty or who left the service under honorable conditions. Rosters to be attached to this Charter as announced by Headquarters, U.S. Marine Corps. The insignia shall be the First Marine Division battle blaze.

II. The organization will hold an annual meeting on 7 August at which time a president and one other member shall be elected as organization officers. Other officers may be from time to time elected by a two-thirds majority of delegates in attendance to satisfy the needs of the organization. There shall be one National Organization with a president, vice-president and others as voted. Other chapters may be formed on application and approval of the National Organization. Local officers shall be elected by majority vote of each chapter. The local chapters shall send one office delegate to the annual meeting of the National organization and he shall represent his chapter on all business. Each local chapter shall have one vote on all organization business. The president of the National Organization shall cast a vote only in case of a tie. Charters will be granted at each annual meeting.

III. The President shall be custodian of the Cognac bottle to be given to the last man living from this organization, this bottle to be displayed at each annual meeting. There shall be but one bottle of Cognac, which the one put in trust on 7 August 1944, in the First National Bank, Atlanta, Georgia. The custody of trust for said bottle shall be for the duration of the national emergency with the Officer in Charge of the Southern Procurement Division, Atlanta, Georgia, at which time the key and deposit receipt will be turned over to the president in office.

IV. Lieutenant General A.A. Vandegrift is hereby elected a charter member of this organization.

*Gus Bruggemann delivers "Last of the First" bottle of cognac to Mgen Whaling, 1965. 1MDA photo*

*From left Jon Paulson, Chairman of the Board, Marines Memorial Association; Don Tenennbaum, Chosin Few member; Maj Gen Mike Myatt, President and CEO, MMC; Bill Boldenweck, Chosin Few member; Bob Easton, VP, Chosin Few Golden Gate Chapter; John Stevens, Chosin Few member.*

*The bottle is in good hands, safely ensconced at the Marines' Memorial Association Headquarters in San Francisco, CA.*

*Sgt Robert Bowen, a staff writer for Leatherneck magazine, escorts the official bottle of Cognac on its way to a bank vault at First and Citizens National Bank of Alexandria, Virginia, not far from the Association's executive offices in 1965. The bottle was insured for $25,000 against theft, willfull destruction or loss. 1MDA photo*

*Marines walking down a jungle trail not knowing what's around the bend, South Vietnam. At the back of the line is the Corpsman for the 1st Shore Battalion. Courtesy of Robert Jeffory Roberts.*

# Stories, Reflections & Memories

# STORIES, REFLECTIONS & MEMORIES

## TRAGEDY AT PELELIU

*By Leopold "Leo" Griego*

The unit departed Guadalcanal on Sept. 4, 1944 to fight the battle of all battles.

Peleliu was one of America's costliest victories in WWII. Fought on a tiny coral island 500 miles east of the Philippines, the assault landing at Peleliu took place on Sept. 15th. A quick two-day crush to victory was anticipated. Instead, American Forces struggled desperately for over two months against 10,900 deeply entrenched Japanese soldiers who had spent six months preparing for the battle. By the time the weary Americans could claim victory, the fight had become one of the war's most costly successes. The 1st Marine Division suffered 6,526 casualties, 1,252 killed and 5,274 wounded. The US Forces suffered one casualty for every Japanese soldier killed—10,900 Japanese were killed.

## SEARCHING FOR THE 1ST MARINE DIVISION IN NORTH CHINA

*By Fred Greguras*

Following World War II, the 1st Marine Division ("**Division**") was part of the III Marine Amphibious Corps ("**III MAC**") that landed in North China for the primary purpose of disarming and repatriating Japanese military and civilian personnel. The Division headquarters was in Tientsin. The Division's regiments were deployed as follows: 1st Marines initially in Tientsin, the 5th Marines were primarily in Peiping and the 7th Marines were assigned to security for coal mines and coal shipments on the Peking-Mukden railroad line. The 11th Marines (artillery) was deployed at several locations in support of the infantry regiments. The 1st and 11th Marine regiments had the responsibility for disarming and repatriating Japanese military and civilian personnel in Tientsin. The 1st Marine regiment was also responsible for the security of the city.

I visited Beijing (Peiping) and Tianjin (Tientsin) in October 2016 to look for places related to the Division's history. I looked for buildings and places that had been used by the Marines as well as places that were part of the Marines landscape. I used old maps and photographs to help me in my search.

Both of the headquarters buildings for the Division have survived in Tientsin. The first headquarters was at the former Italian Consulate and the second headquarters was the former French Municipal Council building, which had been III MAC headquarters before its deactivation in June 1946. The Japanese surrendered to Major General Keller Rockey on Oct. 6, 1945 in a ceremony on the south side of the municipal council building. The 1st Marines were headquartered at the former British Barracks in Tientsin, the 5th Marines at the former German Legation in the former Legation Quarter in Peiping and the 11th Marines at the former French Arsenal in Tientsin. All of these headquarters buildings of the Division's regiments are gone.

### *Tientsin*

My thanks to local historians, Louie Liu and Andrea Klopper, who helped guide me while I was in Tientsin. I stayed at the historic Astor Hotel on Victoria Road (now Jiefang Road) across from Victoria Park and the site of Gordon Hall, the British Municipal Council Building. In 1945, this hotel was the headquarters for the Marines advance party commanded by General William A. Worton, which entered North China 16 days after the Japanese surrender on the Battleship *Missouri* in Tokyo Bay. The story of this advance party is told in the book by William Hook, *Liberating North China-1945*, 2014.

Gordon Hall and Victoria Park were landmarks for Marines in Tientsin in 1945. A Ritz Carlton hotel is now on the site of Gordon Hall, which was mostly destroyed by the 1976 earthquake. Only a small part of Gordon Hall has survived on the west side of Jiefang Road. I visited several other places in the vicinity including the former All Saints Church, where Marines attended services, and the Victoria Apartments across from Victoria Park to the west, which served as an officer's quarters.

Division billets were spread across the city. The former Italian concession was on the north side of the International Bridge where the initial Division headquarters and Headquarters Battalion billets were located. There were billets on the east side of the Haihe River including those for the 11th Marines at the French Arsenal and the 7th Service Regiment. Many billets were on or near the primary north-south road through the city, now Jiefang Road, which in 1945 had different names as it crossed the former concession areas, from south to north, Woodrow Wilson Street, Victoria Road and Rue de France. There were also a number of billets on or near Race Course Road (now Machang Road) just to the west of Jiefang Road. At the south end of Race Course Road was the former racetrack, which was used by the 1st Tank Battalion for a tank park, the 1st Motor Transportation Battalion and as a landing field for small aircraft. The Division field hospital and other billets were in the former Japanese Concession in the west part of the city.

There were two popular American Red Cross Clubs along Jiefang Road in 1945. The Liberty Lounge was located in the former French Club on the east side of Rue de France, the extension of Victoria Road north through the French Concession, and the Amerine Club was located in the former German Club (Club Concordia) on Woodrow Wilson Street. Both of these buildings have survived and are protected as heritage buildings, although the former German Club was damaged in the 1976 earthquake. The Nov. 19, 1945 *Time Magazine*, page 26, reported that the Red Cross "took over the sturdily built German Club and made it into the "finest servicemen's club west of San Francisco." The former French Club is now the Museum of

Finance and the former German Club is a high end restaurant. I was able to tour both buildings. The former German Club has a museum room with a display case dedicated to its time as the Amerine Club. There also were many EM clubs in the city. Some were organized at the Battalion level such as the Headquarters Battalion Club, in the former Italian concession, but several were at the regimental level including the 1st Marines Club along Race Course Road and the 11th Marines Club at the former French Arsenal.

I walked north up Jiefang Road from the Astor Hotel to the former Italian concession. The road still has the look and feel of 1945. There are many buildings along the way that are city heritage sites, which Marines would recognize including the Talati Hotel building, Leopold Building, former French Municipal Council building where the Japanese surrendered, Jardine Matheson building, former French Club and the Imperial Hotel. The distinctive Leopold Building was built in the late 1930s and was the first high rise building in the city. Division Special Services leased the Imperial Hotel as a hostel. Several Marines I've talked to recalled the French Bazaar located west of Jiefang Road. You could purchase about anything there in those days including U.S. military gear. The present name is Quanye Bazaar. The building has been enlarged but retains its 1945 period architectural features.

The former Italian concession contains many buildings connected to the Division's history including the Ermanno Carlotto Barracks on present day Guangming Road, which was the Headquarters Battalion billet, the former consulate which served as the Division's first headquarters building, the Headquarters Battalion EM Club building, the officer's quarters at the Florentine Apartments and the jai alar club building. The EM Club was at the northeast corner of Via Trento and Roma (now Minsheng and Ziyou Roads) and the Florentine Apartments used by Division staff officers was just west across Minsheng from the club. Marine Jay Ruoff indicated that the jai-alai club in the Italian Concession was one of the places where his 1st Separate Engineer basketball team played in the III MAC league in the winter of 1945-46. He called the jai-alar club the "show place" of the venues. The Marines had obtained the club from the Chinese government and converted the inside courts into a basketball court. Going back to the Astor Hotel, I walked south on the new river walkway along the bund from the International Bridge to the hotel. The walkway is a tourist's delight providing great views east across the river as well as of the historic buildings on the former French and British bunds.

There are still three original buildings remaining in the former US Barracks compound on Guangdong Road just south of Machang Road (Race Course Road). This was the Army's 15th Infantry barracks from 1917-1938 and the Marine Barracks from 1938-1941. Post WW II, it was used as a billet for the Division Headquarters Battalion and also for the 1st Signal Battalion. The Tianjin Medical University is currently using the historic buildings and has built a number of new buildings in the compound. Newspapers report that the American flag was raised at the barracks in a ceremony presided over by General Rockey on Oct. 16, 1945. I went into the old recreation hall at the southwest corner where the Marines basketball league played in 1945-46. Basketball is still being played there. The Tientsin Grammar School building just north of the barracks was also a Division billet. The area just west of the barracks along the south side of Race Course Road was known as "Can Do Field," a large recreation area and parade ground. There are many photos of ball games, inspections, parades and other events showing the villas and other residences on the north side of Race Course Road. Today, there is a school building and smaller athletic field on the site of the Can Do Field but the villas and residences that were part of the Marines landscape are still there along Machang Road.

The only building I could find in the race course area that dates back to 1945 was the former country club building. The stables, grandstand and other buildings used as the 1st Motor Transport Battalion billet are gone. The 1st Tank Battalion also had its tank park at the race course. There were a number of houses just north of the race track that were used primarily as senior officer quarters in 1945 but they appear to be gone. The former country club building west of the site of the race course grandstand was a senior officers club. The building, which was damaged in the 1976 earthquake, has been refurbished and is being preserved as a heritage site. It is currently being used as a private club.

I walked west along Nanjing road to search for Division billets in the former Japanese Concession. The former Japanese barracks and Japanese military hospital are gone. The hospital served as the Division Field Hospital operated by the 1st Medical Battalion. It was just south and east across the road from the barracks compound. Both were along present day Nanjing Road near the Anshan Road intersection. Anshan Road has many buildings remaining from the 1945 era. The distinctive Japanese Pavilion at its northeast corner with Nanjing was used by the 1st Medical Battalion as a billet. The building is being preserved as a heritage building. The former Japanese school buildings (high school and primary school) fronting on Anshan and Gansu Roads were used as billets for the 1st Separate Engineer Battalion, the 1st Tank Battalion, units of the 7th Service Regiment and others. According to Marine Fred Bridges, his unit, the 1st Separate Engineer Battalion was billeted in the high school and there was an adjacent Japanese primary school used for other billets. I walked around the entire block and it appears the two school campuses have been consolidated into a single campus. Fred sent me a photograph of a building across the street from his billet which served coffee and had a phone the Marines could use. The building is still there at the southwest corner of Anshan and Gansu. There are also several other buildings along Anshan in the vicinity of the schools that were a NCO Club and quarters for the 1st Medical Battalion and other units.

### *Peiping*

The 5th Marines (less 1/5 and reinforced by 2/11) was the primary Marine unit in Peiping. The regiment was billeted in and around the former Legation Quarter ("Quarter"). The 1st battalion of the 5th Marines garrisoned the Taku-Tangku port area east of Tientsin and the other battalions of the 11th Marines were in Tientsin. The Taku-Tangku port was the main entry port for North China. Rifle companies from 2/5 and 3/5 had security duty at each of Peiping's two airfields. The companies rotated between the Quarter and the airfields.

The geographical setting of the Division in Peiping was centered around two streets running east-west, Chang'an Avenue and Legation Street (now Dongjiaomin Alley) and two north-south streets, Morrison Street (now Wangfujing north of Chang'an) and Hatamen Street (Dongdan north of Chang'an and Chongwenmen Inner Street south of Chang'an). Morrison was two blocks west of Hatamen Street. Chang'an was the north boundary of the Quarter and Legation Street runs through the south side of the Quarter. Morrison Street was almost at the west edge of the Quarter and Hatamen Street was the east edge of the Quarter. The landmark Qianmen Gate ("**Qianmen**") at the south side of Tiananmen Square was the west boundary of the Quarter. In 1945, these were narrow streets with hotels, clubs, bars, restaurants and specialty shops which catered to the Marines and other foreigners. Today, the width of Hatamen is about half a football held at the Chang'an intersection. It narrows as you move north or south but remains much wider in both directions than the street was in 1945. Morrison Street is also much wider and is a modern entertainment and shopping street that becomes a pedestrian mall just north of Chang'an.

I walked up and down both Hatamen and Morrison Streets looking for buildings that were part of the Marines landscape in 1945. At first glance, because of the street widening and modernization, it seemed unlikely I would find anything. I was pleasantly surprised as I walked north on Morrison to find old Chinese buildings on side streets on the east side of Morrison. The St Joseph's Church building on Morrison has survived and is currently known as the Wangfujing Cathedral. I also found 1945 era buildings on the side streets east of Hatamen just north and south of Chang'an.

The former Italian Legation on Rue Marco Polo in the Quarter housed the popular American Red Cross Embassy Club and the Immaculate Conception Catholic Church. This legation was also the billet for companies of the 1st Engineer Battalion and 1st Tank Battalion. The entrance into the legation is still there and there is a historical marker identifying the historical buildings but no access is allowed so I couldn't confirm if the buildings have survived.

The Marines of 2/5 and 3/5 were billeted in the former Marine Barracks and former legation compounds in the Quarter. The Marine Barracks ("**Barracks**") was the home of the Legation Guard before WW II with the mission of protecting the US Legation. The Barracks was a large compound on Legation Street at the southwest corner of the Quarter. It had a hospital, quarters, post exchange, swimming pool, tennis courts and other support facilities. The Marines had a sports field and parade ground on the American glacis in the shadow of Qianmen just west of the barracks. There was a baseball backstop near Qianmen. The glacis was part of the redesign of the Quarter after the 1900 Boxer Rebellion to provide a clear field of fire for defending the quarter. The 1903 era US Legation buildings are still there being used as high end restaurants but the Barracks is gone. The Barracks and American glacis were destroyed as Tiananmen Square expanded.

The larger parade ground used by the Marines and other forces both before and after WW II was the glacis on the east side of the Quarter bordered between foreign legation buildings and Hatamen Street. There was a polo field on this glacis. In his book *China Marine* at page 32, Marine Eugene Sledge mentions there was a parade on the Hatamen glacis on Oct. 19, 1945 and that it was the first Marine parade in Peiping since 1941. The parade included tanks, artillery and other vehicles. After the PLA captured South Air Field in 1949, this glacis was used as a landing held by the nationalists during the PLA siege before the city was captured. The Marine parade grounds and sports fields are gone. The east glacis is covered by buildings except for a small park—Dongdan Park—which is on the site of the polo field. There is also a small recreation area on the east glacis site at the southwest corner of Chang'an and Hatamen.

The Austrian Legation, Belgium Legation and north part of the British Legation used by the 5th Marines are still there. The gates into the French, Japanese and Netherlands Legations also used by the 5th Marines are still there but the 1945 era buildings are gone. The gate into the former British Legation may be the only surviving structure of the 1900 Boxer Rebellion fighting. The former Netherlands Legation was next door to the east from the US Legation and also housed sick bay and the recreation and special services offices. The former Belgium, French, German and Netherlands legations were all along Legation Street.

B Company of the 1st Medical Battalion was billeted at Oliver Jones Hall, a former women's dormitory, at the Peking Union Medical College ("**PUMC**") just north of Chang'an and west of Hatamen. The PUMC still exists as part of Tsinghua University and there are old buildings from the PUMC still remaining. They are just behind (north) of the Grand Hyatt Hotel. The building used for the Marine billet (Oliver Jones Hall) is gone. PUMC was also used by General Marshall beginning in January 1946 for a headquarters and base of operations for his Executive Headquarters for the mission to try to mediate a cease fire between the nationalists and communists. This mission failed and Marshall returned to the US in early 1947.

The Grand Peking Hotel was Hostel No 2 on Chang'an Avenue just west of the present day Grand Hyatt Hotel. The hotel is now known as the Grand Hotel Beijing and has been expanded but the old part, which was used in 1945 still stands. The Crystal Room at this hotel was a favorite liberty destination for the Marines. This hotel housed the representatives of the nationalists, communists and US Army and Marine officers that were part of the Marshall mission mentioned above according to Carrington, *Adventures and Misadventures; The Life and Some of the Times of George W. Carrington, USMC*, 2005, page 73. The nationalist delegation stayed on the first floor, the communists on the second floor and the US delegation stayed on the third floor.

Marines would have walked by several other surviving buildings on a regular basis. St. Michaels Catholic Church continues to be a prominent landmark on Legation Street across from the former Belgium Legation. The distinctive Yokohama Specie Bank building also still stands along Legation Street as does the former French post office. The famous Wagon Lits Hotel, which was across the street from the bank and used as a Marine hostel, no longer stands.

The last units of the Division withdrew from Peiping in June 1947 and from Tientsin in September 1947. It has been over 70 years since the Division landed in North China but its presence can still be seen in both cities.

Semper Fi!

## REFLECTION ON WORLD WAR II

*Corporal Blasco Molle, Headquarters Company*
*2nd Battalion, 7th Regiment, First Marine Division*

I joined the United States Marine Corps on March 3, 1943 and served in the First Division during WW II until Feb. 23, 1946. I greatly valued my time as a Marine; genuine dedication / love of Corps and Country were instilled in each of us as life values, which unfortunately, seem to be lacking in today's U.S. society.

The First Marine Infantry Division was victorious in four major battles between 1942 and 1945—Guadalcanal, Cape Gloucester, Peleliu Island and Okinawa. Each of these victories had significant strategic relevance in winning the Asia-Pacific war against Japan, except for one – the battle of Peleliu.

Initially, the U.S. military believed that the Japanese-held island of Peleliu had significant offensive capability for them to successfully impede General MacArthur's planned campaign to secure the Philippine Islands. However, Admiral Halsey determined, before the US Philippine invasion, that Japan's offensive military strength at Peleliu had significantly diminished and posed no real threat to the planned MacArthur Philippine campaign.

Admiral Halsey reported his findings to Admiral Nimitz, who could have terminated the planned Peleliu invasion. However, he did not.

I fought in the 45-day Peleliu campaign and lived first-hand through the estimated 19,000 casualties and deaths of young Japanese and American soldiers. Each day I fought amidst their bloated, mutilated bodies while inhaling the scent of death and acutely understood that my fate might change at any moment.

To this day, I relive the events of that extended battle over-and-over again in my mind, and I think to myself that the tragic losses of Peleliu were in vain. I wish somehow that history could reverse itself and spare the emotional and physical devastation that occurred for naught.

## THE 32ND ANNUAL JOHN BASILONE PARADE, RARITAN NJ – SEPT. 22, 2013

*Submitted by David West*

During one of my trips with my father driving up Route 206 in Central New Jersey in the mid-1980s, we stopped for a red light at the main intersection in the town of Raritan. We both noticed a small sign indicating that Raritan was the home town of John Basilone, a Marine who had won the Congressional Medal of Honor in WWII. I asked my Dad if he knew of this Marine, not knowing much about Sergeant Basilone at the time, and he acknowledged in his understated way that they had served together in the

*Platoon 136, Marine Barracks, Parris Island, SC, November 1941. Courtesy of David West*

First Marine Division on Guadalcanal and that he was "one tough Marine with a machine gun."

It was also around this time in 1981 that the Town of Raritan started the John Basilone Parade on the third Sunday in September. One distinction of this event is that he is the only enlisted Marine to have an annual parade in his honor, which seems to be in keeping with the fact that he is also the only enlisted Marine to have won the CMOH and The Navy Cross.

As the precursor to these events that you can see in the old newsreels and pictures of the time, was that on Sept. 21, 1943 John's hometown had a "Welcome Home Parade" for him that was attended by over thirty thousand people at the nearby Doris Duke Estate. That was the last time he got to be home while he was back in the States on the War Bonds tour.

Raritan was a very rural farming area when John's family lived there in the 1940s, and today has been blended into the suburban New York metro area, but it still maintains a vibrant "Main Street" with mostly an Italian ethnic identity. Since my son, Brian, lives nearby in Hoboken, I had always wanted to attend this parade with him so that he may better appreciate some of the history of "the greatest generation" that both his grandfathers were fortunate to be a part of.

The parade was held on Sunday, Sept. 22 and it was a perfect sunny crisp day for the expected crowd of several thousand people. Families from many generations and walks of life started lining up along Main Street around 11 AM with their lawn chairs, some residents even had cookouts in their front yards, as the various parade groups assembled at the nearby train station. I had heard that the Raritan Library had a John Basilone Museum room, so my son and I went there before the 1 PM start of the parade. In the room, we found many books, photos and artifacts pertaining to John's life and service. I was shown the "pigtail" stake used to string barbed wire that someone brought back from John's machine gun position on Bloody Ridge.

I had also wanted to see the statue of Sergeant Basilone that was in the park at the other end of Main Street. During our walk down to the park, we passed the reviewing stand where several Marine Officers were mingling with the local citizens. I was aware that General Mark Gurganus was the invited guest speaker, representing the US Marine Corps, and wanted Brian to meet him if possible. We did get the chance and chatted with him for a few moments before continuing on to the statue.

As the parade was about to begin we heard the roar of two vintage WWII Wildcats flying above Main Street to get the crowd's attention to look up as they streamed smoke from their tails. Then came the deafening roar of dozens of "Rolling Thunder" motorcyclists waving flags and banners to kick off the parade. For the next 90 minutes, the crowd of onlookers was treated to a steady march of dignitaries, service organizations, marching bands, military units, and police and fire units.

I had told my son that John Basilone came from a large family, and I was not sure if any of his siblings were still alive. That question was answered when Don Basilone, his younger brother, was introduced and took his place up on the reviewing stand. There were also members of Robert Leckie's family that rode in the parade, as well as several other WWII veterans. As the parade went on and on, I saw my son's eyes get wider and wider as he realized how much the small town of Raritan respects and honors their hometown hero. My wish of keeping history alive had a new convert.

For more information on the life of John Basilone, there are two books that I read this past year. The first is *I'm Staying With My Boys* by Jim Proser with Jerry Cutter (John's nephew). The second, which just came out, is *Voices Of The Pacific* by Adam Makos and Marcus Brotherton, which tells the stories of 15 Marines (still living), several which served with Basilone. One of them was Clinton Watters who was John's, "Best Man" at his wedding and also served one year as Grand Marshall for the Basilone parade. This book gave me many new insights into what my father experienced, but never revealed. Semper Fidelis.

## The Game

*By Dan Silvers*

I was an 18-year-old scout-sniper with Easy Co., 2nd Battalion, 7th Marines alone in the field prior to the Battle for Hill 749. Fog rolled in between the hills separating me from them. The mist made visibility worse. My 3X scope, as worthless as it was to begin with, became sightless. I flipped it off and nervously wiped water droplets off the iron sights with thumb and forefinger. The hilltop directly across was a twin, about the same height with similar vegetation — high underbrush, lots of jutting rocks and scrubby trees. Down below was a little valley. Between us, a small stream flowed out to a larger one. Fortunately for me, there was plenty of cover in case I had to run like hell and get out of there in a hurry. The weather worsened. That was a good omen, meaning more cover.

I was in a prone position behind some jagged rocks. Looking out about 800 yard away was a gaggle of enemy soldiers perched on top. I couldn't really tell how many, but I counted roughly around eight, more or less. Armed with an old WWI Springfield .30 cal. bolt action rifle, I settled into firing position. Adjusting my wet fatigues, I pushed down my torn pants pinching my crotch, and set my steel helmet rim back a notch so I could see my sights better. I waited a few seconds, slowed my breathing, squeezed the trigger and began snipping at them. One shot at a time. No hurry. It took them a few minutes to figure out where I was. Anyway, I wasn't hitting anyone or shooting at anyone in particular, so I don't think they thought I was a big threat…yet. The game was called "pestering". If I was annoying enough, maybe they would abandon what appeared to be a forward patrol outpost. That was my job. Pester the enemy and maybe kill a few. Besides, I wasn't that great of a shot. I was picked because I was "small and fast." No superior physique, fighting skills or marksmanship had anything to do with my selection. I was a PFC. Expendable. So were they.

I kept snipping. They popped their heads up and down like chickens. I popped off a round. They popped down.

No fear of return fire, as I was out of range of their burp guns…the small Chinese-made machine guns called burp guns because when they fired, they made a noise like "buuurrrppp". Soon they had enough. I saw them gathering like bees. Shit! Down the hill they came slowly but surely, intent on getting me. I ducked and ran down the back way and around the corner of the hill about the same time they got to the stream and crossed it. As they moved slowly up, I ran like crazy to the back of their hill, using all available cover. I got to their spot about the same time they got to mine. They looked around. I was gone. Satisfied they chased me away, they relaxed and seemed to be celebrating, at least until I started snipping again.

Now they were REALLY pissed. Clustered like angry bees, down they came. I made sure they saw me duck down like I was going out the back way again. Instead, I waited until they crossed the stream. I watched and figured right. At the base of the hill they split in two groups to head me off at the pass. I waited until they rounded the corners out of sight and ran as fast as I could down the front of the hill, crossed the stream and scampered up to my former position about the same time they reached theirs. They looked around again, trying to figure out where I had gone. Crazy with adrenaline, or testosterone, or plain stupidity, or all three, I slipped a round in the chamber and sent it gleefully off with a haha and a hee hee, a sheer, dumb, instinctive, yet full of apprehension, suicidal act. I couldn't resist!

Now they were beyond pissed. I was done waiting to see what they were going to do next. At that moment an ounce of reason kicked in. Running low on ammo and probably out of luck, too, I split and ran the hell out of there as fast as I could. My heart and head were pounding all the way back to the platoon. I was beyond wet with my own fear-sweat, but then again, I was going to live another day in spite of myself.

## THE WORST DAY/NIGHT OF MY LIFE

*By PFC Gerald J. Williams 1183772*

It all began some time after Jan. 1, 1953. I embarked from San Diego aboard the *USS Nelson M. Walker* with 2,500 Army and 500 Marines aboard. After an uneventful two-week trip, we landed at Inchon, Korea. That is when my ordeal began.

Reveille was at 0300, chow was at 0400. That was the last meal I would have aboard ship. Sailors would later be selling cheese sandwiches for $1.00 each. I, of course, did not bring any money along, thinking what do I need money for in Korea? Boy was I wrong, one of those cheese sandwiches would have tasted pretty good before I debarked the ship many hours later.

They started debarking troops at about 0600, using LCM'S to de-bark the troops. At around 1:00 p.m. they realized this was taking too long, so they brought out a LST and started loading it. I debarked the ship at about 1800. They stacked us in the lower hold standing back to breast. We were dressed in full cold weather clothing, including full field transport pack, helmet and rifle. When the LST was full, they told us to sit down "if you can". The only way to sit was to sit down with our legs spread, then the guy in front would sit between your legs. Now mind you, we were sitting on an ice cold steel deck, in January. When we stood up to get ready to debark the LST, we could hardly stand up. We were totally numb from our butts to our feet; I am guessing it was around 29 degrees. When we debarked the LST, they then gave us a box of C-rations and two rounds of ammunition. I asked the guy handing out the ammo if they were to shoot myself. It was at this time about 16 hours since I had eaten. I do not remember when I ate the C-rations, but they must have tasted pretty good.

We were then put on a train. The car I was in had all the windows broken out, so they would not let us sleep for fear of us freezing. The train trip was very eventful. It would go about a mile forward and a half-mile backward. That, along with kids throwing rocks at the train in the middle of the night, kept us alert. Why weren't these kids home in bed!

After the all-night train ride we arrived at Munsan-ni (the rail head). We were taken off the train and put in trucks to be transported to our outfits. Remember the two rounds of ammo? I was about ready to put one of them to use. (A joke, of course.)

After a short ride in an open truck, only about a mile or two in the freezing cold January early morning, we finally arrived at HQ BN 1st Tank BN. After a quick muster, we were escorted to the mess hall where we were served steak and eggs hot off the grill. The best meal of my life!

After spending 14 months in Korea, 63 years ago, the one thing on my "Bucket List" was to someday return to Korea. This opportunity has come to me via the KWA. On Sept. 19 2016, my wife, my son and I boarded a Korean Airlines Plane to return to South Korea!

## TO THE MARINES AND CORPSMEN OF I CORPS VIETNAM – 1965-1970 THE 50TH ANNIVERSARY: 2015-2020

A thankful and tearful tribute, along with a respectful slow, snappy salute to the living and the dead, Semper Fi – Do or Die – combat Marines and Fleet Corpsmen of I Corps Vietnam.

*Getting some R&R by "Candlelight" in a tent in I Corps. Courtesy of Richard "MoonMan" Mooney*

"The world will little note, nor long remember, your brave and noble selfless courage, nor your selfless warrior service and sacrifice (fraught with armed strife, struggles and suffering), nor your devotion and obligation to your fellow Marines, your Corps and your Country "Lest We Forget", as a Grateful Nation. Semper Fidelis.

*Dedicated by Richard "MoonMan" Mooney, I Corps, '66-67, Ooh-Rah!*

## Crossdraw Laments, "It Was A Crappy War, But It Was The Only One We Had!"

*By Col. P. A Curtis, USMCR (Ret)*

After shipping over from the reserves to active duty in mid-1967, Crossdraw was assigned to Marine Fighter/Attack Squadron, VMFA-323 (The Death Rattlers), who were then stationed at Da Nang in beautiful downtown Vietnam. The

*Echo 2/7 81s on a "Sandbagging" detail. Courtesy of Richard "MoonMan" Mooney*

*Getting some R&R by Red Beach. Courtesy of Richard "MoonMan" Mooney*

*On "Stand Down" in I Corps. Courtesy of Richard "MoonMan" Mooney*

*The "Steel Curtain" 81mm Mortar Crew. Courtesy of Richard "MoonMan" Mooney*

*Getting some R&R by "Sunlight" in a tent in I Corps. Courtesy of Richard "MoonMan" Mooney*

*On "In House" R&R. Courtesy of Richard "MoonMan" Mooney*

*Crossdraw as a ground Forward Air Controller during the Battle of Hue, on a bridge abutment over the Perfume River with mic in hand, calling in an airstrike seemingly about 10 feet from the end of The Kid's nose. Courtesy of P.A. Curtis*

Snakes, flying F-4 Phantoms, then transferred from Da Nang Air Base, and flew out of Marine Corps Air Station, Chu Lai, starting in early '67. The Kid joined the squadron in late August '67 arriving at Tan Son Nhut Airbase, Vietnam, on a Continental Airline 707 flight from San Francisco. He was trucked immediately up Highway One in a convoy of 4x4's. Being a young, (okay, he was 29), tired and stupid replacement pilot, Crossdraw probably thought they couldn't continue the war without him — boy was he wrong. There sat The Kid surrounded by cases of high explosive 20 MM ammo, with the Viet Cong shooting at them! "Welcome to Vietnam."

The Kid's arrival coincided with the closing of the main runway at Chu Li for repairs and lighting, so they took off from the taxiway and recovered on runway 03 which had SATS (Short Airfield for Tactical Support) arresting gear. This was the first extended use of SATS in a combat zone. The SATS concept and tactics were tested for several years, using aluminum panels connected together to form a hard runway surface equipped with a catapult and an arresting gear system. This allowed Marine, fixed-wing aircraft to operate from an airfield much smaller than the typical air base, and allowed them to be quickly positioned much closer to Marines in the fight. This construction took about three weeks or so, but it made a big difference to their night landings, as well as to the wear on the planes. After Commanding Officer, Lt. Col. Miller and his Radar Intercept Officer (RIO) were shot down and became POWs, the squadron was taken over by Lt. Col. Hagman, a GREAT Skipper!

But, things were not always about being the hottest pilot in the sky. As happened to many, Crossdraw was anointed as a short term, rotated-duty, ground Forward Air Controller, (FAC) during the beginning of the Tet offensive. (Not a good idea!) But, having a Marine pilot on the ground, talking to another Marine pilot in the air, calling in 500 pound bombs VERY close to the good guys, IS a good idea, because they spoke the same language and trusted each other. But if they dropped short, it also put The Kid's butt in a sling, big time. He was surrounded and protected by members of the 1st Marine Division, who hopefully appreciated his accurate placement of massive amounts of ordinance.

The Kid is most proud of the work they did in support of the Marines at Khe Sanh and A Shau Valley. His good friend, Senator Max Cleland, a young Army captain at the time, lost both legs and his lower right arm to a grenade at the battle for Khe Sanh, trying to save his men. During their shared speaking engagements, Max often berates The Kid, in jest, for not protecting him from above. Crossdraw always retorts that Max shouldn't pick up grenades, cause they're made to go BOOM! and hurt people. Max went on to become the head of the VA when it still helped our wounded with dignity. Then he was Secretary of State in Georgia, before becoming a United States Senator. Today, he is the secretary of The American Battle Monuments Committee, caring for our war related cemeteries and monuments such as The Punch Bowl in Hawaii, Normandy in France, Flanders Field in Belgium, and over 50 other sites around the world. Over the last decades, The Kid has pushed Max and his chair seemingly thousands of miles all over the world, and enjoyed every minute of doing so. Well, cobble stone streets, curbs and stairs are hard on Max's behind, but what the heck, The Kid is doing the pushin'!

In answering a question that most are afraid to ask, The Kid's favorite ordinance was NAPALM, NAPALM, and more NAPALM, and then the MK 82 snake-eye 500-lb bomb. This is because of some pointy-headed decision made by dolts in Washington, it was decided that the Navy and Marine Corps F-4 Phantoms would not have an internally mounted gun. How can you be a fighter plane without guns? They did use the center

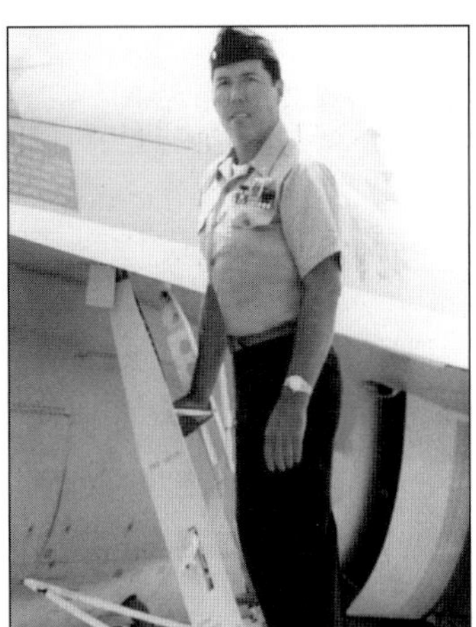

*Col. P.A. Curtis*

*Max Cleland and P.A. Curtis on the Battleship Missouri with a stern lesson in Naval terminology.*

mounted M-61A Gatling gun pod, which hung under the centerline of the plane, when they could steal them from Da Nang (not often). Some of The Death Rattler's planes had the proper equipment and mounts to use these pods. The planes were serviced at CUBI Point in the Philippines, when they could get there for major maintenance. (GOOD duty.) The empty pods were great for Da Nang booze runs, and PX raids.

As Crossdraw didn't drink, he was often charged with declaring a flight anomaly from CUBI, and landed at Da Nang for such activities. He really didn't know who they thought they were fooling, as they had to fly OVER their base at Chu Lai, to get to Da Nang, about 80 kilometers up the road. The Kid remembers his GIB, (The Guy In the Back) calling a brake irregularity on more than one occasion and requesting a landing at Da Nang's MUCH longer runway. Once squared away on the tarmac, and magically discovering that their brakes were okay, The Kid and his GIB could trade whatever they had with Air Force boys in blue, for things the Marines could only dream about, like ice cream, steaks and the odd air conditioner. Da Nang Air Base was shared by the Marines and Air Force, and only the Air Force was strategic, with VERY big planes that could bring in wonderful things from all over the world. Not the Marines, unless you consider Okinawa part of the world.

Before Crossdraw's arrival on station, the squadron's Executive Officer (XO), upon his appointment, had been ceremonially presented with a "borrowed" Air Force blue Jeep that had been painted over in Marine green, and passed down from the beginning of time, from XO to XO, and eventually to The Kid. Under the passenger seat was a small brush and a beat up can of Marine green paint, so that in case of a ding, the Air Force blue could be instantly covered with green. In return, the Marines had nothing the Air Force wanted to steal, except blondes and booze. They traded 'em the booze, and fought 'em for all the blonde, brunette and redheaded Nurses who were in VERY short supply! The Kid has often thought that the grandson of our Viet Cong enemy is still driving the wheels off that Jeep; battered and bruised, partly Air Force blue, mainly Marine Corps green, and not knowing how precious it was to so many.

Looking back 47 years later, the one thing that astounds The Kid, is how he and his fellow pilots made so many low level passes all day, every day, doing their best to protect the mud Marines on the ground, without blowing each other up. It was all in the mumbo-jumbo of fuse timing by their overworked ground crew and an obvious and reasonably clever program the F-4 pilots worked out, but NEVER asked permission to use. Rather than attacking line astern, as their Rules Of Engagement (REO) ordered, which could and did get way to many good Marines shot out of the sky, especially "Tail End Charlie," the last guy to attack, and the focus of all the anti-aircraft fire. The wise pilots would hit the target from different points of the compass, sometimes flying as low as fifty feet. This was obviously very dangerous and needed close coordination from their Forward Air Controllers, flying above them, and directing the action. Otherwise they'd be right over their squadron mate's ordinance when it exploded. ALSO not a good idea! But, it worked perfectly, MOST of the time... Oh, and The Kid's call sign has always been, "Crossdraw," NEVER, EVER "Hollywood!"

## THE TOOLS OF MY TRADE

*By Robert Jeffory Roberts*

Infantry Marines or (Grunts) in Vietnam used their tool, a rifle, to kill the enemy so they could protect their fellow Marines and themselves. When I reported to the 1st Shore Party Battalion, 1st Marine Division, I found out that I would be a Field Radioman attached to the Grunts [Infantry]. I was given my tools—a radio and a .45 sidearm.

As a radioman, I would be part of a (HST) Helicopter Support Team. My responsibilities were coordinating the Infantry Units Re-supply and Medivac Missions. During my first combat operation named Boone, I had my first contact with the enemy in the form of a Vietcong ambush. I had jumped off the trail and moved behind a large rock while firing my .45 automatic pistol. It didn't take me long to fire the three clips (21 rounds) that had been issued to me. After running out of ammo, a feeling of unbelievable frustration took over. I was thinking that I would look up and see a Vietcong looking down at me or that somebody else would be calling in my own Medivac. Fortunately, neither of those scenarios happened, because the Marines won that battle.

As soon as I learned I would be going out on my next combat operation, I immediately headed to the armory and requested additional weapons. I also told the armorer that I was a Marine and having only that .45 pistol was not going to get it done. They came through for me to the point that I felt that I was ready for anything and everything.

On the first day of my second combat operation, named Union that was quickly followed by Union II, everyone was staging and preparing and waiting for the order to move out. I happened to look around and noticed several of the grunts looking at me and chuckling for some reason. One of the grunts approached and told me they had come up with a nickname for me, which was "John Wayne". I laughingly guessed the reason for my new nickname. The reason had to be that I was now armed with a M-14 rifle, five 20 round magazines, of course my .45 pistol, the bayonet for the M-14 rifle, a Marine K-Bar knife, a machete and to top it off, besides my usual allotment of smoke grenades I had several M-26 hand grenades—plus my radio. I believed my radio was my most important tool. I would call in resupply

*Field Radioman Robert Roberts outfitted for the trail.*

missions for food, water and, more importantly, ammo. I also called in medivacs, which I considered to be my most important responsibility—medivacing the wounded to the nearest hospital or Marines killed in action to be sent home to their loved ones.

For many years as a civilian, I had looked for the most important tool that I had used in my life; the same kind of radio that was my tool in Vietnam, and now I can say that I have one and every time I look at it, I can only pray that because of that tool that I used in Vietnam, many of those Marines that I had medivaced are alive to this day.

## THE TEACHER AND THE STUDENT

*By Robert Jeffory Roberts*

I wanted to capture my experience in Vietnam, so I carried a camera with me everywhere I went. This photo is one of 135 photos I shot. Besides being my favorite, I also consider it the most poignant photo in my collection.

The Marine standing in front with the thousand-yard stare was named Campken, from North Carolina. He was on his last combat operation with only a month left in Vietnam. I called him the Teacher.

The young Marine looking over Corporal Campken's left shoulder was on his first combat operation. I called him the Student.

When I first arrived in Vietnam, I had no idea how to do my job; it was basically on the job training. I didn't have a Corporal Campken to teach me how to survive and do my job as a Helicopter Support Team Radioman.

*"The Teacher and the Student" Corp. Campken with his young student looking over his left shoulder. Courtesy of Robert Jeffory Roberts.*

Like all Marines with whom I served, I tried to stay focused on the job at hand, but Corporal Campken made a personal decision to take on another responsibility to help a young Marine who was new to Vietnam. He helped me understand why I was fighting in Vietnam.

To me, Corporal Campken was a true hero.

## 1ST SHORE PARTY BATTALION AND OPERATION SHELBYVILLE

*by Robert Jeffory Roberts*

Who am I? Lance/Corporal Robert "Jeff" Roberts, U.S. Marines, Serial #2180544.

My Unit? Helicopter Support Team or HST Radioman, 1st Shore Party Battalion, 1st Marine Division, which during the Vietnam War was the only unit in the Marine Corps that wore a patch other than the Airwings. It was a small red square patch, worn on the outer side of our trousers at the knee and on the front facing area of our covers or caps and our helmets.

What was my job? I was usually attached to a Battalion Headquarters Company of either the 1st, 5th or 7th Marine Regiments during Battalion sized combat operations and occasionally I was attached to an individual company. My responsibility was a partnership with the Corpsman.

The HST Radioman and the Corpsman were a team dependent on each other to have a successful mission or medivac. While walking during any combat operation, you would find me directly behind the Corpsman. When we had casualties and I heard the call of Corpsman Up, then it became my job to look for the ideal location of an LZ or landing zone, and once I established the LZ, I would get the necessary information from the Corpsman that I needed to give to the Medivac dispatcher.

What was the information? How many Killed in Action (KIA), how many Wounded in Action (WIA), whether I needed a Doctor on the Medical flight, the status of the wounded, which told me if I needed an Emergency, Priority, or Routine Medivac, and what was the status of the LZ—hot, cold, triple canopy on top of a mountain or in a valley. After getting this information, I would then convey

*1st Shore Party BN, across from the Hill 327 "Freedom Hill" complex, Da Nang, South Vietam.*

*Members of the 1st Shore Party Battalion enjoy down time at "China Beach". Robert Jeffory Roberts is pictured fourth from the right.*

it to the Medivac dispatcher, who would later contact me to inform me that the helicopters were on their way. When the helicopters were five kilometers or what we referred to as five klicks out, which meant that they were five minutes away, I would go to the LZ and prepare to throw smoke, when thrown, it would mark the LZ for the pilots. Then after they replied to me that they "Tally Ho" my purple or yellow smoke and I replied back to them the confirmation of my use of purple or yellow smoke, I would then by using hand signals land the two UH -340 "Sea Horse" helicopters into the LZ.

If there were KIA Marines, I would load them into the first helicopter. After the Corpsman were finished treating and stabilizing the WIA Marines, I would load them into the second helicopter. After the loading of the helicopters was finished, I would again aid the pilots by directing them in their taking off from the LZ to turn towards the safest direction. I wasn't trained for this assignment, it became "on the job training" for the duration of my "one year" deployment to Vietnam.

I had approximately thirty-five medivacs over eight major combat operations and a few "No Name or Minor Operations or Extended Patrols." I believe the HST Teams, and specifically the HST Radiomen, were the "UNSUNG HEROES". Although the HST Radioman were considered to be non-combatants, they still were a vital part of any combat operation. They successfully coordinated almost impossible medivacs. Many shed their blood or gave their lives while fighting alongside their Marine brethren. The HST teams were generally overlooked for any medals, promotions or even any recognition.

One such medivac is described in my recollection of Operation Shelbyville below.

## Operation Shelbyville, An Accounting of a Medivac, 25 September 1967

*by Robert Jeffory Roberts*

At approximately 1500 hrs I was informed that there would be an 81 mm mortar mission at approximately 1600 hrs, and that I should call in an emergency resupply request for 81 mm mortar rounds. I quickly called in the resupply mission and the resupply helicopters landed at approximately 1545 hrs. The mortar tube was readied and its rounds were staged beside it.

I believe the mortar mission was for one of the companies, possibly KILO, to enter the tree line and then proceed away from our present position, which was on the bank of the river. The mortar mission's possible intent was that the mortar rounds were to be fired up, over and ahead of KILO Company to a safe position down the trail that they

*An Hoa Marine Combat Base, the starting point of many combat operations. Courtesy of Robert Jeffory Roberts.*

would be traveling so the rounds could possibly clear out any ambushes or snipers.

At approximately 1600 hrs, I had positioned myself approximately eight yards from the mortar tube. I always liked to stand close to any mortar tube during a mortar mission, because after the round is dropped, my eyes would be able to follow it as it leaves the tube, heading upward on its path towards its designated attitude and continue to watch it as it turns downward on its new path towards its predetermined landing zone. However, this mortar mission would be like no other one that I had ever witnessed before.

After watching four rounds successfully leave the tube, the fifth round, when it came out of the tube, made an odd sound. It made an intermittent whooshing sound that immediately alerted the experienced mortar men that it was going to be a short round.

My immediate actions, after hearing the alert of the short round being announced, were motivated by not only my Marine training that I had received prior to coming to Vietnam, but also the on the job self-training that I had developed in honing my skills as a radioman in coordinating as many as 35 previous medivacs, many of them being extremely difficult and challenging. I also had two qualities that one cannot get from training that I believed not only helped me perfect my skills in performing those medivacs, but had many times helped save my life—the first was extremely quick reflexes and the second was the ability to think very fast and make quick decisions under the duress of combat.

As the round was leaving the tube and the immediate report from the mortar team that it was a short round, I noticed that just about everyone was launching themselves to the ground facedown, their hands instinctively going to the backs of their heads. I kept standing and watched the short round. As it sometimes was for me in combat, everything seemed to be happening in slow motion. As the round was in its halfway point of its journey downward, I quickly realized that its destination could possibly be close to KILO Company.

Then immediately after hearing the dreaded, "Corpsman up!", I instinctively turned my head to the right towards where I had my radio set up. As I was running over to get my radio so that I could start the medivac process, I noticed two UH-34D Helicopters, approximately five kilometers southeast and appearing as though they were heading towards Danang. Something was telling me that they were finished with their mission and were probably heading back to base. So, I contacted air control and told them that I had an emergency medivac and was it possible

*CH-46A helicopters used to transport Marines for helicopter assaults, re-supply missions or difficult medivacs. Courtesy of Robert Jeffory Roberts.*

for me to be able to use the two helicopters that I saw heading back in the direction of Danang. They told me to wait one, then after 15 seconds, they called me back and told me that it was a go and gave me their radio frequency and call sign. I immediately contacted the helicopters and after the pilots said that they would help, I turned them around, so they were headed in my direction. I picked up my radio and ran to where the mortar round had landed.

When I arrived, I noticed that there were two KIAs who had been covered with ponchos and what appeared to be five WIAs who were being treated by the Corpsman. Next, after I had selected my LZ, I could hear that the helicopters were close. I looked up and realized that they were fast approaching so I threw a smoke grenade into the LZ. Then I immediately realized that I needed to go and contact the Corpsman, who were working on the WIAs, so that I could write down in my mission book all the information that I needed to give to the pilots—in other words, how many KIAs and WIAs as well as the status of the WIAs. After immediately receiving the information, I spun around and ran back to the LZ, getting there just in time to help them land one behind the other.

The average time for most of my medivacs during previous operations was approximately thirty minutes. A fast medivac would have been fifteen to twenty minutes. After I had landed the two medivac helicopters, I looked at my watch and felt total disbelief. Between the time of the short round impact and the two helicopters touching down was approximately five to six minutes.

I was on the radio talking to the pilot of the first helicopter, giving him the information on the five WIAs, when I looked over and saw that the Corpsman was still working to stabilize them. I then began to get concerned that the helicopters would be on the ground too long and that they might get the attention of a sniper or something worse like getting mortared. So, I quickly decided to load the two KIAs on to the first helicopter.

I approached the first KIA and pulled the poncho from him, spreading it open beside him. Some of his fellow Marines approached and helped me pick him up and place him onto the poncho and we carried him over and put him onto the first helicopter.

I then went to the second KIA. As I approached the poncho covered Marine, I could see that the mortar

*The Marine on the left was in a Helicopter Support Team (HST). In the middle is a Viet Cong 18-year-old girl. On the right is a former NVA soldier who defected under the Chiêu Hoi program and became a Kit Carson Scout. They are waiting for a helicopter to pick up the prisioner. Courtesy of Robert Jeffory Roberts*

*An HST Marine and Kit Carson Scout escort a Viet Cong prisoner on this UH-34D "Seahorse" helicopter. Courtesy of Robert Jeffory Roberts*

round's impact area was right beside him. When I pulled the poncho off him and spread it out beside him, it was as though most of the Marines were seeing what happened to him for the first time. I tried to get the Marines who had helped me with the first KIA to help me with second KIA, but when I asked them to help, they appeared to be so visibly shaken that I don't think that they heard me. So, realizing that I wasn't going to get any help, I got on the radio and made a request to the pilot, asking him if it was possible for the door gunner to come and help me. The door gunner jumped down and ran over and helped me lift the Marine onto the poncho. Then the door gunner and I carried him to the first helicopter.

By then the Corpsman was finished treating the WIAs and Lieutenant Colonel Rockey had restored order and with the help of some Marines, I was able to load the WIAs onto the second helicopter and direct the helicopters safely out of the LZ. Again, I looked at my watch and was surprised in seeing that the medivac from the explosion to the Helicopters leaving the LZ was eight minutes.

Even with what had just happened, I have always wanted the opportunity to be able to thank Colonel Rockey, for his words to me immediately after the medivac—when he came up to me and told me, "Job well done, Marine."

Note: I was able to thank Colonel Rockey forty-four years later at our 1st Marine Division Association Reunion in Alexandria, Virginia in 2011, and with his help I was awarded the Navy and Marine Corps Achievement Medal with the V Device in 2015.

Members of the Southern California Chapter at a Fallujah commemoration, 2014. 1MDA photo

Survivors of Guadalcanal at the 1st Marine Division Reunion, 13-17 August 1986, all members of C-1-5. Pictured l-r: Ralph Dodge, Gerald P. McHale, CWO Butler Metzger, John M. Thomas, Capt Rocco A. Zullo, and Tom C. Panouses. 1MDA photo

Los Angeles Chapter members on the Peleliu Dependence Cruise, 3 September 1981. Pictured l-r: Vic Betcher, Ed McNally, Sig Carlson, Al Lewis, George Hatzikakis, Fidel Hernandez, Jack Sharkey, Bill Becker, Dick Rowland, ?, ?, and Paul Garcia. 1MDA photo

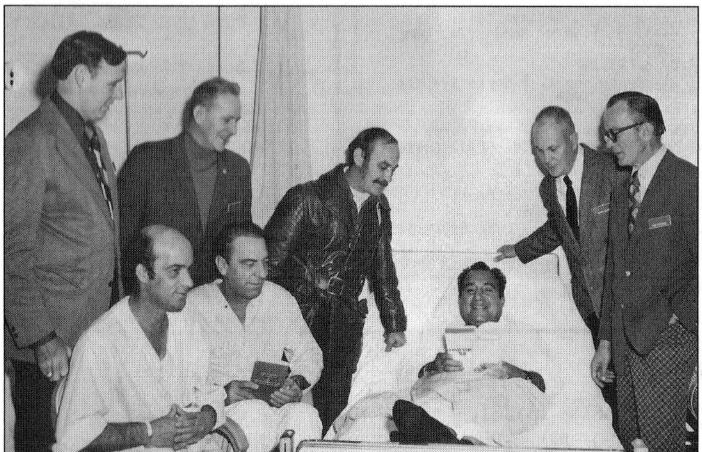

Visiting with patients at Veterans Hospital in Omaha are members of the Omaha Chapter, 1st Marine Division Association. Pictured l-r: Bill Ramsey, President; Col. Don May (ret.); Bill Blum, chairman of the activity; Bernard Zielinski, Chapter Vice-President; and Ray Stavneak, Immediate Past President. 1MDA photo

1st Marine Division Assoc. members from the New York Chapter, ca. 1964. Pictured l-r: William J. Leyden (seated), William L. Pupke, Ralph W. Ernst, Douglas J. Collins, Matthew R. Rousseau, and James F. McEnery. 1MDA photo

# THE OLD BREED NEWS

PUBLISHED IN THE INTEREST OF
THE 1ST MARINE DIVISION ASSOCIATION INCORPORATED
SECOND - CLASS POSTAGE PAID AT ARLINGTON, VIRGINIA

No. 1 January 1975

## "VIETNAM" ADDED TO MARINE CORPS WAR MEMORIAL

— "Vietnam", the 12-year battle in which nearly 13,000 U.S. Marines gave their lives is now burnished in gold forever on the polished black granite of the Marine Corps War Memorial which flanks Arlington National Cemetery

The addition of "Vietnam" was dedicated today in solemn memorial-side ceremonies led by the Commandant of the Marine Corps, Gen. Robert E. Cushman Jr., and Under Secretary the Navy David S. Potter.

"Vietnam" is the first addition to the other 35 major engagements cut into the Memorial since it was erected by Marines and dedicated to pay eternal homage to their battle dead 20 years ago Nov. 10. "Vietnam" takes its place on the Memorial's battle roll — which includes such names as Korea, Iwo Jima, Bataan and Corregidor, Belleau Wood, Vera Cruz, the War Between the States and the Revolutionary War — representing all the major engagements in which Marines have fought and died for nearly 100 of their 199 years of existence

The Memorial itself is a 78-foot high bronze statue depicting the famous "Iwo Jima Flag Raising" atop Mt. Suribachi during one of the toughest tests of Marine valor in World War II. It stands vigilant above the National Capital's skyline to preserve the immortality of fallen Marines of wars past.

During the dedication ceremony, Gen. Cushman, who led the largest force of Marines in the battle for Vietnam for nearly two years, used the inscription from the Tomb of Scotland's Unknown Soldier in Edinburgh to describe the kind of immortality gained by Marines who fell in Vietnam:

They shall not grow old
As we are left to grow old
Age shall not weary them

Cont'd on page 2



*Front page of The Old Breed News, January 1975.*

### Edson Range Chapel Camp Pendleton, California

Dedication service was held on 28 March 1982 for the new Edson Range Chapel. The window, SACRIFICE, was donated as a gift by your Association.

**Schedule of Symbolism**

THE BROKEN ARCH:
Symbolic of untimely death. (The arch has long been the recognized monument to sacrifice and courage)

THE SACRIFICIAL ALTAR:
Old Testament symbol of the perfect obedience shown by Abraham.

THE LION:
Courage! Courage is most often born on a pathway of suffering (thorns) and hardships.

THE RISING SMOKE AND FLAMES:
Recall the zeal, inspiration and youthful fervor of all true martyrs. The rising smoke is also symbolic of prayer ascending to Heaven.

The members attending the tour of Camp Pendleton at the Los Angeles Reunion will have the opportunity to view this stained glass window.

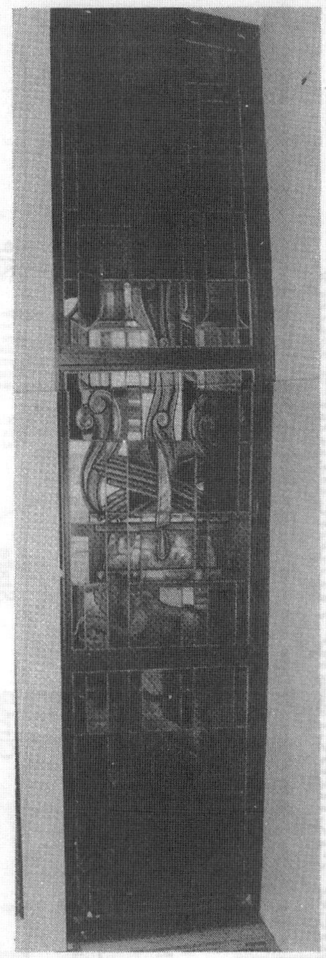

*Stained glass window at the Edson Range Chapel, Camp Pendleton, CA. 1MDA photo*

*Members are all smiles at the Milwaukee, WI reunion, 2013. 1MDA photo*

*The Reckless Memorial is unveiled at the Camp Pendleton Stables by James Vincent (l) and A.G. Studdard. Vincent was the So. California chapter president of the 1st Marine Division Assoc., and Studdard was the association vice-president. The Memorial was placed in honor of Reckless, a pack horse assigned to the 5th Marine Regiment during the Korean War. 1MDA photo*

*Alan Lenzi and James Lee of Great Panes Glassworks in Colorado engrave one of 108 names being added to the Vietnam Veterans Memorial wall in Washington, D.C., 1986 The additional names are those of service members who, while not killed in Vietnam, died in the performance of duties related to combat there. 1MDA photo*

*Paul G. Hymel Jr. (left) and Jorgen V. Jenson, buddies from H-3-11 meet after 38 years at the Milwaukee Reunion, 1984. They had last seen each other in Tientsin, China in 1945. 1MDA photo*

*Minnesota Chapter honors PFC Krause MOH (KIA Peleliu), 1992. 1MDA photo*

*Association members at a meeting in Boston, 1964. Pictured l-r: Larry Reynolds, E. Clark, Major G.C. Fox, Jack Fitzgerald, and Joe Mandell. 1MDA photo*

*Generals Walt, Wieseman, and Davis during a New York Chapter anniversary dinner, 1965. 1MDA photo*

*Members during a reunion in 1991. 1MDA photo*

*1st Marines Bell, Bob Backes and Ysidoro M. Balli (two on the right unknown) while serving somewhere near Peking or Tientsin, China, 1946. 1MDA photo*

*RFV Chapter members Arthur Reinholm, Harry Knox, MG Edward Megarr, Milo Nelson, Col. Eldon Erickson, 1981. 1MDA photo*

*Mrs. Chesty Puller christens the Lewis B. Puller by breaking a bottle of champagne on the ship's bow, 1980. Photo by Sgt. Gerald Blaschke. 1MDA photo*

*Detroit Chapter staff, 1964. Seated l-r: Raymond Kania, Secretary; Richard Lancaster, President; and Kenneth Macabe, Treasurer. Standing: John Cummings, Historian; Albert Watson, Vice-President; Robert Graham, Sergeant-at-Arms; and Walter Wenzel, Membership Representative. 1MDA photo*

*Pictured l-r: "Obie" O'Bryant, "Mike" West, MajGen J.J. McMonagle, Bill Ping, Glen Sinaiko, and SgtMaj "Crow" Crawford. Photo by "Obie" O'Bryant courtesy of 1MDA*

*Northern California Chapter members, 1982. Pictured l-r: George Waselinko, Col. E.L. Erickson, SgtMaj Meyer, Maj Gerry Berry, and LtCol William D. Wischmeyer.*

# THE OLD BREED NEWS

PUBLISHED IN THE INTEREST OF
THE 1ST MARINE DIVISION ASSOCIATION INCORPORATED
SECOND - CLASS POSTAGE PAID AT ARLINGTON, VIRGINIA

No. 4 April 1975

## 1ST MARINE DIVISION BAND TO PERFORM DURING WEST COAST REUNION

The entire West Coast of our Nation is familiar ground for the precisionstepping musical members of the 1st Marine Division Band based at Camp Pendleton, California.

This fine musical organization is kept busy with on-base and off-base schedules that include parades, concerts, daily morning flag raising ceremonies and athletic events.

Training for the Band is not entirely confined to the field of music. Although several hours are devoted to rehearsal weekly, team members follow the rigid military training schedule set up for all Marines. Each musician is qualified on all infantry weapons with special emphasis on the rifle - basic weapon of the individual Marine.

Musical arrangements for the 1st Marine Division Band run the gamut from Beethoven's 5th Symphony to the Tijuana Brass; from Sousa Marches to Broadway show tunes.

The 1st Marine Division Band is presently directed by Chief Warrant Officer Ronald C. Biggs. The Band musicians stand by ready and trained for duty wherever and whenever they may best serve the nation and the Corps.

## HENRY H. BLACK NEW SGTMAJ OF MARINE CORPS

SgtMaj Henry H. Black has been selected by the Commandant of the Marine Corps to become seventh Sergeant Major of the Marine Corps.

A 27-year veteran, Black will assume the post June 1, the day after the present Sergeant Major of the Marine Corps Clinton A. Puckett retires. Puckett has held the post since Feb. 1, 1973.

SgtMaj. Black is presently Marine Corps Development and Education Command Sergeant Major at Quantico, an assignment he has held since December.

Born in Imperial, Pa., Black enlisted in the Corps in April 1948, less than a year after graduating from high school. He was assigned to the 2d Marine Division at Camp Lejeune after completing boot camp and served initially with the 8th Marines, and later the 6th Marines.

Ordered to Korea in 1950, Black joined the 3d Bn., 1st Marines, as the CO's driver. As a Pfc, he earned the Silver Star Medal while serving with a rifle company. Later, Black earned the Bronze Star Medal with Combat "V."

Fifteen years later, while serving as a company first sergeant with the 8th Marines at Camp Lejeune, he landed with the Marines sent to the Dominican Republic.

During the Vietnam conflict, Black completed two tours with line outfits. His first tour, 1966-67, was as first sergeant of Co. A, 1st Bn., 1st Marines. He returned in 1969 for a tour as sergeant major of the 2d Bn., 7th Marines.

SgtMaj Black earned his second and third Bronze Star Medals during his Vietnam tours.

Cont'd on page 2

1

*Front page of The Old Breed News, April 1975.*

*11th Marines Baseball Team, Ballarat, Australia, March 1943. The photo was provided to the Association by Dr. Bill H. Cooke, who is seated at the left end of the bench.*

*This stained glass window was donated to the Edson Range Chapel at Camp Pendleton by the 1st Marine Division Association, 1982. 1MDA photo*

*Six Guadalcanal veterans at the 1stMarDiv reunion in Savannah, Georgia, 1982. Pictured l-r: Sgt. Richard Lyons, MSgt Frank Blakely, Sgt. Frank Smith, General Edwin Pollock, MSgt John Waters, and CWO Bob Nelson.*

*The first annual Weapons Company, 7th Marines Reunion, Memphis, TN, 5-9 June 1985. Pictured l-r: Gill Bolen, Gene Tucker, Tom Giblin, Joe Beckum, Carl Bradley, Paul Pesackis, and Frank Mangino Sal Gelosi is on the tank and Wray Guilbeau and George Bean are kneeling. 1MDA photo*

*Saluting at the sound of taps during a 1st Marine Division memorial service are (l-r) MajGen Bronars, Col Paige, and SgtMaj Schnabel, 1977. 1MDA photo*

*Courtesy of the 1MDA*

*President Heim concludes his acceptance speech and introduces the new officers of the Association, 1981. Pictured l-r: Legal Officer Lester Bales Jr., Treasurer Edwin F. Kelly, Vice President Terrance W. McGuire Jr, 3rd Vice President Stan Roth, 2nd Vice President Jim Forni, Chaplain Earle C. Reynolds, and Seargent at Arms Marc Weinstock. 1MDA photo*

*Distinguished guests at the Anaheim Chapter's 7th Annual Dinner-Dance, 1986. Pictured l-r: Col William E. Barber (MOH), USMC Ret; Mrs. Jone Barber; Mrs. Marilyn Paige; and Col Mitchell Paige (MOH), USMd Ret. 1MDA photo*

*Members of the Boston Chapter at their annual Memorial Mass, 1981. Seated l-r: Russell Webber, Ed McCarthy, Bud Kenney, Pres. Terry McGuire, Fr. James Rogers (Past Nat'l Chaplain), Frank O'Brien, and Dan Regan. Second row: Joe Garland, Herb Hilton, Tony Melnick, unknown, Tom Mulvey, Fred Scalese, Scotty Clements, Watler Marr Sr., unknown, Bud Hall, Dan Casey, and William Sweeney. Top row: Ed Warticki, Jerry Smith, Paul Thomas, Bill Hughes, Martin Elinoff, Henry Horne, and Joe Dean. 1MDA photo*

Almost 1,000 1st Marine Division veterans and their families solemnly viewed the black and white granite Vietnam Memorial where the names of 57,939 dead and missing are engraved, 1984. 1MDA photo

SgtMaj Domenik A. Irrera and retired SgtMaj George F. Meyer present a wreath during memorial ceremonies at the Vietnam Memorial, 1984. 1MDA photo

1stLt Burton Charles Quist and his bride, Catherine Mary (Swallow) Quist, 1970, who met for the first time at the 1964 New York reunion. She is the daughter of Dick Swallow and he is the son of Charlie Quist, both Association life members. 1MDA photo

General Chesty Puller leads a group of Marine veterans down Philadelphia's Chestnut Street, 1961. 1MDA photo

*Executive Secretary George Meyer presenting a charter to members of the Bodfish Chapter at the West Coast Reunion in Brownsville, 1978. 1MDA photo*

*Members of the Alamo Chapter, 1987. Seated, l-r: MSgt Val Martinez (Ret), Maj Ramon "Val" Valadez (Ret), Fidel Gomez. Standing: Robert "Bob" Peterson, Thomas "Tiger" Martinez, 1stSgt V.U. Yruegas (Ret), and Matt M. Davis III. 1MDA photo*

*Rocky Mountain Marines at a plaque presentation honoring the 1st Marine Division, 2003. 1MDA photo*

*Association members march behind the Marine Corps Drill Team and Drum and Bugle Corps during a parade in Detroit, MI, 1959. 1MDA photo*

*OPERA AT TAR SPRINGS John Loomis reports that an opera house is going up next to Chris' Last Change Saloon.*

*W.W. Witherspoon, an observation plane pilot during WWII, finds the mechanical mule's controls unfamiliar, 1965. USMC photo courtesy 1MDA*

*Association Directors' Meeting at the Hotel Sherman, Chicago, IL, 11 May 1953. Sitting l-r: MSgt Homer F. Gable, Maj Thomas H. Barry, Bgen William H. Harrison, LtCol Nathaniel Morgenthal, Col. James J. Keating. Standing: Cmdr Lester M. Lucas, LtCol Harry W. Edwards, Mr. Bertram Z. Lee, Col Paul Drake, 1stLt Alfred Scalcione, Capt Edwin C. Clarke, Capt George H. Slye, Mr. Louis Weiner, Major George P. Hunt, Mr. Reuben Sherman, Maj James V. Donoghue, and Maj Layton W. Bailey Jr. 1MDA photo*

Six Liberty Bell Chapter and MCL detachment members at Smedley Elementary School in Philadelphia, PA, delivering 700 new toys for the Toys for Tots program, 2003. 1MDA photo

Houston "Devil Dogs" (l-r) Judi Hanley, Tom Hanley, Don Morris, Jim Fairbairn, and Tom Vetter, 2003. 1MDA photo

Life Member Frank Turiace at the sign marking the Gunnery Sergeant John Basilone Memorial Freeway at the south lane Basilone Bridge over crossing of the 1-5 freeway on the northern boundary of Camp Pendleton, October 2000. 1MDA photo

"Hail, Hail, the West Coast gang's all here..." as seen in the Old Breed News, ca. 1950s. 1MDA photo

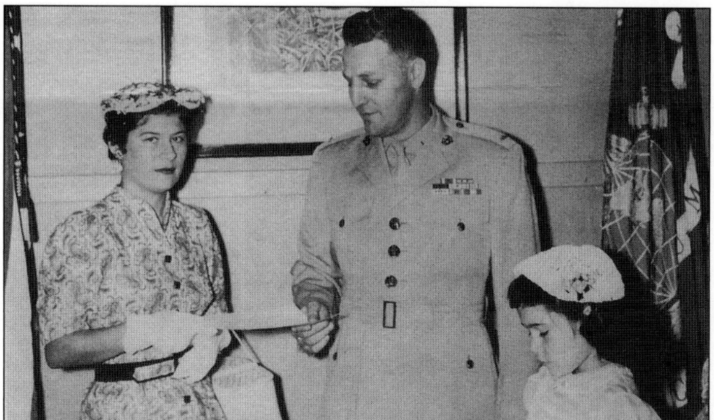

Mrs. Verna Mae Rice (left), widow of Marine Sgt. Oliver Rice, receives the first $1,200 scholarship awarded by the First Marine Division Association from CWO Lawrence A. McCarter at the Naval Reserve Training Center, 1954. Looking on is Rice's daughter, Barbara Lynn. 1MDA photo

Bgen E.A. Montgomery, Commanding General of the Cherry Point Marine Corps Air Station, presents the First Marine Division Association Scholarship award to John T. Stitzel, ca. 1950s. Also pictured is Stitzel's mother, Mrs. Naomi V. Chugg. 1MDA photo

*Four Marines receive the Medal of Honor on 27 October 1953. Pictured l-r: Corporal Alford Lee McLaughlin, PFC Robert E. Simanek, 1stLt Raymond G. Murphy, and 1stLt George H. O'Brien Jr. 1MDA photo*

*Colonel Lew Walt (left) is elected President of the 1st Marine Division Association for the 1957-58 term at the August 10 Business Meeting. He is congratulated by outgoing President, Bgen James J. Keating (Ret). 1MDA photo*

*Lieutenant Generals Puller and Snedeker cast a wreath into the waters of San Francisco Bay, 1964. 1MDA photo*

*Veterans of the 1st Marine Division, meeting in the Island Inn, Westbury, NY, make plans for the formation of the New York Chapter of the 1MDA, 1963. Pictured l-r: William J. Leyden, SgtMaj Charles R. Carr, Maj George F. Pelham, and LtCol Francis R. Kraince. 1MDA photo*

*TSgt L. Lazarko, of "D.I." fame, joins friends in a songfest, ca. 1950s. 1MDA photo*

*Pictured l-r: Ray Meaney, Bob Rohde, President Neal Mishik, Marine Corps League's Chuck LaBerge, and Vice President Tom Vetter, 2001. 1MDA photo*

*Maj Mitch Rios with wife, daughter, father Vince and Cheryl Rios, wins the Bronze Star Medal with Combat "V" in Afghanistan, 2003. 1MDA photo*

*Members of the Old Breed march in Melbourne, Australia during a parade celebrating Washington's Birthday, 1943. 1MDA photo*

*Comrades visit Father Denis O'Brien at the home of Dallas Chapter President, Jim Fairbairn, 2002. Standing l-r: Charlie Britten, Jack Erwin, Walt Schmick, Bob Montgomery, George Barbary, Bob Rohde, Lou Gallio, Neal Mishik, Bob Jebavy. Seated l-r: Marcus Ronquillo, Jim Fairbairn, Joe Walker, Gen Dick Carey, and Father Denis O'Brien. 1MDA photo*

*Medal of Honor recipient Bob Buch at the Robert E. Bush Naval Hospital, Twentynine Palms, California, ca. December 2000. 1MDA photo*

*Retired SgtMaj Gary Truscott with friends from the Southern California Chapters of the 1MDA, 2001. Gary had just become an officer with the Oceanside Police Department. 1MDA photo*

Lady Marines at the Oregon/Columbia River Armed Forces Day Meeting, 2003. 1MDA photo

June Cormier, 1MDA Membership Coordinator, in 2004.

*Officers of "The River Jarheads", 2003. Pictured l-r: George Cary, secretary; Larry Greenwood, 1st Vice President; Karl Dreihaupt, Treasurer; Robert Krause, 2nd Vice President; and Gary Eichhorst, President. 1MDA photo*

*Rocky Mountain Marines at a plaque presentation honoring the 1st Marine Division, 2003. 1MDA photo*

*1st Marine Division Commanding General C.F. Widdecke holds the six millionth artillery round to be fired by the Division's 11th Marine Regiment just before he drops it down the tube, 1970. USMC photo by Cpl John A. Gentry, courtesy 1MDA*

*Dedication ceremony for the Marine Corps War Memorial next to Arlington National Cemetery, 10 November 1954. 1MDA photo*

*Col Barney Barnham (far left), MajGen Mattis (center), and President Neil Mishik, 2003. 1MDA photo*

*Liberty Bell members present wreath at Vietnam Memorial (l-r): Mike Waldron, Rich Gresko, Jim Clendenen, Bruce Boice, Carl Wenhold, and Steve Lakernick.*

*Life Member Jerry Johs, center, presents a Marine officer's sword and scabbard to NROTC Midshipman 1/C C. Benjamin Clayton for demonstrating outstanding leadership. Marine NRTOC instructor Major Joseph M. Grant at right.*

*Marine veterans of Fallujah, April 2004, at a gathering in 2006. 1MDA photo*

*Col Randall Newman swears in new Desert Cities officers (l-r) Quint Villanueva, Jim Martin, Mike Key, Sandy Sandoval, Jim Sullivan, Frank "Doc" Gillette, and Joe Daily. 1MDA photo*

*Blue Diamond Riders: Col Len Hayes (Center), Maj Bill Mimiaga (left) and MSgt Ed Brundage (right), 2008. 1MDA photo*

*Members and guests present at G/3/1's annual Memorial Service at a new Memorial Garden for the First Marines at Camp Horno in Camp Pendleton, 2013. 1MDA photo*

*1st Marine Division Association Headquarters in downtown Oceanside, California.*

*SgtMaj Marty Vasquez with Purple Heart Marines from 3/5. Marty served with the 3/5 in Korea in 1951. 1MDA photo*

*Smaj Juan D. Duff, former Office Manager for the 1MDA, 2004.*

*Col Christopher G. Wright (USMC, Ret) former Executive Director of the 1MDA*

*Liberty Bell members present wreath at the Korean War Memorial (l-r): John Reidenhour, Harry Wiemann, Mike Waldron, Ralph Delaney, and John Heath, 2005. 1MDA photo*

*Old Breed Veterans gather at Division HQ, 2014. 1MDA photo*

*Vietnam veteran John A. Mullan, a staff sergeant with the 1st Battalion, 5th Marine Regiment, gets a spoonfull of vegetables during a special event at Camp Day, 2 February 2006. Photo by Cpl Tom Sloan courtesy 1MDA.*

*Members of California Delta Chapter who assisted in its efforts at Annual Bass Derby: Vic Viera, Joe McKeown, Manny Santos, Ray Bael, and the Air Force Toys for Tots area representative, 2013. 1MDA photo*

*Old Breed Veterans gather at Division HQ, 2014. 1MDA photo*

*President Walt Schmick of the Dallas Chapter, SSGT Roy Knapp, Maj Charles Nicol, Vince Rios (FMDA Vice President), and Bob Montgomery (FMDA Past President) and the annual Christmas dinner, 2014. 1MDA photo*

*Newly installed (2015) President Robert Rohde presents a plaque to outgoing President Edward Aulman (left) at the New York Chapter's installation luncheon. 1MDA photo*

*NY officers, December 1993. Pictured l-r: Neil Mishik, Richard Johnson, Jim Dileo, Ed Aulman, Steve Kraus, John Biagini, and Robert Rohde. 1MDA photo*

*Two veterans from the First Signal Company, 1999. 1MDA photo*

*Beginning with man in red cap with back to camera: Mississippi Chapter's Joe Beckum, C.L. Womack, Wallace Cooper, Bootsie Smitherman, Charles Iverson, and Elwin Ward, 2000. 1MDA photo*

*Pictured l-r: James Fossos, 1st Division CG Gen Daniel Yoo, and AJ Burn at an FMDA reunion, 2015. 1MDA photo*

*Pictured l-r: Jake Aston, Bert Richards, Nathan Getzenberg, and Bill Lynne, 1999. 1MDA photo*

*Women Marines celebrate the birthday of the Corps, NCO Club, Camp Pendleton, CA, 9 November 1994. Pictured l-r: Pat Kelley, Rosemary Albrect, MGySgt Helen Hannah Campbell USMC (Ret), Helen McCarthy, and Harriet Tagye. Courtesy of Obie O'Bryant and the 1MDA*

*Pictured top row, l-r: Sam Cosman, Joe Lorber, and Dick Scheppske. 2nd row: Bob Russell, Phil Hettchen, Virginia Decker, Jim Spurrier, and Ron Bierman. Front row: George Head, Ed Tecco, Mike Sisk, and George Bartram, 1999. 1MDA photo*

*Lou Wiener, Don Ball and Rube Sherman display the Association banner from atop the Willard Hotel in Washington, DC, 25 June 1955. Washington Evening Star photo courtesy 1MDA.*

*General C.B. Cates, former Commandant, delivers a brief address to the "Old Breed" at the 1951 convention banquet in Philadelphia, PA. 1MDA photo*

*Pictured l-r: Michael Mavar, Bill Ping, Paul Baviello, Randy Baviello, and Al Kensley, 23 February 1996. The members were gathered for the Recruit Graduation for Paul's son, Randy. 1MDA photo*

*MajGen Edwin A. Pollock, LtGen O.P. Smith, Gen Lemuel C. Shepherd Jr., LtGen Randolph Pate, and LtGen Gerald C. Thomas during a 1MDA reunion in New York, 1954. 1MDA photo*

*Marine Raiders during a 1MDA conference, 1954. 1MDA photo*

# 1ST MARINE DIVISION ASSOCIATION ROSTER

*Roster of active members as of 26 December 2018, listed by rank (if known), name (last, first, middle), city, state, and service information. Note: Life members are signified by the + symbol; Associate members are signified by the * symbol*

*1STLT* **Aamodt,** John R, Laporte, MN, *C-1-5 VN +*
*GYSGT* **Abbott,** Daniel Wayne, Sequim, WA, *1ST TANK BN 1MARDIV VN +*
*SGT* **Abbott,** Donald E, Tok, AK, *4.2 MTR 1-1 KO +*
*SGT* **Abel,** Daniel G, Cedar Park, TX, *H&S-11MAR KO +*
*SSGT* **Abel,** Jesse M, Vista, CA, *1 MAR COMBAT PHOTO +*
*LTCOL* **Ables,** Charles K, Carlsbad, CA, *7TH MAR, 11TH MAR VN +*
*MAJ* **Ables,** Kathleen V, Carlsbad, CA, *HQ-1MAR CW +*
**Abrams,** Charles (Abe) Michael, Odessa, FL, *FLC III MAF VN +*
*SGT* **Ace,** John Jay, Chino Valley, AZ, *F-2-1 MP CO HQ 1MAR DIV VN*
*PFC* **Achtzehn,** Mel E, Duquesne, PA, *HQ-1MAR WWII CH KO*
*SGT* **Ackerman,** Clinton W, Butler, NJ, *HQ-HQ WWII CH KO +*
*CPL* **Ackerson,** Alvin D, Kimberling City, MO, *D-2-11 KO +*
*SGT* **Ackert,** Phillip E, Half Moon Bay, CA, *B-1-1 KO +*
*CAPT* **Acuff,** Tommy H, Deer Park, TX, *B-1-7 KO +*
*COL* **Adamek,** Edward R JR., Oakdale, MN, *MAG-32 WWII CH KO +*
**Adams,** F R JR., Frederick, MD, *D-2-5 KO +*
**Adams,** John (Jp) P, Arvada, CO, *1 MAW KO +*
*LTCOL* **Adams,** Nate L II, Lexington, VA, *E-2-1 W-3-1 WWII KO VN +*
*SGT* **Adams,** William B JR., Beaverton, OR, *L-3-1 VN +*
*1STLT* **Adamson,** Clarence E, Mckinney, TX, *D-2-7 KO +*
*GYSGT* **Adcock,** Henry L, Trenton, OH, *H&S-2-1 VN +*
*SSGT* **Adler,** Robert Thomas, Peoria, AZ, *WPNS CO 2-1 1MAR DIV KO CW*
*SGT* **Adragna,** Mike, Sterling Heights, MI, *HQ-1ORD KO +*
*MGYSGT* **Adwell,** James R, Oceanside, CA, *G-4 1 MAR DIV SWA CW*
**Adyani,** Kian, Indio, CA, *1ST TANK BN*
*SGT* **Agras,** Demetrio, Brooklyn, NY, *G-3-1 KO +*
*CPL* **Agrelius,** Carl E, Whittier, CA, *F-2-7 WWII KO +*
*SGTMAJ* **Aguilar,** Tony R, Temecula, CA, *E-2-5 L-3-1 VN*
*CPL* **Ahlgren,** Donald E, Lorain, OH, *F-2-1 KO +*
**Ahlgren,** Wesley, Palm Desert, CA, *1MAR*
*CPL* **Ahn,** Heung-Woon, Seoul, Korea, *VN*
*SGT* **Ahrens,** Joseph P, River Vale, NJ, *B-1-5 KO +*
*CPL* **Aichele,** Robert E, Greenwood, IN, *B-1-5 VN +*
*SGT* **Aiken,** Robert G, Cape Coral, FL, *W-2-11 VN +*
*SSGT* **Aitken,** Robert M, New Iberia, LA, *10INF KO +*
*CPL* **Alaimo,** Joseph M, Spring Hill, FL, *C-1-5 KO +*
*SGT* **Alarid,** Jake I, Whittier, CA, *E-2-5 +*
*MRS* **Albert,** Carole, Rochester, NH, *ASSOCIATE **
*CPL* **Albert,** David H, Mequon, WI, *H&S-2-5 ANGLICO 41RM KO +*
*CPL* **Albert,** L E JR., Portland, ME, *K-3- 1 VN +*
*SGT* **Albin,** Francis M, Seattle, WA, *H&S/H-3-5 KO +*
*SGT* **Albright,** Clay A, Tuscaloosa, AL, *1PION 17MAR WWII +*
*SGT* **Alcott,** Henry, Chino Valley, AZ, *TK WWII KO +*
**Alday,** Glenn W, Bellevue, MI, *7SVC CH +*
*SGT* **Aldrich,** Richard C SR., Ware, MA, *A-1TKS KO +*
*SGT* **Aldsworth,** Rick D, Williamstown, WV, *A-1-5 VN +*
*SGT* **Alexander,** Donald W, Springfield, MO, *A-1-5 VN +*
*DR* **Alexander,** Franklin D, San Antonio, TX, *C-1MP FLC VN +*
*CPL* **Alexander,** Wilbert M, Dolomite, AL, *E-2-5 VN +*
**Alfaro,** Martin, Indio, CA, *7MAR*
*PFC* **Alicandro,** Thomas P, Canastota, NY, *F-2-5 WWII +*
*LTCOL* **Allanson,** Wm A, Fairfax, VA, *5TH MARINES KO VN*
*CPL* **Allard,** Edwin W, Dartmouth, MA, *F-2-7 KO +*
*MGYSGT* **Allen,** Arthur III, Menifee, CA, *HQBN HQ-2-11 OIF SWA*
*CAPT* **Allen,** Bill H, Mcdonough, GA, *SIG-5MAR WWII CH KO +*
*SGT* **Allen,** Edward D, Hiawassee, GA, *HQ-1-5 M-3-5 VN +*
*CPL* **Allen,** Elmer R, Wausau, WI, *D-7ENG-PALMS CW +*
*CPL* **Allen,** Gale, Bullhead City, AZ, *AAR69-73*
*SGT* **Allen,** James M, Goodlettsville, TN, *I-3-7 KO +*
*PFC* **Allen,** James P, Spokane Valley, WA, *B-1-5 WWII CH +*
*SGT* **Allen,** John H, Fountain Valley, CA, *HQBTRY-2-11 VN*
*CPL* **Allen,** Paul J, North Wales, PA, *E-2-1 VN +*
*SGT* **Allen,** Robert F, Savannah, GA, *MP-PION KO +*
*CAPT* **Allen,** Robert K, Santa Cruz, CA, *RR-7COMM 1-7MAR VN +*
*SGT* **Allen,** Wesley JR., Jacksonville Beach, FL, *1SHPTY KO +*
*SGT* **Alli,** William E, Bowie, MD, *D-2-1 KO +*
*CPL* **Allison,** James T, Memphis, TN, *A-1-5 KO +*
*MR.* **Allison,** John R, Aledo, TX, *ASSOCIATE **
*CAPT* **Aloise,** Andrew P, Clermont, FL, *H&S-1-5 COMM-HQ SWA +*
*PFC* **Alosi,** Joe P, Cave Creek, AZ, *1 RECON CW +*
*1STLT* **Altenburg,** Laurence M, Rotunda West, FL, *C-1RECON VN*
*LCPL* **Altman,** Ronnie L, Arlington, TX, *H&S BN, H&S CO. SOI*
*CPL* **Alvarado,** Felipe J, San Diego, CA, *1FORRECON CW +*
*SGT* **Alvarado,** Gumercindo G JR., San Antonio, TX, *F-2-7 KO +*
*PFC* **Alvarado,** Lorenzo, Pahrump, NV, *C-1-5 CW +*
*DR* **Alvarez,** Eugene, Ocala, FL, *C-1 AMTRAC KO +*
*CPL* **Alvarez,** Raymond L, Irving, TX, *H-2-5 VN +*
*CPL* **Amato,** Charles A, Locust Grove, VA, *H&S-7MAR KO +*
*SGT* **Amen,** Harold D, Emmett, ID, *F-2-5 KO +*
*SGT* **Amen,** Jerry, Albuquerque, NM, *WPNS-2-5 KO +*
*SGT* **Amen,** Kenneth, Fruitland, ID, *MABS17 KO +*
*COL* **Amery,** Robert S, Springfield, VA, *A-1-5 WWII +*
*SGT* **Ancona,** G, Brownsville, TX, *C-1-5 +*
*TSGT* **Anderson,** Ake L, Bel Air, MD, *H&S-5 WWII +*
*MGYSGT* **Anderson,** Andrew G, Puyallup, WA, *HQ-HQ KO VN +*
*SSGT* **Anderson,** Burton F, Morgan Hill, CA, *D-2-1 1SHPTY KO +*
*CAPT* **Anderson,** Carl W, Alameda, CA, *HQ-5MAR COMM-HQ KO VN +*
*SGTMAJ* **Anderson,** David C SR., Imperial, MO, *SPT 3RD DIV VN +*
*SSGT* **Anderson,** David H, Glendale, AZ, *F-2-5 VN +*
*CPL* **Anderson,** Dennis E, Fairview Heights, IL, *I-3-7 VN +*
*CPL* **Anderson,** Edward Cleve, Ashland, OR, *ALPHA CO, 1ST BN, 1ST MAR VN*
*1STSGT* **Anderson,** Gerald Earl, San Diego, CA, *L & i CO 3RD BN 1MAR REGT VN CW +*
*SGT* **Anderson,** Jack R, Highland Mills, NY, *HQBN KO +*
*SGT* **Anderson,** John M, Haddam, CT, *1ST COMBAT SVC GP KO*
*CPL* **Anderson,** L W, Sacramento, CA, *D-1-26 VN +*
*CPL* **Anderson,** Mark S, Rochester, MN, *TRK CO SVC BN VN*
*SGT* **Anderson,** Norman D, Jensen Beach, FL, *L-3-5 C-1-11 KO +*
*SGT* **Anderson,** Richard C, Springfield, VA, *ATT 7NGF-KMAG KO +*
*SGT* **Anderson,** Robert L, Billings, MT, *H&S/B-1-7 WWII KO +*
*CPL* **Anderson,** U S, Dacula, GA, *1SIG-HQ WWII +*
*SGT* **Anderson,** William L, Chino, CA, *B-1-11 VN*
*MSGT* **Anderton,** Ray "Andy" D, Allen, TX, *RECON CO HQ BN 1ST MAR DIV +*
*MSGT* **Andreas,** Anthony, Oceanside, CA, *HQ-5MAR COMM CO-HQ KO VN +*
*SGT* **Andresen,** Leroy G, Omaha, NE, *H&S-1SHPTY KO*
*GYSGT* **Andrews,** Paul G, Niceville, FL, *B-1 RECON VN*
**Andrews,** Richard J,,, *2ARMAMPH CW +*
**Andrews,** Robert G, Canon City, CO, *D-2-5 KO +*
*CPL* **Andrews,** Robert J, Tallahassee, FL, *I-3-1 VN +*
*LCPL* **Andrews,** Ronald K, Mccordsville, IN, *A-1-11 VN +*
*SGT* **Andrews,** William N, Tulsa, OK, *WPNS-7MAR 3-11MAR WWII CH KO +*
*SGT* **Andrews,** William A. (Joe), North Port, FL, *2/8 CUBA*
*SSGT* **Andróes,** Kenneth A, Dallas, OR, *D-1RECON VN +*
*SGT* **Androvich,** Eddy A, Sayerville, NJ, *H&S-3-7 KO +*
*CPL* **Andrulewicz,** James W, Homer Glen, IL, *L-3-5 VN +*
*CPL* **Angelini,** Richard, Garnet Valley, PA, *G-3-11 VN*
*CPL* **Anger,** Harold E, Midland, MI, *WPNS-7MAR WWII +*
*MGYSGT* **Angerome,** Salvatore P, Miami, FL, *2-11 WWII CH KO VN +*
*LT* **Angioletti,** Louis V, Norwood, NJ, *3-11MAR VN +*
*SGT* **Anglim,** Donald (Don) J, Southbridge, MA, *4.2MRTR-5MAR KO +*
*CPL* **Anglin,** Danny L, Warsaw, IN, *HQ-HQ KO +*
*CPL* **Angstman,** Roderick C, Moorhead, MN, *SIGNAL CO KO +*
*MAJ* **Angus,** Hal M, Escondido, CA, *1CEB CW +*
*SGT* **Anich,** Rudolph S, West Allis, WI, *ORD-ORD KO +*
*SGT* **Anides,** Carl H, Boynton Beach, FL, *RECON CO 1MARDIV KO +*
*CPL* **Aniloff,** Carl, Philadelphia, PA, *K-3-7 +*
*LCPL* **Annaian,** Robert L, Wilmington, MA, *7ENGR CW +*
*SGT* **Antal,** Kenneth M, Hamilton, OH, *A-1-5 VN +*
*LTCOL* **Anthony,** Clarence T, San Diego, CA, *G-2-7 G-2-5 VN +*
*SGT* **Anthony,** Jim, Delphi, IN, *H&S-1MED VN +*
*CAPT* **Antonille,** Russ, Potomac, MD, *COMM CO HQBN CW +*
*SGT* **Apgar,** David, Kutztown, PA, *1ST RECON BN VN*
*CAPT* **Apholt,** Paul Ward, Alton Bay, NH, *1/1 +*

*SGT* **Apodaca,** Alfred R, Littleton, CO, *B-1TK KO* +
*SGT* **Aposhian,** Van L, Lake Forest, CA, *WPNS CO 2-5 KO*
*SGT* **Appleby,** Robert D, Sherwood, AR, *81MM WPNS-3-7 KO VN* +
*CAPT* **Aquino,** Floree J, Bethel Park, PA, *2-11MAR A-1-5 VN* +
*GYSGT* **Arabian,** Gary G, San Clemente, CA, *1SIG CH KO VN* +
*SGT* **Arbogast,** Charles F, Hillsboro, OR, *H-3-1 KO* +
*SGT E-5* **Archer,** Daniel D, Prairie Village, KS, *HQ 1/5 VN*
*CPL* **Archibald,** Peter B, Palm City, FL, *3-7 VN* +
*HM3* **Arkell,** William C, Pendleton, OR, *A-1TK KO* +
*CPL* **Armendariz,** David, Elk Grove, CA, *7COMM CW* +
*SGT* **Armenio,** Anthony P, Douglaston, NY, *HQ-HQ KO* +
*CPL* **Armet,** Ronald D JR., Lindenhurst, NY, *B-1RECON VN* +
*CPL* **Arndt,** Robert Paul, Sun City, AZ, *1ST ANGLICO 1MAR DIV VN*
*CPL* **Arneson,** David D, Onalaska, WI, *H&S-1TK KO* +
*SGT* **Arneson,** John R, Saint Paul, MN, *16 FD C-1-7 WWII KO* +
*SGT* **Arnold,** Charles E, Houston, TX, *HQ-HQ WWII CH* +
*CAPT* **Arnold,** Frederick W, Costa Mesa, CA, *1-7 1-5 VN CW CMC 3-5*
*SGT* **Arnold,** Jason A, Redmond, OR, *E-3D AA BN SOM* +
*GYSGT* **Arnold,** John H, Butler, TN, *D-2-11 KO* +
*SGT* **Arnold,** Lester C, Fostoria, OH, *B-1RECON VN* +
*1STSGT* **Arnold,** M D, Lexington, NC, *F-2-1 KO* +
*SGT* **Arnold,** Ron A, Buffalo, NY, *B-1-1 KO*
*MAJ* **Aronson,** Edgar D, New York, NY, *HQ-1-7 CW* +
*CAPT* **Arseneault,** J D, Warren, NJ, *1-5 VN* +
*CPL* **Arthur,** Fred A, Hubbard, OH, *C-1RECON VN* +
*CAPT* **Arutunian,** Harold, Playa Del Rey, CA, *H-3-1 KO* +
*LCPL* **Ash,** Edward L, Hume, IL, *A-1-5 VN* +
*CPL* **Ashcraft,** F M, Saint. Charles, MO, *DFF-2-7 WWII CH* +
*CPL* **Ashcraft,** Stanley E, Plymouth, MI, *C-1-1 WWII* +
*SGTMAJ* **Ashe,** Eugene, Beckley, WV, *F-2-5 CW* +
*SGT* **Asheim,** Erling (Whitey) PE, New City, NY, *3D BN 1ST MAR KO* +
*CAPT* **Ashley,** Calvin H, Evansville, IN, *G-3-1 HQ-HQ KO VN* +
*SGTMAJ* **Ashton,** Richard E, Hanahan, SC, *1RECON 2-7 VN CW* +
*CPL* **Asp,** Andrew A, Boise, ID, *D-2-11 KO* +
*CPL* **Ast,** Bob A, Emporia, KS, *B-RECON VN* +
*SSGT* **Ast,** Ralph C, Franklin, WI, *1SVC KO* +
*CPL* **Astorino,** Frank, Staten Island, NY, *B-2ND TANK KO* +
*SGT* **Athey,** A S SR., Summerfield, FL, *HQ-2-1 WWII CH* +
*SGT* **Athis,** Franklin T, Gibbstown, NJ, *HQ-HQ KO VN* +
*SGT* **Atkins,** Robert L, Little Rock, AR, *SVC-1ENGR KO*
**Atkinson,** Thomas, Boulder, CO, *AFEM, SOM UN* *
**Attebery,** Bruce A, Oceanside, CA, *RECON KO* +
*CPL* **Attenisia,** John F, Desert Hot Springs, CA, *C-1-7 KO* +
*CAPT* **Atwood,** Theodore O JR., San Diego, CA, *H&S-1-5 VN* +
*LTJG* **Aube,** Karl Eugene, Coarsegold, CA, *HQ BN 1-11 HQ CO 3-1MAR REGT CW* +
*SSGT* **Aubuchon,** C D, Chesterfield, MO, *D-2-11 KO* +
*1STLT* **Aulman,** Edward G, Syosset, NY, *HQ-1-7 VN*
**Ault,** J M, Lafitte, LA, *I/S/O-2-5 VN* +
*DR.* **Austerman,** Jack B DDS, Oklahoma City, OK, *DENT-1MED KO* +
*CPL* **Austin,** Sean N, Winter Park, FL, *B-1-9*
*PFC* **Auwen,** F L, Wellston, OK, *1AMTRAC WWII* +
**Averill,** Bob, Arvada, CO, *1ST MAR DIV TRANSIT VN*
*HM2* **Avey,** Thomas R, San Diego, CA, *I-3-7 1MED VN* +
*CPL* **Ayala,** Ruben S, Chino, CA, *C-1-11 WWII* +
*MR.* **Ayer,** George L, Northport, NY, *B-1-1 WWII* +
*CPL* **Babchak,** Gerald F, Wellsville, NY, *1FLC 1FSR VN* +
*PFC* **Babineau,** William J, Charlton, MA, *TRANS-9MT MABS16 VN* +
**Baca,** John, Julian, CA, *1ST AIR CALVARY DIV USA VN* +
*CPL* **Bacel,** George H, Lakeland, FL, *H&S-1-11 WWII* +
*CPL* **Backer,** David L, Gladstone, OR, *A-2D PLT 1RECON BN VN*
**Backman,** David L, Stayton, OR, *E-2-1 KO* +
*PFC* **Bacon,** Howard C, Miami, FL, *A-1ENGR WWII CH* +
*CPL* **Bacon,** John T, Walnut Creek, CA, *1TK VN* +
**Bader,** Wayne L, Littleton, CO, *L CO HQ 3-7 VN* +
*MGYSGT* **Bael,** Ray J, Stockton, CA, *C-1RECON VN*
*SGT* **Baggerly,** Lawrence A, Commerce Township, MI, *HQ-FMFPAC KO* +
*SGT* **Baggett,** Charles G, Richmond, VA, *H-3-7 KO* +
**Baggett,** Walter (Horace) H, Cairo, GA, *WPNS-1-1 KO* +
*COL* **Baggette,** John C, Port Royal, SC, *I-3-7 VN*
*LCPL* **Bagley,** Edward T JR., Citrus, FL, *I-3-1 H-2-7 VN* +
*LCPL* **Bagrowski,** Daniel S, Burbank, IL, *H&S-2/3-7 5MEB CW* +
**Bagstad,** Charles W, Milwaukee, WI, *M/H&S-3-5 VN* +
**Bagwell,** Benny, Trinity, TX, *A-1-5 WWII KO* +
*PO2* **Bahr,** William K, Port Hueneme, CA, *1FSSG WOT* +
*MAJ* **Bahry,** P T, Carlsbad, CA, *11MAR VN* +
**Baik,** Seung-Mo, Yangcheon-Gu Seoul, Korea
*SGT* **Bailey,** Bartlett, Elizabethtown, NY, *ASST-1-5 WWII KO* +
**Bailey,** Brian H, Sun City, AZ, *WPNS-1-5 WWII KO* +
*SSGT* **Bailey,** Gary Franklin, Waynesville, OH, *C-1-1 1ST MAR DIV KO*
*CPL* **Bailey,** Ian M, Floral Park, NY, *F-2-5 G-2-6 VN* +
*PHM2* **Bailey,** John W JR., Santa Paula, CA, *H&S CO HQBN WWII* +
*MRS* **Bailey,** Naomi F, Santa Paula, CA, *ASSOCIATE* +
**Bailey,** Norman P, Middleton, RI, *H&S-3-5 B-1-7 VN* +
*CWO4* **Bailey,** Oliver W, Saint Petersburg, FL, *HQ-1-1/7 WWII KO* +
*CAPT* **Bailey,** Robert E, Lebanon, MO, *HQ-9ENGR 1ATK VN* +
*GYSGT* **Bailey,** Robert L, Chula Vista, CA, *H&S-3-5 VN CW* +
*CAPT* **Baines,** Bill, Reno, NV, *M-3-1 VN* +
*PFC* **Baioa,** Manuel P, Salida, CA, *E-2-7 1ST MAR DIV VN* +
*COL* **Bair,** Edgar M, San Diego, CA, *AMTRAC-7-RLT VN* +
*GYSGT* **Baird,** Donald W, Jonesboro, GA, *C-1-1 KO* +
*CPL* **Baird,** Fred C, Alexander City, AL, *A-1AMTRAC WWII KO* +
*CPL* **Baird,** Robert A, Knoxville, TN, *A-1-7 KO* +
*SGT* **Baird,** Robert W, Newark, DE, *D-1RECON VN* +
*GYSGT* **Bakas,** Angelone G, North Reading, MA, *B-1 PARSPLTROOP WWII* +
*COL* **Baker,** Chris L, Philadelphia, PA, *1/7 1/5 7TH ENG*
*SGT* **Baker,** Dave E, Rochester, NY, *M-3-1 VN* +
**Baker,** Ferrall L, Coupeville, WA, *G-3-5 KO VN* +
*COL* **Baker,** Horace W, Sheffield, AL, *B-1-1 2-1 VN CW* +
*SGT* **Baker,** James T, Long Beach, MS, *ORD BN KO* +
*SGT* **Baker,** Jerry W, Stanley, VA, *HQ-HQ VN* +
*CPL* **Baker,** William W, Beallsville, PA, *I-3-7 WWII CH* +
*PFC* **Bakke,** Gerald (Jerry) L, Sun City, AZ, *A-1-5 VN* +
*REV.* **Bakken,** Dean Ramon, Becker, MN, *A -1AMTRAC KO* +
*SGTMAJ* **Balderrama,** Bruno, Tustin, CA, *5 MAR KO VN* +
**Baldwin,** Marvin G, Scottsdale, AZ, *WPNS-7MAR WWII CH* +
*CPL* **Baldwin,** Wayne W, Phoenix, AZ, *B-1-5 KO*
*PFC* **Bales,** William R, Estes Park, CO, *HQ-1-7 VN* +
**Balfour,** P D JR., Galena, AK, *C-1-1* +
*SGT* **Ball,** Henry R, Lancaster, KY, *F-2-1 WWII KO* +
*CAPT* **Balmes,** Fred, The Woodlands, TX, *HMH463 1MAW MAG16 VN*
*CAPT* **Baltes,** John F, Stoughton, WI, *HQ-1-11 KO VN* +
*CPL* **Baltes,** John H, Heber City, UT, *I-3-7 KO* +
*MRS* **Bancroft,** Darlene, Philadelphia, PA, *ASSOCIATE* *
**Bang,** Hong S, Downey, CA, *ROKMC KO* +
*SGT* **Banks,** Edward T, Woburn, MA, *HQ-HQ KO*
*SGT* **Barabba,** John M, Gig Harbor, WA, *H-3-7 KO* +
*CPL* **Baranyi,** Edward, Loudon, TN, *C-3AMTRAC WWII* +
*SSGT* **Barber,** Daniel, Palm Desert, CA, *3RD RECON VN*
*SGT* **Barber,** John W, Aliquippa, PA, *H-2-5 VN*
*LCPL* **Barber,** Steven M, Stockton, CA, *H&S-1-5 VN* +
*SGT* **Barbier,** Richard C, White Castle, LA, *COMM-HQ KO* +
*CPL* **Barclay,** Lonnie D, Springfield, OH, *E--2-7 VN* +
*MR.* **Barcus,** Donald W, Tipton, IN, *1SHPTY KO* +
*DR.* **Barfield,** Clyde E, Lemon Grove, CA, *HQ-2-5 HQ-HQ CH* +
*CAPT* **Barkann,** Jeremy A, Princeton, NJ, *I-3-7 KO* +
*HM3* **Barker,** Donald L, Atherton, CA, *I-3-1 E-MED KO* +
*CPL* **Barker,** Frank W, Chicago Heights, IL, *MP CO KO* +
*CPL* **Barker,** J E JR., Polk City, FL, *1SIG HQ WWII* +
*LCPL* **Barker,** Jeffrey H, Aloha, OR, *1/3MAW VN* +
*MAJ* **Barker,** Randy C, Monument, CO, *A-1-1 P-5-11 CW* +
**Barker,** Thomas H, Coto De Caza, CA, *C-1-7 VN*
*SGT* **Barley,** Robert E, Englewood, FL, *1AMTRAC KO* +
*CPL* **Barna,** Joseph D, Raritan, NJ, *L-3-5 VN* +
*COL* **Barnard,** Roger H, Fairfax, VA, *H-3-5 3-7 KO VN* +
*SGT E-5* **Barnard,** Hugh D, Bloomington, IL, *A 1-5 01/1964-06/1965*
*SGT* **Barnes,** Lew R, North Plains, OR, *HMM-362 VN* +
*SGT* **Barnes,** Louis E, San Luis Obispo, CA, *HQ-2-5 CW* +
*1STSGT* **Barnett,** James R, Roseburg, OR, *WPNS-1-1 KO VN* +
*COL* **Barnett,** Peter J, Hollywood, CA, *MAG-16 CW SWA* +
*CPL* **Barnholt,** Edward S, Morrison, CO, *D-1-5 D-2-11 VN* +
*COL* **Barnum,** Harvey C JR., Reston, VA, *2-7MAR VN* +
**Barnwell,** David R, Seville, Spain, *11MAR VN* +
*SGTMAJ* **Barr,** Douglas R, San Diego, CA, *HQ-1/HQ-HQ SWA* +
*CPL* **Barr,** Marvin M, Oberlin, OH, *H&S-8AMTRAC WWII* +
*MSGT* **Barrett,** Mac, San Francisco, CA, *1MAW WWII KO* +
*CPL* **Barrett,** Robert A, Middletown, OH, *HMM-164. HMM-265 VN*

*CPL* **Barrett,** Robert L JR., Powell, WY, *HQHB DIV G-4 VN* +
*COL* **Barrett,** Roscoe L, Norman, OK, *H-3-1 KO VN* +
*SGT* **Barrett,** Terrance J, Wrightwood, CA, *1FSR 1SVC KO*
*SGT* **Barrett,** Thomas M, Cocoa Beach, FL, *C-4-3 KO* +
*HMC/FMF* **Barrier Phd,** Louis J, East Wenatchee, WA, *A CO 1ST ENG BN KO* +
*CPL* **Barrios,** Amador D, Arleta, CA, *1TK HMH163 K-3-5 VN* +
*CAPT* **Barron,** Michael S, Rome, GA, *B-1-5 VN* +
*SGTMAJ* **Barron,** Robert J JR., San Diego, CA, *HQ CO HQ BN G-2 VN* +
*GEN* **Barrow,** R H, Houston, TX, *A-1-1 WWII* +
*SSGT* **Barrows,** George M SR., Jacksonville, NC, *HDQTRS-1-1 KO VN* +
*MAJ* **Barry,** James J JR., Gilford, NH, *HQBN VN* +
*PFC* **Barry,** Robert, Pocatello, ID, *B-1-7 WWII CH* +
*SGT* **Barry,** Roger W, Schuyler, NE, *1MAW VMF-235 KO* +
**Barry,** William H JR., West Hartford, CT, *WPNS-7MAR WWII* +
*HM3* **Barry,** William J, Sandy, UT, *B-1-1 KO* +
*CPL* **Barsomian,** Haig J, Walpole, MA, *G-3-1 KO*
*SGT* **Barson,** Duane K, Herriman, UT, *HQ-HQ CW* +
*SGT* **Bartholomay,** Leon F, Longmont, CO, *HQ-11 VN CW* +
*SGT* **Bartholomew,** Robert N, Oklahoma City, OK, *1RECON KO* +
*CAPT* **Bartley,** James H, Kingwood, TX, *H-3-1 KO VN CW* +
*SGT* **Bartolucci,** Adello R, Niles, IL, *VMJ1 KO* +
*CPL* **Bartram,** George D, Baltimore, MD, *R-2-1 WWII CH* +
*LCPL* **Barvilchak,** Donald J, Myrtle Beach, SC, *D-1-1 VN* +
*SGT* **Base,** Ronald A, Pinehurst, NC, *MAG12-1MAW KO* +
*MAJ* **Basham,** Benjamin E, Warrenton, VA, *G-3-5 C-1-11 KO VN* +
*SGT* **Basile,** James T, Melbourne, FL, *K-11MAR KO* +
*GYSGT* **Basilone,** Michael W, Beaufort, SC, *BAND-HQ-HQ CW* +
*LCPL* **Baskin,** Blake K, Vinita, OK, *B-1-5 CW* +
*SGT* **Bass,** James C, Okeechobee, FL, *D-2-5 KO* +
*HM2* **Bass,** V A, Colonial Heights, VA, *C-1-26 VN* +
*COL* **Batcheller,** Gordon D, Franklin, WV, *H&S/A-1-1 7MAR VN* +
*PFC* **Bates,** Roy L, Winchester, KY, *C-1-7 KO* +
*SGT* **Batherson,** Charles R, Westland, MI, *AT 5MAR KO* +
*GYSGT* **Bauer,** Charles F, Yuma, AZ, *H&S-1-28 B-1RECON CMC VN* +
*MAJ* **Baughman,** Prentiss H, Salina, KS, *TK-HQ WWII CH KO* +
*MSGT* **Baum,** Joseph B, New York, NY, *H&S-3-11 WWII CH KO* +
*SGT* **Baumann,** Donald A SR., Stuart, FL, *B-7MT KO*
*CPL* **Baumgardner,** Gary W, Latrobe, PA, *B-1-1 KO* +
*CPL* **Bautch,** Richard R, Waldport, OR, *B-1ENGR KO* +
*HM3* **Baviello,** Paul M, Corona, CA, *D-1-5 VN* +
*SGT* **Bayer,** Robert M, West Hills, CA, *ISO-HQ VN* +
*LTCOL* **Bayley,** Norman C, Los Angeles, CA, *USS BOSTON WWII* +
*CPL* **Bayuk,** Mark G, Saint Paul, MN, *M-4-11 D-1RECON VN* +
*HM2* **Bazan,** Richard L, Plano, TX, *I-3-5 VN* +
*SGT* **Beach,** Jerry S, Tipton, IN, *A-1-11 KO* +
*SGTMAJ* **Beadle,** Albert E, Laureldale, PA, *D-2-7 KO* +
*SSGT* **Beal,** Norman L, Bryan, TX, *2-5MAR 1MARBDE KO* +
*SGT* **Beal,** R C, American Fork, UT, *M-3-1* +
*SGT* **Beal,** Randy C, Riverton, UT, *B-1-5 M-3-1 VN* +
*SSGT* **Beale,** James I IV, Franklin, VA, *C-1-1 VN* +
*1STLT* **Beall,** Curtis A, Dublin, GA, *81MM HQ-3-1 WWII CH KO* +
*1STSGT* **Bean,** George T, Cherokee Village, AR, *W-1-1 WPNS-7MAR WWII CH KO VN* +
*HM3* **Bean,** Jerry K, Flushing, MI, *C-1-5 VN* +
*MSGT* **Bean,** Robert "Bob" S, Vancouver, WA, *5/11, 3/11*
*CPL* **Bearss,** Edwin C, Arlington, VA, *L-3-7 WWII* +
*SGT* **Beatty,** Robert L, Stephens City, VA, *A-1-5 VN*
**Beaty,** Keith, Oneida, TN, *C-1-7 VN* +
*CPL* **Beaty,** Robert C, Philadelphia, PA, *H&S/B-1-5 VN* +
*SGT* **Beauchamp,** Peter A, Palm Bay, FL, *G-3-1 KO* +
*LCPL* **Beaudoin,** Roger, Marlborough, NH, *2-7MAR CW* +
*SGT* **Beaulieu,** Raymond E, Groton, CT, *H&S-1SHPTY* +
**Beauton,** Alex, Coos Bay, OR, +
*SSGT* **Beauvais,** George E, Yalesville, CT, *1ST CSG 51-53 1STBN 5THMAR KO VN* +
*CPL* **Beaver,** Jay A, Selinsgrove, PA, *A-1-1 VN* +
*CPL* **Bechtel,** W J, Jackson, NJ, *E-2-5 VN* +
*CPL* **Beck,** Gregory T, Texarkana, AR, *1-11 4-11 VN*
**Beck,** Richard G, Brooklyn Center, MN, *C-1ENGR 7MAR CH*
**Beck,** Tom F, Columbus, OH, *B-ENGR KO* +
*SGT* **Beck,** William J, Louisville, KY, *A-1-11 KO* +
*LCPL* **Becker,** Alvin D, Granger, TX, *1-5MAR VN*
*SGT* **Becker,** Danny Joseph, Crystal City, MO, *L-3-5, C-1-5, C-1-7 VN*
*PFC* **Becker,** Harold C, Ham Lake, MN, *HQ-2-5 CH* +
*COL* **Becker,** James S, Port Orange, FL, *HQ-3-1 VN* +
*CPL* **Becker,** Kenneth C SR., Le Mars, IA, *1ARM-AMPH 11MAR VN* +
*LCPL* **Becker,** Michael C, Watertown, SD, *B-1-1 VN* +
*CPL* **Becker,** Thomas, Scarsdale, NY, *A-1-5 VN* +
**Bedford,** Brian J, Matawan, NJ, *WPNS-3-1 CW* +
**Bednar,** Michael J, Haugen, WI, *I-3-5 VN* +
*COL* **Beeler,** Robert A, Sedona, AZ, *A/1/5, 3/5 VN* +
*PHM* **Beers,** Robert N, Central Square, NY, *1SVC WWII CH* +
*CPL* **Beeson,** Vince J, Denver, CO, *11MAR WWII* +
*CPL* **Beffa,** D A, Saint Louis, MO, *A-1-1* +
*3D LTHO GRPH* **Begandy,** Richard, Massapequa Park, NY
*SGT* **Behan,** Frank J, Rego Park, NY, *WPNS CO 2ND BN KO* +
*SGT* **Beheler,** Richard L, Amboy, IN, *E-2-7 VN* +
*LCPL* **Behnke,** Edward E, Madison, SD, *D-1-1 VN* +
*CPL* **Behr,** Arno L, Plymouth, WI, *A-1RECON B-1-7 VN* +
*GYSGT* **Behrens,** Richard H, Greenwood, DE, *H-3-5 CH KO* +
*SGT* **Belfi,** Robert W, The Villages, FL, *I-3-1/5 VN* +
**Belgum,** Richard, Woodland, CA, *1 MAR*
**Beliles,** David A, Sarasota, FL, *5MAR KO* +
*PFC* **Bell,** Freddy L, Cookson, OK, *A/1-5 VN*
*HM3* **Bell,** Gary L, Crawfordsville, IN, *D-1-1 1MED VN* +
*SSGT* **Bell,** Jack B, Richmond, VA, *11MAR 1MAW KO* +
*SGT* **Bell,** John R, O'fallon, MO, *1CSG KO*
*CPL* **Bell,** Samuel A, Baltimore, MD, *H-3-5 KO* +
*SGTMAJ* **Bell,** Wayne R, Temecula, CA, *3AA 1ENGR 11MAR OIF* +
**Bell,** William R, Lumberton, NC, *L-3-1MAR A-1ENGR VN*
*SGT* **Bellamy,** James R, Beckley, WV, *WPNS-1-5 KO* +
*CPL* **Bellando,** Alexander R, Brentwood, NY, *B-1-1 KO*
*CPL* **Belmont,** Christopher W, Cape Coral, FL, *M-3-5 VN* +
*SGT* **Belscamper,** Eugene C, Georgetown, TX, *H&S-1-7 KO* +
*SGT* **Belt,** Ralph F, Palm Bay, FL, *MAG33 KO* +
*SGT* **Belz,** Bob, Indio, CA, *SVCO 1 MAR DIV* +
*CPL* **Belz,** Peter T, Norristown, PA, *I-3-1 WWII CH* +
*CPL* **Bemis,** Forrest W JR., Gilbert, AZ, *A-1-5 WWII* +
*CPL* **Bender,** R H, Monsey, NY, *1ENGR C-1-17 WWII* +
*LTCOL* **Benes,** Edward A, Merced, CA, *B-1-5 VN* +
*SGTMAJ* **Benford,** Larock W, Menifee, CA, *11TH MAR*
*SGT* **Benitez,** Joaquin B, Rescue, CA, *I-3-7 WWII KO* +
**Benjamino,** Mitchell J, Randolph, MA, *1MAR DIV WWII*
*PLTSGT* **Benko,** Stephen E, New Canaan, CT, *HQ-1-1 WWII CH* +
*PFC* **Benner,** Clifford W, Coopersburg, PA, *H&S-1 WWII* +
*TSGT* **Bennett,** Edmund F, Highlands Ranch, CO, *SUP-1TK KO* +
*CPL* **Bennett,** Joseph W, Sewell, NJ, *HQ-11MAR VN* +
*CPL* **Bennett,** Lawrence N, Las Vegas, NV, *C-1-5 WWII CH* +
*PFC* **Bennett,** Rod T, Marshall, MN, *A-1-1 KO* +
*MAJ* **Bennett,** Ronald R, San Diego, CA, *H&S-2-1 HQ-1MAR VN* +
*SGT* **Benning,** Douglas L, Mulberry, FL, *E-1RE-CON VN* +
*SGT* **Benning,** George J, Streator, IL, *WPNS-1-7 KO* +
*MAJ* **Benoit,** Gale F, Yakima, WA, *H&S-1-7 KO* +
*SGT* **Benoit,** Robert E, Exeter, NH, *HQTRS WWII VN* +
*PFC* **Benware,** Eugene M, Chicago, IL, *C-1-5 VN*
*MSGT* **Berardi,** Michael E, Destin, FL, *1-7MAR KO* +
*CPL* **Berentz,** Ronald C, New Matamoras, OH, *HQ-1-7 VN* +
*PFC* **Berg,** William, Naples, FL, *A-1-1 KO* +
*CPL* **Bergart,** Malvin J, Park Ridge, IL, *1-7MAR CW* +
*PFC* **Berger,** Charles P, Chicago, IL, *A-1-5 CW* +
*COL* **Berger,** Spencer S, Auburn, NY, *2-7MAR WWII* +
*SSGT* **Bergeron,** Dennis A, Kenner, LA, *C-1-1 VN* +
**Bergeron,** Joseph W, Mandeville, LA, *HQ-11/5MAR VN* +
*SSGT* **Bergeron,** Robert, Port Ludlow, WA, *7TH MAR KO*
*CPL* **Bergin,** Russell F, Orlando, FL, *1ENGR KO* +
*CPL* **Bergmann,** John E, Burgaw, NC, *B-1-1 KO* +
*SSGT* **Berkeley,** David J, Pocasset, MA, *ATT 1MAR WWII* +
*CAPT* **Berkheimer,** Philip A, Frederick, MD, *1ENGR VN* +
*SGT* **Berkley,** Robert J, East Wenatchee, WA, *H&S-1-1 KO* +
*MSGT* **Bermender,** Carl L, Spring Hill, FL, *WPNS-7MAR WWII KO VN* +
*CPL* **Bernardo,** Joseph A, Avon, MA, *B-1-11 VN* +
**Bernath,** Harold D, Wauseon, OH, *WPNS-7MAR WWII CH* +
*SGT* **Bernhardt,** Thomas J, Phoenix, AZ, *D-1-5 1FSR VN* +
*LTCOL* **Bernier,** Maurice F, Fallbrook, CA, *I/IIIMEF VN* +
*SGT* **Berntson,** Steve L, University Place, WA, *ISO-2-1 1-5MAR VN*
*SGT* **Berot,** Alfred C, Ponchatoula, LA, *10INF KO* +
*MGYSGT* **Bertaut,** Alvin E, Metairie, LA, *K-3-5 A-3-11 SNIPER WWII VN SWA* +
*SGT* **Best,** Dennis M, Voorhees, NJ, *G-2-5 VN* +
*SGT* **Betts,** Warren R, Florissant, MO, *E-2-5 KO* +
*SGT* **Beturne,** David A, Hampden, MA, *M-3-1 VN* +
*SGT* **Bevier,** Richard C, Cordova, TN, *A-1AAMPH KO* +
*MAJ* **Bevilacqua,** Allan C, Grayson, KY, *B-1-5 HQ-4-11 CH KO VN*
**Beyer,** Holly W, Brookings, OR, *ASSOCIATE* +
*HMC* **Beyersdorf,** James B FMF, Pittsfield, VT, *H&S-3-7 1SHPTY VN* +

*CPL* **Beynon,** Evan R, Ho-Ho-Kus, NJ, *HMR-161 KO* +
*SGT* **Bez,** Juan M, Coral Gables, FL, *H-2-5 VN* +
*CPL* **Biagini,** John F, Massapequa Park, NY, *D-1-1 VN* +
*SGT* **Biby,** Robert Thomas, Pacifica, CA, *1ST MASS EVAC CO CW* +
*SGT* **Bickford,** Michael W, Pasco, WA, *H&S/A-1-7 KO VN* +
*LTCOL* **Bickley,** Leroy A, Guilford, CT, *H&S-1-5 VN* +
*LCPL* **Bierman,** John A, Danbury, WI, *C-1-5 VN* +
*SGT* **Bierman,** Robert M, Shipman, IL, *H&S-2-5 VN* +
*PFC* **Biermann,** Ronald R, Linthicum, MD, *B-1TK KO* +
*PLTSGT* **Biernacki,** Leo T, Dolton, IL, *F-2-5 WWII CH* +
*1STLT* **Bigelow,** George W, Allison Park, PA, *B-3AMTRAC VN* +
*MSGT* **Biggs,** James W, Fredericksburg, VA, *HQ-HQ HQ-3-11 SWA* +
*SGT* **Billets,** Richard J, Riverdale, NJ, *1ANGLICO VN* +
*SGT* **Billingsley,** Robert E JR., Rome, GA, *B-1-11 KO* +
*SGT* **Bills,** Terry V JR., Lafayette, LA, *B-1-1 KO* +
*CPL* **Bilsky,** Frank (Skip) R, Iron Mountain, MI, *1-FSR CW* +
*CPL* **Bilyk,** Michael A, Oakland, MI, *H&S-3-7 VN* +
*COL* **Bingham,** Carleton D, Gardnerville, NV, *3-1 CMBT SVC GRP KO* +
*SGT* **Bingheimer,** Peter J, Buffalo, NY, *H-3-7 KO* +
*MGYSGT* **Binion,** Ronald, Oceanside, CA, *H&S/C-1-5 VN* +
*LCPL* **Binkowski,** Frank F, Palm Bay, FL, *A-1-5 VN*
*CPL* **Birch,** Ernest JR., Manchester, MO, *W BTRY 2/11 VN*
*CPL* **Birdsong,** Grady T, Broomfield, CO, *1-27MAR 2-9MAR VN*
*SSGT* **Birkhead,** Claude D, Victoria, TX, *WPNS-3-7 KO* +
*SGT* **Birmingham,** John M, Trussville, AL, *A-1-5 KO* +
*SGTMAJ* **Birnie,** William E, Vista, CA, *3RD BN 1ST MAR DIV*
*CPL* **Bisbee,** Paul B, Innisfil, Ont, Canada, *1 & 2 RECON BLT 115 VN*
*LCPL* **Bishop,** F E JR., Lockeford, CA, *E-2-1 VN* +
*PVT* **Bishop,** Loren J, Cicero, IN, *C-1-1 CW* +
*SGT* **Bishop,** Louis A JR., Chariton, IA, *VN, 7TH COMM BN, HQ CO 27TH MAR VN*
**Bishop,** Robert Daniel, Harvey, LA, *ASSOCIATE* *
*CPL* **Bivens,** Leonard E, Edgewood, MD, *A-1RECON VN*
**Blachura,** K, Eden, NY, *HQ-1-1 VN* +
*SSGT* **Black,** Clyde O, Lovelady, TX, *HQ-3-7 VN* +
*SSGT* **Black,** Harry M, Columbia, MO, *HQ-1-5 WWII CH KO* +
*CPL* **Black,** Jeffrey A, Arvada, CO, *A-1-11 CW* +
*SGTMAJ* **Black,** Troy E, Quantico, VA, *G-2 BN 1MAR, 3 BN 7MAR SWA*
*PFC* **Black,** H S III, Annandale, VA, *H&S-7MAR* +
**Black,** William T II, Las Vegas, NV, *COMM CO KO* +
*CPL* **Blackburn,** Charles E, Mount Vernon, IN, *MT-1SVC KO* +
*LCPL* **Blackburn,** Ron G, Heltonville, IN, *K-3-5 VN* +
**Blackford,** Randall C, Chelsea, MI, *E-2-5 E-1RECON VN* +
*LTCOL* **Blackshear,** William (Butch) B JR., Fallbrook, CA, *1ST TANK BN VN*
*CPL* **Bladstrom,** Walter C, Sarasota, FL, *HQ-HQ KO* +
*OS1* **Blair,** D L, Roseburg, OR, *9ENGR VN* +
*GYSGT* **Blair,** Leo F JR., Mills River, NC, *1SHPTY WWII KO VN*
*CPL* **Blakely,** Charles S, Omaha, NE, *B-3AMTRAC VN* +
*SGT* **Bland,** David P, Los Angeles, CA, *HQ-2-1 CW* +
*SGT* **Blankenheim,** James H, Madison, WI, *H&S-3-5 VN* +
*COL* **Blanton,** Harold L JR., Riverside, CA, *C-1-1 RECON KO* +
*CPL* **Blazer,** John A, Savannah, GA, *G-3-1 KO* +
*MSGT* **Blick,** Joseph A, Jacksonville, NC, *G-3-7 KO VN* +
*MGYSGT* **Blinebury,** Joseph A, Warrington, PA, *5MAR 1FSSG CW VMA131* +
*SSGT* **Block,** George L, Florissant, MO, *HQ-1-7 WWII CH KO*
**Block,** Patrick F, Beaverton, OR, *1RADCOM VN* +
**Bloedau,** Richard K JR., Hays, NC, *5-175 H-3-11 VN* +
*SGT* **Blomeley,** W Scotty, Bradenton, FL, *A-1-1 WWII CH KO* +
*CPL* **Bloomingdale,** Marvin J, Belvidere, IL, *C-1MED KO* +
*CPL* **Blose,** Paul F, Yonkers, NY, +
*CAPT* **Blount,** Earl C JR., Murrells Inlet, SC, *HQBN 1MAR KO VN* +
*CPL* **Blue,** Barry A, Brenham, TX, *H-2-5 VN* +
*CPL* **Blum,** Dale A, Montello, WI, *A-1-11 VN* +
*SSGT* **Blum,** Donald R, Silver Springs, FL, *1AMTRAC KO* +
**Blythe,** Erdman W, Henderson, KY, *WPNS-3-1 KO* +
*SGT* **Boaman,** Charles R, Southern Pines, NC, *3-5MAR KO* +
*PACS* **Boatman,** William Frank, Juneau, AK, *ASSOCIATE* *
*HM2* **Boatman,** William J, Round Rock, TX, *I-3-7 VN* +
*SGT* **Bobar,** W A, Scott Township, PA, *D-2-7 KO* +
*HA1* **Bobst,** Robert F, San Clemente, CA, *K-3-1 WWII* +
**Bodner,** P M, Stony Point, NY, *1TK* +
*TSGT* **Boen,** Chris B, Queensland, Australia, *D-1-5 TK CH KO* +
*SGT* **Bogardus,** Van Ness H III, Grass Valley, CA, *L-3-7 VN* +
*CPL* **Boghosian,** Charles G, Fort Wayne, IN, *I-3-5 WWII CH* +
**Bogusiewicz,** Henry E, Bloomingdale, IL, *VMF(AW) 542 CW* +
*PFC* **Bohach,** Robert L, Peoria, AZ, *F-2-1 KO* +
*CPL* **Bohart,** Richard C, Palm Harbor, FL, *E-2-7 KO* +
*CPL* **Bokemeyer,** Harry L, Houston, TX, *H-3-11 KO* +
*MSGT* **Boland,** Robert F, Chandler, AZ, *K-3-7 L-3-1 VN* +
**Boldt,** Jerome C, Avinger, TX, *4-11MAR VN* +
*LTCOL* **Boler,** Thomas H, Laguna Beach, CA, *AMTRAC WWII KO* +
*2NDLT* **Boley,** James J, Kansas City, MO, *I-3-1 H&S-3-1 KO* +
*LCPL* **Bolfing,** Robert P, Cypress, TX, *C-1TRK VN* +
*SGT* **Bolle,** Charles T, Anaheim, CA, *E-2-11 VN* +
*SGT* **Bollinger,** William R, Port Orange, FL, *H-1-11 KO* +
*CWO4* **Bolton,** Gilbert H, Oceanside, CA, *M-3-7 VN* +
**Bolton,** Jon, Murrieta, CA, *K-3-1 VN CW* +
*CPL* **Bonderud,** Robert J, San Rafael, CA, *C-1TK VN*
*CAPT* **Bondurant,** Richard D, San Juan Capistrano, CA, *C-1-1 MASS-1-1MAW KO CMC VN SWA* +
*CAPT* **Bongiovanni,** Michael C, Sherman Oaks, CA, *3D AABN OIF* +
*PFC* **Bonkosky,** Wayne C, Santa Rosa, CA, *A-1-5 CW* +
*1STSGT* **Bonkowski,** Jerome S, Lombard, IL, *H&S/D-2-7 KO* +
**Bonomo,** Christopher L, San Dimas, CA, *ASSOCIATE* +
*CPL* **Boore,** Lloyd Z, Baltimore, MD, *WPNS-7MAR WWII CH* +
*GYSGT* **Borboa,** Escolastico C JR., Fresno, CA, *H&S/4.2-5MAR KO VN* +
*CAPT* **Borcherdt,** Edward R III, Santa Monica, CA, *B-1-7 SWA* +
*CPL* **Borges,** Saro D, Brooklyn, NY, *G-3-1 KO* +
*SSGT* **Borgio,** William J, Prescott, AZ, *K-3-5 I-3-1 VN*
*CPL* **Borland,** Stephen M, Rio Rancho, NM, *H&S-1RECON CW* +
**Borras,** Joseph (Koch), Grants Pass, OR, *MT-HQ-HQ KO* +
*SGT* **Borst,** John F, Eustis, FL, *D-2-11 KO* +
*SGT* **Bortko,** Walter D, Las Vegas, NV, *A-1-1 KO* +
**Borvansky,** Glenn A, Marseilles, IL, *1-5MAR VN* +
*CDR* **Bosley,** James E, Columbia, SC, *1-7MAR VN* +
**Bosshard,** Steven N, Rohnert Park, CA, *I-3-5-FSR VN* +
*SGT* **Bosstic,** Wilbur E, Chillicothe, OH, *1-1MAR KO VN CMC* +
*CPL* **Bostick,** Bobby J, Muscle Shoals, AL, *HQ-11MAR VN* +
**Bostick,** Calvin T, East Stroudsburg, PA, *A-1TK SWA* +
*CPO* **Bottiggi,** D E, Genoa, NV, *CB* +
*SGT* **Boubel,** George J, San Antonio, TX, *I-3-1 KO*
*CPL* **Bouchard,** Walter P, Bradenton, FL, *HQ-1MED CH* +
*SGT* **Boulden,** Robert G, Burlington, WI, *1SIG H&S-1-1 KO* +
*CPL* **Bouley,** Albert J, San Antonio, TX, *I/M-3-1 WWII* +
*SGT* **Bourgeois,** James A, Lakewood, WA, *D-2-1 KO VN* +
*SGT* **Bovich,** Gary A, Boise, ID, *K-3-5 5MAR DIV*
*CWO3* **Bowden,** Dennis J JR., Norway, ME, *G-2-1 E-2-7 CW* +
*SSGT* **Bowden,** Larry J, Des Moines, IA, *L-3-1 VN* +
*SGTMAJ* **Bowen,** Bruce H, Davidsonville, MD, *ATT 5MAR CW* +
*LTCOL* **Bowen,** James T, Carlsbad, CA, *H&S-2-5 KO VN* +
*CPL* **Bowler,** Gary T, Cape Coral, FL, *H&S-1-7 VN* +
*CPL* **Bowman,** Donald K, Whittaker, MI, *E-2-1 KO* +
*1STLT* **Bowman,** Horace L, Palmyra, VA, *DIV STAFF G-2 KO* +
*2NDLT* **Bowser,** Lionel G, Pocatello, ID, *K-3-5 WWII CH*
*CPL* **Box,** Charles E, Abilene, TX, *C-1-7 WWII* +
*CAPT* **Box,** Robert C, Kansas City, MO, *HQ-HQ KO VN* +
*LCPL* **Boyd,** Donivon L, Onamia, MN, *G-3-11 VN* +
*CPL* **Boyd,** Jeffrey L, Camp Verde, AZ, *A-2ND PCT 1 RECON VN*
*SSGT* **Boyd-Robertson,** Lindsey, Exeter, NH, *4.2 MTR-5 KO*
*SGT* **Boyer,** Gary D, Ferndale, NY, *A-1-1 VN* +
*GYSGT* **Boyko,** Andrew W, Pisgah Forest, NC, *I-3-27 VN* +
*HMCM* **Boyle,** Arthur S, Bristol, WI, *H&S CO 1ST ENG BN* +
**Boyle,** Charles W, Torrance, CA, *B-1-1 WWII* +
*LCPL* **Boyle,** Daniel M, Springhill, FL, *1/1*
*PFC* **Boylston,** Adrian F, Hilton Head Island, SC, *3-11MAR CH* +
*1STLT* **Braatz,** Mark G, San Jose, CA, *2-1MAR VN* +
*CPL* **Brace,** Richard P, La Crescenta, CA, *HQ-11MAR VN* +
*SGT* **Bradley,** Everett G, Bringhurst, IN, *ORD-MAINT-FLC VN* +
*SGT* **Bradley,** John G JR., Lutz, FL, *S&S QTR HQ TRN BN 1MAR DIV WWII CH KO CW* +
*CPL* **Bradley,** Robert D, Fence Lake, NM, *C-1-7 C-1-11 VN* +
*SGT* **Bradley,** Stephen J, Antigo, WI, *L-3-5 VN* +
*CPL* **Bradley,** Walter Herbert, Fitzwilliam, NH, *3D 17 5MM GVN BTRY VN*
**Bradshaw,** William C, Apple Valley, CA, *HQBN CW* +
*CPL* **Brady,** Clifford N, Wellington, FL, *1ARM-AMPH KO*
*LCPL* **Brady,** David Damien, Claymont, DE, *MAG12 CW* +
*CAPT* **Brady,** James H, San Diego, CA, *3-11 OIF* +
*CAPT* **Brady,** James, East Hampton, NY, *D-2-7 KO* +
*SGT* **Brady,** Joseph J, Millsboro, DE, *1TK KO* +
*PFC* **Brake,** Barry B, Roseville, CA, *D-2-1 KO* +

*SGT* **Bramble,** Allen E JR., Abingdon, MD, *E/H&S-2-7 KO* +
*SGT* **Brambora,** Ronald J, Minonk, IL, *A-1-1 CW* +
*CPL* **Brancato,** Salvatore (Sal) G, Branford, CT, *E-2-5 KO* +
*LTGEN* **Brandtner,** M L, Reno, NV, *D-1-5-5MAR VN* +
*CPL* **Brannan,** Gary C, Portland, OR, *C-1ST MAAM BN FMFPAC CW* +
*CPL* **Brannigan,** Donald C, Oak Lawn, IL, *A-7ENGR KO* +
*PFC* **Branson,** Cecil, Mountain Grove, MO, *WPNS-1MAR WWII CH* +
*CPL* **Branson,** Howard A, Brooklyn Center, MN, *1MARBDE CW* +
*CPL* **Bratton,** Raymond W, Chelmsford, MA, *I-3-7 KO* +
**Breault,** Norman P, Jasper, GA, *1MAW 3-11MAR CH KO* +
*SGT* **Breeding,** Patrick Lee, Salina, KS, *2/1 VN*
*CPL* **Brehm,** Lauren P, Traverse City, MI, *HQ-3-7 WWII CH* +
*CPL* **Brendle,** Robert A, New Riegel, OH, *H&S-1-5 VN* +
**Brenenstall,** Steve, Cathedral City, CA, *1 TANK BN*
*SGT* **Brennan,** Francis A, Grove City, OH, *D-2-7 KO* +
*PFC* **Brennan,** James J, West Roxbury, MA, *C-7MAR KO* +
*CPL* **Brennan,** Lawrence E, Scottsdale, AZ, *G-2-1 WWII CH* +
*SSGT* **Brennan,** Vincent R JR., Middletown, NY, *HQ-2-11 VN* +
*GYSGT* **Brennan,** Vincent R III, Congers, NY, *G CO 2 BN 25TH MAR OIF*
*CPL* **Brennan,** William P, Rochester, NH, *B-SHPTY KO* +
*MGYSGT* **Bressell,** Ed, Valencia, CA, *F-2-1* +
*CPL* **Breu,** Dennis L, Stillwater, MN, *A-1-1 WWII CH* +
*1STSGT* **Brewer,** Herb D, Pauls Valley, OK, *A CO 1-5 1-1 VN CW* +
*SGT* **Brewer,** Kevin R, Chesterfield, MI, *MABS24 CW* +
*SGT* **Brewer,** L F, Atlantic, IA, *HQ-11MAR KO* +
*SGT* **Brewster,** Clyde L, Livermore, CA, *G-3-11 WWII* +
*LCPL* **Bricker,** Michael J, Springdale, AR, *C-1-5 VN* +
*CPL* **Bricking,** Ron C, Lexington, KY, *H&S-3-7 CW* +
*LCPL* **Bridge,** Ronald M, Carnegie, PA, *HQ-4-11 VN* +
*PHM2* **Bridges,** Frederick R, Portland, OR, *B CO ENGBN WWII CH*
*CPL* **Brien,** Norman T, Johnston, RI, *1AMPHTRK KO* +
*PFC* **Brieske,** Robert E, Chicago, IL, *W-2-11 BLT 3-1MAR VN* +
*LCPL* **Briggs,** Mark L, Joplin, MO, *A CO-1-5-1 HQTRS CO 1-5* +
*CPL* **Brinker,** Daniel J, Effie, MN, *A-1-5 VN*
*PFC* **Brinkley,** Shery B, Shreveport, LA, *I-3-1 KO* +
**Bristow,** Bruce, Turlock, CA, *3/11*
*SGT* **Bristow,** Byron Woolley, Glendale, AZ, *1/5 VN*
*CPL* **Brittan,** John A, Corsicana, TX, *H-2-5 C-1-1 VN* +
*CPL* **Brittin,** Charles H, Garland, TX, *HQ-1-5 WWII CH* +
*MRS* **Brittin,** Dolores, Garland, TX, *ASSOCIATE* *
*SGT* **Britton,** Harold E, Cascade, MT, *E-2-7 H&S-3-5 CW* +
*1STSGT* **Brixius,** Casper W, Alliance, NE, *MAG 12 1ST MAR DIV KO* +
*PFC* **Broadley,** Leighton S, San Clemente, CA, *B-1-1 WWII CH* +
*GYSGT* **Brock,** T J JR., Arlington, VA, *F-2-1 WWII KO* +
*LTCOL* **Brockish,** Robert F, Louisville, CO, *C-1-1 KO* +
*CPL* **Broe,** Daniel E, Holland, MI, *A/D-1RECON VN* +
*LTCOL* **Broeckert,** Jerry, Brooklyn Park, MN, *HQ-HQ VN* +
*LTCOL* **Broihier,** Michael, Stanford, KY, *I-3-11 CW SOM* +
*CAPT* **Brokate,** George W, Newport Beach, CA, *MAG-13 1ST MAR DIV VN* +
*LTCOL* **Brokaw,** Clifford V III, Southampton, NY, *W-1-7 KO* +
*COL* **Brooke Iii,** George M, Lexington, VA, *3-8IN HOW VN* +
**Brooker,** Paul C, East Boston, MA, *1MAW KO* +
*CPL* **Brookman,** Edwin, Crest Hill, IL, *VMFA-542 MAG-11 1ST MAW VN*
*COL* **Brooks,** Michael A, Fallbrook, CA, *CO-5MAR 2-5MAR CW* +
*GYSGT* **Brooks,** Roosevelt, Memphis, TN, *K-3-5 VN* +
**Brophy,** Brian P, Minden, NV, *K-3-5 VN* +
**Brosnan,** Thomas R, Dix Hills, NY, *COMM KO* +
**Brossette,** Justin W SR., Arabi, LA, *G-3-5 1MAR KO* +
**Brothers,** Ronald E, Hamilton, MT, *D-1-4 SWA* +
*SGT* **Broward,** Ronald D, Davis, CA, *A-1-1 KO* +
*CAPT* **Brower,** Frederick F, Oxford, OH, *H-3-7 KO* +
*CPL* **Brown,** Aaron, Parkland, FL, *B-1MT WWII CH* +
*CPL* **Brown,** Anna T, Santa Monica, CA, *AWRS-7/9 WWII* +
*SGT* **Brown,** Bobby G, Piney Flats, TN, *C-7ENGR VN* +
*SSGT* **Brown,** Cecil L, Santa Fe, NM, *A-1-5 CH KO* +
*LTCOL* **Brown,** David B, Swansboro, NC, *1-5MAR VN* +
*HMC* **Brown,** H B, Melbourne Beach, FL, *C-1-5 WWII CH* +
*CPL* **Brown,** H David, Kansas City, MO, *A-1MED VN* +
*CPL* **Brown,** Herrell E, Pacifica, CA, *D-2-5 KO* +
*SGT* **Brown,** J H, Copperas Cove, TX, *MT-1TKS VN* +
*SGT* **Brown,** James A, Coos Bay, OR, *1ST MAR DIV KO* +
*LTCOL* **Brown,** Jerome W JR., Woodbridge, VA, *ATT 7MAR MCAGTC CW OIF* +
*CPL* **Brown,** Joseph L, Pennsauken, NJ, *B-1-5 VN* +
*SGT* **Brown,** Kenneth E, Florence, SC, *C-1-5 KO* +
*SGT* **Brown,** Max E, Aurora, CO, *1ARMAMPH KO* +
*CPL* **Brown,** Michael L, Porter, TX, *H&S/1-11MAR VN* +
*HM3* **Brown,** Norman Dale, Aurora, CO, *1ST MED BN H&S CO KO* +
*SSGT* **Brown,** Rodger F, Conner, MT, *B-1RECON L-3-7 VN* +
*LTCOL* **Brown,** Ronald J, Novi, MI, *H-2-5* +
**Brown,** Victor W, Mount Joy, PA, *1ENGR WWII CH* +
*CPL* **Brown,** W D, Flushing, NY, *E-2-1* +
*CAPT* **Browne,** Howard S, Williamsburg, VA, *H&S-3-11 KO* +
*CPL* **Browne,** Malcolm W, Houston, TX, *1MAW VN* +
*CPL* **Brownell,** Brian D, Beltsville, MD, *1ALVT VN* +
*SGT* **Bruce,** Bernard P, Loveland, CO, *A-1ENG KO* +
*TSGT* **Bruce,** Harry E, Panorama, TX, *H&S/A-1TK KO* +
*CAPT* **Bruchman,** Roy R, Saint Paul, MN, *MP WWII CH KO* +
*CPL* **Brumbaugh,** Leonard C, Appleton, WI, *HQ-1-11 KO* +
*MSGT* **Brundage,** Edward G, Oceanside, CA, *5TH MAR 7TH MAR SWA CW*
*CPL* **Brunell,** William C, Cape May, NJ, *I-3-7 B-1-11 KO* +
*LCDR* **Brunelle,** David M, Storrs Mansfield, CT, *H&S-1MED VN* +
*SGT* **Brunke,** Harry D, Rancho Santa Margarita, CA, *B C-1-1 1ORD KO* +
**Brunnell,** P E, Oxford, MA, *G-2-5 VN* +
*GYSGT* **Brunner,** Norman J, Orange, CA, *1RECON-5MAR 2/26MAR VN* +
*SSGT* **Brunnert,** Syl F, Florissant, MO, *1MAW KO* +
**Brutinel,** Robert C, Casa Grande, AZ, *2PARA WWII*
*CPL* **Brutzman,** Edward B, Towson, MD, *HQ-3-7 WWII CH* +
*HM3* **Bryan,** Fred N, Louisville, KY, *WPNS-1-5 KO* +
*CPL* **Bryers,** Charles L, Niles, IL, *H&S-7MAR CW* +
*PFC* **Brysky,** G J, Chicago, IL, *HQ-1-11 CW* +
*CPL* **Bryson,** Michael Charles, Sachse, TX, *A CO 1ST RECONN BN OIF*
*COL* **Bubeck,** A Eric, Annapolis, MD, *L-3-7 WWII KO* +
*CPL* **Buchalski,** John F, Portsmouth, NH, *USS TOLEDO KO* +
*HM3* **Buchanan,** James C, Sacramento, CA, *B-1-5 OIF*
*CAPT* **Buchanan,** William L, Mill Valley, CA, *G-2-5 VN*
*CPL* **Buck,** Michael A, Lasalle, CO, *HQ CO (S-4) 5TH MARINE REGIMENT, 1ST MAR DIV*
*SGT* **Buckey,** William F, Grand Island, FL, *1ENGR KO* +
*LTCOL* **Buckley,** Clem, North Augusta, SC, *1TK KO VN* +
*SGT* **Buckley,** James J JR., Alexandria, VA, *G-2-7 VN* +
*COL* **Buckley,** John L JR., Chicago, IL, *F-2-5 MAG/12/33 CH KO* +
*CPL* **Buckmaster,** Robert D, Baltimore, MD, *1AMTRAC KO* +
*PFC* **Buday,** Anthony, Traverse City, MI, *MARDET CV124 KO* +
*SGT* **Budvitis,** Allan V, New Orleans, LA, *C/1/5 CAP 1-4-2 VN*
*HM3* **Buehl,** Robert G JR., Bluffton, IN, *E-1RECON VN* +
*CPL* **Buerger,** Joseph F, Wickliffe, OH, *WPNS-1-5 KO* +
*SGT* **Buethe,** George E, Maricopa, AZ, *I-3-7 VN* +
*CPL* **Buffington,** Donald J, Conrad, MT, *B-1-1 KO* +
*SSGT* **Buffington,** James B, New London, CT, *B-1ENGR KO* +
*COL* **Buhl,** Willard A, Carlsbad, CA, *C0-3-1 1-4MALTCOLR 1MAR SWA OIF* +
*LCPL* **Buist,** M G, Mendon, UT, *HQ-26REGT* +
*CAPT* **Buljan,** Bruce C, Sacramento, CA, *F-2-1 1TK VN* +
*SGTMAJ* **Bulkley,** William C, Twentynine Palms, CA, *HQ-3-4 SWA* +
*SSGT* **Bull,** William A, Mound, MN, *HQ-2-5 VN* +
*HM1* **Bullard,** Jerry M FMF, Johnson City, TN, *HOSP-NSA DANANG VN* +
*BGEN* **Bullard,** John W, Oceanside, CA, *11TH MEU BLT 1/4 BLT 1/5*
*SGT* **Bunnell,** Paul D, Quechee, VT, *HQ-5MAR VN* +
*HN* **Bunner,** Charles D, Asheville, NC, *A-1-1 VN* +
*CPL* **Burbridge,** Ronald L, Emporia, KS, *B-1-7 KO* +
*2NDLT* **Burchfield,** Delmas (Kentucky Colonel) D PHD, Stuarts Draft, VA, *SPLWPNS-11MAR WWII VN* +
*CPL* **Burdett,** Tommy J, Huntsville, TX, *H-2-1 M-3-3 VN* +
*PFC* **Burdette,** Robert B, Knoxville, TN, *1SIG-HQ CH* +
*LCPL* **Burgess,** Harold L, New Baltimore, MI, *K-3-3 B-1-7 VN* +
*SGT* **Burgess,** Philip A, Port Charlotte, FL, *4AAA WWII* +
*SGT* **Burgin,** R V, Lancaster, TX, *K-3-5 WWII* +
*CAPT* **Burke,** Brian T, Edgewater, FL, *1AMTRAC CW* +
*GYSGT* **Burke,** Francis D, San Diego, CA, *ORD-1SVC HQ-1MAR WWII CH KO VN* +
*SGT* **Burke,** Harry L JR., Bloomington, MN, *F-2-7 KO* +
*CAPT* **Burke,** John J III, San Diego, CA, *1-11MAR 1ANGLICO VN* +
*MR.* **Burke,** Kenneth Edward SR., Plant City, FL, *D-1-1-1 D-1-7-1 CW*
*SSGT* **Burke,** William D, Rochester, NY, *1MAW VN* +

*MSGT* **Burke,** William H, San Clemente, CA, *1/2-7MAR VN* +
*MSGT* **Burkhard,** Donald F, Pitman, NJ, *MAG18 1MAW VN* +
*GYSGT* **Burmeister,** George R, Oceanside, CA, *WPNS-1-5 CH KO* +
*SGT* **Burn,** Arthur John, Linwood, PA, *H&S-3-7 VN* +
*PFC* **Burnieika,** Adam Robert SR., Rockland, MA, *E-2-7 VN*
*CPL* **Burns,** Bobby G, Hampton, VA, *VMA121 VMR352 KO* +
*CPL* **Burns,** Donald B, Stockton, CA, *VMF222 MAW7 WWII CH* +
*SGT* **Burns,** Eugene C, Lake Havasu City, AZ, *1 CSG WWII KO* +
*1STLT* **Burns,** Joe W, New Orleans, LA, *I/K-3-7 VN* +
*PLTSGT* **Burns,** Kevin, Champlin, MN, *A-TK WWII CH* +
*SGT* **Burns,** Patrick J SR., Dallas, TX, *H&S 3-5*
*SGTMAJ* **Burns,** Robert L SR., Taylors, SC, *L-3-5 A-1-7 VN* +
*SGTMAJ* **Burns,** Rodney R, Nashville, TN, *M-4-11 WWII KO VN* +
*DR.* **Burnside,** Houston PHD, San Diego, CA, *F-2-1 1AMTRAC WWII CH* +
*GYSGT* **Burris,** Melvin H JR., Paxico, KS, *G-3-5/A-1-7 KO* +
*SSGT* **Burrows,** Charles F, Rincon, NM, *HQ-HQ I-3-2 WWII KO* +
*TSGT* **Burton,** Robert E, Franklin, IN, *WPNS-1-5 WWII KO* +
*CAPT* **Burton,** Ronald (Ron) R, Carlsbad, CA, *H&S/B-1-5 KO VN CW* +
*SGT* **Burzinski,** Gordon J, Manassas, VA, *E-2-1 2-7MAR WWII CH KO* +
*SGT* **Busby,** John F, North Palm Beach, FL, *L-3-5 ZMQ5 WWII* +
**Buschbacher,** Edmund J, Ukiah, CA, *E-2-1 WWII CH* +
*CPL* **Buschbacher,** Frank T, Prescott, AZ, *B-1-7 VN* +
*CPL* **Buschle,** Dennis P, Tully, NY, *A-1-26 E-2-5 VN* +
*PFC* **Bush,** Denzil L, Kirkwood, MO, *L-3-1 WWII* +
*CPL* **Bush,** William H, Youngstown, OH, *H&S/C1-1 KO* +
*LTCOL* **Bushar,** Charles W III, Gladwyne, PA, *2/11* +
*COL* **Bushey,** Keith D, Azusa, CA, *2-1 VN DS CW* +
*CPL* **Butera,** Anthony F, East Meadow, NY, *MAG11 WWII* +
*CPL* **Butler,** Charles E JR., Banning, CA, *D-2-5 KO* +
**Butler,** Irene, Henderson, NV, *ASSOCIATE* +
*COL* **Butler,** Oliver J JR., Lakeside, AZ, *E-2-1 WWII KO* +
*PFC* **Butler,** Walter H, Centerville, MA, *F-2-1 WWII* +
*LTCOL* **Butler,** William O, Sherburne, NY, *B-1-5 C-1-7 CH KO* +
*CPL* **Butt,** Clarence J JR., Gaithersburg, MD, *C-1-7 VN* +
*PHM3* **Butterfield,** Charles E JR., Lakeland, FL, *H&S-11MAR WWII CH* +
*SGTMAJ* **Buttrick,** Walter A, Vancouver, WA, *WPNS-1-1 HQ-HQ KO VN* +
*SGT E-5* **Butz,** Marlin K, Sun City, AZ, *ORDANCE MAINT CO 1ST FSR/FLC VN*
*LCPL* **Butzlaff,** Robert, Arlington, TX, *D/1/5 VN*
*CPL* **Byrne,** James F, San Jose, CA, *G-3-1 KO* +
*SGT* **Cable,** Claude T, Fairview Heights, IL, *1AR-MAMPH KO* +
*GYSGT* **Cabral,** William JR., Westport, MA, *A-1MT VN* +
*LCPL* **Cader,** Bruce M, Santa Rosa, CA, *B-1-5 VN* +
*SGTMAJ* **Cady,** George H, Long Beach, CA, *1RE-CON 1TK KO VN* +
*PFC* **Caggiano,** Gabriel R, Revere, MA, *G-2-1 WWII* +
*PFC* **Cahill,** Hugh M, Huntington Beach, CA, *F-2-7 KO* +
*COL* **Cahill,** Robert E, Cashiers, NC, *1ENGR VN* +
*CPL* **Cahoon,** Richard S, Plymouth, MA, *1/6AM-TRAC WWII* +
**Cain,** James H, Houston, TX, *1MAW* +
*SGT* **Cain,** Patrick M, Owensboro, KY, *OPS-1RA-DIO VN*
*TSGT* **Calaci,** Hugo M, Corona, CA, *VMSB333 MAG33 WWII KO* +
*CPL* **Calderon,** Leonard A, Monterey Park, CA, *I-3-7 VN* +
*CPL* **Calderwood,** Gregg W, Burlington, IA, *1AN-GLICO VN* +
*SGT* **Caldwell,** Overton J, Kerrville, TX, *D-2-1 KO* +
*CPL* **Caldwell,** Robert J, Renton, WA, *D-2-1 KO* +
*SGT* **Calhoun,** Harold E, Clio, MI, *H&S-2-7* +
*SGT* **Calkins,** Robert L, Orland, CA, *MAG33-1MAW KO* +
*CPL* **Call,** Everett R, Springfield, VA, *K-3-1 WWII* +
*SGT* **Call,** Richard W, Milwaukie, OR, *1MT 1MED WWII CH KO* +
*1STSGT* **Callahan,** Frank S, San Diego, CA, *I-3-1 CMC VN* +
*SSGT* **Callahan,** Gerald W, Somers Point, NJ, *1SIG KO CW* +
*1STLT* **Callahan,** James C JR., Swampscott, MA, *B-1-11 H-3-5 KO* +
*CPL* **Callahan,** Larry W, Laurel, MS, *I-3-7 VN* +
*CPL* **Callahan,** William P, Chicago, IL, *I-3-5 VN* +
**Callan,** Kyle "Bill" William, Marion, VA, *H&S CO 1TK BN 1MAR DIV CH* +
*HMC* **Callan,** Richard C, Centennial, CO, *VN*
*CAPT* **Callanan,** John J, Boston, MA, *L-3-1 C-3-11 VN* +
*CWO5* **Callaway,** A N, Bridgeville, DE, *I-3-5 VN* +
*SGT* **Calleja,** Paul J, San Jose, CA, *H-3-1 KO* +
*SSGT* **Callero,** Dolores M, Windsor, CA, *HQBN,HQ DEPT OF PACF*
*SGT* **Camara,** John L, Bayonet Point, FL, *1TK-1RECON KO* +
*SSGT* **Cambrola,** Michael A, Fall River, MA, *B-1AMTRAC KO* +
*CPL* **Cameron,** Billy R, Sanford, NC, *C-1-7 VN* +
*CPL* **Cameron,** Clarence C, Oxford, MI, *COMM HQ KO* +
**Cammisa,** D L, Brooklyn, NY, +
*SGT* **Campbell,** Charles C, Sugar Land, TX, *COMM-HQ VN* +
*MRS* **Campbell,** Dorothy, Brewster, NY, *ASSOCI-ATE* +
*MSGT* **Campbell,** Joseph W, Pittsburgh, PA, *HQ-2-11 CH KO* +
**Campbell,** Kenneth L, Foster City, CA, *E-3-7 KO* +
*SGT* **Campbell,** Louis S, Brooklyn, NY, *W-3-1 KO* +
*LCPL* **Campbell,** M A, Pittsburgh, PA, *1-7 VN* +
*LCPL* **Campbell,** Thomas J, Raleigh, NC, *K-3-5 CW* +
*1STSGT* **Camper,** Sandy H, Cool Ridge, WV, *H-3-11 KO*
*SGT* **Campo,** Emil J, Yakima, WA, *ANGLICO 11MAR WWII CH KO* +
*CPL* **Canjar,** Greg A, Dryden, MI, *HQ-HQ 1MAR VN* +
*CPL* **Cantore,** Joseph F, Elmhurst, IL, *34TH ROT-DRAFT KO* +
*CPL* **Cantrell,** Dan K, Bellingham, WA, *L-3-5 VN* +
*PFC* **Cantu,** J A, Corpus Christi, TX, *C-3-5 CW* +
*CAPT* **Capeci,** Robert L, Brooklyn, NY, *C-1-1 C-1ENGR KO VN*
*CWO4* **Cappadona,** Roy Robert, Durham, NC, *9COMM CW* +
*PFC* **Caputo,** Michael D, Castle Rock, CO, *H-2-1 VN* +
*CPL* **Carbajal,** Joseph R, La Selva Beach, CA, *C-1-5 VN* +
**Cardarelli,** Leo P, Quincy, MA, *E-2-1 WWII CH* +
*LCPL* **Cardenas,** R L, El Monte, CA, *HQ-HQ VN* +
*CPL* **Carder,** Alfred L, Mission, TX, *C-1-5 KO* +
*PFC* **Carey,** C K, Noxen, PA, *D-1-5 WWII* +
*LCPL* **Carey,** Michael P, Pine City, NY, *E CO 2BN 7TH MAR VN*
*LTGEN* **Carey,** Richard E, Plano, TX, *G/WPNS-3-1 KO VN* +
*SSGT* **Carey,** Robert E JR., Cornelius, NC, *1-7MAR VN* +
*SGT* **Carfagno,** Donald A, Ponte Vedra, FL, *B-1-1 KO* +
*CWO4* **Cargill,** W P, Apex, NC, *7CIT -7MAR VN* +
**Carino,** Carolyn Hutchings, Ada, MI, *ASSOCIATE* +
*SGT* **Carista,** Michael D, Dunkirk, MD, *3D LAR* +
*LCPL* **Carl,** David J, Green Island, NY, *B-1-11-1 VN* +
*CPL* **Carlson,** Richard N, Margate, FL, *A-1-1 VN* +
*PFC* **Carlson,** Richard W, Warwick, RI, *E-2-1 KO* +
**Carlton,** Rex A, Prior Lake, MN, *HQ/SVC-2-7 CW* +
*LCPL* **Carman,** Geoffrey J, Woodbury, MN, *L-4-11 CW* +
*GYSGT* **Carmichael,** H C, Tulsa, OK, *WPNS-5-1 WWII* +
*1STSGT* **Carmin,** Charles L, Ellinwood, KS, *D-1-7 CH KO VN* +
*LTCOL* **Carnero,** Manuel JR., Houston, TX, *1-7MAR KO VN* +
*SGT* **Carnes,** Frederick J JR., Fort Lauderdale, FL, *HQ/WPNS-1-5 KO* +
*CPL* **Carney,** Eugene T, Saint Peters, MO, *C-1-1 WWII* +
**Caro,** Robert (Bob), Oxnard, CA, *BAND-HQ KO* +
**Caron,** John P, Oro Valley, AZ, *H&S-3-5 KO* +
*SGT* **Carone,** Michael J, Village Of Lakewood, IL, *A-1-5 KO* +
*HM3* **Carpenter,** C R, Ventura, CA, *H-3-1 1 1CSG KO* +
*SSGT* **Carpenter,** F R, Manchester, NY, *WPNS-3-5 CH KO* +
*SGT* **Carpenter,** Frank P, Pittsford, NY, *C-1-1 1MP KO* +
*CPL* **Carpenter,** Jack W PHD, Burlington, MA, *H&S-1ENG-17 WWII* +
*SGT* **Carpenter,** Lyle D, Lino Lakes, MN, *MAG-25 WWII* +
*1STLT* **Carr,** Bernard RN, Puyallup, WA, *MAG 31 1ST MAR DIV CH* +
*PFC* **Carr,** D B, Buffalo Grove, IL, *HQ-3PHIB WWII CH* +
*LTCOL* **Carr,** John B, Bowling Green, KY, *HQ-3-7 KO* +
*SGT* **Carr,** Robert, Waldport, OR, *1ST ORDN BN 1MAR DIV KO* +
*PFC* **Carranza,** Angel S, San Antonio, TX, *C-1-11 KO* +
*SSGT* **Carrasquillo,** David M, Des Plaines, IL, *HQ-5MAR 1LSB 1FSSG VN* +
*CPL* **Carrelli,** Francis X, Margate, NJ, *I-3-1 KO* +
*LTCOL* **Carretti,** John M, San Clemente, CA, *HQ-1-1 SWA*
*SGT* **Carrigan,** John D, New Bern, NC, *HQ-2-3 5MAR WWII CH KO* +
*SGT* **Carrillo,** John R, Greeneville, TN, *H-2-1 VN* +
*LTCOL* **Carrino,** Albert R, Hanoverton, OH, *A-1-5 KO* +
*SGT* **Carroll,** H Leo, Medford, MA, *C-1-5 WWII CH* +
*CPL* **Carroll,** Robert A, Fresno, CA, *A-1-5 VN*
*SGT* **Carrow,** John P, Wilmington, DE, *A-1-5 VN* +
*SGT* **Carrozzi,** Joe J, Rochester, NY, *A-SHPTY KO* +
*LTCOL* **Carrubba,** Harry D, Las Vegas, NV, *F-2-1 KO* +
*CPL* **Carson,** Edward V, Charleston, WV, *1MAW VN* +
*RADM* **Carson,** H R JR., New Orleans, LA, *CUB-1AERO WWII* +
*SGT* **Carson,** Harry C, Ackley, IA, *B-1-11 KO* +
*COL* **Carter,** Marshall N, Cambridge, MA, *C-1-1 VN* +
*CPL* **Carter,** Nick, Rochester, MN, *L-3-1 VN* +
*SGT* **Carter,** Norville R, Calumet City, IL, *RR/C-7COMM VN* +
*SGTMAJ* **Carter,** Randall, Temecula, CA, *1ST MAR DIV OIF I OIF II* +
*CPL* **Carter,** W F, Greensburg, LA, *F-2-1 CW* +
**Carter,** William (Bill) O, Spring, TX, *2RECON KO* +
*CPL* **Carver,** Glenn E, Lomita, CA, *1PION WWII* +
*SGT* **Cary,** George F, Bullhead City, AZ, *4.2-1-1 KO* +

**Case,** Casey M, Bullhead City, AZ, *1-8IN HOW SP VN* +
*DR.* **Casey,** Donald J, Paradise Valley, AZ, *B-1-8 WWII* +
*CPL* **Casey,** John Charles, Austin, TX, *1ST MED BN CMC CW* +
**Casey,** John J, Phoenix, AZ, *AMED-1-1 WWII CH* +
*CPL* **Casey,** Timothy B, Great Bend, KS, *H&S-1-5 VN* +
*CPL* **Cash,** Joseph Richard, Dawsonville, GA, *C-1-5 VN* +
*HM3* **Cash,** Robert T, Raphine, VA, *I-3-7 VN*
*MSGT* **Cash,** William E, Santa Ana, CA, *H&S-1-5* +
*SSGT* **Cashen,** Joseph L, Alpine, WY, *C-1-5 1CSG KO* +
**Cashman,** Mike F, Seminole, FL, *1CEB VN* +
*COL* **Caspers,** Jeffrey L, Westerville, OH, *HQ-3-11 HQ-5-11*
*SGT* **Cassedy,** John W, Langhorne, PA, *D-1TK KO* +
*SGTMAJ* **Cassell,** Elbert L, Manassas, VA, *1ENGR 1-7MAR CW* +
*CPL* **Cassetta,** Dan, Prescott, AZ, *M-3-7 VN*
*HM3* **Cassidy,** Jack E, Perkinsville, VT, *K-3-1 VN* +
*CPL* **Cassidy,** Mark W, Chicago, IL, *D-2-1 KO* +
*SGT* **Cassidy,** William P, San Francisco, CA, *1MAW KO* +
*SGT* **Castaneda,** Eliseo, East Chicago, IN, *C-1-5 1ST MARDIV 3RD PLT KO*
*MAJGEN* **Castellvi,** Robert F, Camp Pendleton, CA, *CG 1ST MAR DIV* +
*PFC* **Caster,** E.H. H, Fort Bragg, CA, *H-2-5 VN* +
*CPL* **Castile,** James E, West Point, CA, *3-5MAR VN* +
*SSGT* **Castillo,** Al, San Antonio, TX, *I-3-1 WWII KO* +
*CPL* **Castillo,** Arturo "Sonny", Laferia, TX, *WHSKY BTRY 2-11 VN*
*GYSGT* **Castorena,** Pablo, El Paso, TX, *5COMM-HQ MED-SPT VN* +
*PHM2* **Castrogiovanni,** Jack C MD, JD, FCLM, Metairie, LA, *2-1MAR WWII* +
**Catalfu,** Michael S, Corry, PA, *A-1-5 60MM VN* +
**Catavolos,** Archie, Cleveland, OH, *F-2-7 WWII* +
*CPL* **Cathell,** Paul L JR., Stanton, DE, *A/D-1-1 CW* +
**Cathey,** Mary E, Oceanside, CA, +
*MR.* **Catron,** Charles Stuart, Newark, DE, *D-1-26 M-3-7 1FORRECON VN* +
*PFC* **Caulley,** Richard A, Sarasota, FL, *E-2-1 KO* +
*HM3* **Cava,** James D, North Haledon, NJ, *I-3-5 VN* +
*GYSGT* **Cavanagh,** W J JR., New York, NY, *K-3-1 VN* +
**Cavanaugh,** Kenneth W, Waterloo, IA, *C-1-7 KO* +
**Cavanaugh,** Lawrence A, Quincy, MA, *H&S 1-1 KO* +
*SGT* **Cavanaugh,** Thomas D, Careywood, ID, *L-3-1 VN*
*SGT* **Cavin,** Fogel R JR., Albuquerque, NM, *A-1-7 7TH MAR KO* +
*1STSGT* **Cavros,** George P, Brookfield, WI, *SVC-7ENGR WWII KO* +
**Cawley,** John F, Brockton, MA, *B-1RAIDER WWII* +
*CPL* **Caylor,** C W, Dalton, GA, *WPNS-5MAR WWII* +
*SGT* **Cease,** Hank M, Goose Creek, SC, *W-2-1 BLT-3-1 VN* +
*SGT* **Cebula,** John J JR., Olathe, KS, *D-2-7 KO* +
*1STSGT* **Celella,** Philip S, Long Beach, NY, *G-3-5 BRIGADE KO* +
*HM3* **Certo,** Dominic N, Stewartsville, NJ, *E/H-2-7 VN* +
*SGT* **Cesaretti,** Raymond C, Eureka, CA, *C-1-7 KO* +
*CPL* **Cesaroni,** Richard F, Santa Clarita, CA, *H&S-1-5 CW* +
*TSGT* **Cha,** Michael Dae Sup, Buena Park, CA, *KMC KO* +
*CAPT* **Cha,** Wontae, New York, NY, *MC ATT KO* +
*SGT* **Chadwell,** E E, Wichita, KS, *H-2-1 WWII CH KO* +
**Chadwick,** Patrick A, Lynn, MA, *SPT E-ITS CJHP CW* +
**Chai,** Cho O, Hawaiian Gardens, CA, *KMC KO* +
*CPL* **Chaille,** John L, Warrensburg, MO, *H&S CO 1/5 VN*
*SGT* **Chalk,** John R, Palm Harbor, PA, *5/7/11MAR KO* +
*MRS* **Chamberlain,** Lorraine, Twentynine Palms, CA, *ASSOCIATE* *
*SGT* **Chamberlin,** Christopher D, Parsonsfield, ME, *1FSR VN* +
*HM3* **Chamberlin,** William D, Denver, CO, *C-1-5 KO* +
*CPL* **Chambers,** Tony M, England, AR, *I-3-7 G-2-26 VN* +
*SSGT* **Chamerlik,** Hillard M, Skokie, IL, *B-1TK KO* +
*CAPT* **Champion,** E E, Williamstown, NJ, *11MAR WWII* +
*MGYSGT* **Champion,** William L, Sun City, AZ, *HQ-11MAR 3-5MAR KO VN* +
*CPL* **Chan,** Richard G, Oyster Bay, NY, *A-1-5 VN* +
*CPL* **Chandler,** Christopher T, Aurora, CO, *1LAR WOT* +
*MAJ* **Chandler,** James E, Wagener, SC, *C-1 RE-CON VN*
*SGT* **Chandler,** Paul A, New Gretna, NJ, *1CSG KO* +
*COL* **Chandler,** T E JR., Kingwood, TX, *COMM-HQ VN* +
*GYSGT* **Chaney,** W R, Julian, CA, *D-1-9 KO* +
*SSGT* **Chaney,** William M, Greenwood, IN, *B-1-147 WWII* +
*SGT* **Chang,** Franklin R, Honolulu, HI, *D-2-5 KO* +
*HM3* **Chang,** John Son, Surprise, AZ, *C/1/5 VN*
**Chang,** Tae Ok, Los Angeles, CA, *KMC* +
*GYSGT* **Chantiles,** Stavros D, Hubert, NC, *1ST MAW* +
*SGT* **Chapman,** Marvin B, Klamath Falls, OR, *1MAW KO* +
*CPL* **Chapman,** Stewart James, Seekonk, MA, *HQ-3-11-1MAR DIV KO* +
**Chase,** A L, Fairhaven, MA, *G-2-7 WWII KO* +
*TSGT* **Chase,** Maurice Raymond JR., Palo Alto, CA, *B-1TK KO*
*PFC* **Chase,** Milton, Oakhurst, NJ, *H&S-HQ CW* +
*SGT* **Chassey,** Elliott W SR., Plymouth, MA, *HQ-1ARMAMPH KO* +
*SGT* **Chastney,** Ted J, Palm Desert, CA, *A-1-1 H&S-1-1 CW* +
*LCPL* **Chau,** Sergio, Los Angeles, CA, *"C" BTRY 1BN 11TH MAR*
*CAPT* **Chaves,** Jackson B, Peoria, AZ, *L-4-11 KO VN* +
*COL* **Chavez,** Rocky J, Oceanside, CA, *2/11* +
*SGT* **Cheape,** Percy D, Autsin, TX, *D-2-11 KO* +
*SSGT* **Cheek,** Arthur M, Saint Petersburg, FL, *4.5 RKT-11MAR KO* +
*CAPT* **Cheff,** Stanley W, Caledonia, MI, *C-1RECON VN* +
*LTCOL* **Chenoweth Usmcr Nc,** Theodore H, El Verano, CA, *F-2-7 KO* +
*CHAPLAIN* **Cherringt,** E G, Mountain Home, TN, *1/3/6MAR WWII KO VN* +
*SGT* **Chesnut,** Lugene J, Deming, NM, *E-2-1 G-2-7 WWII* +
*LCPL* **Chiarolanza,** Paul M, Langhorne, PA, *MAQ-11-1STMAW, BARRACK JAPAN VN*
*MAJ/04* **Chinea,** Camilo, Miami, FL, *Service Co HQ Bn 1MarDiv*
**Cho,** In H, Studio City, CA, *KMC KO* +
**Cho,** Jae J, Fullerton, CA, *KMC ATT KO* +
*SGT* **Cho,** Jung Gu, Mapo-Gu Seoul, Korea, *COMM RADIO KO VN*
*BGEN* **Cho,** Seong Joo, Los Angeles, CA, *KMC KO* +
**Cho,** Sookeun, Daegu, Korea
*HM2* **Chobot,** Scott (Doc), Baileys Harbor, WI, *A-1-7 VN* +
*SGT* **Chong,** Jerry L ESQ., Sacramento, CA, *M-3-7 VN* +
**Christensen,** Richard B, Berwyn, IL, *E-2-1* +
*SF1C* **Christensen,** Ronald L, Maplewood, MN, *17MAR WWII* +
*GYSGT* **Christiansen,** Arnold J, Orlando, FL, *HQ-3-7 ENG KO VN*
*CPL* **Christiansen,** John B, Gilbert, AZ, *L-4-11 WPNS-7MAR WWII* +
*MGYSGT E9* **Christianson,** Albert E, Sunnyvale, CA, *3/1, 11TH MARINES*
**Christiason,** Mickey A, Cerritos, CA, *ASSOCIATE* *
*SGT* **Christie,** Hilton P, Houston, TX, *4.2 MRTR-1 KO* +
*SGT* **Christie,** Ralph O, Sparks, NV, *C-1MT KO* +
*LTGEN* **Christmas,** George R, Stafford, VA, *H-2-5 CG1MEF VN* +
*SSGT* **Christoffers,** J R, Palm Beach Gardens, FL, *1MAR WWII* +
*SGT* **Christopher,** John P, Revere, MA, *A-1AM-TRAC KO* +
*CPL* **Christopher,** Seaborn W, Dawsonville, GA, *WPNS-7MAR WWII* +
*CPL* **Christy,** Ron K, White Bear Lake, MN, *D-1MT CW* +
*REV.* **Chung,** Sam (Young) Y, Gardena, CA, *KMC VN* +
*MAJ* **Chung,** You J, Los Angeles, CA, *KMC KO* +
*CPL* **Church,** John S, Roswell, NM, *C-1RECON VN*
*MGYSGT* **Churchill,** W A JR., Perrysburg, OH, *H&S/C-1-7 KO* +
*LCPL* **Cima,** Edward George, Pahrump, NV, *1-7 2-7* +
*SSGT* **Ciminelli,** John P SR., Brooklyn, NY, *WPNS-1-5 KO* +
*PFC* **Cinquegrani,** Peter M, Joliet, IL, *1MED WWII CH* +
*CPL* **Cioni,** Robert G, Clearwater, FL, *1WPNS KO* +
*CPL* **Cirelli,** Francis D, Odenton, MD, *B-1-1 VN* +
*CPL* **Citro,** Ralph W, Mantua, NJ, *HQ-11MAR WWII CH* +
*SGT* **Ciullo,** Virgilio J, Venice, FL, *A-3AMTRAC VN* +
*SGT* **Clabo,** Richard D, Bloomington, MN, *F-2-7 KO* +
*LTCOL* **Clancey,** Michael P, Sacramento, CA, *HQ BTRY-1-11 W BTRY-1-11 VN CW* +
*CAPT* **Clancey,** W P, San Marcos, CA, *2-7MAR KO* +
*LTCOL* **Clancy,** J E, San Francisco, CA, *1/2/3 11MAR* +
*SGT* **Clapper,** Joe W, Mesa, AZ, *L-3-1 WWII* +
*SGT* **Clark,** Carl W, Tucson, AZ, *G-3-5 WWI KO* +
*MRS* **Clark,** Charlotte, Edmonds, WA, *ASSOCIATE* *
*SGT* **Clark,** David E, Albion, IL, *H&S-1ENGR VN* +
*CPL* **Clark,** David R, Monmouth, IL, *HQ-11MAR VN* +
*PHM1* **Clark,** James A JR., Oklahoma City, OK, *H&S-1MED H&S-4-11 WWII* +
*1STSGT* **Clark,** Joe T, Owenton, KY, *E-1RECON VN* +
*SGT* **Clark,** John J, Roselle Park, NJ, *1ST RECON BN A CO VN* +
*SGT* **Clark,** John W, Birmingham, NJ, *F-2-7 KO* +
*MAJ* **Clark,** Michael Thomas, Foster City, CA, *1BN 3MARDIV* +
*SGT* **Clark,** Norman F, Tigard, OR, *M BTRY 4TH BN KO* +
*SSGT* **Clark,** Paul F, San Diego, CA, *11MAR KO* +
*CPL* **Clark,** Richard A, North Branch, MN, *2CAG-III MAF VN* +
*LCPL* **Clark,** Richard J, Westfield, NJ, *A-1-1 VN* +
*SGTMAJ* **Clark,** Robert M, Linden, NJ, *A/C/D-1ENGR CW SWA*
*SGT* **Clark,** Ronald A, Coronado, CA, *C-1-5 KO* +
*LTCOL* **Clark,** Ronald A, Purcellville, VA, *2-7MAR VN* +
*CPL* **Clark,** Stephen K, Madison, IN, *HQ-5MAR VN* +
*CPL* **Clark,** William H, Placerville, CA, *1RECON KO* +
*HM3* **Clark,** William S JR., Tacoma, WA, *1ENGR A-1-5 KO* +
*CPL* **Clarke,** David M, Boring, OR, *1MAW VN* +
*HM3* **Claroni,** Paul A, Rutherfordton, NC, *A/C-1-7 VN* +
*SGT* **Clause,** Alan T, Ontario, Canada, *1ENGR SPT CO VN* +

*LCPL* **Claytor,** Thomas R SR., Harrisburg, PA, *A-1ENGR H&S-9ENGR VN* +
*CPL* **Cleary,** R J, Lake Elsinore, CA, *W-2-1 KO* +
*SSGT* **Cleaves,** Mark E, Ocala, FL, *L-3-1 VN* +
*SGT* **Clemans,** Gene H, Spanaway, WA, *K-3-1 VN* +
*MAJ* **Clemens,** W F, Victoria, Canada, *BRIT LIAOFF D-2 WWII* +
*GYSGT* **Clements,** Beauford R, Lake Kiowa, TX, *HQ-3-7 HQ-HQ VN* +
*LCPL* **Clendennen,** Jimmy L, Newtown, PA, *E-2-7 VN*
*CPL* **Clevenger,** Gary D, Excelsior Springs, MO, *B-1ST FSR VN*
*CPL* **Clevenger,** Walter P, Beverly Hills, FL, *H&S/A-1-5 KO* +
*CPL* **Clevenstine,** C E, Pennsburg, PA, *ANGLICO KO* +
*PFC* **Clewis,** W C, Mobile, AL, *7PION* +
*MAJ* **Clifford Ii,** Paul Burton, Dumfries, VA, *1ST RECON BN/ 1ST MAR REG SWA*
*SGT* **Clore,** Gerald J, Corsicana, TX, *D-1-5 G-2-5 VN* +
*CWO4* **Clow,** Jack N, Land O' Lakes, FL, *4-11MAR 3-5MAR KO VN* +
*MSGT* **Cluka,** Daniel, Escondido, CA, *D-7ENGR IIIMAF VN* +
*SGT* **Clulo,** James R, Valley Falls, KS, *COMM-HQ KO*
*SGT* **Clutter,** Albert W JR., Homosassa, FL, *M-3-1 VN*
*MAJ* **Clyatt,** John C, Colorado Springs, CO, *HQ-HQ OIF* +
*CPL* **Clyborne,** Ron, Edmonds, WA, *C-1-5 VN*
*CAPT* **Coan,** Richard M, Carlsbad, CA, *H CO 3D BN 1MAR DIV KO*
*LTCOL* **Coates,** Franklin W, Arlington, VA, *1TK KO* +
*COL* **Coates,** Robert J, San Marcos, CA, *F-2-1 1RECON CW* +
*SGT* **Cobane,** Paul S, Chatham, MA, *H-3-5 KO* +
*SGT* **Cobasky,** Harry R, Cottonwood, AZ, *F-2-5 CW* +
*CPL* **Cobb,** George W JR., Cardiff By The Sea, CA, *HQ-1AMTRAC B-8MT KO* +
*CPL* **Cobb,** Stephen G, Higganum, CT, *L-3-5 VN* +
*SGT* **Cobb,** William, Edwardsville, KS, *K-3-1/5 VN* +
*GYSGT* **Cochran,** Billy O, Asheville, NC, *L-4-11 KO*
*SGT* **Cochran,** Pennelton W JR., Richmond, VA, *A-1-1 VN*
*LCPL* **Cochran,** Wendell P, Pasadena, TX, *3MAW CW* +
*PFC* **Cochrane,** Robert J, Marshfield, MA, *B-1-7 KO* +
*SGT* **Cockrill,** Elward E, Harlingen, TX, *E-2-7 KO* +
*SGT* **Cockson,** Harold F, Columbus, NE, *W-2-11 BLT3-1 VN* +
*SGT* **Codey,** Oscar C, Louisville, KY, *MAG24 C-1-11 WWII CH KO* +
*LTCOL* **Cody,** Richard L, Stafford, VA, *A-1-5 VN* +
*CPL* **Coe,** Hayden M JR., Texarkana, TX, *F-2-1 KO* +
*COL* **Coffman,** Richard W, Potomac, MD, *3/11* +
*SGTMAJ* **Cogan,** Thomas V JR., Springfield, VA, *A-1ENGR VN* +
**Cogswell,** Richard Spencer, Debary, FL, *A-1ENG BN 1MAR DIV KO*
*CPL* **Cohen,** Ivan J, San Diego, CA, *HQ-5MAR 1MAW VN* +
**Cohn,** Alan G, Los Angeles, CA, *HQ-11MAR KO* +
*GYSGT* **Colangelo,** John JR., Neptune, NJ, *1MT KO VN* +
*CPL* **Colbert,** Norman J, Philadelphia, PA, *B-3AMTRAC VN* +
*CPL* **Colburn,** Donald L, Citrus Heights, CA, *E-2-11 CW* +
*MSGT* **Cole,** Alvin R, Cumming, GA, *H&S-7MT CW* +
*SGT* **Cole,** Earl W, Clayton, NY, *3-11 KO* +
*1STLT* **Cole,** Frederick M, Lynn, MA, *C-1-7 KO* +
*MAJ* **Cole,** Jean P, Swannoanoa, NC, *A-1RECON 1ENGR KO VN* +
*SGT* **Cole,** John C, Roy, UT, *I-3-5 WWII KO* +
*SGT* **Cole,** Michael P, Zebulon, NC, *C-1-1 VN* +
*SGT* **Coleman,** Bert (Ernie) E, Cedar Rapids, IA, *C-1-5 VN* +
*SGT* **Coleman,** E D, Tuscaloosa, AL, *M-4-11 WWII CH* +
*CPL* **Coleman,** Henry (Hank) D, Ellisville, MO, *HQ-1PION 17MAR WWII CH* +
**Coleman,** Kathryn, Las Vegas, NV, *B-1-11 WWII* +
*CAPT* **Coleman,** Timothy J, Manlius, NY, *G-2-7 SWA* +
*SGT* **Coles,** Nathan, Lafayette, LA, *H-3-11 VN* +
*MSGT* **Coley,** Jesse E, Norfolk, VA, *K-3-26 VN* +
**Colfax,** Kathleen, North Lauderdale, FL, *ASSOCIATE* +
*SGTMAJ* **Collier,** J T, Beaufort, SC, *G/I-3-1 WWII KO* +
*CPL* **Colligan,** Jerome M, Saint Augustine, FL, *G-3-11 WWII CH* +
*HMC* **Collins,** Elbert H, Portland, OR, *F-2-5 1ST MED BN KO* +
*SGT* **Collins,** James M, West Haven, CT, *B-1RECON VN* +
*PFC* **Collins,** Joseph E, Joliet, IL, *H&S 1BN 7REGT*
*SGT* **Collins,** Michael T, Oak Lawn, IL, *1 RECON BN VN*
*PVT* **Collins,** Mike W, Shelby Township, MI, *1MARDIV VN* +
*SSGT* **Collins,** N L JR., Flanders, NY, *I-3-1 KO* +
*SSGT* **Colson,** Thomas L, Tucson, AZ, *1TK VN* +
*SGT* **Colton,** James F, Westminster, MD, *H-2-5 VN* +
*CAPT* **Colwell,** Stephen B, Carlsbad, CA, *D-1-5 VN* +
*SGT* **Comer,** Robert C PE, NSPE, Rockaway, NJ, *C-1SHPTY KO* +
*SGT* **Cominos,** Nick G, Griffith, IN, *D-1-7 VN* +
*SGT* **Commons,** Merle L, Lawrence, KS, *H&S-1-5 KO* +
*CPL* **Comp,** John Joseph, The Villages, FL, *G-3-1 KO* +
*1STSGT* **Compitello,** Don D, Omaha, NE, *F-2-11 KO* +
*CWO* **Compton,** Bobby Lynn, Glendora, CA, *1ST FSSG BSSG-7*
*SGT* **Compton,** Phillip A, Oakwood Village, OH, *H-2-1 VN* +
*MGYSGT* **Conde,** Felix JR., San Antonio, TX, *B CO 3D AMTRAC BN 1MAR DIV VN CW*
*SGT* **Conde,** Gabriel C, Saint Louis, MO, *A-1-7 KO* +
*CPL* **Cone,** Joseph R, Shelby Twp, MI, *C-1-5 CH* +
*1STLT* **Conklin,** Earl J, Cincinnati, OH, *A-1-7 WWII CH* +
*MAJ* **Conklin,** Leslie R, Anaheim, CA, *HQ CO 7TH ENGINEER BN VN* +
*GYSGT* **Conley,** Peter M, South Portland, ME, *HQ/B-7ENGR VN*
*CPL* **Connell,** Joseph (Joe) R, Westford, MA, *B-7-MT KO* +
*PFC* **Connell,** Richard A, Winter Park, FL, *BAND, HQBN, 1ST MAR DIV*
*CPL* **Connell,** William H, Monticello, GA, *HQ-5MAR HQ-HQ CW* +
*SSGT* **Connelly,** Richard W, Des Moines, WA, *F-2-7 KO* +
*CPL* **Connolly,** Raymond H, Enterprise, OR, *11MAR WWII CH* +
*SGT* **Connors,** Chris J, Crownsville, MD, *A-1-25*
*CPL* **Conrad,** Francis, Orland Park, IL, *SUP-1FSR CW*
*CPL* **Conroy,** Philip W, Apple Valley, CA, *3-11MAR 1SVC KO* +
*MGYSGT* **Consijio,** Lambert JR., Oceanside, CA, *I-3-7 G-3 KO VN* +
*MAJ* **Consodine,** Thomas J, Wichita Falls, TX, *H-S-1-1 KO* +
*CPL* **Constancia,** Peter H, Sierra Vista, AZ, *D-2-13 VN* +
*SGT* **Constantino,** Mathew C, Georgetown, TX, *L-3-5/A-1-7 WWII CH* +
*CPL* **Contreras,** Eduardo, Sherwood, OR, *1ST SHORE PRTY BN 7TH MAR*
*LCPL* **Conway,** Allen J, Frederick, CO, *1FSR VN* +
*GEN* **Conway,** James T, Washington, DC, *HQ-HQ 3-1MAR SWA* +
*SGT* **Conwell,** Phillip A SR., Georgetown, OH, *4.2 MRTR-5 KO* +
*1STLT* **Cook,** C I, Mesquite, TX, *3-5MAR KO* +
*SGT* **Cook,** C L, Sedgewickville, MO, *1ENGR CW* +
*PHM3/C* **Cook,** Earl J, Seal Beach, CA, *C 2* +
*COL* **Cook,** Gorton C, Slidell, LA, *H&S/WPNS-2-1 G3-HQ-HQ KO VN* +
*SGT* **Cook,** John J, Havertown, PA, *C-1-1 KO* +
*LCPL* **Cook,** M L, Dumas, TX, *MP VN* +
*PFC* **Cook,** M P, Wysox, PA, *D-1-5 WWII* +
*SGT* **Cook,** William D, Jasper, GA, *D-2-1 KO* +
*SGT* **Cooksley,** David J, Old Lyme, CT, *W-2-5 1MAR DIV* +
*2NDLT* **Coombe,** Philip W, Lewes, DE, *F-2-7 KO* +
*SGT* **Cooper,** Albert W, Coraopolis, PA, *H&S-106'S 3-1 VN*
*GYSGT* **Cooper,** Billie G, Missoula, MT, *H&S CO 1ST MAR DIV KO VN* +
*WO* **Cooper,** Brian C, Dianella, Australia, *2ND BN 2ND RAR KO* +
*1STSGT* **Cooper,** Charles G, Clayton, IN, *4.2 MTRS WWII KO VN* +
*LCPL* **Cooper,** Lawrence R, Middletown, CT, *A-1-7 VN* +
*GYSGT* **Cooper,** Michael L, Bellingham, WA, *1SHPTY A/D-1-7 VN* +
**Cooper,** Thomas E, Iuka, MS, *F-2-5 WWII CH* +
**Coopersmith,** Craig R, Beaverton, MI, *C-1-5 VN* +
*LCPL* **Copeland,** Michael E, Williamson, SC, *C-1-7 VN* +
*CPL* **Coppola,** Michael C, New Haven, CT, *K-3-1 WWII* +
**Corbett,** A B, Vallejo, CA, *AO-1MAW VN* +
*COL* **Corbett,** Leroy V, Raleigh, NC, *I-3-1 KO* +
*CPL* **Corbett,** Ralph D, Groveland, MA, *1MAW WWII CH* +
**Corbett,** Robert T, Stuart, FL, *F-2-11 KO* +
*SGT* **Corbett,** William J, La Quinta, CA, *H-2-1 VN* +
*PVT* **Corbin,** Dayton C, Oakland, OR, *A-1-7 VN* +
*LCPL* **Corcoran,** J M, Milford, MA, *H-2-1 VN* +
*CPL* **Cordova,** Larry J, Chicago, IL, *L-4-11 VN* +
*GYSGT* **Cordy,** Paul Samuel, Webster, NY, *HQ CO 1ST BN 1ST MAR* +
*CPL* **Corey,** Roger R, Saint Petersburg, FL, *L-4-11 KO* +
*SGT* **Corlew,** James C, Herkimer, NY, *1CSG KO* +
*SGT* **Corley,** Chip, Saint Augustine, FL, *1ST FORCE RECON VN* +
*SGT* **Cornell,** Joseph J, Portland, OR, *E-2-7 KO*
*GYSGT* **Cornick,** Raymond K, Temecula, CA, *B-1PION WWII CH KO VN* +
**Cornish,** Donald J, Los Angeles, CA, *E-2-7 KO* +
*SGT E-5* **Cornstubble,** Ira E, Huntsville, TX, *HMM 262*
*GYSGT* **Cornwell,** Kenneth O, Wenatchee, WA, *A-B-1-5 KO VN* +
*LCPL* **Corona,** Sabino A, Deerfield Beach, FL, *A-1-5 VN* +
*1STLT* **Corpus,** Lazaro, Maxwell, TX, *H&S-1/2-5 VN* +
*GYSGT* **Corrado,** Dominick J, Kelsey, CA, *H&S-1RECON 1FORRECON KO VN* +
**Corrales,** Gregory, San Francisco, CA, *1RECON 1FORRECON VN* +
*CPL* **Correa,** Joseph R, San Antonio, TX, *D-2-7 KO* +
*GYSGT* **Correll,** William J, Millbrae, CA, *C-1-5 WWII CH KO* +
*CPL* **Corrento,** Gerard, Philadelphia, PA, *H&MS36 1MAW VN* +
*CPL* **Corrento,** Jerry JR., Levittown, PA, *A-1FSSG PK* +
*SGT* **Corrie,** Patrick S, Corbett, OR, *1MAW VN SWA* +
*PHM2* **Corry,** Frank FMF, Dublin, GA, *G-2-5 E-2-5 HQ-2-5 WWII CH* +
*SGTMAJ* **Cortez,** Ruben, Vista, CA, *HQ-FSSG VN*
**Corwin,** Robert L, Huntington, NY, *B-1-1 WWII* +
*CPL* **Corzan,** John, Kyle, TX, *H-3-1 KO* +
*CPL* **Cosper,** Patrick, Edgewood, TX, *C-1-5 1MED VN* +
*SGT* **Cossey,** Larry L, Houston, TX, *MAG13/15 VN* +

LCPL **Costa,** Raymond F, Everett, MA, *C-1-7 VN* +

CAPT **Costen,** Laurel M, Pacific Grove, CA, *USN RET* *

MAJ **Cotten,** Richard W, Minneapolis, MN, *4JASCO WWII CH KO* +

CPL **Cotterman,** Kenneth E, Thornville, OH, *B-1RECON VN* +

MR. **Cotti,** Joseph L, Palm Bay, FL, *F-2-7 WWII KO* +

CPL **Cotton,** Rick E, Pace, FL, *A-1-5 VN* +

**Coughlin,** Ann E, Rye, NY, *ASSOCIATE* *

CPL **Coughlin,** Coleman C, Tempe, AZ, *MWSG37 SWA* +

MAJ **Coulter,** Patrick C, Moorpark, CA, *HQ-HQ VN* +

CPL **Countryman,** Leigh F, Saint Paul, MN, *E-2-7 KO* +

CPL **Courage,** A F, Hanover, MA, *2-7MAR VN* +

SGT **Courtney,** B W, Mechanicsville, VA, *C-1-1 WWII* +

SGT **Couser,** Robert H, Orange, TX, *E-2-7 KO* +

CPL **Covanes,** John Nicholas III, Spring, TX, *A-1-7 VN* +

E-2 **Covert,** Harry, Palm Desert, CA, *VMA 241 1MAW CW*

SGT **Covey,** Franklin S, San Diego, CA, *H&S-2LAAM MACS4 MACG18 VN* +

SGT **Covrett,** Ronald B, Fairview Park, OH, *H-2-26-1 VN* +

MGYSGT **Coward,** William L SR., Leesburg, GA, *E-2-7 WWII KO VN* +

GYSGT **Cox,** Barney R, Chandler, AZ, *1 PROV MAR BRIG WWII KO* +

PFC **Cox,** Herschel A JR., Sun Valley, ID, *A-1-5 WWII*

**Cox,** Jerold L SR., Marissa, IL, *3AA BN WWII* +

SGT **Cox,** Jerry D, Hattiesburg, MS, *B-1-1 VN* +

**Cox,** Paul, Berkeley, CA, *HQ-1-26 B-1-5 VN*

SGT **Coxen,** James K, La Grande, OR, *C-1-5 VN* +

DR **Coyle,** Edward J JR., Wallingford, PA, *ASSOCIATE* *

CPL **Coyle,** George T SR., Sayreville, NJ, *D-2-1 KO* +

PFC **Cozza,** Arthur A, East Palestine, OH, *E-2-5 K-3-5 WWII CH* +

MAJ **Cozzens,** Gary W, Capitan, NM, *C-1-7 CW* +

MAJ **Crabtree,** Robert G, Carlsbad, CA, *HQ-1-5 KO VN* +

MAJ **Craddock,** John W, Houston, TX, *G-2-7*

PFC **Craig,** James R, Riverhead, NY, *F-2-1 KO* +

MAJ **Craig,** John, Bordentown, NJ, *5MAR WWII CH KO* +

MRS **Craig,** Marion, Fairfax, VA, *ASSOCIATE* *

MSGT **Cramer,** Harold A, Pasadena, MD, *E-2-11 WWII CH KO* +

SSGT **Crane,** Charles M, Issaquah, WA, *HQ-1SVC KO* +

LTGEN **Craparotta,** Lewis A, Twentynine Palms, CA, *1-7 1-9 1ST MAR SWA OIF CW*

MSGT **Craugh,** Robert J, Canandaigua, NY, *MAG21-1MAR WWII KO* +

CAPT **Craven,** William A, Wills Point, TX, *C-1-1 WWII KO* +

SGT **Cravey,** James D, Stallion Springs, CA, *M-3-5 K-1-4 VN*

SGT **Crawford,** Albert A, Denver, CO, *A-1-11 CW* +

PLTSGT **Crawford,** Alfred E, San Antonio, TX, *E-2-5 WWII* +

SGT **Crawford,** Gerald A, Fort Mohave, AZ, *HENDERSON HALL, 1 MAR WING HHM362*

1STLT **Crawford,** Richard K, Fort Myers, FL, *C-1-5 VN* +

CPL **Crawley,** David P, Rochester, MN, *K-3-1 VN* +

SGT **Creason,** A P, Bellmore, NY, *A-1MED KO* +

PFC **Credo,** E M, Matteson, IL, *G-2-5 VN* +

HM2 **Creely,** Donald A, Port Orange, FL, *MAG12 MWSS-1 KO* +

GYSGT **Crego,** Eugene C, Mesa, AZ, *1FSSG 1MAW VN* +

MSGT **Cressionnie,** Jeff O, Picayune, MS, *HQ-1MARBDE KO* +

COL **Cressy,** Claude 'Nick' N, Colorado Springs, CO, *C 1/5 KO* *

**Creswell,** Thomas W, Greenville, SC, *F-2-5 KO* +

GYSGT **Crimlisk,** John M, Brighton, MA, *C-1-5-26 VN* +

SGT **Crisafulli,** Agostino J, Natick, MA, *W-2-5 KO* +

CPL **Cromer,** Clif A, Blue Springs, MO, *K-3-1 VN*

CPL **Cromer,** Jack C, Covington, GA, *H-3-7 KO*

SGT **Crompton,** James A, Pitman, NJ, *H-3-11 KO* +

1STLT **Cronin,** Daniel J, Coronado, CA, *E-2-11 VN* +

CPL **Croson,** Wayne G, Spokane, WA, *C-1ENGR VN* +

PFC **Cross,** George H, Ballwin, MO, *I-3-5 WWII* +

LCPL **Cross,** Lewis P, Willoughby Hills, OH, *E-2-7 D-1-5 VN* +

CPL **Cross,** Richard F, Bedford, NH, *I-3-1 WWII*

PFC **Cross,** Robert O, Grand Junction, CO, *F-2-5 WWII CH* +

CPL **Croteau,** Joseph L, Lynn, MA, *H&S-1-1 VN* +

PFC **Crouch,** Wyman O, Mcdonough, GA, *G-3-1 KO* +

CPL **Crovo,** Ralph M, Melrose, MA, *E-2-7 WWII*

SGT **Crow,** William R, Wichita, KS, *4JASCO H&S-7MAR WWII CH KO* +

SSGT **Crowe,** Norman W, Tulsa, OK, *1/1*

CWO4 **Crowell,** H W, Riverside, CA, *F-2-1 1MAW WWII KO VN* +

SSGT **Crowley,** Richard L, Naples, FL, *1MAR KO* +

SGT **Crowley,** Robert F, Charleston, WV, *MTACS-2 KO* +

CPL **Cruice,** James J, Tucson, AZ, *I-3-7 WWII KO* +

SSGT **Crumbie,** Watson A, Argyle, TX, *L-4-11 KO* +

CPL **Cruthers,** Melvin F, Burton, OH, *A-1-5 WWII* +

LCPL **Cruz,** Robert E, New York, NY, *A-1-1 B-1-1 VN* +

COL **Cuccio,** Michael T, Stafford, VA, *L-3-1 SWA* +

LCPL **Culbertson,** Walter T, Indianapolis, IN, *C-1MT CW* +

COL **Culkin,** Thomas J, Greensboro, NC, *D-2-7 H&S-1-5 KO VN CW* +

MSGT **Culliton,** Paul J, Hopkinton, MA, *HQ-26MAR VN* +

1STSGT **Culverhouse,** G D, Ladonia, TX, *K-4-11 KO VN* +

CAPT **Cumbaa,** Bill P, Leesburg, FL, *F-2-7 WWII CH* +

**Cummings,** Brenda A, Ventura, CA, *ASSOCIATE* *

SSGT **Cummings,** Dean B, York, PA, *SIG E-1RECON KO* +

SGT **Cummings,** Delano L, Lumberton, NC, *E-1RECON 1MAR VN*

SGT **Cummings,** Larry R, Canyon Country, CA, *B-1-11 E-2-11 VN* +

SGTMAJ **Cummins,** Don R, San Diego, CA, *A-1TK VN* +

SGT **Cupp,** Larry D, Rosharon, TX, *C-1-5 VN*

CPL **Cuppy,** Raymond L, Cerritos, CA, *ASD-1FSR CW* +

PO3 **Curcio,** John B, Dataw Island, SC, *5 MAR KO* +

CAPT **Curran,** John F, Oceanside, CA, *HQ-1-7 VN* +

CAPT **Curran,** Maurice F LLB, JD, Yonkers, NY, *C-1-4 H-3-1 KO* +

SGT **Currin,** Alton L, Birmingham, AL, *RADIO-SIG KO* +

SGT **Curtin,** Dennis M, Raleigh, NC, *E-2-5 VN* +

SGT **Curtin,** John J JR., Quincy, MA, *1TK KO*

TSGT **Curtis,** E J, Los Alamitos, CA, *1ENGR* +

LTCOL **Curtis,** P, Beverly Hills, CA, *FO-1MAW VN* +

**Curtis,** Patrick, Saint George, UT, *2D AIR WING VMFA 323 VN* +

CPL **Curtis,** Ralph C, Sanibel, FL, *H&S-3-1 KO* +

SGT **Curtis,** Roy E, Toms River, NJ, *I-3-7 KO* +

SGT **Cusano,** Thomas C, Seminole, FL, *1ORD H-3-1 KO* +

CPL **Cushman,** Daniel R, Tooele, UT, *H&S 3RD LAR 1ST MAR OIF* +

SGT **Cusick,** Robert J JR., New Bern, NC, *COMM-HQ VN*

CPL **Cuslidge,** Larry D, Bermuda Dunes, CA, *K-3-7 VN* +

SGT **Custodio,** Rigo, Moraga, CA, *C-1-1 KO* +

SGT **Cutright,** Russell R, Shawnee, KS, *HQ-7MAR VN* +

CPL **Dabelstein,** William W, Cathedral City, CA, *C-1-7 KO*

**Dacy,** Douglas C, Kyle, TX, *C-1-5 KO* +

CAPT **D'agostino,** T S, Washington, DC, *5MAR KO* +

SGT **Dahl,** J A, Mankato, MN, *1MAW WWII KO* +

CAPT **Dahlberg,** Karl E, Linden, NJ, *C-1-7 HQ-3-7 VN* +

SGT **Dahlstrom,** Berl D, Malibu, CA, *1DIV, 1ENGR BN, COMM SEC 2543* +

**Dailey,** James F, Cookeville, TN, *HQ-1-1 WWII* +

CPL **Dailey,** Kevin R, West Dennis, MA, *1ARM-AMPH VN* +

SGT **Dailey,** Lester W JR., Fort Wayne, IN, *W-2-1 KO* +

MAJ **Dailey,** Louis, La Quinta, CA, *1MAW, 2MAW, 3MAW, III MAF*

SGT **Dailey,** Paul J, Melrose, MA, *A-1-7 CW*

SGT **Daily,** Joseph A, Thermal, CA, *K-3-1 H&S-1-7 VN* +

**Dake,** James M, Grand Rapids, MI, *H&S-3-1 VN* +

PFC **Dalessandro,** Raymond R, White Plains, NY, *780th FLDARTY KO* +

SGT **Daley,** Eugene J, Sardinia, OH, *1MAW KO* +

SGT **Daley,** Wayne A, Seabrook, NH, *C-1-7 VN* +

CPL **Dalimonte,** Albert P, Aiken, SC, *HQ-2-1 WWII CH* +

SGT **Dall,** Alfred A, Brewer, ME, *MTACS2 KO* +

CPL **Dalrymple,** Gerald F, Saint Petersburg, FL, *A-1-1 KO* +

PFC **Dameski,** Chester, River Edge, NJ, *B-1-1 CH* +

MR. **Damiata,** Joe E, Middlefield, CT, *K-3-1 VN*

SGT **Dana,** James J, Huntington Beach, CA, *D-TK KO* +

CPL **Danberg,** Kale W, Brooklyn Park, MN, *F-2-11 KO* +

SGT **Danehart,** Jerry W, Wheeling, WV, *H&S-3-1 VN* +

SGTMAJ **Danford,** H.(Dirty Dan) D, Cathedral City, CA, *3-5MAR VN* +

MGYSGT **Dangelo,** Philip, Staten Island, NY, *MAG-33-1MAW KO* +

**Dangwillow,** David, Indo, CA, *C-1-12*

PFC **Daniel,** Clovis E, College Point, NY, *H&S-1-1 CH* +

PFC **Dannenbring,** Jack W, Republic, MO, *1MED KO* +

CPL **D'aprile,** Anthony G, Riverside, CA, *1-26MAR VN* +

SGT **Darby,** H J, Portland, OR, *C-1-5 VN* +

1STSGT **Darche,** Michael F, Brockton, MA, *A-1TK CW* +

GYSGT **Dardard,** Joseph A, Saint Francisville, LA, *G-3-5 KO VN* +

MGYSGT **Darden,** Kenneth L, Albuquerque, NM, *WPNS-2-7 KO VN* +

SGT **Dargan,** Thomas J, Weymouth, MA, *B-1-5 VN* +

SGT **Darling,** Stanley H, Holt, MI, *1SVC KO* +

MR. **Darling,** William S, Alameda, CA, *K-3-1 WWII KO* +

CPL **Darnall,** Denny F, Columbus, IN, *F-2-7 WWII* +

SGT **Darre,** John R JR., Winnemucca, NV, *1ANGLICO VN* +

PHM3 **Dascher,** William A, Virginia Beach, VA, *F-2-1 WWII* +

SSGT **Dashner,** J R, Arnold, CA, *B-3TRKS CW* +

CPL **Dauberman,** Edgar L JR., Wiconisco, PA, *E-2-5 KO* +

SGT **Davenport,** William N JR., Cape May Courthouse, NJ, *G2-HQ- HQ VN* +

COL **Davidson,** Darrell U, Jekyll Island, GA, *H&S-9ENGR HQ-HQ VN CW* +

CPL **Davidson,** Frank J, Castleton, NY, *WPNS-1-1 KO* +

CPL **Davidson,** George A, Gaithersburg, MD, *COMM-HQ KO* +

PHM2 **Davidson,** Walter (Doc) L, Scottsdale, AZ, *5RDRS K-3-5 WWII*

*SGT* **Davies,** D O, New Castle, PA, *C-1-1 WWII* +
*SSGT* **Davila,** Raul, Vancouver, WA, *VMO-6 7TH ENGR BN KO VN*
*CPL* **Davis,** Dan Y, Cincinnati, OH, *81MM-1-5 VN* +
*PFC* **Davis,** David J, Dalton Gardens, ID, *I-3-7 VN* +
*SGT* **Davis,** David P, Feasterville-Trevose, PA, *B-1-5 KO* +
*CPL* **Davis,** Dewitt L, Russell Springs, KY, *B-1-27 VN* +
**Davis,** Frank A JR., Fort Lauderdale, FL, *L-3-1 VN* +
*CPL* **Davis,** George I JR., Tallahassee, FL, *A-1ENGR VN* +
*CPL* **Davis,** Gerald L, Temecula, CA, *1ST BN 9TH MARINES*
*SGT* **Davis,** Glenn C, Middletown, KY, *VMO2 HML167 VN*
*SGT* **Davis,** Gordon K, Charlotte, MI, *G-3-1 KO* +
*SGT* **Davis,** James R, Las Vegas, NV, *1MARDIV KO* +
*SGT* **Davis,** Jerry B, Tucson, AZ, *7MAR KO* +
*CPL* **Davis,** Jerry H, Griffin, GA, *L-3-5 VN* +
*CPL* **Davis,** Keven P, Endicott, NY, *LIMA CO 3/1*
*CPL* **Davis,** Larry C, Lake Elsinore, CA, *HQ-HQ CW* +
*MSGT* **Davis,** Logan E, La Quinta, CA, *E-1RECON E-2-1 VN* +
*SGT* **Davis,** Lynn A, Northfield, MN, *F-2-7 KO* +
*MAJ/04* **Davis,** Patrick B, Twentynine Palms, CA, *V17 WPN CO 7TH MAR REGT HQ CO*
*SGT* **Davis,** Richard H, Troy, OH, *B-1AMTRAC KO* +
*COL* **Davis,** Robert E.C., Oceanside, CA, *CO 11TH MAR OIF* +
*SSGT* **Davis,** William J, Welsh, LA, *H-3-7 KO* +
*MGEN* **Davison,** H E, Titusville, FL, *CS HQ-HQ VN* +
*SSGT* **Dawson,** Irven S, West Covina, CA, *TRK -1CSG KO*
*GYSGT* **Day,** Eugene A, Pacifica, CA, *HQ ATT VN* +
*MRS* **Day,** Joan, Needles, CA, *ASSOCIATE* *
*MSGT* **Day,** Larry N, Diamond Springs, CA, *H-2-5 I-3-1 VN* +
*MSGT* **Day,** Oma D JR., Grant, FL, *B/C-1-7 CH KO*
*SGT* **Day,** P, Phoenix, AZ, *I-3-5* +
*SGT* **Deak,** Emil J, Pompton Plains, NJ, *1MAW WWII KO* +
*CPL* **Deamon,** Charles H, Stoneham, MA, *HQ-HQ MT-2-5 WWII* +
*CPL* **Dean,** Billy T, Tyler, TX, *WPNS/H-3-1 KO MOS 0334*
*CPL* **Dean,** Gerald R, Washington, DC, *L-3-1 VN* +
*SSGT* **Dean,** Joseph P JR., Millville, MA, *B-7ENGR VN* +
*CPL* **Dean,** Richard B, Yorba Linda, CA, *C-1TK KO* +
*SGT* **Debie,** Gerard M, Alexandria, VA, *7MAR*
**Debona,** Andrew, Palm Desert, CA, *7 MAR*
*MGYSGT* **Debow,** Chris N, Leesburb, FL, *BAND-HQ SWA* +
*MSGT* **Decarli,** Alfred J, Stafford, VA, *HQ-HQ VN* +
*CPL* **Decker,** Deron H, Batesville, IN, *B-1-5 SWA* +
*HM3* **Decker,** Douglas J, Staunton, VA, *C-1MED VN*
*MSGT* **Decker,** John L, Denver, CO, *F-2-7 M-3-7 VN* +
*PFC* **Decker,** Michael J, Metairie, LA, *6-155HO WWII* +
*LCPL* **Declue,** Gerard F, Saint Louis, MO, *H&S-5MAR F-3-5 VN* +
*PFC* **Dedmond,** Harrison A, Coarsegold, CA, *HQ/G-2-1 CH* +
*SGT* **Deedon,** Eugene E, Clinton, IA, *C-1-5 H-2-7 VN* +
*HON.* **Deen,** Braswell D JR., Atlanta, GA, *K-3-1 WWII* +
*SGT* **Deets,** Samuel R, Havertown, PA, *1ENGR KO*
*SGT* **Deffendall,** Charles V, Evansville, IN, *E-2-5 KO* +
*CPL* **Defilippo,** S P, Middle Island, NY, *9ENGR VN* +
*SGT* **Defina,** Frank W, Shasta Lake, CA, *M-3-1 VN* +
*CPL* **Defusco,** Frank C, Norristown, PA, *HQ-11MAR WWII CH* +
*SGT* **Degiovanntonio,** G, Sicklerville, NJ, *K-3-1* +
*CPL* **Degner,** W O, Palatine, IL, *1MARDIV KO* +
*CPL* **Degrote,** Michael Dennis, Isanti, MN, *I-3-11 I-3-7 VN* +
*PVT* **Deguigne,** Christian, San Mateo, CA, *A-1-5 CW* +
*CPL* **Deibert,** Dennis E, Harrisburg, PA, *I-3-7 VN* +
*GYSGT* **Deighan,** Edgar L, South Daytona, FL, *HQ-4/5-11 WWII* +
**Deka,** Eugene L, Mentor, OH, *A-1MT H&S-2-1 CW* +
*SSGT* **Delagrange,** Edward D JR., Metairie, LA, *1MAW KO* +
*CPL* **Delaney,** James R, Bronx, NY, *4.2 MT -7MAR KO* +
*SGT* **Delaney,** Leo L, San Diego, CA, *1-11MAR VN* +
*SGT* **Delaney,** Ralph M, Williamstown, NJ, *B-1-1 KO* +
*CPL* **Delano,** Steven Alden, Kingston, MA, *H&S 2/5, H&S 3/26 VN*
*SGT* **Delapena,** Gil, Fresno, CA, *I-3-7 KO* +
*PFC* **Delatorre,** Edward V, San Bruno, CA, *WPNS-7 CH* +
*CPL* **Delfavero,** Clement, Sagamore Beach, MA, *C-1-1 WWII* +
*SGT* **Delgiudice,** Felix, East Haven, CT, *E-2-1 CH KO* +
*SGT* **Deliman,** John A, Lorain, OH, *D-1MT KO* +
*SGT* **Dell,** Harry J PE, Moore, OK, *1ST MAR DIV KO*
*CPL* **Dellaquila,** Robert, Turtle Creek, PA, *B-1-5 KO* +
*CPL* **Delligatti,** Patrick P, Toms River, NJ, *VMF-542 WWII* +
*CAPT* **Dellinger,** Harry M, Huntsville, AL, *1ENGR HQ-HQ VN* +
*CPL* **Delorio,** Dominick, Brinnon, WA, *E-2-7 WWII CH* +
*SSGT* **Delossantos,** Pete, Saint Ann, MO, *G-3-1 KO* +
*1STSGT* **Delrio,** Raymond, El Toro, CA, *M-3-1 1ENGR VN* +
*CPL* **Delsignore,** Gino F, New Hyde Park, NY, *HQ-11 MT KO*
**Delucien,** Al SR., Reston, VA, *M-3-5 WWII* +
*SGT* **Deluna,** Henry M, San Antonio, TX, *G-3-5 1PROVMARBDE KO* +
*CPL* **Demartin,** Thomas D, Woodhaven, MI, *K-3-7 VN*
*SGT* **Dembrosky,** Leo J, Erie, PA, *F-2-5 KO* +
*CAPT* **Demeo,** Albert W, Extetor, RI, *11th Marines*
*CAPT* **Deming,** Angus, New York, NY, *E-2-5 KO* +
**Demmery,** Dean S, Matthews, NC, *H&S/D-1RECON VN* +
*SGT* **Dempsey,** Roy D, Woodlyn, PA, *MAG13 1ANGLICO VN* +
*CPL* **Demrest,** Edward G, Canyon Country, CA, *B-1AMTRAC* +
*SGTMAJ* **Denecke,** Kenneth E, Oceanside, CA, *1ENGR CW* +
*1STLT* **Denes,** Barry L, Villa Park, CA, *1-5TH MAR REG VN*
*SGT* **Denham,** Richard A, Brewster, MA, *H&S-7MT KO* +
*MAJ* **Dennis,** Jeff, Lafayette, CA, *VMF311-VMF214 KO* +
*CPL* **Dennis,** John E, West Burlington, IA, *C-1MT WWII* +
*PFC* **Dennis,** M G, Irvington, VA, *1RECON CH* +
*PFC* **Dennis,** William J, Eutaw, AL, *B CO-1ST TANK BN KO* +
*SGT* **Dennison,** Walter K JR., Baltimore, MD, *MT-3-7 KO VN* +
*CPL* **Denoyer,** Eugene A, Minocqua, WI, *H&S-5MAR CH*
*SGT* **Denton,** Donald D JR., Ashland, VA, *H&S-1RADIO VN* +
*MGYSGT* **Denton,** Glenn E JR., Bakersfield, CA, *G-2-7 VN* +
**Denton,** Howard E, Sun City, CA, *ASSOCIATE* *
*PFC* **Depp,** Robert R, Owensboro, KY, *SCOUT/SNIPERS HQ-1MAR VN* +
*SGT* **Deroma,** Florindo F, Hyde Park, MA, *A-1AT VN* +
*CPL* **Derrico,** T M, Shrewsbury, MA, *9DEF WWII* +
*SGT* **Desanno,** Michael J, Oxnard, CA, *ANGLICO/SIG KO* +
*CPL* **Desilva,** Alan B, Houston, TX, *CMR-11MAR VN* +
*CPL* **Despain,** Gary R, Poway, CA, *D-1ST BN 5TH MARINES VN*
*CAPT* **Destefano,** George J, Islip, NY, *C-1-5 VN* +
*PFC* **Detherage,** Kenneth C, Jackson, MO, *M-3-5 WWII* +
*CPL* **Dethloff,** Harvey F JR., Manchester, MI, *G-3-1 KO* +
*1STSGT* **Devasto,** Richard R, Winter Park, FL, *1-1MAR KO VN* +
*GYSGT* **Devereaux,** Maurice A, Carson City, NV, *B-1-5 KO* +
*SGT* **Devine,** Edward J, San Francisco, CA, *VMF-214 MAG12 KO* +
*CPL* **Devine,** John G, Ashland, PA, *VMF(N)541 WWII*
*LCPL* **Devine,** John J, Massapequa, NY, *A-1RECON VN* +
*SGT* **Devito,** Albert C, Indian Wells, CA, *I-3-1 KO* +
*LCPL* **Devivo,** Michael P, Waterbury, CT, *C-1-1 VN* +
**Devlin,** Philip J, Zavalla, TX, *HMR161/162 MAG 16 KO* +
*CPL* **Dewey,** Duane E, Hawthorne, FL, *E-2-5 KO* +
*MSGT* **Dey,** Jerry M, Bigfork, MN, *C-1AMTRAC KO* +
*LCPL* **Diabo,** Arthur B, Quebec, Canada, *M-3-5 VN* +
*MSGT* **Diaz,** Luis, Deltona, FL, *F-2-1 KO VN* +
*CPL* **Diaz,** Wilfred, Los Angeles, CA, *C-1-11 KO* +
*CPL* **Dibbs,** Leonard A, Wilmington, DE, *D-7TH EN BN VN*
*PFC* **Dibiase,** Ronald F, Ocala, FL, *1-1 1-7* +
*TSGT* **Dickens,** George E, Elizabeth, CO, *1SPLW-PNS 3DEF WWII* +
*MAJ* **Dickerson,** Donald L, Hendersonville, TN, *K-3-5 H&S-1stTKS VN* +
*SGT* **Dickerson,** John G, Baltimore, MD, *WPNS-3-5 KO* +
*SGT* **Dickerson,** William J, Bartlesville, OK, *HQ-2-5 E-2-5 WWII CH* +
*CPL* **Dickey,** Perry J, Bartlesville, OK, *D-2-7 KO* +
*HON.* **Dickinson,** Perry G, Ravenna, OH, *G-2-1 WWII* +
*CPL* **Dickson,** William K, Locust Grove, VA, *A-1RECON VN* +
*SGT* **Dieduardo,** Patrick, Ledgewood, NJ, *7MAR WWII* +
*PFC* **Diefenbach,** Russell E, Aurora, IL, *81MM HQ-3-1 WWII* +
*SGT* **Diez,** Charles G, Pasadena, CA, *1 155 HOW BN C BTRY KO*
**Diffee,** William B JR., Bakersfield, CA, *4.2 MTRS-5 KO* +
*COL* **Diggs,** Alphonso Buster JR., San Marcos, CA, *1ST MARINE DIVISION*
*MSGT* **Diggs,** Warren J, Southfield, MI, *VMF-124 WWII* +
*CPL* **Dike,** Chris L, Ben Wheeler, TX, *81MM-1-5 VN* +
*CPL* **Dike,** Norman L, Hollister, CA, *B-1-7 WWII CH*
*SGT* **Dileonardo,** Frank C, Valley City, OH, *4.2-5MAR KO* +
*CPL* **Dilorenzo,** Mario, Victor, MT, *B-1-5 CW* +
*SGT* **Dilorenzo,** Michael D, Concord, CA, *9COMM CW* +
*CPL* **Dimascio,** Joseph A, North Cape May, NJ, *A-1-1 KMC KO* +
*MAJ* **Dimenna,** Jerome L, Larchmont, NY, *3RD BN 5TH MAR MAG-13*
**Dini,** Ray J, Addison, IL, *C-1MED WWII*
*CPL* **Dinoski,** Robert A, Port Richey, FL, *WPNS-3-5 KO* +
*LTCOL* **Dinsmore,** Jeffrey S, Murrieta, CA, *3RD BN 1ST MAR DIV HQ SWA*
*CPL* **Dintelman,** Robert C, Milton, WA, *HQBN CH* +

CPL **Dinuzzo,** Bruce C, Orient, NY, VMA-223 MAG-12 VN+

LCPL **Dipaola,** Sal, Farmingdale, NY, 9TH MAB CW VN

SGT E-5 **Dischler,** Kyle, Riverside, CA, 2 TANK BN H&S, C CO+

LTCOL **Disher,** William H, San Diego, CA, F-2-5+

LCPL **Distefano,** Joseph A, Farmingdale, NY, HQ CO HQ BN 1MAR DIV VN

PFC **Ditch,** William A, Ridgely, MD, I-3-7 KO

LT **Dito,** Raymond E, San Rafael, CA, SCOUT-HQ-1MAR VN+

LTCOL **Dixon,** A King II, Laurens, SC, 1RECON VN+

GYSGT **Dixon,** Eugene "Gene" W, Traverse City, MI, A/WPNS-1-5 KO+

SGT **Dixon,** Gregory S, Warrington, PA, D/1/5 VN

PFC **Dixon,** William T, Elk Grove, CA, E-2-5 CH

SGT **Dlouhy,** Robert G, Ellensburg, WA, H&S-2-5 KO+

CPL **Dlugosh,** John R, West Branch, MI, I-3-11 VN+

**Dobeck,** Sean R, Escondido, CA, 1ST MAR DIV STAFF SWA

1STSGT **Dobson,** Paul R, Roland, AR, C-1-11, I-3-5 KO VN CW+

SGT **Dobson,** Richard J, Garden City, MI, H-2-26 VN+

SGT **Doerksen,** Kenneth Eugene, Blanchard, OK, H&S, M CO, 3/5 VN

PFC **Doerscher,** Edwin H, Bennett, IA, C-1-1 KO+

CAPT **Doffin,** James E, North Charleston, SC, H&S-2-1 VN

MSGT **Doherty,** Donald W, Moyock, NC, A-1-5 VN+

CPL **Doherty,** John J, Myrtle Beach, SC, C-1-7 KO+

**Doherty,** Paul D, Lynnfield, MA, F-2-5 B-1-5+

CAPT **Dohse,** Gunther, Chimacum, WA, C-1-5 3AT KO VN+

SGT **Dolan,** James S, Lakewood, CA, 1RECON VN+

GYSGT **Dolgner,** Dennis R, West Allis, WI, E-2-1 SWA CW+

SGT **Dolph,** Paul William, Upland, CA, HQCO 7TH 1MARDIV CW+

CPL **Domier,** Jerome D, Visalia, CA, HQ-1-1 KO+

CPL **Domke,** Gary, North Port, FL, 1MT 1FSR/FLC VN+

SGTMAJ **Domyan,** Andrew J, Oceanside, CA, E-2-1 VN+

SGT **Don,** Harold, Tucson, AZ, W-1-1 KO+

SGT **Donaho,** Peter M, Normangee, TX, D-2-1 KO+

PFC **Donahue,** Theodore C, Milton, MA, L-3-1 WWII+

SGT **Donaldson,** Darrell K, Crowley, TX, H&S/C-1-1 KO+

COL **Donegan,** Darryl A, Huntington Beach, CA, H&S-1MAR CW+

LCPL **Donlan,** Dennis K, Katy, TX, BAND-H&S-HQ VN+

CPL **Donnelly,** George E, Fall River, MA, A-1-5 KO

**Donnelly,** James M, Kim, CO, D-1-5 VN+

CPL **Donohue,** Richard J, Monroe Twp, NJ, ANGLICO-1-5MAR KO+

1STSGT **Donovan,** C J, Portland, ME, G-3-1ENG KO VN+

PFC **Donovan,** John F, Valley Stream, NY, A-1-5 KO

CPL **Donovan,** Laurence P, Orange, MA, H&S-3-5 H&S-1TK CW+

SSGT **Donovan,** Richard M, Hubert, NC, H&S-3AMTRAC C-1TK VN+

MAJGEN **Donovan,** Timothy E, Oceanside, CA, 1TK 1SVC SWA+

SGT **Doody,** Eric L, Westminster, MA, HQ-MABS12 CW+

SGT **Doody,** Henry L, Winchendon, MA, MAW-BAND KO+

CPL **Dorsey,** Charles R, Athens, GA, B-1-1 KO+

SGT **Dorsey,** Don P, San Marcos, TX, SCT/SNPR HQ-1MAR VN+

SGT **Dorst,** James J, Claremont, CA, AMMO-1ORD KO+

**Dostert,** Donald, Saint Paul, MN, I-3-1 WWII+

SGT **Doty,** Donald H, Fall River Mills, CA, I-3-11, H&S 3-11 KO+

LCPL **Doty,** Richard C, Deltona, FL, G-2-5 VN

SGT **Doucette,** Ralph F, Celebration, FL, MABS24 VN+

SGT **Dougherty,** James E, Eagleville, PA, B/D-1-5 VN+

**Dougherty,** Thomas G, Jim Thorpe, PA, B-1AVNENGR WWII+

**Dougherty,** Thomas J, Novato, CA, F-2-7 VN+

LCDR **Doughty,** Douglas H JR., Penscola, FL, E/F-2-5 VN+

HM1 **Douglas,** George J, Auburn, CA, E-2-1 KO+

SGT **Dovale,** John E, Naperville, IL, I-3-12 A-1-11 VN

MRS **Dowd,** Louise Mae, Fair Oaks, CA, ASSOCIATE*

SSGT **Dower,** Kenneth Earl, San Diego, CA, G-2 HQ-HQ WWII KO

**Dowling,** Daniel R, Beaufort, SC, E-2-1 VN+

CPL **Downer,** James C, Traverse City, MI, G-2-5 VN+

CAPT **Downing,** David B, La Quinta, CA, 3-7MAR VN

SSGT **Downs,** Bruce L, Palmer, AK, H&S CO 2-7 VN+

BGEN **Downs,** Michael P, Alexandria, VA, HQ-5 F-2-5 VN+

SGTMAJ **Downs,** Paul A, Gulfport, MS, E-2-5 BRIG WWII KO+

SGT **Downs,** Robert P, Hilton Head Island, SC, MP-HQ CW+

SGT **Doyle,** Richard P, Beach Haven, NJ, AT-7MAR KO+

CPL **Dozier,** John J, Kill Devil Hills, NC, C-1-11 KO+

**Drainville,** Richard D, Warren, MI, K-3-5 F-2-5 WWII CH+

CPL **Drake,** Raymond E, Louisville, KY, HQ-1-7 1SIG CH+

MSGT **Drasky,** Raymond G, Central City, CO, H&S-3-7 VN+

**Drawhorn,** Josiah, Mohave Valley, AZ

SGT **Dray,** Jack W, Oceanside, CA, S-2 HQ-11 KO+

**Dreher,** Robert L, Simi Valley, CA, 7COMM CW+

SGT **Dreves,** Arthur F, Oviedo, FL, C-1-1 WWII CH+

SGT **Drew,** Richard M, Glenwood Springs, CO, A-1-1 VN+

SGT **Dreyer,** Douglas W, Corona Del Mar, CA, C-1-1-1+

CPL **Dreyer,** Leonard H CPA, Yorba Linda, CA, C-7COMM VN CW+

**Driscoll,** Francis W, Dorchester, MA, 1FSR KO

COL **Driscoll,** John A, Belleville, NJ, C-1-5 KO

CAPT **Drobny,** Donald D, Bluffton, SC, VN A CO & B CO 1/5 VN

PFC **Droeger,** W H, Greenwood, IN, H/W-3-1 KO+

**Drogus,** Robert, Beaver Falls, PA, 1AT KO+

CAPT **Drollinger,** Harry Ben, Mckinney, TX, B-1-5 VN+

LCPL **Druckemiller,** Phillip J, Prague, OK, H&S-2-1 VN+

LTCOL **Drummond,** Milton D JR., Richmond, VA, A-1ENGR KO VN CW+

CPL **Du Four,** Willie P, Boston, MA, 9DEF SPL WPNS WWII+

GYSGT **Dube,** Joseph A, Winder, GA, WPNS-5MAR WWII CH+

SSGT **Dubose,** Billy A, Rock Hill, SC, D-1-5 VN+

CPL **Duca,** Eugene J, Ridge, NY, L-3-7 WWII+

PFC **Ducasse,** Richard C, Middleboro, MA, G-2-5 VN+

CPL **Dudek,** Ron G, Lake Geneva, WI, 1TKS VN+

MAJ **Dudman,** William R, Chico, CA, HQ-1MAR VN+

**Dudon,** Andrew R, Rio Rancho, NM, HQ-11MAR H&S-1-1 VN+

SGT **Due,** Jorgen C, Bend, OR, 5-7 MAR KO+

CPL **Duenas,** Andrew C, Battleground, WA, MARINE LIAISON NHCP

SGTMAJ **Duff,** Juan D, Oceanside, CA, HQ-HQ HQ-7MT SWA+

SGT **Duffy,** William A, Lady Lake, FL, D-2-5 KO+

SSGT **Dugan,** Robert Eugne, Costa Mesa, CA, D CO 2-5 KO+

CWO3 **Dugan,** Walter L, Cape Coral, FL, 11-7MAR WWII CH KO+

SGT **Duh,** Joseph W, Piscataway, NJ, HQ-11MAR KO+

CPL **Dula,** Dorian A, New Market, MD, C-1-5 VN

SGT **Dullinger,** Art J, Hamilton, MT, VMF-214 1MAW VN

HM3 **Dumas,** William T, Cottage Grove, TN, B/C-1-7 KO+

SGT **Dumong,** John J, Los Osos, CA, D-2-11 CW+

SSGT **Dunaway,** John L, Sharpsburg, KY, HQ-1SVC KO+

CAPT **Dunbar,** Martin W, North Richland Hills, TX, E-2-11 F-2-11 E-2-5 VN+

MGYSGT **Duncan,** Charles E JR., Charleston, SC, A-1-5 KO VN+

MSGT **Duncan,** John A, Silver Spring, MD, HQ-1-11 KO

GYSGT **Duncan,** Thomas E, Roanoke, VA, C-1-7 KO+

**Dunford,** Don R, West Lafayette, IN, F-2-1 KO+

COL **Dunlap,** Greg Ray, Idyllwild, CA, 1ST LAR

SGT **Dunn,** George H, Dedham, MA, 1ORD KO

PFC **Dunn,** Gerald W, Saugus, CA, I-3-1 CW+

SGT **Dunn,** Timothy, Denver, CO, H-2-1 VN+

CPL **Dunn,** William T, Reedville, VA, C-1-7 1ST MAR DIV

**Dunne,** Kay, Westminster, CO, ASSOCIATE

MR. **Dunne,** Robert W, San Jose, CA, H-3-1 KO+

SGT **Dunning,** Charles A, Pontiac, IL, COMM-HQ KO+

HM3 **Dunning,** John M, Cottonwood Heights, UT, B-1-5 VN

SGT **Dupont,** Robert T, San Mateo, CA, 1CSG KO+

COL **Dupre,** Paul J, Port Hueneme, CA, 7MAR WWII CH KO VN+

**Durall,** Dean D, Mapleton, UT, ATT H&S-16AA WWII+

LCPL **Durand,** R. William, Rochester, NY, DRUM AND BUGLE CORPS

SGT **Durni,** Robin A, Albany, NY, FOX CO 2-5 VN+

SGT **Dust,** Gregory P, Prescott Valley, AZ, HQ-1-11 CAP-D-3 VN+

CPL **Dust,** Robert M, West Branch, MI, K-4-13 VN+

CPL **Duty,** Denis D, Tustin, CA, 3-5 1MAR DIV DST STORM

1STLT **Dutz,** Michael, Parlin, NJ, I-3-5 KO+

SGT **Duvall,** Carl C, Kansas City, MO, H-3-1 KO+

CPL **Dybowski,** Robert V, Shelby Township, MI, B-1-1 WWII CH KO+

CAPT **Dye,** Dale A, North Hills, CA, HQBN 1MARDIV H-2-5 VN

CPL **Dyer,** Norman, Old Orchard Beach, ME, D-2-5 KO+

CWO3 **Dykes,** Hugh G III, Oceanside, CA, HQ-11TH MAR B-1-4+

CPL **Dyson,** James V, West Roxbury, MA, I-3-5 KO+

**Dzielenski,** Cynthia, Terryville, CT, ASSOCIATE*

CPL **Eagleblanket,** William A, Hattiesburg, MS, A-1-5 SWA+

DR **Eames,** Frederick G, Waterville, ME, HQ CO 7MAR+

PHM2 **Earhart,** Harry W, Fairfield Bay, AR, C-1-1 WWII+

**Earle,** Robert, Ithaca, NY, 4JASCO-1ASCO WWII CH+

SGT E-5 **Easley,** Robert D, Valrico, FL, D CO 1ST MAR DIV

SGT **Easly,** Ernest M, La Pine, OR, HQ-3-11 KO+

COL **Easterday,** Steven G, Portland, OR, HQ-7ENGR 1MAR CW+

CAPT **Eaton,** William M, Broomfield, CO, E-2-7 VN

CPL **Eaves,** Earl J, Deltona, FL, ORD-5-7 KO+

LCDR **Ebbitt,** David M MD, Greencastle, PA, H&S-1LAR CW+

SGT **Eberle,** Robert A, East Stroudsburg, PA, 11MAR 7MAR CH KO+

*SGT* **Ebert,** Clyde R, Portland, OR, *C-1ST AMTRAC BN WWII KO*
*CAPT* **Ebert,** Robert W, Louisville, KY, *I-3-7 G-2-7 KO VN* +
*CPL* **Ebner,** Lyle E, Chaparral, NM, *I-3-5 WWII CH* +
*SSGT* **Echave,** Ralph A, Snohomise, WA, *1MED KO* +
**Eckert,** Bud, Hayward, CA, *L-3-1 VN* +
*SGT* **Eckert,** James O, Millstadt, IL, *H&S-11MAR KO* +
**Eckert,** Ray L, Hummelstown, PA, *B-1-1 KO*
*SGT* **Economy,** James T, Roanoke, VA, *H&S-1-5 KO* +
*SGT* **Edelmann,** Bruce A, New Kent, VA, *H&S-1-7 SWA* +
*SGT* **Eder,** Anthony A, Waterford, WI, *HQ-1MAR VN* +
*SGT* **Eder,** Harry A, Media, PA, *4.2-1MAR H&S-3MAR CH* +
*CPL* **Edmond,** R, Waynesboro, GA, *HQ-3-11 KO* +
*MGYSGT* **Edmunds,** James P, Chula Vista, CA, *G-3-5 KO* +
*MAJ* **Edson,** Herbert R, Ellenton, FL, *5MAR VN* +
*SGT* **Edwards,** Delbert E, Ottawa, KS, *HQ-1FAG VN* +
**Edwards,** John C, Colonial Heights, VA, *E-2-5 1MP-HQ WWII CH* +
*SGTMAJ* **Edwards,** John L, Elk River, MN, *A-1-5 VN* +
*SGT* **Edwards,** Orace L, Arlington, TX, *G-3-1 KO* +
*CPL* **Edwards,** Raymond F, East Bridgewater, MA, *A-1ENGR VN* +
*PFC* **Edwards,** Robert A, Wichita, KS, *H&S-3-11 WWII CH* +
**Efaw,** Cary R, Zelienople, PA, *H&S-1RECON VN* +
*SGT* **Egan,** John M, Concord, CA, *USS SAN FRANCISCO WWII* +
*PFC* **Eggeman,** H J, Fort Huachuca, AZ, *A-1-7 KO* +
*SGT* **Eggen,** Arthur E, Pacifica, CA, *VMFA-323 VN*
*CPL* **Eggleston,** Robert J, Salcha, AK, *D-2-1 KO* +
*CPL* **Ehrlich,** Raymond, West Palm Beach, FL, *1-1MAR WWII* +
*CPL* **Ehrlich,** Robert L, Arbutus, MD, *I-3-1 KO*
*CAPT* **Eickenhorst,** David I, Apo, AP, *HQBN G-3 DIV SCH 1MAR DIV* +
*COL* **Einsidler,** Michael A, San Diego, CA, *1-1 HQ CO HQ BN VN* +
*DR. 1STLT* **Eisenbach,** Charles R II, Newberg, OR, *D CO., 1ST RECON BN VN* +
*E-6 SSGT* **Eisler,** John P, Winterhaven, FL, *2/1 3RD MARINES*
*CPL* **Ekins,** Junior, Newton, IA, *I-3-1 WPNS WWII* +
*SGT* **Ekker,** Charles M, Ellijay, GA, *F-2-5 VN* +
*CAPT* **Eklund,** Stephen A, Fernandina, FL, *7COMM HQBN VN* +
*SGT* **Elbert,** Thomas J, Grafton, OH, *SNIPER-HQ-5MAR VN* +
*CPL* **Eledge,** Jerome R SR., Council Bluffs, IA, *C-1-5 VN* +
*CAPT* **Eley,** Thom, Anchorage, AK, *1st RADIO 1-1 VN*
*LCPL* **Eley Iii,** G W III, Jackson, MI, *3-1MAR VN* +
*SGT* **Eliason,** Orval M, Bullhead City, AZ, *K-3-5 CH*
*PFC* **Elliott,** Donald K, Longwood, FL, *I-3-7 KO* +
*PFC* **Elliott,** L A, Stockton, CA, *8MAR-2MAR WWII* +
*LTCOL* **Elliott,** Richard M, Richardson, TX, *1ENGR-1PION KO* +
*CPL* **Elliott,** William Dennis, Hixson, TN, *D-1-7 VN* +
*CPL* **Ellis,** Fred C, Roanoke, VA, *K-3-5 WWII* +
*HM3* **Ellis,** George I, Jackson, MO, *G-2-1 VN* +
*MAJ* **Ellis,** George M, San Clemente, CA, *HQBTRY-11 C-1-11 SWA* +
*CPL* **Ellis,** Glendal R, Evansville, IN, *A-1-1 KO* +
*GYSGT* **Ellis,** Iron Bob, Cape Coral, FL, *1RECON-HQ KO* +
*SGT* **Ellis,** Laurel Glynn, Wills Point, TX, *H-3-11 KO* +
*CPL* **Elmore,** Joshua E, Escondido, CA, *B-1-5 OIF* +
*CPL* **Elsea,** Danny D, Winter Haven, FL, *G-2-5 VN* +
*SGT* **Elsner,** R A, Phoenix, AZ, *H&S-11MAR KO* +
**Emanuelson,** William C, Chicora, PA, *E-1RECON VN* +
*SSGT* **Emhoolah,** Parker, Lawton, OK, *2-7MAR KO VN* +
*1STSGT* **Emme,** Robert D, Rushville, IN, *L-3-5 CW* +
**Enfinger,** Alan C, Pensacola, FL, *B-1-RECON VN* +
*SGT* **Engel,** Edward N, Hawthorne, NV, *C-1-5 VN* +
*SGT* **England,** Oscar M, Page, ND, *WPNS-2-1 KO* +
*PFC* **English,** James T, Benton, AR, *L-4-11 VN* +
*CPL* **Engman,** Joseph M JR., Mosinee, WI, *HQ/F-2-1 VN* +
**Ennis,** Clarence 'Bud' A, Trenton, MI, *H&S-1MAR WWII CH*
**Enos,** Leonard F, Esparto, CA, *B-1-5 KO* +
*SGT* **Enright,** Richard N, Raynham, MA, *HQ BTRY-1ST BN-13TH MAR- 1ST MAR VN*
*SGT* **Epperson,** H R JR., Melbourne, FL, *C-7-1 KO VN* +
*CPL* **Epstein,** David H, Overland Park, KS, *HQTRS KO*
*COL* **Erdmann,** Hal L, Waukesha, WI, *B-1-1 KO* +
*SSGT* **Erens,** Richard E, Central Point, OR, *H&S-3-5 HQ-1MAR SWA*
*CPL* **Erickson,** Jack R, San Carlos, CA, *I-3-5 WWII KO* +
*HM3* **Erickson,** Mark W, Anaheim, CA, *A-1-5 VN* +
*LTCOL* **Erickson,** Randall L, Irvine, CA, *2-7 VN* +
*MR.* **Erickson,** Richard L, Wenatchee, WA, *B-7ENGR VN*
*SGT* **Erskine,** John W, Satellite, FL, *C-1-5 VN* +
*SGT* **Erwin,** Robert S, Canaan, CT, *1 ENG BN 1MAR DIV*
*SGT* **Escalera,** Jason C, Wildomar, CA, *C CO 1ST LAR BN*
*PFC* **Escamilla,** Manuel JR., Fontana, CA, *B-7-1-1 KO* +
*HM2* **Eschbach,** Herb H, Amenia, NY, *1ARMAMPH VN* +
*CPL* **Escher,** Sidney E JR., Slidell, LA, *H-3-1 KO* +
*SSGT* **Espino,** Tony S, San Antonio, TX, *E-2-5 KO* +
*CPL* **Espinoza,** Felipe JR., Grand Terrace, CA, *H&S-2-5 VN*
*MGYSGT* **Espinoza,** Frank A, San Antonio, TX, *A-1-1 VN* +
*LTCOL* **Estrada,** Albert A, Alta Loma, CA, *E-2-1 CJHP* +
*SGT* **Estrada,** Ramon, Montebello, CA, *H&S-3-27 H&S-1RECON VN*
*CPL* **Etheridge,** William S, Cedar Hill, TX, *H&S-3-7 VN* +
*MSGT* **Eubank,** Richard L, Lahaina, HI, *C-1RECON VN* +
*SGT* **Evans,** Albert B, Weston, MA, *HQ-3-1 81MM WWII CH* +
*CPL* **Evans,** Art W, Long Beach, CA, *L-3-1 VN* +
**Evans,** Cecil H, Olathe, KS, *C/D-1-7 WWII* +
*SGT* **Evans,** David B, Norwood, NC, *C CO 1ST RECON BN H&S CO 1ST MAR VN*
*G 2-5 1ST MAR 014* **Evans,** Eanos T, Newport Beach, CA, *G-2-5 WWII CH KO* +
*MGYSGT* **Evans,** Edward M, Nashville, TN, *HQ-HQ VN* +
*SGT* **Evans,** Francis E, Ava, NY, *H&S-11MAR KO*
*CPL* **Evans,** G L, Martinsburg, WV, *1RADIO VN* +
*CPL* **Evans,** James L, Meriden, CT, *H&S-7MAR KO* +
*LCPL* **Evans,** Jimmie L, Danville, IL, *HQ-HQ VN* +
*CPL* **Evans,** Richard A, Dayton, OH, *D-2-7 KO* +
*CPL* **Evans,** William R JR., Central Point, OR, *H-3-5 KO* +
*CPL* **Eversole,** W E, Williamsport, OH, *WPNS 2-7* +
*SGT* **Every,** John O, Bloomville, NY, *WPNS-3-7 KO* +
*COL* **Ezell,** Don D, Fort Worth, TX, *HQ-11 H-3-5 WWII CH KO VN* +
*PFC* **Fabian,** Golda Faye, Tigard, OR, *USMCWR, MWSS-4*
*HM2* **Fabian,** James R, Pensacola, FL, *A/B-1-5 VN* +
*CPL* **Fabregas,** Peter H, Massapequa Park, NY
*GYSGT* **Facchini,** Dennis R, Plymouth, MA, *B-1-1 KO*
*MAJ* **Fackler,** James W, New Hope, MN, *C-1MED B-1-7 WWII CH*
*SGT* **Facopoulos,** Michael T, Ronkonkoma, NY, *MOTOR TRNSPORT 7BN CW*
**Fadde,** Harry C, Cold Spring, NY, *H&S-1-1 CH* +
*SGT* **Fairbairn,** James M, Richardson, TX, *A-1-5 KO* +
*CPL* **Fairbanks,** Carter E, Bullhead City, AZ, *1STMD 1970-1971*
*1STLT* **Fairchild,** C.T., Round Rock, TX, *A-1-11 WWII CH KO* +
*CAPT* **Falk,** Allen E, Aberdeen, NJ, *HQ-HQ VN* +
*CPL* **Fall,** L G, Church Point, LA, *1-7MAR WWII CH* +
*COL* **Fallon,** Mike O, Paradise Valley, AZ, *1ST RECON BN VN*
*CPL* **Fallon,** Robert M, Medford, NJ, *COB 1ST MT BN 1MARDIV VN*
*SGTMAJ* **Fantau,** Steven A, Jacksonville, NC, *F-2-1 OIF*
**Farias,** Felix & Penny, New Braunfels, TX, *GOLD STAR PARENTS* +
*PFC* **Farias,** Hector JR., Laredo, TX, *1-14INF CW* +
*MSGT* **Farmer,** Allen E, Richmond, VA, *H&S-3-5 HQ VN SWA* +
**Farmer,** Charles W, Louisville, KY, *G-3-11 WWII* +
*MAJ* **Farmer,** Robert D, Oceanside, CA, *1RECON M-3-1 KO VN* +
*SGT* **Farnsworth,** W J, Riverton, UT, *1-5 MAR VN* +
*SSGT* **Farnum,** William E, Chepachet, RI, *7MT KO* +
*CPL* **Farr,** Bruce J, Powell, TN, *G-3-1 KO* +
**Farrar,** Stanley G, West Paris, ME, *WPNS-5MAR WWII* +
*SGT* **Farraye,** Louis E, Portage, MI, *H&S-1st90MM AAA KO* +
*RADM* **Farrell,** Eugene H, San Antonio, TX, *BB42 USS IDAHO WWII* +
*SGT* **Farrell,** John F, Utica, NY, *HQ-HQ KO* +
**Farrell,** Joseph J, Redondo Beach, CA, *17MAR KO* +
**Farrell,** Thomas F, Bay Shore, NY, *H-3-1 KO*
*1STLT* **Farrell,** William L, Palo Cedro, CA, *RECON-MAW VN* +
*LCPL* **Farrington,** John J, Clark, NJ, *VMO6 G-2-7 VN* +
*1STSGT* **Farritor,** John F, Vista, CA, *H&S 1-11 KO*
*CPL* **Faughnan,** Eugene P, Valley Stream, NY, *I-3-5 VN*
*SGT* **Faulkner,** Scott N, Las Vegas, NV, *H&S-3-5 VN* +
*GYSGT* **Faulkner,** Taylor, Saint Louis, MO, *1ST MAR DIV* +
*1STLT* **Faust,** Frank B, Lilburn, GA, *H-2-5 VN* +
*SGT* **Fee,** James J JR., Mary Esther, FL, *A-1ENGR MABS17 KO*
*CPL* **Feeney,** William J SR., Somerdale, NJ, *L-3-7 WWII* +
*SGT* **Fehrle,** Thomas Lee, Oklahoma City, OK, *C-1-7 1ST MAR DIV KO* +
*CPL* **Feickert,** Douglas P, Perkinsville, VT, *1MP CW* +
*SGT* **Feickert,** Paul R, Emmett, ID, *FLSGA VN* +
*SGT* **Feight,** Randahl D, Brownwood, TX, *I-3-7 VN*
*SGT* **Feil,** Donald R, Buena Park, CA, *1FSR CW* +
*SGT* **Feinhor,** J L, Alva, FL, *H-3-7 KO* +
*PFC* **Feist,** Robert M, Alexandria, VA, *IIIMAC WWII* +
*SGT* **Feith,** Henry J JR., Ellenville, NY, *ANGLICO E-2-5 KO* +
*CPL* **Fekken,** Nick A, Pentwater, MI, *C-1-1 VN* +
*PM3* **Feldman,** Morris, Sherman Oaks, CA, *L-3-5 WWII* +
*CPL* **Felsen,** Daniel, Midvale, UT, *HQ-1SVC 2LANSPT CW* +
*SSGT* **Felser,** Max J JR., Palmdale, CA, *MWCS-38* +
*CAPT* **Feltman,** Oneil Buck, Arley, AL, *HQ-HQ VN* +
*CPL* **Fenech,** Joseph G, Chelsea, MI, *H&S-1-5 VN* +
*CPL* **Fenkner,** Alfred E SR., Kenmore, WA, *F-2-1 KO* +
*SGT* **Fenlon,** David C, Carson City, NV, *H&S-1MT 1MAR KO* +

*LCDR* **Fennerty,** Michael B, Portland, OR, *2/11 1ST MAR DIV*
*SGT* **Fenske,** Lyle R, Waskish, MN, *A-3AMTRAC VN* +
*GYSGT* **Fenton,** Robert A, Granite Bay, CA, *A-1-11 I-3-7 KO* +
*CWO4* **Ference,** Daniel B, Chittenden, VT, *ATT 8MAR H&S-2-25 CW*
*CPL* **Ferguson,** Earl E II, Independence, MO, *A-7ENGR VN* +
*CWO3* **Ferguson,** Joseph H, Santa Ana, CA, *VMF214 1MAW WWII KO VN* +
*SGT* **Ferguson,** Roger J, Sparks, NV, *C-7ENG VN* +
*SGT* **Fernandez,** Larry O, Tampa, FL, *H&S-1-5 VN* +
*SSGT* **Fernquest,** Donald E, Portola Valley, CA, *1ANGLICO KO* +
*LTC* **Ferran,** Thomas D, Colorado Springs, CO, *M-3-7 SNIPER VN* +
*CAPT* **Ferrari,** Henry A, Plymouth, MA, *MTACS-2 KO*
*SSGT* **Ferrer,** Victor M, Kapolei, HI, *COMM-HQ SWA* +
*CWO3* **Ferrier,** James S, Milwaukee, WI, *H&S-1-5 CMC* +
*SGT* **Ferrigno,** Lawrence, Stafford, VA, *4.2-7MAR KO* +
*CPL* **Ferris,** Carlton L, Rio Rancho, NM, *HQ-1ENGR KO* +
**Ferris,** Ian, Dunnloring, VA, *F-2-1 VN* +
*CAPT* **Ferry,** Richard T, Vero Beach, FL, *H&S-3-5 KO* +
*SGT* **Fetters,** Lee W, Covina, CA, *RECON KO* +
*SGT* **Feuerherm,** Richard J, Camarillo, CA, *C-1-5 KO* +
**Fick,** Kenneth C, Toms River, NJ, *HQ-1MAR KO* +
*CAPT* **Fick,** Nathaniel, Washington, DC, *B-1-1 B-1RECON OIF* +
*SGT* **Field,** Robert V, Kingman, AZ, *WPNS-1-5 KO* +
*SGT* **Field,** Stephen J, Buffalo Grove, IL, *HOWZ-11MAR VN* +
*SGT* **Fielden,** B N, Las Vegas, NV, *HQ-1MAR WWII* +
*SGT* **Fielden,** Donald F, Grand Saline, TX, *A-1-1 VN* +
*CPL* **Fieseler,** Edward L, Ruthven, IA, *I-3-1 WWII CH* +
*A3C* **Filippone,** Angelo, Flushing, NY, *315 AIR DIV KO*
*1STSGT* **Filkins,** Fred W, Prescott, AZ, *1ENGR WWII CH KO VN* +
*CAPT* **Finamore,** Theodore III, Culver City, CA, *H&S-1-9 H&S-1-1 CW* +
**Finch,** William J, Somerville, MA, *F-2-7 VN* +
*MRS* **Fincher,** Olga V, Palm Harbor, FL, *ASSOCIATE* *
*PFC* **Finegan,** J R, Bluewater, NM, *I-3-1 WWII* +
*SGT* **Finestead,** James B, Ogden, IA, *B-9-7 SWA*
*CPL* **Fink,** C W, Auburn, CA, *E-2-5 WWII* +
*1STLT* **Finn,** Don R, San Clemente, CA, *E-2-12 SWA* +
*SGT* **Finn,** John P, Queens, NY, *D-1-26 VN* +
*SGTMAJ* **Finn,** Michael (Mickey) J, Oceanside, CA, *K/M-3-5 VN* +
*GYSGT* **Finnegan,** William H, Independence, MO, *G-2-1 WWII KO* +
*SGT* **Finney,** James L, Decherd, TN, *1TK WWII* +
*1STSGT* **Finstad,** Carl D, River Falls, WI, *H&S 1ST MAR REG KO* +
*COL* **Fischer,** Robert, Arvada, CO, *ATT 1-9MAR 1MARBDE VN* +
*CWO3* **Fishel,** Jeffery D, Chula Vista, CA, *WPNS-1-1 OIF*
*SGT* **Fisher,** Bernard M, Bay Pines, FL, *D-2 1MT WWII* +
*SGT* **Fisher,** Bobby P, Houston, TX, *WPNS-1-7 KO*
*LTCOL* **Fisher,** Carl J, Virginia Beach, VA, *HQ-5MAR HQBN VN* +
*CPL* **Fisher,** Clayton I JR., Henderson, NV, *B/D-1-7 WWII* +
*HM2* **Fisher,** Earl, Anthem, AZ, *A-1-5 VN*
*CPL* **Fisher,** Foyea, Miami, FL, *H&S-1-5 VN* +
*MRS* **Fisher,** Laura, Anthem, AZ, *ASSOCIATE* *
**Fisher,** R L, Bellevue, WA, *C-1-7 WWII* +
*SGT* **Fisher,** Roland W, Littlestown, PA, *1REGT KO* +
*SGT* **Fisher,** Ronald D, Eugene, OR, *H&S-1-7 VN* +
*SGT* **Fitch,** Jerry L, Las Vegas, NV, *1-5MAR WWII KO* +
*SGT* **Fitch,** Robert R JR., Hamilton, NJ, *h-2-1 f-2-7* +
*SGT* **Fitzgerald,** Edward G, Westfield, MA, *H-3-5 KO* +
*GYSGT* **Fitzpatrick,** Peter J JR., Salem, OR, *D-9ENGR 1CSG KO VN* +
*CPL* **Flaherty,** James M, Saint Louis, MO, *I-3-7 B-7MT KO* +
*LCDR* **Flaherty,** M. B, Golden, CO, *CVW-9 1ST MAR DIV VN* +
*CPL* **Flaherty,** Robert E, Saint Louis, MO, *1ST MAW, MGCIS3, MACG2 KO* +
*COL* **Flaherty,** Thomas J, Hillsboro, OR, *G-2-27 VN*
*CAPT* **Flatland,** Richard JR., San Mateo, CA, *1MAW WWII KO* +
*SGT* **Flavin,** Daniel T, West Lafayette, IN, *1-3-7 VN*
*SGT* **Fleishman,** Barney, Oceanside, CA, *HQ-1MT WWII CH KO* +
*LCPL* **Fleming,** George J, Cocoa Beach, FL, *SVC-9ENGR VN* +
*SGT* **Fleury,** A J, Buena Park, CA, *1-1MAR* +
*CPL* **Florence,** Joseph K, Wethersfield, CT, *H-3-1 KO* +
*GYSGT* **Florentine,** Gerard C, Randolph, MA, *1 RECON VN*
*CPL* **Florentino,** Michael J, Hillsborough, NJ, *K-3-5 VN* +
**Florentino,** Thomas M, Winthrop, MA, *H&S-1-7 VN* +
*CPL* **Florez,** B J, Sunnyside, UT, *C-11MT* +
*SSGT* **Flournoy,** W V, Red Bluff, CA, *HQ-1-11 KO* +
*SGT* **Floyd,** Barry L, Sundance, WY, *H-3-11 VN* +
*SSGT* **Floyd,** Elbert F, Parachute, CO, *MAG-14 1MAW WWII* +
**Floyd,** Eric, Palm Desert, CA, *1 MAW*
*GYSGT* **Fluegel,** George A, Duluth, GA, *A/B/C-3AMTRAC VN* +
*CPL* **Fluke,** Robert (Duke) D SR., Los Angeles, CA, *B-1-7 VN* +
*SGTMAJ* **Flynn,** Daniel J, Buffalo Grove, IL, *2-5MAR 3-7MAR 1MAW VN* +
*SGT* **Foate,** David E, Madeira Beach, FL, *COMMCO-HQBN KO* +
*CPL* **Folco,** Glen F, Martinsville, IN, *1ENGR 1FSR VN* +
*CPL* **Foley,** Daniel R, Roswell, NM, *7ENGR HQ-1FSSG CW* +
**Foley,** Don, La Quinta, CA, *1 MAW*
*SGT* **Folk,** Norman E, Northumberland, PA, *W-1-11 VN*
*CPL* **Fonte,** Joseph R, Metairie, LA, *E-2-5 KO* +
*CPL* **Foote,** Bradford L, La Pine, OR, *K-3-5 C-1-1 E-2-7 VN* +
*CPL* **Ford,** Martin X, Wollaston, MA, *G-3-1 KO* +
*SGT* **Ford,** Patrick R, Union, WA, *SVC-7ENGR VN* +
*CPL* **Ford,** Richard E, Quincy, MA, *G-3-1 KO* +
*COL* **Ford,** Wesley W, Saint Cloud, FL, *AT-1-1 KO* +
*CPL* **Fore,** Richard V, Los Lunas, NM, *A-1-7 KO* +
*CPL* **Forester,** Denver B, San Marcos, CA, *AMMO-1FSR VN* +
*SSGT* **Forgie,** Harry J, Turtle Creek, PA, *B-1-1 MAW CH KO* +
*CPL* **Forman,** Joel J, Culver City, CA, *C&E BN CW* +
*CPL* **Formisano,** Jerry A, Mount Vernon, NY, *C-1-7 KO* +
*SGT* **Forrest,** James A, Wasco, CA, *F-2-7 KO* +
*CPL* **Forslin,** Thomas C, Fremont, WI, *H&S-3-11 WWII* +
*CPL* **Fosnaught,** William F, The Villages, FL, *7ENGR VN* +
*CPL* **Foss,** David, Walnut Creek, CA, *HMS MAG-11 CMC* +
*SGT* **Fossos,** James A, Des Moines, WA, *B-1RECON VN* +
*CPL* **Foster,** Charles A, Tonawanda, NY, *WPNS-2-1 KO* +
*MSGT* **Foster,** M.L., Oceanside, CA, *SVC-HQ VN CW* +
*CPL* **Foster,** Thomas R, Grand Junction, CO, *HQ-HQ VN* +
*SSGT* **Fournier,** Raymond L, Shepherdstown, WV, *MAG11 WWII* +
*CAPT* **Fowkes,** David W, Winter Park, FL, *D-2-5 KO*
*1STSGT* **Fowler,** Charles O, Vista, CA, *1FORREC VN* +
*REV.* **Fowler,** Frank L JR., Hot Springs, AR, *MARDET KO* +
*SGT* **Fowler,** Johnnie R, Linn, MO, *HQ-11 CW* +
*SGT* **Fox,** Billy E, Wilton, CA, *HDQ CO 1ST BASE DEPOT, 1MAR DIV WWII* +
*SGT* **Fox,** Charles W, Ripon, CA, *A -1SHPTY KO* +
*HMCM* **Fox,** Mike, Houston, TX, *I-3-5 KO VN* +
*SGT* **Foy,** William L JR., Marion, IN, *C-7MT SVC-9ENG VN* +
*CPL* **Fraleigh,** Pat F, Poughkeepsie, NY, *A-1-1 VN* +
*SGT* **Francis,** James M, Jackson, MO, *A CO 1ST TANK BN 1ST EOD PIT*
*CPL* **Frank,** Jack E, Parker, CO, *B-3AMTRAC WWII* +
*LCPL* **Frank,** James M, New Milton, WV, *D-9ENGR VN* +
*MSGT* **Franklin,** David M, Dacono, CO, *7ENGR BN VN* +
*SGT* **Franklin,** John J, Lakewood, NJ, *B-1ENGR KO* +
*CPL* **Franklin,** Marvin E, Wellman, TX, *H&S-8AMTRAC WWII CH* +
*SGT* **Franklin,** Ted L, Florence, MT, *B-1-5 3TK VN* +
*MAJ* **Franklin,** Woody Griffith, Alpine, WY, *COMM-HQ 1MAR VN* +
*COL* **Frazier,** Michael M, Oceanside, CA, *HQ-2-11 CW*
*LCPL* **Frazier,** Michael S, Thornton, CO, *B-1-1 VN* +
**Frechette,** Ronald P, Auburn, ME, *2-7MAR 1SHPTY VN* +
*CPL* **Frederick,** Hart, Highland, IN, *H&S/B--155GUN KO* +
*MR.* **Frederickson,** A.L. (Rick), Marshalltown, IA, *H&S-5 3-5 WWII CH KO* +
*SGT* **Freeh,** Edwin J JR., Saint Petersburg, FL, *A-1TK KO* +
*CPL* **Freeman,** Bruce A, Justin, TX, *3 MAW 269 Gun Runner*
*CPL* **Freeman,** Stephen Max, Rockwall, TX, *H&S CO 1RECBN, 1MARDIV VN* +
*SGT* **Freeman,** William A JR., O'fallon, MO, *1RECON HQBN VN*
*CAPT* **Frei,** Jason R, Saint Charles, MO, *5-11, 1-11-OIF* +
*PFC* **Frenaye,** John W, Palm City, FL, *G-2-1 WWII* +
*CPL* **French,** Horace Wells "Red", Port Charlotte, FL, *E-3-E-4* +
*MGYSGT* **French,** Robert D, Fallbrook, CA, *3/7, 1STMARDIV HQ 6-3*
*SGT* **Frerichs,** Roger A, Bassfield, MS, *A-3AMTRAC VN* +
*PhM3* **Friede,** Eldon L, Blair, WI, *E-2-7 C-1MED WWII CH* +
*PFC* **Friedman,** Wayne V, Tucson, AZ, *HQ CO 1ST BN 5TH REG* +
*SGT* **Fritz,** Allen A, Huntingburg, IN, *M-3-1 VN* +
*SSGT* **Fritz,** Rudolph J, Naperville, IL, *A/WPNS-1-7 WWII KO* +
**Frizelle,** Cynthia A, Bullhead City, AZ, *ASSOCIATE* *
*1STLT* **Froats,** Lorne, Indian Wells, CA, *1MT WWII KO* +
**Frost,** Bill L, Kansas City, KS, *F-2-7 KO* +
*CAPT* **Frost,** Jack C, Mesa, AZ, *7MT KO* +
*CPL* **Fry,** Kenneth L, Davenport, IA, *B-3AMTRAC VN*
*PHM3* **Fry,** Meredith W PE, Anderson, IN, *G-2-5 WWII* +
*SGT* **Fuerst,** Paul D, Sebastopol, CA, *W-1-11 VN* +
*CPL* **Fuhlrodt,** Warren D, Blair, NE, *F-2-1 WWII* +
*SGT* **Fukuoka,** Ronnie M, Westminster, CA, *G-3-11 KO* +
*CPL* **Fulford,** Floyd E, Palmyra, VA, *B-1-5 KO* +

**Fulkerson,** Glen M, Michigan City, IN, *G-2-7 VN* +
*CAPT* **Fulkerson,** Jimmie H, Jonesboro, AR, *C-1-7 VN* +
*COL* **Fulks,** James A, Parkton, MD, *B-1-1 VN SWA* +
*LTCOL* **Fuller,** Jeffrey, Oceanside, CA, *1MARDIV G3 FIRES*
*SGT* **Fullerton,** Scott A, Leavenworth, WA, *H&S/A-1-5 VN* +
*LCPL* **Fulton,** Bob, Lake Havace City, AZ, *1ST MAR DIV (SUPPLY) HDQ KO* +
*PFC* **Fulwider,** Ed D, Pacifica, CA, *G/H&S-2-1 WWII CH* +
*COL* **Funston,** G D, Wichita Falls, TX, *H&S/L-4-11 KO* +
*CWO3* **Furgal,** Michael L, Monroe, WI, *9ITT VN* +
*GYSGT* **Furlong,** Richard D, San Diego, CA, *A-1-9 1RECON VN* +
*SGT* **Furlong,** Tim, Cotopaxi, CO, *B-3AMTRAC VN* +
*SGT* **Furr,** John (Johnny) D, Boswell, IN, *K-3-5 VN* +
*CPL* **Gabaldon,** John S, Thousand Oaks, CA, *C-1TK BN 1MAR DIV WWII* +
*SGT* **Gable,** Robert H, Scottsdale, AZ, *I-3-11* +
*LCPL* **Gabriel,** Keith A, Appleton, WI, *F-2-11 VN* +
**Gaeta "Doc",** Louis C, Bethesda, MD, *A-1-5 CACL4 7COMM VN* +
*CPL* **Gaffney,** Harry J JR., Lafayette Hill, PA, *HQ-9MAR VN* +
*1STSGT* **Gaines,** Robert L, Las Cruces, NM, *F-2-7-1 CH KO* +
*CAPT* **Gainey,** Paul M, San Marcos, CA, *1MARDIV*
*CPL* **Galinski,** Richard L, Junction City, OR, *K-3-5 VN* +
*SSGT* **Gall,** John F, Saint Petersburg, FL, *C-1-5 W-3-7 KO VN* +
*SGTMAJ* **Gallagher,** Don W, Winchester, CA, *1-5 1MAR DIV*
*GYSGT* **Gallagher,** Thomas C, Roseboro, NC, *1SVC KO* +
*LCPL* **Gallagher,** William M, Tehachapi, CA, *H-2-11 VN* +
*MAJ* **Gallant,** Ray A, Anchorage, AK, *1AMTRAC 1PION WWII KO* +
*CPL* **Galle,** Michael J, Fort Mohave, AZ, *VMA 223*
*CPL* **Gallio,** Louis A, Manvel, TX, *1TK CW* +
*CPL* **Gallo,** G T, Sarasota, FL, *1ORD WWII* +
*SGT* **Galt,** Ed P JR., Montgomery, AL, *H&S-1-7 VN* +
*1STSGT* **Galvan,** George E, Atascadero, CA, *WPNS 1-7 KO VN* +
*SGT* **Galvez,** Alan A, Bellefontaine, OH, *MAG-12 1MAW VN*
*1STLT* **Galyean,** Michael L, Winter Park, FL, *C-1-5 VN* +
*SGT* **Gambrel,** Herschel H, Indianapolis, IN, *D-2-1 A-1-2 KO* +
*CPL* **Gandara,** George R, Lake Villa, IL, *E CO 2-1* +
*CAPT* **Ganeles,** Burton F, San Marcos, CA, *HQ-5MAR ELMACO-1FSR WWII CH KO VN* +
*CPL* **Gangloff,** Robert L, Harmon, IL, *C-1-7 VN* +
*CAPT* **Gannon,** Daniel J, Ankeny, IN, *M CO 3/5*
*HM2* **Gant,** Bruce B JR., Morrow, GA, *E-2-5 VN* +
*SSGT* **Garaway,** Marvin, Green Valley, AZ, *5MAR KO* +
**Garbarini,** Charles, Palm Desert, CA, *2MARDIV*
*CPL* **Garber,** A L, Wichita, KS, *I-3-7 VN* +
*CPL* **Garcia,** Augustine L, Corpus Christi, TX, *E-2-1 CH KO* +
*SGT* **Garcia,** Gilberto C, Corpus Christi, TX, *B-1-7 CH KO* +
*SGT* **Garcia,** Michael L, Lancaster, CA, *2/7*
*SGT* **Gardiner,** Charles R, Cmch, NJ, *WPNS-2-5 KO* +
*SGT* **Gardner,** Jimmy C, Cullman, AL, *D-2-7 KO* +
*CPL* **Garofano,** Dominick D, Mountain View, CA, *L-3-7 WWII* +
*GYSGT* **Garren,** Raymond M, Hunlock Creek, PA, *HQ-1-1 CH KO VN* +
*SGT* **Garrett,** Franklin D, San Antonio, TX, *III MAF VN 2-5-1* +
**Garrett,** Randall H, Amarillo, TX, *K-3-1 WWII CH* +
*SGT* **Garrett,** Wilford A, Russellville, AR, *B-1-7 KO* +
*1STLT* **Garris,** Preston F, La Grange, NC, *B-1-5 VN* +
*LCPL* **Garrison,** Larry A, Superior, MT, *H-2-1 VN* +
*CPL* **Garvey,** David J, Wallingford, PA, *I-3-7 VN* +
*SGT* **Garza,** Jesse, San Antonio, TX, *VMF513 1MAW KO* +
*CPL* **Garza,** Manuel R JR., Corpus Christi, TX, *1MT KO* +
*CPL* **Gasche,** Bob T, Gainesville, FL, *D-2-7 KO* +
*SGT* **Gastelum,** Ralph A, Chandler, AZ, *WPNS CO 2-1-1 KO*
**Gatchell,** G Gordon JR., Lincoln, MA, *1CSG KO* +
*SSGT* **Gates,** Damon E, Williamsburg, VA, *FOX CO 2-11 VN* +
*SGT* **Gates,** Robert L, Urbandale, IA, *H-3-7 KO* +
*SSGT* **Gaugenmaier,** Robert L, Carefree, AZ, *E-2-7 KO* +
*PFC* **Gavan,** Edward J, Grand Rapids, MI, *I-3-5 WWII CH KO* +
*SGT* **Gaynor,** W A, Claymont, DE, *H&S-1-5 KO* +
**Gearhart,** Charles Gordon, Santa Margarita, CA, *SVC-1ENGR KO* +
*CPL* **Geddie,** Larry C, Spring, TX, *G-2-5 VN* +
*SGT* **Gehrlein,** Gordon A, Erie, PA, *1MAW CW* +
**Geier,** Raymond R, Florence, KY, *K-3-5 VN* +
*CPL* **Geiger,** Milton A JR., Phoenixville, PA, *F-2-1 VN* +
**Geiger Rajich,** Ralph J, Superior, WI, *M-4-11 WWII* +
*CPL* **Geist,** Robert E, Lancaster, PA, *3-26 2-27 VN* +
*SGT* **Gelb,** David R, Malaga, WA, *B/H&S-1-5 KO* +
*SGT* **Geldert,** George B, Winthrop Harbor, IL, *I-3-5 KO* +
*MAJ* **Gelles,** T N, Scranton, PA, *2-1/7MAR* +
*PFC* **Gemma,** Nicholas J, Syracuse, NY, *A-1-1 KO*
**Genninger,** Andrew P, Fallbrook, CA, *H-3-5 WWII CH KO* +
*SSGT* **Genochio,** Frank A, Santa Clara, CA, *1SIG-HQ WWII* +
*SGT* **Genrich,** Jon C, Greenville, TX, *WPNS/H-3-7 KO* +
*1STSGT* **Gentry,** John H JR., Loveland, OH, *B-1-7 F-2-7 VN* +
*SGT* **George,** Nicholas, Rowley, MA, *G-3-7 KO* +
*SSGT* **Gerace,** Joseph B, Boca Raton, FL, *HQ-7MAR KO*
*CPL* **Geraci,** Emile A, Gretna, LA, *B-1-5 KO*
*GYSGT* **Gerdau,** Michael T, La Pine, OR, *HQ-HQ HQ-2-7 VN* +
*CPL* **Gerding,** Geoffrey J, Covington, KY, *H&S-3-1 VN*
*CPL* **Gerheim,** Earl C, Spokane, WA, *ISO-3-5 VN* +
*LTCOL* **Gerlach,** Howard L, Fairfax, VA, *HQ-1 5RECON 3-5MAR VN* +
*SGT* **Gerlach,** J.B. (Hank), Napa, CA, *SIG COMMSPT-HQ KO* +
*CPL* **Germano,** Joseph, Mamaroneck, NY, *COMFIBPAC WWII* +
*CPL* **Germeraad,** Jacob, Vacaville, CA, *81MM-2-1 VN CW*
*CPL* **Gero,** Herman P, Brook Park, OH, *HQ-1 1ORD CH KO* +
*GYSGT* **Gerstner,** Raymond C, Cotopaxi, CO, *B-AMTRAC LAAM WWII KO VN* +
*SGT* **Gervase,** Nicholas G, Scottsdale, AZ, *I-3-1 KO* +
*CAPT* **Gest,** J S, Avon, CT, *I-3-11* +
*SGT* **Geurts,** Gary F, Green Bay, WI, *A-1-1 KO* +
*CPL* **Geyer,** Richard M, Port Orange, FL, *3SEPMED C-1-6 C-1-22 WWII* +
*LCPL* **Giambrocco,** Rocco E, Pepperell, MA, *H&S/M-3-5 VN* +
*CPL* **Giantvalley,** Alan J, Pittsburg, CA, *C-1-7 VN* +
*CPL* **Gibeau,** P E, Rapid City, SD, *HQ-1-11 KO* +
*CPL* **Gibney,** Ronald F, Chiloquin, OR, *A-1-11 1-1MAR VN* +
*CAPT* **Gibney,** William A, Pittsfield, MA, *HQ-11 KO VN*
*CPL* **Gibson,** Donald A JR., Richmond, TX, *WPNS-1-5 KO* +
*SGT* **Gibson,** Holland (Hoot) M JR., Raleigh, NC, *H&S-3-5 KO* +
*MGYSGT* **Giddens,** Billie Leon, Houston, TX, *H&S-1-5 H&S-3-1 VN* +
*MGYSGT* **Giese,** Kenneth A, Arvada, CO, *1818 AACS KO*
*CPL* **Giguere,** William P, Bedford, NH, *RECON-HQ KO* +
*SGTMAJ* **Gilbert,** Arthur N, Burbank, CA, *D-1-5 WWII KO VN* +
**Gilbert,** Gregory, Winterhaven, CA, *C-1-7 1RECON VN* +
*SGT* **Gilbert,** Stephen J, Los Angeles, CA, *1AMPHIBTRAC KO* +
*CPL* **Gilbertson,** Walter A, Litchfield, MN, *JASCO-1-7 WWII CH* +
*CPL* **Gilday,** Scott R, Marengo, IL, *K-3-5 VN* +
*CPL* **Gilker,** Donald E, Loveland, OH, *H-3-7 CH* +
*CPL* **Gill,** Jerry M, Savannah, GA, *W-1-5 KO* +
*SGT* **Gill,** Marlin D, San Mateo, CA, *HQCO 1-7* +
*CPL* **Gill,** Truman F, Tuleta, TX, *K-4-11 WWII* +
*CPL* **Gillen,** William F JR., Waveland, MS, *A-1-1 KO* +
*COL* **Gillespie,** Frank E, Warrenton, VA, *G-3-11 CW* +
*SGT* **Gillett,** David D, Bloomington, MN, *H&S-1ENG CW* +
*PFC* **Gillette,** Dennis C, Spokane, WA, *C-1-7 1ST MAR DIV* +
*SCPO* **Gillette,** Frank G USN(RET.), Desert Hot Springs, CA, *1ST MED BN 1ST MAR DIV CW VN*
**Gillick,** Fredrick (Fred) F, Saint Clair Shores, MI, *L-4-11 KO* +
*SSGT* **Gilliland,** Harold H, Tucson, AZ, *A-1AMTRAC KO* +
*CPL* **Gilling,** Richard A, Bokeelia, FL, *H-3-7 KO* +
*SGT* **Gilmore,** James H, Coshocton, OH, *1ENGR VN* +
*CPL* **Gilpin,** Hershel O, Scott City, MO, *K-3-7 WWII CH* +
*1STLT* **Gilwee,** William J JR., Cupertino, CA, *C-1-7 KO* +
*SGT* **Gin,** Henry, Oakland, CA, *AD Grp-HQBN/CMC* +
*CPL* **Girod,** Walter D, Minneapolis, MN, *E-2-11 WWII CH* +
*LCPL* **Girrens,** Charles M, Bentley, KS, *TOW-1TK CW* +
*E-6 SSGT* **Glade,** Devin S, Fallbrook, CA, *3RD AA-BN H&s CO*
*MAJGEN* **Glasgow,** Harold G, Brentwood, TN, *HQ-2-1 KO VN* +
**Glasgow,** Marc H, Brecksville, OH, *9ENGR G-2-5 VN* +
*LCPL* **Glasgow,** Peter H, Canton, MI, *A/C-1-1 VN* +
*SGT* **Glasner,** Robert A, Pikesville, MD, *C-1-7 VN* +
*SGT* **Glass,** Irvin, Naples, FL, *A-1-6 CW* +
*SGT* **Glass,** James W, Sun City Center, FL, *H&S-5MAR KO* +
*SGT* **Glass,** Stephen D, Whittier, CA, *I - H&S-3-1 CW* +
*SGTMAJ* **Glass,** Stuart D, San Clemente, CA, *1/4, 2/5, 1CEB, 1/11* +
*CWO2* **Glasser,** L B, South Windsor, CT, *F-2-5 VN* +
*SSGT* **Glassford,** Frank, Spring Hill, FL, *D&H&S-1-1-VN* +
*SGT* **Glatz,** George J JR., Crescent, PA, *B-1-1 WWII KO* +
*CPL* **Glaze,** Dennis L, Whittier, CA, *C-1-AT CW* +
*SGT* **Glazzy,** Michael J, San Jose, CA, *MGCI S3-1MAW KO* +
*CPL* **Gleason,** Raymond P, Cleves, OH, *C-1-1 VN* +
*CAPT* **Glenn,** James P, Clovis, CA, *C-1-1 VN* +
*CAPT* **Glore,** J W, Whitefish, WI, *HQ-3-5 VN* +
*TSGT* **Glover,** Cleveland W, Stuart, FL, *WPNS-2-1 KO*
*1STLT* **Glover,** John N, Newberry, SC, *K-4-11 VN*
*SGT* **Goas,** Robert F JR., Johnstown, PA, *I-3-1 WWII* +
*TSGT* **Gober,** Bill, Sheffield, AL, *B-1AMTRAC KO* +
*SGT* **Goble,** Joe O, Conover, NC, *B-1-7 WWII* +
*CPL* **Goblet,** James P, North Fort Meyers, FL, *A-1ST155GUN C-1ST75AAA KO* +

*CPL* **Goff,** Arthur G JR., Braidwood, IL, *SVC-1AMTRAC CW* +
**Gogerty,** Daniel J, Allyn, WA, *I-3-5 KO* +
*HMC* **Gognat,** Joseph H, Indianapolis, IN, *HQ-2-7 VN* +
*MR.* **Gohn,** Steven, Savannah, GA, *G-2-5 CW* +
*CPL* **Gold,** Frank E, Stroudsburg, PA, *H&S-5MAR WWII CH* +
*GYSGT* **Gold,** Kenneth G, Houston, TX, *3-1MAR H-3-7 CH KO* +
*LCPL* **Goldberg,** Bruce W, Commerce City, CO, *H&S-1-7 VN* +
*SGT* **Golden,** David T JR., Charlottesville, VA, *F-2-1 KO* +
*SGT* **Golden,** Roger E, New Port Richey, FL, *B-1-1 VN* +
*CPL* **Goldstein,** Jerome L, Lynbrook, NY, *B-3AMTRAC CW* +
*MR.* **Goldston,** Richard NEIL, Boise, ID, *1-3-7 VN* +
*CAPT* **Goldszer,** James F, Rye, NY, *NAV HOSP CAMP PEND OIF* +
*SGT* **Gomer,** Richard H, Gilroy, CA, *H-3-7 WWII KO* +
*CPL* **Gomez,** J, Los Angeles, CA, *H&S-17MAR WWII* +
**Gonder,** John A JR., Fort Worth, TX, *H&S-3-1 VN* +
*CPL* **Gonzales,** Alfred F SR., Saint Bernard, LA, *WPNS-1MAR KO* +
*LCPL* **Gonzales,** Armand A, Salinas, CA, *1ST TKS VN*
*CPL* **Gonzales,** Edward V, San Antonio, TX, *F-2-7 KO* +
**Gonzales,** Guillermo (Bill), Chino Hills, CA, *H&S-2-11MAR WWII KO*
*SGT* **Gonzales,** John A, Houston, TX, *1ST MAR 7TH MAR VN*
*COL* **Gonzales,** Lawrence D, Watsonville, CA, *3-CAG* +
*SGTMAJ* **Gonzales,** Michael E, Oceanside, CA, *3-5 1-5 11TH MARINES*
*LCPL* **Gonzales,** Raymond A, Santa Paula, CA, *C-1-7 VN* +
*PVT* **Gonzales,** Ricardo MIGUEL, Shingle Springs, CA, +
*SGT* **Good,** Rodney W, Hughes Springs, TX, *L-3-1 VN* +
*SGT* **Good,** William D, New York, NY, *I-3-1 KO* +
*CPL* **Goode,** Lemuel C, Fresno, CA, *WPNS-1-7 WWII KO* +
*GYSGT* **Goodell,** M.C. (Charlie) JR., Virginia Beach, VA, *HQ- HQ VN* +
*LCPL* **Goodenough,** Neil M, Stuart, FL, *1ST FSR/FLC*
*CPL* **Goodfield,** David A, Carpinteria, CA, *C-1RECON CW* +
*CPL* **Gooding,** Leslie A, Lexington Park, MD, *I-3-11 WWII CH* +
*SGT* **Goodman,** William W, Nashville, TN, *COMBAT PHOT KO* +
**Goodrich,** D J, San Antonio, TX, *F-2-7* +
*PFC* **Goodrich,** Forrest R, East Longmeadow, MA, *B-1PION CH* +
*GYSGT* **Goodrum,** Raymond, Binghampton, NY, *1ST MAR DIV OIF* +
*MSGT* **Goodspeed,** Troy E, Hacienda Hgts, CA, *HQ-3-7 HQ-3-1 CW* +
*PFC* **Goodwin,** Andy JR., Pala, CA, *K-3-26 VN* +
*CWO4* **Goodwin,** Gene C, Tyler, TX, *G-3-11 WWII CH* +
*SGT* **Goodwin,** Jay S, Corpus Christi, TX, *BRAVO CO 1ST BN 1ST MAR DIV VN*
**Goodwin,** Paul M, Palm Desert, CA, *B-1-1 B-1MED KO* +
*SGT* **Goorey,** Richard L, Riverside, CA, *MWSG17 VN* +
*SGTMAJ* **Gordon,** Carroll SR., Randallstown, MD, *2-7 1MAR VN SWA* +
*SGT* **Gordon,** David G, Orlando, FL, *H&S/B-1-7 D-2-5 WWII KO* +
*CPL* **Gordon,** John A, Saint John, WA, *C-1-5 WWII* +
*MSGT* **Gordon,** Winford F, New Elm, MN, *HQ-FT-FMFPAC KO VN* +
**Gore,** Charles E, Sherman Oaks, CA, *I-3-7 WWII KO* +
*SGT* **Gorman,** James D JR., Middlesex, NJ, *W-2-5 KO* +
*CAPT* **Gorski,** D T, Depew, NY, *1MAR VN* +
*SGT* **Goshko,** Stephen SR., Crest Hill, IL, *A-1SPLWPN WWII* +
*MAJGEN* **Gossell,** William H, Farmes Branch, TX, *1ST MAR DIV* +
*SGT* **Gotham,** Frederick O, Camden, NY, *WPNS-3-1-KO* +
*SGT* **Gothard,** William A JR., Jacksonville, FL, *D-2-5 KO* +
*COL* **Gottlich,** Robert P, Hunt, TX, *HQ-1-7 WPNS-2-7WWII CH KO* +
*SGT* **Gough,** Walter J, Stockton, CA, *C-1MT KO* +
*PFC* **Goughler,** M D, Mcelhattan, PA, *C-1-11 KO* +
**Gouka,** Henry JR., West Des Moines, IA, *H&S-17MAR 1ENG WWII* +
**Gould,** Arthur J, East Greenwich, RI, *C-1-7 WWII CH KO* +
*COL* **Goulet,** David G, Sparta, WI, *A-1-9 G-3-1MAR DIV*
*SGT E-5* **Goulet,** John Gregory, Ventura, CA, *7TH COMM BN VN*
*CPL* **Gourley,** Byron B, Lynnwood, WA, *A-1-5 MAG31 WWII KO* +
*CPL* **Gower,** Ernest M JR., Stroudsburg, PA, *AMMO-SUP VN* +
*SGT* **Gracia,** Henry L, Niagara Falls, NY, *WPNS-2-1 KO*
*COL* **Gracida,** Joaquin C, Oceanside, CA, *K-3-5 H&S-2-7 VN* +
*SGT* **Grady,** Patrick P, Scottsdale, AZ, *B-1RECON C-5RECON VN* +
**Graebel,** Donna, South Elgin, IL, *ASSOCIATE* +
*CPL* **Graf,** Edward L, San Antonio, TX, *F-2-5 KO CW*
*MR.* **Graff,** John P, Austin, TX, *1-1MAR VN* +
**Graham,** C B, Newport, NC, *F-2-5 HQ-HQ VN* +
*CPL* **Graham,** Jay L, Arlington, TX, *H&S-1TK KO* +
*GYSGT* **Graham,** Leo G, Hillsboro, OR, *B-1ENGR KO* +
*SGT* **Grailer,** John J, Las Vegas, NV, *1RECON CW* +
*SGT* **Gramkow,** Raymond C, River Edge, NJ, *D-2-1 KO* +
*SGT* **Grana,** David R, Willard, OH, *H&S-1-5 VN* +
*SGT* **Granberry,** Robert R, Magnolia, TX, *11MT VN* +
*CPL* **Grandusky,** Steve, Webster, NY, *B-1RECON VN* +
*SGT* **Grant,** Marvin F, Cincinnati, OH, *G-2-5 WWII CH* +
*GYSGT* **Grasmick,** Alexander, Washington, DC, *L-3-5 WWII* +
*CPL* **Grass,** Thomas J, Metaline Fall, WA, *RECON 5MAR WWII CH* +
*MGYSGT* **Graustein,** Charles F, San Antonio, TX, *HQ-HQ-FLC WWII VN* +
*LCPL* **Graustein,** W H, Arlington, VA, *L-3-5* +
*PFC* **Graves,** Donald A, Keizer, OR, *CMR-2-11 KO* +
*1STSGT* **Gray,** Billy F, Greensboro, NC, *H-3-11 KO*
*SGT* **Gray,** Joseph I, Michigan City, IN, *1MAW KO* +
*SGT* **Gray,** Robert P, Summerfield, FL, *I-3-7 WWII CH KO* +
*LCPL* **Gray,** Ron, Clarkston, WA, *TRUCK CO HQ 1ST SSR FMF*
*SSGT* **Grayden,** Ed B, Minneapolis, MN, *1SIG WWII* +
*1STLT* **Greco,** Vince, San Marcos, CA, *HQ-ENGR KO* +
*CPL* **Green,** Donald J, Port Wentworth, GA, *H&S-2-7 VN* +
*SGT* **Green,** Gene L, Valencia, CA, *G-3-11 KO* +
*TSGT* **Green,** Glen R, Aurora, NE, *3-5 2-7 KO* +
*CPL* **Green,** James M, Lima, OH, *C-1-5 VN*
*CAPT* **Green,** James R, Beaufort, SC, *HQ-1TK KO VN* +
*CPL* **Green,** Jerald R, Houston, TX, *A-1ENGR E-2-1 WWII CH KO* +
*SSGT* **Green,** Leonard W JR., Baltimore, MD, *1CSG KO* +
*SGTMAJ* **Green,** Ollie M, San Francisco, CA, *I-3-5 VN* +
*CPL* **Greene,** James D, Albuquerque, NM, *E-2-5 VN* +
*SGT* **Greene,** John D, Santa Paula, CA, *I-3-5 KO* +
*LT* **Greene,** Laurence W JR., Laramie, WY, *MEDBN WWII KO* +
*LTCOL* **Greene,** S. Dale, Alpharetta, GA, *C-1-5 VN* +
*HM2* **Greenough,** James A, Chino Valley, AZ, *ASSOCIATE*
*GYSGT* **Greenwood,** Larry M, Fort Mohave, AZ, *DETB-1FSG VN* +
*SGT* **Greenwood,** Rick, Albuquerque, NM, *L-3-5 C-1-7 VN* +
*COL* **Greenwood,** Thomas C, Arlington, VA, *WPNS-3-9 7MAR CW* +
*MR.* **Greenwood,** William F, Tumwater, WA, *A-1-7 WWII KO* +
*CPL* **Greer,** Delbert T, Dublin, CA, *7TH COM CW*
*CPL* **Gregesich,** George J, Rhinelander, WI, *C-1-5 VN* +
*CPL* **Gregori,** Louis M, Penfield, PA, *A-1-5 VN* +
**Gregory,** James H, Charleston, SC, *I-3-7 5MAR VN* +
*CAPT* **Greguras,** Fred M, Los Altos, CA, *H-2-5 VN* +
*CPL* **Greig,** Ronald J, Far Rockaway, NY, *WPNS/A-1-5 KO* +
*MR.* **Gren,** Fred L, Sun City, AZ, *F-2/3-1MAR VN* +
*SGT* **Gresko,** Richard W, Newtown, PA, *H&S/I-3-5 VN* +
*COL* **Gressly,** Donald A, Vista, CA, *ADC 3AA 2-1MAR VN* +
*LCPL* **Grewing,** Jeffrey A, Fair Oaks, CA, *H&S-3-7 VN* +
*CPL* **Grgurich,** John M, Saint James, MO, *MAG-12 1MAW VN* +
*PFC* **Griego,** Leopoldo, Los Ranchos, NM, *A-1-5 WWII*
**Griffin,** Charles W, Nashville, TN, *E-2-7 KO* +
*SGT* **Griffin,** Darrell D, Hemphill, TX, *HQ-1-11 L-4-11 CW* +
*SGT* **Griffin,** Eugene J, Metuchen, NJ, *D-1-7 KO* +
*SGT* **Griffin,** Farris F, Pittsburgh, OK, *HQ-1-11 KO* +
*CPL* **Griffin,** Jesse L JR., Lancaster, CA, *H&S-1TK VN* +
*CPL* **Griffin,** Michael E, Monson, MA, *K-3-7 VN* +
*SSGT* **Griffin,** Robert E, Albany, OR, *B-1AMTRAC KO* +
**Griffis,** Gwynn W, Warsaw, OH, *81MM-1MAR KO* +
*CAPT* **Griffith,** John A III, Jacksonville, FL, *HQ-11MAR KO VN* +
*MAJ* **Griffith,** Ray C, Rock Hill, SC, *HQ-1-5 KO VN* +
**Grill,** J B, Newark, OH, *SPLWPN WWII* +
*CPL* **Grimala,** Paul L, Exbridge, MA, *M-3-7 VN* +
*SGT* **Grimes,** Alfred, Carson City, NV, *H&S-1-1 WWII* +
*SGT* **Grimes,** Donald L, Tucson, AZ, *A-1-11 KO* +
*SGT* **Grimes,** James F, Jefferson, OR, *D-1TK KO* +
*LTCOL* **Grimm,** Edward A, Lake Ridge, VA, *H&S-1-1 VN CW* +
*PFC* **Grinell,** Eric, Las Vegas, NV, *C-1-7 VN* +
*PFC* **Grissom,** Charles C, El Paso, TX, *11MAR CH* +
**Groh,** Darwin W, Seal Beach, CA, *5/7/11MAR CMC* +
*CPL* **Gron,** Frank M, Concord, OH, *C-1-1 VN* +
**Groos,** Alfred J, Palm Coast, FL, *1MAR CH KO* +
*LTCOL* **Groseclos,** Jerry M, Wasco, CA, *A/D-1RECON VN* +
*SGT* **Gross,** Anton C, Hackett, AR, *1MAB CW* +
*CPL* **Gross,** Robert W, Orlando, FL, *A-1-5 KO* +
*SGT* **Grosshans,** Karl H, Lodi, CA, *HQ-5MAR VN* +
*LCPL* **Grossi,** Daniel P, Staten Island, NY, *A&B-1-7 VN* +
*SGT* **Grossman,** Norman W, Woodstock, GA, *I-3-1 KO* +
*PFC* **Grossmann,** Louis W, San Mateo, CA, *O-5-11 H-3-11 WWII* +
*SGT* **Grote,** Lloyd W, Papillion, NE, *H&S-9ENGR VN* +

*SGT* **Grover,** Robert T, Temecula, CA, *4.2-5MAR KO* +
*SGT* **Grubar,** Patrick E, Washington, DC, *WPNS-3-5 CW* +
*CPL* **Grubbs,** Ronald L, Henryville, IN, *H&S-9ENGR VN* +
*GYSGT* **Gruenberg,** Arthur, Eden Prairie, MN, *1MARDIV KO* +
*SGT* **Grueneich,** Dennis R, Bismarck, ND, *E-2-7 VN* +
*CPL* **Gruetzmacher,** Curtis L, Goliad, TX, *A-1RECON VN* +
**Gruhl,** Werner M, Columbia, MD, *HQ-1-11 KO* +
*MSGT* **Grunder,** H L, Sherman Oaks, CA, *C-ENGR 7MAR WWII CH KO* +
*LTCOL* **Gruning,** Charles R, Oceanside, CA, *D-2-5 H&S-1-5 KO VN* +
*SGT* **Gruver,** Kenneth N, Germantown, OH, *H&S CO 2-7 KO* +
*SGT* **Guaraglia,** Concetta R, San Leandro, CA, *ATT 2SIG KO* +
*SGT* **Guarino,** Fred J JR., Curwensville, PA, *M-3-1 K-3-1 WWII* +
*CAPT* **Guenther,** Daniel B, Morrison, CO, *H&S/A-3AMTRAC VN* +
*SGT* **Guerena,** Joe L SR., Chula Vista, CA, *B-1-5 WWII CH* +
**Guerra,** A A, Carrollton, TX, *1MED* +
*SGT* **Guerra,** Ambrose M, Cupertino, CA, *A-1-5 VN* +
*CPL* **Guerra,** Geary A, Rosemead, CA, *1ST FSSG 3RD FSSG CW*
*SGTMAJ* **Gugle,** Larry E, Jackson, TN, *HQ-11MAR HQ-HQ VN* +
*SGT* **Gugler,** Wallace C, Mesa, AZ, *DIV HQ WWII CH* +
*1STLT* **Guhl,** Alfred H, Tucson, AZ, *M-3-27 VN* +
*SGT* **Guice,** Gerald (Jerry) P, New Orleans, LA, *F-2-7 KO* +
*CPL* **Guiles,** Donald P, Auburn, CA, *ECHO 2ND 7MAR*
*PFC* **Guiles,** Thurman C, Irving, TX, *I-3-7 KO* +
*SGT* **Guillaume,** Stan L, Fort Lauderdale, FL, *I-3-5 A-1-5 VN* +
*MSGT* **Guise,** R G, Riverside, CA, *7 COMM KO VN* +
*CPL* **Guisto,** Paul A, Sonoma, CA, *4th Div USMCR*
*CPL* **Gullette,** Kenneth E, Corsicana, TX, *A-1-1 KO* +
*MSGT* **Gummow,** James R, Iberia, MO, *SIG 3/5 KO* +
*TSGT* **Gunn,** James F, Pompano Beach, FL, *HQ-1TK CH KO* +
*SGT* **Gustafson,** Walter H, Englewood, CO, *VMF223 KO* +
*CPL* **Guterba,** H J, Canfield, OH, *L-3-7 VN* +
*SGT* **Gutermuth,** John, Norwood, MA, *D-2-1 KO VN* +
*CPL* **Guthrie,** Bruce G, Morongo Valley, CA, *G-2-7 VN* +
*LCPL* **Guthrie,** Jerry, Guymon, OK, *S&H CO 2-4 1MAR DIV CW* +
*CPL* **Gutierrez,** David R, San Bernardino, CA, *1FSR VN*
*CPL* **Gutierrez,** Henry E, Laredo, TX, *WPNS-2-1 KO* +
*SGT* **Gutierrez,** Ramiro R, Sonora, CA, *A-1ENGR KO* +
*SGT* **Gutzler,** J.W., Woodburn, OR, *E-2-7 KO* +
*SSGT* **Guyer,** Richard S, Glen Mills, PA, *HQ-7MAR 1SHPTY KO* +
*CPL* **Guzzi,** Richard S, Denton, TX, *HQ CO HQBN CW*
**Gwizdak,** Stanley B, Orlando, FL, *A-1AMTRAC WWII* +
*CAPT* **Ha,** Young CHANG, Charlotte, NC, *3FSSG* +
*CPL* **Haas,** Dennis B, Pollock Pines, CA, *E-1RECON VN* +
**Haas,** W. Pete, Denville, NJ, *H&S-1 KO* +
*CAPT* **Haase,** George M SR., Slidell, LA, *HQ-11MAR VN* +
*HM2* **Habell,** David F, Orange Park, FL, *B-1-5 C-1MED ICU VN* +
*CPL* **Haberman,** Bernard HAROLD, Edgewater, FL, *1TK CH* +
*SGT* **Hackett,** James P, Valencia, CA, *11MAR VN* +
*1STSGT* **Hackett,** Thomas F, Cleveland, OH, *H&S-3-1 KO* +
*PFC* **Hadaway,** James J JR., Waycross, GA, *ENG-5MAR WWII CH* +
*MGYSGT* **Hadley,** Michael R, Severn, MD, *M-4-11 HQ-1-11 VN* +
*CPL* **Hagan,** Michael W, Everett, WA, *D-2-11 VN* +
*1STSGT* **Hager,** John F.H, Port Saint Lucie, FL, *A/S-1MT-1DIV WWII KO* +
*GYSGT* **Hagins,** Jack A, New Port Richey, FL, *WPNS-1-5 MP-HQ KO* +
*MSGT* **Hagler,** Raymond A, Vacaville, CA, *1MP 1SHPTY KO VN*
*CAPT* **Hagman,** Thomas A, Moorpark, CA, *3-5 3-7MAR CW* +
**Hahn,** Philip E, Elyria, OH, *W-3-1 KO* +
*LTGEN* **Hailston,** Earl B, Beaufort, SC, *1RECON VN* +
*SSGT* **Haldeman,** Edwin D, Harvard, IL, *1MAR KO* +
*CPL* **Haldeman,** John R, Pine Grove, PA, *D-1-5 VN* +
*QMC* **Hale,** Allan D, Pacifica, CA, *USCG*
*PFC* **Hale,** Ronald, Red Oak, TX, *I-3-1 KO* +
*SGT* **Hale,** William (Pete) DAVID, Mill Creek, WA, *C-1-7 KO*
*MGYSGT* **Hall,** Bobby L, Oceanside, CA, *HQ-5MAR LAV-ITB VN SWA* +
*GYSGT* **Hall,** Bradley, Chaska, MN, *HQBN G-6 1ST MAR DIV OIF* +
*HM3* **Hall,** Charlie, Palm Desert, CA, *1STBN 1ST-MAR BRAVO VN*
*SGT* **Hall,** E E, Boardman, OH, *HQ-9ENGR VN* +
*PFC* **Hall,** Edward L, Naples, FL, *I-3-7 WWII* +
*CAPT* **Hall,** J C, Victoria, Australia, *SVC-1MAW WWII KO* +
*SGT* **Hall,** James D, Montgomery, TX, *MT-3-11 KO* +
*CPL* **Hall,** John (Duke) R, Johnson City, TN, *L-4-11 5MAR VN*
*LCPL* **Hall,** Raymond M, Page, AZ, *1RECON VN* +
*GYSGT* **Hall,** Richard L, New Boston, TX, *A-1-5 VN* +
*SGT* **Hall,** Robert D, Bellingham, WA, *AMMO-ORD WWII KO* +
*CPL* **Hall,** Robert E JR., Scotia, NY, *WPNS-2-5 KO*
*SGT* **Hall,** Robert M, Little Rock, AR, *D/E-2-11 KO* +
*CPL* **Hall,** Wayburn J, Franklin, TX, *HQ-2-1 WWII CH* +
*LCPL* **Hall,** William, Clifton Park, NY, *C-1-7 VN* +
*SGT* **Hallas,** Francis J, Moreno Valley, CA, *H&S/A-1-1 VN* +
*1STLT* **Halsey,** John H, Las Vegas, NV, *H&S-2-7 VN* +
*SSGT* **Halstead,** Duane K, Van Nuys, CA, *VMF-312 KO* +
*SGT* **Hamblen,** Calvin H, Gorham, ME, *M-4-11 KO* +
*1STSGT* **Hamblen,** D. (Woody) N, Oceanside, CA, *1FORRECON KO VN* +
*CPL* **Hamblin,** Lawrence O, Hesperia, CA, *A-1-17 WWII CH*
*SGT* **Hambrick,** Samuel T, Alvin, TX, *HQ-2-11 KO* +
*1STLT* **Hamerslough,** Herbert L, Palo Alto, CA, *G-2-1 WWII* +
*COL* **Hamill,** James G, Edmond, OK, *1ST TANK BN 1STMARDIV* +
*SGT* **Hamilton,** Eugene M, Bloomsburg, PA, *11MAR WWII*
*SGT* **Hamilton,** George A, North Lauderdale, FL, *WPNS-3-1 KO* +
*CPL* **Hamilton,** William E, Live Oak, FL, *L-3-5 WWII CH* +
*PVT* **Hamilton,** William W, Bidwell, OH, *1MAW CW* +
*MAJ* **Hamlin,** D J, Los Angeles, CA, *HQ-5MAR CW* +
*CPL* **Hammen,** Walter A, Everett, WA, *E-2-7 KO* +
*SGT* **Hammontree,** Ralph H SR., Dalton, GA, *E-2-11 KO* +
*SGT* **Hancock,** Billy J, Gig Harbor, WA, *D-1TK KO* +
*CPL* **Hancock,** Marc A, Las Vegas, NV, *G-2-27 VN* +
*CPL* **Hand,** Jeffrey T, Neptune, NJ, *B-1-1 VN* +
*SGT* **Handley,** Robert W, Bonita Springs, FL, *D-9ENGR VN* +
*CPL* **Handy,** Harry F, Salem, OH, *VN*
*SSGT* **Handzo,** George JR., Wilkes-Barre, PA, *A-1-1/A-1-5 KO VN* +
*SGT* **Hane,** Thomas R SR., Edina, MN, *D-1-5 VN* +
**Hanke,** Phyllis, Port Saint Lucie, FL, *ASSOCIATE* +
*SGT* **Hanks,** Robert C, Houston, TX, *H-3-11 KO* +
*CPL* **Hanle,** Fred, Clifton, NJ, *A-1-5 KO*
**Hanna,** Bob C, Spring, TX, *H&S-2-1 CW* +
*PFC* **Hannah,** Glen G, Peoria, IL, *A-1AMTRAC WWII* +
*PFC* **Hanner,** Allen W, Bellwood, NE, *E-2-5 WWII CH* +
*LTCOL* **Hanner,** Norman F, Eureka, IL, *1MAW VN* +
*CPL* **Hannon,** James M, Buffalo, NY, *B-1-7 KO* +
**Hanrahan,** Bernard, Virginia Beach, VA, *USS STORMES KO* +
*SGT* **Hansberry,** Edward H, Pennsville, NJ, *B-1-17 WWII* +
*GYSGT* **Hansen,** Arne H, Seatac, WA, *HQ-2-4 HQ/B-1TK KO VN* +
*CPL* **Hansen,** Jeremiah E, Oregon City, OR, *L-3-1 OIF*
*SGT* **Hansen,** Jerry A, Manhattan Beach, CA, *A-1-7 KO* +
**Hansen,** John A JR., Keene, NH, *H&S-1-5 D-1-5 VN* +
*SGT* **Hansen,** Keith W, Duluth, MN, *1MAW KO* +
*SSGT* **Hanshaw,** Delbert G, Rossville, GA, *H-3-5 11MT KO VN* +
*CPL* **Hanson,** Edwin R, Pahrump, NV, *WPNS-2-1 KO* +
*SGT* **Hanson,** Larry M, Elgin, IL, *B-1RECON VN* +
*CAPT* **Hanway,** Stephen S, Grand Haven, MI, *M-3-1 VN* +
*CPL* **Harakal,** Jack J, Stamford, CT, *H-3-7 KO* +
*SGT* **Harbin,** Kurt B, Las Vegas, NV, *K-3-1 SWA* +
*SGT* **Harbin,** William H, Martinez, CA, *VMA121-MAG12 HQ-3-7 KO* +
**Hard,** Robert W, Garrison, NY, *VMA212 KO* +
**Hardell,** John, Indio, CA, *1MAW*
*1STLT* **Hardy,** M A, Austin, NV, *3-7MAR VN* +
*SGT* **Hardy,** Patrick O, Silsbee, TX, *H-2-5 VN* +
*MSGT* **Hare,** John F, Hubert, NC, *H&S C-1RECON VN* +
*SGT* **Hargrove,** J D, Anson, TX, *E-2-7 KO* +
*GYSGT* **Harlan,** Robert E, Austin, TX, *H&S-3-5 KO* +
*COL* **Harley,** William, Washington, DC, *B-1-5 VN* +
*SGT* **Harmon,** Clyde A JR., Portland, OR, *HQ-HQ CW* +
*CPL* **Harmon,** Walter J, Campbell, CA, *G-3-5 I-3-7 KO* +
*GYSGT* **Harmon,** Wayne E, Indianapolis, IN, *1ST BN 11TH MAR OIF*
*CPL* **Harms,** Joel E, Denver, CO, *1ST MAR DIV K-31*
*SGT* **Harper,** James P, Ann Arbor, MI, *F-2-5 VN* +
*TSGT* **Harper,** James V, Hedgesville, WV, *HQ-1-7 HQ-5MAR VN* +
*SSGT* **Harper,** Jessie R, Porter, TX, *H-3-5 4PROV RKT- 11MAR WWII CH KO* +
*SGT* **Harper,** Wayne T, Andersonville, TN, *1FLD ARTY VN* +
*COL* **Harrell,** J E, Austin, TX, *WPNS-2-5 WWII KO VN* +
*CAPT* **Harrell,** James S, Mobile, AL, *H&S-2-11 KO VN* +
*CPL* **Harrington,** Charles L, Westfield, NJ, *A-1-1 WWII CH*
**Harrington,** John G, Chelmsford, MA, *1SVC VN* +
*COL* **Harrington,** Michael H, Houston, TX, *C/1/11* +
*COL* **Harrington,** Myron C JR., Charleston, SC, *D-1-5 VN* +
*GYSGT* **Harris,** Calvin E JR., Sun City West, AZ, *I-3-7 VN* +
**Harris,** Eddie D JR., Columbus, GA, *A-1-7 VN* +

CPL **Harris,** Eddie LOUIS, Columbus, GA, *F-2-11 VN* +
LCPL **Harris,** James TRUETT, Alta Loma, CA, *HQ-9ENGR VN*
CPL **Harris,** Jerry L, Dodd City, TX, *3RD MAF-FORC 1MARDIV VN*
MAJ **Harris,** Ronald ELLIS, Santa Maria, CA, *C-1ST RECON BN VN CW*
CPL **Harris,** William E, Pataskala, OH, *7TH COMM BN, 5TH NOP @29 PALMS VN*
LTCOL **Harris-Inman,** Terry E, Gulf Breeze, FL, *1/7ENGR VN* +
SSGT **Harrison,** Edward A, Lapel, IN, *M-4-11 KO* +
CPL **Harrison,** Harold K, Lewisburg, WV, *I-3-5 KO* +
CPL **Harrison,** Jimmy W, Milledgeville, GA, *I-3- 5 KO* +
SGT **Harrison,** John E JR., Richmond, VA, *C-1-5 KO* +
CPL **Harrison,** Karl C, Fort Pierce, FL, *B-1-5 VN*
MS **Hart,** Bridget, Corolla, NC, *
PVT **Hart,** David L, Cincinnati, OH, *SVC-7ENGR VN* +
COL **Hart,** Franklin A JR., Saint Simons Island, GA, *CO-3-7 CO-1-5 VN* +
LTCOL **Hart,** James A, Walnut Creek, CA, *3-5 VN*
MR. **Hart,** Patrick J, Springfield, VA, *4TH MAR CEB 1ST MAR DIV 5TH BN*
CPL **Hart,** Ronald G, Leona, TX, *COMMSPT-7COMM CW* +
MGYSGT **Hartig,** George H, Baltimore, MD, *CSG KO* +
LCPL **Hartman,** John A, Portland, OR, *B-1-7 VN* +
CPL **Hartman,** Roger JEAN, Oklahoma City, OK, *WPNS CO-1-7 KO* +
SGT **Hartmayer,** Raymond F, La Mesa, CA, *H&S CO 1-5 CW* +
CPL **Harty,** D T, South Boston, MA, *F-2-11 VN* +
CPL **Harty,** Ralph W, Poplar Bluff, MO, *B-1-5 KO* +
**Harvath,** James M, Plover, WI, *7TH COMM BATT VN*
CAPT **Harvey,** David T, Reno, NV, *B-1-7 VN*
MR. **Harvey,** John S JR., Acton, MA, *11/5MAR KO* +
GYSGT **Harvey,** Quillie L, Philadelphia, PA, *1/2-1MAR SWA CW* +
CPL **Harvey,** Richard J, Littleton, CO, *A-1-5 1MAR DIV KO* +
SGT **Harville,** Victor L, De Queen, AR, *H&S HQ-11MAR KO* +
COL **Harwood,** R M, Seguin, TX, *A BTRY 1AAA* +
1STLT **Haskel,** Merwin R, Hartsdale, NY, *I-3-5 KO* +
SGT **Hassick,** Paul F, Bethlehem, PA, *D-2-7 KO* +
CPL **Hassler,** Robert D, Hamlet, NC, *B-1-1 VN* +
SGT **Hastings,** James E JR., Bellingham, MA, *M-3-7 VN* +
LCDR **Hatch,** Philip B JR., Portland, ME, *1ANGLI-CO VN* +
GYSGT **Hatfield,** P M, Port Royal, SC, *Unit?? WWII KO VN* +
GYSGT **Hattox,** Jerry R, Manavel, TX, *HQ-2-7 VN* +
SGT **Hauber,** Walter J, Gillette, WY, *AMMO-1ORD KO* +
CPL **Haugan,** Gil D, Brandon, SD, *F-2-1 KO* +
CPL **Hauge,** Melvin A, Elmore, MN, *K-3-1 WWII* +
GYSGT **Havelka,** Ken A, Yorkville, IL, *B-1-9 B-1RE-CON VN CW* +
SGT **Havens,** Gerald R, Woodstock, IL, *H&S-1-5 VN* +
**Hawke,** James W, Brunswick, OH, *B-1TK WWII CH*
SSGT **Hawkins,** Charles A, Coon Rapids, MN, *3-7 1ST MAR DIV* +
SSGT **Hawkins,** Dave E, Santee, CA, *H&S-2-7 G-3-1 CH KO* +
SGT **Hawkins,** Elmer J, Daytona Beach, FL, *SIG-HQ WWII* +
SSGT **Hawkins,** Thomas J JR., North Hollywood, CA, *MAG-36-1MAW CW* +
SGT **Hawley,** Claude L, Bakersfield, CA, *B-1RE-CON KO* +
MGYSGT **Hay,** Forrest W, Kingwood, TX, *SVC-1-11 C-7ENGR KO VN* +
MR. **Hay,** William A, Huntington Beach, CA, *HQBN 1ST MAR DIV KO* +
CAPT **Haydock,** Robert A, Lebanon, VA, *I-3-1 KO* +
SSGT **Hayes,** Harry W, Geneva, Switzerland, *C-1RECON VN* +
BGEN **Hayes,** James M, Fairfax, VA, *1/2-11MAR KO* +
COL **Hayes,** Leonard C, Oceanside, CA, *3-7 3-5 2-1 VN* +
SSGT **Hayes,** Robert D, Snellville, GA, *1ANGLICO KO* +
MAJ **Haynes,** John L, Monticello, FL, *B-1-1 EOD-FLC WWII CH KO VN CMC* +
CPL **Haynie,** Robert C, Galt, CA, *ORD WWII KO* +
CAPT **Hayward,** Leo J, Larkspur, CO, *HQ/E-1-1 CMC* +
SGT **Heald,** James E, Milford, NH, *E-2-1 KO* +
SGT **Healey,** James F, Pensacola, FL, *AMMO-1-1 KO* +
PFC **Healy,** Gerald P, Largo, FL, *WPNS-1REGT WWII* +
SGT **Healy,** James L, Kokomo, IN, *8AMTRAC WWII* +
PFC **Healy,** Peter N, Huntington Beach, CA, *WPNS-1-1 KO*
COL **Hearnsberger,** Brian, Laguna Vista, TX, *AC/S G-4 1ST MAR DIV* +
SGT **Heath,** Eldon E, Springfield, OH, *K-4-11 KO* +
SGT **Heath,** Joe R, Seattle, WA, *HQ-1SIG KO* +
PFC **Heath,** John P, Bellmawr, NJ, *A-1-1 KO* +
SSGT **Heath,** Philip HAROLD, Granite City, IL, *G-3-1 KO* +
SGT **Heath,** Ronald J, Long Beach, CA, *K-3-5 VN* +
SGT **Heathcoat,** C H, Upland, CA, *HQ-1-11 VN CW* +
CPL **Hebert,** Thomas J, Opelousas, LA, *HQ-1-7 VN* +
CPL **Hefling,** J T, Pebble Beach, CA, *B-1ENGR CH* +
MAJGEN **Hegarty,** Joseph P, Sarasota, FL, *C-1-11 1ASCO WWII* +
CPL **Hegg,** R L, Miami, FL, *HQ-HQ VN* +
SSGT **Heidenreich,** W G, Port Richey, FL, *H&S-3-7 CW* +
**Heim,** Diane D, Silver Spring, MD, *ASSOCIATE*
CPL **Hein,** Allen E, Portland, OR, *1MARBDE H&HS3 VN*
**Hein,** Robert R, Redford, MI, *H-3-7 KO* +
**Hein,** Rosemarie ANN, New Hyde Park, NY, *AS-SOCIATE* *
CPL **Heine,** David L, Las Vegas, NV, *4/2 MORTAR CO HQ CO 1ST MAR REG 1ST MARDIV* +
HMC **Heinen,** Ronald E, Dayton, TX, *G-3 HQBN OIF* +
CPL **Heinzel,** John R, Rogers City, MI, *HML107/367 VN* +
LCPL **Heis,** Mel R, Cleves, OH, *L-3-1 VN* +
CPL **Heitur,** Val, San Anselmo, CA, *C-1-5 KO* +
SGT **Helfers,** Edward R, Hankins, NY, *B-1-7 KO* +
COL **Hellman,** Robert S, Carlsbad, CA, *HQ-1EN-GR 7ESB SWA* +
LCPL **Helsel,** Gary L, Sarasota, FL, *HQ-7MAR CW*
CPL **Hemenway,** Charles W, Lakeland, FL, *E-2-7 WWII* +
CPL **Hemstreet,** John M, Newark, CA, *A-1-5 VN*
LTCOL **Henderson,** Mark D, Colorado Springs, CO, *HMM 764 OIF* +
1STSGT **Henderson,** William B, Silver Springs, NV, *F-2-5 H-2-1 VN* +
SGT **Hendrickson,** William (Bill) E, Portland, OR, *1-7 3-1 VN*
LCPL **Hendrix,** Danny, Addison, TX, *HQ-2-26 E-2-7 VN* +
CPL **Hendrix,** Edmond G, Saint Joseph, MO, *E-2-5 KO* +
CAPT **Henehan,** Michael J, Wilmington, NC, *2ND BN 5TH MAR VN*
COL **Henley,** Robert J, Pagosa Springs, CO, *1-11-11 KO VN CW WOT* +
PFC **Hennessy,** Robert A, New York, NY, *C-1-7 KO* +
SGT **Hennings,** Charles R, Yuma, AZ, *A-1MT KO* +
SGT **Henrikson,** L H, Arlington, SD, *B-1-1 KO* +
LTCOL **Henry,** Clark G, San Francisco, CA, *H&S-3-5 G-3-1 KO VN* +
SSG **Henry,** Johnson B USA(RET.), Gueydan, LA, *HQ-1ORD KO* +
CAPT **Henry,** Joseph JAMES, Olympia, WA, *DEL-TA CO 1BN 5MAR, H&S CO 1BN 5MAR VN*
CPL **Henry,** Robert W, Saint Petersburg, FL, *L-3-5 VN* +
SGT **Henry,** Terrence W SR., Coplay, PA, *D-1-7 VN*
PHM2 **Henseler,** Kenneth J, Yankton, SD, *I-3-5 WWII* +
**Hensell,** Jimmie J, Bedford, IN, *D-1RECON VN* +
MR. **Hensley,** Franklin D, Baldwin, FL, *A-1-5 E-2-1 VN* +
SGTMAJ **Hensley,** Troy L, Wingate, TX, *1/5, 2/5 VN* +
PFC **Henson,** Amos G, Vienna, WV, *G-2-1 CH* +
SSGT **Henson,** G R, Pittsburg, CA, *COMM-HQ VN* +
CAPT **Herberger,** Melvin E, Tonawanda, NY, *H-2-5 VN* +
SGT **Herbst,** James W, Hollis, NY, *7COMM-1TK VN* +
LTCOL **Hering,** John C, Carlton, OR, *D-2-11 A-1-11 VN SWA* +
RM3 **Herman,** Irvin H, Indianapolis, IN, *4JASCO 1ASCO-HQ WWII*
MAJ **Hernandez,** Angel G, Port Saint Lucie, FL, *5COMM IIIMAF VN* +
E-6 **Hernandez,** Antonio, Houston, TX, *5MAR, 9MAR CH KO* +
**Hernandez,** David, El Paso, TX, *G-2-5 WWII* +
**Hernandez,** Eulalio J, Chicago, IL, *STGNG-CJHP CW* +
**Hernandez,** J S, Sylmar, CA, *F-2-11 1MARDIV VN* +
SGT **Hernandez,** Ralph P, La Mesa, CA, *VMA251-MAG12 KO* +
SGT **Hernandez,** Raul JR., Oregon, OH, *A-1AT VN* +
PFC **Hernandez,** Ruben, Harlingen, TX, *HQ-HQ WWII CH* +
SGTMAJ **Herndon,** Robert N, Dallas, OR, *HQ-HQ 1LSB VN SWA* +
SGT **Herold,** William A, Pearl City, IL, *1SR MAR 2ND MAR KO* +
SGT **Herrera,** Daniel JR., Mesa, AZ, *1-4MAR KO CW* +
PHM1 **Herrera,** Jesus, San Antonio, TX, *F-2-7 WWII CH* +
**Herrera,** Robert, Amarillo, TX, *K-3-5 VN*
CPL **Herrmann,** Daniel V, Egg Harbor Twp, NJ, *H-2-1 WWII* +
CPL **Herron,** James H, Dubuque, IA, *G-3-5 KO* +
SSGT **Hershey,** Ron P, Kettering, OH, *H&S-RECON 5MAR KO* +
SGT **Hertz,** Aaron L, Ocala, FL, *H-3-7 1ST MAR DIV KO* +
**Herzberg,** John C, Saint Charles, MO, *VMA-121 MAG-12 VN*
SGT **Herzog,** William F, Arlington, TX, *H-3-1 KO* +
**Heslin,** Vincent E, Okeechobee, FL, *E-2-5 KO* +
CAPT **Hess,** Leroy R, Racine, WI, *WPNS-2-1 WWII KO* +
SGT **Hesseling,** John R, Brownsville, TX, *B-1-7 KO* +
LCPL **Hessler,** Joseph T, Springfield, MO, *C-11MT VN* +
HM2 **Hessman,** J F, Rockville, MD, *G-3-5 KO* +
SSGT **Hettchen,** Philip C JR., Perry Hall, MD, *H&S-7MAR H&S-4-11 WWII CH*
SGT **Heuman,** Robert L, O'fallon, MO, *W-2-11 BLT3-1 VN SWA* +
CPL **Hewitt,** David F, Santa Monica, CA, *S-5-5 VN* +
**Hewitt,** Harold K, Keizer, OR, *DIV HQ KO* +
CPL **Hibarger,** Walter JAMES, Weston, MO, *A 1/5 VN*
CPL **Hibbard,** H R, Clinton, NY, *G-2-5 WWII* +
MSGT **Hibbs,** Lewis C SR., Skyesville, MD, *1ENGR KO* +
CPL **Hibbs,** Wayne R, Cypress, TX, *HQ-HQ 1AM-TRAC KO* +

*COL* **Hichborn,** Hal D, Manhattan Beach, CA, *D/ HQ-1ENGR KO* +
*CPL* **Hickey,** Gary T, Ridgefield, NJ, *K-3-5 VN* +
*MAJ* **Hickey,** Stewart M, Bedford, PA, *D-3TK 7MAR SWA* +
*SGT* **Hickey,** Thomas E, Hudson, FL, *HQ-3-1 KO* +
*MSGT* **Hickman,** Gilbert, Indianapolis, IN, *7COMM CW* +
*CAPT* **Hickman,** John L, Victor, MT, *1-5MAR VN* +
*CAPT* **Hickox,** Charles R, Dallas, TX, *K-3-7 WWII CH* +
**Hicks,** Alfred L, Hollis, NY, *C-1-1 KO* +
*MSGT* **Hicks,** John T, Greeneville, TN, *VMGR 152 3DMAW VN* +
*CPL* **Hickson,** William W, Philadelphia, PA, *L-4-11 3-8IN HOW HQ-1-11 VN* +
*SGTMAJ* **Hidalgo,** Juan M JR., San Diego, CA, *1ST TK BN 3D AABN OIF*
*SGT* **Hiett,** Nathaniel G, Corpus Christi, TX, *ORD BN KO*
*CPL* **Higaki,** Harry Y, Soquel, CA, *1ST PLT 11MAR VN* +
*PFC* **Higginbotham,** George J, Biloxi, MS, *E-2-5 WWII CH* +
*COL* **Higgins,** Martin C, Virginia Beach, VA, *E-2-7 1RECON VN* +
*PFC* **Higgins,** Thomas F, Quincy, MA, *D-1SVC KO* +
*CPL* **Higgins,** Thomas F, Buffalo, NY, *I-3-11 KO* +
*COL* **Hilgers,** Jack W, Virginia Beach, VA, *H&S-3-5 VN* +
*SGT* **Hill,** Clarence L, Greeley, CO, *1ORD KO* +
*LCPL* **Hill,** James E, Plano, IL, *7COMM VN* +
*CAPT* **Hill,** Kevin S, Allen, TX, *D-2-12 SWA* +
*CPL* **Hill,** Robert B, San Antonio, TX, *H&S/I-3-7 VN*
*LTCOL* **Hilliard,** Frank P, Anchorage, KY, *HQ BN CW* +
*GYSGT* **Hillis,** Eric L, Fpo, AE, *FOX CO 2/7 MARINES SWA*
*CPL* **Hilton,** Charles W JR., Baltimore, MD, *H&S/ A/C-1RECON VN* +
*SGT* **Hilton,** Herbert L, Framingham, MA, *WPN-1-1 KO* +
*CPL* **Hilton,** Howard R, Richfield, MN, *HQ-1MAR CW*
**Hilton,** Steven A, Great Falls, MT, *C-1-5 VN* +
*MRS* **Hinds,** Barbara, Walpole, MA, *
*PFC* **Hines,** Garion L, Louisville, KY, *3/27 M/CO 3/5 I/CO*
*HM3* **Hinkle,** Johnny DEWAYNE, Oregon, MO, *BAS HQ BAT SCT SNIPER HQ BAT VN*
*CPL* **Hinman,** Dennis A, Los Angeles, CA, *1MAR VN* +
*CPL* **Hinson,** Willis A, Hernando, MS, *H-2-7-1 WWII* +
*CPL* **Hintacutan,** Ismael S, Waianae, HI, *H-3-7 KO* +
**Hinton,** Calvin, Pacifica, CA, *A-1-11 WWII CH* +
*SSGT* **Hintz,** Jackie E, Phoenix, AZ, *D-2-7 KO* +
*CPL* **Hinz,** John G, White Bear Lake, MN, *H&S-3-5MAR VN* +
*SGT* **Hirdler,** Arthur L, Houston, TX, *1BRDG-7ENGR VN* +
*LTCOL* **Hirt,** Paul L, Falls Church, VA, *HQ-4-11 3-11MAR WWII CH KO VN* +
*CWO3* **Hitchborn,** Charles D, Smithville, MO, *E-2-5 KO* +
*CAPT* **Hitchcock,** T W, North Hollywood, CA, *9DEF WWII* +
**Hoaglund,** Jeffrey, Spokane, WA, *2-4 5TH MAR* +
*CPL* **Hoban,** Peter D, Medford, MA, *H-2-1 VN 68-69 VN* +
*CPL* **Hobbs,** Jimmie L, Burley, ID, *SPT/STOR-3BN-MCSC CW* +
*CPL* **Hobeck,** Joseph C, Daly City, CA, *1ENGR KO* +
*TSGT* **Hoch,** Elvin A, Moreno Valley, CA, *C-1-11 WWII* +
*SGT* **Hockenberry,** Robert T, Meadville, PA, *H&S-2-7* +
**Hockensmith,** Bob, Leesburg, VA, *M-3-1 VN* +
*CPL* **Hockensmith,** Lowell E, Des Moines, IA, *C-1TK KO*
*SGT* **Hodapp,** Philip H, Cleveland, MN, *G-3-11 KO* +
**Hodges,** Jack C, Fanning Springs, FL, *HQ- 4-11 KO* +
*LTCOL* **Hodges,** Thomas A, Lancaster, PA, *C-1-5 A-1-7 WWII CH KO VN* +
*CPL* **Hodges,** William D, Panama City, FL, *8RAD-SEC USA VN* +
*PFC* **Hodshire,** Frank L, East Moline, IL, *H&S-4-11 KO* +
*SSGT* **Hodson,** Lowell M, Niles, MI, *A-1-7 KO* +
*LCPL* **Hoel,** Rod L, San Diego, CA, *K-3-5 VN*
*HM3* **Hoepner,** Joseph A, Hastings, MN, *M-3-7 VN* +
*1STLT* **Hoey,** William CHRISTOPHER, Maitland, FL, *H-2-5 VN*
*SGT* **Hoffman,** Francis (Frank) H, Easton, PA, *H&S-2-7 KO*
*LCPL* **Hofstetter,** George J, Downey, CA, *E-2MAR VN* +
*MRS* **Hogan,** Margaret, Haines City, FL, *ASSOCIATE* *
*CPL* **Hogg,** David S, Dover, MA, *1CSG KO* +
*CPL* **Hogquist,** John A, Saint Cloud, MN, *B-5 E-2-5 KO*
**Hogrefe,** A L, Placerville, CA, *HQ-2-11 VN* +
*SGT* **Hohmann,** Tom H, Riverside, CA, *G-2-5 VN* +
*CPL* **Holan,** Arthur R, Mentor, OH, *VMJ1-MAG33 KO* +
**Holbrook,** Richard T, Muskegon, MI, *C-1-5 A-1-7 WWII CH KO* +
*LTCOL* **Holcomb,** Ward A, Battle Ground, WA, *F-2-5 G-2-1 CW* +
*SGT* **Holcombe,** Horton W, Palm Bay, FL, *A-1-1 KO* +
*LTCOL* **Holcroft,** Calvin D, San Diego, CA, *7COMM WWII CH KO VN* +
*SSGT* **Holder,** Edward L, Jacksonville, NC, *M-3-1 KO VN* +
**Holguin,** Michael, Joshua Tree, CA, *5 MAR, 1 LAR*
*PFC* **Holl,** Daniel W, Farrell, PA, *F-2-5 KO* +
*SSGT* **Holland,** George C, Moore, SC, *C-1-7 VN* +
*SGT* **Holland,** John J, Englewood, CO, *1MAW VN*
*CWO4* **Holland,** William M, Bakersfield, CA, *H&S/B-1-1 SWA* +
*SSGT* **Holley,** Keith S, Piscataway, NJ, *9TH COMM VN* +
*MSGT* **Hollier,** Anthony R, Broussard, LA, *G/I-3-11 KO VN* +
*CPL* **Hollier,** Fred SR., Erwin, TN, *G-2-5 WWII* +
*CPL* **Hollier,** Fred JR., San Antonio, TX, *D-RECON VN* +
*CAPT* **Hollingsworth,** Jesse C, Miamisburg, OH, *H-2-5 A-1-5 WWII* +
*LCPL* **Holloran,** Thomas A, Queens Village, NY, *2-1MAR VN* +
*LCPL* **Hollub,** Gilbert (Sonny) H JR., Buda, TX, *E-2-26 VN* +
*CPL* **Holm,** Blair I, Highland, CA, *1-5 HQ 5MAR KO* +
*PFC* **Holmberg,** Arwed C, Oroville, CA, *C-1-1 WWII* +
*SGT* **Holmberg,** Harvig E III, Green Valley, AZ, *ASSOCIATE* +
*MGYSGT* **Holmes,** J C, Huntsville, AL, *HQ-7-2-7-KO CW* +
*GYSGT* **Holmes,** Jack A, Granbury, TX, *C-1-5 H-2-7 KO VN* +
*SGT* **Holmes,** Ken P, Paris, TX, *1MED KO VN* +
*GYSGT* **Holmes,** Kenneth R, Mount Center, CA, *7COMM VN* +
*SGT* **Holmes,** Nile H, Las Vegas, NV, *1st Eng Bn D Co. KO* +
*CPL* **Holmes,** Richard A, Stevensville, MT, *HQ-HQ CW* +
*SGT* **Holmes,** Robert J, Kingsville, MD, *D-2-1 KO* +
*SGTMAJ* **Holsapple,** Kenneth R, Mission, TX, *HQ-1MAR HQ-3-5 VN* +
*COL* **Holt,** Edward Y JR., Norfolk, VA, *H-3-5 I-3-5 KO* +
*CPL* **Holten,** James C, Reno, NV, *COMM-HQ KO* +
*SGT* **Holterhaus,** Donald P, Fort Madison, IA, *H&S-H&S-5 FSSG VN*
*MGYSGT* **Holtry,** G H, Palmdale, CA, *H-2-1 F-2-7 VN* +
*CPL* **Holtz,** John, Pacifica, CA, *I-3-5 VN* +
*SSGT* **Holtz,** Olen GARLAND, Abilene, TX, *1SIG H-3-5 KO* +
*SGT* **Holtzer,** Robert C, Sun Valley, NV, *D-1TK KO* +
*SGTMAJ* **Holub,** Robert W, Ewa Beach, HI, *A-1-1 HQ-5 CW SWA*
*PFC* **Holup,** R W, Perth Amboy, NJ, *F-2-7 WWII* +
*COL* **Holzapfel,** William R, Elizabeth, NJ, *H&S-3-7 KO* +
*SGT* **Homan,** Alfred G, Pierce, NE, *I-3-7 VN* +
*CPL* **Honan,** William L, Chester, CT, *C-1-5 VN* +
*COL* **Hong,** Sa E, Los Angeles, CA, *KMC KO* +
**Hood,** Jasper E, West Hills, CA, *F-2-5 WWII* +
*SSGT* **Hooge,** Michael, Paris, TX, *HQ-1 HDBN 1ST MAR DIV OIF* +
*CPL* **Hoogendoorn,** Warren G, Dorr, MI, *E-2-1 VN* +
*CPL* **Hook,** Douglas WAYNE SR., Lake City, FL, *HQ-3-1 WWII CH* +
*MAJ* **Hooker,** Daniel L, Pearl River, NY, *HQ-2-1 CW* +
*CPL* **Hooker,** John R, Norwalk, OH, *F-2-7 VN* +
*PFC* **Hooker,** William H, Fairhope, AL, *A-1-7 KO* +
*MAJ* **Hoolan,** J P JR., Williamsburg, VA, *HQ-1-1 VN* +
*CPL* **Hooper,** William A, Pacifica, CA, *G-2-5 H&S-3-26 VN* +
*MSGT* **Hoover,** Charles W, Middleburg, FL, *WPNS-3-7 1MAR DIV FMF KO* +
*SGT* **Hoover,** Gary G, Grass Valley, CA, *A-1-1ST REG CW KO* +
*SSGT* **Hoover,** Harry R, Pismo Beach, CA, *3MAW KO* +
*1STSGT* **Hope,** Harold (Harry), Creve Coeur, MO, *H&S-3-7 KO* +
*SSGT* **Hope,** R M, Arlington, VA, *H&S-1MAR* +
**Hopfer,** Albert V, Ripley, WV, *C-1-7 WWII* +
*MAJGEN* **Hopgood,** M T JR., College Station, TX, *E-2-1 VN* +
*CPL* **Hopkins,** A. Norman, Pioneer, CA, *B-1-7 KO* +
*SGT* **Hopkins,** Ted A, Casa Grande, AZ, *HQ/G-2MAR KO* +
*CAPT* **Hopkins,** W B, Roanoke, VA, *H&S-1-1 WWII KO* +
*MGYSGT* **Hoppe,** Charles R, Mequon, WI, *HMM364-MAG36 VN* +
*SGT* **Horne,** James ROBERT, Fayetteville, NC, *B 1/5 VN*
*CPL* **Horner,** David E, Indianapolis, IN, *A-1-11 KO* +
*PFC* **Horstmyer,** Harry E, Wilmington, DE, *A-1-1 CH* +
*LCPL* **Horton,** William W, Arlington, TX, *2-11MAR VN* +
*SGTMAJ* **Horvath,** David D, Morehead City, NC, *H&S-3-7 VN* +
*SGT* **Horvath,** Gordon C, Dearborn Heights, MI, *1CSG KO* +
*PFC* **Horvath,** Joseph JR., Anaheim, CA, *K-3-7 WWII* +
*CPL* **Hoskins,** H E, Fairfield, IA, *K-3-1 WWII CH* +
*GYSGT* **Hoth,** Edward W, Hazlet, NJ, *E-2-1 KO* +
*COL* **Houck,** G W, San Diego, CA, *1-11MAR KO VN* +
*SGT* **Houck,** Martin J, Great Falls, MT, *F/G-2-7 WWII KO* +
*CPL* **Houghtaling,** Robert W, Warwick, RI, *WPNS-1-1 KO* +
*SGTMAJ* **Houle,** Joseph L, Jacksonville, NC, *3-1MAR VN* +
*GYSGT* **Houlette,** Delbert RAY, Las Vegas, NV, *11TH MAR 5TH MAR* +
*SGT* **House,** William L, Crandall, TX, *SUP-1CSG KO* +
*CPL* **Houser,** James D, Crestone, CO, *E/H&S-7MAR KO* +
*SSGT* **Houston,** Robert A, Orange Park, FL, *W-4-11 C-1TK WWII CH* +
*CAPT* **Houston,** William M, Denver, CO, *1-11 CW* +

*GYSGT* **Hovey,** Kurt E, Bergland, MI, *C-1-4 SWA* +
*CPL* **Howard,** George P JR., Pittstown, NJ, *4JAS-CO 3-7MAR WWII CH* +
**Howard,** James A, Lombard, IL, *A-1 RECON VN*
*CPL* **Howard,** Leon P III, Frenchtown, MT, *H&S-3-7 VN* +
*COL* **Howard,** Michael C, Hillsboro, OR, *B-1ENGR CW* +
*SGT* **Howard,** Michael J, Little Egg Harbor, NJ, *C-1-7 KO*
*HM2* **Howard,** Philip D, West Grove, PA, *HQ-3-5 SHR PTY VN CW*
*CPL* **Howard,** Robert K, Clovis, CA, *L-3-5 VN* +
*SSGT* **Howdyshell,** Charles E JR., Middlebrook, VA, *1ST RECON BN VN* +
*CPL* **Howe,** Edward L, Seminole, FL, *L-3-1 WWII CH* +
*CPL* **Howe,** F A, Newport, NH, *A-1-5 WWII* +
*SGT* **Howe,** Nelson C, Walterboro, SC, *B-1-5 KO* +
*SGT* **Howell,** Elliott M, Arroyo Grande, CA, *HQ-HQ CW* +
*PFC* **Howell,** Larry P, Katy, TX, *3-1MAR 9 ENGR VN* +
*CPL* **Howell,** Ralph LAMAR, Akron, OH, *C-1AMPH TRAC BN KO* +
*MGYSGT* **Hoxworth,** Terry L, Tallahassee, FL, *I-3-1 VN SWA* +
*SSGT* **Hoyer,** William J, Canby, OR, *K-3-7 H&S-1MAR CW* +
*CPL* **Hoyer,** William P, Milwaukee, WI, *F-2-11 H&S-1-5 VN* +
*CPL* **Hubanks,** Edward W, Redding, CA, *1RECON 3-7MAR VN* +
**Hubbard,** James C, Dearborn, MI, *HQ-1-5 WWII CH* +
*SGT* **Hubert,** Mike A, Arnold, MO, *T-5-11 CW* +
*CPL* **Hubler,** John HARRY, Gallatin, TN, *FLC RLT7 VN* +
*SGT* **Hubster,** Morris JR., Holland, IN, *1MAW VN* +
*PFC* **Hudgens,** Lawrence W, Pueblo, CO, *WPNS-2-1 H&S-3-5 CW* +
*LTCOL* **Hudson,** Floyd G, Callao, VA, *W-2-5 G-2 WWII KO VN* +
**Hudson,** John H, Gresham, OR, *A/B-1ENGR KO*
*CPL* **Hudspeth,** Gene T, Tucson, AZ, *B-1-5 VN* +
*CPL* **Huegel,** Roland C, Catasauqua, PA, *B-1RE-CON 1FORRECON VN* +
*SSGT* **Huff,** Hugh L, Yuba City, CA, *HQ-3-1 KO* +
*SSGT* **Huffman,** David D, Phillipsburg, NJ, *H&S-3-1 KO* +
*LCPL* **Huffman,** David L, Parkersburg, WV, *M-3-7 VN* +
*SGT* **Huffman,** Gary L, Pine Grove, CA, *HQ-1-11 VN* +
*SSGT* **Huffman,** Gary L, West Augusta, VA, *1RE-CON 1ANGLICO VN* +
*SGT* **Huffman,** John C, Farmington, NM, *HQSQDN 1MAW KO* +
*CPL* **Huffman,** Larry K, Eddyville, OR, *A-1RECON VN* +
*DR* **Huggins,** Gerald A, Las Cruces, NM, *G-3-11 KO*
*PFC* **Hughes,** Billy H, Houston, TX, *A-1-5 KO* +
**Hughes,** Charles "Doc" W PHD, Arkadelphia, AR, *3-7 KO*
*CPL* **Hughes,** Dana T, Whiting, NJ, *5TH DEF BN, ZMQ-3 WWII* +
*CPL* **Hughes,** Denny, Imperial, PA, *H&S-3-1 VN*
*SGT* **Hughes,** Gregory K, Marina Del Rey, CA, *MAG16-1MAW VN* +
**Hughes,** Thomas H, Peachtree City, GA, *TK CH KO CW* +
*LCPL* **Hughes,** Frederick E, Crossville, TN, *1/5 VN*
*SGT* **Hulet,** Richard W, Kelseyville, CA, *2-5MAR VN* +
*MR.* **Hull,** C W, Pleasant Hill, TN, *C-1-5 CW* +
*SSGT* **Hullinger,** William F, Fort Wayne, IN, *SVC-1TK KO* +
*SSGT* **Humberson,** Joseph E JR., Elkridge, MD, *HQ-3-1 KO* +
*LTGEN* **Hummer,** Steven A, Apo, AE, *1-1MAR CW*
*PFC* **Humphrey,** Dora J, Georgetown, IL, *B-1-5 WWII* +
*SGT* **Humphrey,** James B, Akron, OH, *1ANGLICO KO* +
*CPL* **Humphrey,** Kenneth G, Emory, TX, *H&S-2-5 VN* +
*LCPL* **Humphrey,** Patrick C, Triangle, VA, *1 TANK, HQCO-3-5*
*SGT* **Humphrey,** Paul D, Honeoye, NY, *1ST 90AAA KO* +
*CPL* **Hundshamer,** F X, Carlsbad, CA, *1SVC 1MAR WWII KO* +
*SGT* **Hunt,** Lucky J, Rockwall, TX, *B-1TK C-7TK CH KO* +
*SGT* **Hunt,** Robert M, Las Vegas, NV, *1ST MAR DIV 11TH MAR* +
*PFC* **Hunter,** Blair, Sarasota, FL, *HQ-DSS KO* +
*SGT* **Hunter,** Daniel T, Dickinson, TX, *F-2-5 KO* +
*PVT* **Hunter,** Harmon P, Nova Scotia, Canada, *B-1-5 WWII* +
*SSGT* **Hunter,** James A, Flint, MI, *AMMO-1ORD KO* +
*MAJ* **Hunter,** James B JR., Charlotte, NC, *F-2-1 WWII* +
*LTCOL* **Hunter,** W Dean, Palm Desert, CA, *VMF-312 CMC KO VN CW*
*HMZ* **Huntington,** Richard H JR., Mountain View, CA, *G 2/5 FMF VN*
*SGT* **Huntsinger,** W C, San Diego, CA, *C-1-5 KO* +
*CPL* **Hurley,** John T, Fargo, ND, *I-3-11 KO*
*SGTMAJ* **Hurley,** Michael J, Naples, FL, *COMMHQ 1-25 VN SWA* +
*SGT* **Huseby,** Krist III, Tacoma, WA, *I-3-7 A-1-1 VN* +
**Hussey,** Eugene P, Fircrest, WA, *HQ-1-7 KO* +
*PFC* **Hussion,** C L, Indianapolis, IN, *M-3-1 WWII* +
*SSGT* **Huszanyik,** Joe JR., Cleveland, OH, *5-DEF AAA WWII* +
**Huther,** Ralph J, Kirkwood, MO, *HQ-ENGR WWII CH KO* +
*SSGT* **Hutt,** Leroy, Beverly, MA, *B-1SHPTY KO* +
*CPL* **Hyatt,** Daryl W, Tulsa, OK, *HQ-3-7 VN* +
**Hyder,** Lester J, Corpus Christi, TX, *G-2-1 VN* +
*SGT* **Hyder,** Thomas M, Phoenix, AZ, *2-7 A-1ST RECON VN* +
*MR.* **Hyland,** James F, South Weymouth, MA, *1BRDG-7ENGR VN* +
*CPL* **Hymel,** Paul J, Metairie, LA, *H-3-5 KO* +
*CAPT* **Hyun,** Kee-Tae, Daejeon, Korea, *VN*
**Iglesias,** Rudolph, San Diego, CA, *G-2-5 WWII* +
*LCPL* **Ignas,** James J, Philadelphia, PA, *A-1-7 VN* +
*MGYSGT* **Iliffe,** George W JR., Oceanside, CA, *2-11 3-11 VN SWA* +
*SGT* **Illman,** Paul E, Kansas City, MO, *L-3-1 VN* +
*MR.* **Imfeld,** Louis A, The Villages, FL, *G-2-1 WWII* +
*MRS* **Immerman,** Carolyn, Baldwinsville, NY, *AS-SOCIATE* +
*CPL* **Improta,** Ned R, Washingtonville, NY, *7MT KO* +
*PVT* **Inda,** Jack J, Oak Creek, WI, *C-1AMTRAC KO* +
*LCPL* **Indie,** Arthur E JR., Redding, CA, *L-3-1 VN* +
*CAPT* **Ingebrand,** George B, Edina, MN, *C-1-5 KO* +
*CPL* **Ingebrigtson,** Paul J, Waubun, MN, *F-2-1 WWII* +
*SGTMAJ* **Ingle,** Jerry V, Brownsville, TX, *1FORRE-CON CMC VN* +
*SSGT* **Ingram,** Jerry W, Shawnee Mission, KS, *C-1TKBN CH* +
**Ingram,** Robert R, Jacksonville, FL, *C-1-7 VN* +
**Innis,** James R, Santa Ana, CA, *1SVC BN KO* +
*CPL* **Intall,** John F, Bayside, NY, *A-7 MT VN* +
*PFC* **Ireland,** James H, North Hollywood, CA, *H&S-11MAR CH* +
**Irvin,** Melvin E, Santa Clara, CA, *ENGRSPT-1EN-GR VN*
**Irwin,** Dorothee, Palm Springs, CA, *FOX 14TH BN*
*LTCOL* **Irwin,** Jim, Palm Springs, CA, *1/5 2/5 1ST SVC BN*
*CPL* **Irwin,** Thomas J, Saint Louis, MO, *1ST LOGIS-TICS COMMAND, VN*
*CAPT* **Isenhour,** William D, Southfield, MI, *H&S-2/5 S-4 VN* +
*SGT* **Isky,** Mike, Manchester, NJ, *1-5MAR 1ENGR WWII KO* +
*LTCOL* **Istel,** Jacques A, Felicity, CA, *1MAW KO* +
*CPL* **Iverson,** B G, San Angelo, TX, *H&S-5MAR WWII CH* +
*SGT* **Jablonski,** Joseph C, Washinton, DC, *VM06-1MAW PK*
*SGT* **Jabusch,** W G, Graham, WA, *3-26 1MAW VN* +
*MAJGEN* **Jackson,** Anthony L, Fallbrook, CA, *1ST MAR (C.O) 5TH MAR*
*HA1* **Jackson,** Charles L, Edinburg, PA, *E-2-7 WWII CH*
*SGT* **Jackson,** Craig L, Wake Forest, NC, *D-1-5 VN* +
*CPL* **Jackson,** Horace T, Mobile, AL, *1ENGR 1MT CH KO* +
*SSGT* **Jackson,** James O, Greenville, GA, *1SVC KO VN* +
*LCPL* **Jackson,** Joseph P, Loudonville, NY, *L-4-11 C-1-11 VN* +
*CPL* **Jackson,** Lawrence H, Spokane, WA, *F-2-1 WWII CH* +
*SSGT* **Jackson,** Ray D, Tempe, AZ, *MTACS2 MAG33 KO* +
*SGT* **Jackson,** Robert M, Las Vegas, NV, *B-1-1 VN* +
**Jacobs,** Cornelius, Far Rockaway, NY, *H-2-1 VN* +
*1STSGT* **Jacobs,** Michael J, Triangle, VA, *2-9-3-5*
*CPL* **Jacobsen,** George C, Brooklyn, NY, *H&S-11MAR WWII CH* +
*CAPT* **Jacobsen,** Raymond F, Inver Grove Heights, MN, *155-11MAR VN* +
*SGT* **Jacoby,** Charles J, Ozark, MO, *L-4-11 KO* +
*MR.* **Jager,** Leroy F, Buffalo, ND, *HQ-1-11 KO* +
*SSGT* **Jahn,** Herbert L, Lake Forest, CA, *B-1-11 KO* +
*1STSGT* **Jainnini,** Al SR., Susquehanna, PA, *F-2-23 KO* +
*CPL* **Jakob,** Erwin E JR., Browns Mills, NJ, *E-2-1 VN* +
*SSGT* **James,** John C, Marion, IL, *H-2-11 10RD KO VN* +
*SGT* **James,** Ray C, Wapato, WA, *A-1RECON KO* +
*MR.* **James,** Theadore, Death Valley, CA, *SVC-HQ CW* +
*DR (CDR)* **James,** Thomas L, Miami, FL, *DENTAL CO WWII KO* +
*CPL* **James,** William E, Dallas, TX, *A-1-5 VN* +
*PFC* **Jamieson,** Richard E, Spokane, WA, *E-2-5 KO* +
*CAPT* **Janes,** Dustin F, Portland, OR, *C-7MT H&S-3-5 CW* +
*SGT* **Janes,** Robert C, Elk Grove, CA, *E-2-5 KO* +
*COL* **Janiczek,** Rudolph M, Apo, AP, *1ST MAR DIV/ HQBN* +
*SSGT* **Jankowski,** Wallace A, Roswell, GA, *RADIO SIG KO* +
*LCPL* **Janssen,** Alan J, Arbor Vitae, WI, *C-1-1 1ST MAR DIV VN*
*ADJ3* **January,** James E, Salinas, CA, *MAG11-1MAW VN* +
*1STSGT* **Jaques,** Charles E, Belgrade, ME, *C-1-1 I-3-7 CH VN* +
*HM2* **Jardine,** Paul, Fair Heaven, VT, *B-1-25-1MAR DIV OIF WOT OEF*
*CPL* **Jarrett,** James E, Cosby, MO, *H-3-1 KO* +
*CAPT* **Jarrett,** Larry E, Garland, TX, *1ST MAR DIV 3RD MAR DIV* +
*SGT* **Jarrett,** Robert T, Englewood, FL, *A-1-7 WWII* +
*PFC* **Jarson,** Lloyd M, Oak Grove, MN, *C-1-5 WWII* +
*SGT* **Jarvis,** Gary E, Jacksonville, FL, *D-1-27 VN* +
*LCPL* **Jaunal,** Greg R, Denham Springs, LA, *1LAR 2/1 CW* +
**Javins,** Paul, Milwaukee, WI, *C/1/5 VN*
*HM1* **Jeffrey,** Harold F, Palm Desert, CA, *C-1-5 CW* +
*SGTMAJ* **Jeffrey,** Louis B, Ocala, FL, *1ENGR-11MAR WWII KO VN* +
*CPL* **Jeffries,** Merle L, Saint Joseph, MO, *H&S 2-5 VN*

GM1 **Jeffries,** Robert R, Lawndale, CA, *A12-A19 UDT WWII* +
**Jenkins,** Charles E, Beaver Falls, PA, *D-1-5 VN*
LTCOL **Jenkins,** Clarence E, Mashpee, MA, *H&S-3-7 WWII KO VN* +
**Jenkins,** Dale G, Medway, OH, *WPNS-3-1 KO* +
SGT **Jenkins,** Gerald L, Staten Island, NY, *C-7ENGR VN* +
**Jenkins,** Kenneth L, Paducah, KY, *D-1-11 H&S-1-5MAR VN* +
LCPL **Jenkins,** Richard EUGENE, Glendale, CA, *HQ CO HG BN 1ST MARDIV* +
PFC **Jennings,** Leonard J, Los Angeles, CA, *D-1-5 CW* +
HM2 **Jennings,** Lewis, Sycamore, IL, *1/5 VN*
**Jensen,** Dane K, Huntington Beach, CA, *I-3-7 CW* +
SGT **Jensen,** Gale R, Roy, UT, *D-2-7 KO* +
CWO2 **Jensen,** Robert G, Beaumont, CA, *E-2-1 KO* +
**Jerabek,** Rita, Shawano, WI, *GOLD STAR MOTHER* +
**Jerome,** George N, Griffith, IN, *COMM-H&S VN* +
CPL **Jerome,** Robert D, Ankeny, IA, *MP D-2-7 H&S-7MAR KO* +
CPL **Jesser,** Wayne H, Wickenburg, AZ, *H-3-5 KO* +
**Jevne,** Franz P III, Indian Wells, CA, *HQ-HQ VN* +
CPL **Jimenez,** Edward, San Antonio, TX, *B-1MT KO* +
**Jimerson,** Floyd B, Shreveport, LA, *HQ-1-2-11 KO* +
CPL **Jimms Jimenez,** Ben F, Lincolnwood, IL, *F-2-1 G-3-11 CH KO* +
CPL **Jocham,** R G, Daniels, WV, *WPNS 1-1 KO* +
MSGT **Johann,** John C, Victor, MT, *E-2-7 K-3-1 KO VN* +
SGT **Johannes,** Karlos R, Palmdale, CA, *M-3-1 VN* +
SGT **Johns,** Charles R, Brownsburg, IN, *1FORREC VN* +
SGT **Johns,** William C, Santa Fe, TX, *I-3-5 KO* +
CPL **Johnsmiller,** Robert W, Carlsbad, CA, *I-3-2 WWII*
SGT **Johnson,** Addison J JR., Roxboro, NC, *E-2-7 VN* +
LCPL **Johnson,** Allan Dean, Boulder City, NV, *C-1-5 VN*
NCCM (SW) **Johnson,** C R, Grass Valley, CA, *A-1-1 WWII KO VN* +
1STSGT **Johnson,** C T, Warwick, RI, *G-3-1 KO VN* +
CPL **Johnson,** David G, Santa Rosa, CA, *G-3-7 KO* +
CPL **Johnson,** Dietel R, Coon Rapids, MN, *C-1ENGR KO* +
SGT **Johnson,** Donald C, Hibbing, MN, *HQ-4-11 KO* +
SGT **Johnson,** Donald D, Denver, CO, *K-4-11 KO* +
CPL **Johnson,** Gerald E, Bisbee, AZ, *HQ-11MAR WWII CH* +
1STLT **Johnson,** Harold A, Saint Cloud, MN, *H-3-5 KO* +
HM2 **Johnson,** John L, Tulsa, OK, *VMO2 HMM163 VN* +
SGT **Johnson,** Johnny M, Richmond, KY, *WPNS/C-1-5 KO* +
PFC **Johnson,** Kenneth H, Center Moriches, NY, *H-3-1 KO*
SGT **Johnson,** Kenneth R, Claremont, CA, *1SHPTY KO* +
SGTMAJ **Johnson,** L C, Vista, CA, *WPNS-1-1 KO* +
MAJ **Johnson,** Michael O, Bremerton, WA, *C-9ENGR VN* +
**Johnson,** Orville C, Detroit Lakes, MI, *I-3-5 WWII CH* +
SGT **Johnson,** Perry S III, Henderson, CO, *1TK 9ENGR VN* +
SGT **Johnson,** R G, Lantana, FL, *HQ-HQ VN* +
**Johnson,** Richard D, Vallejo, CA, *G-3-1 KO* +
SGT **Johnson,** Robert J, Council Bluffs, IA, *E-2-7 KO* +
CPL **Johnson,** Rodney S, Fort Smith, AR, *I-3-5 VN* +
CPL **Johnson,** Steve, Danville, CA, *HQ-3-5 WWII CH* +
CPL **Johnson,** Timothy SHANE, Windermere, FL, *1 MARDIV 1ST RECON BN HQ*
SGT **Johnson,** Virgil W, Woodbridge, VA, *52DEF WWII* +
GYSGT **Johnson,** Wesley R, Belleville, MI, *1-1/5MAR 3-71FORRECON KO VN* +
**Johnsrud,** Norman W, Covina, CA, *E-2RAIDER WWII CH* +
SSGT **Johnston,** Nathan K, Minden, NV, *3/7 OIF*
TSGT **Johnston,** Richard A, Live Oak, FL, *F-2-1 4.2 WWII CH KO* +
CWO5 **Johnston,** Robert W, Melbourne, FL, *H&S-2-23 OIF* +
CPL **Johs,** Jerry, Raymond, WA, *L-3-1 VN* +
SGT **Jones,** Alan R, San Carlos, CA, *K-3-5 M-3-1 VN* +
**Jones,** Allen L, Santa Rosa, CA, *C-1AMTRAC WWII* +
CPL **Jones,** Andrew C, Mohave Valley, AZ, *K-3-5*
CPL **Jones,** Bill J, Midland, TX, *B-1MT VN* +
SSGT **Jones,** Dale L, Lynwood, CA, *HQ-1SHPTY KO* +
PHM2 **Jones,** Darrell S JR., El Paso, TX, *H&S-1MED WWII CH* +
SGT **Jones,** Gerry L, Carefree, AZ, *1ST RECONN WWII KO CH* +
SGT **Jones,** Gordon H, Bellingham, WA, *D-2-5 KO* +
**Jones,** Henry O III, Cordele, GA, *ASSOCIATE* +
PFC **Jones,** J BRUCE, San Francisco, CA, *E-2-7 WWII CH* +
CPL **Jones,** Jim J, Warwick, RI, *D-1RECON VN* +
TSGT **Jones,** John H, Burlington, IA, *1MAW WWII* +
SGT **Jones,** Joseph W JR., Cleveland, OH, *H&S-5MAR KO* +
CPL **Jones,** Richard T, Baltimore, MD, *B-AMTRAC KO* +
SGT **Jones,** Richard W, Clovis, NM, *C-7ENGR VN* +
CPL **Jones,** Robert A, Stow, MA, *ORD SVC* +
SGT **Jones,** Robert F, Baton Rouge, LA, *I-3-7 VN* +
SSGT **Jones,** Robert H, Centennial, CO, *C-1ST TK KO* +
**Jones,** Roderick L. Donald, Fairfax, VA, *A-1-1 WWII KO VN* +
GYSGT **Jones,** Sam E, Irwin, PA, *E/F-2-5 KO VN* +
SGTMAJ **Jones,** Wilbur L, Lakewood, CA, *G-3-1 H-3-1 WWII KO VN* +
CPL **Jordan,** Alfred ROBERT, Clearwater, FL, *D-2-5 KO* +
SSGT **Jordan,** Billy J, Oxford, MS, *HQ-2-11 KO* +
MAJ **Jordan,** Michael J, Yorba Linda, CA, *7ENGR IMEF SWA* +
**Jordan,** Richard T, East Falmouth, MA, *1SCOUT-1TK 1PION WWII* +
SGT **Jorgensen,** Gordon J, Modesto, CA, *WPNS-3-5 KO* +
COL **Jorz,** Raymond R, Mentor, OH, *E-2-5 KO* +
CPL **Joseph,** David M, Apple Valley, CA, *1MAW VN* +
PFC **Joseph,** Ira ADRIEN, Auburn, WA, *AMMO CO 1ORD BN KO* +
LCPL **Joseph,** Sylvester SR., Shively, KY, *G-2-1 VN* +
GYSGT **Josif,** Paul E, Akron, OH, *7SVC CH* +
**Joslin,** Loren E, Maryville, TN, *H&S-6 AMTRAC WWII* +
SGT **Joy,** Ralph EDWARD, Lakeside, AZ, *2ND LGT SPT CO* +
HMC **Joyce,** John T, Randolph, MA, *1MED 1TK KO VN* +
CPL **Joyce,** Stephen F, Marlton, NJ, *W 2/11 VN*
CAPT **Ju,** Chang D, Los Angeles, CA, *1-1MAR KMC KO* +
LTCOL **Judge,** Bruce, Stafford, VA, *HQTRS 11 MAR SWA*
CPL **Julson,** Paul B, Dodgeville, WI, *C-1-5 VN* +
SSGT **Juneau,** Paul F, Concord, NC, *WPNS-3-7 I-3-7 KO* +
1STLT **Jung,** D H, Canyon Country, CA, *ROK 1MARDIV CW* +
**Jung,** Jacob A, Valencia, CA, *1-5MAR CW* +
CPL **Jungen,** Lee MICHAEL, Appleton, WI, *1ST RECON 1ST MAR DIV*
SGTMAJ **Jurinski,** J N, Port Orchard, WA, *B-1-AMBN KO VN* +
CPL **Kaczmarek,** Walter P JR., Woodbridge, NJ, *H-2-5 VN* +
SGT **Kadlub,** Joseph J, Palm Harbor, FL, *A-1TK KO* +
GYSGT **Kahl,** Howard R, Rathdrum, ID, *H-2-1 1FSR VN* +
CPL **Kalk,** Richard E, San Marino, CA, *9TH REGT 1MAR DIV* +
CAPT **Kammeier,** Cyril L, Inwood, WV, *HQ-HQ NAG-MACV KO VN* +
CPL **Kamnetz,** Richard A, Muskego, WI, *H&S-1AMTRAC KO* +
SGT **Kane,** Darrell JAMES, Appleton, WI, *HQ COM 7TH COMM BN VN*
GYSGT **Kane,** Harold W, Livingston, NJ, *B-1-7 KO* +
CPL **Kane,** John J JR., Littleton, CO, *C-1-7 KO* +
CAPT **Kane,** Robert F, Newbern, NC, *F-2-5 VN* +
SGT **Kang,** Chen-Bok, Jongno-Gu Seoul, Korea, *KO VN*
SGT **Kania,** Randall C, Pinckney, MI, *7TH ENGR VN* +
SGT **Kania,** Richard M, Brighton, MI, *VMFA115 VN* +
**Kanigowski,** Alfred (Al) J, Troy, MI, *H&S-1TK WWII CH* +
LCPL **Kankkonen,** William M, Astoria, OR, *MABS12 VN*
CPL **Kanner,** Jeffrey S, Raleigh, NC, *HQ-HQ VN* +
2NDLT **Kappel,** R W, Pittsburgh, PA, *B-1-17 WWII* +
CPL **Kappeler,** Harvey S, Pittsburgh, PA, *C-1-7 VN* +
MAJ **Karlson,** Kenneth E, Florence, MT, *MAG-11 1MAW VN* +
CAPT **Karp,** Warren S, Woodland Hills, CA, *1PROV DMZ KO*
**Karski,** Greg M, Bullhead City, AZ
LTCOL **Karsten,** Ronald F, Oregon City, OR, *1ST CBT ENGR BN VN*
SSGT **Kasdorf,** Glenn A, Pewaukee, WI, *DIV RECON CO KO* +
1STLT **Kassin,** L A, Topeka, KS, *11MT* +
**Kastelic,** Robert, Ontario, CA, *HQ-HQ* +
**Kauffman,** George M, Port Charlotte, FL, *I-3-1 VN* +
1STSGT **Kauffman,** Russell W, Orlando, FL, *H&S-1-1 HQ-1ENGR VN* +
LTCOL **Kaufman,** Larry A, Salem, OR, *C-1-7 VN* +
**Kaufman,** Robert B, Seminole, FL, *E-2-5 KO* +
SGT **Kavanaugh,** M J, Mercer Island, WA, *WPNS/D-2-1 KO* +
SSGT **Kay,** Thomas, Flint, MI, *D-2-11 WWII KO* +
SGT **Kay,** Victor J, Schaumburg, IL, *HQ-HQ KO* +
LCPL **Kaylor,** James N, Newport Beach, CA, *E-2-26 3CAG VN* +
**Kazmierczak,** Henry J, Chicago, IL, *D-2-11 KO* +
**Kearney,** John P, Fort Lauderdale, FL, *HQ-1-7* +
LTCOL **Kebelman,** Frank L III, Oceanside, CA, *1ENGR SWA* +
CAPT **Keckler,** R C, Irvington, NY, *HMM-364 VN* +
**Keefe,** T, Bronx, NY, *5MAR WWII* +
CPL **Keel,** Bill J, Bellingham, WA, *MED-MT WWII CH KO* +
SGT **Keeler,** R A, Saint Louis, MO, *1MAW VN* +
COL **Keeley,** John M, Oldsmar, FL, *5MAR-HQ WWII CH KO VN*
CPL **Keeling,** John MARVIN, Houston, TX, *C-1-1 VN* +
MGYSGT **Keely,** James L, Oceanside, CA, *K-3-5 K-3-1 H&S 3-1 VN* +
CPL **Keen,** Daniel H, Sycamore, IL, *MP-1MAR VN* +
CPL **Keen,** James B, San Juan Capistrano, CA, *H&S-2-5 H&S-1-1 CMC* +
SGT **Keen,** John (Jack) B, Philadelphia, PA, *HQ-2-5 CW* +
SP4 **Keenan,** Charles, Houston, TX, *101ABN ATT VN* +

*SGT* **Keenan,** Gerald K, Longmont, CO, *A-1-11 KO*
*CAPT* **Keenan,** John F, Floral Park, NY, *M-3-7 VN*
*MSGT* **Keene,** David E, Randleman, NC, *TRK-1FSR/FLC VN+*
*MR.* **Keffer,** Gerald D, Grove City, OH, *COMM-HQ KO+*
*SGT* **Keffer,** James M, Erie, CO, *WPNS-2-1 KO+*
*SSGT* **Kegley,** Frederick P, Keansburg, NJ, *G-3 F-2-7 KO VN+*
*MAJ* **Keister,** Charles F, Harrison, TN, *A/C-1-11 KO+*
*CPL* **Keith,** Charles W, Roslindale, MA, *E-2-5 KO+*
*CPL* **Keith,** Robert R, Needham, MA, *HMM361/261 VN+*
*SGT* **Keithley,** Austin T, Hamilton, MT, *SPT 4MARDIV CW+*
*SGT* **Kellam,** Richard L, Shelbyville, IN, *HQ-1-11 KO+*
*SGT* **Kellems,** Norman A, Littlerock, CA, *H&S 2-1 CW+*
*SGT* **Keller,** Charles L, Brook Park, OH, *ORD-1SVC KO+*
*CAPT* **Keller,** Dale H, Sandy, OR, *4.2-1MAR KO+*
**Keller,** Darrel, Grand Saline, TX, *I-3-7 VN+*
*SGT* **Keller,** John D, Fpo, AP, *5COMM VN+*
*SGT* **Kelley,** Arthur R, Marstons Mills, MA, *1MAW WWII CH KO+*
*GYSGT* **Kelley,** George E, Salem, OR, *1SVC FLC KO VN+*
*SSGT* **Kelley,** Kenneth, Tucson, AZ, *HQCO MAG25 WWII+*
*SGT* **Kelley,** Robert F, Roxbury, MA, *H-3-1 KO+*
*COL* **Kelley,** Terrell T, El Paso, TX, *I-3-1 VN+*
*CAPT* **Kelley,** Thomas W, Childs, MD, *DIV CHAPLAIN+*
*SGT* **Kelley,** William E, Cohasset, MA, *WPNS-2-5 KO*
*CPL* **Kelligher,** Lewis H, Philipsburg, PA, *1ENGR VN+*
*SGTMAJ* **Kellogg,** Alan J JR., Kailua, HI, *G-2-5 VN+*
*SGT* **Kelly,** David C, Farmington, NM, *SUP-1ORD KO+*
*MGYSGT* **Kelly,** Donald L, Port Angeles, WA, *H&S-1-7 VN+*
*SGT* **Kelly,** Everett L, Houston, TX, *A-1-5 H&S-2-7 VN*
*PFC* **Kelly,** James J, Nutley, NJ, *B-1-5 VN*
**Kelly,** James J, Hopewell Jct, NY, *B-1RECON VN+*
*BGEN* **Kelly,** John F, Washington, DC, *ADC HQ 1LAR 3-4MAR WOT+*
*CPL* **Kelly,** John W, Grove City, OH, *E-2-7 KO+*
*TSGT* **Kelly,** Patricia A, Springfield, VA, *ASSOCIATE+*
*CPL* **Kelly,** Terence P, North Weymouth, MA, *HQ-3-11 1FAG VN+*
*SSGT* **Kendall,** Terry D, Lodi, CA, *I-3-7 CW+*
**Kennedy,** Alan J, Florissant, MO, *D-1-1 CW+*
*SSGT* **Kennedy,** Manert H, Boulder, CO, *D-2-1 KO+*
*LCPL* **Kennedy,** Martin E, Tyler, TX, *D-1-5 7MAR CW+*
**Kennedy,** William P, Torrance, CA, *1-1MAR VN+*
*2NDLT* **Kenney,** George S, Beverly, MA, *F-2-5 KO+*
*CPL* **Kenny,** Richard L, Oviedo, FL, *I-3-5 VN+*
*CPL* **Kenny,** Thomas D, New Rochelle, NY, *D-MT-7 KO+*
*SGT* **Kensil,** Alan J, Cedar Springs, MI, *H&S-3-1 VN+*
*MAJ* **Kent *********,** Donald E, Emerald Isle, NC, *HQ-2-1 WWII CH KO VN+*
*CPL* **Kenyon,** O P III, Wakefield, RI, *F-2-1 VN+*
*PVT* **Kepalas,** Juozas D, Seminole, FL, *D-1RECON VN+*
*GYSGT* **Kerley,** James E, Ann Arbor, MI, *WPNS-2-5 KO VN+*
*MSGT* **Kerlin,** Jessel JAMES, Vernal, UT, *C-1-6 MABS-12 1ST MAW VN+*
*CPL* **Kerr,** Brian, Phoenix, AZ, *VN FOX CO. WPNS PLT VN*
*SGTMAJ* **Kerr,** Charles L, Moody, AL, *G/H/S-3-11 WWII+*
*CPL* **Kerr,** Ronald N, Fort Mohave, AZ, *3-1MAR VN+*
*CAPT* **Kerrigan,** Thomas G, Roselle Park, NJ, *L-3-1 VN+*
*LTCOL* **Kershaw,** Charles W, Carlsbad, CA, *A-1RECON VN SWA*
*LTCOL* **Kerzic,** Robert L, Dauphiin Island, AL, *H&S-1-5 S-3 VN+*
*SSGT* **Kerzman,** Lawrence O, Santa Ana, CA, *B-1-11 KO+*
*CPL* **Kessler,** Charles W, Tucson, AZ, *L-3-7 WWII CH+*
*SGT* **Kessler,** Henry W, Rock Hill, SC, *1 CSG KO+*
*SGT* **Kessler,** J T, Napa, CA, *D-2-7 KO+*
*SSGT* **Kettner,** Donald H, Glendive, MT, *1ST MAR DIV 11TH MAR KO+*
*DR* **Kever,** Gus P, Ponca City, OK, *E-2-7 KO+*
*SSGT* **Key,** Bert W, Sandy, OR, *B-2-7, 7TH MT*
*SGT* **Kibler,** Kenneth L, Hunker, PA, *B-532ENGR 2ENGRSPCLBDE KO*
*CAPT* **Kicklighter,** Rod C, Ocala, FL
*LCDR* **Kidd,** Bobby J, Barbourville, KY, *2LAAM VN+*
*SGT* **Kidd,** Richard L, Vinton, VA, *HQ/H-3-1 KO+*
*CPL* **Kidder,** John L, Tucson, AZ, *A-1-5 KO+*
*CPL* **Kiger,** James C, Orange, CA, *HQ-11MAR CW+*
*GYSGT* **Kilbride,** Vincent J, Rialto, CA, *C-1-7 WWII VN+*
*SGT* **Killeen,** Gerald C, Bonita Springs, FL, *WPNS-3-1 KO+*
**Killough,** Charles W, Lawndale, NC, *I-3-7 VN+*
*SSGT* **Kim,** Chang-Gn, Inchon Metro, Korea, *D-7 BULLDOZER ENGR KO VN*
*SGT* **Kim,** Chulkyung, Seoul, Korea, *KO VN*
*LTCOL* **Kim,** Edward H, Roland Hgts, CA, *KMC ATT KO+*
*COL* **Kim,** Ho Y, Los Angeles, CA, *KMC-50-53 KO+*
**Kim,** Jin, Los Angeles, CA, *KMC KO VN+*
*BUCK SGT* **Kim,** Jong-Ku, Daegu, Korea, *ROKMC 2ND BRIGADE 5TH BN HQ CO VN*
**Kim,** Jun B, Los Angeles, CA, *KMC KO+*
*COL* **Kim,** Kab J, Los Angeles, CA, *KMC ATT KO VN+*
*SGT* **Kim,** Ki H, Poway, CA, *D-2-7 KO*
**Kim,** Kyo WON, Northridge, CA, *KMC KO+*
**Kim,** Moon W, Garden Grove, CA, *KMC KO+*
*CAPT* **Kim,** Paekun, Los Angeles, CA, *ROKMC KO+*
*CAPT* **Kim,** Paul M, Los Angeles, CA, *3MAW CW+*
**Kim,** Phillip, Waukegan, IL, *ROC MC VN*
*BUCK SGT* **Kim,** Wang-Ju, Jung-Gu, Seoul, Korea, *ROKMC 2ND BRIGADE 2ND CO VN*
*GYSGT* **Kim,** Yong-Sam, Gyeongnam, Korea, *VN*
*M SGT* **Kim,** Yong-Soo, Seoul, Korea, *ROKMC REGT CMBT TEAM 1-2-3RD PLT*
**Kim,** Yoo Kyung, Ku-Seoul, Korea, *S-2 KO+*
*MR.* **Kim,** Young Y, Bethel, AK, *KMC VN+*
*SGT* **Kimker,** Al T, Bellingham, WA, *HQ-7MAR VN*
*MAJ* **Kinder,** Joseph D, Brawley, CA, *E-2-5 HQ-HQ VN+*
*CPL* **Kindred,** Linn E, Le Claire, IA, *SCOUT-SNIPER VN+*
*SGT* **King,** Arthur P.C., Carlsbad, CA, *A-1-7 KO+*
*MAJ* **King,** Carl E, The Woodlands, TX, *H-2-1 VN+*
*CPL* **King,** Charles L, Pearland, TX, *A-1ENGR WWII CH+*
*SSGT* **King,** Edward L, Glen Burnie, MD, *1ENGR A-3-5 KO+*
*SGT* **King,** James HAYES JR., Columbus, OH, *A/1/7 VN*
*CAPT* **King,** Kenneth M, Vonore, TN, *C-1RECON VN+*
*CAPT* **King,** Reed T, Northridge, CA, *1ST MARDIV*
*SGT* **Kingston,** Charles E JR., Abita Springs, LA, *H&S-3-5 KO+*
*SSGT* **Kinkade,** Roger N, Kellyville, OK, *1ST MAR DIV KO+*
*SSGT* **Kinnear,** Elwyn L, Anoka, MN, *D-7ENGR WWII KO VN+*
*LT* **Kinney,** John E, Austin, TX, *HQ-1-11 VN+*
*CPL* **Kinsey,** Stephen L, Yakima, WA, *A-11MT VN+*
*MGYSGT* **Kinsherf,** John F JR., Halifax, MA, *MAG 36/39 SWA+*
**Kinzel,** Robert C, Pollock Pines, CA, *M-3-1 VN+*
*SGT* **Kipp,** John G, Chino Valley, AZ, *H&S-1SHPTY KO+*
*CPL* **Kirby,** Charles L, Rogers, AR, *F/HQ-2-5 WWII+*
*SGT* **Kirby,** James F, Burnsville, MN, *H&MS12-MAG12 KO*
**Kirby,** John B, Aurora, OH, *3-155GUN-11MAR VN+*
*SGT* **Kirk,** Sidney E, Santa Ana, CA, *SIG/MP CH KO+*
*SGT* **Kirker,** Tom J, Anaheim, CA, *E-2-5 B-1-1 KO+*
*SGT* **Kirsch,** Warand R, Laguna Hills, CA, *WPNS-1-7 KO+*
*DR.* **Kirschke,** James J, Paoli, PA, *H-2-5 81MM VN+*
*TSGT* **Kirst,** Kenneth M, Metairie, LA, *VMF143/451 KO+*
*LCPL* **Kistler,** Randy A, Middlebury, IN, *D-2-11 VN+*
*CPL* **Kittinger,** Jack L, Long Beach, CA, *HMR462 CW+*
*SGT* **Klapack,** John S, Reseda, CA, *1ENGR 1MAW WWII+*
*CPL* **Klawon,** Jay, Hamilton, MT, *HMM163-MAG30 CW+*
*CAPT* **Klein,** Edwin A, Nacodoches, TX, *Q/R-5-11 SWA+*
*CAPT* **Klemm,** Wilbur C JR., Springfield, VA, *HQ-1-11 HQ-HQ CW+*
*SSGT* **Klemmer,** Donald R, China Township, MI, *ANGLICO KO+*
*SSGT* **Klenk,** George M, Florissant, MO, *1MAW KO+*
*MAJ* **Klie,** Timothy F, Blythewood, SC, *E/2/5 VN*
*CAPT* **Kliewer,** Edward, San Antonio, TX, *HQ-1-7 HQ-3-11 VN+*
*SGT* **Knapp,** Robert W SR., South Boston, MA, *A-1-6 F-2-1 KO+*
**Knee,** Robert W, Naples, FL, *1-2MAR VN+*
**Knickerbocker,** Charlie K, Indian Wells, CA, *1MAW*
*SSGT* **Knight,** Steven M, Palmyra, IN, *K-4-11, 1ST MAR DIV VN*
*CPL* **Knisley,** Leland F, Salinas, CA, *B-1-17 B-1ENGR WWII+*
*HM2* **Knispel,** Ray W, Edinburg, OH, *HQCO 5TH MAR VN+*
*LTCOL* **Kniss,** Gary J, Beaverton, OR, *F-2-1 VN SWA+*
*CPL* **Knoll,** George A, Rosemead, CA, *A-3 155HOW WWII+*
*SGT* **Knopf,** David H, Columbus, GA, *H-2-7 VN+*
**Kocan,** John P, La Quinta, CA, *1MAW CW+*
*SGT* **Koch,** Charles W, Phoenix, AZ, *WPNS-1-5 KO+*
*CPL* **Koch,** Douglas K, Sioux Falls, SD, *D-2-5 CH KO+*
*LCPL* **Kocourek,** Charles J, Franklin, WI, *H&S/B-1-5 VN*
*LCPL* **Koel,** Eric D, Denver, CO, *G-2-5 G-2-9 CW+*
*CAPT* **Kogut,** Allen S, Glen Burnie, MD, *L-3-1 CW*
*SSGT* **Kokal,** Ron E, Virginia, MN, *HQ-3-5 KO+*
*SGT* **Kokofski,** Stanley C, Enfield, CT, *A-1- 5 WWII+*
*TSGT* **Kolba,** Joseph J JR., Yonkers, NY, *H&S-1-5 KO+*
*SGT* **Koletis,** Thomas, Westbrook, ME, *F-2-1 CH+*
**Komel,** Stanley J, Elmhurst, IL, *A-1AMTRAC WWII+*
*1STLT* **Komenda,** Joe E JR., Santa Maria, CA, *B-1-1 VN+*
*LCOL* **Kong,** Sang H, Santa Monica, CA, *KMC KO+*
**Kong,** Sun Taek, Anaheim, CA, *KMC KO+*
*SGT* **Koonce,** Elbert E, Mountain Home, AR, *G-3-5 WWII CH KO+*
*CPL* **Kopec,** Stanley J, Bayonne, NJ, *I-3-1 KO+*
*SGT* **Kopetz,** Harold F, Oregon, WI, *H&S/A-1ENGR WWII CH+*
*SSGT* **Kopko,** Larry EDWARD, Kent, OH, *1ST FSR/FLC, RED BEACH, SUPPORT CO*
*LCPL* **Kopping,** Phillip B, Carmichael, CA, *B-1-1 CW+*

*CPL* **Korb,** John M, Fond Du Lac, WI, *H-1-5 KO* +
*SGT* **Korsen,** Steven S, Scarsdale, NY, *A-1-7 KO* +
*SGT E-5* **Koss,** Michael T, Oklahoma City, OK, *3/5*
*SSGT* **Kostecki,** James A, Missoula, MT, *B-1-5 C-1AMTRAC CH KO VN* +
*SGT E-5* **Kostek,** James H, Fort Mohave, AZ, *SUP-FLSGA-FLC VN* +
*CPL* **Kotsovos,** James L, Beaverton, OR, *1MARDIV, 3MARDIV VN*
*HM2* **Kovacs,** Albert JR., Downingtown, PA, *A-1-7 VN* +
*CPL* **Kowalski,** P S, Sacramento, CA, *G-3-11 KO* +
*CPL* **Kozer,** Jack J, Las Vegas, NV, *W-1-7 KO* +
*MGYSGT* **Kozina,** Mark M, Oceanside, CA, *COMM-HQ 1MAR OIF* +
*SGT* **Kozlowski,** Larry J, Santa Rosa, CA, *C-1-5 VN* +
*CPL* **Kozlowski,** Robert A, Traverse City, MI, *B-1-11 WWII CH* +
*SGT* **Krajcovic,** Paul, Fort Myers, FL, *D-2-1 KO* +
*MRS* **Kramer,** Mary, El Cajon, CA, *ASSOCIATE* *
*SGT* **Krampe,** Donald E, Murrieta, CA, *B-1AMTRAC KO VN* +
*MGYSGT* **Krause,** Robert RUSSELL, Bullhead City, AZ, *5MAR WWII CH KO VN* +
*CPL* **Kraynick,** Mike, San Jose, CA, *SPLWPNS-11MAR WWII* +
*CWO4* **Krebs,** Frederic T, Denver, CO, *HQ BN WWII KO* +
*SSGT* **Krebsbach,** Marvin D, Universal City, TX, *H&S-1TK CVL104 KO*
*SSGT* **Kreidell,** Mark F, Kennesaw, GA, *5MEB CW* +
*E2-CWO4* **Kreitz,** Donald B, Huntington Beach, CA, *MAINT CO1 CSG 29 PALMS DET KO* +
*SSGT* **Kreller,** William L JR., Baltimore, MD, *1ANGLICO KO* +
**Krieger,** Chris M, Bradenton, FL, *B-SVC/9ENGR VN* +
**Krieger,** Paul L, Fullerton, CA, *A-1-11 KO* +
*CPL* **Kronaizl,** James E, Vermillion, SD, *K-3-5 WWII* +
*CPL* **Krueger,** Dave, Napa, CA, *M-3-5*
*CDR* **Krulak,** Victor H JR., San Diego, CA, *H&S-3-5 1-7MAR VN* +
*SGT* **Krumm,** Gene (Eugene) D, Wellsville, NY, *D-1AMTRAC KO* +
*SGT* **Kubicki,** Donald L, Sunrise Beach, MO, *F-2-11 KO* +
*CPL* **Kuchar,** John P, Metuchen, NJ, *H&S-2-5 VN* +
*1STLT* **Kuchman,** Trevor C, Carlsbad, CA, *2/1 1ST MARINES*
*MAJ* **Kuehl,** Marcia A, Capistrano Beach, CA, *MAG39 CW* +
*SGT* **Kuehn,** Thomas J, Minden, NV, *F-2-1 VN* +
*CPL* **Kuenster,** Edmond F, San Diego, CA, *KO, 5TH MAR HEAVY WPNS KO* +
*CWO2* **Kues,** Edwin J, San Diego, CA, *1ST TANK BN KO VN* +
*SGT* **Kuhen,** Gerald, Middlefield, OH, *C-9ENGR VN* +
*CPL* **Kuhne,** James R, Parkers Praire, MN, *B-1-9 B-1-1* +
*PFC* **Kuhnke,** Herbert L, Huntington Beach, CA, *G-2-5 CH KO* +
*CPL* **Kulka,** Thomas F, Elk Grove Village, IL, *K-3-1 E-2-7 VN* +
*SGT* **Kumaus,** Dan C, Palmdale, CA, *WPNS CW* +
**Kung,** Kug SUH, Nobeisville, IN, *ROKC VN* +
*CPL* **Kunz,** Fred R, Whiteland, IN, *1FSR VN* +
*SSGT* **Kurandt,** Kurt J, Mesa, AZ, *H&S-1MAR SWA* +
*GYSGT* **Kuras,** Paul T, San Antonio, TX, *VMA212-MAG12 WWII KO VN* +
*CPL* **Kurtz,** Eric L, Bakersfield, CA, *7TH MTR TRN-SPT CW* +
*HM2* **Kurtz,** Robert M, Emmaus, PA, *5MAR 1TK CW*
*CPL* **Kurtz,** James, Erin, TN, *C 1/5 VN*
*SSGT* **Kushner,** Jerry S, Raleigh, NC, *H&S-1AMTRAC KO*
*HON.* **Kuykendall,** Steven T, Long Beach, CA, *HQ-11MAR 1ANGLICO VN* +
*PFC* **Kvavli,** C S, Elmhurst, IL, *HQ-7 1DIV BAND WWII* +
*TSGT* **Kvoriak,** Joseph R, Chagrin Falls, OH, *A-1ENGR 17MAR WWII* +
*CAPT* **Kwon,** Eung-Chang, Michucolgu Incheon Metro-City, Korea, *INFANTRY 2MD DRILL UNIT KO VN*
*CWO5* **Kyzer,** Vincent, Oceanside, CA, *1ST MARDIV GUNNER*
*SGT* **Laber,** William R, Somersworth, NH, *E-1RECON 1MAR VN* +
**Labranche,** Joe G, Rockland, ME, *B-1-5 VN* +
*TSGT* **Lack,** Lawrence J JR., Cornelia, GA, *C-1ENGR KO* +
*CPL* **Lacki,** Stephen, Lewiston, NY, *F-2-1 KO* +
*HMC* **Lacy,** Henry E, Rio Vista, CA, *I-3-1 9DEF WWII KO* +
*LCPL* **Ladan,** John L, Seattle, WA, *C-1-1 H&S-1-7 VN* +
*CPL* **Ladner,** Thomas, Bristol, PA, *C-1-5 VN*
*SGT* **Lafayette,** William J, Pikeville, TN, *C-1TK KO* +
**Lafiosca,** John F, Raymondville, TX, *C-1MT WWII* +
*CPL* **Lafley,** John D, Noel, MO, *H-2-5 VN* +
**Laghezza,** William A, Oakdale, NY, *1ARMAMPH KO* +
*SGT* **Lahait,** C J JR., Troy, NY, *1ENGR 3-11 WWII CH KO* +
*SSGT* **Lahm,** John O, Cape Coral, FL, *I-3-1 WPNS-3-5 WWII CH KO* +
*MAJ* **Lain,** Bobby D, Round Top, TX, *B-1-1 VN* +
*COL* **Laine,** Elliott R JR., Virginia Beach, VA, *C-1TK KO* +
**Laing,** William H MD, PHD, London Ontario, Canada, *A-1MED-5 WWII* +
*SGTMAJ* **Laird,** Loren R, Salina, KS, *A-1RECON VN* +
*MSGT* **Laird,** Thaddeus A, Westminster, CA, *WPNS-1-5 WWII KO* +
*SSGT* **Laird,** William S, Navasota, TX, *H&S-1MT WWII* +
*SGT* **Lake,** Rick G, Fullerton, CA, *G-2-23RD REGT 4MAR DIV*
*HM3* **Lakernick,** Steve "Doc" P, Macungie, PA, *B/C-1-1 1MAW 1RECON VN* +
*SGT* **Lamb,** Joseph P, Hope, RI, *I-3-7 VN*
*CAPT* **Lamb,** Robert H, Richmond, VA, *C-1-1 VN* +
*SGT* **Lambdin,** Louis C, Fort Collins, CO, *E-2-5 KO* +
*SGT* **Lambert,** Albert N, Piedmont, OK, *D-2-5 KO* +
*MRS* **Lambert,** Carla, Golden Valley, AZ, *ASSOCIATE* *
*SSG* **Lambert,** Norman H, Galloway, OH, *H&S-1-5 KO* +
*CPL* **Lambert,** Robert J, White Pigeon, MI, *1RECON WWII* +
*GYSGT* **Lambson,** Dale W, Garfield, AR, *C-7MT WWII KO* +
*MRS* **Lancaster,** Sharon A, Windcrest, TX, *
*LCPL* **Lancaster,** Tom J, Windcrest, TX, *A-1-5 VN*
*SGTMAJ* **Lance,** Robert F, Gretna, LA, *D-2-7 A-1-1 KO VN* +
*MAJ* **Land,** Edward J JR., Woodbridge, VA, *HQ-HQ VN* +
*SSGT* **Land,** William, Randolph, MA, *F-2-7 VN* +
*LCPL* **Landerman-Moore,** Norman J, Anacortes, WA, *5TH MAR REGT 2ND BN CW* +
*CPL* **Landry,** Cecil J, Prairieville, LA, *L-3-1 VN*
*CPL* **Landry,** Edward M, West Lynn, MA, *4.2-1-11 VN* +
*LCPL* **Landt,** Charles P III, Fayetteville, NC, *W-3-11 VN* +
*1STLT* **Lane,** Charles Ray, New Orleans, LA, *1FLC VN* +
*TSGT* **Lane,** Samuel R, Plantation, FL, *MAG-11-14 WWII* +
*CPL* **Lang,** Daniel P, Omaha, NE, *7MT KO* +
*LCPL* **Langan,** Ed J JR., Orlando, FL, *K-3-27 VN* +
*CPL* **Langdon,** Robert J, Albuquerque, NM, *1ANGLICO VN* +
*CPL* **Lange,** Lawrence MICHAEL, The Woodlands, TX, *W-2-11 VN*
**Lange,** Robert, Las Vegas, NV, *L-3-5 VN* +
*SSGT* **Langfitt,** Leroy F, Winchester, CA, *2-26 MAR VN* +
*1STSGT* **Langford,** James L, Carlsbad, CA, *I-3-7 VN* +
*SGT* **Langheim,** John J, Springfield, IL, *MAG12 VN* +
*SSGT* **Langley,** Charles, Glendale, KY, *A-1-11 KO* +
*SGT* **Lanham,** D C, Torrance, CA, *E-2-5 KO*
*HM3* **Lansbury,** W R, Huntingdon Valley, PA, *E-2-5 VN* +
*SGT* **Lansford,** William D, Playa Del Rey, CA, *2RAIDER WWII* +
*CPL* **Lantz,** Joseph R, Baltimore, MD, *T&R COM. / MCDS 1MARDIV* +
*SGT* **Lanza,** Andrew F, Staten Island, NY, *11MAR KO* +
*CPL* **Lanzillotto,** Charles W, Eastchester, NY, *H&S 1SHPTY VN*
*SGT* **Laporte,** Arthur T, Hudson Falls, NY, *I-3-7 WWII KO* +
*SGTMAJ* **Lara,** Steven J, Oceanside, CA, *3AA 1-1MAR HQ-11MAR SWA* +
*CAPT* **Laramy,** Robert E, Savannah, GA, *G2-HQ VN* +
*CPL* **Large,** Richard L, Lincoln, NE, *B-1-5 KO* +
*MSGT* **Larimer,** Robert H, Bakersfield, CA, *H&S-1/7MAR WWII CH* +
**Larios,** Robert A SR., San Antonio, TX, *FLSG VN* +
*MAJ* **Larkin,** James A, Jamaica, NY, *A/B-1-5 KO*
*CAPT* **Larkin,** James T, Old Greenwich, CT, *H&S-1-5 KO* +
*CAPT* **Larkin,** Joseph V, San Diego, CA, *1ST MOTOR TRNSPT BN KO* +
*LCPL* **Larsen,** Arne W, Tempe, AZ, *7TH COMM VN*
*SSGT* **Larson,** Gerald O, Great Falls, MT, *HQ-3-11 VN*
*CPL* **Larson,** Lloyd D, Coon Rapids, MN, *K-3-5 VN* +
*CAPT* **Larson,** Norman W, Roseville, CA, *SVC SQU MAG 23 1MAW WWII*
*SSGT* **Larson,** R W, Cambridge, MN, *E-1-5* +
*CPL* **Larson,** Stanley T, Windom, MN, *C-1-5 VN*
*CPL* **Larue,** Roger T, Overbrook, KS, *D-1RECON VN* +
**Lasco,** Robert C, Antioch, IL, *E-2-1 WWII* +
*CPL* **Lasco,** Tom S, Antioch, IL, *F-2-5 VN* +
*1STSGT* **Laskey,** James R, Cumberland, RI, *7TH MAR VN*
*CPL* **Lasley,** James H, Bethel, OH, *3/71ST MAR DIV FMF H&S CO WIRE PIT VN*
*LCPL* **Lasley,** James, Billerica, MA, *A-1-5 VN*
*MR.* **Lassere,** Donald J SR., New Orleans, LA, *B-1-5 KO* +
*SGT* **Lassere,** Lloyd J, New Orleans, LA, *B-1-5 KO* +
*SGT* **Laswell,** Michael C, Indianapolis, IN, *A-1-5 VN* +
*SGT* **Latham,** Kenneth W, Reedville, VA, *WPNS-2-5 KO* +
*LTCOL* **Lathrop,** Michael E, Chesapeake, VA, *3D AABN HQBN CW OIF*
*1STSGT* **Latimer,** Richard L, San Diego, CA, *A-1TK KO* +
*LCPL* **Latour,** Steven A, Duluth, MN, *H&S-RECON VN* +
**Latta,** James, Crystal Spring, PA, *B-1-5 VN*
*CPL* **Latvala,** James C, Two Harbors, MN, *5MAR A-1MT 2-5 VN* +
*CPL* **Laubach,** James T, Houston, TX, *B-1-7 WWII CH* +
*SGT* **Laufer,** Kenneth J, Lake Winnebago, MO, *D-2-5 KO* +
*PFC* **Laurice,** Salvatore J, Oakland, NJ, *I-3-7 KO* +
**Laurino,** Albert A, Plymouth, MA, *K-3-1 WWII* +
*GYSGT* **Lauve,** George H SR., Wenatchee, WA, *B-1-5 WWII* +
*CPL* **Lavin,** Karl Franz, Ramsey, NJ, *MIKE BATT 4-11 VN*
*PFC* **Lavine,** Alfred E, Forest Hills, NY, *A-1AMTRAC 3-7MAR KO* +
*LTCOL* **Law,** Arthur K, Oceanside, CA, *B-1-1 VN* +
*SGT* **Law,** Chuck E, Mentor, OH, *G-2-5 VN* +
*HM2* **Lawrence,** Wesley H, Wilton, NH, *K-3-7 VN* +

*LCPL* **Laws,** Melvin R, Houston, TX, *C-1TK CW* +
**Lawson,** Raymond G, Troy, MI, *E-2-7 WWII CH* +
*CPL* **Layman,** Thomas M, Petersburg, MI, *I-3-7 VN* +
*PFC* **Lazarus,** Lester, Ho-Ho-Kus, NJ, *E-2-1 KO* +
*CPL* **Le Beau,** Robert C, Vacaville, CA, *1ST FLSG A VN* +
*CPL* **Leach,** Andy F, Aurora, CO, *1st TANKS* +
*SGTMAJ* **Leach,** John H, Cynthiana, KY, *3-155GUN VN* +
*SGT* **Leach,** Lewis B JR., Vista, CA, *G-2-27 A-1-4 HQ-1MARBDE VN*
*CWO3* **Leach,** Patrick, Bristol, CT, *HQCO HQBN VN*
*SGT* **Leach,** Steve M, Horseshoe Bend, ID, *AT-1TK SWA* +
*CAPT* **Leach,** Thomas I, Harrisonburg, VA, *K-3-5 VN* +
*LTCOL* **Leahy,** Kevin M, Oceanside, CA, *1ST BN 4TH MAR 1ST FSSG*
*SGT* **Leal,** Daniel D, Paso Robles, CA, *I-3-7 KO* +
*MGYSGT* **Leather,** James H, Brick, NJ, *1 CSG KO* +
*PFC* **Leatherman,** Everett L, Seymour, MO, *E-2-7 WWII* +
*SGT* **Leavitt,** Howard J, Riverside, CA, *HQ-7MAR KO* +
*SGT* **Leblanc,** Carroll T, Marrero, LA, *MCSD KO* +
*MR.* **Leblanc,** Richard S, Rockledge, FL, *1-3-9 VN*
*PFC* **Lecourt,** Donald A, Barataria, LA, *H&S-8IN HOW CW* +
*CPL* **Ledbetter,** Clay E, Missoula, MT, *ATT2-9MAR 15MEU SWA* +
*PFC* **Leddy,** James P, Dix Hills, NY, *H-3-7 KO* +
*LCPL* **Leddy,** John F, Pearl River, NY, *D-1-26 VN*
*CWO4* **Lee,** Bert Z, Tucson, AZ, *H&S-1 WWII CH KO* +
*DR.* **Lee,** Billy (Bill) E, Montgomery, AL, *K-3-1 WWII CH* +
*MGSGT* **Lee,** Bradley D, Pala, CA, *11TH MARINES*
*CPL* **Lee,** Chang-Woo, Gangseo-Gu Korea, Korea, *VN*
*SSGT* **Lee,** Charles R, Woodbridge, VA, *H&S/D-1-5 VN*
**Lee,** Corkie "Jim", San Marcos, CA, *ASSOCIATE* +
*LTCOL* **Lee,** Do S, Los Angeles, CA, *ROKMC KO VN* +
*CPL* **Lee,** Don S, Seal Beach, CA, *K-3-7 VN* +
*CPL* **Lee,** Gary R, Sandwich, IL, *1SHPTY VN* +
*1STLT* **Lee,** Hee-Il, Gangnam-Gu Seoul, Korea, *MAR 1ST BRIGADE KO VN*
*CPL* **Lee,** Ho G, Inchon City, Korea, *ROK MC VN* +
*GYSGT* **Lee,** Hyo-Jin, Pyeongtaek-Si Gyeonggi-Do, Korea, *VN*
*BUCK SGT* **Lee,** Hyup-Kil, Dongiak-Gu Seoul, Korea, *ROKMC 2ND BRIGADE HQ CO VN*
*PFC* **Lee,** James R, San Marcos, CA, *I-3-7 KO* +
*SGT* **Lee,** Jin-Hee, Dobong-Gu Deoul, Korea, *MAR 1ST REGT 3RD BN KO VN*
*SGT* **Lee,** John J, Valley Stream, NY, *A-1-5 VN* +
*LCDR* **Lee,** John T, Apo, AE, *1-1MAR 1ENGR CW* +
*CAPT* **Lee,** John Y, Vienna, VA, *HQ-1MAR KO* +
*BGEN* **Lee,** Jong TAE, Choon Chun, Kangwon Province, Seoul, Korea, *ROKMC KO* +
*1STLT* **Lee,** Kenneth I, Lynnwood, WA, *2-5MAR TF-XRAY VN* +
*COL* **Lee,** Kyu-Chul, Seoul, Korea, *2ROKMARBDE VN*
*LTCOL* **Lee,** Man C, Carson, CA, *KMC KO* +
*CPL* **Lee,** Otis W, Baton Rouge, LA, *D-2-7 KO* +
*CPL* **Lee,** Paul R, Hunt Valley, MD, *G-2-5 VN* +
*CPL* **Lee,** Robert A, Maywood, CA, *HQ-HQ WWII KO* +
*SGT* **Lee,** Sang W, Los Angeles, CA, *ROKMC KO* +
*SGT* **Lee,** Sang-Kyu, Euiwang-Sigyeonggi-Do, Korea, *MAR SEOHAE 41 CO KO VN*
**Lee,** Shang Hyun, Hermosa Beach, CA, *KMC KO* +
*MAJ* **Lee,** Thomas I, Hillsborough, CA, *D-2-7 KO CW* +
*SGT* **Leedom,** Randy J, Hillsboro, OR, *B-1-5 VN* +
*PFC* **Leek,** Harvey E, Summerfield, FL, *C-1AMTRAC WWII* +
**Leeka,** David L, Tallahassee, FL, *K-3-7 VN* +
*HN* **Leeson,** N J, Elmwood Park, IL, *G-3-1 KO* +
*CPL* **Legrand,** Stephen L, Oro Valley, AZ, *K-3-5 VN* +
**Lehman,** Howard, Catherdral City, CA, *1 ITR BN*
*CPL* **Lehman,** Robert C, Sewaren, NJ, *I-3-5 KO* +
*SGT* **Leiser,** James K, Valley, WA, *K-3-1 VN* +
*GYSGT* **Leister,** Clarence V, Surprise, AZ, *1MP M-3-7 VN* +
**Leistler,** Myron J, North Bend, OH, *E-2-1 KO* +
*SSGT* **Leitch,** Richard M, Keansburg, NJ, *G-2-7 MPCo SU#1-SVC VN* +
*SGT* **Leitner,** Gregory C, Peoria, IL, *C-1-5 VN* +
*SGT* **Lemay,** Evarist A, Warwick, NY, *E-2-5 KO* +
*SGT* **Lemos,** William J, Daphne, AL, *1ENGR 1SHPTY WWII CH KO* +
*SSGT* **Lenhart,** Bernie L, North Fort Myers, FL, *H&S-1ENGR 6MAR WWII KO* +
*1STLT* **Lenihan,** J. David, Marietta, GA, *C/D 1-5 VN*
*SGT* **Leon,** Jim E, Albuquerque, NM, *ROK MAR VN* +
*SGT* **Leon,** Joseph J, Mesquite, NV, *1SIG KO* +
*LCPL* **Leonard,** David A, Albuquerque, NM, *3FSSG CW* +
*SSGT* **Leonard,** James H, Brockton, MA, *I-3-11 VN* +
*1STLT* **Leonard,** Robert F, Redlands, CA, *A-1-7 WWII CH KO* +
*GYSGT* **Leonesio,** Cleveland J JR., Turlock, CA, *3D-4.5-11MAR VN* +
*CPL* **Leonhard,** Robert D, Portland, IN, *H&S-1AMTRAC KO* +
*PFC* **Lepine,** Jack J, Barnesville, MD, *HQ-2-7 WWII CH* +
*CPL* **Lepori,** A J, Sacramento, CA, *WPNS-5 WWII* +
*SGT* **Lepsche,** Thomas G, Milaca, MN, *B-1/2 LAAM VN* +
*COL* **Lethin,** Clarke R, Fallbrook, CA, *E-2-7 HQ-5MAR SWA OIF* +
*GYSGT* **Levesque,** Donald A, Birmingham, AL, *L-3-5 VN* +
*HN* **Levine,** Jeffrey JAY R., Milford, CT, *E-2-7 VN*
*PFC* **Levitt,** Harry P, Overland Park, KS, *E-2-7 KO* +
**Levy,** Steve A, Cedarville, CA, *B-9ENGR VN* +
*SGT* **Lewis,** Donald J, Orange, CT, *HQ-1SIG KO*
*PHM2* **Lewis,** Frances A, Canoga Park, CA, *ATT WWII* +
*SGTMAJ* **Lewis,** James A, El Cajon, CA, *A-1-7 B-1LAR CW* +
*SGT* **Lewis,** Paul E, Urbana, IL, *G-2-5/MSG BN CW* +
*LTCOL* **Lewke,** Carl A, Cathedral City, CA, *1ST FSSG*
**Lheureux,** David R, Spencer, MA, *1-5MAR CW* +
**Lheureux,** Robert H, Sanford, NC, *D-2-11 F-2-11 VN* +
*PFC* **Liberatore,** Dominick B, Yonkers, NY, *E-2-1 WWII CH* +
*SGT* **Liberatore,** Frank V, Winter Park, FL, *E-2-1 A-1-1 WWII CH KO* +
*SGT* **Liberty,** George G, Apple Valley, CA, *1/2-1MAR KO* +
*PFC* **Libri,** Anthony P, Media, PA, *H&S-1 AVNENG WWII* +
*PFC* **Licht,** Carl N, Brooklyn, NY, *I-3-1 KO* +
*MAJ* **Lichtenberger,** James B, Blairsville, GA, *A-1-5 WWII KO* +
*CPL* **Licker,** S Robert, San Dimas, CA, *A-1-7 KO* +
*COL* **Liddle,** Chester A JR., Alexandria, VA, *1ST MAW VN* +
*MR.* **Lidholm,** Lyle E, Watertown, WI, *A-1ARM-AMPH KO* +
*COL* **Lieber,** Marc C, Sagumore Beach, MA, *1ST MAR DIV*
*CPL* **Lieberman,** James M, Webster, NY, *L-3-1 WWII* +
*LTCOL* **Lietzow,** Jay H, New Hope, MN, *3/5* +
*SGT* **Lightle,** Sherman J, Port Charlotte, FL, *C-1SHPTY KO* +
*HM3* **Ligos,** George, Fair Lawn, NJ, *B-1-5 KO* +
*COL* **Lilley,** John R II, Catharpin, VA, *E-2-7 KO* +
**Lillian,** Fred A, Kirkland, WA, *A-1TK KO*
*COL* **Lillie,** Jay C, Milwaukie, OR, *HQ-3-5 7ENGR VN* +
*HM3* **Lillig,** Ralph E JR., Pocatello, ID, *B-1-7* +
**Lilly,** Leroy H, New Hope, MN, *C-1-1 KO* +
*BUCK SGT* **Lim,** Hyo-Keun, Gyeongsan-Si, Gyeongbuk-Do, Korea, *ROKMC 2ND BRIGADE HQ CO*
*SSGT* **Lim,** Richard, Los Angeles, CA, *HQ-HQ* +
*SGT* **Lima,** Anthony M, Weymouth, MA, *D-2-5 KO* +
*SGT* **Limburg,** Charles A, Indio, CA, *COMMCO HQBN 1ST MAR DIV* +
*SGT* **Limner,** Karl EDWARD, Caledonia, NY, *1CSG 1KMCAG KO* +
*MGYSGT* **Limpic,** Mark S, Gladstone, MO, *L-3-5 HQ-5MAR VN* +
*PFC* **Lince,** George R, Rome, NY, *A-1-7 WWII KO* +
*CAPT* **Lindberg,** Charles S, Brookfield, CT, *HQ/D-2-11 KO* +
*CPL* **Lindgren,** Robert J, Anaheim, CA, *1TKS VN* +
*TSGT* **Lindholm,** Thomas C, Ventura, CA, *1MAW WWII* +
*DR* **Lindley,** J R, Las Cruces, NM, *HQ-HQ KO* +
*SGT* **Lindquist,** E D, Big Bear City, CA, *1-5 2-5 VN* +
*MSGT* **Lindsay,** Charles W, Denton, TX, *VMSB234 WWII* +
*PFC* **Lindsay,** Douglas R SR., Phoenix, AZ, *1ST DIV 1ST REG HDQ CO CH*
*CPL* **Lindsay,** Edward F, Peoria, IL, *G-2-7 VN*
*SGT* **Lindsay,** Frank R JR., Rochester, NY, *A-1-5 CH* +
*SGT* **Lindstrom,** Joshua E, Clarksville, TN, *H&S 1/5 1MARDIV*
*MAJ* **Linkes,** Leonard P, San Antonio, TX, *VMO2 HMM163 VN* +
*1STSGT* **Linkous,** Donald E, Dayton, OH, *A-1AMTRAC KO* +
*SGT* **Linscott,** Donald W JR., Auburn, ME, *11MAR KO* +
*CAPT* **Linsert,** Henry, Alexandria, VA, *3-11MAR VN* +
**Linvill,** C E, Porter, IN, *MP CO VN* +
**Lippa,** David A, Laguna Niguel, CA, *L-MARSPT VN* +
*HM2* **Lippincott,** Jeffry L, Wilmington, DE, *G-2-5 VN* +
*HM2* **Lipscomb,** Joseph H JR., Tualatin, OR, *3-1-1 KO*
**Lisowski,** Harry J, Medina, OH, *B-1-7 VN* +
*SSGT* **Little,** L R, Safety Harbor, FL, *H-3-5 KO* +
*COL* **Livingston,** Gordon M.B. SR., Jamestown, RI, *H&S-3-7 4-11 CH KO VN* +
*1STSGT* **Livingston,** Herbert H, Colstrip, MT, *H-2-5 MAW WWII KO VN* +
*MAJGEN* **Livingston,** James E, Mount Pleasant, SC, *H-2-5 H&S-3-7 KO VN* +
**Locker,** Melvin E, Paramount, CA, *SLCU30 WWII* +
*MGYSGT* **Loewy,** Kurt, Oceanside, CA, *1-5-HQBN KO VN* +
*DT2* **Lofgren,** Gordon CARL DDS, Mcfarland, WI, *7TH MAR REGT KO* +
*CPL* **Lofurno,** Nicholas L, Fort Payne, AL, *A-1TK WWII* +
*HM3* **Logalbo,** Frank A, Clarence, NY, *USHS COMFORT SWA* +
*SGT* **Logerfo,** Gustave J, Douglaston, NY, *WPNS-3-1 KO* +
*GYSGT* **Lohdamm,** William A, Willingboro, NJ, *H-3-1 KO* +
*CAPT* **Lohmeyer,** William J III, Smyrna, GA, *A-1-11 VN* +
*SGT* **Lomascola,** Leonard JR., North Haledon, NJ, *E-2-11 VN*
*CPL* **Lombard,** Eduardo A, Miami, FL, *2-7MAR C-1ENGR VN* +
*PFC* **Lombardi,** Mario, Millbrae, CA, *C-1-5 KO* +
**Lombardo,** Carlo D, Chicago, IL, *I-3-7 VN* +
*CPL* **Lombardo,** Phil J, Green Acres, FL, *HQ-HQ KO* +
*SGT* **Londos,** Edward M, Palos Heights, IL, *G-3-5 KO* +
*CPL* **Long,** Albert E, Lake Havasu City, AZ, *1SIG WWII* +

*SGT* **Long,** Delford H JR., Elk River, MN, *F-2-1 KO* +
*CPL* **Long,** Don J.L, Hollister, MO, *2ND BN-11MAR KO* +
*PFC* **Long,** James D, Conway, SC, *C-1-7 KO* +
*MAJ* **Longtin,** Ronald A JR., Sequim, WA, *C-1-5 VN*
*SGTMAJ* **Loo,** Lawrence KT, San Diego, CA, *HQ-2-11 KO VN* +
**Loomis,** Evelyn "Lindy" J, Pismo Beach, CA, *ASSOCIATE* +
*COL* **Looney,** Patrick GERARD, Apo, AE, *RCT-5 3-5 OIF* +
*PLTSGT* **Loose,** Wilford J, Coldwater, MI, *HQ-1-5 WWII CH KO* +
*LCPL* **Lopes,** L M, Norwood, MA, *F-2-5 VN* +
*SGT* **Lopez,** Alfredo, Gallup, NM, *A-1-5 VN* +
*Sgt* **Lopez,** David E, Anaheim, CA, *H-2-1 VN* +
*E-6 SSGT* **Lopez,** Eduardo, Cedar Hill, TX, *CSSG-11 & SPMAGTF SWA*
*CPL* **Lopez,** Edward R, Moreno Valley, CA, *C-1-1 VN* +
*1STLT* **Lopez,** John K, Stanford, CA, *HQ-HQ KO* +
*SGT* **Lopez,** Johnny, San Antonio, TX, *B-1-7 KO*
*CPL* **Lopez,** Jose I, San Antonio, TX, *HQ-1MT KO* +
**Lopez,** Joseph M. Mike, Boca Raton, FL, *ASSOCIATE* *
*HM2* **Lopez,** Lupe L, Wapato, WA, *I/H&S-3-1 SWA* +
*MGYSGT* **Lopez,** Ramon, Lathrop, CA, *5TH MAR REG HQ'S BN G-4 SWA*
*CPL* **Lord,** Jeb S JR., Calhoun, LA, *HQ/C-1-7 WWII CH* +
*1STSGT* **Lord,** John J JR., Livingston, TX, *C-1-3 K-3-7 VN* +
*SGT* **Lossing,** Bradley J, Aliquippa, PA, *G2-HQ-HQ CW* +
*MGYSGT* **Lotman,** William B, Baltimore, MD, *G-2-7 VN* +
*SGTMAJ* **Lott,** Ira J, Oceanside, CA, *H&S/WPNS-2-9 1TK CW* +
*SGT* **Lotzgesell,** Robert E, Buffalo, IN, *A-1-5 WWII CH*
*GYSGT* **Lotzkar,** Fred, Sparta, NJ, *1ST RECON 5TH MAR VN* +
*SGT* **Lou,** Tin S, Greenwood, MS, *ALU-G2-HQ VMO3 CH* +
*E-5 HM2* **Loudermilk,** John "Doc", Shepherdsville, KY, *C 1/5 VN*
*SGT* **Loughran,** Eugene P, Park Ridge, NJ, *D-2-5 KO* +
**Loughrey,** T J JR., Dushore, PA, *L-3-26 VN* +
*SGT* **Lounders,** Richard A, Tampa, FL, *H&S-1-1 VN* +
*SSGT* **Loupe,** Sydney S, Fullerton, CA, *D-2-5 KO*
*SGT* **Lovas,** John J, Mckinney, TX, *12DEF CL56 USS COLUMBIA WWII* +
*LCPL* **Love,** George H JR., Latrobe, PA, *H&S-3-1 VN* +
*SGT* **Loveless,** Bobby A, Oklahoma City, OK, *B-1AT-5MAR CW* +
**Lowe,** Archie F, Wasilla, AK, *A-1RECON WWII* +
*CPL* **Lowe,** Walter, Higley, AZ, *2-5 KO* +
*CPL* **Lowe,** R L II, Martinsburg, WV, *H&S-3-7* +
*SGT* **Lowery,** William T, Asotin, WA, *C-1-1 VN* +
**Lownes,** Richard E, Pasadena, CA, *H-3-11 HQ-2-10 KO* +
*SSGT* **Loyd,** Gerald L, Fort Wayne, IN, *B-1SHPTY KO* +
*CPL* **Loyd,** Tom R SR., Aurora, CO, *M-3-7 VN* +
**Loza,** Basilio Z JR., Weslaco, TX, *H&S-1-1 WWII* +
*PFC* **Lozano,** George R, Santa Ana, CA, *A-SPLW-PNS WWII* +
*CPL* **Lubbock,** Jim L, Adkins, TX, *D-1RECON VN* +
*SSGT* **Lucal,** R D, Lansing, MI, *VMF-121* +
*LCPL* **Luchinske,** Bernard D, Jackson, WI, *M-3-27 K-3-5 VN* +
*SGT* **Lucido,** Larry M, Dallas, TX, *B-1-1 KO* +
*MSGT* **Lucy,** William E, El Paso, TX, *4-11 CH* +
*CPL* **Luebke,** Gerald R, Oregon, WI, *E-2-7 VN* +
*SGT* **Luetke,** James I, Red Wing, MN, *I-3-7/1 VN* +
**Lufkin,** Neil E, Newbury, VT, *H-3-5 KO* +
*SGT* **Luhan,** Charles JR., Chicago, IL, *11ENGR 1-1MAR VN* +
*COL* **Lukeman,** John ROBERT, Oklahoma City, OK, *MASS2-MACG2 KO* +
*MR.* **Lund,** Guy E, New Orleans, LA, *4-11MAR CW* +
*SGT* **Lundeen,** Charles W, Joliet, IL, *W-2-1 F-2-1 KO*
*SGT* **Lundy,** P V JR., Mclean, VA, *1ORD* +
*SGT* **Lunn,** Matthew E, Anoka, MN, *HMM163-MAG16 MSGDET-G CW* +
*HM3* **Lunsford,** Paul E, Yerington, NV, *I-3-11 KO* +
*HM3* **Lunsford,** Thomas J, Torrance, CA, *G-2-9 CW* +
*SGT* **Lupfer,** Michael S, Aiken, SC, *H&S-1FSR CW* +
*CAPT* **Lupori,** James A, Riverside, CA, *M-3-1 F-2-5 VN* +
*SGT E-5* **Lutes,** Randal A, Eagle River, AK, *VMFA 115, VMFA 314 VN*
*CPL* **Lydens,** Peter F, Mount Airy, NC, *SUP-1CSG KO*
*SGT* **Lydon,** Thomas P, Plainville, MA, *D-1TK KO* +
*CPL* **Lynaugh,** Philip J, Stillwater, MN, *F-2-7 KO* +
*CPL* **Lynch,** E J, Bloomfield Hills, MI, *K-3-5 WWII CH* +
*CPL* **Lynch,** Gerard L, Gaithersburg, MD, *D-1-1 VN*
*PFC* **Lynch,** John D, Oak Forest, IL, *1/3/4* +
*CPL* **Lynch,** John H, Peekskill, NY, *I-3-1 VN* +
*SGT* **Lynch,** Raymond F, Cranford, NJ, *VMJ1-MAG33 KO* +
**Lynch,** Susanne IRENE, Portage, IN *
*MSGT* **Lynn,** Michael J, Yorba Linda, CA, *H&S 2-5 VN*
*SGT* **Lyon,** Arthur J, Staten Island, NY, *G-2-5 VN* +
*SGT* **Lyons,** Albert B, Newport, RI, *D-1ENGR KO* +
*SGT* **Lyons,** Billie J, Largo, FL, *B-1-7 VN* +
*SSGT* **Lyons,** Daniel E, Garden Grove, CA, *I-3-11 G-3-12 VN* +
*LT* **Lyons,** Jack A, Hearne, TX, *MTACS-2 KO* +
*SGT* **Lyons,** James T, Santa Rosa, CA, *A-3AMTRAC VN* +
*LCDR* **Lyons,** Richard M, Chula Vista, CA, *1-1MAR VN* +
*SSGT* **Lyons,** William L, Glendale, CA, *I-3-1 KO CW* +
*CAPT* **Lysaught,** Jerome P, Rochester, NY, *C-1-1 KO* +
*SSGT* **Lyshall,** Arnold P, Seattle, WA, *H&S/A-1-7 CH KO* +
*SSGT* **Lytle,** George R, South Point, OH, *HQ-4-11 VN* +
*SSGT* **Maass,** Kenneth L, Watertown, WI, *C-1AM-TRAC KO* +
*CPL* **Macaitis,** Robert B, Salem, OR, *H&S-11MAR KO CW* +
*MSGT* **MacArtie,** George R, San Diego, CA, *MTACS 1RECON/SVC/FSR HQ KO VN* +
*SGT* **MacCain,** William R, Garnet Valley, PA, *G-3-1 KO* +
*1STLT* **Macchia,** E J, Boca Raton, FL, *5MAR KO* +
*SSGT* **MacDermott,** Donald F, Murrieta, CA, *A-1ENGR WWII KO* +
*SSGT* **MacDonald,** James A, Canton, MI, *WPNS-3-7 KO* +
**MacDonald,** James B, Hemet, CA, *3MAR VN* +
*SSGT* **MacDonald,** Steven W, Carver, MA, *1RE-CON VN* +
*GYSGT* **MacElrath,** Clyde ROBERT, Alamo, NV, *B-1-7 CH KO VN* +
*SGT* **Macey,** Patrick J, Tonasket, WA, *C-1RECON VN*
*SSGT* **MaCarlane,** Donovan, Yucaipa, CA, *HQ-HQ HQ-1MAW WWII KO* +
*CPL* **Machamer,** Lance K, Kailua, HI, *G-2-5 VN* +
*MRS* **Mack,** Dolphine M, Longview, WA, *ASSOCI-ATE* *
*CPL* **Mackey,** Alexander W, Philadelphia, PA, *H&S-1-26 VN* +
*SSGT* **Mackey,** John W, Galesburg, IL, *A-1-11 VN* +
*SGT* **Mackin,** David J, Ilion, NY, *D-MCB133 VN*
*SGT* **MacLaren,** Thomas E, Oxnard, CA, *B-2-5 KO* +
*SGT* **MacLean,** Douglas A, Uniontown, OH, *4.2 MORTARS 1MAR DIV KO* +
*SGT* **MacMichael,** Joseph W JR., Marlton, NJ, *B-1SHPTY KO* +
*CAPT* **MacMurtrie,** J A JR., Collegeville, PA, *3-11MAR SWA* +
*SSGT* **MacNichol,** Robert B, Rancho Santa Margarita, CA, *B-1-5 VN* +
*CPL* **MacQueen,** William D, Westwood, MA, *D-7MT KO* +
*1STLT* **Madden,** G M, De Graff, OH, *HQ BN VN* +
*CWO4* **Madden,** Thomas P, Hudson, NH, *A-1-5 KO* +
*CPL* **Madel,** Frank J, Valencia, CA, *E-2-7 KO* +
*1STLT* **Madenford,** E C, Reading, PA, *HQ-HQ VN* +
*SGT* **Mader,** Edward C, Detroit, MI, *MB536 MP-HQ KO* +
*SSGT* **Madsen,** Earl A, Palm Springs, CA, *4.2 MORTARS-1MAR KO*
*CPL* **Maese,** Leo D, Collegeville, PA, *HQ BTRY-3-11 VN*
*MGYSGT* **Maffioli,** Len, Murrieta, CA, *B1SVC-1 TANK KO CW* +
*SSGT* **Magallanes,** Jerry ISMAEL, Fullerton, CA, *I MEF OIF*
**Magazine,** Sheldon, Rancho Mirage, CA, *WPNS-1 WWII* +
*SGT* **Magiera,** Andrew J, Chicago, IL, *F-2-7 WWII* +
*SGT* **Maginn,** Edward D, Secane, PA, *A-FLC VN*
*SGT* **Magnan,** Duane L, Centralia, WA, *M/4/11* +
*CWO2* **Magner,** Richard M, Newark, DE, *D-2-11 VN* +
*SSGT* **Magnussen,** Milton R, Redding, CT, *B-1-5 VN* +
**Maguda,** Edward D, Orange City, FL, *A-1MT 7ENGR MAINT-1FSR VN* +
*PFC* **Maguire,** Stuart B, Wrentham, MA, *H&S-1-1 CW* +
*LTCOL* **Mahler,** Donald C, Fairfax, VA, *H&S 2-1 VN* +
*CAPT* **Mahlum,** Thomas J, Jacksonville, NC, *M-3-5 VN* +
*CPL* **Mahon,** Brandon LEE, Galeton, PA, *1-4 1-9 OIF*
*PFC* **Mahoney,** J F, Fort Lauderdale, FL, *G-3-7 B-2-5 KO* +
*SGT* **Mahoney,** James M, Windham, NH, *WPNS-1-25 SWA* +
*LCPL* **Maier,** Richard F JR., Chicago, IL, *E-2-1 CW*
*CPL* **Mailhes,** John B, Keithville, LA, *A-1-5 TRK CO 1FSR CMC*
*SSGT* **Main,** Robert V, Surfside Beach, SC, *WPNS-3-7 KO*
*SGT* **Majka,** John W, Syracuse, NY, *H&S-1-5 VN* +
*SGT* **Makaneole,** Kawelo S, Indianapolis, IN, *B-1RECON B-1-1 VN* +
*SGT* **Maker,** Bill T, Salinas, CA, *K-3-7 CW* +
*CPL* **Malast,** John C, Fountain Valley, CA, *MIL POL MCAS EL TORO CW*
*CPL* **Malboeuf,** Paul J, Fitchburg, MA, *K-3-5 VN*
**Maldonado,** Bill D, Mineola, NY, *B-1TK B-2TK CW* +
*SSGT* **Maldonado,** Robert P, Bell, FL, *I-3-7 VN* +
*GYSGT* **Malecki,** Norbert J, Benicia, CA, *HQ-1EN-GR KO VN* +
*SGT* **Maling,** George W, Sun City Center, FL, *H-3-5 KO* +
*SGT* **Mallah,** Robert A, Pleasant Hill, CA, *M-4-11 VN* +
*SGT* **Mallery,** Michael R, La Pine, OR, *H&S-3-1 VN* +
*LCPL* **Malm,** Christopher, Durham, NC, *H-2-5 VN*
*LTCOL* **Malone,** George M, Reno, NV, *A-1-9 VN* +
*PFC* **Malone,** O F, Pleasant Hill, CA, *B-3DEF WWII* +
*CPL* **Malone,** Thomas M, Bethlehem, PA, *A-1-17 WWII*
*CAPT* **Maloy,** Raymond LEE, Pensacola, FL, *Div-LnO* +
**Mammele,** Edwin A, Lady Lake, FL, *H&S-3-7 KO* +
**Manahan,** Harold B, Omaha, NE, *HQ-3-11 KO* +
*CPL* **Mancini,** Frank M, Goldsboro, MD, *I-3-7 VN* +
*CPL* **Mane,** Louis P, New Berlin, WI, *HQ-1PION WWII CH*
*SGT* **Mangan,** Paul C, Des Moines, IA, *F-2-1 VN* +
*CPL* **Maniates,** Ted G, Bakersfield, CA, *H-3-7 KO* +

CPL **Manion,** Thomas L, Bellville, OH, SCOUTS-1-5 VN +
LCPL **Manipole,** David A, Kerrville, TX, D-1-7 VN +
CPL **Mankowski,** Jon E, Portland, OR, H&S-1-5 VN +
SSGT **Manley,** D D, Ellicott City, MD, H&S-3-9 SWA +
MSGT **Manley,** Thomas C, Norfolk, VA, 1-5MAR VN +
SSGT **Mann,** Charles H, San Francisco, CA, HQ CO 1ST PIONEER BN VN +
CWO4 **Mann,** Frederick D, Mcallen, TX, CUB1 WWII +
HM3 **Mann,** James P, Valencia, CA, 3-11 VN
CPL **Manns,** Bruce M, Enfield, NH, A-1AT B-1TK VN +
CPL **Manny,** Leo F, Cape Coral, FL, L-4-11 WWII CH +
PFC **Manoogian,** John A, Canton, MI, 1AMTRAC WWII CH +
**Manott,** Emil C, Dumont, NJ, E-2-7 KO +
SGT **Mansfield,** G H, Kingston, MA, K-3-7 WWII +
SGT **Mansfield,** John E, Pennsburg, PA, H&S-7MT VN
PFC **Mantei,** Mark J, Appleton, WI, I-3-7 VN +
PFC **Manteufel,** Thomas W, Huachuca City, AZ, A-1-1 KO +
SGT **Manuello,** Tonio S, Sterling, CO, WPNS-1-9 SWA +
SGT **Manzella,** Samuel J, Gretna, LA, B-9ENGR VN +
SGT **Maquinalez,** Vincent VAL, Santa Maria, CA
MRS **Marascio,** Wanda, San Diego, CA, ASSOCIATE *
CPL **Marasco,** Philip N, Maryland, NY, A-1-13 VN +
SGT **Marascola,** Richard M II, Diamond Bar, CA, 1ANGLICO CW +
SSGT **Marascola,** Richard, West Covina, CA, WPNS-2-1 CH KO +
**Marcelynas,** Richard C, Olympia, WA, H&S CO 3/1 VN
CPL **Marchand,** Roland T, Corona, CA, 1-5 VN +
LTCOL **Marek,** Jerry V, Llano, CA, C-1-7 L-3-5 VN +
CPL **Margraf,** Eugene A, Findlay, OH, H&S/H-3-7 KO +
SGTMAJ **Mariner,** Daniel MICHAEL, Antioch, CA, HQBN 1MAR DIV OIF
HMC **Marino,** J P, North Fort Myers, FL, 3-5MAR KO +
GYSGT **Mariscal,** Carlos, Salinas, CA, 1-1
SGT **Mark,** Donald J, Webster, NY, HQ-2-11 WWII CH KO +
SGT **Markley,** William H, Mesa, AZ, HMG 3-7 KO +
LCPL **Markowski,** Walter W, Livonia, MI, C-1-5 VN
SSGT **Marks,** David C, Kingman, AZ, B-1-5 VN +
COL **Marletto,** Michael P, Fallbrook, CA, 2/HQ-11MAR OIF +
SSGT **Marley,** Bruce C, Jacksonville, FL, SIG KO +
COL **Marlow,** V N, Malone, NY, 3-11MAR +
PLTSGT **Marmet,** John W, Glenmont, OH, K-3-5 WWII +
**Marolda,** Theodore R, Winsted, CT, A-1AMPHTRK WWII +
MGYSGT **Marotz,** Robert W, Roseburg, OR, HQ-11TH WWII CH KO +
LCPL **Marquardt,** Barry L, Santa Clara, CA, C BTRY 1ST LAAM BN, B BTRY 2ND LAAM BN VN
SSGT **Marquez,** Leo, Selma, CA, C-1-1 KO +
SGTMAJ **Marquez,** Roque E, Aurora, CO, 4JASCO WWII CH KO VN +
SGT **Marquis,** Armand H, Beverly Hills, FL, D-1TK KO +
LTC **Marr,** Clayton E, Richmond, VA, B-1ENGR WWII CH +
PFC **Marr,** James, Rochester, NY, H-3-5 KO +
CPL **Marr,** Walter J JR., Hopkinton, MA, B-9ENGR VN +
CAPT **Marrin,** Thomas P JR., Glendale, AZ, M-3-7
SGT **Marroquin,** Charles, Benbrook, TX, H-3-7 KO +
PFC **Marsh,** George W, Clinton, MA, B-1-5 WWII +
COL **Marsh,** John O, Cynthiana, KY, H&S/D-2-7 C-1-1 KO VN +

**Marshall,** David A, Santa Ana, CA, 1MAW CW +
CPL **Marshall,** Gary P, Chino Hills, CA, K-3-5 HQ-5MAR CW +
CPL **Marshall,** John V, Cincinnati, OH, HQ-1-7 KO +
SGT **Marshall,** Robert, Mill Creek, WA, M-4-11 VN +
GYSGT **Marshall,** Stephen R, Spotsylvania, VA, WPNS-2-5 CW +
SGTMAJ **Martello,** Herbert P JR., Gretna, LA, K/L-3-5 H&S-2-1 VN +
CPL **Martillaro,** Mark W, Elk Grove Village, IL, 1MAW/MAG-12/H&MS-12/CRYOGENICS TECH
SGT **Martin,** Don R, Camarillo, CA, C-11MT VN +
CPL **Martin,** Ernest LEON JR., Sacramento, CA, W 2/1, BIT 3/1 VN
SGT **Martin,** George R SR., Edgewater, MD, M-3-7 VN +
MGYSGT **Martin,** James R, Gaffney, SC, 1RADIO 1FSSG VN +
CAPT **Martin,** Jimmie D, Ventura, CA, RECON WWII CH KO +
CPL **Martin,** Joe W, Raleigh, NC, C-1-11 WWII +
SSGT **Martin,** Leonard P, Beverly Hills, FL, HQ-1TK KO +
**Martin,** Leroy C, Rivervale, NJ, H-3-7 KO +
CPL **Martin,** Leroy, Lafayette, OR, B-1TK +
**Martin,** Rick, Edgewood, NM, 1RECON VN
PFC **Martin,** Robert E, Las Vegas, NV, HQ-3-5 WWII +
PFC **Martin,** Sherman E, Chester, IL, HQ-4-11 KO +
CPL **Martin,** Thomas J, Santa Maria, CA, H-3-7 WWII KO +
SGT **Martin,** Waldo G JR., Morro Bay, CA, H&S-1MT 17MAR WWII CH +
LCPL **Martinez,** Frank W, Northridge, CA, E-3RECON VN +
CPL **Martinez,** Ignacio H, San Antonio, TX, G-2-5 VN +
**Martinez,** Jesse J, Union City, CA, HQ-11MAR KO +
MSGT **Martinez,** Joe, Atascadero, CA, A/D-1TK KO VN +
SGTMAJ **Martinez,** Joseph JR., Jacksonville, NC, D/1/1 1965, H/2/7 1970-1971 VN
SGT **Martinez,** Juan T, Corpus Christi, TX, W-1-11 3-3MAR VN +
CPL **Martinez,** Manuel F JR., South San Franciscoo, CA, H-3-5 KO
SGT **Martinez,** Ralph (Jim) J, Portland, OR, F-2-5 KO +
CPL **Martinez,** Raymond L, Sylmar, CA, VMA211 1MAW CW +
CPL **Martinez,** Robert "Bob" N, Sylmar, CA, H-3-11 KO +
PFC **Martucci,** Harry W, Huntington, CT, H-3-7 KO +
LCPL **Marx,** Eddie III, Beaver Falls, PA, K-3-1 VN +
CPL **Marzano,** John, White Plains, NY, C-3-7 WWII CH +
CPL **Masch,** Robert J, Wind Lake, WI, SVC-HQ VN +
PFC **Masi,** Victor A, Granada Hills, CA, 11 MAR WWII +
SGT **Masino,** Bernard W, Altoona, PA, A-1-7 VN +
SGT **Mason,** D R, Platte, SD, 4.2-7MAR KO +
HMCM **Mason,** Donald E, San Antonio, TX, B+A 1ST BN 7TH MAR KO
GYSGT **Mason,** James L, Mankato, MN, 2-1 VN +
SGTMAJ **Massaro,** John R, Orem, UT, B-1-5 H-3-5 KO VN +
CPL **Mast,** Vince, La Quinta, CA, 1ST SHORE PARTY BN
**Masters,** Lyle W, Stanford, IL, HQ-1MAR VN +
**Masterson,** Daniel R, Darien, NY, 1ST MAR DIV 2ND MAR DIV KO +
CPL **Masterson,** Thomas M, Plainfield, IL, HQ CO 1/1, HQ BTRY 1/11
LCPL **Mastripol,** J V, Bowie, MD, A-1-5 VN +
SGT **Mateo,** L M, South Lake Tahoe, CA, D-2-5 KO +
SSGT **Materna,** Rick H, Plymouth, MN, C-1-5 G-2-3 VN +

SGT **Mateyko,** Edward J, Oceanside, NY, 3DEF 12AAA WWII +
**Matheny,** Robert W SR., New Franken, WI, BMU ATT 1MAR WWII KO +
HM3 **Matheson,** James, Fort Wright, KY, F-2-1 KO +
SGT **Mathews,** E L, East Falmouth, MA, 1ENGR KO +
LCDR **Mathews,** Mary A, El Paso, TX, NAVMED VN +
CPL **Mathiesen,** Richard D, Sunapee, NH, WPNS-2-5 KO +
MAJ **Mathis,** Don E, Evensville, TN, HQ-11/27MAR VN +
MAJ **Mathis,** Jack D, Atlantic Beach, FL, RECON VN +
LCPL **Mathues,** Timothy I, Solana Beach, CA, 1-7 FLSG VN +
**Matsumoto,** Ralph "Lil Pineapple", Gardena, CA, B-1-1 KO +
SGT **Matthews,** George B, Chico, CA, G-2-5 A-1-5 WWII CH KO +
SGT **Matthews,** John M, Vero Beach, FL, D-1-1 VN +
CPL **Matthews,** Lawrence R JR., Stuart, FL, A/B/H&S-3AMTRAC VN +
LCPL **Matthews,** Phillip A, Bay City, MI, L-3-5 VN +
CPL **Mattine,** Robert W, Albuquerque, NM, L-3-7 OIF +
GEN **Mattis,** James N, Richland, WA, CG-1MARDIV CO-1-7 SWA OIF +
SGT **Mattis,** John L, Camp Hill, PA, 4.2-1MAR KO +
**Matye,** Nick W, Granada Hills, CA, H&S-2-4 +
CPL **Mauger,** Michael E, Powell, OH, C-1-5 VN +
CPL **Mauldin,** Wade L, Norwood, NC, C-1ENGR WWII CH +
SGT **Mavar,** Michael P, Long Beach, CA, D-1-5 VN +
CAPT **Mawe,** Richard W, Auburn, IN, L-4-11 B-1-11 CW CMC +
HM3 **Mawhinney,** Robert J, Fort Collins, CO, H&S/I-3-5 CW +
CPL **Maxheimer,** Milton JOHN, Patterson, CA, M-4-11 CW
SSGT **Maxwell,** D Edward, Wickenburg, AZ, 1MAW WWII +
SGT **Maxwell,** Guy R, Cocoa, FL, I-3-7 VN +
**Maxwell,** Paul C JR., Orrtanna, PA, D-2-5 KO +
SGT **Maxwell,** Robert C, Saint Joseph, MO, B-1ENGR KO +
**May,** Billy E SR., Mustang, OK, D-1-5 VN +
CW3 **May,** Charles W, Astoria, OR, ARMAMPH KO +
CPL **May,** Irvin A, Willoughby, OH, H-3-7 KO +
CPL **Mayette,** Michael D, Massena, NY, 2-1 CW +
SGT **Mayeux,** Michael L, Bourg, LA, L-3-26 VN +
SGT **Mayhew,** Roland D, Topeka, KS, G-3-11 C-1-7 B-1-7 VN
CPL **Mayhew,** Timothy G, Mass City, MI, K-3-26 K-3-1 VN +
TSGT **Mazzia,** William L, Salinas, CA, 3-5MAR CW +
SGT **Mazzone,** Richard W, Winthrop, MA, H&S-2-7 KO +
LCPL **McAllister,** Charles W, Martinsburg, WV, K-3-1 VN +
SGT **McAllister,** Conrad O, Winter Park, FL, H-2-5 1MAW VN +
CWO5 **McAlpine,** Kenneth Guy, Phoenix, AZ, 7ESB 1LAR 1MARDIV G-4 OIF OEF +
SGT **McAndrews,** Edward T, Brunswick, OH, C-1-5 KO
LCPL **McAndrews,** Edward, Riverton, NJ, 1RECON VN +
SGT **McAniff,** John T III, Winchester, VA, 7COMM BN 1MARDIV VN CW
CAPT **McBride,** Edward T, Rio Rancho, NM, MP-HQ/FSSG CW +
**McBride,** Tom J, State College, PA, F-2-1 WWII CH
COL **McCabe,** Thomas M, Phoenixville, PA, HQ-11MAR KO +
**McCaleb,** C F JR., Weslaco, TX, 1RECON +

*TSGT* **McCall,** Louis R, Bellevue, TX, *I/WPNS-3-7 KO +*
*PVT* **McCalla,** W.W., Studio City, CA, *R-2-5 WWII +*
*PFC* **McCargo,** Louis P, Brown Deer, WI, *L-3-5 WWII +*
*CWO4* **McCarter,** Lawrence A, Smithfield, VA, *1ENGR WWII KO VN +*
*CAPT* **McCarthy,** J R, North Fort Myers, FL, *C-1-11 KO +*
*CAPT* **McCarthy,** Joseph H, Naples, FL, *HQ-11MAR WWII CH KO +*
**McCarthy,** Mac A, Malta, NY, *H-3-11 VN +*
*HM2* **McCarthy,** Thomas F III, Metairie, LA, *HQ-3FSR VN +*
*SGT* **McCarthy,** Tom E, Carlsbad, CA, *M-3-7 VN +*
*CAPT* **McCartney,** J R, Front Royal, VA, *MAG-16 1MAW VN +*
*COL* **McCartney,** Stephen M, Warwick, RI, *E-2-1 1-25MAR VN SWA +*
*CPL* **McCarty,** Donald F, North Las Vegas, NV, *WPNS-2-5 KO +*
*SGT* **McCarville,** Ronald E, Porterville, CA, *K-3-5 VN +*
*CPL* **McCauley,** Ben F, Ravenswood, WV, *HQBN SECURITY KO +*
*GYSGT* **McCauley,** Richard A, Acworth, GA, *SVC-1SVC-FLC VN +*
*MSGT* **McChesney,** Chester H, Colbert, GA, *B-1SHPTY E-2-5 VN +*
*PFC* **McClaran,** Jack, Rio Vista, CA, *L-4-11*
*SGT* **McClendon,** William M, Kingwood, TX, *B-1-11 VN +*
**McClintock,** Earl L, Champaign, IL, *1MARDIV KO +*
*CPL* **McClory,** Robert J, Andover, MA, *1SIG HQ-5MAR KO +*
*SGT* **McCloskey,** John F JR., Colma, CA, *D-7MT CW*
*COL* **McClung,** Jim W, College Station, TX, *H-2-7 VN +*
**McClure,** Jack S, Santa Ana, CA, *A-1MED 7MT KO +*
*SGTMAJ* **McColley,** Robert L, Oceanside, CA, *1-5MAR VN +*
*COL* **McCollum,** Mike, Dallas, TX, *G-2-1 VN +*
*HA1* **McCombs,** Jack, Palm Beach Gardens, FL, *G-1-1 WWII +*
*MSGT* **McCorkle,** John F, Morganton, GA, *11MAR FLSGB KO VN +*
**McCormack,** Bert W, Santa Barbara, CA, *1-1 KO*
*CPL* **McCormack,** John F, Miller Place, NY, *E-2-4 VN +*
*CPL* **McCormack,** W Frank, Flagstaff, AZ, *1RECON-28MAR VN +*
*SSGT* **McCormick,** John P, Fannin, TX, *1PROVAAA KO +*
*CAPT* **McCormick,** Len G, Houston, TX, *HQ-HQ KO +*
**McCoy,** Charles A, Moreno Valley, CA, *3DEF WWII KO +*
*SGTMAJ* **McCoy,** James H, Jacksonville, NC, *F-2-5 VN +*
*PFC* **McCrary,** H W, Luxemburg, WI, *F-2-1 KO +*
*SGT* **McCrary,** James W, Dallas, TX, *MAG-23 VMF224 WWII +*
*SGT* **McCrary,** Patrick E, Pace, FL, *A-1-5 VN +*
*SGT* **McCreless,** John D, Gadsden, AL, *C/1/7 VN*
*HM2* **McCrory,** Jack E, Corona, CA, *D-2-5 C-1MED KO +*
*CPL* **McCrossen,** John P, Belle Chasse, LA, *A-1-11 VN +*
*BGEN* **McCulloch,** William L, Alexandria, VA, *B-1-1 H-3-7 WWII CH KO VN +*
*CPL* **McCurry,** Holbrook E, Annandale, VA, *H&S-3-5 VN +*
*CPL* **McCurtain,** Jim T, Big Spring, TX, *B-1-7 KO +*
*SGT* **McCuskey,** Denzil H, Danville, CA, *F-2-7 KO +*
*SGT* **McDavid,** Robert P, Irondale, AL, *W-2-11 3-1MAR VN +*
*SGTMAJ* **McDermott,** Mac, Yuma, AZ, *A-1-5 VN +*
*MSGT* **McDevitt,** Homer Jackson, Irvine, CA, *HQ-1MAW KO +*
**McDonald,** David J, West Linn, OR, *F-2-5 VN +*
*SSGT* **McDonald,** Francis E, Rnch De Taos, NM, *SER-HQ-1 WWII KO +*
**McDonald,** J P, Rapid City, SD, *HQ-4-11 +*
*CAPT* **McDonald,** Kenneth M, Allentown, PA, *C-1MED BN VN +*
*SGT* **McDonald,** R H, Ellington, CT, *D-2-11 KO +*
*DR.* **McDonald,** Stanford L, Kankakee, IL, *H&S/A-1-5 KO +*
*CPL* **McDonald,** William H, Houston, TX, *D-1-5 WWII +*
*1STLT* **McDonell,** Mike G, Hilton Head Island, SC, *HQ-11MAR VN +*
**McDonnell,** Patrick (Mac) H, El Cajon, CA, *1MAW KO +*
*MAJ* **McDonough,** F M, Oakhurst, NJ, *RECON VN +*
*SGT* **McDonough,** Joseph T, Newport News, VA, *I-3-9 CW +*
*GYSGT* **McDowell,** Gerald, Eureka, CA, *1BRDG-7ENGR-IFSR-FLC VN +*
*CPL* **McEachern,** Robert A, Warren, MA, *GSM-MAINT-1ESR/FLC VN +*
*LCPL* **McElyea,** James (Jd) D, West Frankfort, IL, *1ST BN 13TH MAR 1MAR DIV VN*
*SGT* **McEnery,** James F, Ocala, FL, *K-3-5 WWII +*
*CPL* **McEntire,** John E, Holden Beach, NC, *VN*
*CPL* **McEvoy,** John F, Keizer, OR, *B-1ENGR KO +*
*CPL* **McEvoy,** Steven P, Deer Park, NY, *HQ-2-11 VN*
*TSGT* **McEwen,** C D, Long Beach, CA, *N-5-11 WWII KO*
*SGT* **McEwen,** Gerald, Chattanooga, TN, *WPNS-2-1 WWII /KO +*
*SGT* **McEwen,** Joseph C, Noblesville, IN, *C-1-5 VN +*
*MAJ* **McFadden,** John P, South Fork, CO, *VMF(N)542 KO +*
*SSGT* **McFall,** F P, La Place, LA, *AT-7MAR +*
*SGT* **McFarland,** E C, Houston, TX, *F/HQ-3-11 KO +*
**McFarland,** J W, Andover, NJ, *1 MAW VN +*
*DR* **McGannon,** R F, Norwalk, CT, *1AMTRAC +*
*CPL* **McGary,** Raleigh E, Newburgh, IN, *H&S/B-1-1 KO +*
**McGee,** Edward J, Austin, TX, *17MAR WWII +*
*MAJ* **McGee,** Edward T JR., Allen, TX, *1RECON VN +*
*CPL* **McGee,** William R, Columbus, OH, *MP-1MAR KO +*
*CPL* **McGehee,** Bill J, San Antonio, TX, *HQ-1-5 WWII +*
*SGT* **McGehee,** Cecil D, Tahoe City, CA, *WPNS CO 1-7-1 KO +*
*PHM2* **McGhee,** Harold D, Tucson, AZ, *1-1MAR CH +*
*SGT* **McGlone,** Randall K, Grayson, KY, *L-3-1 VN +*
*CPL* **McGowan,** John J, Evergreen Park, IL, *H&S-1-1 KO +*
**McGowan,** John R, Carbondale, IL, *HQ-11MAR WWII CH +*
*PFC* **McGrail,** John E, Brimley, MI, *D-2-1 KO +*
*SGT* **McGreevey,** Jack P, Carteret, NJ, *G-3-11 WWII CH KO +*
*PVT* **McGrew,** Kenneth L, Dayton, OR, *K/M-4-11 VN +*
*SGT* **McGroary,** Allan L, Lanesboro, MA, *C-1-5 VN +*
*SSGT* **McGuinness,** Raymond F, Mentor, OH, *C-1-11 KO +*
*MSGT* **McGuire,** Daniel J, Zion, IL, *K-3-5 CW SWA*
*CPL* **McGuire,** John F, Newark, DE, *B-1-7 VN SWA*
*PFC* **McGuire,** Michael J, Leominster, MA, *1TKBN I-3-7 KO +*
*PFC* **McGuire,** Ray F, Clearwater, FL, *WPNS-3-7 KO +*
*LCPL* **McGuire,** Terry W III, Willmington, NC, *WPNS-3-7 CW +*
*SSGT* **McHaney,** Charles E, Malaga, WA, *A-1MT WWII CH KO*
*HM1* **McHugh,** Jerome ROBERT, Lake Ariel, PA, *I-3-1 VN +*
*SSGT* **McInerney,** Brendan J, Wantagh, NY, *A-3AA CW +*
**McInerney,** John T, Wantagh, NY, *1-3MAR OP-CON VN +*
*SGT* **McKay,** Harry L, Pasadena, TX, *H-2-5 VN +*
*PFC* **McKay,** John G, Mechanicsville, VA, *HQ-A-1-7 WWII CH +*
*SGTMAJ* **McKelvey,** James A, Oceanside, CA, *L-3-5 E-2-5 VN +*
*SSGT* **McKenna,** Dale D, Simi Valley, CA, *G-3-1-60MM KO*
**McKeown,** Frank J JR., West Palm Beach, FL, *G-3-7 1MAR KO +*
*GYSGT* **McKernan,** Thomas A, Clinton, CT, *D-1-1 HQ-2-5 VN +*
*SGT* **McKillips,** Douglas F, Sherwood, OR, *VMA223 VN +*
*CPL* **McKillop,** James E, Fresno, CA, *4TH JASCO 2-5 +*
*SSGT* **McKinney,** John M, Prescott, AZ, *HQ/D/E-2-11 KO +*
*SGT* **McKinnon,** John JR., Lady Lake, FL, *H&S-1AMTRAC KO +*
*CPL* **McKinnon,** Melvin D, Lebanon, OR, *D-1-5 3PLT VN +*
*SGT* **McLauchlan,** Jack H, Allyn, WA, *D-2-1 KO +*
**McLaughlin,** B D, Tujunga, CA, *A-1-7 VN +*
*CPL* **McLaughlin,** John J, Medford, MA, *HQ-HQ KO +*
*CPL* **McLaughlin,** Thomas C, Mankato, MN, *E-2-5 VN +*
*SGT* **McLean,** Barry R, Whittier, CA, *D-2-11 KO +*
*SGT* **McLean,** Charles A, Scituate, MA, *1ST FORCE SVC REGT VN*
*1STLT* **McLean,** Robert D, Colorado Springs, CO, *HQBN KO +*
*SGT* **McLendon,** J D, Pensacola, FL, *G-3-1 KO +*
*1STLT* **McLeod,** John K, Santa Ana, CA, *B-1-1 KO +*
*SSGT* **McLeod,** Philip W, San Leandro, CA, *WPNS-2-1 WWII CH KO +*
*STS3* **McLeod,** Tom R, Texarkana, TX, *1ST MAR DIV HISTORIAN VN +*
**McLeroy,** Richard W, Sharpsburg, GA, *E-2-1 B-SHPTY KO +*
**McMackin,** Douglas K, Litchfield Park, AZ, *C-7ENGR VN +*
*LCPL* **McMahan,** Larry K, San Antonio, TX, *1 MAR DIV*
*CPL* **McMahon,** Arthur L, Vail, AZ, *A-1-11 KO +*
**McMahon,** Charles G, Glenmoore, PA, *H-2-5 VN +*
*1STLT* **McMahon,** Dennis J, Canfield, OH, *E-2-7 H&S-2-7 VN +*
*SGT* **McMahon,** John E, Clearfield, PA, *E-2-11 VN*
**McManigal,** William L, Harker Heights, TX, *HQ-HQ CW +*
*LTCOL* **McManus,** J D, Peoria, IL, *H&S-5MAR HQ CH KO +*
*CPL* **McManus,** John A, Vicksburg, MI, *I-3-7 1MAR DIV VN*
**McMillan,** Grace, Huntley, IL, *ASSOCIATE **
*CPL* **McMillan,** Richard L, Huntley, IL, *HQ/A/C-1-7 KO*
*CPL* **McMinn,** E L, Elkridge, MD, *D-2-7 KO +*
*MAJGEN* **McMonagle,** James J, Vista, CA, *CG H-3-5 KO VN CW +*
*SSGT* **McMullin,** Perry V, Locust Grove, GA, *H&S-1-5 VN +*
*CAPT* **McMurray,** Daniel D, Toledo, OH, *B-1-7 VN*
**McMurray,** R H, Webster Groves, MO, *HQBN WWII CH +*
*CPL* **McNabb,** Charles L, Rossville, GA, *D-2-11 KO*
*CPL* **McNally,** Daniel J, Simi Valley, CA, *WPNS-1-9 1MAR CW +*
*SSGT* **McNally,** Edward J, Simi Valley, CA, *HQ-17MAR WWII CH +*
*CAPT* **McNamara,** Michael K, Edmond, OK, *HQBN VN +*
*SGTMAJ* **McNeive,** Francis T, Jacksonville, NC, *G-3-1 KO VN +*
*CPL* **McPeek,** Marshall (Mac), Milford, NJ, *C-1-5 VN*
*MSGT* **McPhail,** William T, Glen Burnie, MD, *A-1ENGR WWII CH KO +*
*SSGT* **McPherson,** Lewis E, Dallas, TX, *1CSG KO +*

*CPL* **McPherson,** William MORGAN III, Glendora, CA, *H&S 1/5 VN*
*1STSGT* **McPhetres,** William A, Surprise, AZ, *1ANGLICO KO* +
*CPL* **McRay,** Roy C SR., Cassoday, KS, *A-1AMTRAC KO* +
*SGT* **McVey,** Warren L, Spring Hill, KS, *A-1-7 KO* +
**McWilliams,** D. (Mac) G, Fair Oaks Ranch, TX, *H&S-5MAR WWII CH* +
*SGT* **Mead,** Duane D, Tyler, TX, *C-1-1 KO* +
**Mead,** Lee N, Smithtown, NY, *D-2-11 I-3-1 KO* +
*CPL* **Meade,** John F, South Glens Falls, NY, *F-2-5 KO* +
*SFC* **Meade,** Michael L, Garden City, ID, *ENGR-MAINT-1FSR HQ-1-1 VN* +
**Meagher,** Robert E, North Branford, CT, *MAINT-1ORD KO* +
*1STSGT* **Meaney,** Raymond W, South Richmond Hill, NY, *1MAW KO* +
**Medal,** Lou H, El Dorado Hills, CA, *WPNS-2-5 KO* +
*MSGT* **Medina,** Edgar JOE, Roseville, CA, *M-3-1 VN* +
*CAPT* **Mednis,** Alfons J, Willow Grove, PA, *W-3-1 KO VN* +
*CAPT* **Meegan,** George B, Tempe, AZ, *1RECON I/L-3-26 VN*
*CPL* **Meehan,** Bernard M, Danbury, CT, *C-1-5 KO* +
*CPL* **Meehan,** James J, Port Chester, NY, *D-1-1 VN* +
**Meenach,** Donald L, Circleville, OH, *E-2-11 KO* +
*MGEN* **Megarr,** Edward J, Napa, CA, *D-2-5 KO* +
*CPL* **Mehigan,** J.J., Watertown, MA, *1AMTRAC MT CW* +
*SGT* **Meier,** Ernest B, Shoreline, WA, *E-2-5 KO*
*CPL* **Meier,** Kenneth F, Granbury, TX, *F-2-1 KO* +
*LTCOL* **Meier,** Paul N, Fairfax, VT, *C-1-5 VN CW*
*2NDLT* **Meikle,** J W, Mount Shasta, CA, *WPNS/C-1-7 KO* +
*SGT* **Meiners,** Leonard F, Saint Clair, MO, *A-1AR-MAMPH KO* +
*LTCOL* **Melanphy,** Sean M,, CA, *1ST MAR DIV G4*
**Melbourne,** R E, San Luis Rey, CA, *AMPHIB-CB#1 KO* +
*GYSGT* **Mell,** Frank E JR., San Marcos, CA, *1 MAW KO VN* +
*LCPL* **Mellon,** Ross S, South Dennis, MA, *L-3-7 VN* +
*SGT* **Mellott,** G A JR., Riverside, CA, *MAINT-1FSSG CW* +
*GYSGT* **Mellott,** George A SR., Riverside, CA, *G-3-5 KO* +
*1STLT* **Melnick,** Gregory E JR., Winter Park, FL, *D-1-5 B-1RECON VN*
*SGT* **Melton,** Howard L, Moneta, VA, *B-1-11 VN* +
**Melton,** Peter G, Houston, TX, *HQ VN* +
*PFC* **Melton,** Robert L III, Mesquite, TX, *C-1-5 VN* +
*SGTMAJ* **Memmer,** Howard J, Pleasanton, CA, *D-2-11 WWII VN* +
**Memorial Club,** Marines, San Francisco, CA, +
**Menagh,** Philip J, Lake Oswego, OR, *
*PFC* **Menary,** Joseph W, Williamsburg, IA, *F-2-1 KO* +
*PFC* **Mendez,** Gustavo C, Scottsdale, AZ, *I-3-1 KO* +
*CPL* **Mendivil,** Manuel H, Los Angeles, CA, *G-2-7 VN* +
**Mendoza,** Jose G, Chula Vista, CA, *4.2 1MAR KO* +
*MR.* **Menge,** Henry J, New Port Richey, FL, *ORD 1CSG KO* +
*CPL* **Mennie,** G K, Detroit, MI, *1FORREC* +
**Mennis,** Jack, Allison Park, PA, *H&H5 MCAS*
*CAPT* **Menzelos,** Soterios (Sam) J, Rancho Palos Verdes, CA, *K-3-5 WWII CH KO* +
*LCPL* **Merboth,** John M, Waldwick, NJ, *F-2-5 VN* +
*CPL* **Mercer,** James W.D.L SR., Levittown, PA, *E-1RECON VN* +
*MSGT* **Mercier,** Paul ROBERT, Lutts, TN, *FLSU1-FLC 9MAB VN* +
*SSGT* **Meredith,** Donald P, Hawthorne, FL, *E-2-5 KO* +
*SGTMAJ* **Meringolo,** Albert A, Washington, DC, *WPNS-3-5 KO* +
*1STLT* **Merna,** Gerald F, Arlington, VA, *WPNS/HQ-1-5 E-2-5 KO VN* +
*CPL* **Meseure,** John F, Van Nuys, CA, *C-1-7 KO* +
*SGT* **Messina,** Samuel V, Canonsburg, PA, *1SVC KO* +
*CPL* **Metoyer,** David I, Fontana, CA, *K-3-1 VN* +
*SGT* **Mets,** Gerald T, Ventura, CA, *1ORD KO* +
**Mettler,** Michael, Rye, NY, *MAG25-MADS1 WWII* +
*SGT* **Meunier,** Philip N, Washington, ME, *HQ COM CO 5TH MAR VN*
*MAJ* **Meyer,** Larry D, Richmond, VA, *A-1-5 CW SWA* +
*CAPT* **Meyers,** John F, Oceanside, CA, *C-1-1 CH KO* +
**Meytrott,** W B, Pennington, NJ, *B-1-7 VN* +
*CWO* **Meza,** Michael, San Clemente, CA, *7MAR WWII CH KO* +
*PFC* **Michael,** Robert A, Elberta, MI, *B-1-1 WWII* +
*MGYSGT* **Michalak,** William N, Kailua, HI, *2-1 5MAR OIF* +
*LCPL* **Michalski,** Steve W, Saint Louis, MO, *D-1-1 CW* +
*SSGT* **Michaud,** E R, Canton, MA, *MT-7MAR KO* +
*SGT* **Michell,** William J, Hicksville, NY, *COMM CO. 7TH COMM BN VN*
*MSGT* **Mickle,** George W, Vista, CA, *COMM CO HQBN 1MARDIV KO CW* +
*SSGT* **Middaugh,** F E, Galesburg, IL, *HQ-1-11 KO* +
*SGT* **Mielke,** James H, Appleton, WI, *SVC-1ENGR KO* +
**Mignano,** Ernest (Doc) R, Brooklyn, NY, *L-3-1 VN* +
*CPL* **Mikel,** Albert (Bill) W, Redford, MI, *81MM HQ-3-1 WWII CH* +
*MAJ* **Mikolajczak,** Frank E, Triangle, VA, *9COMM SWA* +
*CPL* **Milano,** Anthony A, Johnston, RI, *E-2-7 VN*
**Milburn,** Jerome B, Baltimore, MD, *A-7MT KO* +
*MAJ* **Miley,** George P, Menomonee Falls, WI, *E-2-5 CW* +
*MR.* **Miller,** Andrew T, Jupiter, FL, *B-1-7 KO* +
**Miller,** Carl W, Indialantic, FL, *B-1-5 VN* +
*HM2* **Miller,** Charles T, Saint Albans, WV, *K-4-11 VN* +
*CPL* **Miller,** Charles W, Willow Street, PA, *HQ/A-1-7 VN* +
*CPL* **Miller,** David M, Loveland, OH, *L-3-5 VN* +
*SGT* **Miller,** Edward D, Milton, MA, *HQ-1MAR KO* +
**Miller,** Fern A, Golden Valley, AZ, *ASSOCIATE*
*LCPL* **Miller,** Gary D, Erdenheim, PA, *HQ-26MAR VN* +
*LT* **Miller,** George W, Charleston, SC, *B-1-1 CH* +
*SSGT* **Miller,** Guy L III, Indianapolis, IN, *1SVC KO*
*CPL* **Miller,** Herbert L, Scottsdale, AZ, *A-1-1 KO* +
*WO1* **Miller,** J W, Katy, TX, *1RECON VN* +
*PFC* **Miller,** Jack L, Sun City West, AZ, *4-8INHOW(SP) A-4-11 CW* +
*CAPT* **Miller,** James R, Saratoga, CA, *VMF224 F-2-11 WWII KO*
*MRS* **Miller,** Jeanette, Phoenix, AZ, *ASSOCIATE*
*CPL* **Miller,** John J, Sutter, CA, *HQ-26MAR VN* +
*1STSGT* **Miller,** Joseph M, Oswayo, PA, *H&S/K/M-3-7 VN* +
*HM3* **Miller,** Larry L, Pierre, SD, *C-1-5 1MED VN* +
*CPL* **Miller,** Larry V, Golden Valley, AZ, *1ST RE-CONBN 1ST MAR VN* +
*PFC* **Miller,** Murray A, Berrien Springs, MI, *H-3-7 KO* +
*CPL* **Miller,** Robert J, Orland Park, IL, *175 GUN-11 MAR-VN*
*1STLT* **Miller,** Robert S III, Virginia Beach, VA, *29CA VN* +
*SSGT* **Miller,** Roy, Bend, OR, *H&S-1-5 1PROV-MARBDE KO* +
*SGT* **Miller,** T L, Chicago, IL, *M-3-1 VN* +
*MAJ* **Miller,** W D, Pauma Valley, CA, *A-1ARMAM-PH KO* +
*CAPT* **Miller,** W E, Phoenix, AZ, *VMCJ-1MAR VN* +
*PFC* **Miller,** W J, Wollastom, MA, *K-4-11 KO* +
*CPL* **Miller,** William J, Boring, OR, *E-2-7 KO* +
*1STSGT* **Millett,** Robert J, Canyon, TX, *M-4-11 VN*
*GYSGT* **Milligan,** Otis D, Austin, TX, *F-2-1 G-2/3-5 KO VN* +
*SGT* **Mills,** John D, Evansville, IN, *H/I-3-7 KO* +
*LCPL* **Mills,** Thomas F, Dry Ridge, KY, *B-2-7 KO* +
*MAJ* **Mills,** William F, Winchester, VA, *F-2-5 KO VN* +
*LCPL* **Milsop,** Daniel, Hockley, TX, *I-3-5 VN* +
*MAJ* **Mimiaga,** William R, Costa Mesa, CA, *M-4-11 VN SWA* +
*CAPT* **Mincey,** David L JR., Lizella, GA, *11MAR VN* +
*CAPT* **Miner,** G M, Wenatchee, WA, *C-1-5 CW* +
*SSGT* **Mink,** Michael T, Hubert, NC, *MAG-16-OIF* +
*SSGT* **Minnery,** James W, Elyria, OH, *7ITT VN*
*SGT* **Minor,** William T, Euclid, OH, *E-2-7 KO* +
**Minter,** H C JR., Telford, PA, *E-2-7 KO* +
*SGT* **Minter,** Roland T, Oxford, WI, *7TH REG. 1ST MARDIV KO* +
*MR.* **Mirabella,** Joseph P, Morehead City, NC, *HQ-3-5 WWII* +
**Miratsky,** Tony JR., Omaha, NE, *BAND CSG KO* +
*CPL* **Misch,** George J, Mentor, OH, *A-1-5 WWII CH* +
*CPL* **Mish,** Erik P, Buffalo, NY, *G BTRT, 2 BN 11MAR SWA*
*LCPL* **Mish,** V G, Niagara Falls, NY, *HQ PLT-PMC, 1ST FSR CW*
*GYSGT* **Mishik,** John P, Woodstock, GA, *1MAW CW*
*GYSGT* **Mishik,** Neal P, Staten Island, NY, *A-1 ENGR KO* +
*SGT* **Mitchell,** Gary E, Avondale, PA, *E-2-5 VN*
*LCPL* **Mitchell,** Jack B, Woodland, CA, *M-3-1 VN* +
*SGT* **Mitchell,** Richard G, Hudson, MA, *K-3-5 VN* +
*SGT* **Mitchell,** Richard S JR., Elk, CA, *F-2-1 G-3-7 WWII CH KO* +
*SGT* **Mitchell,** Robert J, Houston, TX, *B-1-7 KO*
*LTCOL* **Mitchell,** Robert L, Orange, CA, *A-3MT KO VN* +
*HM2* **Mitchell,** Thomas J, Laurel, MD, *K/L-3-5 VN* +
*PFC* **Mitnick,** Norman, Philadelphia, PA, *H&S 1MAW WWII CH*
*SGT* **Mittendorf,** Donald R, Scottsdale, AZ, *G-3-7 KO* +
**Mixon,** John D, Bakersfield, CA, *B-TK WWII KO* +
*LTCOL* **Modder,** Donald J, Annandale, VA, *1ENGR HQ-HQ SWA* +
*CPL* **Modisette,** Joe L, Little Rock, AR, *E-2-7 KO* +
*CPL* **Moeller,** Gus A, Leesburg, FL, *I-3-7 KO* +
*CPL* **Moffatt,** George H, Palm Desert, CA, *SEA GNG AMTRAC*
*CPL* **Moffet,** Michael R, Jamestown, OH, *W BTRY 2-11, 4-11 HQ*
*COL* **Moffett,** J W, Mission Viejo, CA, *1-7 2-5-1 VN* +
*COL* **Moffett,** John C, Dallas, TX, *1-11MAR VN CW* +
*PFC* **Moffett,** Miller F, Goodrich, TX, *E-2-5 WWII CH* +
*CPL* **Mohn,** Gerald K SR., Reading, PA, *F-2-17 WWII* +
*LTCOL* **Moisuk,** John JR., Richardson, TX, *5-11MAR SWA CW* +
*GYSGT* **Molina,** John JR., San Jose, CA, *B-1-9 I-3-1 CW* +
*CPL* **Molle,** Blasco M, Collingswood, NJ, *HQ-3-7 WWII CH* +
*TSGT* **Mollo,** Salvatore F, Oxnard, CA, *B-1-7 KO* +
*PFC* **Mollon,** Leslie, Novi, MI, *H&S-1ENGR CH* +
*CPL* **Moloy,** Ronald J, Blue Springs, MO, *B-1-7 WWII KO* +
*SGT* **Molsbee,** John R, El Dorado, AR, *MACG-2 KO* +
*CPL* **Molstead,** David A, New Boston, MI, *C-1-5 VN* +
*HMCS* **Monaco,** Martin L, Sarasota, FL, *A-1ARM-AMPH E-1MED KO VN*
**Monahan,** Henry, Palm Desert, CA, *1 MAW MAG 52*

*SGT* **Monahan,** Richard J, San Rafael, CA, *3RD MAW WWII* +
*CPL* **Monahan,** Terrence P, Dudley, MA, *B-1TK VN* +
*CPL* **Moncrief,** Dwayne L, Olympia, WA, *A-1-5 VN* +
*CAPT* **Monroe,** Anthony A, Belmont, CA, *A-1-5/7 VN* +
*HM3* **Monroe,** Bradford H JR., Grantham, NH, *F-2-7 KO* +
*ARM 1/C USN* **Monroe,** Charles E, Riverside, CA, *VT8 TORPEDO WWII* +
*PFC* **Monroe,** Richard A, Fenton, MI, *M-3-1 VN CW*
*CPL* **Monroe,** Thomas E, Saint Louis, MO, *HQ CO 3RD BN 24TH MAR*
*SGT* **Montecino,** Sidney G, Metairie, LA, *H&S-1MAR KO* +
*CPL* **Monteverde,** Christopher Roman, Las Vegas, NV, *H&S-3-5 CW* +
*SGT* **Montgomery,** Donald L, Thousand Oaks, CA, *1MP-H&S-HQBN KO* +
*CPL* **Montgomery,** John A, Houston, TX, *COMM SPT CO-7-1*
*MRS* **Montgomery,** Rita, Dallas, TX, *ASSOCIATE* *
*LTCOL* **Montgomery,** Robert R, Dallas, TX, *B-1TK WWII KO VN* +
**Montgomery,** Robin L, Brookfield, CT, *A-1-5 WTB QUANTICO VN*
**Montgomery,** Tamara O, Souderton, PA, *ASSOCIATE*
**Monti,** Konrad P, Burbank, CA, *A-1-21 24DIV KO* +
*PFC* **Montoya,** Dennis C, Seal Beach, CA, *H-3-5 KO* +
*SGT* **Montoya,** Scott C, La Puente, CA, *2ND BN 23 MAR OIF*
*SMSGT* **Moody,** Henry C, Leesville, LA, *B-1-1 KO* +
*SGT* **Moody,** J E, San Benito, TX, *MT-2-1 KO* +
*CAPT* **Mook,** David, Newbury Park, CA, *HQ-HQ 3AMTRAC VN* +
*CPL* **Moon,** Deuk-Yong, Gyeongsangnam-Do, Korea, *VN*
**Moon,** Don E, Katy, TX, *MAG-36&37-MAW VN* +
*CPL* **Mooney,** Richard (Moon-Man) B, Floral Park, NY, *81MM/E-2-7 VN* +
*SGT* **Moore,** Allen E, Hood River, OR, *SVC/SUP-1SVC KO* +
**Moore,** Charles L, Lake Worth, FL, *1MED-1RECON WWII VN* +
*GYSGT* **Moore,** Colvin C, Bandera, TX, *REG 5MAR KO* +
*LCPL* **Moore,** David L, Oceanside, CA, *C-1-5 VN* +
*LCPL* **Moore,** Eric L, Aliso Viejo, CA, *B-1-5 OIF* +
*LTCOL* **Moore,** Jacques J JR., Richmond, VA, *3-7MAR CW* +
**Moore,** James E, San Antonio, TX, *E-2-7 HQ-HQ KO VN* +
*CPL* **Moore,** Jerry P, San Antonio, TX, *C/1/11, H&S 3rd Med 1/9, 3MAW*
*MAJ* **Moore,** Lawrence R, Catalina, AZ, *A-1SHPTY 1MAR KO* +
*MAJGEN* **Moore,** Marc A, Escondido, CA, *3-1MAR ADC-CG KO VN* +
*CPL* **Moore,** Neal E, Long Beach, CA, *H&S-1FSSG 1ENGR CW* +
*SGT* **Moore,** P L, Fremont, CA, *H&S-3AMTRAC CJHP* +
*TSGT* **Moore,** Richard, Cibolo, TX, *9TH ENG*
*CAPT* **Moore,** Ronald D, Chowchilla, CA, *D-1MP VN* +
*PFC* **Moore,** Russell L, Woody, CA, *B-1-5 WWII* +
*MSGT* **Moore,** William E, Pittsburgh, PA, *E-2-5 KO* +
*CPL* **Moorehead,** Gerald A, Granger, IA, *H-2-7 VN* +
**Moran,** Edward J, Wilmington, DE, *I-3-11 KO* +
*SGT* **Moraza,** Pete JR., Santa Maria, CA, *SUP-1SVC KO* +
**Morbitzer,** Edward A JR., Richardson, TX, *ASSOCIATE* *
*MRS* **Morehead,** Barbara, Kokomo, IN, *
*SGT* **Moreno,** David C JR., San Antonio, TX, *1MAR VN* +
*CPL* **Moreno,** Emanuel R, Sun City, CA, *WPNS-1-5 KO* +
*SGT* **Moreno,** Michael G, Rosemead, CA, *1FSSG CW* +
*PFC* **Morey,** Floyd, San Leandro, CA, *B-1-1-1 CH* +
*PFC* **Morey,** William A, Monroe, NH, *H-2-1 VN* +
*SGT* **Morgan,** Evert L, Lindsay, CA, *M-3-1 VN* +
*SSGT* **Morgan,** Mitchell P, Oceanside, CA, *HQ-HQ 1ST SVC BN* +
*CPL* **Morgani,** Wilmer J, New Orleans, LA, *H-3-1 KO* +
*LCPL* **Morgret,** Andrew J, Memphis, TN, *1ST MAR DIV BAND* +
*CPL* **Morie,** Lawrence M, Ferguson, MO, *MAG16-1MAW CW*
*SGT* **Morley,** Cephas R, Chatfield, MN, *HQ-11MAR KO* +
*SGT* **Morley,** Peter J, Hazlet, NJ, *B-1-7 CW* +
*SGT* **Morrell,** Haskel L, Bristol, TN, *I-3-7 KO* +
*GYSGT* **Morris,** Anthony G, Conrad, MT, *A-1-1, 1ST RECON VN* +
*SGT* **Morris,** Douglas K, Sussex, NJ, *H&S/D-2-11 VN* +
**Morris,** Frank T, Prescott, AZ, *HQ-2-1 WWII CH* +
*CPL* **Morris,** Glenn A, Thornton, CO, *3-7MAR 2-5MAR VN* +
*SSGT* **Morris,** James THURMAN, Bakersfield, CA, *VMFAF 122 VMF AW 235 VN* +
*CPL* **Morris,** Joe T, Satsuma, FL, *H&S 5MAR WWII CH* +
*CPL* **Morris,** Robert M, Lee's Summit, MO, *4.2-7MAR KO* +
*SGT* **Morris,** Troy, Cambridge, MD, *C-1-5-VN* +
*SGT* **Morris,** William H, Rock Hill, SC, *H&S-2-7 VN* +
*MSGT* **Morrison,** Donald F, Easthampton, MA, *1MAW WAR/ERA* +
*SGT* **Morrison,** Ellis A, Hillview, KY, *G-2-5 VN* +
*MAJ* **Morrison,** John R, Spring, TX, *A/B-1-11 VN*
*SGT E-5* **Morrison,** Ronald L, Fogelsville, PA, *HQ 1ST MAR DIV 5TH MAR REGT*
*CPL* **Morrissey,** W P, Burlington, MA, *A-1-5 KO* +
*LTCOL* **Morrow,** John A, Libertyville, IL, *3-5MAR CW*
*CPL* **Mortensen,** James H, Vacaville, CA, *H&S/A-1-5 KO* +
*PFC* **Mortensen,** Noland M, Littleton, CO, *D-2-1 KO* +
*1STSGT* **Mortenson,** Carl R, Burnsville, MN, *1MAW WWII KO* +
*CPL* **Morton,** Clyde D, Daytona Beach, FL, *1ANGLICO 1-5MAR KO* +
*SGT* **Morton,** Richard B, Redwood City, CA, *RECON G-3-7 KO* +
*CPL* **Mosbrucker,** Gene J, Portland, OR, *2-4 1MAR BRGDE FLT MAR*
*2NDLT* **Mosca,** Edward J JR., Miami Gardens, FL, *SEC CO 1ST CMB SVC GRP KO*
*SGT* **Moschin,** Robert S, Phelan, CA, *ORD-SVC KO* +
*MSGT* **Mosemak,** Michael, Gulfport, MS, *G-3-11 WWII KO VN* +
*CPL* **Mosher,** Arthur F, Derry, NH, *H-2-5 H&S 3-5 VN*
*E-5* **Mosis,** Dirk P III, Boerne, TX, *B-1TK CW* +
**Mosqueda,** Edward M, Tustin, CA, *K-3-7 VN* +
*SGT* **Moss,** Kerry B, Cocoa, FL, *H-2-7 H&S-3-7 VN* +
*MAJ* **Mossler,** Al H, Woodbridge, VA, *HQ-4-11 VN* +
*LCPL* **Moszcienski,** Stanley F, Bernville, PA, *1DN 5MAR 1MARDIV* +
**Mothershed,** W, Garden Grove, CA, *3D-175 GUN WWII* +
**Moyer,** Patrick, Bullhead City, AZ, *1/7MT CJHP* +
*CAPT* **Moyse,** R A, Wimborne, England, *RM-41 KO* +
*MSGT* **Muceus,** Jerry B, Manzanita, OR, *1TK 2-7MAR VN* +
*1STSGT* **Mueller,** C R, Gulf Shores, AL, *H&S-1-7 CW* +
*COL* **Mueller,** Joe N, Chatsworth, CA, *G-2-7 CW* +
*PFC* **Mueller,** John C, Baltimore, MD, *SVE-1SVC CH* +
*CPL* **Muhl,** Jonathan P, Stony Creek, NY, *B-1ST RECON BN 1-7 CW*
*SGT* **Muhs,** Fred W, Highland Village, TX, *HQ-4-11 VN* +
*SGT* **Muir,** Donald W, Middlesex, NJ, *4.2/H-3-7 KO* +
*SSGT* **Mulcahy,** Richard N, Ofallon, MO, *1SIG-1CSG WWII KO* +
*SGT* **Mulkey,** Jess O, Monroe, GA, *HQ-2-5 CH* +
**Mullan,** Catherine M, Mesa, AZ, *
*SSGT* **Mullan,** John A, Mesa, AZ, *C-1-5 VN* +
**Mullen,** John M, Irving, TX, *3-11MAR 2-9MAR VN* +
*CPL* **Mullen,** Thomas W, Sioux City, IA, *H&S-3-5 VN* +
*HM3* **Mullins,** Thurman G, Lebanon, TN, *D-1RECON VN* +
*LCPL* **Mullis,** Arthur C, Roanoke Rapids, NC, *B-1-5 VN*
*CPL* **Mulrain,** Charles B, Pembroke, MA, *B-1-7 WWII* +
*MGYSGT* **Mulvihill,** Matthew J JR., Fountain Valley, CA, *F-2-7 H&S-1MEF SWA CW* +
*SGT* **Munro,** Robert M, Salem, MA, *F-2-5 KO* +
*CAPT* **Muraki,** Yoshiyuki C, Portland, OR, *B/A-1ENGR SWA CW* +
*PFC* **Murdock,** John M, Gainesville, GA, *H&S 1/5 C1/5 VN*
*CPL* **Murfin,** Walter L, Beaverton, OR, *1ST MAR DIV*
*MAJ* **Murkey,** M.F., Timonium, MD, *1-SHPTY KO* +
*SGT* **Murphy,** Braeden D, Lyndon, KS, *2AA OIF* +
*CPL* **Murphy,** David J, Hancock, MI, *1ST MAR VN*
*SGT* **Murphy,** Donald R, Flushing, MI, *C-1-11 KO* +
*COL* **Murphy,** Edward S, Yuma, AZ, *A-1-5 MT KO* +
*PFC* **Murphy,** Harry J, Circle, MT, *H-3-7 HQ-2-11 KO*
*PFC* **Murphy,** Jack MCKINLEY, Princeton, WV, *D-1-1-3RD MAR DIV VN*
*MAJ* **Murphy,** James L, Los Osos, CA, *1ST ENG DIV 1ST MAR DIV KO VN* +
*CPL* **Murphy,** John J, Jamestown, CA, *DIV BAND KO CW* +
*SGT* **Murphy,** John J, Santa Maria, CA, *HQ-1-11 1LAI SWA* +
*SGT* **Murphy,** Joseph M, Scarsdale, NY, *G-3-5 KO* +
*SSGT* **Murphy,** L E JR., Malvern, AR, *1TK-1FSR KO VN* +
*FTM1* **Murphy,** Michael J, Ridgecrest, CA, *CG11 USS CHICAGO VN* +
*CPL* **Murphy,** Patrick A, Fulton, MS, *I-3-11 CW* +
*SGT* **Murphy,** Robert E, Northglenn, CO, *C-1SHPTY KO* +
*MAJ* **Murphy,** Vincent B JR., Far Hills, NJ, *C-1-5 KO* +
*PFC* **Murray,** J P, Billerica, MA, *H&S-5MAR F-2-17 WWII* +
*SSGT* **Murray,** Robert J, Independence, OR, *RECON-1MAW VN* +
*SSGT* **Murtagh,** John J, Slingerlands, NY, *C-1 4.5-11MAR KO* +
**Murtaugh,** Thomas H JR., Woodbridge, NJ, *NBG-1-CB* +
*CAPT* **Musilli,** John A, Boyes Hot Springs, CA, *5-1MAR KO* +
*CPL* **Musk,** Norman E, Windsor, CT, *HQ-1-5 KO* +
*PFC* **Mussatto,** C R, Melrose Park, IL, *B-1-5 KO* +
*CPL* **Mussehl,** Ralph E, Lewiston, MI, *I-3-7 VN*
*SGT* **Musser,** Edward N, Fairview Heights, IL, *H&S/D-2-5 KO* +
*SSGT* **Musser,** Eldon JR., Phoenix, AZ, *1MAW KO* +
*SGT* **Muster,** Frederic P, Leland, NC, *E-2-5 L-3-4 VN* +
*SGT* **Muszel,** Sam, Flushing, NY, *I-3-7 VN* +
*MAJGEN* **Myatt,** James M, San Francisco, CA, *HQ-HQ VN SWA* +
*SGT* **Myers,** James D, North Olmsted, OH, *B-1-5 C-1-7 VN*
*CPL* **Myers,** James D, Tulsa, OK, *I-3-5 VN* +
*SGT* **Myers,** John D, Columbus, OH, *A-1 ENGR KO* +
*CPL* **Myers,** John E, Hilton Head Island, SC, *C-1-5TH REGT KO* +

*CPL* **Myrick,** Joseph N, Lakebay, WA, *HQ-HQ VN* +
*SGT* **Nadeau,** Pierre J, Lino Lakes, MN, *AT-1MAR KO* +
*SGT* **Nally,** Joseph F, Brooklyn, NY, *3AMTRAC WWII* +
*PHM3* **Napier,** Burnett, Frankfort, KY, *HQ/B-1-1 WWII CH* +
*GYSGT* **Naples,** Dominic J, Damascus, MD, *E-2-5 H-3-3 KO CW* +
*CPL* **Naples,** Jan S, Brooklyn, OH, *AMMO-1ORD KO* +
*LCPL* **Napolitano,** Thomas, Chicago, IL, *COMM-HQ VN* +
*CPL* **Nardolillo,** John A, Latham, NY, *C-1-4 D-1-4*
*CPL* **Nardolillo,** Peter C, Albany, NY, *1AT-1FSR VN* +
*CAPT* **Naremore,** W D, Shreveport, LA, *B-1-11 E-2-11 VN*
*LTCOL* **Nargele,** Dominik G, Arlington, VA, *HQ-HQ 5MAR VN* +
*MAJGEN* **Nash,** Gordon C, Chocowinity, NC, *HQ-7MAR H&S-1-7 CW* +
*LTGEN* **Natonski,** Richard F, Washington, DC, *1-5, HQBN CW-OIF* +
*COL* **Navarre,** R. STEWART, Rancho Santa Margarita, CA, *5MAR 2-7MAR CW SWA* +
*SSGT* **Nave,** Richard P, San Rafael, CA, *C-1AMTRAC KO* +
*CPL* **Naylor,** David H, Richmond Bc, Canada, *A-1-5 VN* +
*CPL* **Neace,** Stephen R, Wichita, KS, *C-1-5 VN*
**Neal,** C E, Rockledge, FL, *C-1-1 WWII KO* +
*CPL* **Neal,** K L, Ruston, LA, *H&S-2-7 VN* +
*SGT* **Neal,** Robert F, Oceanside, CA, *HQ-3-11 VN* +
*SSGT* **Near,** Francis J, Rome, GA, *F-2-1 WWII KO* +
*PFC* **Near,** Robert V, Athol, ID, *4.2-1-1 KO* +
*CPL* **Neas,** Edward F, Rahway, NJ, *A-1-1 VN* +
*CPL* **Neeson,** James P, Las Vegas, NV, *C-1ENGR KO* +
*CPL* **Neff,** Robert H, Gresham, OR, *B-1-1 G-2-7 CW* +
*CPL* **Negri,** E, Peoria, AZ, *S-1COMB KO* +
*SGT* **Negron,** Victor JR., Palm Beach Gardens, FL, *G-3-7 KO* +
*SGT* **Nehila,** J F JR., Phillipsburg, NJ, *ANGLICO-7 KO* +
*BGEN* **Neil,** Mike I, San Diego, CA, *D-1-7 VN* +
*MAJOR* **Neilson,** Roger B, Virginia Beach, VA, *G/3/7 KO VN*
*SSGT* **Nelson,** A T, Webster, SD, *SVC BN KO* +
*CPL* **Nelson,** Arthur J, Port Saint Lucie, FL, *VMO6 KO* +
*LCPL* **Nelson,** Daniel T, Bronx, NY, *D-1-1 VN* +
*SGT* **Nelson,** Darrell L, Mountain View, CA, *K-3-5 VN* +
*CPL* **Nelson,** Donald K, West Des Moines, IA, *WPNS 2-7*
*CAPT* **Nelson,** Scott A, Westlake Village, CA, *A/C-1-5 VN*
*SGT* **Nelson,** Wallace S, Fair Haven, VT, *B-1TK KO* +
*SGT* **Nelson,** Willard G, Anchor Point, AK, *G-2-5 K-3-1 VN* +
*CPL* **Nemec,** Frank J, West, TX, *B-TKS WWII CH* +
*SGT* **Nerenberg,** Leonard I, Concord, CA, *F-2-1 E-2-11 KO*
*MSGT* **Nesbit,** Louis LEON, Cedaredge, CO, *HQ CO, HQBN, 1STMARDIV*
*SGT* **Nesmith,** Stephen A, San Dimas, CA, *H&S-1MT VN* +
*SGT* **Nettekoven,** Arnold A, Appleton, WI, *A-1ARMAMPH KO* +
**Neuberger,** Harold C, Brookings, SD, *1MAW WWII CH KO*
*CPL* **Neuens,** E P, Fredonia, WI, *D-1TK KO* +
*CWO4* **Nevgloski,** Alexander J, Hubert, NC, *H&S-1-4 SWA* +
*CPL* **Nevin,** Charles W, Florence, MT, *1AMTRAC VN* +
*LCPL* **Newcomer,** Crist L, Chambersburg, PA, *A-1-5 VN*
*SSGT* **Newlin,** James R JR., Franklin Park, IL, *C-1-11 D-2-11 VN* +
*SGT* **Newman,** Raymond C, Roy, WA, *E-2-12 VN* +
**Newsom,** Anthony D, Framingham, MA, *K-3-3 F-2-9 VN* +
*CWO4* **Newsome,** Charles P JR., Sacramento, CA, *1AMTRAK 1 TK KO VN* +
**Newsome,** James D, Bedford, TX, *1ANGLICO 1SIG KO* +
*SGT* **Newton,** Harvey S, Ormond Beach, FL, *K-3-5 VN* +
*CPL* **Newton,** Michael A, Peabody, MA, *C-1-1 VN* +
*CPL* **Newton,** Warren D, Andrews, SC, *B-1-5 VN* +
*SGT* **Nichols,** Richard F, San Bruno, CA, *1/3MAW VMA332 KO* +
*CPL* **Nichols,** Robert, Seminole, FL, *H-3-7 KO* +
*CPL* **Nicholson,** James E MD, Rockwall, TX, *G-3-7 KO* +
*SGT* **Nick,** Daniel W, Caldwell, ID, *MAG12-MABS12/MAG16-KO* +
*PFC* **Nickels,** Harold, Bristol, VA, *I-3-1 WWII* +
**Nickerson,** Donald H, Stoughton, MA, *M-3-5 VN*
*1STLT* **Nickerson,** Les M, Atwater, CA, *B-1-1 VN* +
*1STLT* **Niehoff,** Ralph J, Cincinnati, OH, *A-1-1 KO* +
*PLTSGT* **Niehues,** Otto V, Morgan Hill, CA, *MP CO WWII CH KO* +
**Nielsen,** H D, Glendale, AZ, *C-1-5* +
*CAPT* **Niemann,** Harry C III, Holland, PA, *MACS3-1MAW KO* +
**Niner,** Francis R, Monkton, MD, *C-1ENGR KO* +
*CPL* **Nissen,** Don R, Burbank, CA, *G-3-7 WWII KO* +
*CPL* **Nix,** Ira L, Houston, TX, *A-1-5 KO* +
*SGT* **Nixon,** Dennis R, China Spring, TX, *A-1ENGR 1BRDG VN* +
*SGT* **Nixon,** Patrick B, Hanover, MD, *HQRS HC 1MAR DIV VN*
*SGT* **Niziol,** Charles, Kingwood, TX, *C-1-5 VN* +
*SGT* **Noa,** Michael S, Bayport, NY, *C-1-1 VN* +
*MAJ* **Noble,** Charles H JR., San Antonio, TX, *7/10MAR KO* +
**Noble,** F C, Santa Ana, CA, *1MAW VN* +
**Noble,** Frederick, North Syracuse, NY, *C-1-5 KO* +
*MAJ* **Nobles,** E T, Corvallis, MT, *MAG25 WWII CH KO* +
*1STSGT* **Nocifora,** James R, Woodbridge, VA, *2-11 WWII KO* +
*CPL* **Nolan,** Robert E, Norwood, MA, *H-3-7 KO* +
*SGT* **Noonan,** Robert S, Greenwood, IN, *F-2-7 KO* +
*CPL* **Noonkester,** Dan A, Bedford, TX, *S-2 L-3-5 VN* +
*CPL* **Norheim,** Eugene L, Rocklake, ND, *AMMO KO* +
*HM2* **Norman,** Howell L, Lascassas, TN, *C-1-5 VN*
*PHM2* **Norman,** William E, Springfield, OH, *C-1MED WWII* +
*LTCOL* **Norquist,** Brent R, Portland, OR, *HQ-1TK HQ-7MAR OIF SOM* +
*CPL* **Norris,** Charles H, Burbank, CA, *USS WORDEN COM PAC FLET VN* +
*CPL* **Norris,** Joseph F, Urbandale, IA, *A-3AMTRAC CW* +
*SGT* **Norris,** Lenver E, South Bend, WA, *HQ-1ENGR KO VN* +
*CPL* **Norris,** Richard D, Pass Christian, MS, *G-3-5 KO* +
*HMC (SS)* **Northern,** T K, Livonia, MI, *A-1-1 KO* +
*LTCOL* **Norton,** Bill, Vista, CA, *1ST BN 7TH MAR 1ST RECON BN*
*COL* **Norton,** Donald V, Carol Stream, IL, *SUP-1SHPTY KO* +
*SGT* **Norton,** K E, Tewksbury, MA, *1MAW KO* +
*CPL* **Norton,** Lawrence M, Quincy, MA, *H-2-5 VN*
*1STLT* **Norton,** P A, Glen Arm, MD, *F/H&S/G-2-7* +
**Norwood,** Janet, Pflugerville, TX, *GOLD STAR MOTHER* +
*SGTMAJ* **Nottingham,** Arthur W, Yuma, AZ, *G-2-7 HQ-2-5 VN* +
*CPL* **Novelli,** Theodore F, Pioneer, CA, *1TK VN* +
*LCPL* **Novicki,** Kenneth A, Palm Coast, FL, *C-1-5 VN* +
*CPL* **Novotney,** Lawrence S, Markleton, PA, *C-1-7 KO* +
*HM3* **Novotny,** Stuart M, Austintown, OH, *A-1-1 VN* +
*LCPL* **Nowik,** Thomas E, Bolingbrook, IL, *K-3-1 VN* +
*SGT* **Nunez,** Peter Peter, Houston, TX, *RECON KO* +
*CPL* **Nuno,** Arturo, Arroyo Grande, CA, *A-1AMTRAC KO* +
*CPL* **Nutley,** Bruce F, Felicity, OH, *HQ-1RECON VN* +
*CAPT* **Nuzum,** Kathleen A, Fredericksburg, VA, *COMM-H&S CW* +
*CPL* **Oakes,** Melvin L, Elmira, NY, *M-3-5 VN* +
*SGT* **Oakes,** Phillip L, Shoreline, WA, *1SVC-H&S KO* +
*SSGT* **Oaks,** Duane A SR., Lubbock, TX, *H&S-3-5 VN* +
*CPL* **Obrecht,** Jaime L, Lincoln, NE, *F-2-13 HQ-4-11 VN*
*LCDR* **Obrien,** A, Newport, RI, *B-1-5 USN SEALS* +
*PFC* **Obrien,** Frank J, Holbrook, MA, *1AMTRAC WWII* +
**Obrien,** Joseph A, Fort Lauderdale, FL, *CBMU-1 KO* +
**Obrien,** William J, Revere, MA, *C-1-7 WWII* +
*CPL* **O'Brien,** Francis R, Tucson, AZ, *K-3-1 WWII* +
*CPL* **O'Brien,** John M, Murphy, NC, *C-1-5 VN* +
*CPL* **O'Brien,** Michael J, Springfield, OH, *C-1-5 1MAR DIV VN*
*CW3* **O'Brien,** Kerry, Fairfield, CA, +
*CPL* **Oburke,** Robert S, Duncanville, TX, *WPNS-3-1 KO* +
*GYSGT* **Occhi,** Edison C, Berlin, CT, *SVC-11MAR WPNS-2-1 KO* +
*SGT* **Ockman,** Robert J JR., Metairie, LA, *1ANGLICO KO* +
*CPL* **O'con,** Roland G, Kerrville, TX, *A-1-7 KO*
*SGT* **Oconnell,** Brendon T, Reston, VA, *K-3-4/9 SOM* +
**Oconnell,** George R, Warrenton, VA, *TK VN* +
**Oconnell,** James J JR., Toms River, NJ, *SIG-1SIG KO* +
*LCPL* **Oconnell,** Paul E, Stoughton, MA, *M-3-5 VN* +
**Oconnell,** T B, New Rochelle, NY, *1PION CH* +
*SGT* **Oconnor,** Donald M, Lake Ridge, VA, *4.2-5MAR KO*
*CPL* **Oconnor,** George R, La Grange Park, IL, *G-3-1 KO* +
*CPL* **Oconnor,** John B, Orland Park, IL, *A/C-1PION WWII CH* +
*SGT* **Oconnor,** Kevin J, Midlothian, VA, *SPT LMSB VN*
*1STLT* **Oconnor,** William T III, Dallas, TX, *F-2-7 KO* +
*SGT* **O'Connor,** Arthur W JR., Fairfax, VA, *B-1AMTRAC KO* +
*SGT* **O'Connor,** James E, Gaylord, MI, *I-3-1 1RECON KO* +
*CPL* **O'Connor,** Richard G, Phoenix, AZ, *H&S CO 1-5 VN*
*SGT* **O'Connor,** Thomas J, Spotswood, NJ, *1ARMAMPH KO* +
*SGT* **Odell,** Herb W, Fort Worth, TX, *WPNS-3-7 KO* +
*SSGT* **Odom,** Arthur P, La Mirada, CA, *COMM-HQ VN* +
*SSGT* **Odom,** Arthur P, La Mirada, CA, *COMM-HQ VN* +
*SGT* **Odom,** Philip L, Houston, TX, *F-2-1ST REGT VN*
*SGT* **Odonnell,** John E CPA, Brielle, NJ, *H&S-1SHPTY VN* +
*SSGT* **Odonnell,** John P, Philadelphia, PA, *H&S-1SHPTY KO* +
*SSGT* **Odonnell,** Robert R, Gilford, NH, *F-2-5 KO* +
*SGT* **O'Donnell,** Francis G JR., Jefferson, LA, *WPNS-3-7 KO* +
*MAJGEN* **O'Donohue,** Daniel J, Camp Pendleton, CA, *CG 1ST MAR DIV*
*CPL* **Ofarrell,** Arthur S, Grand Junction, CO, *I-3-7 VN* +
*SGT* **Ogilvie,** James A, Ashland, WI, *C-1MT VN* +

*SGT* **Ogle,** Alan L, Solon, OH, *B-1-7 VN* +
*MSGT* **Oh,** Byong H, Grand Prairie, TX, *ATT-ROK-MC KO* +
*CPL* **O'Halloran,** Thomas L, Phelps, WI, *S CO 1ST TANK BN 1MARDIV KO*
*COL* **Okeefe,** John J, Missoula, MT, *7MAR 1AT KO VN* +
*SGT* **O'Keeffe,** John S, Worthington, OH, *E-2-5 VN* +
*COL* **O'Kelley,** James T PHD, PE, Keswick, VA, *9ENGR VN* +
*SGT* **Okraski,** Francis C, Minonk, IL, *H-3-7 KO* +
*SSGT* **Oksnee,** Carl H, Gardnerville-Florence, WI, *H&S-2-5 H&S-1-9 VN* +
**Oldenburg,** Richard W, Tehachapi, CA, *HQ-3-5 BAND-HQ KO* +
*1STSGT* **Oldland,** Harry G, Uniontown, PA, *B-1-1 VN* +
*PFC* **Olds,** James S, Wentachee, WA, *K-3-1/5/7 WWII* +
*CAPT* **Oleary,** Francis T, East Boston, MA, +
*CPL* **Oleary,** John A, El Cerrito, CA, *D-1ENGR KO* +
*SSGT* **Oleary,** Sean P, San Rafael, CA, *E-2-5 CW* +
*LTCOL* **O'leary,** Raymond J, Cody, WY, *F-2-7 3-7 KO VN* +
*LCPL* **Olenski,** Paul F, Gold Canyon, AZ, *C-1RE-CON VN* +
*CPL* **Olges,** Raymond J, Louisville, KY, *7SVC WWII CH* +
*CAPT* **Oliphant,** Don W, Rancho Santa Fe, CA, *2-5 VN* +
*CPL* **Oliva,** Angelo A, Auburndale, FL, *1MAW KO* +
*SGT* **Oliva,** Franklin T, Phelan, CA, *M-3-1/5 VN* +
*CPT* **Oliver,** B, Madison, NJ, *G-2-1 VN* +
*SGT* **Oliver,** Peter K, Lakeville, CT, *HQ-1-5 HQ-3-5 VN* +
*MSGT* **Olivero,** Phil A, Castaic, CA, *H&S H&S-IMEB SWA* +
*LTGEN* **Olmstead,** Stephen G, Annandale, VA, *G-3-1 KO VN* +
**O'Loughlen,** Patrick, Boise, ID, *BAKER 1/7 KO*
*1STSGT* **Oloughlin,** Mark J, Santee, CA, *L-3-1 A-1-1 SWA OIF*
*SSGT* **Olsen,** John C, Anacortes, WA, *I-3-5 VN* +
**Olsen,** Robert, Vista, CA, *F-2-1 CH KO* +
*SGT* **Olson,** Gilbert L, San Diego, CA, *A-1-11 D-2-7 CH KO* +
*SSGT* **Olson,** Randall A, Jamestown, ND, *1TK VN* +
**Olson,** Robert E, Duluth, MN, *F-2-5 A-1-7 WWII CH KO*
**Olson,** Van C, Saukville, WI, *F-2-27 VN* +
*SSGT* **Oneal,** C M, Queens, NY, *COMM-1 WWII KO VN* +
*CAPT* **Oneil,** Christopher W, Aguanga, CA, *L-3-5 HQ-3-1 OIF* +
**Oneil,** Lester R, La Quinta, CA, *A-1-7 KO* +
*SSGT* **Oneill,** James V, Congers, NY, *HQ-17MAR HQ-1SIG WWII CH* +
*SGT* **O'Neill,** Richard B JR., East Sandwich, MA, *COMMSPT-HQ KO VN*
*CAPT* **O'Neill,** Thomas G JR., San Jose, CA, *11TH MEUSOC 1ST LSB SOM*
*1STSGT* **Oppenheimer,** S J, Yuma, AZ, *TK MAW KO VN* +
*SSGT* **Orlof,** Ronald M, Virginia Beach, VA, *1MARDIV VN* +
*SGT* **Orman,** Robert T, Reno, NV, *F-2-5 K/G-2-2 WWII KO* +
*LTCOL* **Orourke,** James M JR., Mccomb, MS, *HQ-HQ VN* +
*PFC* **Orr,** James L, Flushing, MI, *RECON KO* +
*MGYSGT* **Ortamond,** Kim, Twentynine Palms, CA, *1FSSG* +
*CPL* **Ortega,** Zataniel, Chicago, IL, *D-1-7 VN* +
**Orth,** John, Jacksonville, FL, *H-3-7 KO* +
*CPL* **Ortiz,** Edward G, Hemet, CA, *A-1-5 VN* +
*LCPL* **Ortiz,** John R, Hagerstown, MD, *ANTI-TANK CO 1ST TANK BN 1969 VN*
*PFC* **Orzyp,** Robert A, Chicago, IL, *I-3-1 WWII* +
*MRS.* **Osborn,** Ruth A, Oceanside, CA, *HQCO,1STMARDIV* +
**Osborne,** Harry (Gene) E, Montgomery, TX, *G-3-7 KO* +
*CPL* **Osborne,** Robert J, Feasterville-Trevose, PA, *3-1-1 KO*
*LTCOL* **Oss,** Merton J, Lynwood, WA, *H-3-7 KO* +
**Ostrom,** Mike, Palm Desert, CA, *2BD BN 12 MAR*
*SGT* **O'Sullivan,** M, Anaheim, CA, *C-1-KOREA* +
*LTCOL* **Otoole,** Patrick E, Port Jefferson Station, NY, *H&S-1-5 VN* +
*CPL* **Otoole,** William A, Blue Beu, PA, *1AMTRAC CW* +
*SGT* **Otto,** Robert M, Newburgh, NY, *H&S-8AM-TRAC WWII* +
*CAPT* **Otto,** William R, Fort Worth, TX, *G-3-11 VN* +
*CPL* **Ottoway,** Dean R, Fulton, NY, *L-3-7-1 VN* +
*CPL* **Oudsteyn,** J D, Chicago Ridge, IL, *7MAW WWII CH* +
*SGT* **Ourso,** W J, Clinton, LA, *W-2-7 1MAR CH KO* +
*SGT* **Outerbridge,** Robert A, Fort Lauderdale, FL, *WPNS-3-5 KO* +
*SGT* **Overman,** Mark P, Granville, OH, *A-1-5 VN* +
*MSGT* **Overstreet,** Coy, Dickens, TX, *1ENGR KO VN* +
*SGT* **Overton,** Ronald V, Grand Ledge, MI, *A-1RECON VN*
*PFC* **Owen,** Dennis R, Fallbrook, CA, *ANGLICO-1SIG KO* +
*SGT* **Owen,** Robert L, Concord, MA, *1SIG M-4-11 WWII* +
*SGT* **Owen,** Vincent P, Suffolk, VA, *HQ-1-5 HQ-1MAR VN* +
*SGT* **Owen,** William K, Reston, VA, *H&S-2-1 VN* +
*LTCOL* **Owens,** James L, Rockville, MD, *H&S/WPNS-2-5 VN* +
*COL* **Oxnam,** Herbert R, Tucson, AZ, *RECON I-3-7 KO* +
**Pace,** William A, Monticello, AR, *7TH ENG COMBAT PLT 1MARDIV*
**Pace,** William S, Bethesda, MD, *1ENGR WWII* +
*SGT* **Pacheco,** Samuel SR., Ottawa, KS, *B-1-7 KO* +
*SGT* **Pacheco,** Samuel II, Ottawa, KS, *3 MAW MCAS EL TORO*
*SGT* **Pack,** Jon H, Prescott, AZ, *A-1-5 VN* +
*CPL* **Pacura,** Thomas A, Omaha, NE, *FLSUA-FLC 2-5MAR VN* +
*SGT* **Padgett,** Richard L, Gaithersburg, MD, *C-1MT KO* +
*SGT* **Padilla,** Alvin G JR., Harlingen, TX, *A-1-7 KO* +
*CPL* **Padilla,** Bernabe F, Wichita, KS, *1FSR VN*
*CPL* **Padusnak,** Ludwig J, Edgewater, FL, *D-1-5 WWII* +
*HM3* **Page,** James (Jim) R, Aurora, OR, *HMM263-MAG11 VN* +
*CPL* **Page,** Randall A, Newport, NH, *E-2-7 VN* +
*LCPL* **Paget,** Michael W, Apple Valley, CA, *L-3-11 L-4-12 VN* +
*CPL* **Pahler,** Francis J, Paso Robles, CA, *1PARA BN WWII* +
*MSGT* **Pahler,** J J, Arroyo Grande, CA, *VMSB132 MAG11 WWII* +
*MRS* **Paige,** Marilyn, Palm Desert, CA, *ASSOCIATE* *
*SGT* **Palermo,** Charles N, Ocean City, NJ, *HQ-HQ WWII* +
*CPL* **Pallatto,** Anthony E, Oakmont, PA, *E-2-7 VN* +
*LTCOL* **Palmer,** Charles B, Vista, CA, *HQ-HQ KO VN* +
*CPL* **Palmer,** Robert D, San Rafael, CA, *WPNS-1-5 KO* +
*SGT* **Palmer,** Robert F, Houston, TX, *HQ-1-11 KO* +
*CPL* **Palmer,** Russell L, San Jacinto, CA, *SERV BN WWII KO* +
*PFC* **Palmieri,** P P, Stratford, CT, *SPLWPNS* +
*SGT* **Palomino,** Manuel J, San Diego, CA, *RE-CON-HQ KO* +
*SGT* **Pang,** Henry, Vallejo, CA, *H&S-2-7 KO* +
*SGT* **Pankey,** Hugh A, Lubbock, TX, *B-1-5 VN* +
*PFC* **Pantelis,** Constantine G, Key West, FL, *7MAR WWII* +
*LTCOL* **Pape,** Richard A, Springfield, VA, *A-1-1 KO VN* +
*CPL* **Pape,** Robert J, Flagler Beach, FL, *HQ-7MAR KO* +
*MGYSGT* **Pappas,** George, Oceanside, CA, *WPNS-7MAR WWII KO VN* +
*PHM3* **Pappas,** Harry R, Stoneham, MA, *VMF 121-MAW WWII* +
*SGTMAJ* **Paradine,** Ralph A JR., Huntsville, AL, *1-9MAR SWA* +
*CPL* **Paradise,** Herman J, Manchester, CT, *HQ-3-5 WWII* +
**Paradise,** James H, Pearson, GA, *HQ-3-7 F-2-5 WWII* +
*CAPT* **Parascandola,** Ciro A, Alexandria, VA, *A/WPNS-1-7 PK* +
*CPL* **Parascandola,** Ciro 'Charlie' A, West Babylon, NY, *I-3-5 KO* +
*COL* **Parish,** Preston S, Kalamazoo, MI, *A-1-7 WWII* +
*SGT* **Park,** Bong Y, Alea, HI, *HQ-2BDE (ROK) VN* +
**Park,** Chong Keun, Norwalk, CA, *ROKM CH VN* +
*1STSGT* **Park,** Dung HWA, Seoul, Korea, *ROK MC KO* +
**Park,** J C, Los Angeles, CA, *KMC KO* +
**Park,** Jik BANG, Los Angeles, CA, +
*BGEN* **Park,** Jung SOO, Kwangju City Kyongki-Do, Korea, *2MARBDE ROKMC VN* +
*LT* **Park,** Lee C MD, Baltimore, MD, *MED MT KO* +
**Park,** Yong CHU, Los Angeles, CA, *KMC VN* +
*SGT* **Parker,** Aaron R, Palisade, CO, *SPT SCH-1TR-CJHP VN* +
*CAPT* **Parker,** Cecil N, Ventura, CA, *1MAW VMA251 KO VN* +
*SGT* **Parker,** Charles W, Granite City, IL, *AMMO-1ORD KO* +
*CWO4* **Parker,** Dutch E, Bonsall, CA, *HQBN HQCO-1 FMF OIF* +
*LCPL* **Parker,** Paul E, Framingham, MA, *C-1-5 KO*
*CWO* **Parker,** William J JR., Coinjock, NC, *D-2-11 WWII CH KO VN* +
*M SGT* **Parkhurst,** Timothy A, Newport, NC, *WEAPONS CO, 3/5 SWA*
*SGT* **Parks,** Frank E, Plainfield, IN, *C-1-5 VN*
*LCDR* **Parks,** Joe "Doc" FMF, Delran, NJ, *A-1-7 C-1MED WWII KO VN* +
*SGT* **Parlin,** Thomas S, Redmond, OR, *C-1-7 CW* +
*PFC* **Parquette,** Frank S SR., Montgomery, AL, *B-1-7 CH*
*CPL* **Parra,** Samuel, Oceanside, CA, *F/2/1*
*CPL* **Parrish Iii,** Raymond L, Westminster, CA, *E-2-26 VN*
*SGT* **Parry,** David L, Yankton, SD, *WPNS-3-5 KO* +
**Parry,** Doris, Santa Ana, CA, *ASSOCIATE* *
*1STSGT* **Parson,** Kenneth L, Indianapolis, IN, *H-2-1* +
*MGYSGT* **Parson,** Robert L, Fort Smith, AR, *HQ-1-11 WWII KO VN* +
*SGT* **Parson,** Stanley S, Baltimore, MD, *A-1-1 WWII KO* +
*LCPL* **Parsons,** Roland F, Kenosha, WI, *C-1SHPTY CW* +
*COL* **Partee,** Richard A, Palm Desert, CA, *H&S-1RECON CW* +
*SGT* **Partridge,** Robert C JR., San Diego, CA, *A-1TK CW* +
*SGT* **Partusch,** Leonard L, Cincinnati, OH, *F-2 B-1-11 WWII CH*
*MSGT* **Parungo,** Edward J, Raleigh, NC, *H-3-7 KO VN* +
*CPL* **Pasbjerg,** John C, Buckley, MI, *I-3-5 HQ-1-1 VN* +
*PFC* **Pate,** C E, Aliceville, AL, *C-1-5 WWII CH* +
*CPL* **Patrick,** Samuel E, Astoria, OR, *F-2-3 CW* +
*SGT* **Patt,** Dave A, Sitka, AK, *9ENGR VN* +
*CPL* **Patterson,** Donald J, Herron, MI, *G-3-11 HQ-1FAG CW* +
*GYSGT* **Patterson,** John H, Lodge Grass, MT, *1AMTRAC KO VN* +
**Patterson,** Pasco P, Holly Pond, AL, *G-3-7 KO* +
*HM3* **Patton,** Sherrel D, Tampa, FL, *HQ-7ENGR VN* +

*SGT* **Pauley,** Dwight E, Scott Depot, WV, *C CO, 1ST ENG VN*
*GYSGT* **Paulhamus,** Harry M, Fort Mohave, AZ, *HQ-HQ KO VN* +
*SGT* **Paulson,** Daryl S, Bozeman, MT, *3-5MAR VN* +
*PFC* **Pauly,** William O, Tamarac, FL, *F-2-1 7MT KO* +
*PVT* **Pavenski,** Thedore S, Peabody, MA, *H&S-1AMPHTRAC WWII* +
*SGTMAJ* **Paxton,** Bill E, Santee, CA, *F-2-5/7 VN* +
*SSGT* **Paxton,** Gene H, Grand Rapids, MI, *A-1-1 KO* +
*CAPT* **Paxton,** Jack T, Wildwood, FL, *1ST PROV HIS PLT KO VN CMC CW* +
*MAJGEN* **Paxton,** John M JR., Springfield, VA, *C-1MAR 3-5MAR CW* +
*SGT* **Payne,** Alfred C JR., Wellington, FL, *W-2-11 VN* +
*CPL* **Payne,** Charles T, Dedham, MA, *B-1-5 KO* +
**Payne,** Harold GREGORY, Montgomery, TX, *ASSOCIATE* +
*HM3* **Payne,** Richard L, Tacoma, WA, *F-2-1 1CSG KO* +
*CWO* **Payseur,** O J, Worton, MD, *B-2-11* +
*SGT* **Paz,** George, El Paso, TX, *G-3-5 KO* +
*CPL* **Peabody,** Ted E, Tucumcari, NM, *C-1ENGR WWII CH* +
*MAJ* **Pearce,** James T, Piedmont, SC, *D-2-11 WWII* +
**Pearson,** Bob P, North Easton, MA, *I-3-7 MP CSG KO* +
*SGT* **Peck,** Nelson N JR., Rochester, NY, *HQ BTRY-3-11 VN* +
*COL* **Peeler,** John J, San Antonio, TX, *I-3-1 WWII KO VN* +
*SGT E-5* **Peeler,** Phillip S SR., Lee's Summit, MO, *A 1/5 VN*
*CPL* **Peeler,** Phillip S JR., Austin, TX, *USA 1/43 ADA*
*CPL* **Peer,** William F, Los Angeles, CA, *H-3-7 HQ-2-11 KO* +
*SGT* **Pegelow,** Donald R, Castro Valley, CA, *WPNS-3-5 KO* +
*CPL* **Peitsmeyer,** Steven W, Grove City, OH, *G-2-5 VN* +
*MAJ* **Pelkey,** James D, Milwaukee, WI, *HMH-462, MAG-36 VN*
*SGT* **Pella,** James V, Pittsburgh, PA, *E-2-5 KO*
*CPL* **Pellegrini,** A R, Bedford, NH, *HQ-1PION WWII* +
*CPL* **Pelletier,** Gillman J, Scottsdale, AZ, *C-1-11 WWII CH* +
*CPL* **Pellow,** Robert H, New Brighton, MN, *WPNS-2-7 KO*
*SGT* **Pelosi,** Robert F, Center Moriches, NY, *1SHPTY KO* +
*SGTMAJ* **Pemberton,** Robert N, Glen Cove, NY, *H&S-17MAR FMF CW* +
*CPL* **Pena,** John H, San Jose, CA, *I BTRY 2-1*
*SGT* **Pendleton,** Neal F JR., Covington, LA, *1ANGLICO KO* +
*SGT* **Penfold,** Donald L, Lady's Island, SC, *H-3-1 KO* +
*SGT* **Penick,** John R SR., Winchester, CA, *H-3-7-KO* +
*MAJ* **Penkethman,** Dean A, San Antonio, TX, *B CO 1-4 1MAR* +
*CPL* **Pennington,** Donald R, Tullahoma, TN, *WPNS-1-5 KO* +
*CPL* **Penor,** Albert R, Farmington, NM, *C-1-1 WWII CH* +
*MSGT* **Peplinski,** B, Northville, MI, *1MARDIV WWII KO VN* +
*LTCOL* **Percy,** Stephen, Waterford, CT, *H&S-2-1 F-2-1 HQBN KO* +
*CPL* **Peregory,** L E, Newark, CA, *VMF-513 KO* +
*SGT* **Pereira,** Joaquin M, San Leandro, CA, *F-2-5 WWII* +
*1STSGT* **Perez,** Aurelio D, Corpus Christi, TX, *I-3-5 KO* +
*CPL* **Perez,** Gil, Whittier, CA, *B CO 1ST RECON VN*
*CPL* **Perez,** Henry B, San Antonio, TX, *G-2-5 VN* +
*HM2* **Perez,** Vic R, Juneau, AK, *K/I-3-5 VN* +
*SSGT* **Perfetto,** Sid R, Croghan, NY, *H&S-2-7 VN*
*SGT* **Perillo,** John J, Wappingers Falls, NY, *7TH MAR 1ST TK BN VN* +
*MSGT* **Peringer,** James N, New Smyrna Beach, FL, *B-1-7 1ST CIT VN* +
*HM3* **Perkins,** Lawrence J, Hamburg, NY, *1ST BN 5TH MAR VN*
*HM2* **Perkins,** Ray M, South Dennis, MA, *C-1-1 VN* +
*E-6* **Perkioniemi,** Robert E, Riverside, CA, *H&S 2/7, 3 FSSG*
*CPL* **Permenter,** Roy ALLEN, Surprise, AZ, *E-2-1 CW* +
*CPL* **Pernetti,** Jim M, Portland, OR, *MCMWTC L-3-1/HQ CamPen*
*CPL* **Perron,** George W, Franklin, MA, *C-7th MT BN KO* +
*SGT* **Perry,** Frank H, Franklin, TX, *H&S BTRY 2D LAAM BN VN*
*CAPT* **Perry,** Frank L JR., Cincinnati, OH, *H&S-2-7 KO* +
*1STLT* **Perry,** J A JR., Novato, CA, *1MAW* +
**Perry,** L A, Safety Harbor, FL, *D-2-5 KO* +
*SGT* **Perry,** Robert W, Manhattan Beach, CA, *2-4 H&S 3RD MAR VN* +
*SGT* **Perry,** Thomas M, Greenwood, FL, *A-3AMTRAC VN* +
*SGT* **Perry,** William E, Colorado Springs, CO, *HQ-1MAR CW* +
**Persing,** Norman V, Old Bridge, NJ, *4.2-7MAR KO* +
*SGT* **Peruta,** Edward A, Rocky Hill, CT, *I/K-3-5 VN* +
*PFC* **Peruzzi,** R W, Sterling Heights, MI, *B-1-1 CW* +
*SGT* **Pessein,** Howard J, Post Falls, ID, *D-1ENGR KO* +
*SGT* **Pete,** Eugene J, Chauvin, LA, *L-3-1 VN* +
*LCPL* **Peterman,** Gerald L, Ocala, FL, *B-1-5 VN* +
*PFC* **Peters,** Charles W, Aiken, SC, *H&S-8AMTRAC WWII* +
**Peters,** G E, Playa Del Rey, CA, *H&S-5MAR CW* +
*LCPL* **Peters,** James E, Cleveland, TN, *D-1-5 VN* +
*CPL* **Peters,** Philip C, Poughkeepsie, NY, *B-1RECON VN* +
*SGT* **Peters,** S E JR., Oklahoma City, OK, *HQ-2-5 WWII* +
*CPL* **Peters,** William L, Titusville, NJ, *C-1MT KO* +
**Peterson,** Carol J, Elgin, IL, *ASSOCIATE* *
*CPL* **Peterson,** Daniel L, Payson, UT, *A-1AMTRAC CW* +
*SSGT* **Peterson,** David H, Hitchcock, TX, *SVC-49FA-7DIV KO* +
*LCPL* **Peterson,** Douglas R, Babbitt, MN, *F-2-5 VN* +
*TSGT* **Peterson,** Eugene J, Brooklyn Park, MN, *1MAW WWII KO*
*MSGT* **Peterson,** Laurence H, Oceanside, CA, *A-1-7 G-2-1 VN* +
*SGTMAJ* **Peterson,** Randal E, Downey, CA, *1-3 VN OIF* +
*SGT* **Peterson,** Robert P, Roseville, CA, *MABS33 KO* +
*SGT* **Peterson,** Wayne D, Beecher, IL, *WPNS-2-7 KO* +
**Petray,** Edmund L, Des Plaines, IL, *WPNS-1-5 KO* +
**Petroff,** Richard, Palm Desert, CA, *1 ENG BN*
*CAPT* **Petronzio,** John A, Beverly, MA, *B-1-1 H-2-7 KO VN* +
*COL* **Petronzio,** Nicholas C, Beverly, MA, *HQ-HQ OIF* +
*GYSGT* **Petros,** David B, Edgewater, FL, *M-3-5 WWII KO* +
*CPL* **Petrosian,** Martin V, Fresno, CA, *E-2-7 VN*
*SGTMAJ* **Petrovich,** David J, Henderson, NV, *1TK 7MT SWA* +
*PFC* **Petrovski,** Vincent J, Clarendon Hills, IL, *A-1SPLWPNS WWII* +
*SGT* **Petterson,** Robert F, Beloit, KS, *I-3-7 KO* +
*SGT* **Pettigrew,** Don W, Gainesville, TX, *M-3-1 VN* +
*CAPT* **Pettit,** Kenneth E, Alpine, CA, *SVC WWII KO VN* +
*LCPL* **Pettlon,** Kenneth R, Maryville, MO, *H&S-1TK-1MAR VN* +
*SGT* **Petzak,** Rodney R, Reno, NV, *B-1TK KO*
*SGT* **Peveto,** Alfred L, Vidor, TX, *I-3-1 KO* +
*CPL* **Pfannkuche,** Edward L JR., Streamwood, IL, *MARDET- CA124 KO* +
*PVT* **Pfeiffer,** George A, Woodland Hills, CA, *B-1-1* +
*PHM3* **Pfeiffer,** John J, Bergenfield, NJ, *D-1MED WWII CH* +
*PFC* **Pharis,** C P, Hearne, TX, *H&S-11 CH* +
*PFC* **Pharis,** W C, Silsbee, TX, *K-3-7 WWII* +
*LTCOL* **Phillips,** George R, Signal Mountain, TN, *1MAW WWII KO VN* +
**Phillips,** Howard W, Brea, CA, *B-1ENGR WWII CH KO* +
*MAJ* **Phillips,** Paul, Yardley, PA, *A-1AMTRAC WWII* +
*DR* **Phillips,** Sidney C, Theodore, AL, *H-2-1 WWII* +
*PFC* **Phillips,** William E, Lake Oswego, OR, *HQ-1-1 WWII CH* +
*CPL* **Phillips,** Woodrow N, Pecos, TX, *IRECON VN* +
**Phipps,** Edward J, Sausalito, CA, *1ANGLICO KO* +
*PFC* **Pianko,** Edward J, Metuchen, NJ, *H&S-1-5/7/11 WWII CH*
*GYSGT* **Picarello,** Michael R, North Weymouth, MA, *I-3-5 KO VN* +
*LTCOL* **Piccola,** Frank J, Middle Island, NY, *A-7ENGR CW*
*PFC* **Piciulli,** Joseph R, Port Saint Lucie, FL, *H&S-4-11 CH* +
*MGYSGT* **Pickering,** Charles D, Englewood, FL, *H&S-6MT SWA* +
*CPL* **Pickett,** William E, Framingham, MA, *A-1-1/7 CW* +
*GYSGT* **Pierce,** Charles Chuck H, Bakersfield, CA, *H&S CO-1-5 KO* +
*CPL* **Pierce,** Lawrence D, North Bend, OR, *D 2/11 VN*
*SSGT* **Pierce,** Robert W, West Linn, OR, *SPT COMCARDIV1 KO*
*SGT* **Pietrykoski,** David P, Dingmans Ferry, PA, *1ANGLICO VN* +
*HM3* **Pike,** H L, Orleans, MA, *1-5MAR CW* +
*SGT* **Pileggi,** Vito P, Stayton, OR, *E-2-7 KO* +
*CPL* **Pilewski,** Francis (Frank) J, Erie, PA, *B-1-17 H&S-1ENGR WWII* +
*CPL* **Pilyer,** Denver L JR., North Attleboro, MA, *C-1-1 WWII CH KO* +
*SGT* **Pine,** Robert J, Newport, RI, *A-1-5 VN*
*CPL* **Pinedo,** Joe A, Thermal, CA, *MAG26 VN*
**Pingley,** Ronald L, Elkins, WV, *F-2-7 VN* +
*CAPT* **Pinnell,** Murry C, Oceanside, CA, *A-1-7 D-1-5 KO VN* +
*CPL* **Pippi,** Christopher R, Whitney, TX, *1AMTRAC VN* +
*LCPL* **Pistol,** Raymond, Las Vegas, NV, *C-1-5 VN* +
*SSGT* **Pitt,** Donald S, Chadds Ford, PA, *B-1-1 KO*
*HM3* **Pittman,** William E, Arlington, VA, *HQ-1-5 VN* +
*SGT* **Pitts,** Michael, Middletown, OH, *M-3-1 VN* +
*LCPL* **Pitts,** Philip W, Dallas, TX, *T CO HQBN OIF* +
*CPL* **Placko,** Edward C, Oregon, OH, *H-3-7 KO* +
*SSGT* **Plaine,** Boyd C, San Carlos, CA, *WPNS-7MAR KO* +
*MSGT* **Plannette,** Herbert L JR., Central Point, OR, *HQ-HQ HQ-5MAR VN* +
*CPL* **Playford,** Michael, Los Angeles, CA, *H&S-1-5 VN* +
*MGYSGT* **Plott,** Samuel C JR., Springfield, VA, *G-3-11 WWII CH KO VN* +
*CPL* **Plushanski,** Fred, Asbury, NJ, *H&S-1MAR KO* +
*PLTSGT* **Plyler,** Paul J, Miami, FL, *WPNS-7MAR WWII KO* +
*LCPL* **Pobi,** George, Vancouver, WA, *1COMM 1FSSG E-2-1 CW* +
*CPL* **Poelstra,** Eugene R, Armour, SD, *CW* +
*PFC* **Poirier,** Daniel E, Tucson, AZ, *G-2-1 WWII KO* +

*CPL* **Polaske,** Eugene P, Berlin, CT, *H&S-1MT CH* +
*SGT* **Polasko,** John M, Hopewell Junction, NY, *HQ-HQ VN* +
*LCPL* **Politi,** Salvatore F, Surprise, AZ, *M-3-7 VN* +
*SSGT* **Polkinghorn,** Norman G, The Villages, FL, *E-2-7 WWII CH* +
*SSGT* **Pollard,** Carl M JR., Sealevel, NC, *B-1AM-TRAC KO* +
*HMC (SWP)* **Pollard,** John C, San Diego, CA, *D-1-5 CW* +
**Pollicino,** Joseph G, Albany, NY, *L-3-5 VN* +
*PFC* **Pollins,** David L, Arlington, MA, *2-5/11MAR VN* +
*CAPT* **Pollock,** Leonard, Beechurst, NY, *H-2-7 VN IRAQ*
*PFC* **Polsgrove,** Joseph S, Palmetto, FL, *A-1-5 KO* +
*SGT* **Polson,** Robert ALEX, Seattle, WA, *SVC-4-11 KO* +
*CPL* **Pomakis,** Mike, Winter Garden, FL, *M/I-3-7 VN* +
*CPL* **Pompel,** Ron, Gresham, OR, *HIMS--24 MAG 24 HIMS-33*
*CPL* **Pompeo,** John N, Seattle, WA, *E-2-7 KO* +
*SGTMAJ* **Pompos,** Anthony J, Twentynine Palms, CA, *3/7, 1/5, 7MAR*
*SGT* **Ponder,** Chuck C, Salem, OR, *H-3-7 KO* +
*SGT* **Pondish,** Paul A, Huntsville, TX, *C-1-1 VN* +
*SGT* **Pontious,** Rodrick STANLEY, Warren, PA, *C-1-5 VN*
*CPL* **Pool,** James C, Saint Louis, MO, *DELTA 1/5 VN*
*SGT* **Poole,** Samuel T JR., Falling Waters, WV, *HMM364/165 VN* +
**Poorman,** D, Johnson City, NY, +
*CPL* **Pope,** Harlan B, Wichita Falls, TX, *B-1-5 KO* +
*LTCOL* **Popelka,** Michael E, Southlake, TX, *HQ-11MAR VN* +
*LCPL* **Poplawsky,** Donald J, Phelan, CA, *B-1-7 CW* +
*PFC* **Popovich,** Peter, Pittsburgh, PA, *SIG-7SVC WWII CH* +
*MGYSGT* **Popp,** Kenneth J, Waco, TX, *M-4-11 D-2-5 KO* +
*CPL* **Poppe,** George W, Yukon, OK, *H-3-5 WWII* +
**Porcari,** John, Long Island City, NY, *H&S-1-1 WWII CH* +
*SGT* **Portenier,** Robert A, Topeka, KS, *A-1TK VN* +
*SGT* **Porter,** Donald EARL, Norwich, CT, *H&S CO 1ENG BN 1MAR DIV KO* +
*LCPL* **Porter,** Joseph F, Golden, CO, *ORD-MSGM-1FSR CW*
*COL* **Porter,** Robert B, Tehachapi, CA, *VMF 121 WWII* +
*CAPT* **Porter,** Terrell B, Big Bear Lake, CA, *HQTS CO-9TH ENGR BN VN* +
*CPL* **Porter,** William E JR., Saint Charles, IL, *2-11MAR VN* +
*SSGT* **Posey,** Ronald L, Norresundby, Denmark, *B-1-5 D-1-1 VN*
*SSGT* **Pospisil,** Richard E, Monterey, CA, *MACG3 KO CW* +
*MAJ* **Poss,** Willard B, Houston, TX, *M-3-5 D-1-7 VN CW CMC* +
*HM3* **Poth,** M RICHARD JR., FMF, Huntsville, TX, *A-1-5 VN*
*CPL* **Pottner,** M R, Mason, OH, *AT-5MAR KO* +
*SGT* **Poulin,** Robert A, Anza, CA, *C-1-5 VN* +
*1STSGT* **Poulin,** Robert C SR., Anza, CA, *2ND BN 11TH 1MAR DIV*
*SGTMAJ* **Poulk,** Russell K, Rockport, TX, *H-3-1 WWII KO VN* +
*CPL* **Poulson,** James S, Gas City, IN, *COMM-H&S-1FLC/FSR VN* +
*CPL* **Poutz,** William E, Parma, OH, *E-2-7 KO* +
*LTCOL* **Powalski,** Cathy M, Temecula, CA, *H&S-HQ* +
*SGT* **Powell,** Truman O, Tyler, TX, *2-7MAR 1-5MAR VN* +
*CAPT* **Power,** Pierce J, Tierra Verde, FL, *D-2-1 1AMTRAC KO* +
*CPL* **Powers,** Calvin A, Mount Carmel, TN, *I-3-11 WWII CH*
*LCPL* **Powers,** Dwight T, Amityville, NY, *FLC-1-27 VN* +
*SGT* **Powers,** John W, Independence, OH, *E-2-5 KO*
*CPL* **Powers,** Thomas J, Newell, WV, *G-3-1 KO* +
*SGT* **Powers,** William E, Junction City, KS, *E-2-1 VN* +
*CPL* **Powless,** Gary A, Beatty, OR, *H&S-1-26 9MAB VN*
*SGT* **Praeuner,** Robert Eugene, Fritch, TX, *COMM CO 7TH COM BN VN*
*CPL* **Prasch,** Harry R, Maple Shade, NJ, *IST BRIDGE CO, 7TH ENG BN VN*
*PFC* **Pratt,** Kenneth A, Winsted, CT, *G. CO. 3/7 1STMARDIV KO* +
*SGT* **Prax,** Eldon A, Haslet, TX, *2/5 MSSG-35*
*CPL* **Precour,** James E, Vallejo, CA, *D-1ENGR KO* +
*CPL* **Preseren,** Alan J, Oswego, IL, *A-1-5 VN*
*CPL* **Pressnall,** David C, Sacramento, CA, *G-2-5 WWII* +
*MAJ* **Preston,** Harry L, San Antonio, TX, *K-3-5 CW*
**Preston,** Paul J, Alexandria, VA, *H-3-11 WWII* +
*CPL* **Prial,** Philip J JR., New Smyrna Beach, FL, *H&S-1-1 KO* +
*SGT* **Price,** Dewitt, Commerce, GA, *C-1-5 VN* +
*COL* **Price,** Donald L, Sierra Vista, AZ, *A-1-7 VN* +
*MSGT* **Price,** J O, Shelby, NC, *MP-1-1 CH* +
*MAJ* **Price,** Samuel ANTHONY, San Diego, CA, *3-1 1-4 13TH MEU OEF*
*CPL* **Price,** Stephen J, El Paso, TX, *H&S-1-1 VN* +
*LCPL* **Pries,** Richard H, Corrales, NM, *1-1 OIF* +
*SGT* **Prijatel,** Emil, Whitestone, NY, *H&S-4-11 WWII* +
*SGT* **Prince,** Jack, Rancho Mirage, CA, *G-3-1 CH KO* +
*SGT* **Prince,** Jack, Rancho Mirage, CA, *H-3-7 KO* +
*SGT* **Prince,** Roger R, Centennial, CO, *WPNS-3-1 KO* +
*CPL* **Prindle,** David N, Rochester, MN, *H&S-1TK VN* +
*SGT E-5* **Pringer,** Robert H, Broken Arrow, OK, *ALPHA 1/5-64-65*
*SGT* **Pritchard,** Bob, Palm Desert, CA, *ANGLICO*
*CAPT* **Pritchard,** John E, Pensacola, FL, *G-2-7 A-1-5 VN* +
*CPL* **Procassini,** Anthony J, Ann Arbor, MI, *I-3-1 WWII* +
*SGT* **Prochaska,** Wayne LEE, Woodinville, WA, *HQBTRY-11 H&HS1-1 CMC*
*SGT* **Procter,** Donald, Altadena, CA, *H&S-1-11 WWII* +
*SGT* **Progen,** Donald H, Westminster, MA, *VMGR152 VN*
**Pronevitz,** Edward P, Hicksville, NY, *HQ-3-5 WWII CH* +
*CPL* **Prosper,** C A, Nutley, NJ, *L-3-1-VN* +
*LTCOL* **Prosser,** Lloyd H, Oceanside, CA, *9TH ENGR BN 1ST ENG BN VN*
*SSGT* **Proulx,** James D, Orange Park, FL, *D-2-1 KO VN* +
*SSGT* **Provence,** Joe K, Ocala, FL, *F-2-5 KO* +
*1STSGT* **Provenza,** Charles S, Bayonet Point, FL, *H&S CO 3-5 KO*
*1STLT* **Provine,** Carl R, Yelm, WA, *1ST MAR DIV KO* +
*CPL* **Provost,** N R, Princeton, IL, *H&S-3-5* +
*SSGT* **Pruden,** James C, Tooele, UT, *K-4-11 KO* +
**Pruitt,** Hugh, Jonesborough, TN, *F-2-5 KO* +
**Pryer,** Wilford E, Tulsa, OK, *L-4-11 KO* +
*SGT* **Puente,** Raul, San Antonio, TX, *4.2MM G-3-5 KO*
*SSGT* **Puente,** Candice,,, *1st MARINE DIV*
*SSGT* **Puentes,** Robert J, Teaneck, NJ, *VMA251-MAG12 KO*
**Puentes,** Robert, Cathedral City, CA, *1 FSSG 1MARDIV*
*SGT* **Pugh,** Joe R, Dallas, GA, *16 FIELD DEP WWII* +
*LCPL* **Pullen,** Kenneth N, Diamond Head, MS, *M-4-11 VN* +
*SGTMAJ* **Pulley,** Frank E, Murrieta, CA, *E-2-11 CW* +
*CAPT* **Pullis,** Roger MICHAEL, Lake Arrowhead, CA, *K-3-5 VN* +
**Purcell,** William M, Evergreen, CO, *A-1-1 VN* +
*LCPL* **Purdy,** Howard L, Vinton, IA, *H-2-7 CW* +
*CPL* **Purnick,** James M, River Falls, WI, *AT-1MAR KO* +
*SGT* **Puro,** Gary A, Decatur, MI, *ATT-E-2-11 VN* +
**Putrino,** Gary A, Omaha, NE, *E-1RECON VN* +
*MAJ* **Pye,** Leslie JOHN, Blenheim, New Zealand, *B SQN 1ST ROYAL TK REGT KO VN*
*GYSGT* **Qualters,** John J, Ward Hill, MA, *H&S/K-3-7 VN* +
*PFC* **Quandt,** Robert R, Bloomingdale, IL, *WPNS-3-5 KO*
**Quant,** H E, Burleson, TX, *E-2-7 1LAAM VN* +
*CPL* **Quattrocchi,** R A, Smyrna, GA, *I-3-7 KO* +
*SGT* **Queen,** Emmett W, Seffner, FL, *WPNS/K-3-5 VN* +
*GYSGT* **Queen,** William H, Lexington, KY, *B-1-26 VN* +
*SGT* **Queener,** Herman R, Oak Ridge, TN, *H&S-1MAR WWII KO* +
*SGT* **Quick,** Lealand T, Bellingham, WA, *B-1-5 VN* +
*SGT* **Quickel,** James L, Carlisle, PA, *5MAR CH* +
*SGT* **Quigley,** Jack, Emerson, NJ, *B-11 MT VN* +
*SGT* **Quijano,** Carlos R, San Antonio, TX, *G-3-7 KO* +
*SGT* **Quinlin,** Robert J, New Egypt, NJ, *F-2-1 KO* +
*SGT* **Quinones,** Anthony, Superior, WI, *D-1MT 1SVC KO* +
*CPL* **Quinones,** Edwin, Eastampton, NJ, *HMA169 HMLA267 SWA* +
*SGT* **Quirk,** Robert M, Saugerties, NY, *G-3-5 KO* +
**Rabinowitz,** Jack, Palm Desert, CA, *1 MAR BRIGADE*
*CPL* **Rabtoy,** Marvin G, Wolcott, CT, *HQ-11MAR KO* +
*CAPT* **Raccuia,** Hugo A, Orange, CT, *VMO-6 KO* +
*1STLT* **Racely,** Edward W, Brewster, MA, *HQBN KO* +
*SSGT* **Racine,** John J, Springfield, MA, *HQ-2-11 A-1-11 VN* +
*CPL* **Rackliffe,** Thomas L, Maple Heights, OH, *I-3-11 CW* +
*SGT* **Radakovich,** George R, Grand Junction, CO, *HQ-5MAR HQ-7MAR VN* +
*LCPL* **Raddatz,** Raymond W, Charleston, SC, *E-2-7 CW* +
*SGT* **Radford,** Arthur R, Garden Grove, CA, *L CO 3-5 VN* +
*CAPT* **Raffel,** Richard R, Saint Louis, MO, *4-11 KO VN* +
*CPL* **Raftery,** John J JR., Schaumburg, IL, *F-2-7 KO* +
*SGT* **Ragni,** Joseph V, Washington, MI, *H-3-7 KO* +
*CPL* **Raible,** M H, Flushing, NY, *L-3-27 1MAR* +
*CPL* **Raimo,** David P, Campton, NH, *F-2-7 I-3-1 VN* +
*CPL* **Rainbolt,** C MICHAEL, Medford, NJ, *1FSR VN* +
**Rainbow,** Harvey A, Gnadenhutten, OH, *WPNS-1-5 KO* +
**Raley,** H L JR., Seattle, WA, *B-1-11 WWII CH* +
*HM* **Ramirez,** Mario H, San Fernando, CA, *1ST MAR DIV*
*SSGT* **Ramos,** Angeles, Dallas, TX, *C-1-1 KO* +
*SGT* **Ramos,** Bonifacio J, Fresno, CA, *D-2-1 KO* +
*LCPL* **Ramos,** Mark A SR., West Sacramento, CA, *HQ CO 5TH MARINES* +
*LCPL* **Ramsey,** Daniel D, Las Vegas, NV, *L-3-1 VN* +
*SGT* **Ramsey,** Edward E, Indianapolis, IN, *CSG KO* +
*MAJ* **Ramsey,** Robert (Bob) J, Marion, NC, *HQBN KO VN* +
*1STLT* **Ramsey,** William R, Bakersfield, CA, *1RECON VN* +
*PHM1* **Randall,** Charles A, Phoenix, AZ, *MAG11/14 1MAW WWII* +
*SGT* **Rangel,** Frank J, Saint Paul, MN, *AT-5MAR KO* +
*CPL* **Rankin,** Lucien T, Nevada City, CA, *H&S-2-26 VN* +
*MAJ* **Raphael,** Maurice, Bastrop, LA, *B-1-5 WWII* +
*HM2* **Rappolt,** Richard T SR., Sioux Falls, SD, *5MAR KO* +

*MGYSGT* **Raskin,** T S, San Diego, CA, *ANGLICO-COMM KO VN* +
*SGT* **Rasmussen,** Albert W, Tacoma, WA, *WPNS-2-1 KO* +
*CPL* **Ratcliff,** Carlos G, Sulphur, LA, *1RECON*
*SGT* **Ratcliffe,** Edward K, Greene, RI, *C-1-5 VN* +
*CAPT* **Rathbun,** Edward C, San Rafael, CA, *H&S-3-7 VN* +
*PFC* **Ratner,** Joseph, Hempstead, NY, *ABLE 1ST MARBN 1MAR*
*SGT* **Rau,** John H, Metairie, LA, *H&S-1TK KO* +
*CPL* **Rauwald,** Gerald M, Green Bay, WI, *1SEPSUR 1ST90AAA KO* +
*SGT* **Raventos,** John A, Washington, DC, *B-1EN-GR CW* +
*SGT* **Ray,** Corbit A, Castro Valley, CA, *D-2-7 KO* +
**Ray,** John J JR., Danvers, MA, *HQ-5 I-3-7 KO* +
*CPL* **Ray,** John J, Lanoka Harbor, NJ, *G-3-7 KO* +
*CPL* **Ray,** Ronald K, Adrian, MI, *C-ENGR WWII CH* +
*SSGT* **Ray,** Tom, Louisville, KY, *H&S-3-5 KO* +
*COL* **Rayfield,** Richard M, San Antonio, TX, *MASS3 SWA*
*CAPT* **Raymond,** Lionel A, Bristow, VA, *H&S-2-7 VN* +
*CPL* **Raymond,** Peter T, Conowingo, MD, *F-2-5 CW* +
*CAPT* **Rayner,** J W, Southsea Hants, England, *41 RM KO* +
*SGT* **Re,** Robert, Saddle River, NJ, *SVC-2-11MAR KO* +
**Read,** M L, Angleton, TX, *1RECON F-2-11 VN* +
*CPL* **Reale,** Paul, Staten Island, NY, *1MAW-VMJ1 KO* +
*SGT* **Reams,** Gregory P, Acton, CA, *1MAR CW* +
**Reardon,** Daniel M, Plantsville, CT, *A-1ENGR VN* +
*SGT* **Reardon,** E P, Staten Island, NY, *2-17MAR WWII* +
*LCPL* **Reardon,** James D, Atlantis, FL, *H&S 1ST-BN-1STMAR*
**Reardon,** Joseph A, Uxbridge, MA, *H&S-4-11 KO* +
*PFC* **Reber,** Ralph R, Erie, PA, *A-1ENGR WWII* +
*PVT* **Rebich,** Sam, Aliquippa, PA, *1MT CH* +
*SGM* **Reclosado,** Joaquin C JR., El Centro, CA, *H&S-3-5 KO* +
*MGYSGT* **Redburn,** Richard D, Las Vegas, NV, *E-2-5 KO VN* +
*CPL* **Redden,** Zachary M, North Bennington, VT, *3/1*
*SGT* **Reddig,** Darrel R, Tehachapi, CA, *MCTU#1 CW* +
*PFC* **Redner,** R A, Ringwood, NJ, *D-1-1 WWII* +
**Reece,** Belynda M, Palm Desert, CA, *9TH COMM BN* +
*CPL* **Reed,** Bart B, Fresno, CA, *WPNS-1-5 CW* +
*SSGT* **Reed,** Bruce J, Albert Lea, MN, *G-3-11 KO* +
*CPL* **Reed,** D K, Oktaha, OK, *PION-17MAR* +
*SGT* **Reed,** Jack E, Oceanside, CA, *ANGLICO* +
*SSGT* **Reed,** Jerry P, Tomball, TX, *1MAW VN*
*MAJ* **Reed,** Joseph D, Beaver Island, MI, *H-3-1 KO* +
*CPL* **Reed,** M W, Anaheim, CA, *M-3-7 VN* +
*PVT* **Reed,** Michael R, Atwaterspring Valley, CA, *1-7 SWA* +
*CPL* **Reed,** R H, Syracuse, NY, *C-1AMTRAC WWII* +
*CPL* **Reed,** Richard O, Minter City, MS, *HQ-1-11 KO* +
*SGT* **Reed,** William F, Montrose, CA, *1ANGLICO KO* +
*SGT* **Reedy,** Joseph B, East Moline, IL, *F-2-1 VN* +
*CPL* **Reehl,** William F, Louisville, KY, *C-1-11 WWII CH* +
*CPL* **Reese,** Leonard D III, Tatum, TX, *C-1-5 VN*
*CAPT* **Reeside,** John B, Santa Barbara, CA, *H&S-3 1MARDIV VN* +
*LTCOL* **Regal,** John E, Troy, VA, *A-1/K/L-3-1 VN* +
*MSGT* **Regalot,** Rene P, San Diego, CA, *D-1RE-CON VN*
*CPL* **Regan,** Gerald D, Burke, VA, *C-1-5 VN*
*1STLT* **Regan,** J PATRICK, Brunswick, OH, *B-11MAR* +
*MAJ* **Reich,** Nathaniel N, Fullerton, CA, *2ND BN 11TH REGT KO VN* +
*CPL* **Reichelderfer,** Charles O, Lima, OH, *WPNS-2-1 KO* +
*SSGT* **Reicher,** Stephen A JR., Dayton, OH, *HQ-5MAR VN* +
*SGT* **Reid,** Donald F, San Francisco, CA, *WPNS-3-7 KO* +
*SGTMAJ* **Reid,** Eddie, Lake Elsinore, CA, *1-1-MAR 1TK OIF*
*GYSGT* **Reid,** James H, Green Mountain, NC, *A-1ENGR CH KO* +
*MGYSGT* **Reidenhour,** John P, Pottstown, PA, *C-1-5 KO* +
*PFC* **Reil,** William H, Dorchester, MA, *B-1-7 KO* +
*COL* **Reilly,** George P, San Jose, CA, *M CO-3-5 1MAR DIV CW* +
*TSGT* **Reilly,** John L, Santa Ana, CA, *HQ-4-11 KO* +
**Reilly,** Joseph H, Novato, CA, *4.2MRTR 1MAR KO*
*REV. DR.* **Reilly,** Leonard F, Zelienople, PA, *C-1-1 CH KO* +
*SGT* **Reinholm,** Eric A, San Jose, CA, *ATT 1BTO* +
*SGT* **Reininger,** Werner W, San Antonio, TX, *WPN-3-5 KO* +
*SGT* **Reis,** John J, West Roxbury, MA, *B-1-5 VN* +
*CPL* **Remine,** John, Friant, CA, *1st ANGLECO FMF*
*2NDLT* **Renaghan,** Joseph F, Glen Cove, NY, *L-3-27MAR VN* +
*SSGT* **Render,** Ronald P, Valparaiso, IN, *1TK KO* +
*PFC* **Rendon,** Raul R, San Antonio, TX, *HQ-1 B-1-7 CH KO* +
*CPL* **Renner,** Charles E, Goodyear, AZ, *107 MM MTR BTRY 2-11 VN* +
*SGT* **Rennie,** Donald D, Cadillac, MI, *WPN-3-7 KO* +
*LTC* **Reno,** Clarence, Riverside, CA, *USA MED ATT:WWII* +
*SGT* **Renshaw,** Reed M, Bozeman, MT, *D-1ENGR KO* +
*CWO4* **Renteria,** Albert R, Perris, CA, *BLT-3-1, BLT-1-1 SWA* +
*HM2* **Resare,** Robert C, Tigard, OR, *I-3-7 1ORD KO*
*LTCOL* **Reuter,** Erland, North Las Vegas, NV, *H&S/A-1-5 CW* +
*SGT* **Revak,** Bernard E, San Diego, CA, *B-1-1 KO* +
*GYSGT* **Reynar,** Waverley C, Leduc, Canada, *H-2-7 K-2-5 VN* +
*COL* **Reynolds,** Claude L, Roanoke, VA, *F-2-1 KO* +
**Reynolds,** Irvin H, Upper Marlboro, MD, *D-1RAIDER WWII* +
*CPL* **Reynolds,** Larry L, Brockton, MA, *1-4.5RCKT KO* +
*SGT* **Reynolds,** Moses J, Philadelphia, PA, *L-3-1 VN* +
*MRS* **Reynolds,** Reba, Morrow, GA, *ASSOCIATE*
*SGT* **Reynolds,** Thomas C JR., Wilmington, DE, *AT-1-1 KO* +
*CPL* **Reynolds,** William E, San Clemente, CA, *SPT MCSC-ALBANY CW*
*1STLT* **Rhatigan,** William F, Pocasset, MA, *I-3-5 VN* +
*CPL* **Rhoads,** Stephen D, Seminole, FL, *81MM-2-5 VN* +
*PFC* **Rhodes,** Charles R, Stanton, MI, *C-1-7 WWII CH* +
*CPL* **Rhudy,** Porter O, Saulsbury, TN, *B-1-7 WWII* +
*CPL* **Rice,** Browne B JR., Houston, TX, *WPNS-7MAR WWII* +
*PFC* **Rice,** Earl F, Reno, NV, *A-1-7 WWII CH* +
*CPL* **Richard,** Daniel P, Napa, CA, *WPNS-1-7-KO* +
*GYSGT* **Richard,** John M, Lake Charles, LA, *AM-MO-1ORD HQ-IIIMAF KO VN* +
*CPL* **Richard,** Joseph D, Port Arthur, TX, *H-3-7 VMF213 WWII KO* +
*SGT* **Richards,** Harry D, Lebanon, PA, *D-2-11 WWII* +
*SGT* **Richards,** James L, Redding, CA, *A/C-1RE-CON VN* +
*CPL* **Richards,** Mark A, Dixon, CA, *B-1MT VN* +
**Richards,** Morris W JR., Scottsdale, AZ, *H-3-7 KO* +
*SGT* **Richards,** Richard L, Tomball, TX, *M-3-27 VN* +
*PHM2* **Richards,** William BERT, Oxford, NJ, *3/6ARMAMPH F-2-5 WWII CH*
*SGT* **Richardson,** David E, Miami Springs, FL, *HMH463 VN* +
*GYSGT* **Richey,** Weldon L JR., Springtown, TX, *1LSB CW*
*PLTSGT* **Richter,** Sherman, Saint Louis Park, MN, *B-1-7 KO* +
*CAPT* **Rickert,** John H, Rye Beach, NH, *E-2-7 H-3-11 VN* +
*SGTMAJ* **Rideout,** V R, North Little Rock, AR, *F-2-5* +
*CPL* **Rider,** R J, Tonawanda, NY, *C-1-11 I-3-1 VN* +
*SGT* **Ridgeway,** Ray M, Rogue River, OR, *A-1-7 KO* +
*SGT* **Ridley,** Donald D, Reno, NV, *1TK KO* +
*SGT* **Rienhardt,** Allen P, Syracuse, NY, *B-1-7 VN* +
*CPL* **Rierdon,** Thomas P, Jacksonville, FL, *G-2-5 SWA* +
*SGT* **Rieth,** Terence J, Westwego, LA, *B-1AM-TRAC KO* +
*MGYSGT* **Riggle,** Andrew J, Saint Charles, MO, *VMFA542 1ST MAW MAG11 VN*
*CPL* **Riggs,** James R, Santa Clara, CA, *A-1-7 WWII* +
*MAJ* **Riggs,** Robert K, Winchester, VA, *WPNS-2-5 H&MS15 H&S-5MAR KO VN* +
*SSGT* **Rigoni,** Vincent E, Napa, CA, *1CSG KO* +
*CPL* **Riha,** Frank D, Newbury, CA, *B-1-1 WWII* +
*SGT* **Riley,** James C, Libertyville, IL, *INDIA CO 3RD BN 1ST MAR* +
*CWO4* **Riley,** Michael R, Humble, TX, *A-1-7 VN SWA*
*CAPT* **Rimes,** John H, Naples, FL, *E-2-1 KO* +
*SGT* **Rinard,** Arthur C, Placentia, CA, *3AABN-KO* +
*1STSGT* **Rincon,** Bert Q, Tucson, AZ, *A-1-1 1MAR KO* +
*2NDLT* **Rine,** John H, Ocean View, DE, *F-2-7 VN* +
*MSGT* **Rinehart,** R L, Little Rock, AR, *HQ-3-11* +
*CWO* **Ring,** Edwin R, Punta Gorda, FL, *WPNS-3-5 M-3-1 KO* +
*SGT* **Ringler,** George DANIEL, Blairsville, PA, *MAG33 KO* +
*PFC* **Rinken,** Robert M, Honeoye Falls, NY, *4.2-1-11 VN* +
*SGTMAJ* **Riojas,** Frank, Arlington, TX, *DIV SGT-MAJ VN* +
*CPL* **Riordan,** James D, Country Club Hills, IL, *1ST RECON BN VN*
*CPL* **Riordan,** Walter F, Kodak, TN, *A 1/5*
**Rios,** Brianna L, Gainesville, VA, *
*MRS* **Rios,** Cheryl, Haslet, TX, *ASSOCIATE* *
**Rios,** Frances R, South San Francisco, CA, *ASSOCIATE* *
*CAPT* **Rios,** Mitchell D, Gainesville, VA, *HMM462 CW* +
*SGT* **Rios,** Vincent, Haslet, TX, *A-1-5 VN* +
*CPL* **Rios,** Pete V, Pittsburg, CA, *IRAQ*
*MSGT* **Risch,** Stephen R, Eufaula, AL, *HQ-HQ VN* +
*1STLT* **Rishell,** C G, Columbia, MD, *D-1-7 VN* +
*CPL* **Ritcher,** Albert R, Mansfield, OH, *HQ-3-1 81MM KO* +
*LCPL* **Ritchie,** J S, Saint Francisville, LA, *E-2-11 CW* +
*SGT* **Ritchie,** William D, Des Plains, IL, *H&S-7MAR WWII CH KO* +
*SGT* **Ritter,** Harold T, Wilmington, DE, *HQCO HQBN 1ST MAR DIV KO*
*PFC* **Ritter,** M W, Hinsdale, IL, *155GUN BTRY WWII* +
**Rivers,** Larry W, Celebration, FL, *E-2-7 VN* +
*SGT* **Roach,** Joseph E, Houston, TX, *B-1-7 KO* +
*1STSGT* **Roach,** Robert W JR., Fallon, NV, *H&S 2-7 VN* +
**Roadifer,** Roy E, Custer, SD, *HQ-7MAR WWII CH* +
**Roan,** Charles C, South Williamsport, PA, *C-1-7 KO* +
*CPL* **Roan,** William B JR., Miami, FL, *D-1-1 VN* +
*MGYSGT* **Roane,** Lawrence H, Beaufort, SC, *HQ-1-1 KO VN* +
*SGT* **Robb,** James L, Willcox, AZ, *VMA311 MAG12 VN* +

*PFC* **Robbins,** James F, Vernon Hills, IL, *A-1-5 CH* +
*CPL* **Robbins,** Richard J, Santa Rosa, CA, *3RD AMPH TRAC BN*
**Roberge,** Larry S, Berlin, NH, *9ENGR VN* +
*CPL* **Roberts,** Arthur H, Savannah, GA, *G-3-1 KO* +
*LTCOL* **Roberts,** C R JR., Lockhart, TX, *1TK WWII KO* +
*SGT* **Roberts,** Charles H, Sunrise, FL, *R 2ND 2ND ITR CW CMC* +
*COL* **Roberts,** Darryl F, Ardmore, OK, *A-1-11 VN* +
*GYSGT* **Roberts,** Donald E, Santa Clara, UT, *H&S-1RECON HQ-7MAR VN* +
*PFC* **Roberts,** Donald L, Sharpsburg, GA, *1SERV CH* +
*LCPL* **Roberts,** R J, Lawndale, CA, *H&S-1SHPTY VN* +
*SGT* **Robertson,** C W SR., Wichita, KS, *D-2-5 KO* +
*CPL* **Robertson,** Gordon H, Barrington, RI, *B-1-1 KO* +
*CAPT* **Robertson,** Roland GENE, Garden City, ID, *HDQS CO IST MAR DIV*
*SGT* **Robertson,** W M, Wilton, CA, *155GUN 3-11MAR WWII KO* +
**Robertson,** William C, Mio, MI, *C-1-5 KO* +
*CPL* **Robichau,** Norman E, West Hills, CA, *1AM-TRAC KO* +
*PFC* **Robinson,** Alvin M, Indianapolis, IN, *1-7MAR VN* +
*PFC* **Robinson,** Bob S, Portland, OR, *F-2-5 CH*
*SGTMAJ* **Robinson,** Cliff, Lutz, FL, *DIV SGTMAJ KO VN* +
*PFC* **Robinson,** E M, Oshkosh, WI, *C-1-1 VN* +
*LTCOL* **Robinson,** Gilford G, Orlando, FL, *2/1, 1/5 VN*
*SGT* **Robinson,** Howard L, Orlando, FL, *HQ-HQ HQ-11MAR KO* +
*CAPT* **Robinson,** J D, Leesburg, VA, *K-3-1 VN* +
*CPL* **Robinson,** Jack W, Snellville, GA, *C-1-1 KO* +
*SGT* **Robinson,** James L, Bullhead City, AZ, *1ST ENGR, 1MAW VN* +
**Robinson,** Norman C, Neptune, NJ, *HQ-1-5 WWII CH* +
*SGT* **Robinson,** Richard S JR., Oceanside, CA, *MASS 3 3RD FAAD PLT*
*CPL* **Robinson,** Robert D, Swartz Creek, MI, *M-3-1 VN* +
*SGT* **Robles,** Ernest Z, Novato, CA, *I-3-7 KO* +
*CPL* **Roche,** Michael D, Aurora, IL, *HQ-1MAR VN* +
*SGT* **Rockhill,** David E, Grandview, MO, *HQ-1-11 KO* +
*CPL* **Rockhold,** Greg, Hobbs, NM, *3AMTRAC CW* +
*LCPL* **Rockman,** Jeremy PATRICK EDD, Black River Falls, WI, *E-2-1 2CAG VN* +
*PFC* **Rockwell,** Harry D, Colliers, WV, *HQ-1-1 VN* +
**Rodack,** Michael, Wappingers Falls, NY, *B-1TK KO*
*CPL* **Rodarte,** John R, Bullhead City, AZ, *1MAW HMW 463, MAG 16 VN*
*SGT* **Rodda,** Stephen C, Elko, NV, *1MAW VN* +
*PFC* **Rodeschin,** William M, Newport, NH, *WPNS-7MAR WWII CH* +
*CPL* **Rodgers,** Goodloe (Woody) H, Saint Augustine, FL, *1 AMTRAC KO* +
*LCPL* **Rodgers,** Leroy E, Ortonville, MI, *B-1-9 K-3-1 VN* +
*1STSGT* **Rodrequez,** Eugene, Oakdale, CT, *G-3-7 2-11MAR CH KO VN* +
*SGT* **Rodriguez,** Fernando, Signal Hill, CA, *C-1-5 CW* +
*LCPL* **Rodriguez,** Jimmie, Houston, TX, *H&S-1-5 VN* +
*GYSGT* **Rodriguez,** Juan J, Corpus Christi, TX, *E-2-7 H-3-7 KO*
*CPL* **Rodriguez,** Julio, Laverne, CA, *M-3-7 1MAR DIV VN*
*CPL* **Rodriguez,** Richard R, San Clemente, CA, *1 PION CW* +
*CAPT* **Roe,** James D, Lodi, CA, *1SVC REGT KO* +
*MAJ* **Roe,** Patrick C, Lopez Island, WA, *H&S-3-7 KO* +
*Capt* **Roe,** Ronald R, Danville, CA, *A-1-1 CMC* +
*SGT* **Rogers,** Billy D, Oklahoma City, OK, *C-1-11 KO* +
*CPL* **Rogers,** Cebert R, Charleston, WV, *A-1-5 KO* +
*PVT* **Rogers,** Frank J, Oneonta, NY, *I-3-11 WWII CH* +
*HM2* **Rogers,** J R, Dublin, GA, *I-3-7 KO* +
*SGT* **Rogers,** Joseph A, Waco, TX, *D-1ENGR 7MAR KO* +
*SSGT* **Rogers,** R E, Waianae, HI, *B-1TK KO* +
*MRS* **Rohde,** Elena, Bethpage, NY, *ASSOCIATE* *
**Rohrback,** Thomas V, Santa Barbara, CA, *B-1-1 KO* +
*SGTMAJ* **Rohrs,** Francis E, De Bary, FL, *I-3-1 KO VN* +
*SSGT* **Rolando,** Victor R, Bennington, VT, *M-4-11 KO* +
*LCPL* **Rolke,** William C, New Berlin, WI, *K-3-7 VN* +
*1STLT* **Rolleri,** M J, Arlington, VA, *2-7MAR* +
*CPL* **Rollette,** Donald L SR., Linthicum, MD, *H&S 11ENGR* +
*SGT* **Rollins,** James E, Sewanee, TN, *K-3-7 VN* +
*SGT* **Rollins,** Kenneth R, Pasadena, MD, *H-3-5 KO* +
*CPL* **Rolston,** Glen N, Henderson, NV, *H&S-1-5 VN* +
**Roman,** George J, Vidor, TX, *5MAR KO* +
*SGT* **Romanino,** Enrico S, Riverbank, CA, *HQ-11MAR KO* +
*CPL* **Romano,** S J, Rochester, NY, *1-1MAR WWII KO* +
**Romero,** A LEWIS, Aptos, CA, *81MM-3-1 WWII CH* +
*CPL* **Romine,** Gordon L, Tulsa, OK, *ORD-1CSG KO* +
*PFC* **Rommel,** Michael L, Sacramento, CA, *L-3-7 SVC VN* +
*CPL* **Romo,** Jose GABRIEL, Fontana, CA, *HQ BTRY REGT 12 MAR CW*
*CPL* **Roney,** James A, Carlisle, PA, *B-1-7 KO* +
*SGT* **Roney,** Walter L, Woodsboro, MD, *9DEF WWII* +
*SGTMAJ* **Rood,** John C JR., Wilmington, NC, *B-1-1 KO VN* +
*CPL* **Roos,** Gary A, Austin, TX, *MP-H&S-1FSSG SWA* +
*SGT* **Roper,** William I, Mount Olive, AL, *B-1-5 WWII* +
*SGT* **Rosati,** Dominick R, Syracuse, NY, *I-3-7 KO* +
*SGT* **Roscoe,** James S, Conway, SC, *FDC-2-11MAR KO* +
*EMR* **Rose,** D S, Clarksville, TN, *CB VN* +
*COL* **Rose,** Daniel R, Stafford, VA, *MEW33-MAG33 SWA* +
*MGYSGT* **Rose,** L A, Ballston Lake, NY, *3-7MAR* +
*COL* **Rose,** Murray F, Ashburn, VA, *A-1-17 1ENGR-SHPTY WWII KO* +
*CPL* **Rose,** Richard D, Des Moines, IA, *I-3-7 VMR953 WWII KO* +
*SSGT* **Rosegrant,** Robert D, Monticello, AR, *HQ-E-2-7 VN*
*PHM1* **Rosen,** Seymour M FMF, Haydenville, MA, *B-1-1 WWII CH* +
*PLTSGT* **Rosenheim,** Sidney, Silver Spring, MD, *F-2-11 H&S-2 WWII* +
*MR.* **Rosenmiller,** Alan J, San Carlos, CA, *B-1-5, 2-23 OIF* +
*PFC* **Ross,** Albert M, University City, MO, *G-3-7 KO* +
*SSGT* **Ross,** B D, Somerset, NJ, *PION WWII CH KO* +
*1STLT* **Ross,** Charles A, La Place, LA, *HQ-9ENGR VN* +
*SGT* **Ross,** George, New Lenox, IL, *MP-RECON 2-1MAR CW* +
**Ross,** John J, Alexandria, VA, *D-2-11 KO*
*SSGT* **Rossell,** Robert A, Southampton, NJ, *B-1-5 H-3-5 KO* +
*PFC* **Rossetti,** Robert M, Stone Harbor, NJ, *MAG11 WWII* +
**Rotar,** Daniel G, Clinton Township, MI, *E-2-5 VN* +
*MGYSGT* **Roth,** Allen RICHARD, Huntington Beach, CA, *A-1-1 11MAR CH KO VN* +
*COL* **Roth,** Earl F, Kissimmee, FL, *4.2-7MAR E-2-7 WWII CH KO VN* +
*SSGT* **Roth,** Edward J, Ringwood, NJ, *H&S-2-5 KO* +
*SGTMAJ* **Rothove,** L J, Yorba Linda, CA, *I/K-3-7 VN* +
*SGT* **Rotton,** Luther C JR., Birmingham, AL, *SVC-3-11 KO* +
**Rousseau,** Cyril J, Scottsdale, AZ, *E-2-1 CW* +
*CPL* **Rousseau,** Matthew R, Stuart, FL, *B-1-5 WWII* +
*CPL* **Rowe,** James H II, Mcsherrystown, PA, *A-1RECON VN* +
*HM1* **Rowe,** Marshall A, Alta Loma, CA, *H-2-1 7COMM VN* +
*SGT* **Rowland,** Thomas E, Henderson, NV, *HQ 1ST MAR DIV* +
*E-3* **Rowland,** William E II, The Villages, FL, *1ST RECON BN A CO*
*SGT* **Roy,** Joseph L, Vero Beach, FL, *A-1-5 KO* +
*PFC* **Roy,** Ronald, Lowell, MA, *1SHPTY VN* +
*HN* **Rozanski,** Leonard J, Oak Creek, WI, *A-1-5 VN* +
*CAPT* **Rozyskie,** Elwin A, Mobile, AL, *I-3-1 KO* +
*SGT* **Rubio,** Manuel JR., Lucerne Valley, CA, *G-2-1 C-1-5 VN* +
*SSGT* **Ruckdeschel,** Harold R III, Oxford, IN, *CAG* +
*SGT* **Rudoi,** Wesley, San Francisco, CA, *7TH MAR REGT VN*
*CPL* **Rueckert,** Roger F, Vancouver, WA, *H&S-1-5 H&S-2-1 CW* +
**Ruffoni,** Dino, Torrance, CA, *3 BN 12 MAR*
*SSGT* **Ruger,** Dj, Oregon City, OR, *2/7 1RECON 3/11 1FSSG VN*
*LCPL* **Ruggles,** Floyd A, North Saint Paul, MN, *RECON VN*
*CPL* **Ruman,** P A, Houston, TX, *H&S-3AMTRAC WWII* +
*LTCOL* **Rumburg,** Kenneth P, Glendale, CA, *E-2-11 KO* +
**Ruminski,** Florence F, New Cumberland, PA, *ASSOCIATE* *
*SGT* **Runge,** Charles E, Reading, MA, *H&S-11MAR KO* +
*SGT* **Runion,** Ronald L, Wellington, OH, *E-2-1 VN* +
*SGT* **Ruperd,** Walter R, Kansas City, KS, *B-1-7 MAG14 CW* +
*SGT* **Rushing,** Kenneth P, Vidalia, LA, *H&S CO 3D AABN* +
*SGT* **Rusinko,** Paul, Yonkers, NY, *G-3-7 KO* +
**Russ,** John, Irvington, AL, *G-3-7 KO* +
*MGYSGT* **Russell,** Danny R, Mohave Valley, AZ, *2-7MAR CW*
*CPL* **Russell,** Donald, Frankfort, IL, *K-3-7 B-1-3 VN*
*SGT* **Russell,** John F, Vancouver, WA, *HQ CO MAR CORPS BAND VN*
*LCPL* **Russell,** Ronald E, Highwood, MT, *C-1-7 VN* +
**Russo,** Angelo D, Waltham, MA, *D-1-7 WWII* +
*1STLT* **Rutherford,** Robert E, Madison, IN, *I-3-11 1-7MAR KO* +
*COL* **Rutledge,** Earl R, Las Vegas, NV, *D-2-7 3/51MAF KO VN* +
*CPL* **Ruud,** Kenneth E, Coon Rapids, MN, *F/H-2-1 KO* +
*1STSGT* **Rux,** Lee, San Antonio, TX, *B-1-7 KO* +
*SGT* **Ruzza,** V, Rotterdam, NY, *G-2-5 VN* +
**Ryan,** Bernard F, Shoreham, NY, *HQ BN KO* +
*CPL* **Ryan,** E R, Lansing, MI, *A-1TK WWII* +
*CAPT* **Ryan,** Hewitt F, Tuscaloosa, AL, *A-1-5 KO* +
*CPL* **Ryan,** John H IV, Minonk, IL, *H&S-1ST TK BN VN*
*SSGT* **Ryan,** Joseph D, Greenwood Village, CO, *G-3-7 KO* +
*SGT* **Ryan,** Patrick L, Green Valley, AZ, *C-1TKS KO* +
*PFC* **Ryan,** Peter V, Tequesta, FL, *B-1-5 CH KO* +
*MR.* **Rybczyk,** Stanley M, Memphis, TN, *HQ/D-1-7 WWII* +
*SSGT* **Ryff,** John V, Chambersburg, PA, *AT-7MAR KO* +

**Saathoff,** John J, Sevierville, TN
CPL **Sabourin,** Joseph A, Saint Louis, MO, C-1TK WWII CH+
LCDR **Sack,** Kent L, Pacheco, CA, 1HOSP VN+
SGT **Saco,** J T, Manchester, MA, SCOUT DOGS VN+
PVT **Sada,** Victor, Miami, FL, A-1-5 VN+
DR **Saddler,** John L JR., Ontario, CA, A-1AMTRAC WWII+
CPL **Sadler,** Jack D, Bonham, TX, H-3-7 KO+
COL **Sadler,** Woodson A, Lexington, VA, HQ-HQ CW+
SSGT **Sadowski,** John S, Moorpark, CA, HQ-11MAR KO VN+
**Sadowski,** Pauline, West Allis, WI, ASSOCIATE*
**Sager,** George A JR., Healdsburg, CA, I-3-7 VN+
MAJ **Sager,** William H, Arlington, VA, K/I-3-1 WWII+
**Sahlein,** Hugo F, Pasadena, CA, 1-1MAR 4JASCO WWII CH+
CPL **Sakowicz,** William J, New Britain, CT, WAR DOG PLT WWII+
SGT **Sakura,** Mark I, Woodinville, WA, HQ-26MAR D-2-11 VN+
SGT **Salas,** Joseph I JR., San Diego, CA, E-2ND BN 7TH MAR KO+
PHM3 **Salazar,** Frank JR., Houston, TX, 1MED WWII KO+
CPL **Salazar,** Gabriel, Cheyenne, WY, A-1-11MAR KO+
SGT **Salazar,** Raymond A, San Jose, CA, G-3-11 KO+
CPL **Salerno,** Bart D, Wildwood Crest, NJ, 1MED KO+
CPL **Salerno,** John J, Oak Brook, IL, A-1-5 KO+
CPL **Salimbene,** Roger, Barnegat, NJ, H-3-5 KO+
PVT **Salisbury,** Roland "Bud" M, Mount Vernon, OR, L-3-7 WWII+
CPL **Salomone,** Joseph RONALD, Venice, FL, VMF 224 1ST MAW KO
SSGT **Salter,** Ledarby, Shreveport, LA, ANGLICO-2-5 KO+
LCPL **Saltinas,** Edward A, Riverhead, NY, A-TKS KO+
HM3 **Saltsman,** Henry C JR., Taft, CA, 1ENGR VN+
SGT **Saltzman,** Joseph W, Yarmouth Port, MA, G-2-26 1-7MAR VN+
SGTMAJ **Sammartino,** Anthony, Oceanside, CA, DIV HQ HQBN
TSGT **Sampson,** Louis F, Seabrook, NH, A-1MT WWII KO+
SGT **Sampson,** W A, Saddle Brook, NJ, 1SVC WWII CH KO+
**Samra,** Sammy S, Rialto, CA, 1ENGR KO+
SGT **Sams,** Louis, Frankfort, KY, H-3-7 KO+
HM2 **Samuelson,** L D, Farmington, UT, A-1MED VN+
SGT **San Souci,** Albert G, Surprise, AZ, 1-1MAR 1TK VN+
**Sanchez,** Henry, Palm Desert, CA, 2 BN 26TH MAR
SGT **Sandall,** Walter J, Green Valley, IL, 7COMM CW+
**Sanders,** Gordon P, Rome, GA, 1MAR WWII CH KO+
**Sanders,** Stephen M, Broken Arrow, OK, 1RECON VN+
CAPT **Sanderude,** Kenneth G, Bend, OR, A-1TK WWII CH+
LCPL **Sandlin,** Bill R, Irvine, CA, 1ST MAR DIV+
LCPL **Sandoval,** Ramon, Highland, CA, B-1MED VN
E-3 **Sandoval,** Sandy, Corpus Christie, TX, 1 BN 5 MAR
1STLT **Sandro,** Pete M, Newport Beach, CA, 3RD RECON BN 3 MAR 3-28 VN
CPL **Sanford,** Roger T, Garden Grove, CA, 3RD MARDIV OKINAWA-MAG15 ELTORO+
MAJGEN **Sangalis,** C D, Schererville, IN, I-3-7 1SVC CH KO+
PFC **Sangiorgio,** Frank P, Newark, NJ, B-1-7 WWII+
GYSGT **Santiago,** Paul, Jackson, NJ, HQ-1-5 HQ-3-11 ANGLICO 1SIG KO+
**Santor,** Kenneth F, Reno, NV, C-1-1 KO+
CPL **Santos,** Eugene JR., Martinez, CA, H-3-7 CH KO+
SSGT **Santos,** Jack A, Brentwood, CA, WPNS-3-1 KO+
SSGT **Santos,** Manuel F, Rio Vista, CA, 1ST RADIO BN VN
SGT **Santos,** Robert B, Shrewsbury, MA, 1ST SHORE PTY-KO
**Santos,** Sandra, Rio Vista, CA, ASSOCIATE*
SSGT **Santos,** Thomas, Ironwood, MI, ORD CO, 1ST SER BN, 1MAR DIV CH+
SGT **Sappington,** Michael F, Saint Louis, MO, HQ-11MAR CW+
**Saraceno,** C.P., Redondo Beach, CA, G-2-1 VN+
PFC **Saraceno,** Victor J, Portland, OR, 4.5 RKT F-2-11 KO+
SGT **Sarazin,** Arthur M, Eastham, MA, 1ANGLICO KO+
CAPT **Sargeant,** Robert A, Rio Vista, CA, 1ST PIONEER BN, 1ST FORCE SVC REG+
SGT **Sarlls,** Anthony G, Aurora, CO, 1MAW VN+
GYSGT **Sarmento,** Ernest A, Atascadero, CA, 5/7MAR KO VN+
HR **Sarniguet,** Claire E, Saint Louis, MO, FIELD MED SVC SCH+
SGT **Sarros,** George S, Schererville, IN, I-3-1 WWII KO+
CPL **Sartain,** Ronald B, Silver Spring, MD, G-2-7 VN+
LT **Satterfield,** Frank G III, Houston, TX, D/C-1-5 VN
SGT **Saulnier,** Ralph J, New Bedford, MA, COMM KO+
MAJ **Sauls,** R G, Marshall, NC, E-2-5+
PFC **Saunders,** William D, Bondurant, WY, 4JASCO WWII CH+
**Savacool,** Herbert A, Newton, NJ, A-1-7 KO+
CPL **Savage,** B J, Westminster, CA, B-1-7 B-1-5 VN+
CPL **Savage,** George E, Cypress, TX, SPT 3ANGLICO KO+
SGT **Saverno,** Ronald J, Parma, OH, F-2-1 KO+
SGT **Savino,** Daniel M, Freehold, NJ, WPNS-2-1 KO+
CAPT **Sawyer,** William F, Oceanside, CA, H&S CO 3RD BN 7TH MAR HQ CO 7TH MAR VN+
COL **Saxton,** Patrick JAMES, Kailua, HI, 1AMTRAC KO VN+
CPL **Saxton,** Ray A, Brighton, CO, K-3-5 WWII+
SGT **Sayles,** Peter HERBERT, Sebastian, FL, H&S CO 1/5 VN
COL **Saylor,** Bennett W, Oceanside, CA, HQ-11MAR C/S-HQ OIF+
CPL **Scafidi,** John N, Jersey City, NJ, K-3-5 VN
LCPL **Scalf,** Paul W, Holland, MI, F-2-11 VN+
**Scarborough,** A L, Virginia Beach, VA, C-1AMTRAC KO+
1STSGT **Scarborough,** Daniel P, Roberts, ID, A-1-7 H&S-2-5 WWII KO VN+
PFC **Scardena,** Joseph L, Livingston, NJ, WPNS-1-7 KO+
PVT **Scarlato,** Salvatore, Hauppauge, NY, H&S/B-1SHPTY KO+
**Schaefer,** Lois A, Bottineau, ND, ASSOCIATE*
CPL **Schaeffer,** John T, Machesney Park, IL, C15
CAPT **Schaffner,** Harry, La Quinta, CA, 4TH DIV RESERVE
CAPT **Schaller,** Donald F, Scottsdale, AZ, E-2-11 KO+
SSGT **Schassen,** John C, La Pine, OR, 1ST FORCE RECON-2-4 VN
SGT **Schauble,** Albert E, Saint John, WA, H&S-7MAR KO+
MSGT **Schaudel,** George L, Woodbridge, VA, WPNS-1-1 KO VN+
CPL **Schaustal,** Leonard J, Santa Clarita, CA, FMFPAC CW+
MSGT **Scheese,** Richard A, Dugway, UT, 3-11MAR KO VN+
SGT **Scheffki,** Marvin H, Phoenix, AZ, HQ-11 KO+
**Scheidel,** David C, Oklahoma City, OK, HQ-7MAR VN+
MAJ **Scheiern,** Michael L, San Pedro, CA, 1-1MAR HQ-11MAR SWA+
SGT **Schelb,** Bernard L, Longview, WA, HQ/K-4-11 KO+
CPL **Schera,** Ciro D, Bergenfield, NJ, D-1-7 WWII+
MSGT **Scherer,** Jerry B, Billings, MT, 1AMTRAC1TK KO VN+
SGTMAJ **Schickel,** James JOSEPH, Fontana, CA, 3-9 3D ANGLICO OIF+
**Schiff,** Jon, Coronado, CA, 5 MAR
SGT **Schilb,** F L, Prairie Home, MO, A-1TKS KO+
TSGT **Schilke,** Donald LEE, Englewood, FL, MAG-33, MACS-21 KO+
SGT **Schiller,** Richard A, North Jupiter, FL, COMMCO-HQBN CW+
CPL **Schimmel,** Wayne M, Winfield, MO, 175 GUN BTRY VN+
SGT **Schlagel,** Richard L, Clinton Township, MI, C-1-5 VN+
LCPL **Schlagenhauf,** Johnny J, Dallas, NC, HQ-7-1 VN+
CPL **Schlesinger,** Barry M, Fresno, CA, B-1-5 1ST MAR DIV
CWO5 **Schley,** Walter H JR., Kansas City, KS, B-7MT VN SWA+
**Schlicher,** Marvin D, Beech Grove, IN, E-1RECON VN+
CPL **Schlupp,** William, Hainesport, NJ, A-1-11 WWII+
CDR **Schluter,** Greg, Oceanside, CA, 2-5 1-11 OEF
SGT **Schmalzbauer,** James D, New Brighton, MN, MAG15 VMF253 KO+
**Schmick,** Laudine THERESE, Arlington, TX, ASSOCIATE*
LTCOL **Schmick,** Walter C JR., Arlington, TX, 11MAR CW+
SGT **Schmidt,** Dale G, Cincinnati, OH, G-3-5 KO+
**Schmidt,** John R, Hastings, NE, H-3-5 KO+
PVT **Schmidt,** John R, Elmira Heights, NY, H&S/C-1TK WWII CH+
CPL **Schmidt,** Randall B, Medina, OH, K-3-1 VN+
**Schmidt,** Robert K SR., Glenburn, ME, B-1-1 1RECON VN+
SGT **Schmidt,** Robin A, Columbus, OH, F-2-1 KO+
SGT **Schmirler,** Wayne E, Neenah, WI, 1SHPTY VN+
CPL **Schmitz,** Robert A, Bella Vista, AR, AT 5MAR KO+
CAPT **Schmitz,** William V, Newton, NJ, F-2-7 1FORREC KO VN
GYSGT **Schmoyer,** A H, Central Valley, CA, 11MAR WWII KO VN+
CPL **Schnautz,** Rene D, Evansville, IN, C-1-5 WWII CH+
**Schnautz,** Robert L, San Diego, CA, C-1-1 WWII KO+
GYSGT **Schneider,** Brian W, Joshua Tree, CA, HQCO-3-4 OIF+
**Schneider,** Fred R, Milwaukee, WI, C CO 1ST ENG BN
MAJ **Schneider,** Robert I JR., Reading, PA, K-3-7 VN
SSGT **Schneider,** Ronald D, Novato, CA, F-2-7 KO+
CPL **Schneider,** William H, Tucson, AZ, H&S-11MT VN+
SGT **Schoenecker,** John L, Cocoa Beach, FL, HQ-1-7 WWII+
SSGT **Schoenfeld,** John E, Cincinnati, OH, H&S-2-1 1ST MAR DIV KO+
MAJ **Schoon,** John E, Rickreall, OR, 7ENGR KO+
HMC **Schoonover,** Edward N, Charlotte, MI, D-2-5-MED KO VN+
SSGT **Schott,** E M, Yakima, WA, G-3-5 KO+
SGT **Schraub,** Billie B, Seguin, TX, G-3-7 KO+
TSGT **Schreiber,** August J, Dillon, MT, H-3-11 WWII+
CAPT **Schroeder,** Frederick W, Carlsbad, CA, HQ/B-1-7 KO+
SSGT **Schroeder,** George E, Wichita, KS, H&S-1-11 H&S-1ENGR CH+
**Schroeder,** Kenneth, Elma, NY, HQ-5MAR VN+

*CPL* **Schroeder,** R J, Delray Beach, FL, *L-4-11 CW* +
*GYSGT* **Schuff,** Leroy E, Neenah, WI, *D-2-5 2LAAM KO VN* +
*CAPT* **Schultz,** Carl A, Fenton, MO, *3-5MAR VN*
*SGT* **Schultz,** E R, Tiffin, OH, *F-2-7 H&S-2-7 KO* +
*MSGT* **Schultz,** G L, Orlando, FL, *B-1-1 VN* +
*TSGT* **Schultz,** Gene L, Hudson, WI, *C-1-7 KO* +
*CPL* **Schultz,** George E, Conway, SC, *1AMTRAC WWII* +
*SGT* **Schultz,** George W, Bunnell, FL, *H&S-5MAR KO* +
**Schultz,** Harold, Palm Desert, CA, *G-3-7 KO* +
*GYSGT* **Schultz,** Henry E, Aiken, SC, *HQ-HQ 2-11MAR KO VN* +
*SGT* **Schultz,** Johnie A, Langley, OK, *A-1-1 KO* +
*CPL* **Schultz,** Richard D, Seattle, WA, *VMF121 WWII CH* +
*LCPL* **Schultz,** Wayne A, North Judson, IN, *SUP DPI CW* +
*LCPL* **Schulz,** Miriam, Linden, NJ, *H&S BN*
*CPL* **Schulze,** Francis T, Bristol, CT, *FLSG-B-1FLC VN* +
*SGTMAJ* **Schum,** Ray, Palm Springs, CA, *1MAR DIV WWII KO RVN*
*LCPL* **Schussler,** Kenneth W, Orland Park, IL, *B-1-5 VN* +
*SGTMAJ* **Schutzman,** Bernard M, Rhinebeck, NY, *H&S-3-5 KO* +
*CAPT* **Schwab,** Carl P, Rockford, IL, *H-3-5 KO*
*TSGT* **Schwab,** John F, Surprise, AZ, *HQ-HQ 11TH MAR KO*
*SGT* **Schwab,** Lyle P, Orchard Park, NY, *ANGLICO-1SIG KO*
*CPL* **Schwartz,** Art B, Seal Beach, CA, *WPNS-3-5 KO* +
**Schwartz,** J W, Houston, TX, *MT-1MAR VN* +
*SSGT* **Schwartz,** Ralph G, Bowling Green, KY, *C-1TK VN, 1ST & 3RD PLT VN*
*SSGT* **Schwarz,** Harold F, Saint Paul, MN, *HQ-3-11 KO* +
*LCPL* **Schwarz,** Phillip S, Dubuque, IA, *B CO 1CEB*
*LTCOL* **Schwarzkopf,** Michael A, Atlanta, GA, *A-1TK SWA* +
*CAPT* **Schwetje,** Craig R, San Diego, CA, *B-1RECON OIF* +
*PFC* **Scibetta,** J T, Jersey City, NJ, *A-1-7 CW* +
*LTCOL* **Scofield,** Jeffrey P, Dumfries, VA, *E-2-11 OIF* +
*PFC* **Sconiers,** Edward L, Ellenwood, GA, *WPNS-3-5 KO* +
*SSGT* **Scott,** A E, Yuma, AZ, *HQ-1-5 KO* +
*CPL* **Scott,** Carl F, Eldwood, IN, *B-1-7 WWII* +
*CPL* **Scott,** George W, Portland, OR, *HQ-1MAW KO* +
*CPL* **Scott,** Harold R, Saint Louis, MO, *H&S-7MAR DMZ KO* +
*SGT* **Scott,** Jason, Highlands, NJ, *HQBN 1ST MAR DIV SWA* +
*SGT* **Scott,** Kelly F, Lake Oswego, OR, *B-1RECON 1MAR VN* +
*CPL* **Scott,** Lynwood V, Riverview, FL, *H&S-3-5 VN* +
*SGT* **Scott,** Richard L, Jacksonville, FL, *HQ-3-11 VN* +
*SGT* **Scoville,** Dennis H, Walnut, CA, *WPNS/G-3-5 KO* +
**Scroggs,** Donald D, Bellingham, WA, *B-1-5 WWII CH* +
*CAPT* **Scurich M.A. J.D,** Rick, Merced, CA, *1-5 2-5 VN*
**Scurlock,** Loren E, Los Angeles, CA, *K-4-11 KO* +
*CPL* **Seagrave,** Alan F, Chula Vista, CA, *A-1-5 KO*
*CAPT* **Seale,** Thomas F III, Northport, AL, *7th COMM BN 1st MAR DIV* +
*CAPT* **Search,** George B, Green Valley, AZ, *1TK KO VN*
*COL* **Seaton,** James B III, Oceanside, CA, *1-11MAR HQ-HQ OIF* +
*CPL* **Seberger,** George C, Garden Valley, CA, *A-1-5 KO*
*CPL* **Sebetto,** Raymond A, Lambertville, MI, *H-3-1 KO* +
**Seddio,** A D, San Francisco, CA, *COMM 1MAR VN* +
*CPL* **Sedrowski,** Timothy S, Roseville, MI, *L-3-5 VN* +
*CPL* **Seeley,** Bernard J, Port Richey, FL, *A-1-7 KO* +
*PHM3* **Seeley,** John E, Kihei Maui, HI, *C-1MED BN WWII* +
*CPL* **Sehrt,** James W JR., Redding, CA, *D-1-7 VN* +
*CPL* **Seifert,** Lee R, Copperton`, UT, *B-1-5 VN* +
*SGT* **Self,** Donald M, Ringgold, GA, *4-11MAR KO* +
*CPL* **Sells,** Ronald M, Port Lavaca, TX, *3 AMTRAC VN* +
*CPL* **Semrau,** Dennis E, Wind Lake, WI, *H-3-1 KO* +
*CPL* **Sena,** Joseph G, Clearwater, FL, *H&S-1TK WWII* +
*CPL* **Sena,** Salvatore V SR., Newington, CT, *2MAW VN* +
*2NDLT* **Senatore,** Thomas J, Cape Coral, FL, +
*CPL* **Senneke,** David W, Naperville, IL, *A-1-5 VN*
*COL* **Seo,** Byoung M, Los Angeles, CA, *KMC KO* +
*SGT* **Seppala,** Gary M, Ypsilanti, MI, *E-2-26 VN* +
*SGT* **Serrano,** Jesus J, Calexico, CA, *1st LSB, 1ST FSSG* +
*SSGT* **Sessums,** Richard C, Reno, NV, *I-3-7 KO* +
*MSGT* **Sewell,** C R, Phoenix, AZ, *HQ-5MAR WWII KO* +
*LTCOL* **Sewell,** Leonard G, Augusta, GA, *1SIG KO* +
*PFC* **Seyffarth,** William C, Hicksville, NY, *H&S-11MAR CH* +
*SGT* **Seymour,** Eldridge E, Yulee, FL, *H&S-1AMTRAC CW* +
*SGT* **Shafrath,** James L, Bastrop, TX, *L-3-1 VN* +
*GYSGT* **Shank,** L G, Stafford, VA, *H-2-1 HQ-2-7 KO VN* +
**Shannon,** J W, Pacifica, CA, *3-17MAR* +
*LCPL* **Shannon,** Patrick J, Leesburg, FL, *I-3-5 VN* +
*SGT* **Shannon,** Patrick T, Pittsburgh, PA, *B-1-1 KO* +
*SGT* **Sharkey,** Daniel J, Toms River, NJ, *ANGLICO 2-5 KO* +
*DR* **Sharow,** Ralph J, Goodlettsville, TN, *1TK VN* +
*1STSGT* **Sharp,** James A JR., Goodyear, AZ, *F-2-7 HQ-HQ KO VN* +
**Shave,** W M, Farmingdale, NJ, *B-1-1 VN* +
*CPL* **Shaw,** Edward A, Nokomis, FL, *C/D-1RECON VN* +
*CPL* **Shaw,** Gerald, Wantagh, NY, *H&S-1-11 WWII CH* +
*CPL* **Shaw,** Ronald J, Thousand Palms, CA, *E-2-7 KO* +
*CPL* **Shaw,** William C JR., Minneapolis, MN, *HQ-1MT WWII CH* +
*LCPL* **Shea,** Michael S, Chanhassen, MN, *MAG16 1MAW VN* +
*CPL* **Shea,** William J, Backus, MN, *2 AAA/AW KO* +
*LCPL* **Shearouse,** A.J., Cameron, NC, *C-1-5 VN*
*CPL* **Shedd,** Donald C, Wallingford, VT, *A-1-5 WWII* +
**Shedd,** Wesley M JR., Shrewsbury, MA, *M-3-7 VN* +
*CPL* **Shedlov,** William L, Los Alamitos, CA, *H&S-1SPLWPNS KO* +
*CAPT* **Sheehan,** John F, Anza, CA, *D-1-7TH MAR G-2-5TH MAR* +
*MGYSGT* **Sheehan,** John H, Merrimack, NH, *HQBN G-3 VN* +
*MR.* **Sheldon,** Donald T, Brooklyn, NY, *D-2-7 KO* +
*PFC* **Shelkin,** Barry D, Alexandria, VA, *B-1-5 WWII CH KO* +
*COL* **Shelley,** G L III, Northfield, VT, *D-2-11 KO VN* +
*LCPL* **Shelton,** Fred L, Fort Worth, TX, *I-3-5 VN*
**Shelton,** Joseph M, Scottsdale, AZ, *HQ-2-1 VN* +
*PFC* **Shelton,** Larry J, Petersburg, IN, *I-3-7 KO* +
*MR.* **Shelver,** Jack D, Twentynine Palms, CA, *C-1-1 F-2-1 1PROVMP KO* +
*SGTMAJ* **Shepard,** Melvin, Wildomar, CA, *CHARLIE BTTRY, 1BN, 11MAR*
*CAPT* **Shepard,** Robert, Palm Desert, CA, *3RD MAR AIR WING* +
*LCPL* **Shepard,** Sekou, New York, NY, *C-1MP VN* +
*SGT* **Sheridan,** James R, West Caldwell, NJ, *H&S/E-2-11 WWII CH KO* +
*SGTMAJ* **Sheridan,** Norman L, Willis, TX, *B-1TANK VN* +
*SGT* **Sherman,** Dennis S, San Antonio, TX, *H&S/C-1-1 VN* +
*CPL* **Sherrick,** Russell J, Renton, WA, *E-2-7 VN* +
*SGT* **Shields,** Charles J, Arlington Heights, IL, *HQ BN 1ST MAR DIV KO* +
*1STSGT* **Shields,** Donald G, Saint Louis, MO, *1/8 - PNDC PORTSMOUTH, NH KO*
*CAPT* **Shifflette,** Leonard R, Harrisonburg, VA, *A-1-7 KO VN*
*CAPT* **Shifter,** Ernest, Laguna Hills, CA, *C-1-11 WWII KO* +
**Shim,** Johnny, Los Angeles, CA, *KMC* +
*LTCOL* **Shinkle,** Brian T, Albion, IL, *2-24 24 MEU* +
*SSGT* **Shipley,** Edward L JR., Peru, IA, *HQ-HQ WWII CH* +
*LT.* **Shipp,** Leslie N, San Antonio, TX, *H&S CO 1ST BN 1ST MAR REG SWA*
*LCPL* **Shipp,** William G, Huntington Beach, CA, *F-2-5 VN* +
*CPL* **Shipps,** James D, Huntington Beach, CA, *M-3-7 HQ CO, HQBN WWII CH* +
*MSGT* **Shivers,** J JR., Baltimore, MD, *H&S COMMPHOT WWII CH* +
*MAJ* **Shockley,** James G, Victor, MT, *7th COMM CW* +
**Shoemaker,** Mac, La Quinta, CA, *FSSG 3MARDIV*
*PFC* **Shofner,** Lee R, Knoxville, TN, *WPNS-2-7 KO* +
*SGT* **Sholl,** Vinton H, San Antonio, TX, *WPNS-1-5 KO* +
*LCPL* **Shomody,** Robert A, Camp Pendleton, CA, *C-1LAR CW* +
*1STLT* **Shore,** Ed SAMUEL, Merville, TN, *B-1-27 A-1-5 VN*
*SGT* **Short,** Michael JAMES, Gahanna, OH, *C-1-5 VN*
*SGT* **Shove,** Michael J, Somonauk, IL, *H&S-1MT VN* +
*SSGT* **Shraga,** George N, Clifton, NJ, *E-2-5 VN* +
**Shultz,** J H, Sunnyvale, CA, *11MAR* +
*GYSGT* **Shumaker,** August J, Fredericksburg, VA, *E-2-5 KO VN* +
*CAPT* **Shumaker,** James C, Elizabeth, PA, *HQ/B/D/BRDG-7ENGR VN* +
*PFC* **Shurtleff,** George H, Rochester, MA, *1PION BAND WWII* +
*CPL* **Shutts,** Lewis, Bullhead City, AZ, *MARDETC-VA61 VN* +
*CPL* **Siatkowski,** E J, Fort Myers, FL, *11DEF* +
*CAPT* **Sick,** Milt, Fort Myers, FL, *G-2-5 VN*
*MGYSGT* **Siegmann,** Duane P, Oceanside, CA, *2-1 3-7 DIV SCHOOL OIF*
*SGT* **Siev,** Israel, Ozone Park, NY, *I-3-1 WWII KO VN* +
*LTCOL* **Sifuentes,** Raul A, Dumfries, VA, *HMM 163 HMM164 VN* +
*CPL* **Siggins,** Gordon D, Grand Rapids, MI, *C-1-11 WWII CH* +
**Sigourney,** A R, Boston, MA, *A-1-7* +
*LCPL* **Sikkema,** Richard A, Grand Rapids, MI, *E-1RECON VN*
*CPL* **Silins,** Andris J, West Barnstable, MA, *K-3-7 VN* +
*CAPT* **Silliker,** Gordon L JR., June Lakes, CA, *RAD-COMM-HQ VN* +
*MGYSGT* **Silva,** Albert A, Oxnard, CA, *3-1 1-5 7TH MAR OIF*
*SGT* **Silva,** Chris B, Rosenburg, TX, *A-1SVC VN* +
*MAJ* **Silva,** Donald A, El Cajon, CA, *C-1-1 CH KO* +
*MSGT* **Silva,** Martin, El Paso, TX, *1MED 1RECON CW* +
*PFC* **Silvers,** Dan W, Plymouth, MN, *E-2BN 7MAR* +
*PFC* **Simanek,** Robert E, Farmington Hills, MI, *5MAR KO* +
*MSGT* **Simerman,** John D, Hernando, FL, *F-2-11 1MAW KO VN* +
*SGT* **Simmons,** Edwin B, Missouri City, TX, *A-1-5 G-2-7 VN* +

*CAPT* **Simon,** Edward J, Ramsey, IN, *K-4-11 KO VN* +
**Simoneau,** Robert A, Woodland Hills, CA, *1MAR VN* +
*SGT* **Simons,** Charles N, Annapolis, MD, *I-3-1 WWII KO* +
*PFC* **Simons,** Melvin L, Weatherford, TX, *B-1-11 WWII CH* +
*SGTMAJ* **Simpson,** David W, Portland, OR, *A-7ENGR CW* +
*CPL* **Simpson,** Donald, Spring Hill, FL, *H&S CO 2-5 KO* +
*SGT* **Simpson,** William W, Irving, TX, *G-3-1 KO* +
*CPL* **Sims,** Merle E, Decatur, IL, *D-2-1 KO* +
**Sims,** N L, Lyons, NJ, *E-2-7 KO* +
*MSGT* **Sims,** Pierre A, Claymont, DE, *4MAW VN SWA* +
*SSGT* **Sims,** Richard R, Atlanta, GA, *1-7MAR WWII CH KO* +
*GYSGT* **Sincock,** William F, Florence, AL, *B-SHORE PTY KO CW* +
**Sinderhoff,** Lee, Montrose, CA, *L-3-5 WWII KO* +
*SGT* **Singer,** Charles, Lake View Ter, CA, *K-3-5 HQ-2-5 VN* +
*SGTMAJ* **Singer,** Robert F, Fredericksburg, VA, *C-1-1 VN* +
*SGT* **Singleton,** William H, Louisville, KY, *M-4-11 KO*
*SGT* **Sinkfield,** Eddie J, Cincinnati, OH, *HQ-HQ 1-1 VN* +
*CAPT* **Sinn,** Donald F, San Jose, CA, *G-2 ATT 310 CIC WWII KO* +
*SGT* **Sinnett,** Robert S, Seaford, DE, *B-1-7 KO* +
*SGT* **Sinnicki,** John G, Barnegat, NJ, *1SIGCO WPNS-1-7 KO* +
*SGT* **Sisk,** Michael D, Baltimore, MD, *11MT VN* +
*SGTMAJ* **Siverson,** Paul W, Jacksonville, NC, *A-1-1 G-2-7 VN* +
*MSGT* **Six,** Ralph K, Harrisville, WV, *G/WPNS-3-1 KO* +
*SGT* **Sixbery,** Ken W, Bullhead City, AZ, *HQ-1-5 KO* +
*CPL* **Sizer,** W R, Windsor Locks, CT, *1MAW KO* +
*CAPT* **Skalski,** Stanley A, Homewood, IL, *MAG 11/16 VN* +
*CPL* **Skellchock,** Robert B, Woodland, CA, *F-2-7 VN* +
*HM1* **Skidmore,** Michael, Igo, CA, *A1/9, E2/5*
*CPL* **Skinner,** C J, Rochester, NY, *A/C-1-7 CH* +
*SGT* **Sklar,** S. Buddy, La Quinta, CA, *NSG CO G 1MAR DIV*
*BGEN* **Sklenka,** Stephen D, Oceanside, CA, *7MAR*
*CPL* **Skortz,** Alan R, Bartlett, IL, *MACS2-MACG28 CW* +
*SGT* **Skrabits,** Walter STEVEN, Little Falls, NJ, *3D AMTRAC KO*
**Skrha,** Steve, Oak Brook, IL, *G-2-5 WWII* +
*LCPL* **Skurnicki,** Thomas F, Wisconsin Dells, WI, *COMMSPT-7COMM VN* +
*GYSGT* **Slagle,** Louis E, Miami, FL, *B-1RECON VN* +
*SGTMAJ* **Slate,** Ron E, Temecula, CA, *2-5MAR HQ-1MAR VN*
*CPL* **Slater,** Jonathan B, North Myrtle Beach, SC, *B-1-5 VN*
*CPL* **Slater,** Robert J, Excelsior Springs, MO, *A-1-1 WWII CH* +
*MR.* **Slattery,** John, West Keansburg, NJ, *E/WPNS-2-7 KO* +
*1STLT* **Slavec,** Anthony P, Denver, CO, *1CSG WWII KO* +
*SGT* **Slavens,** Joseph C, Leavenworth, KS, *WSKY BTRY 3-11 1ST MAR VN* +
*CPL* **Sledd,** Herbert D JD, Lexington, KY, *C-8AMTRAC WWII CH* +
*LCPL* **Slee,** Ron F, Seattle, WA, *HQ-5MAR SVC-9ENGR VN* +
*SGT* **Slepsky,** Larry, Saline, MI, *K-4-11 KO* +
*SGT* **Slevin,** James J, Hawley, PA, *W-2-7 KO* +
*SGT* **Slifka,** Robert W, New Middletown, OH, *WPNS-3-7 KO* +
*HM2* **Slingluff,** Robert D, Baltimore, MD, *L CO 3RD PLT BAS 3RD BN VN* +
*SSGT* **Slovak,** Robert S, Corpus Christi, TX, *G-3-7 KO CW CMC*
*CPL* **Small,** Richard M, Defiance, OH, *I/M-3-7 WWII* +
*SGT* **Small,** William W, Newark, CA, *I-3-7 KO* +
*CPL* **Smalley,** Haskell L, Benton, CA, *G/I-3-1 KO* +
*SGT* **Smart,** Delbert D, Reno, NV, *C-1AMTRAC KO* +
*SGT* **Smart,** Harry C, San Antonio, TX, *E-2-7 KO* +
*PFC* **Smart,** William E, Tomball, TX, *G-3-7 KO* +
*SGT* **Smiley,** Edward P III, Baton Rouge, LA, *A-1-5 1MED VN* +
*SGT* **Smith,** A G, Los Angeles, CA, *1TK* +
*SGT* **Smith,** C RUSS, Livonia, MI, *H&S-1-5 KO* +
*SGT* **Smith,** Charles G, Canyon Lake, CA, *1-5MAR 1FSR VN* +
*CAPT* **Smith,** Charles W JR., Warrenton, VA, *E-2-5 KO VN* +
*CPL* **Smith,** Clifford O JR., Dale City, VA, *B-1-27 VN*
**Smith,** Daniel B, Aberdeen, MD, *B-1-1 WWII CH* +
*SSGT* **Smith,** Daniel P, Oceanside, CA, *VMCJ-3 VMCJ-1 1MAR VN* +
*CAPT* **Smith,** Donald F, Hickory, NC, *I-3-1 HQ-HQ KO VN*
*SGT* **Smith,** Donald K, Wilmington, DE, *D-2-7 KO* +
*SGT* **Smith,** Donald L, Portland, OR, *HQ BN 1ST MAR DIV KO VN* +
*SGT* **Smith,** Edward S, Chicago, IL, *1SVC KO*
*SGT* **Smith,** Gerald E, Medway, MA, *1TK* +
*SSGT* **Smith,** Glenn C, Manchester, PA, *H&S-3-5 VN* +
*LCOL* **Smith,** Harold BILL, Dallas, TX, *AMMO, 4/11, K BTRY 4/11 KO* +
**Smith,** Harold E, Little Rock, AR, *M-3-5 WWII* +
*CPL* **Smith,** Harry H, Sparks, MD, *I-3-7 KO* +
*SGT* **Smith,** Homer FRANK, West Palm Beach, FL, *H&S-1-1 WWII* +
*2NDLT* **Smith,** J D, Bristol, RI, *C-1-1 VN* +
*CAPT* **Smith,** J VAL, Pottsboro, TX, *F-2-7 KO* +
*SSGT* **Smith,** James O JR., Overland Park, KS, *H&S-3-1 KO* +
**Smith,** James R, Houston, TX, *1PROVMARBDE KO* +
*SGT* **Smith,** James, Fairfax, VA, *1RAIDER H&S-5MAR WWII* +
*SSGT* **Smith,** James (Greg) G, Boynton Beach, FL, *H&S-2-5 VN* +
*LCPL* **Smith,** John E, Middletown, NJ, *L-3-7 VN* +
*MGYSGT* **Smith,** Joseph D, Pompano Beach, FL, *B-1RECON VN* +
*1STLT* **Smith,** Keith L, South Haven, MN, *I-3-1-1 VN* +
*CPL* **Smith,** Lloyd T, San Francisco, CA, *M-3-1 VN* +
*HMCM* **Smith,** Malvin W, Roselle, IL, *C/D-1MED KO VN* +
*CPL* **Smith,** Martin J, Oakland, CA, *I-3-7 VN* +
*CPL* **Smith,** Paul R, Dana Point, CA, *3D ENG BN 3MAR DIV VN* +
*SSGT* **Smith,** R K, Lynnwood, WA, *RADIO-SIG KO* +
*LTCOL* **Smith,** R L, Quantico, VA, *HQ-11MAR VN* +
*1STSGT* **Smith,** Raymond L, White Bear Lake, MN, *HQ/C-1-7 KO VN* +
*SGT* **Smith,** Richard B, Hemet, CA, *E-2-7 KO* +
*SGTMAJ* **Smith,** Richard W, Oceanside, CA, *DIVSGTMAJ 2-11MAR SWA CW* +
*MAJ* **Smith,** Robert H, Oceanside, CA, *1TKS-1-1 KO VN* +
*PFC* **Smith,** Robert L, Rogersville, TN, *C-1-5 KO* +
*1STLT* **Smith,** Robert N, Washington, DC, *RECON KO VN* +
**Smith,** Robert (Smitty) S, Hanover, MA, *C/H-3-7 KO* +
*CPL* **Smith,** Ron M, Houston, TX, *MAINT-1CSG KO* +
*CPL* **Smith,** Ronald J, La Pine, OR, *H&S-11MAR KO* +
**Smith,** Sharon BRADSHAW, Virginia Beach, VA, *
*LTCOL* **Smith,** Thomas B, El Paso, TX, *H&S-1-7 KO* +
*CWO* **Smith,** Thomas J, Rathdrum, ID, *WPNS-1-5 KO* +
*SGT* **Smith,** Thomas J, Belleville, NJ, *A-1-1 KO* +
*PFC* **Smith,** Thomas J, Shawnee, OK, *MAG12 KO* +
*PFC* **Smithson,** Michael W, Anaheim, CA, *1MAR VN* +
*SGT* **Smithson,** Sidney J, Lakewood, CA, *VMCJ1/3 VN* +
*E-3* **Smithwick,** Wayne T, Depere, WI, *G-2-7 K-3-5 1ST MAR DIV*
*CAPT* **Smola,** James F, Silver Spring, MD, *E-2-7 KO* +
*CAPT* **Smoley,** Brian A, Silverdale, WA, *1ST MAR DIV STAFF HQBN SWA*
*SGT* **Smothers,** K P, Shingle Springs, CA, *1MAW VN* +
*SSGT* **Smothers,** Sean N, Shingle Springs, CA, *MAG16/39 SWA* +
*SGT* **Smuts,** Joseph E JR., Modesto, CA, *MACS-1 KO* +
*MGYSGT* **Snarski,** Anthony P, Saint Clair Shores, MI, *H&S-3-7 VN* +
*SSGT* **Snell,** Arthur J JR., Appleton, WI, *1/1*
*HMCM* **Snider,** David L, Poinciana, FL, *D-1RECON 1MED VN*
*SGT* **Sniras,** Albin R, Orlando, FL, *K-4-11 WWII CH KO* +
*SGT* **Snook,** Staley L, Edgerton, MO, *A-1-1 CH* +
*MGYSGT* **Snow,** Charles C, Crane Hill, AL, *AT-5MAR CH KO* +
*PFC* **Snow,** Robert M, Newport, NH, *1AMTRAC WWII* +
*CPL* **Snowden,** Ernest, Clay City, KY, *L-3-5 WWII* +
*MGYSGT* **Snowden,** Howard C, Twentynine Palms, CA, *H&S-1-7 HQ-1RECON VN* +
*LCPL* **Snyder,** D K, Montebello, CA, *ENGR VN* +
*SGT* **Snyder,** Harvey E, Bensenville, IL, *1MAR CW* +
*SGTMAJ* **Snyder,** James W, Kettering, OH, *C-1MT 1SHPTY KO VN* +
*SGT* **Snyder,** Thomas F, Nazareth, PA, *MT 1TKS VN* +
*PFC* **Snyder,** William E, Cincinnati, OH, *L-3-1 WWII* +
*CPL* **Soard,** Charles E, Aza Kongo, Japan, *1/2-5MAR VN* +
*PFC* **Socarras,** Manuel, North Arlington, NJ, *C-4-11 CW* +
*SGT* **Soda,** William R, Dunstable, MA, *K-3-7 CW VN* +
*SGT* **Soetaert,** Thomas J, Emporia, KS, *CAG 2-4MAR VN* +
*LCPL* **Sokolosky,** William D, East Brunswick, NJ, *M-3-5 VN* +
*CPL* **Sokoluk,** Arthur, Hamtramck, MI, *I-3-7 KO* +
*LTCOL* **Solis,** Gary D, Alexandria, VA, *3AMTRAC VN* +
*PFC* **Soltis,** Ronald A, Mason, MI, *SVC VN* +
*MSGT* **Son,** Kyu-Pyo, Seongnam Si, Kyeon-Ki-Do, Korea, +
*SGT* **Sondergaard,** Donald L, Long Beach, NY, *B-1-5 KO* +
*HM2* **Sonderman,** Joe, Columbus, OH, *H-2-5 VN* +
*HM3* **Sonderman,** Milton J, Saint Charles, MO, *1MAW KO*
*CAPT* **Song,** Jae S, Rancho Palos Verdes, CA, *ROKMC VN* +
*CPL* **Soper,** Earle W JR., Alexandria, VA, *A-1-5 CH* +
*CWO3* **Soper,** Harold G, Brainerd, MN, *AT-7MAR KO* +
*COL* **Soper,** Martha P, Edenton, NC, *ATT 1-7MAR SWA* +
*CPL* **Soper,** Rudy F, Lublin, WI, *I-3-5 WWII CH* +
*SSGT* **Sopp,** Richard A JR., Chesterfield, MO, *B-1-1 CH KO*
*MGYSGT* **Sora,** Allan M, San Diego, CA, *G-2-5 K-3-5 KO VN* +
*HM3* **Sorace,** Edward F, Elizabethtown, KY, *A-1-1-1 VN*
*SGT* **Sorenson,** William P, Zimmerman, MN, *B-1-7 KO*
*CPL* **Sorrells,** Jon H, Tyler, TX, *E-2-5 VN* +
*LT* **Sothoron,** W. Haddox, Selbyville, DE, *BN SURGEON 3-5 CW* +

*CPL* **Soto,** William T SR., Carson, CA, *D-2-7 KO*
*SSGT* **Soucie,** Gary J, Presque Isle, ME, *H&S CO III MAF DANAGE VN* +
*CPL* **Soufrine,** Sanford (Sandy), Woodbridge, CT, *H-3-1 B-1-1 KO* +
*SSGT* **Sousa,** Frank, Granby, MA, *ATT-1ANGLICO KO* +
*CAPT* **Southall,** James B USMC(RET.), Carlsbad, CA, *I-3-1 KO VN*
*MSGT* **Southworth,** W E, Mission Viejo, CA, *1MAW WWII CH KO* +
**Souza,** William, New Bedford, MA, *K/M-3-1 WWII* +
*MGYSGT* **Sova,** Thomas C JR., Perry Hall, MD, *1AVNENGR WWII KO VN* +
*SGT* **Sowell,** Henry B, Willis, TX, *C-3AMTRAC KO* +
*CPL* **Sowers,** Tom E, Atchison, KS, *4.5-11MAR KO* +
*SGTMAJ* **Sowers,** William T, Camp Pendleton, CA, *1ST MAR DIV*
*CPL* **Spada,** Salvatore, Wrightwood, CA, *G-2-1 CMC CW* +
*GYSGT* **Spagnuolo,** Charles P, Holt, MI, *1MAW 3MAW KO VN* +
*SGT* **Spann,** Martin B, Simi Valley, CA, *H&S 1/5*
*CPL* **Spano,** Andrew E, Hendersonville, TN, *K-3-5 WWII CH* +
*SGT* **Spano,** Bob, West Chester, PA, *M-3-5 VN CW* +
*SGTMAJ* **Sparks,** Cooper L, Shongaloo, LA, *B-1-1 CH KO VN* +
*SGT* **Sparrow,** J A, Stamford, CT, *L-3-7-MAG36 VN* +
**Speach-Mastriano,** Angela, Brewerton, NY, *ASSOCIATE* +
*CPL* **Specht,** Joseph A, Lakewood, NJ, *ANGLICO-1MAR KO*
*SGT* **Specht,** M H, Park City, MT, *A-1-1 CW* +
*SGT* **Speckels,** Ben H JR., Pasadena, TX, *B-1-11 KO*
*LCPL* **Speer,** Gary, Chelsea, MI, *MAG-16 1MAW WWII* +
**Speights,** Robert J, Austin, TX, *A-1ENGR KO* +
**Speller,** R E, Penndel, PA, *8th AF 380th FW CW* +
*SGT* **Spencer,** Charles J, Bartow, FL, *L-3-27 HQ-3-1 VN* +
*CPL* **Spencer,** Lionel D, San Francisco, CA, *K-3-1 HQ-HQ WWII CH* +
**Speranzo,** Americo, Randolph, MA, *12SVC CH* +
*MGYSGT* **Sperling,** Mark A, Menifee, CA, *HQ SVC BN, 1MARDIV OIF*
*SGT* **Sperling,** Ronald A, Stratford, CT, *1COMBAT SVC KO* +
*SSGT* **Spicer,** Frank D, Fairfax, VA, *1ORD KO* +
*CAPT* **Spivey,** Buddy B, North Little Rock, AR, *A-3AMTRAC D-1-7 VN* +
*CPL* **Spivey,** Lacey N, Nashville, TN, *HQ-2-5 VN* +
*CPL* **Spradling,** Brian H, Longmont, CO, *D-1-5 VN* +
*CPL* **Spraggins,** Willie J, Alexander City, AL, *HQ-3-7 WWII CH* +
*HM1* **Sprague,** Arthur Y, Honolulu, HI, *C-1-5 KO* +
*CPL* **Sprague,** Edward C, Inman, SC, *E-1RECON VN* +
*LTCOL* **Sprague,** Zane E, Lakeside, CA, *H&S-3-11 WWII KO VN* +
*SGT* **Sprenkle,** Ronnell M, York, PA, *H&S-5 KO* +
*SGT* **Spring,** Edmund, Fredericksburg, VA, *MATCU66-MAG11 CW* +
*SSGT* **Springer,** Lucky J, Tujunga, CA, *C-1-5 VN* +
*MSGT* **Sprinkle,** Gary B, King, NC, *C-1-5 VN* +
*CPL* **Spurlock,** Harold R, Fort Pierce, FL, *HQ-11MAR KO* +
*SGT* **Spurr,** Daniel S, Monponsett, MA, *1-5MAR VN* +
**Squires,** Richard W, Pembroke, MA, *I-3-7 KO* +
**Squitieri,** Sophie, Howard Beach, NY, +
*GYSGT* **St. Andrew,** Karl R, Coatesville, PA, *B-1-5 CH KO* +
*SSGT* **Stacey,** William C, Strongsville, OH, *G-3-1 KO* +
*CPL* **Stack,** John R, Highland Beach, FL, *A-1-5 VN*
*SSGT* **Stahl,** A J, Bayville, NJ, *WPNS- 2-7 KO* +
*SGT* **Stahl,** David W, Philadelphia, PA, *F-2-5 CW* +
*SSGT* **Stahlman,** William R, Sebring, FL, *SVC-1ENGR KO* +
*COL* **Stallings,** George R, Mesa, AZ, *M-3-5-1PA-RA WWII* +
*SSGT* **Stallkamp,** Joseph E SR., Newport, KY, *3-155GUN F-2-11 VN*
*LTCOL* **Stankus,** Henry W, Chesapeake, VA, *2-5MAR 3-1MAR WWII CH KO* +
*CPL* **Stanley,** Eldon L, Garden City, KS, *H-3-7 KO* +
*1STSGT* **Starks,** Joe N, Oklawaha, FL, *B-1-1 VN* +
*SGTMAJ* **Starkweather,** Homer C, Lone Oak, TX, *HQ-2-11 VN* +
*COL* **Starling,** Christopher C, San Francisco, CA, *1/1 DELTA & WPNS CO*
*CAPT* **Starr,** J W, San Francisco, CA, *5MAR WWII* +
*MR.* **Starr,** Maurice J, Sherman Oaks, CA, *RECON KO* +
*SGT* **Stasio,** James T, North Bellmore, NY, *C-1SHPTY KO*
*PFC* **Stauffer,** John A, Fairhope, AL, *H&S-4DEF WWII* +
*SGT* **Stearns,** Joseph GEORGE, Belfast, ME, *E-2-5 KO* +
*CPL* **Stearns,** Mike L, Victor, MT, *C-1MT VN* +
*SGT* **Steed,** Rodney E, Camarillo, CA, *1MT KO* +
*LTGEN* **Steele,** Martin R, Tampa, FL, *A-1TK VN* +
*SGT* **Steen,** Walter H, Sarasota, FL, *F-2-7 KO* +
*LCPL* **Stefan,** Steve T, Newton, MA, *C-7COMM VN* +
*SGT* **Stefanowicz,** Harvey J, Warminster, PA, *HQ-2-7 CH* +
*COL* **Steffensen,** Robert E, Prescott, AZ, *1ENGR HQ-HQ CW* +
*SGT* **Stegall,** William S, El Paso, TX, *VMA 533* +
**Stegmueller,** Bernard A, Willow Springs, IL, *H-2-5 VN* +
*CPL* **Steiger,** Donald J, Lolo, MT, *1ENGR CW* +
*CPL* **Stein,** Lawrence L, Baltimore, MD, *D CO 1-5TH MAR VN*
*SGT* **Steinbach,** Phillip R, Potosi, MO, *HQ-2-7 1RECON CW* +
*GYSGT* **Steinbacher,** Lary C, Pleasant Lake, IN, *FLSG-B VN* +
*SGT* **Stella,** Marc, Anchorage, AK, *A-1-1 WWII CH* +
*SGT* **Stenger,** Joseph J, Buffalo, NY, *2-5MAR WWII CH* +
*SSGT* **Stephan,** Clarence L, Saint Clair Shores, MI, *H-3-1 KO* +
*SGT* **Stephens,** Timothy E, Riegelsville, PA, *B-1-11 VN* +
*1STSGT* **Stephens,** William L, Alexandria, VA, *E-2-5 KO*
*LCPL* **Stephenson,** Don M, Belton, TX, *2d REPL CO VN* +
*SGTMAJ* **Stephenson,** Paul, Carlsbad, CA, *1AMTRAC 2-5 MAR KO VN* +
*CPL* **Steppe,** P A, Nottingham, MD, *WPN-3-1 KO* +
**Stern,** Edward I, Hilton Head, SC, *B-1-1 CW*
*LCPL* **Stern,** Loyal DAVID, Lake Saint Louis, MO, *H & S-2-5 CW*
**Sternowski,** A R, Lawndale, CA, *E-2-5* +
*SGT* **Sterns,** Carl E, Norman, OK, *A-1ENGR* +
*CAPT* **Stettler,** George, Cathedral City, CA, *1 MAW EL TORO* +
*MAJ* **Stevens,** Arnold T JR., Osyka, MS, *G-2-1 VN* +
*MRS* **Stevens,** Joanne S, San Francisco, CA, *ASSOCIATE* +
*SGT* **Stevens,** John H, San Antonio, TX, *1ST TANK BN CO D, G-3RD BN 1MARDIV KO*
*LTCOL* **Stevens,** John R, San Francisco, CA, *A-1-5 HQ-7 MAR WWII CH* +
*SGT* **Stevens,** John, Boise, ID, *L-4-11 KO* +
*GYSGT* **Stevens,** Roger A, Burnet, TX, *H&S-3-7 VN* +
*SGT* **Stevens,** Victor A, Dexter, MI, *1/ 5MAR KO* +
*SGT* **Stevenson,** John H, Tulsa, OK, *H&S-1ENGR VN* +
*CPL* **Stevenson,** Matthew M, Wausaukee, WI, *BAND-HQ VN* +
*SGT* **Stevenson,** Richard H, Tucson, AZ, *H&S/E-2-7 VN* +
**Stevenson,** Valerie N, South San Francisco, CA, *ASSOCIATE* +
*CPL* **Stevenson,** William E, South San Francisco, CA, *BRAVO CO, 5 TANKS, 5 DIV*
*CPL* **Stevison,** Ellsworth E, Westbrook, CT, *B-8AMTRAC-1 WWII CH KO* +
*LCPL* **Stewart,** Daniel L, Los Angeles, CA, *A-1-1 VN* +
*SGT* **Stewart,** Frank J, Ipswich, MA, *H-2-1 WWII* +
*MSGT* **Stewart,** W M, Deland, FL, +
*MGYSGT* **Stewart,** W V, Fuquay Varina, NC, *SV-CENGR KO* +
*CPL* **Stewart,** Wallace T, Sebastopol, CA, *B-1-1 MP-HQ KO* +
*DR.* **Stiles,** Curt H PHD, Wilmington, NC, *HQ-HQ VN* +
*BGEN* **Stiles,** William A, Mclean, VA, *H&S-17MAR E-2-5 WWII VN* +
*SGT* **Stillwell,** Robert K, Lakeland, FL, *E-2-7 KO* +
*SGT* **Stimac,** Frank J JR., Munising, MI, *L-4-11 KO*
*CPL* **Stine,** Alton E, Cincinnati, OH, *L-3-1 WWII* +
*1STSGT* **Stine,** Arthur M, Okawville, IL, *I-3-1 KO VN* +
*SGT* **Stiteler,** Ed, San Antonio, TX, *I-3-7 VN* +
*HM3* **Stitzel,** Mark P, Shoreview, MN, *C-1-7 VN*
**Stix,** Charles N, Cincinnati, OH, *3 ARMAMPHIB WWII* +
*MR.* **Stodder,** Page W.T, Chicago, IL, *HQ BN KO* +
*HM3* **Stoeffler,** Walter K, Eugene, OR, *I-3-7 KO*
*SGT* **Stoess,** Ray H, Louisville, KY, *1MP KO* +
*GYSGT* **Stofiel,** John F, Vancouver, WA, *K-3-5 VN* +
*SGT* **Stohldrier,** Chris W, Center Barnstead, NH, *1AMTRAC 4MAR VN* +
*SFC* **Stokley,** William J, Lehigh Acres, FL, *F-2 H-3-5 CH KO* +
*CPL* **Stone,** Leonard J SR., Damascus, MD, *H-3-5 KO*
*E-3* **Stone,** Michael ALLAN, Atlanta, MI, *BRAVO 1/5 VN*
*SGT* **Stone,** Michael P, Pasadena, CA, *VMA 133 4TH MAW*
*LCPL* **Stoner,** Donald E, Lititz, PA, *H&S-1-26 VN* +
**Stott,** John E, Palm Desert, CA, *HQ-2-11 WWII KO* +
*LTCOL* **Stougard,** Larry D, Johnston, IA, *7MAR CW* +
*SGT* **Stouppe,** Gerald F, Kerrville, TX, *F-2-1 KO* +
*SGT* **Stout,** D R, Anaheim, CA, *HQ-7MAR KO* +
*LTCOL* **Stout,** Jay A, San Diego, CA, *VMFA451 SWA* +
*SGT* **Stovall,** Charlie W, Houston, TX, *B-1-7 1SVC WWII KO* +
*PFC* **Stowers,** Carl L, Butler, KY, *E-2-7 WWII* +
*MR.* **Stoya,** John B, Manchester, NJ, *F-2-5 WWII CH* +
*SSGT* **Strain,** Thomas S, San Dimas, CA, *VMO-2 1 MACE VN* +
*CPL* **Strait,** F JEFF JR., Florence, MT, *H&MS13 VN* +
*1STLT* **Strates,** E JAMES, Orlando, FL, *HQ-1-1 KO* +
*CAPT* **Straus,** David J, San Antonio, TX, *E/F-2-5 WWII CH KO* +
*SGTMAJ* **Streete,** Theodore E, Port Orchard, WA, *2-7MAR H&S-3-1 VN* +
**Streit,** Mary, Jupiter, FL, *ASSOCIATE* +
*MR.* **Streitz,** William L MD, Roseburg, OR, *7/11MAR VN* +
*SGT* **Striker,** Andy (Andrew John Steinbach), San Diego, CA, *D-1ENGR KO* +
*HM2* **Strode,** Gerald M, Woodinville, WA, *BRAVO 1/5 VN*
*CWO3* **Strong,** David P, Beaumont, CA, *B-1-26 VN* +
*CPL* **Strong,** Joseph M, Brick, NJ, *A-1-1 VN* +
*1STSGT* **Stroud,** Kenneth E, Las Vegas, NV, *L-4-11 G-3-11 KO VN* +
*PVT* **Stroud,** Walter J, Apo, AP, *1PROVTRK KO* +
*TSGT* **Struble,** K R, Exira, IA, *MAW WWII* +
*SGT* **Strunk,** Allen D, Las Vegas, NV, *1MAW KO* +
*CPL* **Strunk,** R M, Lancaster, PA, *ORD-FSR VN* +
*SGT* **Stuart,** George M, Kearney, MO, *L-3-1 VN* +
**Stubbs,** Jack R JR., Colonie, NY, *K-3-1 VN* +
*SSGT* **Studenny,** Dennis C, Broken Arrow, OK, *G-2-5 VN* +

SGT **Stueck,** Michael H, Lincoln, NE, G-2 VN +
CPL **Stuertz,** John R, Lincoln, NE, 5TH MAR VN
CPL **Stump,** Edward P, Avon, IN, I-3-7 VN +
GYSGT **Sturdevant,** Roger K, Saint Louis, MO, 1MAW KO VN +
**Sturgill,** James JR., Cincinnati, OH, H&S-3-5/I-3-5 KO +
HM2 **Sturiano,** Jack V, Island Park, NY, HQ-2-1 VN +
SGT **Stutler,** Edward L, Memphis, TN, FLSGB-FLC VN +
SGT **Suarez,** Richard A, San Francisco, CA, I-3-7 WWII CH KO +
SGT **Suden,** Ronald S, Clatonia, NE, 1-4 11TH MAR VN
SGT **Sulentic,** Emil L, Council Bluffs, IA, H-3-1 F-2-5 KO +
1STLT **Sullivan,** Edmund S, Alexandria, VA, WPNS-2-5 3LAR PK +
SGT **Sullivan,** Francis V, Howell, NJ, M-3-6, E-2-7 VN
CPL **Sullivan,** G M, Evansville, IN, M-3-7 VN +
CPL **Sullivan,** Harold F, Middlebury, CT, H-3-5 KO
CPL **Sullivan,** James D, Philadelphia, PA, A-1-1 VN +
**Sullivan,** Jerry D, Cornelia, GA, H&S-1-5 VN +
SGTMAJ **Sullivan,** John A, Jacksonville, NC, W-1-11 M-4-11 KO VN +
LCPL **Sullivan,** John L, Wautoma, WI, MWSG17 D-2LAAM VN +
GYSGT **Sullivan,** John W, Stanton, CA, 1MAW VN +
GYSGT **Sullivan,** Lisa A, Bullhead City, AZ, 1MAW CW
SGT **Sullivan,** Philip J, New Milford, NJ, B-1-7 KO +
PM2 **Sullivan,** Robert E, Texas City, TX, F-2-5 WWII KO +
LTCOL **Sullivan,** Thomas C, Huntersville, NC, HQ-HQ G-2-7 VN +
CPL **Sullivan,** William P JR., Port Chester, NY, D-1-5 VN +
**Summers,** Craig D, Cheektowaga, NY, SVC-9ENGR VN +
CPL **Summers,** Roger W, Timberville, VA, B-1-5 VN
**Summers,** William J, Philadelphia, PA, K-3-5 WWII +
GYSGT **Summerville,** Harry S, Jacksonville, FL, F-2-1 ENGR CSG CH KO +
SGT **Sundberg,** Edgar L, Kailua Kona, HI, A-1-5 WWII +
LCPL **Sunderlin,** David E, Niagara Falls, NY, C-1-1 VN +
SGT **Sundquist,** Craig D, Castle Rock, CO, 1ST SHORE PARTY BN VN
CPL **Supernaw,** Kenneth N, Wilbraham, MA, HQ-2-11 WWII CH +
SGT **Sustaita,** Manuel A, Houston, TX, B-1-7 VN
HM2 **Suszko,** August GUS, Poway, CA, D-2-7 KO
**Suter,** R G, Waldwick, NJ, D-2-7 KO +
HM2 **Sutton,** Harold S, Nashville, TN, I-3-7 KO +
SSGT **Sutton,** James F, Crestwood, KY, HQ E-2-5 CH +
SSGT **Sutton,** Paul L, Ocean View, NJ, H&S-1-7 VN +
CPL **Sutton,** William C, Lake Katrine, NY, SVC-HQ VN +
SGT **Suzenski,** Edmund W, Suffield, CT, F-2-5 WWII CH +
MSGT **Svandrlik,** S J, Honolulu, HI, 1KMC ADV GRP KO +
COL **Svenson,** O IVAR JR., Vero Beach, FL, G/I-3-11 3-7MAR KO CMC VN +
PFC **Swan,** Frank, Escondido, CA, A-1-7 KO +
SSGT **Swan,** Gerald L, Fresno, CA, 4.2-7MAR KO +
SSGT **Swann,** David C, Santa Maria, CA, SVC-MT CH KO +
GYSGT **Swanson,** A W, Inglis, FL, A-1-7 +
1STLT **Swanson,** Donald L, Dallas, TX, 1MT KO +
CAPT **Swanson,** Ernest R, Lewes, DE, HQ-3-4 CH +
**Swanson,** Walter L, Woodland Hills, CA, 1ENGR KO +

SGT **Swap,** Charles R, Ramsey, MN, H-2-5 HQ-HQ VN +
CPL **Sweeney,** Daniel J SR., Gilbert, AZ, C-1RECON VN +
CPL **Sweeney,** Jerome V, Boston, MA, A-1-1 KO +
LCPL **Sweeney,** Robert R, Red Bank, NJ, A-1-7 KO +
**Sweeney,** W P, Fair Haven, VT, B-9ENGR VN +
SGT **Sweet,** Richard G, Derby, NY, H&S-1-5 VN +
LTCOL **Sweitzer,** Merrill A JR., Jersey Shore, PA, HQ-1-7 VN +
CPL **Swickard,** David G, Boise, ID, H&S-2-7 M-3-1 VN +
SGTMAJ **Swindle,** John A, Lacey, WA, A-1-11 E-2-11 KO VN +
SGT **Swisher,** Daniel, Fairbanks, AK, F-2-5 +
LTCOL **Switzer,** Dan G, Indianapolis, IN, K-4-11 KO +
PFC **Swoszowski,** E J, Boca Raton, FL, M-3-1 WWII +
LCPL **Symanski,** Theodore E, Edison, NJ, B-1TK KO +
PHM3 **Symonowicz,** Edwin F, Jefferson, MA, D-1MED WWII +
SGT **Sypko,** Theodore P, Independence, MO, K-3-5 VN
CAPT **Szabo,** Peter J, Benicia, CA, 1ENGR VN +
CPL **Szczepanski,** Victor L, Auburn, NY, I-3-5 WWII CH +
CPL **Szlachta,** Richard J, Halifax, MA, G-2-5 VN +
CPL **Szula,** Michael P, Ridott, IL, WPNS-1-7 KO +
CAPT **Szymkowicz,** John T, Washington, DC, HQ-3-7 VN +
SGT **Taber,** Lawrence ERVIN, Lakeland, FL, D-1-5 VN +
SSGT **Tachis,** Thomas F, Corte Madera, CA, C-1AMTRAC WWII KO +
LCPL **Tadei,** Alexander G, Seaside, OR, 2ND BN 4TH MARINES
CPL **Tagert,** Jesse D, Pearl, MS, H&S-1-5 81MM VN +
SSGT **Tagupa,** Alfred, Kaneohe, HI, D-2-7 KO VN +
GYSGT **Tall Bear,** Alvin, Shawnee, OK, F-2-7 1ST RECON 1MAR DIV KO +
SGT **Tallick,** Thomas P, Arvada, CO, 11MAR VN
CPL **Tam,** Gail E JR., Fruitland, ID, 1FAG CW +
CPL **Tamer,** Edward, Brighton, MA, B-1TK +
**Tamucci,** Jacqueline, Fort Lauderdale, FL, ASSOCIATE +
SGT **Tancke,** Frederick W, Glendale, AZ, M-3-5 VN +
**Tangeman,** Karl K, Winchester, VA, M-3-1 WWII +
CPL **Tangney,** Thomas N, Pendleton, OR, MARDET ROCHESTER KO +
CPL **Tardif,** Robert G, Coral Gables, FL, HQ-2-5 WWII CH +
CPL **Tarnow,** Rodney J, Knox, IN, 2-4 CW +
CPL **Tarr,** Harold M, Cassville, MO, 11MT VN +
LCPL **Tarrant,** Brian P, Belmar, NJ, 1MT 1FSR CW +
1STSGT **Tarter,** Albert J, Oviedo, FL, E-2-5 H-3-5 CH KO +
1STSGT **Tarver,** Willie A, Wetumpka, AL, L-4-11 3-155 VN +
PFC **Tarvin,** Harold L, Chesterfield, IN, H/F-2-7 WWII +
COL **Tashjian,** Robert C, Smithland, KY, H&S-1/7 VN +
SGT **Tasnady,** Roger W SR., Kenvil, NJ, E-2-7 VN +
SSGT **Tassinari,** Henry L, Walnut Creek, CA, H&S-HQ CW +
GYSGT **Tate,** Edwin H, Sierra Vista, AZ, 1ST MOTOR TRNSPT H&S KO +
CPL **Tate,** Ralph A, Chattanooga, TN, H-3-7 KO +
COL **Tate,** William A, Winter Park, FL, HQ/K-3-1 KO VN +
CPL **Tatrow,** Milford A, Arlington, TX, F-2-5 VN +
**Tavone,** Marie, Elmwood Park, NJ, ASSOCIATE *
SSGT **Taylor,** Bobby G, Lubbock, TX, HQ-11MAR KO +
SGT **Taylor,** Dick D, Bakersfield, CA, H&S-1-5 2-5MAR CW +
SGT **Taylor,** Don R, Bakersfield, CA, 1AMTRAC 1RECON +

PHM3/C **Taylor,** Hal, Sitka, AK, A-1MT WWII CH
**Taylor,** Harold G, New Providence, NJ, E-2-5 WWII +
MAJ **Taylor,** James J, Northport, AL, A-2 1st RECON VN +
SGT **Taylor,** John T, Troy, IL, C-1AVNENGR WWII +
SGT **Taylor,** Raymond H, Iselin, NJ, B-1RECON VN +
SGT **Taylor,** Richard W, Palm Desert, CA, D-2-11 KO +
MSGT **Taylor,** W M, San Diego, CA, H&S-7 WWII KO +
GYSGT **Taylor,** Willis E, Tucson, AZ, 1COMM-HQ VN +
SGT **Taylor,** Zack, San Juan Capistrano, CA, A-1ENGR 3-5MAR KO +
1STLT **Teague,** Frank J, Hingham, MA, M-3-1 VN
SGT **Teefey,** William J, Midlothian, VA, HQ-3-7 WWII KO +
SGT **Tekhelet,** Israel A, Lakewood, CO, A-1-1 VN +
TSGT **Temple,** Gordon E, West Chester, PA, 1SIG-WPNS-7 WWII CH KO +
CPL **Templeton,** John R, Queen Creek, AZ, A-1-5 E-2-9 VN +
CPL **Templeton,** John T, Mountain Home, AR, L-3-5 F-2-7 VN +
**Tenholder,** Thomas J, Eureka, MO, C-7COMM CW +
MAJ **Tenney,** Joseph R, Fullerton, CA, K-3-5 VN +
HM3 **Teno,** Richard A, Ayer, MA, D-1-1 VN
**Tepe,** Robert F, Cincinnati, OH, W-1-11 VN +
**Teply,** Roy W, Mesa, AZ, C-1-1 WWII KO CH +
MRS **Terhune,** Cleta A, West Fork, AR, *
CPL **Terrebetzky,** Peter, Maspeth, NY, HQ-2-11 VN +
LT **Terrebonne,** Burnick J JR., Metairie, LA, HQ-11MAR CW +
SGT **Terrell,** Franklin D, Capitol Heights, MD, L-3-9 VN +
CAPT **Terrio,** Frank C, Staten Island, NY, L-3-7 VN +
SGT **Territo,** Peter R, Harvey, LA, HQ-3-5 1SVC KO +
SGT **Terry,** Andrew "Andy", Boerne, TX, 1ST SHORE PTY 1MARDIV VN
SGT **Tevis,** John L, Phoenix, AZ, H&S-2-7 KO +
**Thacher,** Frank G, Centerville, MA, VMO-6 1MAW KO +
SGT **Thackston,** Willard C, Crossville, TN, 1CSG KO +
MGYSGT **Thalassites,** L G, Palm Harbor, FL, C-1ENGR WWII KO +
SGT **Tharp,** Robert E, Sapulpa, OK, 2-1MAR CW
LCPL **Thaxton,** Jack W, Robstown, TX, K-3-26 I-3-1 VN +
SSGT **Thayer,** Douglas J, Alturas, CA, WPNS-2-5 KO +
**Thayer,** Robert L, Mccook, NE, AT-7MAR KO +
SGT **Thibault,** David L, Byron Center, MI, 2-5MAR 7COMM-9MAB VN +
**Thibodeau,** A E, Morgan City, LA, I-3-1 KO +
GYSGT **Thibodeaux,** James P, Kenner, LA, H&S/E-2-11 KO +
CPL **Thiel,** James E, Appleton, WI, M-3-1 G-2-5 VN
CPL **Thilman,** Robert J, Indianapolis, IN, 4.2 MRTR 5MAR KO +
1STLT **Thinschmidt,** Donald M, Holland, MI, C CO 1ST BN 5TH MAR VN
SGT **Thom,** Roland W, Ellsworth, WI, C-1TK KO +
SGT **Thomas,** F B, Colonial Beach, VA, A-9ENGR VN +
**Thomas,** George M, Lemont, IL, ASSOCIATE *
TSGT **Thomas,** James M FMF, Fernandina Beach, FL, C-1PION WWII KO +
CPL **Thomas,** Kenneth L, Idaho Falls, ID, A-1-7 HQ-7 KO +
TSGT **Thomas,** L E, Panama City, FL, 1MAW WWII +
SGT **Thomas,** Ray H, Shawnee-Mission, KS, H&S/H-3-7 KO +
MSGT **Thomas,** Walter J, Dearborn, MI, 16FLD DEP-7MAR WWII +

*HMC* **Thomas,** William A, Beech Grove, IN, *C-1-7 WWII KO* +
*LCPL* **Thomas,** William, Whiting, NJ, *HQ BTRY 3-11 VN*
*PFC* **Thompson,** Alfred C, Diamond Springs, CA, *5MAR WWII CH* +
*MRS* **Thompson,** Chris, Saint George, UT, *ASSOCIATE* *
*CAPT* **Thompson,** David J, Wayne, PA, *M-3-1 VN*
*SGT* **Thompson,** Don C, Rowlett, TX, *D-2-5 KO* +
*MAJ* **Thompson,** Earl W, Brentwood, CA, *A-1-7 WWII CH KO* +
*CPL* **Thompson,** Elton E, Poteau, OK, *1SIG WWII CH* +
*SGT* **Thompson,** Eugene B, Coeur D'alene, ID, *HQ-1MAW VMF214 KO* +
*SGT* **Thompson,** Harold J, Orland Park, IL, *G-2-5 WWII CH* +
*SGT* **Thompson,** Olin E, San Diego, CA, *H&S-1-1 KO*
*COL* **Thompson,** Robert H, Fredericksburg, VA, *G/I-3-7 1-5MAR KO CMC VN* +
*SGT* **Thompson,** Thomas M, Severna Park, MD, *S-2-11 KO* +
*MGYSGT* **Thompson,** Wilbur E, Paducah, KY, *HQ-HQ 11MAR KO VN*
*CPL* **Thompson,** William D, Hampton, FL, *C-1-5 VN* +
*LT* **Thomson,** P V, Wakefield, RI, *H&S-HQ-5 WWII* +
*SSGT* **Thomson,** Richard W, Johnston, RI, *A-1-27 VN* +
*CPL* **Thomson,** Robert W, Valrico, FL, *D-2-5 KO* +
*SSGT* **Thorndyke,** Kenneth P, Davenport, IA, *D-2-7 KO* +
*SGT* **Thornton,** Robert J, La Jolla, CA, *H-3-7 KO* +
*CPL* **Thoroe,** Richard W, Itasca, IL, *K-4-11/13 VN*
*LCPL* **Thorpe,** R C, Nevada City, CA, *HQ-3-1 CW* +
*SGT* **Thorsnes,** David J, Portland, OR, *H&S-1FSR-FLC HQ-1MARBDE VN* +
*CWO3* **Thrasher,** Carlos M, Arlington, TX, *HQ-27MAR 7MEB CW* +
*SGT* **Thrasher,** Harold L, Clovis, NM, *C-1-5 VN* +
*MAJ* **Throm,** Robert B, Phoenixville, PA, *1 KMC KO VN* +
*SGT* **Throop,** Paul A, Lexington, KY, *H&S-1MAR KO* +
**Thurman,** Paul M, Tucson, AZ, *G-2-5 VN* +
**Thurston,** Duane R, Omaha, NE, *1 FSR CW CMC*
*CPL* **Thyen,** Robert N, Saint Cloud, MN, *A-1-11 CMC CW* +
*MRS* **Tibbetts,** Sandra, West Melbourne, FL, *ASSOCIATE* *
*PH1* **Tickle,** William Y, Metairie, LA, *B/E-1MED WWII* +
*MSGT* **Tidwell,** Charles L, Murrells Inlet, SC, *E-2-7 KO VN* +
*MR.* **Tiedemann,** Danny R, Alta, CA, *
*CPL* **Tiedemann,** Tommy, Boise, ID, *A-1-5 VN*
*LTCOL* **Tierney,** Mark F, Lake Ridge, VA, *M-3-7 VN* +
*SSGT* **Tierney,** Richard K, Ozark, AL, *I-3-7 KO* +
*PVT* **Tifft,** Donald M, Jackson, MI, *C-1-17 WWII* +
*CPL* **Tillery,** Calvin C, Broken Arrow, OK, *H&S-1-5 KO* +
*SSGT* **Timmins,** William J, Rockland, MA, *I-3-1 KO* +
*SGT* **Timmons,** Burl K, Midland, TX, *WPNS-2-5 KO* +
*CWO4* **Tindall,** Donald L, Martinez, CA, *C-1-1* +
*SSGT* **Tinklepaugh,** Clyde L, Hudson, NY, *B-1-7 WWII CH*
*COL* **Tinling,** Jerome B, Alamogordo, NM, *MTACS-2 KO* +
*SGT* **Tintiangco,** John J, Lincolnshire, IL, *G-3-7 4.2-7MAR KO* +
*SGT* **Tipton,** Jesse E, Compton, CA, *H&S-2-1 VN*
*SGT* **Tisdale,** Ed L, Norfolk, VA, *DIVRECON KO* +
*CPL* **Tkacik,** Albert, Fairfield, VA, *HQ-1MARBDE VN* +
*1STSGT* **Todd,** Alexander G, Las Vegas, NV, *C-1RECON RECON-HQ CW* +
*LCPL* **Todd,** Alton C, Mendota Heights, MN, *B CO 3RD AMTRAC BN* +
*COL* **Todd,** John R, Oceanside, CA, *B-4-11 HQ-HQ VN SWA* +
*COL* **Tokarz,** Anthony P, Bristol, RI, *I-3-7 VN* +
*CAPT* **Tole,** Glenn L, Wichita Falls, TX, *C-1-11 WWII KO* +
*CPL* **Tolentino,** Thomas J SR., Menife, CA, *C-1-11 CW* +
*SGT* **Toller,** Oscar DARBY JR., Yulee, FL, *H&S 2-7 K-3-8 VN*
*COL* **Tolleson,** Frederic L, Seattle, WA, *E/2/7 HQ 7MAR KO VN* +
*SGT* **Tom,** Dennis L, Columbus, OH, *B-1-5 VN* +
*MSGT* **Tom,** James K, Kailua Kona, HI, *G-3-7 H&S-FLC KO VN* +
*SSGT* **Tomchik,** F.G., Monroe, CT, *HQBTRY 1-11* +
*CPL* **Tomeo,** Joseph, Brea, CA, *1ST ENG BN VN*
*SSGT* **Tomlinson,** Kenneth D, Oceanside, CA, *H&S-2-9 VN* +
*MGYSGT* **Tompkins,** Robert R SR., Dupont, WA, *B CO 3RD LVT BN VN*
*CPL* **Tomsche,** Don G, Little Canada, MN, *WPNS-3-5 KO* +
*SSGT* **Toner,** Robert J, Fair Haven, VT, *1SHPTY KO*
*SGT* **Tonge,** Fred W, Salem, MA, *K-3-7 VN* +
*CPL* **Tonkyn,** Michael S, Spokane, WA, *C-1-5 VN*
*LTGEN* **Toolan,** John A, Falls Church, VA, *1MAR SWA OIF* +
*PFC* **Toomey,** Paul V, La Habra, CA, *G-2-7 WWII* +
*MSGT* **Topham,** William J, Needham, MA, *FLC 1-25MAR VN SWA* +
*HM3* **Toppel,** Edward USN, Encino, CA, *B-1-7 KO* +
*PFC* **Torgrimson,** Stanely O, Portland, OR, *A-8AMTRAC WWII* +
*SGTMAJ* **Torizzo,** Arthur T, San Marcos, CA, *1FORRECON 4.2-HQ-7MAR KO VN* +
**Torres,** Frank, Santa Ana, CA, *A-1-5 KO VN* +
*PFC* **Torres,** Michael, Chicago, IL, *G-2-7 CW* +
*SGT* **Torres,** Ruben, Oceanside, CA, *1/1 SCOUTS CW*
*MGYSGT* **Toth,** Paul A, Saint Petersburg, FL, *MAG 12 KO* +
**Touchette,** Robert D, Oviedo, FL, *5 DENTAL CO 1 DENTAL CO VN*
*CPL* **Toups,** Ronald E, Marrero, LA, *C-1-7 VN* +
*SSGT* **Tower,** Gerald L, San Mateo, FL, *F-2-7 WWII CH KO* +
*1STLT* **Towle,** Alex C, Essex, MA, *1ENG HQ-1MAR VN* +
*SGT* **Towner,** Gilbert, Lapwai, ID, *ANGLICO-2-5 CH KO* +
*CAPT* **Townsend,** Arnold J, Saratoga Springs, NY, *H&S-7MAR WWII* +
*CPL* **Townsend,** James S, Pleasant Hill, CA, *COMP B 1ST BN 5TH MAR VN*
*CPL* **Tracey,** John J, Bronx, NY, *I-3-1 KO* +
*SGT* **Tracy,** Richard T, Franklin, OH, *H-2-5 G-2-5 WWII* +
*LCPL* **Trafas,** Peter C JR., Long Beach, CA, *1-5 VN* +
*SSGT* **Trahan,** Joseph V, Gonzales, LA, *VMF223 MAG11 CH KO* +
*CAPT* **Traiser,** Richard E, Freeport, ME, *B-1TK 1-7MAR VN* +
*MSGT* **Trammell,** William M JR., Oxnard, CA, *H&S-1-5 C-1-11 VN* +
*CPL* **Tramonte,** Oreste A, Marshfield, MA, *1CSG KO* +
*SGT* **Trapp,** William B JR., Metairie, LA, *10INF KO* +
*LTCOL* **Traynor,** Andrew F JR., Manassas, VA, *B-1AT VN CW VN* +
*CAPT* **Trebon,** Iver W, Temecula, CA, *H&S-1-5 VMA121 KO* +
*MAJ* **Tredup,** James D, Tacoma, WA, *A-1-5 D-1-5 WWII* +
*CAPT* **Tremblay,** Dr Richard E, Bellevue, WA, *3.5IN-11MAR KO* +
*SGT* **Trenck,** Eric W, Murrells Inlet, SC, *I-3-7 KO* +
*LCPL* **Trimm,** Phillip R, Potsdam, NY, *A/D-1-5 VN* +
*PFC* **Triplett,** Gerald S, Clinton, MS, *TF-38 CV-36 WWII CH* +
*SGT* **Triplett,** L H JR., Germantown, MD, *K-3-1 VN* +
*SGT* **Troboy,** William W, Lufkin, TX, *HQ-1SVC WWII KO* +
**Trocio,** M W, Gardena, CA, *1MAW* +
*SGTMAJ* **Trope,** William S, El Paso, TX, *G-3-7 1ENGR CH KO VN* +
*CPL* **Trosko,** John M, Flint, MI, *7COMM CW* +
*GYSGT* **Trosper,** Ralph M, Mullins, SC, *7MT VN* +
*CPL* **Trousdale,** James M, Orange, CA, *1ST ENG BN H&S CO A CO* +
*PFC* **Trowbridge,** Duane D, Virginia Beach, VA, *H-3-1 KO*
*SGT* **Trucks,** Joseph L JR., Bensalem, PA, *1CSG 1ENGR KO* +
*SSGT* **Trueblood,** Harley J, Anderson, IN, *D-1TK KO* +
**Trueworthy,** Michael U, Scarborough, ME, *H&S-1-7 VN* +
*SGT* **Truitt,** John T, Metamora, IL, *SVC-7MAR KO* +
*CPL* **Trumble,** William M, Oregon City, OR, *MAB12 MAG12 1STMAW* +
*PFC* **Trumbull,** Byron W, Meadville, PA, *1ENGR-17MAR WWII* +
*SSGT* **Tryon,** Richard W JR., Mont Clare, PA, *E-2-5 KO* +
*GYSGT* **Tsareff,** Thomas C, Speedway, IN, *155GUN KO* +
*CPL* **Tsegeletos,** George H, Sonoma, CA, *I-3-1 KO* +
*SGT* **Tsuda,** Thomas T, Kailua, HI, *H-3-7 KO* +
*SGT* **Tucker,** Billy RAY, Bullhead City, AZ, *2ND MARDIV*
*CPL* **Tucker,** Charles R, West Hartford, CT, *HQ-1ENGR KO* +
*MAJ* **Tucker,** Fred, Madison, TN, *G-2-7 VN* +
*MAJ* **Tucker,** G.B., Nevada City, CA, *HQ-1/7MT MWSG17 CH KO VN* +
*SGT* **Tuczak,** Joseph R, Dextur, MI, *1MAR CW* +
*CPL* **Tuller,** John B, Westervile, OH, *A-1-7 VN* +
**Tullis,** Harold W, Sherman Oaks, CA, *SVC-HQ CW* +
*SGT* **Tuminaro,** Raymond D, Easton, PA, *D-2-11 KO* +
*CPL* **Tungate,** John E, Cincinnati, OH, *4.2-7MAR KO*
**Tuohy,** Dennis J, Bethany, CT, *1/1 VN*
*HM2* **Tura,** Thomas L, Kingston, MA, *A-1-1 VN*
*MGYSGT* **Turano,** Louis M, Whiting, NJ, *HQ-3-11 1MAW CH KO VN* +
*SSGT* **Turiace,** Frank A JR., Marina Del Rey, CA, *C-1-5 KO* +
*CPL* **Turnberger,** Thomas L, Plantation, FL, *A-1-26 VN* +
*CPL* **Turner,** Charles EDWARD, Diamond Bar, CA, *C-1-1 CW* +
*SGT* **Turner,** Dale L, Newhall, CA, *A-1-5 9MT VN* +
*SGT* **Turner,** Gary L, Strasburg, CO, *ORD KO* +
*SGT* **Turner,** Ira B, Langhorne, PA, *H&S-1SHPTY KO* +
*CPL* **Turner,** Richard G JR., Missoula, MT, *2-1MAR 1RECON VN* +
*PLTSGT* **Turner,** William D, Rowlett, TX, *G-2-1 WWII* +
*CPL* **Turner,** William E, Van Nuys, CA, *H&S CO 3RD AMTRAC BN VN* +
**Turner,** William JR., Louisville, KY, *H-3-7 KO* +
*MR.* **Turpin,** Daniel M, Beavercreek, OR, *B-1RECON VN* +
**Tveit,** Thomas, La Quinta, CA, *2BN 5MAR*
*TSGT* **Twork,** M E, Pinconning, MI, *HQ-1-5 WWII KO* +
*COL* **Twyman,** Gayle F, Friendswood, TX, *HQ-HQ 3-26MAR VN* +
*PFC* **Tyde,** Albert W, Wacunda, IL, *RECON-HQ KO* +
*SSGT* **Tyler,** Blaine L, Portland, OR, *1ST MAW 1ST MAR DIV*
*CPL* **Tynan,** Charles M, Levittown, NY, *G-3-1 KO* +
*CAPT* **Tyndall,** John G III, Redwood, CA, *2-1MAR HMH463 VN* +
*CAPT* **Tyson,** Francis D, Scranton, PA, *C-1-4 HQ-HQ K-3-26 CH KO VN* +
*SGT* **Tyynismaa,** Victor J, Lake Havasu City, AZ, *C-1-5 VN* +

*MAJ* **Uehling,** William V, Arlington, VA, *HQBN VN* +
*PFC* **Ulibarri,** Arsenio G, Springerville, AZ, *D-1TK KO* +
*SSGT* **Ullman,** Albert F, Woodbridge, VA, *WPNS-1-7 KO* +
*CPL* **Ulreich,** Walter M, Park Ridge, IL, *C-1TK WWII CH* +
*CPL* **Ulrich,** Kenneth T, Lower Gwynedd, PA, *D 1/26 M 3/7 VN* +
*SSGT* **Ulsh,** A J, Mullica Hill, NJ, *1ENGR WWII CH KO* +
*SGT* **Underhill,** H W, Guilford, CT, *1MAW WWII* +
*GYSGT* **Underhill,** H, San Diego, CA, *11MAR CH KO VN* +
*SGT* **Underwood,** Phillip G, Magnolia Springs, AL, *L-3-5 VN*
*CPL* **Underwood,** Ray E JR., New Boston, MI, *H&S-1RECON VN* +
*SGT* **Unger,** F T, Alexandria, VA, *SPLWPNS WWII* +
*CPL* **Unger,** William T, Oceanside, CA, *2-1MAR VN* +
*SGT* **Unruh,** Melvin L, Otis, OR, *HQFMFPAC KO* +
*MRS* **Urrutia,** Virginia, Watsonville, CA, *ASSOCIATE* *
*CPL* **Uscier,** Jeffery H, Aurora, CO, *VN*
*SSGT* **Usher,** Richard L, Robertsville, MO, *H-3-11 KO* +
*LCPL* **Uzanas,** Philip A JR., Manchester, CT, *MWCS-1 VN* +
**Vaca,** Robert, Harbor City, CA, *1AMTRAC KO* +
**Vadino,** George T, Issaquah, WA, *AMMO-1ORD KO* +
**Vadus,** Joseph R, Potomac, MD, *MP-HQ WWII* +
*SGT* **Vagell,** Robert J, Toms River, NJ, *HQ-1ENGR D-2-5 KO* +
*CAPT* **Vagnetti,** John W, Fairfax, VA, *F-2-5 D-2-11 VN* +
*SGT* **Vail,** Gary D, Oakland, CA, *VMF314 MAG11 KO*
*MAJ* **Valadez,** Ramon V, San Antonio, TX, *F-2-7 KO* +
*LCPL* **Valdez,** Alfonso G, Arleta, CA, *3FAAD CW* +
*CPL* **Valentine,** Ronald M, Chicago, IL, *VN, COMM SUPPORT CO, 7TH COMM BN*
*SGT* **Van Abel,** John P, Port Saint Lucie, FL, *1RECON VN* +
**Van Court,** William T, Highlands Ranch, CO, *USS NEW ORLEANS WWII*
*LTCOL* **Van Fleet,** Duane "Dutch", Columbia, MS, *G-2-9 D-1-7 VN* +
*COL* **Van Hoomissen,** George A, Portland, OR, *1ST MAR DIV G-2 HQ KO* +
*SGT* **Van Houtte,** Michael FRANK, La Mirada, CA, *M CO-3-1 VN* +
*SSGT* **Van Leuvan,** Edward J, Westbury, NY, *G-2-3 1FORRECON VN* +
*SGTMAJ* **Van Waes,** Frank W, Lowden, IA, *7-11MAR KO VN* +
*SGT* **Vanacore,** Frank M, El Dorado Hills, CA, *B-1-7 C-RECON CW* +
*LTCOL* **Vanairsdale,** James B, Saint Augustine, FL, *E-2-7 KO VN* +
*SSGT* **Vanartsdalen,** Frank C, Cape May Court House, NJ, *E-2-1 KO* +
*CPL* **Vanavery,** Lawrence R, Glendale, CA, *HQ-7MAR CW* +
*SGT* **Vance,** John C, Dallas, TX, *H&S-2-7 KO* +
*SGT* **Vance,** Randolph H JR., Flatwoods, KY, *H&S-2-5 2-1 VN* +
*SGT* **Vandegrift,** Charles A, Leiston, England, *A-7MT KO* +
*SGT* **Vanderels,** E M, Rochester, NY, *G-2-RNLMC WWII* +
*PFC* **Vanderhoof,** Harley D, Mulberry, FL, *A-1-1 WWII* +
*CPL* **Vandiver,** John D, Burnsville, MN, *H&S-3-7 KO* +
*CAPT* **Vandruff,** Roscoe W JR., Phoenix, AZ, *C-1-1 KO VN* +
*CPL* **Vandyke,** S DOUGLAS, Salem, OR, *G-3-1 KO* +
*SSGT* **Vanmeter,** Herman G, Louisville, KY, *K-4-11 KO* +
*SGT* **Vano,** John J JR., Parma, OH, *G-3-11 KO* +
*SGT* **Vanort,** John R, Steger, IL, *E-2-5 KO* +
*CPL* **Vansickle,** Perry E, Westerville, OH, *H&S-1-17 WWII* +
*SGT* **Vanvoorhis,** Charles D, Marion, OH, *A-1-5 VN* +
*CPL* **Vanwaes,** George A, Canandaigua, NY, *G-2-7 MP VN* +
**Varano,** Marshall B, San Diego, CA, *1ENGR KO* +
*GYSGT* **Vardell,** Karol W, Walters, OK, *H&S-1TK KO* +
*CPL* **Varela,** Gabriel R, Mchenry, IL, *VMA (AW) 242, MAG11 VN*
*SGT* **Varley,** George A, Exeter, NH, *F-2-7 WWII CH* +
*SSGT* **Varley,** Thomas H, Louisville, KY, *H&S REG-1 KO* +
*SGT* **Varnes,** Robert L, Sheridan, IL, *G-3-7 KO* +
*SGT* **Varnum,** Raymond A, Santa Rosa, CA, *1AR-MAMPH H&S- 3AMTRAC VN* +
*SGT* **Vartikian,** Harold B, Livingston, CA, *C-1-7 KO* +
*SGT* **Vaselakos,** Pete, Georgetown, TX, *RECON-HQ KO* +
*CPL* **Vasper,** Edmund A SR., Aiea, HI, *H&S-1-5 KO* +
*SGTMAJ* **Vasquez,** Martin V, Oceanside, CA, *I/WPNS-3-5 KO* +
*PVT* **Vass,** Douglas M, Marydel, DE, *L-3-1 VN* +
*SSGT* **Vass,** Joseph A JR., Quinton, VA, *1ENGR KO* +
*SSGT* **Vattimo,** Charles J JR., Winchester, CA, *HMLA367 CW OIF* +
*SGT* **Vattimo Feickert,** Sandra D, Winchester, CA, *MALS39 CW* +
*SSGT* **Vattuone,** Vic H, Palm Desert, CA, *1RECON VN* +
**Vaughan,** Eddie L, Brownsville, TX, *I-3-26 VN* +
*CPL* **Vaughn,** Jerald M, Conroe, TX, *K-3-5 VN*
*CPL* **Vaught,** Larry R, Ladoga, IN, *I-3-5 H-2-1 VN* +
*SSGT* **Vecchio,** Philip J, Providence, RI, *C-1-5 VN* +
*CAPT* **Veideman,** Robert A, Ludlow, MA, *RAD-HQ HQ-2-1 CW* +
*MGYSGT* **Veintimilla,** Carlos, Oceanside, CA, *E-2-5* +
*SGT* **Velasco,** Guadalupe JR., Flagstaff, AZ, *F-2-5 VN* +
*CPL* **Ventre,** F C, Ossipee, NH, *H&S-1/7MAR* +
*BGEN* **Verbeck,** Guido F JR., Vineyard Haven, MA, *A/L-4-11 WWII* +
*1STSGT* **Vermurlen,** Robert C, Grand Haven, MI, *C-1RECON WWII KO VN* +
*SSGT* **Vernier,** D J, Phoenix, AZ, *834TH AIR DIV* +
*SGT* **Vertacnik,** Robert A, West Newton, PA, *H&S/G-3-7 KO* +
*LTCOL* **Vetter,** Thomas M SR., Dana Point, CA, *H&S-4-11 KO* +
*PFC* **Vezaldenos,** Gus K, Manteca, CA, *1AT-7MAR KO* +
*SSGT* **Vicari,** Robert A JR., San Francisco, CA, *I-3-11 KO* +
*DR.* **Vick,** Charles GORDON JD, DD, Moscow, TN, *IMAC VMO3 WWII* +
*SSGT* **Vick,** Timothy ROBERT, Gresham, OR, *1ST FORCE SVC REGT*
*CPL* **Victory,** Russell E, Visalia, CA, *HQ-7ENGR VN* +
*CPL* **Vienot,** Robert B, Burlingame, CA, *F-2-5 WWII NC* +
*GYSGT* **Vigil,** Paul A, Mcallen, TX, *H&S-2-1 VN* +
**Vilbig,** Gerard R, Little Neck, NY, *WPNS-1-7 KO*
*SGT* **Vilionis,** Victor J, Dollard-Des-Ormeaux, Canada, *HQ-7MAR VN* +
*SSGT* **Villalobos,** Jesse P, San Antonio, TX, *81MM H&S KO VN* +
*SGT* **Villano,** Richard S, Gilroy, CA, *HQ-7COMM VN* +
*SSGT* **Villanueva,** Quintin L JR., Palm Desert, CA, *H&S WPNS-2-1 KO* +
*LCPL* **Vimarco,** Dominic C JR., Chicago, IL, *K-3-5 VN* +
*TSGT* **Vinski,** John JOSEPH, Jupiter, FL, *1SHPTY KO* +
*COL* **Visser,** Eric P, Alexandria, VA, *3-11 VN CW* +
*GYSGT* **Vissers,** John C, West Palm Beach, FL, *E-2-7 A-1AT CMC VN* +
*CPL* **Vital,** Edward, Sunnyvale, CA, *SVC BN 1LGT SUPT CO CMC* +
*SGT* **Viterbo,** Jules R, Nederland, TX, *H&S-3-1 KO* +
*1STLT* **Vitucci,** Kenneth J, Austin, TX, *B-1-5 VN* +
*LCPL* **Viviano,** Bob J, Alton, IL, *C-1-5 2/3-CAG VN* +
*1STSGT* **Viviano,** Peter J, Rio Rancho, NM, *M-3-1 VN* +
*COL* **Vogel,** Frederick J, Herndon, VA, *HQBN RECON VN* +
**Vollendorf,** Keith A, Drums, PA, *C-1-5 VN* +
*SGT* **Vollentine,** Gerry L, Erie, PA, *H&S-1-5 H&S-1RECON VN* +
*PFC* **Vollmayer,** John W, Reno, NV, *H-11MAR WWII CH* +
*CPL* **Voltolina,** Albert F, Metairie, LA, *AT-1MAR KO* +
*SSGT* **Von Oiste,** James J, Port Jefferson, NY, *A-1-5 KO*
*1STSGT* **Von Rinteln,** Frank T, Port Deposit, MD, *W-1-7 KO VN* +
*SSGT* **Vonhinken,** Fred H JR., Roscommon, MI, *1SIG KO* +
*SGT* **Vortisch,** Christian FRANK JR., Hope Mills, NC, *H&S-7MAR CH* +
*CPL* **Voswinkel,** William H, Lago Vista, TX, *1AAA 1AAV-1MAR KO* +
*LCPL* **Vriner Vrinios,** Louis (Lampros) G, Houston, TX, *MTM MTR TRSPT BN VN* +
*SGTMAJ* **Vrmeer,** Howard D, San Leandro, CA, *1MAW WWII CH KO VN* +
*MAJ* **Vuky,** Paul T, Beaverton, OR, *I-3-1 VN* +
*SGT* **Vyvial,** Elgin W, La Marque, TX, *B-1-7 KO* +
*MGYSGT* **Wabeck,** J F, San Diego, CA, *1ORD H&S-HQ* +
*SGT* **Wada,** Robert M, Buena Park, CA, *HQ/D-1TK KO* +
*SSGT* **Wadalavage,** George, Glendale, NY, *1ENGR WWII CH* +
*TSGT* **Wade,** Edward D, Lebanon, NH, *VMSB234 WWII* +
*CPL* **Wade,** Larry STEVEN, Wolverine, MI, *K-3-5 1RECON CB VN* +
*SGT* **Wade,** Robert B, Deadwood, OR, *E-2-7 KO* +
*SSGT* **Wadlow,** Joseph J, Sewickley, PA, *M-3-1 VN* +
*SGT* **Wafer,** George E JR., Centennial, CO, *D-2-7 KO* +
*HMCS* **Wager,** Charles J, Hubert, NC, *H-2-5 1ANGLICO VN* +
*CPL* **Wagner,** Donald F, Vero Beach, FL, *F-1-1 WWII*
*SGT* **Wagner,** Edward J, Dunedin, FL, *AT-7MAR KO* +
*CPL* **Wagner,** G C JR., Lakewood, WA, *155 MMGUNBN WWII* +
*PFC* **Wagner,** Gilbert R, Pahrump, NV, *1MAR KO* +
*LTCOL* **Wagner,** Joseph P, Las Vegas, NV, *H&S-2-11 WWII* +
*CAPT* **Wagner,** Junior S, Manhattan, KS, *HDQ-11 WWII CH KO* +
*GYSGT* **Wagner,** K J, Castaic, CA, *F-2-1 KO VN* +
*CAPT* **Wagoner,** Robert L, Moneta, VA, *W-2-11 VN* +
*CPL* **Wahlbeck,** Robert E, Poplar Grove, IL, *G-2-5 D-2-7 WWII CH KO* +
*SSGT* **Waite,** Bruce W, Ocala, FL, *A-2MAR 1/3RECON VN* +
*SGT* **Waite,** Robert W, Ocala, FL, *B-1LAR SWA* +
*CPL* **Walczyszyn,** Michael, Staten Island, NY, *A-1-1 VN* +
*CPL* **Walden,** Richard T, Bremerton, WA, *L-3-1 WWII* +
*MGEN* **Waldhauser,** Thomas D, Oceanside, CA, *CG 1ST MAR DIV* +
*LCPL* **Waldie,** Ronnie, Garland, TX, *B-1-11 E-2-1 VN* +

*CPL* **Waldron,** Kenneth CLARK, Roanoke, VA, *E-2-7 1MAR DIV VN*
*GYSGT* **Waldron,** Michael W, Newton, PA, *H-3-7 HQ-11MAR KO VN* +
*SGT* **Walker,** Allen W, Hillsboro, OR, *G-2-1 VN* +
*CPL* **Walker,** Heward R, Reno, NV, *HQ 11MAR WWII CH* +
*PFC* **Walker,** Horace H, Rockport, TX, *B-1-6 WWII* +
*LCPL* **Walker,** John D, Lake Havasu City, AZ, *1RECON A-SNIPER VN* +
*CPL* **Walker,** Joseph B, Hammonton, NJ, *A-1SHPTY VN* +
*SGT* **Walker,** Michael LYN, La Quinta, CA, *VMA-214*
**Walker,** Mike, Meridian, ID, *3 CAG*
**Walker,** Ray L, Franklin, TN, *A-1-5 KO* +
*1STLT* **Wallace,** Frank E III, Martinez, CA, *HQ CO HQBN CW*
*CPO* **Wallace,** Frank A, Santa Maria, CA, *7MAR VN* +
*CPL* **Wallace,** Patrick J, Milwaukee, WI, *C-1TK VN* +
*MACM (SW)* **Wallace,** Thomas C, Garden Grove, CA, *SUPPORT VN* +
*SGT* **Wallace,** William M, Lansdale, PA, *5-7-COMM, 3RD MAF VN* +
*SSGT* **Wallach,** Alfred E, New Haven, MO, *A-1ENGR KO* +
*SSGT* **Walling,** William C, Des Moines, IA, *F-2-5 WWII KO* +
*CAPT* **Walsh,** Bennett W, Beufort, SC, *WPN/L-3-1 CW* +
*CAPT* **Walsh,** Daniel M III, Springfield, MA, *L-3-1 VN* +
*MR.* **Walsh,** Edward M, Aledo, IL, *H&S 3/5 VN*
*CPL* **Walsh,** Gerald S, Wauwatosa, WI, *WPNS-3-1 KO* +
*CPL* **Walsh,** James M, Deland, FL, *M-3-1 VN* +
*SGT* **Walsh,** Patrick J, Evanston, IL, *I-3-7 VN* +
*LTCOL* **Walsh,** Robert L, South Burlington, VT, *2 -7MAR VN* +
*COL* **Walsh,** Thomas C JR., Great Mills, MD, *A CO 3RD AAV BN*
*SSGT* **Walsh,** J JR., Miami, FL, *I-3-1 WWII* +
*MR.* **Walter,** Thomas P, Sunset Hills, MO, *7COMM BN VN* +
*CPL* **Walters,** Richard S, Solon, OH, *B CO. 1ST BN 5TH MAR VN*
*SSGT* **Walther,** Douglas S JR., Red Bank, NJ, *I-3-7 KO VN* +
**Walz,** Nicholas, Palm Desert, CA, *HMM 362, 261*
*SGT* **Wandrie,** David F, Port Hope, MI, *HMM165 VN* +
*SSGT* **Ward,** C C, Mcallen, TX, *HQBN KO* +
*SGT* **Ward,** Ernest M, Lynchburg, VA, *C-1-5 VN* +
*SGT* **Ward,** Gerald A, Zephyrhills, FL, *HQ-HQ VN* +
*LTCOL* **Ward,** Henry A, Greenville, MI, *1ANGLICO VMF 323 KO* +
*CPL* **Ward,** Howard N, Panama City Beach, FL, *HQ-HQ WWII CH* +
*1STLT* **Ward,** Lawrence G, Alexandria, VA, *3-7MAR ENGR-11 KO VN* +
*CAPT* **Wardlaw,** Craig M, Charlotte, NC, *A-7ENGR VN* +
**Ward-Llewellyn,** T P, Oxnard, CA, *H&S-2-7 VN* +
*CPL* **Warne,** Earl W, Middlefield, OH, *R-2-5 WWII CH* +
*SGT* **Warner,** Leslie A, Lyndhurst, NJ, *WPNS-3-7 KO* +
*CPL* **Warner,** Nial W, Sparrow Bush, NY, *E-2-7 WWII* +
*CPL* **Warner,** William R, Keene, NH, *H-2-7 VN* +
*SGT* **Warnes,** Gordon C, Salem, SC, *SPT-1SVC 1/3-1MAR 5/7MAR KO*
*1STLT* **Warr,** R. NICHOLAS, Auburn, CA, *C-1-5 VN* +
*COL* **Warren,** Bruce H, San Antonio, TX, *H&S-5MAR WWII CH VN* +
*SGT* **Warren,** C E, Bakersfield, CA, *B-1-5 WWII KO* +
*CPL* **Warren,** Robert E, Oregon City, OR, *D-1-5 VN*
*LCPL* **Warren,** W L, Herndon, VA, *E-2-7 CW* +
**Warzeka,** P J, Cincinnati, OH, *1-9MAR CW* +
*SGTMAJ* **Waschkowsky,** Peter D, Concord, CA, *HQ-11MAR KO* +
*MRS* **Waselinko,** Anita, Santa Clarita, CA, *ASSOCIATE* +
*GYSGT* **Washington,** Walter L, Oceanside, CA, *VMGR 152 VMGR 352 VN* +
*GYSGT* **Wasilewski,** Ron E, Flower Mound, TX, *M-3-7 VN*
*CPL* **Waterfield,** Kelly M, Mill Valley, CA, *C-1-1/5 CW* +
*CAPT* **Waterhouse,** Mark D, Pleasant Valley, CT, *HQ/C-1ENGR VN* +
*LCPL* **Waterman,** Wayne P, Honolulu, HI, *B-1-26 VN* +
*COL* **Waters,** Herbert RAY, North Dartmouth, MA, *MAR AIR SPT SDN 1ST MAW KO* +
*CPL* **Watkins,** Herbert S, Manchester, NH, *A CO 1ST MAR 1ST MAR REGT*
*SGT* **Watkins,** John, Haines City, FL, *B-1-7 KO* +
*SGT* **Watkins,** Kenneth H, Fort Worth, TX, *MP-5MAR KO* +
*CAPT* **Watkins,** Price I, Pasadena, CA, *SIG BN WWII KO VN* +
*GYSGT* **Watso,** Jack M, Denver, CO, *HQ-HQ BAND KO* +
*CDR* **Watson,** Donald JR., Burlingame, CA, *1MED KO* +
*PFC* **Watson,** James E, Lantana, FL, *HQ-1ARM-AMPH KO* +
*LTCOL* **Watson,** Leah B, Fredericksburg, VA, *HQ-HQ CW* +
*SGT* **Watson,** Robert L, Orange, CA, *C-1-5 KO* +
*2NDLT* **Watson,** William A, Middlesboro, KY, *G-3-7 KO* +
*LTCOL* **Watson,** William P III, Rancho Penasquitos, CA, *CW, 1ST DIV SUPPORT GROUP*
*SGT* **Watterson,** Kenneth W, Terrell, TX, *G-3-11 VN* +
*CPL* **Watts,** Ronald C, Bartlesville, OK, *L-3-7 VN* +
*CPL* **Watts,** Thomas D JR., Hampton, VA, *L-4-11 VN* +
*SSGT* **Wax,** Joseph L, Baton Rouge, LA, *H&S-1MAR KO* +
*CAPT* **Wear,** Brad, Plano, TX, *A/C-1-7 CW* +
**Weatherell,** John C, Saint Petersburg, FL, *1MAW KO* +
*SGT* **Weaver,** A L, Quincy, MA, *1MAW KO* +
*CPL* **Webb,** Harold E, Sunny Side, GA, *A-1-5 VN* +
*CAPT* **Webb,** James H JR., Falls Church, VA, *D-1-5 VN* +
*MAJ* **Webb,** John N, Coral Gables, FL, *C-1-5 KO* +
*CPL* **Webb,** Larry P, Hope Hull, AL, *M-3-7 VN* +
*LCDR* **Webb,** Thomas EDWARD, Oceanside, CA, *11TH MAR REG MAG 39 SWA SOM* +
*SGT* **Webb,** W L. PAT, Nashville, IN, *E-2-5 KO* +
*MSGT* **Webber,** C B, Petaluma, CA, *2MAR ATT WWII* +
*SGT* **Weber,** Donald C, Willowick, OH, *E-2-7 KO* +
*LTGEN* **Weber,** Joseph F, College Station, TX, *HQ-11MAR CW* +
*CPL* **Weber,** Robert A, Miami, FL, *F-2-1 G-3-8 CH* +
*CAPT* **Weber,** Stanley E, Portland, OR, *HQ-1TK WWII CH KO* +
*SGTMAJ* **Weber,** W H, Asheville, NC, *SVC TK KO* +
*GYSGT* **Webster,** Albert E JR., Willis, TX, *3-9MAR KO VN* +
*CAPT* **Webster,** J M, Plymouth, MA, *B-1-11 VN* +
*HM3* **Webster,** William, Muskogee, OK, *1ARM-AMPH KO* +
*PFC* **Weckerly,** Frank W JR., Bluffton, SC, *1MAR KO* +
**Wedemeyer,** Eleanore F, Petaluma, CA, *ASSOCIATE* *
*CPL* **Weeden,** Willie H JR., Pittsburgh, PA, *B-1-7 C-1-6 VN* +
*SGT* **Weglinski,** Tony N, Reading, PA, *I-3-11 VN* +
*SGT* **Wehby,** Bernard A, Hendersonville, TN, *F-2-7 KO* +
*SGT* **Weigel,** Rex A, Hilo, HI, *I-3-1 VN* +
*1STSGT* **Weightman,** Robert L, Pinehurst, ID, *B-1-1 CH KO VN* +
*CWO4* **Weimer,** Wayne W, Kansas City, MO, *CWO-4 FOX-2-11 KO* +
*CPL* **Weinberg,** James A, Longwood, FL, *1-26 VN*
*SGT* **Weinrich,** Harold W, Perryville, MO, *B-TK KO* +
*LTCOL* **Weinsaft,** Keith S, Buffalo, NY, *1MARDIV G3, HQ BN SWA*
*SGT* **Weinstein,** Lewis E, Cranston, RI, *1ORD KO* +
*SSGT* **Weisberger,** Arthur J, Sierra Vista, AZ, *PIO-1-7 KO*
*BGEN* **Weise,** William, Springfield, VA, *G-3-5 KO VN* +
*GYSGT* **Weisgerber,** William D, Milpitas, CA, *I-3-7 KO* +
*SGT* **Weishuhn,** Harvey L, Saginaw, MI, *H&S-2-1 VN* +
*SGT* **Weisler,** Richard J, Hollywood, FL, *1 ARM-AMPH KO* +
*PFC* **Weiss,** George J JR., Marine, MN, *K-4-11 WWII CH* +
*SSGT* **Weitman,** Michael D, Tillamook, OR, *CIT VN* +
*SSGT* **Welch,** Michael J, Des Moines, IA, *H&S 2-7 VN* +
*SGT* **Welch,** Norman J, Muskegon, MI, *A-7ENGR D-1ENGR KO* +
*GYSGT* **Welch,** William R, Port Charlotte, FL, *G-3 D-1-1 VN* +
*GYSGT* **Weliver,** John A, Fort Myers, FL, *VMO-6 KO* +
*PFC* **Weller,** Paul G, Reno, NV, *WPNS-3-1 KO* +
*GYSGT* **Wells,** Adolphus W JR., Culver City, CA, *I-3-7 HQ-HQ KO VN* +
*CPL* **Wells,** D R JR., Middletown, NY, *H&S-1-7 VN* +
*MAJ* **Wells,** E F, Arlington, VA, *D-1-5 VN* +
*LTCOL* **Wells,** Jack D, Cupertino, CA, *H-3-11 VN* +
*SGT E-5* **Wells,** Larry Ward, Houston (Kingwood), TX, *D CO 1ST MP BN 1MAR DIV VN*
**Wells,** Thomas (Tommy) G, Denham Springs, LA, *C-1-3 WWII* +
*SGT* **Welsh,** Mike, Los Altos, CA, *B-1-5 VN*
*CPL* **Welter,** Terry L, Oregon City, OR, *MABS11-MAG11 VN* +
*SGT* **Wendorf,** Clarence W, Wauwatosa, WI, *1ANGLICO HQ-5MAR KO* +
*SSGT* **Wendt,** Richard A, New Lenox, IL, *H&S-1RECON VN* +
*MRS* **Wenhold,** Harriett, Lansdale, PA, *ASSOCIATE* *
*SGT* **Wenzel,** Walter E, Rogers City, MI, *B-1-5 KO* +
*CAPT* **Werckle,** Robert E, Lebanon, TN, *G-3-1 KO* +
*CPL* **Wermuth,** Delbert S, Carmel, CA, *C-1-1 WWII KO* +
*MAJ* **Werner,** Herb (Fritz) J, Chula Vista, CA, *HQ-HQ 4.2-5MAR KO VN* +
*SSGT* **Werntz,** Theodore E, Groveport, OH, *H&S-3-1 VN* +
*MSGT* **Werntz,** William R SR., Mishawaka, IN, *I-3-7 1MAW KO VN*
*LTCOL* **Wersell,** William J, Nokomis, FL, *G-3-7 WWII KO VN* +
*SGT* **Wesche,** Fred W, Carmichaels, PA, *I-3-5 VN* +
*CAPT* **West,** Bing, Newport, RI, *1-7 VN* +
**West,** David F, Westbrook, CT, *ASSOCIATE* *
*SGT* **West,** Kenneth D, Grand Blanc, MI, *SUP-1SVC KO* +
*MSGT* **West,** Samuel E, Gulfport, MS, *H&S-2-7-CH-KO* +
**Westfall,** Dominic, Twentynine Palms, CA, *B-1-5 VN* +
*CPL* **Westlund,** Robert L, Damascus, OR, *HQ-3-11 KO* +
*SGT* **Westover,** Del R, Dallas, OR, *L-3-27 K-3-7 VN* +
*SGTMAJ* **Westwick,** Earl R, Algonquin, IL, *HQ-1FSSG 1MAW VN SWA* +
*MSGT* **Wetherbee,** Donald A, Media, PA, *H&S-7MAR G-1 CH KO* +
*CPL* **Wetzel,** Kenneth W, Newport, PA, *WPNS-3-1 CW* +
**Wheeler,** John R, Bourbonnais, IL, *B-1-5 VN* +

*SGT* **Wheeler,** Neil S, Huntington, MA, *1AMTRAC CW* +
*SGT* **Whelan,** E F, Charlestown, MA, *1-5/7MAR KO* +
*PFC* **Whelehan,** Walter L JR., Las Vegas, NV, *HQ-1-1 WWII CH* +
*SGT* **Whetzel,** Thomas R, Canyon Country, CA, *HQ-HQ-1MAR VN* +
*MAJ* **Whipp,** James T, Tucson, AZ, *1ST SERV BN 7TH COMM BN*
*SGT* **Whisennand,** Arthur L, Colorado Springs, CO, *TK H-3-7 WWII CH KO* +
**Whitaker,** Bruce W, Cresaptown, MD, *D-1-5 VN* +
*CPL* **Whitaker,** Elbert C, Elm Grove, WI, *VMF223 H&MS11-MAG11 CW* +
*LCPL* **White,** Arnold G JR., Rochester, NY, *L-4-11 VN* +
*REV.* **White,** Don E, Yucca Valley, CA, +
*SGT* **White,** Douglas F, Bountiful, UT, *1FSR/FLC VN* +
*SGT* **White,** Edward E, Daphne, AL, *H&S/G-2-1 VN*
*PFC* **White,** Eugene C, Vinton, VA, *WPNS-3-7 KO* +
*LCPL* **White,** Harold E, Fernandina Beach, FL, *HQ-HQ 1MAW VN* +
*CPL* **White,** Harry G JR., Marianna, PA, *1st BRIDGE CO 7TH ENGR VN* +
*LTCOL* **White,** Jean P, Vista, CA, *I-3-7 KO VN* +
*SGT* **White,** Joe L, Mishawaka, IN, *D-1-5 A-1-1 VN* +
*GYSGT* **White,** John L, Tampa, FL, *G-2-1 WWII KO* +
*COL* **White,** Robert D, Cameron Park, CA, *H-7MAR KO VN* +
*MAJ* **White,** Robert "Bob" W, Marietta, GA, *11 MAR* *
*SGTMAJ* **White,** Robin D, Plainfield, IN, *WPNS-2-5 CW* +
*PFC* **White,** Stewart E, Indianola, WA, *E-2-7 KO* +
*SGT* **White,** Thomas C, Pompano Beach, FL, *K-3-7 VN* +
*COL* **White,** W V, Nokesville, VA, *1MAR VN* +
*SGT* **White,** William G, Hot Springs, AR, *HQ-2-11 KO* +
*SGT* **Whiteaker,** Jack S, Nipomo, CA, *C-1-7 WWII CH* +
*CAPT* **Whited,** Robert L, Carlsbad, CA, *G-2-7 H&S-5MAR KO VN*
*SGT E-5* **Whitehead,** Samuel D, Boring, OR
*CPL* **Whitman,** Lester E, Jonestown, PA, *3RD BN 26TH MAR VN*
*HM2* **Whitman,** Robert S, Boone, IA, *D-1-26 C-1MED VN* +
*SGT* **Whitmer,** Maurice P, Millville, CA, *D-1-5 VN* +
*CWO3* **Whitney,** Dallas C, Cape Carteret, NC, *HQ-5/11MAR SWA* +
*BM1C* **Whitt,** Joseph V, Bethel, OH, +
*CWO2* **Whitten,** Morris E, Vacaville, CA, *HQ-HQ KO* +
*CPL* **Whitten,** William K, Indianapolis, IN, *L-3-1 WWII* +
*SSGT* **Whitters,** Paul R, Platte City, MO, *HQBN 1ST MAR DIV KO* +
*COL* **Whitters,** Robert A, Talent, OR, *HQBN OIF* +
*HM2* **Wickman,** Robert C, Keizer, OR, *I-3-7 KO* +
*SSGT* **Wiebe,** Lavern, Lincoln City, OR, *ANGLICO-5MAR KO*
*COL* **Wiedhahn,** Warren H, Annandale, VA, *4.2 MRTR 5MAR CH KO VN* +
**Wiegel,** Gregory B JR., Newbury, MD, *H-2-1 H-2-7 VN* +
*SGT* **Wiegert,** Steven D, Santa Rosa, CA, *D-1-5 VN* +
*PFC* **Wiegmann,** Daniel L SR., Huntertown, IN, *F-2-5 VN*
*LTCOL* **Wieler,** Eric H, Vero Beach, FL, *HQ-4-11 VN* +
*CPL* **Wiesley,** Russell D, Waukee, IA, *G-2-1 VN* +
*CPL* **Wihl,** Louis J, Albuquerque, NM, *H&S-5MAR WWII CH* +
*HM2* **Wiken,** Leslie E LPN, West Palm Beach, FL, *M-3-5-1MED VN* +
*MSGT* **Wilcox,** Ralph M, Fredericksburg, VA, *1AVNENGR WWII* +
*CPL* **Wilder,** Gordon T, Berkeley, CA, *E-2-5 CH* +
*GYSGT* **Wilder,** James R, Cocoa, FL, *C-1RECON VN* +
*SGT* **Wiley,** Charles F, Placentia, CA, *WPNS-2-1 KO* +
**Wiley,** Linn, La Quinta, CA, *VMF-AW 513*
*SGT* **Wiley,** Richard D, Portland, OR, *H&S-2-1 KO* +
*GEN* **Wilhelm,** Charles E, Villa Rica, GA, *CG 1MARDIV VN SWA* +
*CPL* **Wilker,** James A, New Richland, MN, *C-1RECON VN* +
*MAJGEN* **Wilkerson,** H L, Greensboro, NC, *A-1-7 CO-1MAR WWII CH KO VN* +
*LTCOL* **Wilkerson,** Richard J, San Jose, CA, *US7THFLT VN* +
*PFC* **Wilkes,** Roy G, North Barrington, IL, *1-29MAR C-BRIDGE WWII CH* +
*SSGT* **Wilkins,** Barney F, Benton, LA, *1TK WWII KO* +
*SGT* **Wilkins,** Raymond L, Dayton, TX, *HQ-HQ VN* +
*SGT* **Wilkinson,** Lawrence ROBERT, Oak Park, IL, *HQ 1-13 VN*
*PFC* **Wilkinson,** Raymond H, Ashby, MA, *H&S-1ENGR WWII* +
*LCPL* **Wilkinson,** Wayne R, Elk Grove, CA, *MABS16 CW* +
*CPL* **Willard,** Larry W, Advance, NC, *D-7ENGR VN*
*SGT* **Williams,** Clayton A, Coral Gables, FL, *WPNS-1-5 KO* +
*PFC* **Williams,** D B, Rutland, MA, *L-3-1 WWII* +
*MR.* **Williams,** Daniel R, Georgetown, TX, *HQ-2-11 VN*
*SGT* **Williams,** Dewey W, Clinton Twp, MI, *C-1-7 E-2-1 WWII CH KO* +
**Williams,** Don M, Bellville, TX, *L-3-5 CW* +
**Williams,** Ezra F, Ofallon, MO, *I/3/7 H/3/7 KO*
*SGT* **Williams,** George L, Topeka, KS, *11MAR CH KO* +
*CWO3* **Williams,** Gordon H, Boise, ID, *F-2-7 KO VN* +
*MR.* **Williams,** Gordon H, Rochester, NY, *A-1/3AMTRAC VN* +
*SSGT* **Williams,** Gordon R, Carmine, TX, *K-4-11 KO VN* +
*SSGT* **Williams,** Jack W, Plymouth Meeting, PA, *SPLWPNS WWII* +
*SGT* **Williams,** James D, Central City, PA, *G-3-7 KO* +
*COL* **Williams,** James L, Oceanside, CA, *1RECON 3-5MAR VN*
*LCPL* **Williams,** Jamie J, Allentown, PA, *2/1 H, 2/4 G, WEAPONS-MGO*
*PVT* **Williams,** Jobert M.A., Crossville, TN, *B-1-5 WWII* +
*SGTMAJ* **Williams,** Joel Stanley, Mars Hill, NC, *B 1/5 VN*
*SGT* **Williams,** John F JR., Centennial, CO, *C-1AT VN* +
*PFC* **Williams,** Lafayette, Chicago, IL, *F-2-5 VN*
*SGT* **Williams,** M R, Winters, TX, *1MAW KO* +
*SGT* **Williams,** Marcus L, Honolulu, HI, *C-1-11 WWII* +
*CPL* **Williams,** Mason D, El Segundo, CA, *AM-TRACS 1MAW KO* +
*LCPL* **Williams,** Paul J, Fort Mohave, AZ, *1ST 8' HOWITZER 3D 155 HOWITZER*
*CPL* **Williams,** Richard F, Palm Harbor, FL, *C/1/5 VN*
*1STSGT* **Williams,** Robert E, Georgetown, TX, *I-3-7 WWII CH KO* +
*SSGT* **Williams,** Robert V, Albuquerque, NM, *HQ-1-5 WWII* +
*CAPT* **Williams,** Samuel M, Glen Rose, TX, *VN, ECHO CO 2ND BN 5TH MARINES VN* +
**Williams,** Thomas P, Vermontville, MI, *H&S-1/2-26 VN* +
*SGT* **Williams,** Warren E, Elko, NV, *WPNS-2-5 KO* +
*CPL* **Williams,** Michael SCOTT, Boulder Creek, CA, *7TH MTN BN 1ST FSR*
*CPL* **Williamson,** Charles B, Washington, PA, *C-1-1 VN* +
*CPL* **Williamson,** Johnny M, Louisville, KY, *I-3-7 KO* +
*SGT* **Williamson,** Mark T, Garretson, SD, *C-1RECON VN* +
*COL* **Williamson,** Tren A, Sequim, WA, *7TH MAR KO VN* +
*MSGT* **Willis,** Bill M, Louisville, KY, *MAG16-1MAW VN* +
*CAPT* **Willis,** Raymond E, Tustin, CA, *C-1-5 HQ CO 5TH MAR VN* +
**Wills,** John M, Huntsville, AL, *ASSOCIATE* +
**Wills,** Martha W, South San Francisco, CA
*SGT* **Willson,** Lewie R, Eaton, NY, *H-3-7 KO* +
*SGT* **Wilmoth,** Dennis A, Conroe, TX, *7MAR VN* +
*CPL* **Wilson,** B L, Los Fresnos, TX, *B-1ARMAMPH WWII* +
*CPL* **Wilson,** D L, Rising Sun, MD, *HQ-1-11* +
*SGT* **Wilson,** George M, Hillsboro, OR, *C-1-7 WWII CH* +
*SGT* **Wilson,** Irvin R, Fallon, NV, *A-1-5 VN* +
*SGT E-5* **Wilson,** James C, Trinity, TX, *11MAR* +
*LCDR* **Wilson,** John A, Milpitas, CA, *3-1MAR USS-TOLEDO KO* +
*SSGT* **Wilson,** John J, King Of Prussia, PA, *A-1MT D-2-5 KO* +
*CPL* **Wilson,** Ken, San Antonio, TX, *W-1-13 VN* +
*CPL* **Wilson,** Michael T, Marietta, GA, *H&S-3-5 VN* +
*SGT* **Wilson,** Neil E, Oliver Springs, TN, *D-1-7 VN* +
*COL* **Wilson,** Paul E, Winter Park, FL, *1ST 3RD MAR DIV WWII CH KO VN* +
*CPL* **Wilson,** Richard W, Annapolis, CA, *K-3-5 VN*
*SGT* **Wilson,** Robert D, Waterville Valley, NH, *WPN-1-25 SWA* +
*SGT* **Wilson,** Rube G, Jonesboro, GA, *E-2-5 H&S-1-28 VN* +
*SGT* **Wilson,** Stephen P, Brooksville, FL, *B-1-11 E-2-1 VN* +
*SGT* **Wilson,** Warren E, Lanham, MD, *HQ-HQ VN* +
*SGT* **Wilt,** Howard E, Williamsport, PA, *F-2-11 KO* +
*MAJ* **Winburne,** E R, Cordova, TN, *F-2-7 KO* +
*MRS* **Winchester,** Marianna, Rockville Centre, NY, *GOLD STAR MOTHER* +
*CPL* **Winder,** Roy L, Britton, SD, *G-3-5 KO* +
*SGT* **Windett,** Edward L, North Aurora, IL, *A-1-7 KO* +
*CWO2* **Winfield,** Robert L, Virginia Beach, VA, *C-1-7 KO VN* +
*SSGT* **Wing,** Kenneth L, Mount Vernon, MO, *H&S/A-1TK FLSGB-FLC VN* +
*CPL* **Wingo,** E M JR., Odessa, TX, *HQBN-MAW VN* +
*CPL* **Winkler,** Eugene E, Torrance, CA, *WPS-2-7 KO* +
*CPL* **Winkler,** Kenneth E, Lincoln, NE, *B-1MED 5MAR WWII CH* +
*CPL* **Winn,** Omer H, Jacksonville, FL, *1ST SIG BN 1MAR DIV KO* +
*1STSGT* **Winsett,** Hulan H, Fort Collins, CO, *H&S-1SVC B-1MT CW* +
*MRS.* **Winsett,** Linda V, Aurora, CO, *ASSOCIATE* *
*PLTSGT* **Winsler,** John A, Rossville, TN, *M-4-11 WWII* +
*SGT* **Winslow,** George S, Portland, OR, *3-8IN BTRY-11MAR VN*
*LTC* **Winston,** Herbert T, Miami Shores, FL, *K-3-1* +
*SGT* **Winston,** Willis H, Wake Forest, NC, *H-2-7 WWII* +
*GYSGT* **Winter,** John B, Bloomington, MN, *MG-CIS-1 KO* +
*CPL* **Winters,** Albert R, East Liverpool, OH, *W-3-7 KO* +
*CPL* **Winters,** Stephen J, Merrick, NY, *E-2-5 VN* +
*SGT* **Winterwerp,** Carl J, Port Orange, MD, *G-3-1 KO* +
*LCPL* **Wirgau,** Timothy J, Philadelphia, PA, *HHS MCAS IWAUKUNI CW*
*MSGT* **Wirth,** John A, Joliet, IL, *MAG21 WWII* +

*COL* **Wischmeyer,** William D, Austin, TX, *I/L-3-1 VN CW* +
**Wise,** Bill JR., Surfside Beach, SC, *SVC-9ENGR VN* +
*SGT* **Wishart,** John W, Whiting, NJ, *B-1-1 KO* +
**Wisneski,** Joseph J, Bridgeport, CT, *A-1-7 VN* +
*CPL* **Wisniewski,** Fred W, Lockport, IL, *I/H&S-3-1 KO* +
*CPL* **Wisocki,** Joseph JOHN, Bella Vista, AR, *VN, HQ, 1-5, 1-9, 106 PLT VN*
*CPL* **Wissinger,** John E JR., Frankfort, OH, *L-3-1 VN* +
**Withee,** Jan, San Clemente, CA, *ASSOCIATE* +
*CAPT* **Withrow,** Max D, Mission Viejo, CA, *B-1ENGR* +
*SSGT* **Witkowski,** Eugene A, Garden Grove, CA, *1ANGLICO KO* +
*CPL* **Wittie,** Lawrence, Rio Rancho, NM, *K-4-11 KO* +
**Wittig,** Judge, Boerne, TX, *HQ-HQ VN* +
*LCPL* **Wityak,** Thomas A, Southbury, CT, *M-3-5 VN* +
*SSGT* **Wodrich,** Stephen W, Marietta, GA, *Bco 3RD AMTRAC BN VN*
*LTCOL* **Wodtke,** Ronald P, Maple Grove, MN, *1MEF VN SWA* +
*MAJ* **Wogan,** Christopher M, Tucson, AZ, *5MAR VN* +
*LCPL* **Wogan,** Michael P, Beverly, MA, *HQ/A/B-9ENGR VN* +
*PVT* **Wojahn,** Paul W, New Ulm, MN, *C-1PION-17 WWII* +
**Wolff,** R, Chicago, IL, *W-2-5* +
*SGT* **Wolford,** Keith L, Duncannon, PA, *H-3-11 KO* +
*CPL* **Wolski,** G J, Sault Ste Marie, MI, *HQ-3-11 CW* +
**Womack,** Bert E.M. JR., Denver, CO, *1-5 KO* +
**Won,** Gary E, Danville, CA, *H&MS-42 MAG42 VN* +
**Wong,** Herbert C, State College, PA, *H&S/G/H/I-3-1 KO* +
*COL* **Wonson,** Craig R, Newport, RI, *3-5MAR OIF* +
**Woo,** Je C, Huntington Beach, CA, *ROKMC VN* +
*GYSGT* **Wood,** Dillon L, Santa Rita, GU, *D-2-5 KO* +
*SGT* **Wood,** Frederick C, Liverpool, NY, *H&S-9ENGR VN* +
*COL* **Wood,** Leonard E, Reno, NV, *G-3-5 KO VN* +
*SGT* **Wood,** Lewis E, Dallas, TX, *M-4-11 VN* +
*PFC* **Wood,** W Gordon SR., Tucson, AZ, *K/L/HQ-3-5 WWII CH* +
*MRS* **Woodard,** Audrey V, Idaho Falls, ID, *ASSOCIATE* *
*SGT* **Woodcock,** Earl J, Boone, IA, *HQ-HQ KO* +
*LTCOL* **Woodier,** William H, Bristow, VA, *B-1RECON VN SWA* +
*CAPT* **Woodley,** Charles L, San Mateo, CA, *K 3/16 5MAB, I 3/1 1MARDIV VN*
*MAJ* **Woodman,** Michael D, Oviedo, FL, *H&S-3-1 CW* +
*CPL* **Woodrow,** Matthew A, Honolulu, HI, *HQ-HQ KO* +
*SGT* **Woods,** James R, Tonganoxie, KS, *SUP-1SVC KO* +
*SGT* **Woods,** Joseph D, Huntington Beach, CA, *C-1-7 KO* +
*PFC* **Woods,** Larry E, Rushville, IN, *1SIG-HQ WWII*
**Woods,** Robert J SR., Grand Forks, ND, *K-3-5 WWII* +
*CPL* **Woods,** Thomas (Woody) W, San Antonio, TX, *C-1-5 SWA CW* +
*GYSGT* **Woods,** William N, Oceanside, CA, *1ST MAW 3MAW VN* +
*SGT* **Woolery,** Joe M, Minden, NV, *A-1-1 CW* +
*SGT* **Woolley,** Byron B, Glendale, AZ, *1/5 VN*
*SGT* **Wooten,** Lawson L, Richmond, TX, *E-2-7 VN* +
*SGT* **Wootton,** Tommy J, Whittier, CA, *1ANGLICO KO* +
*CPL* **Work,** G H, Aurora, CO, *C-6-AMTRAC WWII* +
*PFC* **Worth,** P JR., Waukee, IA, *1MAW WWII* +
*SSGT* **Worthy,** John M JR., Mesquite, TX, *M-4-11 KO* +
*SGT E-5* **Woulfe,** Thomas E, Palm Desert, CA, *1MARDIV HQ BATT, 7TH COMM, 3RD MARDIV*
*PFC* **Woznick,** Lawrence E, Woodsfield, OH, *A-1-5 VN* +
*SGT* **Wright,** Alfred J, Greenwood, IN, *C-1-7 KO* +
*CPL* **Wright,** Keith D, Vancouver, WA, *H-2-5 VN* +
*SGT* **Wright,** William L, Melbourne, FL, *C-1TK VN* +
*PSGT* **Wrobleski,** Henry M, Rochester, MN, *C-1-17 WWII* +
*SSGT* **Wuerth,** Paul H, Coquille, OR, *HQ-MAG33 KO* +
*SGT* **Wuestenfeld,** Robert 'Gene' E, Fountain Hills, AZ, *B-1-11 CW*
**Wyatt,** E RAY, Upland, IN, *I-3-7 VN* +
*CPL* **Wylie,** Scott, Westport, CT, *HQ-2-5 CW* +
*1STSGT* **Wyman,** Ron E, Huntington Beach, CA, *1ST MAR 5TH MAR KO VN CMC CW* +
*LCPL* **Wyne,** W L JR., West Palm Beach, FL, *M-3-26 VN* +
*CPL* **Wynn,** Charles MARTIN, Somerville, NJ, *A/C-1AMTRAC KO* +
*PFC* **Wyrick,** Donald H, Tulsa, OK, *B-1-5 KO* +
*SGT* **Yager,** Alan M, Houston, TX, *MED-1-32INF-7DIV KO* +
*SGT* **Yancey,** James H, Fort Valley, GA, *1-5MAR 2-1MAR VN* +
*SGT* **Yancey,** Owen D, Yucca Valley, CA, *E-2-11WWII CH KO* +
*SGT* **Yapp,** George J JR., Mokena, IL, *E-2-5 VN* +
*CPL* **Yarbrough,** J A, Victorville, CA, *1TKS VN* +
*PFC* **Yarbrough,** R F, Fulton, TX, *K-3-7 WWII* +
*SGT* **Yarbrough,** R W, Glen Rose, TX, *1ARMAM-PH-11MAR VN* +
*CWO2* **Yates,** Christopher S, San Clemente, CA, *1-4/5MAR SWA*
*CPL* **Ybarra,** Frank, Palm Desert, CA, *3TH/4TH MARINES*
*CPL* **Yencich,** Joseph JR., Bothell, WA, *E-2-5 VN* +
**Yeon,** Kim H, Glendale, CA, *KMC KO* +
*PFC* **Yi,** Joseph C, Des Plaines, IL, *SHR PTY 1MAR DIV KO*
*SGT* **Ylizaliturri,** Frank R, Granada Hills, CA, *MP-HQ CW* +
*SGTMAJ* **Ynacay,** Robert S, San Bernardino, CA, *KO VN* +
*SGT1ST CLASS* **Yoo,** Byung-Sup, Gyeonggi-Do Korea, Korea, *KO VN*
*SGT* **Yoo,** Chuck, Tehachapi, CA, *KMC KO VN* +
*CAPT* **Yoo,** Tae-Young, Seocho Gu Seoul, Korea, +
*CAPT* **Yoon,** Pil J, Rancho Palos Verdes, CA, *KMC KO* +
*LTCOL* **Yorck,** David C, San Diego, CA, *L-3-1 H-2-9 I MEF VN SWA* +
*SGT* **York,** Hillous, Franklin, KY, *C-1-5 VN* +
*CPL* **York,** Joseph K, Killingworth, CT, *W-3-7 KO* +
*HM2* **York,** R L, Pahrump, NV, *F-2-27MAR VN* +
*PFC* **York,** Thomas M, Balboa Island, CA, *B-1-5 VN* +
*CPL* **Young,** Charles E, Annapolis, MD, *I-3-11 KO* +
*SSGT* **Young,** Clarence M, Pontiac, MI, *A-1-5 VN* +
**Young,** Dai OH, Garden Grove, CA, *KMC* +
*CWO5* **Young,** Howard, San Ramon, CA, *MAG26 SWA* +
*SGT E-5* **Young,** James P IV, Lugoff, SC, *SPT CO 7 ENG SPT BN 1FSSG OIF*
*CPL* **Young,** James T, Gray, TN, *H&S-COMM-7MAR CW* +
*CAPT* **Young,** Paul R, Adin, CA, *B-1RECON VN* +
*CPL* **Young,** Phil A, Santa Monica, CA, *A-1-7 VN* +
*SGT* **Young,** Richard A, Grants Pass, OR, *L-3-1/5 VN CW* +
*CPL* **Youngblood,** Louis P, Metairie, LA, *10INF KO* +
*SGT* **Youngdeer,** Robert S, Cherokee, NC, *E-1RAIDERS 1MAR WWII CH* +
*SGT* **Youngren,** Allan M, Cherry Valley, CA, *H&S-1TK KO*
*1STSGT* **Yruegas,** Valente U, San Antonio, TX, *D/E/H-2-5 KO VN* +
**Yu,** Chris, Torrance, CA, *ROKMC VN* +
*CAPT* **Yu,** Wha S, Seoul, Korea, *ROKMC VN* +
**Yu,** Young S, Granada Hills, CA, *KMC VN* +
*SGTMAJ* **Zacker,** Mike G, San Diego, CA, *HQ/A-C-1-11 VN* +
*LCPL* **Zadian,** Michael O, Los Angeles, CA, *C-1MAAM CW*
*CPL* **Zaeff,** Eugene D, Toledo, OH, *D-2-11 CH KO* +
**Zagone,** William SR., Palm Desert, CA, *AMPHIB*
*CPL* **Zagorski,** Julius F, Hilton Head, SC, *I-3-11 WWII* +
*SGT* **Zajackowski,** Florian J, Milladore, WI, *D-1-1 KO* +
*CPL* **Zakian,** Charles, Jupiter, FL, *H&S-3-5 VN* +
*SGT* **Zaletta,** Cyril M, Mesa, AZ, *17ENGR HQ-HQ WWII CH*
*LCPL* **Zalpis,** James L, Longview, WA, *E-2-7 VN* +
*CPL* **Zamora,** E.J., Harlingen, TX, *1MAG KO* +
*CPL* **Zang,** Michael T, Brooklyn, NY, *M-3-5 VN* +
*SGT* **Zavis,** Kenneth, Westmont, IL, *E-2-1 CW* +
*CAPT* **Zeferjohn,** David A, Topeka, KS, *A-1-11 SVC-HQ KO VN* +
*CPL* **Zeis,** Roger R, Lakewood, CA, *H&S-3-26 VN* +
*SGT* **Zelasco,** Matthew W, Stockton, IL, *F-2-5 M-3-5 VN*
*CAPT* **Zell,** Richard M, Homosassa, FL, *A-1-5 VN* +
*HN* **Zelvin,** Bruce D, Bristol, PA, *MAR AIR GRP 11&16 1MARDIV VN*
*PFC* **Zembriski,** Stanley P JR., Mahwah, NJ, *H&S/I-3-7 KO* +
*HM3* **Zender,** Matthew (Matt) D, Meggett, SC, *K-3-5 VN* +
*CPL* **Zenner,** Mike W, Lenexa, KS, *HQ-5-7MAR VN* +
*LTCOL* **Zetzman,** Wayne P, Lenexa, KS, *1RECON CW* +
**Zidel,** Dan, Palm Desert, CA, *2MARDIV*
*CPL* **Zielinski,** M JOHN, Philadelphia, PA, *G-3-11 WWII* +
*SGT* **Ziemann,** Charles A, South Pasadena, CA, *F-2-5 VN* +
*CPL* **Ziemnick,** James A, Calumet, MI, *C-11MT VN* +
**Zien,** Carl J, New Berlin, WI, *C-1-1 CH KO* +
*CPL* **Zienkiewicz,** Robert F, Little Ferry, NJ, *I-3-7 KO* +
*SGT* **Zigulis,** Andrew P, Mountain View, CA, *E-2-7 KO*
*SSGT* **Zimman,** Sidney H, Oceanside, CA, *VMSB 341* +
*SGT* **Zimmerman,** James N, Murrells Inlet, SC, *D-1ENGR KO* +
*COL* **Zink,** Russell TODD, Westlake Village, CA, *3/9 7MAR 1MARDIV*
*SGT* **Zinnell,** A O, Brazoria, TX, *A-1-1 KO* +
*CPL* **Ziolkowski,** Ben, Racine, WI, *B-1-5 WWII CH* +
*LTCOL* **Zitz,** Kenneth W, Waialua, HI, *B-1TK VN* +
*CAPT* **Zoellin,** Max K, Johnson City, TN, *C-11MT VN* +
*SGT* **Zoutis,** Theodore C, Carlsbad, CA, *M-3-1 VN* +
*CPL* **Zuehl,** Richard L, Eden Prairie, MN, *G-2-3 HQ-3MAW CW* +
*MGYSGT* **Zugaj,** Frank B, Oceanside, CA, *COMM-HQ VN, 3-7MAR CMC* +
*COL* **Zumwalt,** Orlow R, Gaithersburg, MD, *H-3-7 KO* +
*SGT* **Zuspan,** Glenn A, Pine Bluff, AR, *HQCO-2-7 VN* +
*SGT* **Zweifel,** V G, Coopersburg, PA, *ORD BN KO* +

*Marines finishing training at Parris Island, SC. Photo by Alfred T. Palmer courtesy Library of Congress*

# Biographies

**DANIEL G. ABEL** was born July 16, 1933, Karlsruhe, ND; enlisted in the Marine Corps in 1952 and completed boot camp training at MCRD San Diego. Volunteered to serve in Korea and was assigned to Headquarters Battery, 11th Marines, 1st Marine Division. Deployed to Korea and after one year returned to Camp Pendleton. During my time in the Marine Corps, achieved the rank of sergeant and was awarded numerous medals/awards: PUC, GDCON, NDSM, KDS, KPUC, UNSM and RKWSM; completed active duty in 1955 and was assigned to inactive Reserves and received an Honorable Discharge in 1960.

Enrolled in college under the G.I. Bill and graduated with a BS degree in Engineering/Business from UCLB (University of California, Long Beach) in 1963 and subsequently received Master of Business Administration degree, 1977.

During my professional career as an aerospace engineer, I worked on the Apollo Program until man landed on the Moon in 1969 and later worked on unmanned satellites, Global Positioning Satellites (GPS) and retired in 1993 as Program Manager working 35 years in aerospace.

My wife Margery and I both have had prior marriages and together have six children and seven grandchildren.

**EDWIN WARNER ALLARD** was born March 23, 1932 in New Bedford, MA. After graduating from Holy Family high school in 1950, he enlisted and took Boot Camp at Parris Island. He received additional training at Camp Pendleton, CA.

He served in Korea and as a result of his service received the Combat Ribbon, KPUC with 5 stars, AFJC with Star, and Korean Ribbon with 3 stars.

He stated his memorable experience was coming home from Korea.

He was discharged at Quantico, VA with the rank of Corporal, and later worked for Standard Times Newspaper.

**MASTER GUNNERY SERGEANT ARTHUR "ARTIE" ALLEN III** was born and raised in Miami, Florida on 11 July 1967 and graduated from Miami Central High School in June 1985. He entered recruit training on 3 February 1986 at Marine Corps Recruit Depot, Parris Island, South Carolina. His first assignment was to Headquarters Battery, 2nd Battalion, 11th Marine Regiment, 1st Marine Division, Camp Pendleton, California as a Field Wireman.

Allen's duty station assignments included Marine Wing Communications Squadron 18, 1st Marine Aircraft Wing (1988 Okinawa, Japan); 9th Communication Battalion, I Marine Expeditionary Force (1989 & 1994 Camp Pendleton, CA); Marine Wing Communications Squadron 48, 4th Marine Aircraft Wing (1998 Fort Sheridan, Highwood, IL); Company M, Third Recruit Training Battalion, Marine Corps Recruit Depot (1992 San Diego, CA); 7th Communication Battalion, III Marine Expeditionary Force (2001, 2008-2016, Okinawa, Japan) and Communications Company, Headquarters Battalion, 1st Marine Division (2004 Camp Pendleton, CA)

Allen's combat deployments include Operations Desert Shield/Desert Storm (1990-1991 9th Communication Battalion, I Marine Expeditionary Force-Forward, Saudi Arabia and Kuwait); Operation Iraqi Freedom 05-07 (2006-2007 9th Communication Battalion, Multi-National Force-West, Camp Blue Diamond, Ar Ramadi, Al Anbar Province); and Operation Enduring Freedom (2009-2010 Headquarters United States Forces-Afghanistan, Kabul, Afghanistan).

Master Gunnery Sergeant Allen's awards and decorations include the Legion of Merit, Defense Meritorious Service Medal, Meritorious Service Medal (with gold star in lieu of 2nd award), Navy and Marine Corps Commendation Medal (with gold star in lieu of 2nd award), Navy and Marine Corps Achievement Medal (with gold star in lieu of 5th award), Joint Meritorious Unit Award, Navy Unit Commendation (4th Award), Meritorious Unit Commendation (3rd award), Good Conduct Medal (10th award), National Defense Service Medal (2nd award), South West Asia Service Medal (3 stars), Afghanistan Campaign Medal (1 star), Iraqi Campaign Medal (2 stars), Global War On Terrorism Service Medal, Korea Defense Service Medal, Military Outstanding Volunteer Service Medal, Sea Service Deployment Ribbon (14th award), Drill Instructor Ribbon, Non-Article 5 NATO/ISAF Medal, Kuwaiti Liberation Medal (Saudi Arabia), and the Kuwaiti Liberation Medal (Kuwait). He has a multitude of other forms of appreciation, commendation, honors and recognition.

Master Gunnery Sergeant Allen retired on 1 September 2016 after serving nearly 31 years of honorable & faithful service. He resides in Menifee, CA where he enjoys his volunteerism activities in veteran services, Habitat for Humanity, and a Docent for the Marine Corps Recruit Depot Museum Foundation, San Diego, CA.

Artie's professional affiliations include the Armed Forces Communications and Electronics Association (AFCEA), Veterans of Foreign Wars (VFW), West Coast Drill Instructor Association, Marine Corps Association & Foundation and the 1st Marine Division Association, Southern California Chapter.

Artie is married to the former Sabrina Rene Beasely of Memphis, Tennessee. He has a son, A'ntron Lee age 27 and a daughter, Alexyss Reene age 19.

**MARK T. AMANN** was born July 17, 1948, the son of Earl J. and Jean B. Oppeau Amann. He graduated from Buchanan High School in Troy, MO, with the class of 1968. On his 20th birthday anniversary, July 17, 1968 he joined the US Marines. Dec. 31 of that same year, he received his orders for Vietnam. He was assigned to Headquarters Battalion 1st Marine Division. On Aug. 12, 1969 in Quang Nam Province he was killed by small arms fire.

Military Rites were held for Vietnam War casualty B Marine PFC Mark T. Amann, Aug. 23, 1969. Full military honors were given PFC Amann. Six Marines, in dress blues, carried the flag-draped casket between two rows of VFW and VFW Auxiliary members, who stood at attention to the funeral coach. PFC Amann received a 21 gun salute at the Hawk Point Cemetery where he was laid to rest followed by the playing of Taps. The flag was folded and presented to the parents of the young Marine. The entire service was supervised by Sgt. Greg Higgins, USMC, who was PFC Amann's escort.

PFC Amann had three sisters - Susan, Penny and Kris and two brothers, Craig and Kurt. Now Kurt and Kris are the only siblings left to remember their dear brother, Mark.

On Dec. 29, 2001 Kris left this message on the Virtual Wall. "I will always remember you, I was only 5 years old but I do know how much you did love me. I still hold you close to my heart and my memories!" *Submitted by Kris (Amanda) Watt, sister.*

**SGT. DONALD J. ANGLIM** was born in Brooklyn, NY on Dec. 25, 1932. He lost his parents at an early age, was raised in boarding schools and Spring Lake, NJ. He graduated from Asbury Park, NJ high school in 1950. After serving in the New Jersey National Guard from Jarl 1949 to June 1950, he joined the Marine Corps Aug. 1, 1950. He went to boot camp at Parris Island and had 4.2 Mortar training in the 2nd Marines at Camp Lejeune, 1950 to Dec. 1951. He was an FO for 4.2 Mortars, 5th Marines in Korea February 1952 to February 1953. He was shot in the abdomen by "friendly fire" on March 15, 1952. His last duty station was Marine Barracks, Brooklyn Navy Yard. He had the honor of carrying the American Flag in a ticker tape parade for the "Angel of Diem Bien Phue" in April 1954.

After his discharge on Aug. 1, 1954, he worked in a bank and at night went to The Television Workshop of New York to learn TV Broadcasting. His TV career was from 1956, as an engineer, to 1973 as Program Manager. While at WKRC in Cincinnati, he became friends with a fellow Marine, Glenn Ryle Schnitker, who was the host of a children's program for 30 years. He produced and directed a documentary, "Skipper Ryle goes to Washington." The high light was going to be a private meeting with Vice-President Humphrey, but for Don it was the laying of a wreath at the Tomb of the Unknown Soldier by S.Sgt. Glenn Ryle Schnitker, a Marine combat veteran of WW II and Korea and directed by Sgt. Donald Anglim, a Marine combat veteran of Korea.

Don lives in Southbridge, MA with his wife, Carol. Between them they have 10 children, 31 grandchildren and seven great-grandchildren.

**JOHN W. BAILEY** was born in Missouri in 1925. His family moved to California during the dust bowl in 1934. He was attending Santa Paula Union High School, when in December 1942 John talked his dad into signing the papers to al-

low him to enlist in the Navy at age 17. He said, "It feels just like I am signing your death warrant," but like so many fiercely patriotic, loyal, proud Americans John was anxious to join the fight for our country! He entered Navy boot camp Company 43-15 at NTC San Diego, CA on Jan. 7, 1943. At the end of boot camp he was assigned to Hospital Corps School in Balboa Park, San Diego, CA where they were expected to learn two years of medical training in about eight weeks. John was then sent to the Naval Hospital on Mare Island, CA for "hands-on" training. Upon returning to San Diego he went through Marine Boot camp (tougher than Navy boot camp!) and field med training at Camp Elliott.

John was assigned to the 1st Marine Division at New Caledonia and joined them in Brisbane, Australia. The war took them to Guadalcanal (staging), Australia, Pavuvu (rest camp), New Guinea, New Britain and to their bloody and devastating battle on Sept. 15 – Oct. 30, 1944 (where because of the massive life toll, he served with the 1st, 5th and 7th Marines), and finally to Okinawa. Along with caring for the injured and dying, John was assigned to Grave Registration and received an accommodation in the prestigious *Navy Corpsmen's Magazine* for having only three Marines left unidentified in over 4,000 identified. He also received four Battle Stars and two Presidential Unit Citations.

Through all the devastation, there was also comradery and antics. Like the time he was court martialed by General Chesty Puller for shooting a bullet through a General's tent, but then getting a battlefield promotion.

John was discharged as a PhM 2 on May 30, 1946 and like all others that have experienced war, says he would never be the same. "But God blessed my return through my marriage to my beautiful wife, Naomi, to whom I've been married for 71 wonderful years, and the gift to raise four loving children and see my dear grandchildren and great-grandchildren.:

In 2001 John wrote the book, *ISLANDS OF DEATH - ISLANDS OF VICTORY*, to help preserve for future generations the horrors of war and the bravery of those that served. The true heroes of war remain in their final resting places far from home and must never be forgotten.

Even though he has been legally blind for almost 15 years, he still enjoys his friends of VFW Post 2043 in Santa Paula, CA and his brothers and everyone he have met through the FMDA. He is proud and humbled when they call him "Doc." "I've always said that I joined the Navy to avoid being drafted by the Army, and ended up having the honor of serving as a Corpsman with the greatest men of the 1st Marine Division. "Semper Fi until I die."

**FERRALL L. BAKER** was born in Clayton, ID; spent his early life with his parents on an Idaho Cattle Ranch. Attended primary school and graduated from high school in Challis, ID.

He enlisted in the US Marine Corp September 1948, attended recruit training (boot camp), San Diego, CA. On completion of "Boot Camp," he was assigned to the 1st Provisional Marine Brigade, stationed on Guam. After returning to the States and stationed at Camp Pendleton, CA, he was again assigned to the 1st Provisional Marine Brigade as a Machine Gunner, G CO 3rd Battalion and departed for Pusan, Korea, 1950. Participated in campaigns in the Pusan Perimeter, 1st and 2nd Naktong River Operation, landed on the island of Wolmi-do with the 3rd Battalion. 5th Marine, involved in all operations in landing at Inchon and the capture of Seoul, Korea. Participated in the action at the Chosin Reservoir, as a member of G CO 3rd Battalion. 5th Marine at Ydam-Nie, November-December 1950. Returned to the States and was stationed at Camp Pendleton, CA.

During his 30 year career, he has served with the 1st, 2nd and 3rd Martin Divisions, 1st Marine Aircraft Wing and Post and stationed through the world. He completed two tours of duty in Vietnam with the 3rd Marine Division. For four years was Senior NCO in charge of Security for the President of the US, President Richard Nixon when the President would visit MCAS, El Toro, CA and the Summer White House at San Clemente, CA. Spent eight years on recruiting duty, four years in Alabama and NCOIC Recruiting Station, Charlotte, NC.

His personal military decorations include Bronze Star with Combat V, Naval Commendation Medal with Combat V, Naval Achievement medal, four Presidential Unit Citations and over 20 other ribbons.

Ferrall retired as a Marine Master Gunnery Sergeant with 30 years Marine Corp Service at MCA Station, El Toro, CA. Received his degree in Business Management. He resides with his family – daughters Sarah, Jennifer and Kate – in Laguna Niguel, CA and Whidbey Island, Coupville, WA.

**DON "BARNEY" BARNARD** was born Aug. 4, 1945 in Hinsdale, IL. After graduating from Bettendorf High School, he enlisted in June 1963. He earned a BA in Business in 1970 from St. Ambrose College (now University.

After Boot Camp at Camp Pendleton, he also attended NCO School. He was stationed at Camp Pendleton, Camp Hensen, Okinawa and Da Nang, Vietnam from July 1965 to May 1966.

For his service, he received the Good Conduct medal, Vietnam Service medal and National Defense Service medal.

Barnard says he met several lifelong friends while in service and his memorable experience was leaving Da Nang in May 1966. He was discharged as Sgt. E-5 at El Toro, CA.

He was a business analyst for State Farm Insurance from 1970 to 2005, when he retired. Now he volunteers with AMBUCS, Relay for Life and Midwest Food Bank.

Don and Glenda have two children, Britt and Amanda.

**DOUGLAS R. BARR** was born in Plainfield, NJ on July 28, 1942. He enlisted into the U.S. Marine Corps at Raritan, NJ after graduation from Westfield High School. He served Active Duty in the USMC from 1962-1992, with the rank of Sergeant Major upon his discharge.

He served a tour in Vietnam from 1966-67, and was part of Operation Eagle Claw (US hostages rescue attempt) in 1980. Other assignments include: 11th MEU, SgtMaj, July 1987-July 1990; 1st Marines, SgtMaj, July 1990-March 1991 during the Gulf War (Desert Shield/Desert Storm); and 1st Mar Div, SgtMaj, March 1991-July 1992. MOS: 9999 / 8511 / 6014.

His awards include: LOM, MSM, NMCM w/V, NMCAM, CAR w/star, MCGM w/10 stars, NDSM w/star, VSD w/3 stars, SASM w/2 stars, MCDIR w/2 stars, RVCM, and KLM.

SgtMaj Barr graduated from Southern Illinois University (B.S.) in 1993 and earned a master's degree from National University (MBA) in 1995. He retired from National University, EA, Assoc. Regional Dean, Military and VA.

**RANDY C. "BUSHMAN" BEAL** was born July 14, 1948 in Provo, UT. He graduated from Altamont High School and attended Salt Lake City Community College.

On Nov. 14, 1966 he enlisted at Salt Lake City and went to Boot Camp at MCRD. He also received training in TRAC VEH REP MAN, Mil Policeman Scol, Civil Action Program and Landmine Warfare.

Beal was stationed at Camp Pendleton, Lejeune, Vietnam and at Pax River. He served with I Corps, at Hue City and Baxter Garden.

He received the National Defense Service Medal, Vietnam Campaign Medal w/device, Combat Action Ribbon, Vietnam Service medal with 3/stars, RVN Cross of Gallantry w/palm and frame, Purple Heart Medal w/2 stars and Good Conduct Medal.

Beal was discharged as Sgt. on Aug. 12, 1970 at MCRD.

After retirement in 1996, he spends his time gardening.

Andy, Tim, Rachelle, Kim, Anna Marie and Carrie - the children of Randy and Michelle - have given them 14 grandchildren.

**COLONEL VAN D. BELL, JR.** USMC Retired, was born Aug. 25, 1918 in Atlanta, GA. He died June 3, 2009 in Tupelo, MS. In a career that started at the Marine Corp Recruit Depot at Parris Island, SC in 1936, he served 39 years. Colonel Bell rose from Private to Master Sergeant and up the officer ranks to Colonel. A China Marine and a three war veteran, he participated in the battles of Guadalcanal, Bougainville, Guam and Okinawa in WW II.

His service in the First Marine Division started in the Korean War as a Company Commander with a Company First Battalion, Seventh Marines. His service in Korea would be marked by the awards of the Navy Cross and Silver Star medals. During the Vietnam War he would serve as the beloved Battalion Commander of the First Battalion, First Marines. For service in Vietnam, he would again be awarded the Navy Cross and Silver Star.

His distinguished service to country, Corps and the Marines he commanded in three wars made him the most decorated and respect Marine of his era.

His most significant decorations include two Navy Crosses, two Silver Stars, Legion of Merit with Combat V, Bronze Star Medal with Combat V, five Purple Hearts, Combat Action Ribbon, four Presidential Unit Citations, four Navy Unit Citations and three Marine Corps Good Conduct Medals.

Colonel Bell is buried at Arlington National Cemetery in Washington, DC among the nation's honored dead.

Semper Fidelis.

**JOHN ALLISON BLAZER,** born April 18, 1930 in Nashville, TN had a widely diverse service from August 1948 when he enlisted at Parris Island, SC to discharge on July 10, 1953, Washington, DC after 107 days spent aboard Naval vessels, two amphibious landings (plus two on maneuvers) and 227 days in combat/combat zones.

He received training at Fort Bragg, NC (Parachute School); Camp Lejeune, NC and Marine Corps. Institute. He was also stationed at Newfoundland, Canada; Puerto Rico; Japan; Inchon, Korea; California, Texas and Washington, DC.

He was awarded the Purple Heart Medal, Combat Action Ribbon, President Unit Citation, Joint Meritorious Unit Award, Good Conduct Medal, Navy Occupation Service Medal, National Defense Service Medal, Korean Presidential Unit Citation, United Nations Service Medal and ROK War Service Medal. He earned the Airborne Basic, Expert Rifleman and Expert Pistol Badges.

From 1962 to retirement in 1996, he was a psychologist/psychotherapist/diagnostician, working in Texas, Tennessee and Georgia.

Blazer has published 21 books on genealogy and family history.

He and Harriett Bragdon Crevis Blazer have one child, Allison Kristine Blazer and one grandchild, Rafael Blazer Carrillo.

**JOSEPH "JOE" A. BLINEBURY JR.** was born in 1946 in Philadelphia, PA. After graduating from Cardinal Dougherty high school, he enlisted in April 1966 in Pennsylvania and took Boot Camp at Parris Island. He also was trained in survival and safety equipment.

During his career, he was stationed at MCAS Beaufort, SC; NAS Willow Grove, PA and Camp Pendleton, CA SOI. He was discharged at MGy SGT. in March 1999.

Professional affiliation was Delaware Valley/Philadelphia Stand Down.

Since discharge in 1999, he has assisted in working with homeless veterans.

Joe and wife, Carol, have two children, Gary and Bonnie and one grandchild, Austin Battaglia.

**DENNIS L. BREU** born in Searles, MN on 10 April 1926. Enlisted in 1943 at age 17, prior to graduating from high school. Completed boot camp at MCRD San Diego, followed by infantry training at Camp Pendleton, CA. Dennis stated that the only buildings he saw at Camp Pendleton were the ranch house and barns, that all Marine Corps facilities at that time were in tents.

After completing training, Dennis traveled across the Pacific via troop ship with hundreds of replacement Marines, arriving on Pavuvu in the Solomon Islands in early October, 1944. When the Division returned from the battle of Peleliu a few weeks later, Dennis was assigned to Alpha company 1st Battalion, First Marines.

Dennis went ashore with the Division on Okinawa 1 April 1945. Alpha company encountered no opposition until 13 April when they came under intense enemy fire, sustaining approximately 90% casualties, including all officers and NCO's. Following the war, he served in China for a year, being involved in skirmishes with Communist Chinese forces. He was discharged in 1946. Dennis married LaVaun Warner, raising daughters Shelley and Renee, in Stillwater, MN. Employed by Univac Corporation, where he was awarded twelve patents from the U.S. Patent Office during his career. Passed away 25 June 2016.

**MICHAEL L. BROWN** was Michael L. Brown was born on 16 June 1,946 in Davin, West Virginia and raised in the tri-state area of West Virginia, Kentucky and Ohio. Upon graduation from Woodward HS, Cincinnati, Ohio in June 1964, he began his enlistment in the Marines at MCRD, San Diego, CA and after completing basic infantry training, was assigned to the 1st Marine Division at Camp Pendleton, California.

In February 1966 he departed San Diego with BLT 3/5 and spent a few months training in Okinawa before landing at Chu Lai, Vietnam on May 27, 1966. Mike started his Vietnam tour in the communications section with the 11th Marines and went on to be a Scout/Sniper for the 1st Marines. During his 14 months in Vietnam he participated in numerous combat activities including Operations; Cheyenne, Apache, Oakland, Washington, Colorado, Cannon, Suwanee, Troy, Prairie, Coffee, Teton, Madison, County Fair, Trinidad I, Trinidad II, Glenn, Shasta II, Arcadia, Stone, Searcy, Lafayette, Independence, Canyon, Union and Calhoun. While in Vietnam, he was awarded a Meritorious Mast, National Defense Service Medal, Vietnam Service Medal w/1*, Vietnam Campaign Medal w/device and the Good Conduct Medal.

After serving over three years in the 1st Marine Division, he returned from Vietnam and was released from active duty at El Toro MAS, El Toro, CA in July 1967, he went on to earn a BS in Chemical Engineering from LSU in 1973 and spent his entire career in the energy industry. He married his wife Shirley on Aug. 30, 1967 and they have three sons - Jason, Daniel and Stephen and eight grandchildren.

**HOWARD S. BROWNE** was born July 1, 1925 in Ponca City, OK. After graduation from high school he attended University of Oklahoma and Northwestern University School of Medicine.

After AC DO in 1949 at Bremerton, WA he was FMSS at Camp Lejeune in 1951. For his service, he was awarded the Navy Commendation w/V, Korean Service, Combat Ribbon PUC w/star, and Korean PUC.

He retired in 1969 as Capt. MC USN.

Howard and Doris (Cox) have four children – Stephen, Catharine, Elizabeth and Alastair and two grandchildren, Jerzy Brown and Joelyta Ilona Browne.

**PFC GABRIEL ROBERT CAGGIANO,** 2nd Battalion, Company G (later Company E), 1st Marines, 1st Marine Division was born and raised in Boston, Massachusetts. He was the sixth child of Michele Caggiano and Italia Lanzilli. He was 16 and ½ when Pearl Harbor was bombed. He decided to leave school and join the marines to go fight for his country. He was turned down because of his age but was able to finally join in October 1943 when he was old enough to do so.

Mr. Caggiano received his training at Parris Island, South Carolina then transferred to Camp Elliot, California to be deployed to the South Pacific where he spent nearly two years between 1943 and 1945. He was part of, and participated in, some of the worst battles of the South Pacific—Guadalcanal, Okinawa and Pelelieu. While on Okinawa on May 9, 1945 he volunteered to draw enemy fire while the wounded could be moved. He was hit by a mortar, blown off a ridge and wounded. He was awarded a purple heart and three battle ribbons.

Following his discharge from the Marine Corps in October 1945, Mr. Caggiano took advantage of the GI Bill and attended Suffolk University and

Suffolk University Law School where he received his LLB and JD. Mr. Caggiano was licensed to practice within the courts of the Commonwealth of Massachusetts, the U.S. District Court and U.S. Supreme Court. Following a brief employment with Employer Insurance Company, Mr. Caggiano went into the private practice of law. He left private practice to join the administration of Governor John A. Volpe as Chief Legal Counsel, Massachusetts Department of Public Works and successfully prosecuted the corrupted practice of the Department of Public Works Waterways division. He returned to the private practice of law until 1965 when he was re-appointed by Governor John A. Volpe as Director of the Bureau of International Trade within the Massachusetts Department of Commerce where he remained for four years. Mr. Caggiano was an advisor to Governor Volpe on international trade matters; he welcomed foreign dignitaries and traveled extensively representing the Commonwealth of Massachusetts throughout Europe in an effort to promote exports. He was an advocate of free trade. He was responsible for holding international trade seminars and bringing together business leaders, bankers, manufacturers and government officials in an effort to educate small and medium-sized businesses on how to export their products. In 1969 Mr. Caggiano returned to the private practice of law as trial attorney from which he retired in 2005 at age 80.

Mr. Caggiano was an avid skier who enjoyed skiing in Switzerland, France, Italy and Austria as well as California, Colorado, Utah and the Green Mountains and White Mountains of Eastern United States and Canada. Mr. Caggiano was also a competitive sailor in the United States and Bermuda. He enjoyed ballroom dancing.

Mr. Caggiano passed away on August 2, 2016 at age 91. He was survived by his beloved wife Ninetta (Torra) of Revere, Massachusetts; son Gabriel Caggiano, Jr. of California, freelance reporter, former White House reporter and former war correspondent during Desert Storm;

Daughter, Michelle Rosmarin, MBA, retired entrepreneur; Son Marshall Caggiano, Associate General Counsel of the Department of Homeland Security and retired Colonel from the U.S. Air Force; Daughter Gabrielle Clemens, attorney, Vice President – Wealth Management - Certified Divorce Financial Analyst (CDFA™) UBS. He was also survived by granddaughter Elise Rosmarin of New York; grandsons Marshall and Maxwell Clemens of Weston, Massachusetts; granddaughter Gabrielle Caggiano of Maryland; and step grandchildren Nikki, Justina and Mary.

**CLARENCE CAMERON** was born August 26, 1935 in Highland Park, MI, and enlisted on August 6, 1953 at Detroit, MI. Boot camp was at San Diego, CA, Plt 285, with additional training at Camp Pendleton Machine Gun School and water cooled .30 Cal. in Korea.

He was assigned to the 1st Marine Division HG BN Comm. Co. Wire Platoon in Korea from 1954-55, and came home with the Division in 1955 on the *General Meig*. He spent 1955-56 at Camp Pendleton before his discharge on Aug. 6, 1956 with the rank of Corporal.

Cameron received the National Defense Service, Korean Service, Korean Presidential Unit Citation, United Nations Service, Korean Defense, and Good Conduct awards. He is a life member of the 1st Marine Division Association., Commander of the North Oakland County Young Marines (active), American Legion Post 108 in Oxford, Michigan, and the VFW.

He retired from the U.S. Postal Service after 39 years as a carrier and building maintenance superintendant. He also worked as Director of Golf at Heather Hills Golf Course in Romeo, MI, and coached girl's golf at Romeo High School for 19 years.

He is married to Margaret and they have four children – Clifford (Air Force Master Sgt. Ret.), Dody, Bonnie, and Penny – and seven grandchildren.

**JOSEPH A. CAPITO** was born on December 26, 1931 and raised on the Lower Eastside of New York City. Joe attended PS 12 and the School of Industrial Arts. At the age of 17, Joe joined enlisted in the Marine Corps with his mother's permission. He went to Camp Lejune, NC and Parris Island, SC for military training, and was eventually deployed to Korea.

"While serving with the 1st Battalion, 1st Marines, 1st Marine Division, FMF, (in the Field), on November 22, 1950, Corporal Capito's platoon was ordered to assault and seize Hill 1088. Advancing up the icy-treacherous slopes of this hill, Corporal Capito's squad met with heavy enemy small arms fire and automatic weapons fire. During this action Corporal Capito was slightly wounded, nine men serving with his squad were killed and two wounded seriously, leaving himself and one man fit for duty. Realizing that the Chinese-held bunker directly above him was delivering heavy fire toward his comrades and taking a heavy toll of lives, he knew it had to be destroyed. Corporal Capito, with disregard for his own personal safety, assaulted said bunker by himself and succeeded in destroying it with a hand-grenade. Taking it upon himself to see that damage had been done with the grenade, Corporal Capito leaped into the remains of the emplacement there meeting face to face with two Chinese communist soldiers. Corporal Capito proceeded to destroy the two enemy soldiers with his bayonet, thus completely demolishing the main artery of the enemy defense. This personal sense of duty led to the complete seizure of this strategically important enemy held position. Corporal Capito's actions were in the traditional spirit of the United States Marine Corps." Corporal Capito was awarded the Purple Heart and Silver Star Medal for Conspicuous Gallantry Above and Beyond the Call of Duty.

After serving his country, Joe settled in New Jersey then moved to California, where he worked at the Elks club as bartender and is especially remembered by hosting "JOE's Italian Night."

Joe "Sarge," as he was called by his friends, passed away June 18, 2003 and is survived by his three children, grandchildren and great grandchildren, his sisters Josephine, Cookie and Gracie, nieces, nephews and cousins. Joe Sarge was, and still is, our hero!

**FATHER VINCENT R. CAPODANNO "THE GRUNT PADRE"** — Fifty years ago on the 4th of September 1967, the "Grunt Padre", Fa-

ther Vincent Capodanno, a Maryknoll Missionary, a Vietnam Navy Chaplain of combat "Grunt Marines," the posthumous recipient of the Medal of Honor, the Bronze Star (with combat V for Valor), and the Purple Heart, a "Servant of God" on the path of Sainthood, was killed in action on Operation Swift in I Corps, Que Son Valley, Vietnam.

Fifty years later, Fr. Capodanno (Saint Semper Fidelis) remains a "Living Saint" and "Spiritual Comrade" to Marines and Corpsmen "of every climb and place." The "Grunt Padre's" service and sacrifice, along with his "Honor, Courage and Commitment", were "always faithful" (Semper Fidelis) to God, Corps and Country. *Dedicated by Richard "MoonMan" Mooney, I Corps Vietnam, '66-67.*

**CHARLES W. CARTER** was born Dec. 30, 1927 in Washington, DC. He graduated from Veteran's High School in 1949 and received an AA degree from M.D. University.

After enlistment on Nov. 1, 1945 he took Boot Camp at Parris Island. He was stationed at Tanggu, China; Nagasaki, Japan and Washington, DC.

Memorable experience included at the Tanggu, China 1st Division ammo dump, when the Chinese raided it and killed six Marines.

Carter was discharged at Washington, DC on Nov. 11, 1948 with the rank of Cpl.

After retirement in 1985 he has served as a store proprietor and court bailiff.

He and wife, Joan, have child, Craig and two grandchildren, Cory and Denny.

**JOHN L. CHAILLE** was born in Ross, CA on Dec. 27, 1946. After spending most of his early years in nearby San Anselmo, graduating from Sir Francis Drake High School and attending the College of Marin, he joined the US Marine Corps in 1966.

Once he completed training in southern California (MCRD, San Diego; 2nd ITR and BIT, Camp Pendleton) he embarked on the *USNS Upshur* from San Diego. Arriving in Vietnam in March 1967, John joined the 106 Platoon, H and S Company, 1st Battalion, 5th Marines near Chu Lai. Over the next 10 months he spent various amounts of time in and around Hill 54, Snaggletooth, Chu Lai, Tam Ky, Nui Lac Son, Hill 51 (Que Son), Hoi An, Horseshoe, Phu Loc 6, and Da Nang.

On Jan. 15, 1968 he was wounded south of Phu Loc along the Bowling Alley. Over the next three months he recovered, initially in Da Nang before going to Yokosuka Naval Hospital in Japan

and then Oak Knoll Naval Hospital in Oakland, CA prior to being discharged from active duty.

He then went back to school attending College of Marin, Kentfield, CA; Humboldt State University, Arcata, CA (BA, Zoology); University of Nevada, Las Vegas; South Dakota School of Mines and Technology, Rapid City (MS, Geology (Paleontology)); University of Rochester, NY and the University of Texas at Austin (PhD, Geological Sciences). After getting his degree in Austin, he remained there for a few years before moving to Warrensburg, MO, where he lives with his wife, Sally.

**GEORGE WARREN COBB JR.** served in the US Navy Reserve - December 1948 to January 1951. Enlisted into the US Marine Corps in Buffalo, NY on Jan. 13, 1951.

After boot camp at Parris Island, he went on to Camp Pendleton for Infantry Training prior to shipping out to Korea. He served in H & S Company 1" Amtrac Battalion as a truck driver in Korea from July of 1951 to July of 1952. Participated in action against enemy forces in south, central and western Korea from Aug. 6, 1951 to July 2, 1952.

On returning from Korea, he spent the balance of his three year enlistment with the 8th Motor Transport Battalion, Fleet Marine Force at Camp Geiger, Jacksonville, NC. Carolina. Honorably discharged from Camp Lejeune, NC Sept. 10, 1953.

In the fall of 1953, he enrolled at the University of Rochester, graduating in June of 1957. After graduation, he joined IBM in Rochester as a salesman. Shortly thereafter he was assigned to the Johnstown, PA, IBM office as a sales rep. In 1961, he was promoted to sales rep at The Pennsylvania State University Campus, State College, PA.

In January of 1971, he transferred to the IBM Federal Office in Washington, DC as the IBM sales rep for the National Institutes of Health.

His IBM days ended in 1973 when he took a sales position with a start-up California company that was marketing a new concept in typewriting - the Lexitron Corp. In the fall of 1977 he left Lexitron to join Exxon Enterprises and a company called Qyx in Lionville, PA. In April of 1979 he got an offer from a good friend and former IBM Manager to go to San Diego and join him in marketing telephone systems.

Barbara and Cobb moved to Cardiff by the Sea, CA, in 1979.

In 1982, he joined Grubb & Ellis as a commercial real estate broker. After 14 years, he retired from Grubb & Ellis in August of 1995.

Cobb has five children: Ty, Jonathan, George, Sandy and Kris. In addition, he now has eight wonderful grandchildren.

Retirement has been very good to Barbara and George. They have been fortunate to be able to travel a great deal. Cobb has been a volunteer at the Cardiff by the Sea Elementary School, and a docent at the Camp Pendleton Marine Corps Base...serving the Mechanized Museum, the Ranch House and Las Flores.

**MANVILLE P. COOK** was born on March 8, 1924 in Rome, PA. He graduated from Rome High School in 1941. He joined the Marines July 14, 1941 and was a rifle and pistol marksman.

He served with the First Marine Division in the Asiatic-Pacific area from May 20, 1942 to Dec. 9, 1944. He participated in action against the enemy at Guadalcanal from Aug. 7, 1942 to Dec. 9, 1942; at Cape Gloucester from Jan. 1, 1944 to

May 7, 1944; Palau Islands Sept. 15, 1944; Russell Islands October 1944; Brooklyn Navy Yard from Feb. 2, 1945 until discharge Sept. 6, 1945.

Manville also had five brothers who served in WW II at the same time.

Returning home, he ran his farm in Rome and was a US Rural mail carrier. He passed away Sept. 29, 2006. He is survived by his wife, Sherry and children – Wayne, Mark, Robert and Thomas (deceased 1962) and Faye; eight grandchildren and five great-grandchildren.

**DR. HERSCHEL A. COX JR.** enlisted at Seattle, WA Nov. 10, 1942. Recruiting had selected 63 men for Seattle's own platoon.

Six months guard duty at Whidbey Island, Washington Naval Air Station before advanced training in San Diego, 1943 before troopship to New Caledonia where he was assigned to A Company, First Battalion, Fifth Regiment, First Division as a barman.

He saw combat in New Britain, was wounded in Banzai attack with rifle bullet up right forearm and out the elbow. Shipped to New Guinea Hospital then by hospital ship to Sidney, Australia for surgery. Next hospital at Mare Island, CA. Was discharged July 13, 1944.

He enrolled at University of Washington, received B of S 1948. Followed with dental school and graduated 1953. Retired from private practice in Seattle August 1994 and moved to Sedona, AZ for five years until his wife developed Alzheimer's disease. Better medical care in Orange County, CA for five years. Full time care was available in Seattle for 10 years.

Cox now lives in Sun Valley, ID. In addition of hobbies of skiing, hunting and motorcycling, he participated in trapshooting. In 1964 he participated in the US Olympic tryout finals at Fort Benning, knowing he would not make the team although he had been A and Double A state champion. In August for the last 14 years, he and his daughter, along with different family members, have skied in Chile.

**GORDON KARL DAVIS** was born Nov. 6, 1935 in Lansing, MI and enlisted on Nov. 18, 1952 in Detroit, later receiving his GED. He was the third highest shooter in his basic training platoon and his first duty station was at Camp Del-Mar, CA as a weapons instructor.

Davis fought in Korea and was an NCO, 2nd Squad leader in George Co., 3rd BN, 1st Marines. While there he was shot in his right arm at the DMZ by a North Korean sniper.

He was awarded the National Defense Service Medal, U.N. Service Medal, and Korean Service Medal.

Davis was discharged from active duty on Aug. 1, 1955 from G Co., 3rd BN, 1st Marine Division, Camp Pendleton, CA.

As a civilian he worked for Abrams Instrument Corp. as a machinist, Charlotte Crown Kamper as a quality control inspector, worked in cabinet making and as a prosthetic technician making arms and legs for amputees, and now is a self-employed auctioneer.

**KYLE DISCHLER** was born in Madison, WI on May 16, 1979, graduating from River Valley High School in 1997. He enlisted in the USMC on August 4, 1997 and was sent to MCRD San Diego for basic training and later completed the Advance Tank Tech Course.

Dischler (Sgt D) was stationed at Camp Lejeune, NC, and was deployed as part of the Invasion of Iraq in 2003. He was discharged on November 16, 2004 at Camp Lejeune with the rank of E-5 Sgt. He was awarded the Marine Corps Good Conduct Medal (2nd award), Combat Action Ribbon (Iraq), Global War on Terrorism Expeditionary Medal, Sea Service Deployment Ribbon, National Defense Service Medal, and Presidential Unit Citation.

He is a Fire Engine Fabricator, Security Professional, NRA Instructor, Executive Protection Professional, Training Director Security, and Manager DeCA Commissary. Professional affiliations include: National Rifle Assoc., Disabled American Veterans, National Order of the Trench Rats, 1st Marine Division Assoc., Marine Corps Association and Foundation, Marine Corp Recruiting Depot (MCRD) Museum Foundation, Wounded Warrior Project (WWP), and Iraq and Afghanistan Veterans of America (IAVA).

He is married to Minette O'Bryan.

**WILLIAM T. DUNN** was born in Roanoke, VA on March 10, 1932 and spent the first 18 years of my life there. I grew up during the Depression and money was very hard to come by. I got his first newspaper route when I was 12 and I was working in a drugstore when I was 14. When I was 16, two friends from high school asked me to go with them to join a Marine Reserve unit. One was 18 and they

signed him up. The other was 17, but he had a letter from his parents giving him permission to join. The sergeant then looked at me and asked if I wanted to join. I said, "I might as well." He asked how old I was and I said 18. Next, it was raise your hand, take the oath and sign right here. I'm still listed with the Marine Corps as two years older than I am.

My two-year enlistment started Feb. 13, 1949. We were paid $30.00 every three months. I did not go to either summer camp in 1949 or 1950 and later this turned out to be a blessing. I finished high school on June 10, 1950 and the war in Korea broke out on the 25th.

Our reserve unit was activated in the latter part of July 1950. We marched down Roanoke's main street at 7:00 a.m. on a Sunday morning and boarded a troop train for California. The train trip ended up being five days of sea stories, poker playing, and beer drinking. When we arrived at camp Pendleton, all veterans and anyone who had been to two summer camps went one way and the rest of us went another. The first group boarded ships the latter part of August and made the Inchon landing on Sept. 15. The rest of us went to an accelerated training program. It was eight weeks of boot camp and four weeks of advanced training, then we shipped out to Korea.

We left San Diego on Dec. 6, 1950 and arrived in Korea before Christmas. There were four of us from our old reserve unit on the ship. Two of the four never made it back alive. I was assigned to the 1st Shore Party Battalion. We moved all types of supplies everywhere and I ended up running a "gook train." No offense intended, but that is what we called our 15 to 20 South Korean employees. These men were willing to carry water, ammo and C-rations up to the lines on their A-frame packs. I never knew what we paid them, but in addition to the hard and heavy work carrying all that weight up some very steep and frozen hills, it was also very dangerous due to mines and mortars. In my four months that I was with them, I know of six that we lost.

One day, after a real bastard of a climb up a frozen mountainside, we finally got supplies to the outfit that we were looking for at about 4:00 in the afternoon. With darkness approaching, the company commander strongly suggested that we spend the night next to his command post and leave early the next morning. I agreed, since you didn't want to be out after dark with a lot of Koreans and some very nervous Marines.

About midnight, all hell broke loose with a full-scale counterattack by the Chinese. My partner and I were ordered to help out, so we climbed over the ridge line and fought with the company all night. They kept the valley lit with flares. This was my first experience at seeing so many people die. By dawn the attack was over, so I went back over the hill to get my "gook train," but they were all gone. A joke got started that I had forgotten to set my brakes correctly and my "train" rolled back down the mountain.

In February 1951, my enlistment was up and I was informed that I was now COG (convenience of the government), which meant that my enlistment had been extended by one year.

In the spring of 1951, a truck that I was riding in hit a mine and I ended up spending about five weeks on the hospital ship *Repose*, which was docked at Pusan. One morning I was told that I had been signed off the ship, was fit for duty and was to go back to my outfit. I had nothing but the pajamas that they had furnished me. I was told to go down to the quartermaster's deck and draw some fatigues, but they didn't have any weapons on board ship. They didn't know where my outfit was, but they guessed that it was some hundreds of miles north and that it was up to me to find it. I thumbed rides on trucks, got a hop on a cargo plane (C-47) and actually stole a 45-automatic pistol for my protection. I literally begged for food from different outfits. Four days later, I found my battalion. No one had notified them that I had been signed off the ship.

The Chinese spring offensive had caused such heavy casualties that they were asking for volunteers for the rifle companies. So in May 1951, I transferred into Charley Company, 1st Battalion, 7th Marines. From there on, until I finally came home, it was one hill after another. We were constantly getting replacements for the guys we lost and once someone was killed, his name was never mentioned again.

The summer and fall found us trying to take as much new ground as needed in order to straighten the lines. The peace talks were going on and we were using psychological warfare. We had to endure Chinese music coming from our loud speakers, trying to get them to surrender. We also dropped millions of "safe passage" leaflets from planes. The leaflets that floated to our side were used for toilet paper. They brought up dozens of big searchlights and reflected them off the clouds. This would light up the valley between us almost like daytime. If you were in a rifle company at that time and were on the lines, you were either trying to take new high ground or sending out daily probing patrols. The company would send out a platoon-size patrol every day. Since there were three platoons per company, you caught a patrol every third day. You didn't volunteer, you just went. I later estimated that I had been on at least 40 of these patrols.

We had a feeling that we owned the day, but they owned the night. That was when they would usually attack. We had Chinese come to the foot of our hill and shout up in good English, "Hey, Marine, you die tonight. We kill you, you f------ Marine." When we couldn't see them, we threw grenades. I threw an awful lot of grenades. It really was rare when we were on the line that they didn't probe sometime during the night, looking for a weak spot.

By now, I had heard from home that eight members of my old reserve unit had already been killed and that a close friend had lost both legs at the Chosin Reservoir, The odds were really not in your favor if you were in a Marine rifle company at that time. I knew that our company was referred to as "Suicide Charley" and I took it for granted that it was because of so many men that we were losing. It was not until years later that I learned my company earned that name from a stand they had made at Guadalcanal in WW II.

In the fall of 1951, our entire company, with a platoon of engineers, jumped off to take a small hill that the Chinese were using to stage night attacks. The plan was to secure the hill, plant mines all over it, and return to our lines. I was a corporal at the time and I was responsible for a four-man fire team. On the way, we got into a minefield that the Chinese had left for us and one of my men lost both legs. I stayed with him until we got a corpsman to take over. I then caught up with the rest of the company, which was now at the base of the Chinese-occupied hill. The company spread out to about the length of a football field and then we started up. Not a shot had been fired until we got about two-thirds of the way up and then they opened up with mortars. I had been under mortar fire many times, but nothing like this. They walked the fire back and forth, up and down and had the range down perfect. We tried to dig, but the ground was hard shale rock and we got nowhere. I tried checking on my other two guys and I couldn't get a response from a new replacement named Dave Munson. I crawled over to him and found him dead. My last fire-team member was now calling for a corpsman, so I went to his aid and found that he had a nasty but minor head wound.

Our company was trapped on the side of that hill getting incoming fire for over five hours. It was too much exposure between the hill and our lines, so we had to wait it out until we could get air support. Finally, four Air Force P-51s came in with napalm and burned them out. When we got back to our lines, my platoon had 16 men standing. We had a full platoon of 41 that morning. I lost my whole fire-team and we hadn't fired a shot.

I came off the lines the last time about the middle of December and on Christmas Eve, they told me that I was going home. I left Korea on Jan. 2, 1952, after riding all night in a canvas-covered truck in zero-degree weather, in order to get to the coast. On Feb. 13, 1952, I received an honorable discharge from the Marine Corps. I was 19 years old with three years of reserve and active duty and I couldn't vote or buy a bottle of beer.

We all left home together, but we came back one at a time. This was in February and my mother had left the Christmas tree up for me. Within an hour of arriving home, my friend who had lost both legs at Chosin came by and the party started.

I brought with me the names of five Marines that I was with when they were killed. I thought that it just might ease some pain if the parents could talk to someone who was with their son when he died. About a week after coming home, I drove to Richmond, VA and looked up the parents of Dave Munson. He was an only child and his parents were two of the finest people I had ever met. But there were so many questions and so many tears that when I left their house I threw the list with the remaining names away. It had just been too emotional.

In the fall of 1952, I started using my GI Bill and enrolled at Virginia Commonwealth University in Richmond. I went to work for Esso Standard Oil Company while still in college. I was married in 1953 and we have three children and six grandchildren. My wife and I retired early and we live on the Virginia side of the Chesapeake Bay. My life has turned out so good that I would not want to change anything in my past. However, very few days go by that I don't think about all the friends I lost in Korea and how young we all were. Bill Dunn lives in Reedville, VA.

**JOHN C. EDWARDS** was born in Petersburg, VA May 8, 1929. After a brief stint in the Virginia State Guard, he enlisted in the Marines Aug. 1, 1946 at age 17. Edwards was assigned to Platoon 272, 3rd Recruit BN, MB Parris Island, SC. After boot camp he was assigned to Camp Pendleton Nov. 3. He joined the 110th Replacement Draft and embarked aboard the *USS General*

*William Mitchell* at San Diego Nov. 21 and sailed Nov. 22 for Guam, arriving Dec. 8, stopping en route at Naval Base Pearl Harbor for several days. Then embarked aboard the *USS President Adams* and sailed Dec. 9 for Tako Bar, China. Along the way destroyed as a Japanese mine, arriving Dec. 20. Edwards was assigned to the 1st Military Police Co., HQ., BN., 1st Marine Division as a brig chaser in Tientsin, China.

On April 4-5, 1947 a raiding part of 350 communists attacked an ammunition supply point at Hsin Ho and five Marines were KIA and 16 WIA (6 communists KIA, 20-30 WIA) in the last major clash between 1st Division Marines and communist forces.

The 1st M.P. Co. departs Tientsin May 5, and merged with the 5th Marines in Peiping (withdrawal and redeployment from China). Before he left Tientsin for Peiping while on guard duty at the rail line (heavy equipment) outside the city, after dark, it was not unusual to hear small arms fire in the distance. The 5th Marines embarked on board the *USS Bronx* at Chinwangtao, China May 12 and sailed May 14 for Guam, arriving May 20. The 5th Marines joined the 1st Provisional Marine Brigade then forming on the island. Edwards was assigned to E Co., 2nd Bn., 5th Mârines as a Machine Gun crewman. After Guam he was assigned via Govt. Air to H & S BN., FMF PAC in Hawaii Aug. 21 and returned to the States via Govt. Air at MB Nav. Sup. Ctr. (MBNS) Oakland, CA Oct. 7. On Oct. 30 was assigned via Govt. Air to MB US Naval Base, Charleston, SC and was honorably discharged June 15, 1948.

Edwards married Betty Goodman and has one daughter, Pamela and two grandchildren, Amanda and Daniel. Retired from the US Postal Service with 39 years of service. He is a law enforcement badge collector and life member National Sheriffs' Association and former Texas Rangers Foundation (Sergeant). Some of his honors: (Honorary) Deputy US Marshal; Deputy (Walking Tall) Sheriff, McNairy County, TN; Admiral in the Texas Navy; an Honorary TEXAN AND A KENTUCKY COLONEL.

**CORPORAL JERRY EPPARD, USMC,** arrived March 14, 1966 at Marine Corp Recruit Depot, San Diego, CA where he took my Basic Training in Platoon 172. He received orders for Camp Lejeune where in a matter of weeks he was sent back to Camp Pendleton for training for Vietnam.

Eppard arrived in Vietnam the 1st of October 1966 and was assigned to Delta Company 1st Bn. 5th Marine Reg. 1" Marine Division. The battalion was based on Hill 54, 10 Kilometers from Chu Lai airport. Delta Company ran several operations from Hill 54. The last part of 1966 sometime early in 1967 3rd Platoon was sent to Chu Lai Airfield to guard the airstrip. The Army relieved us - while we had been eating C-rations they set up a mess hall and were grilling steaks the first day - we couldn't believe we were from the same country.

The last of April 1957 we started Operation Union 1. On May 12th we took many casualties when we were ambushed by a NVA unit. We went right into Union II where we encountered a NVA unit again and we lost our Platoon Commander Second Lt. Larry Chmiel and Platoon SSgt David Dixon on June 2, while inflicting heavy casualties on the enemy.

Eppard was wounded June 16, 1967 in the Quang Nam Province near Nui Loc Son. "I'm able to write this because of Navy Corpsman Raymond (Doc) Gallegos and the great doctors in Chu Lai and aboard the *USS Repose*." After returning to the USA Eppard was sent to Great Lakes Naval Hospital. After several months he was sent to Philadelphia Naval Hospital for about nine months, where he was retired from the Marine Corp.

**RADM EUGENE FARRELL. USN (RET)** was born in Bosque County, TX, April 17, 1918. He enlisted in the USN in 1936 as an Apprentice Seaman. In 1938 he was one of 87 Sailors and Marines who passed the entrance exams for the USNA and were admitted to the Academy. He graduated with his Class of 1942 Dec. 19, 1941 and reported for duty in the *USS IDAHO BB-42* at Norfolk, VA, the same day. He served on her until April 20, 1945, as Main Battery Fire Control Officer during the assault and occupation of the Aleutians, Gilberts, Marshalls, Marianas, Western Carolines, Iwo Jima and Okinawa. For directing his ship's Main Battery fire in support of the First MarDiv in Peleliu and Okinawa, he was awarded an Honorary Lifetime Membership in the First MarDiv Association.

After WW II, his four sea commands culminated with the President's National Ship, *USS NORTHAMPTON*. Ashore, as the J-6 of JCS, the nation's highest military office, he participated in planning the air strike on Hanoi that ended the Viet Nam War. His decorations include the Navy and Air Force Commendation Medals, the Meritorious Service Medal and four Legions of Merit.

**ROBERT MELBOURNE FEIST** was born Nov. 20, 1924 on a small farm in Caseyville Township, IL. He enlisted in the Marines Dec. 8, 1942 in St. Louis, MO. After attending boot camp and radio school in San Diego, he was assigned to the newly forming Radio Intelligence Platoons. He participated in two WW II campaigns: Bougainville and Peleliu. Duty stations included New Caledonia, Guadalcanal and Sasebo, Japan. He was discharged Dec. 11, 1945, in Great Lakes, IL.

Financially assisted by the G.I. Bill, he received a bachelor's degree in English from Illinois College, and a master's degree in journalism from the University of Missouri. He was employed as a writer for newspapers and public relations agencies and retired from the US Department of Agriculture Information Division. An avid sports fan he also played second base for teams participating in amateur baseball and softball leagues. Along with his wife he took part in organized bicycle tours for years. He lives in Alexandria, VA with his wife, the former Ruth Eckert Nielsen of Copenhagen.

**GEORGE L. FIREHAMMER** was born May 1, 1944 at St. Joseph, MI. After graduating in 1962 from Concordia High School he attained a B.A. in 1966 from Concordia Sr. College.

In May 1966 he enlisted at Cleveland, OH. Boot Camp was at OCC, Quantico, VA. He had additional training at Language School at Monterey, CA.

He was stationed at III MAF RVN and Quantico, VA. Firehammer served in RVN Alanbrook.

For his service, he was awarded the P.H., CAR, RVN medals.

Firehammer was discharged on Dec. 10, 1969 at Quantico, VA with the rank of 1st Lt.

**RICHARD JOHN FEUERHERM** was born in Newark New Jersey on July 21, 1930. He was second to the youngest of nine children.

He graduated from Essex County High School and enlisted in the Marine Corp on April 11, 1948.

He went to Parris Island, SC and trained as a rifleman in which he became "Expert."'

He was transferred to Camp Pendleton June 16, 1949 before leaving for his tour of duty in Korea. He was selected for Sgt. in 1950.

He was involved in the capture and securing of Seoul. Participated in the Wonsan-Hungnam-Chosin Campaign. Due to Sub Zero Temperatures, he sustained frost bite injury to his fingers and feet in front line action against an organized enemy. He was discharged from the Marines April 11, 1952.

He returned home to Newark, NJ and was married to his childhood sweetheart, Emma Tavares April 11, 1953.

He began working for Flying Tiger Airlines in 1954 and carved out his career there. He was a self-taught engineer/load master and developed new ways of shipping cargo. He consulted for Flying Tiger Airlines and loaded cargo all over the world. He retired from Fed Ex in 1999.

Most recently he was living near his only daughter and son-in- law in Camarillo, CA. He had two grandchildren.

Richard passed away on Sept. 27, 2017 at the age of 87.

**MARVIN L. FOSTER** was born March 17, 1940 at Chicago, IL and graduated from Englewood High School in 1958. He earned an Assoc. in Arts degree from MiraCosta College, Oceanside, CA, in 1980, and an Assoc. in Science degree from MiraCosta College in 1983. He enlisted in the USMC in 1958 with basic training at Parris Island, SC. He also received Infantry Training at Camp LeJeune, NC, the Mountain Leaders' Train-

ing Course at Bridgeport, CT, and the Embarkation/Logistics Training Course at Okinawa, Japan.

Foster spent a total of 18 months, boots-on-the-ground, in Vietnam. Other stations included: Marine Barracks Subic Bay, Philippines; 1st Marine Division, Camp Pendleton, CA; 3rd Marine Division, Okinawa, Japan; 5th Marine Division, Camp Pendleton, CA; and Inspector-Instructor Staff, Gulfport, MS.

Awards include the Navy Achievement Medal, Combat Action Ribbon, Presidential Unit Citation, and various service and unit awards. His memorable experiences include his promotion to Sergeant in 1965 and commanding the General's Meritorious Mast in 1968.

Foster was discharged on August 28, 1978 (USMC, MSGT, Retired). He was employed for 17-1/2 years by North San Diego County Transit District, serving as a bus operator, radio dispatcher, and retiring as a transit supervisor in 2001.

He served for six years as a Public Commissioner on the Oceanside-Government Parks and Recreation panel, and two years as a member of the City of Oceanside-Government Senior Citizen Standing Committee.

His first wife, Dorothy D. Foster, is deceased, and he is now married to Joyce Lavely-Foster. They have one child, Chandra Pugh, and two grandchildren.

**THOMAS "TOM" C. GALLAGHER** was born Jan. 7, 1928 at Shaler Township, PA. He enlisted in the US Navy in January 1944 and was stationed at Sampson Naval Training Center and Samara, Philippines before being discharged July 4, 1946. On Oct. 13, 1946 he enlisted in the US Marine Corps, Boot Camp was at Parris Island. He was also stationed at 5th Service Depot (Guam); Barstow, CA; Korea; Camp Lejeune, NC; Pittsburgh, PA and Quantico, VA before retiring on Oct. 30, 1966 as GySgt. He attended Supply School and Chemical Warfare School.

Gallagher received the Navy and Marine Corps Commendation "V," Navy Unit Commendation, Marine Corps Good Conduct 4B, American Campaign Medal, Asiatic Pacific Campaign, WW II Victory Medal, National Defense Service Medal 1B, Korean Service Medal 3B, Republic of Korea PUC Medal, UN Service Medal and Republic of Korea War Service.

Thomas and Vivian have four children – Debra Jean, Clarence, Cynthina Lynn and Thomas C. Grandchildren are Thomas J. Gallagher, Melissa and Nick Gwinn, ____ and Robin Hudson. Great-grandchildren are Kelissa and Collin Gallagher, Nataly Gwinn, London Gwinn, Madelyn Gwinn and Joshua Hudson.

**CHARLES R. GARDINER,** born April 14, 1932, Camden, NJ. Raised in South Jersey. Attended Haddon Heights High School in New Jersey, graduated in 1950 and was employed by RCA in Camden, NJ, worked on assembly lines building television sets. The Korean War was on so I decided to quit and enlist in the US Marine Corps,

which I did on April 24, 1951. After Boot Camp at Paris Island I was assigned to Engineers School at Camp Lejeune for eight weeks.

My next duty station was Camp Pendleton for Advance Infantry Training and Cold Weather training at Pickle Meadows.

On Feb. 1, 1952 I embarked onboard *USNS GEN WM WEIGLE* (17th Replacement Draft) for Korea. Eventually I was assigned to Weapons Company 2nd Bat. 5th Marines 81-mm Mortars. After 12 months in Korea I returned home to the good old USA aboard the *USNS GEN WALKER.* I was promoted to Corporal in Korea and Sergeant in Quantico.

My last duty station was Quantico where I was Honorably Discharged April 23, 1954. After being discharged from the Regular Marine Corps, I enlisted in The Marine Corps Reserve April 30, 1955, 155mm Howitzer BN at The Philadelphia Navy Yard. The training nights interfered with my night school so I transferred to VMF 218 NAS Willow Grove, PA and was Honorably Discharged April 29, 1958.

I had the privilege of having two of my sons, Charles and Louis, attend The Marine Military Academy in Harlingen, TX for one year.

**DOMINICK A. "DOM" GATTA** was born May 6, 1923 in Brooklyn, NY. He enlisted in July 1940 and after Boot Camp at Parris Island, also trained as Field Artillery Crew Man. He served with "D" Battery, 2nd Battalion, 11th Marines from July 29, 1940 to Aug. 23, 1945. He served in Cuba (October 1940 – April 1941) and the South Pacific Area (June 1942 – July 1944). Also participated in action at Guadalcanal, British Solomon Islands from Aug. 7, 1942 to Dec. 14, 1942; at Cape Gloucester New Britain Area Sept. 26, 1943 – Feb. 10, 1944 and Palaria New Britain March 6, 1944 – March 15, 1944.

Corporal Gatta was a member of the Marine Corps Boxing Team (1940-1941) and was selected as the "Most Outstanding Welterweight" representing the USMC Team in the "Golden Gloves (North Carolina and New York City). He boxed professionally after the war – 39 straight wins as a middleweight.

Gatta received a Presidential Unit Citation, Navy Marine Corps Commendation, Good Conduct, American Defense Service Medal, Asiatic Pacific Campaign, WW II Victory Medal and American Campaign Medal.

Dominick (deceased November 2010) and wife Helen (deceased) had two children, Sgt. Rocco J. Gatta, USMC and Marianna. Grandchildren are James; 1st Ronald D. Winchester, (USMC/USNA (2001), KIA Iraq, Sept. 3, 2004) and Kristine. Great-grandchildren are Ronald James, Anthony and Brian.

**ROBERT LOUIS GAUGENMAIER,** aka "Gaugie," was born in Pierre, SD on May 23, 1928. He graduated from Ft. Pierre High School in 1946 and enlisted in the USMC at Omaha, NE Sept. 18, 1946.

His first tour of duty was in the Pacific area from Oct. 3 1947 until March 11, 1949. He was honorably discharged and continued in the US Marine Corps reserve effective Sept. 18, 1949.

That same month he entered the University of Southern California. His education was interrupted with a call back to active duty in February of 1951. From Camp Pendleton he was sent into combat in Korea and served with the 7th Marines (E-2-7), receiving a Purple Heart and was discharged with the rank of Staff Sergeant in March of 1952.

Working for himself, his business career led him into the field of aviation when he developed an aircraft docking system to park commercial jets. RLG Docking systems has over 900 installations at airports worldwide.

Gaugie died Feb 7, 2016 at his home in Carefree, AZ, leaving his wife of 48 years, Judie and sons: Jon of Albuquerque, NM and Kent of Los Angeles, CA.

**GORDON A. "PETE" GEHRLEIN** was born Aug. 19, 1936 at Erie, PA. After graduation from Academy High School he enlisted on Sept. 29, 1955 at Cleveland, OH. After Boot Camp at Parris Island, he also received additional training at Courthouse Bay – Diesel and M.C. Corr. Schools – Diesel.

"Pete" was stationed at Parris Island, Camp Lejeune and Iwakuni, Japan. He received the Good Conduct medal and 10 others.

Memorable experience was being given a meritorious promotion to Sgt. (E-4) in Japan.

Gehrlein was discharged at Great Lakes, IL on Sept. 29, 1958 with the rank of Sgt. E-4.

Professionally he was in food and refreshment ending for 45 years, founding AAA Vending on Jan. 6, 196. After retiring in 2006, he spends his time fishing, doing yard work and amateur carpentry.

"Pete" and Martha M. have three children: Kenneth, Katherine and Gary and one grandchild, Victoria.

**NATHAN A. "ARTIE" GILBERT** was born Oct. 17, 1920 at Detroit, MI. He graduated from Central High in 1938 and attended University of Chicago (1940).

Gilbert enlisted Oct. 17, 1941 and took Boot Camp at Parris Island, SC. He was a Parris Island drill instructor. He landed at Guadalcanal Aug. 7, 1942

Gilbert stated he had received many awards/ medals.

After discharge in October 1946 as M/Sgt. he worked for the State of Michigan as an investigator.

Artie and wife, Ana Rodas Gilbert, had three children: Denise, Ron and Dennis and two grandchildren, Nicholas and Tiffany.

**JOHN A. GONDER JR.** was born Dec. 30, 1947 at Birmingham, AL. After graduating from Ramsey HS, 1967 he attained a B.S. Computer Science at East Texas State Univ., 1986.

Gonder enlisted at Birmingham, AL on June 3 1969. After Boot Camp at MCRD, Parris Island, SC he had additional training as 0351 Anti-Tank Assault Man and MCI Marine NCO, Okinawa, 1970.

Stationed at Camp Lejeune, NC; Guantanamo Bay, Cuba; Philippines; Okinawa; Southern I-Corps, RVN; Camp Pendleton, CA; Camp Lejeune, NC he participated in Operation Upshur Stream (1971), Quang Nam, RVN (1971); Operation "Hoang Dieu" 103, RVN (1971); Operation Imperial Lake, RVN (1971) and Operation Scott Orchard, Quang Nam, RVN (1971).

He received: NDSMI- VSM w/2*, Combat Action Ribbon and VCM w/60 Device.

Memorable experiences were: served with Weapons Platoon, H&S Company, 3rd Bn, lst-Mar, 1* MarDiv in RVN. Performed duties as a gun leader for a 106 Recoilless Rifle in RVN. Performed duties as a fire team leader during infantry operations.

Gonder was discharged June 2 1972 at Camp Lejeune, NC.

Professionally he worked at Jobs Northrop Grumman – Engineer and Lockheed Martin – Engineer. Since retiring in 2008, he enjoys Shooting Sports and Home Defense and his Australian Shepherd Maverick.

John's spouse is Danita.

Has volunteered as Training Officer (7 years), Supply Officer (2 years) Young Marines, Tarrant County, TX

**ROBERT P. "BINK" GOTTLICH** was born April 2, 1925 in Panama City, Canal Zone. After graduating from Corpus Christi High School he also attended Texas A&M University.

Gottlich enlisted on Feb. 10, 1943 at Houston, TX and after Boot Camp at Parris Island, attended C&S School and Cold Weather Survival School.

He was stationed at Quantico; Camp Lejeune; Camp Pendleton; Corpus Christi, TX; Peyio Beach, China and El Toro.

After participating in the Pacific, China and Korea, he says his memorable experiences were OIC, Cold Weather Survival/Escape and Evasion School at Fallon, NV.

Colonel Gottlich was discharged at San Antonio, TX.

Professionally he was Executive VP for Church's Fried Chicken. After retirement in 19 67, he has been an exotic game rancher.

He and Glenda have four children: Rob, Peggy, Matt and Todd. Grandchildren are Rob III, Caleb, Leah, Matthew, Garrett, Elizabeth, Brittany, Sam, Shelton, Cardo, Kyle and Audrey.

**LOUIS M. GREGORI** was born in DuBois, PA in 1947. Following his graduation from Bennetts Valley High School in 1966, he enlisted with the Marine Corps. He went to Boot Camp at Parris Island. In December 1966, he was assigned to A/1/5 and sent to Vietnam. Among his medals

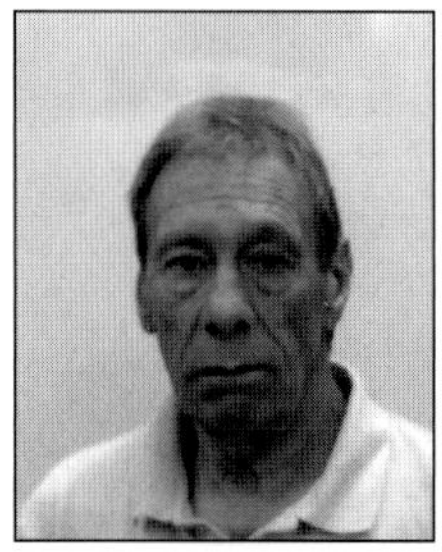

received while serving in Vietnam was a Purple Heart. He took part in Operation Union 1, Union 2 and Operation Swift, which were awarded a Presidential Unit Citation. Returning from Vietnam, he was assigned to Camp Lejeune, took part in a MedCruise and returned to Camp Lejeune until his discharge on April 1, 1969 with rank of Cpl.

He worked for the International Union of Operating Engineers for 47 years and retired in 2007. He and his wife Ruth have two children and two grandchildren. He enjoys hunting, fishing, golfing, gardening and wine making.

**LEOPOLDO "LEO" GRIEGO** was born April 29, 1924 at Albuquerque, NM. On Dec. 11, 1942 he enlisted at San Diego, CA. He received Rifle Sharpshooter training on Jan. 21, 1943.

Stationed in San Diego, he participated in New Britain (Dec. 29 to May 5, 1941), Russell In. (May 7, 1944 to Aug. 22, 1944), Guadalcanal B.S. and the tragedy of Peleliu. On Sept. 15, Leo's unit landed on Orange Beach 1 and 2. Their objective was take over the runways. Leo was wounded on Sept. 16, 1944. He was evacuated to the Russell Islands for recuperation and more military training in preparation for the invasion of Okinawa. His should wound was not healing properly. His Captain transferred Leo stateside to Mare Island, CA.

After a few months at Mare Island, he was honorably discharged on Sept. 6, 1945 as Private First Class.

Leo was in civil service for 25 years. Since retiring, he spends 3 hours a week swimming.

Leo and his wife, Sharon Housel, have two children, Matt and Brandon Griego.

**ALFRED J. "FRED" GROOS**, born Jan. 2, 1931 in New York, enlisted on July 11, 1948. After boot camp at Parris Island, he received Communication training.

He was stationed at Treasure Island, CA; Camp Catlin, HI; Tsingtao, China with stops at Guam, Philippines and Japan; Camp Pendleton; South Korea and to Portsmouth, NH where he was discharged on July 12, 1952 with the rank of Sgt.

After participating in battles in China, Japan and Korea he received the China Medal, Korean Medal and Good Conduct Medal.

He worked on Wall Street for 10 years, at Prudential Insurance for 10 years and as sales manager in New Jersey for 26 years. After retiring in 1987 his activities are golf, bowling and traveling.

He and Audrey were married 60 years before her death in 2014. They had six children: son, Alfred and daughters: Karen, Robbin, Linda, Laura and Cindy. They have 13 grandchildren: Amanda, Allison, Caroline, James, Tara, Heather, Jessica, Matthew, Craig, Kevin, Ryan, Meghan and Michael. Great-grandchildren are Eli, Emerson and Bentley.

**DANIEL "TRIGGER" GROSSI** was born May 21, 1949 at Staten Island, NY. After graduating in 1968 from McKee High School, he enlisted on April 29, 1969. After Boot Camp at Parris Island, he had training in CUPP (Combined Unit Pacification Program).

Grossi was stationed at Camp Lejeune, Camp Pendleton and Da Nang, Vietnam.

He served in Vietnam from October 1969 to September 1970 as a machine gunner 0331, also was attached to a Combined Unit Pacification Program.

Awards he received were the CAR, Vietnam Service, PUC and Vietnam Campaign.

Grossi was discharged with the rank of E-3 on Sept. 17, 1970 at Camp Pendleton, CA.

He served with the New York City Fire Department for 25 years, retiring June 1, 2003.

He owns a 1967 Pontiac GTO and enjoys car shows and old movies.

He and Rose have two children, Daniel Jr. and Rosemarie.

**DAVID "DAVE" T. HARVEY,** born Dec. 14, 1941 at Berkeley, CA graduated from Robt. Louis Stevenson School in 1959; attended Stanford University, 1963 earning a B.A. and M. of Forestry from Yale University in 1969.

Enlisting through Stanford NROTC he attended Boot Camp at Quantico, VA. He also received Mtn. Warfare Training, Bridgeport, CA; attended Raid School and Vietnamese language at Okinawa. He was stationed at Camp Pendleton and Camp Pulgas.

He participated in engagements at Chu Lai, Vietnam and Starlight, Piranah, Da Nang as aide to Brig. Gen. L. E. English. He received the Bronze Star w/Combat "V."

Memorable experiences were night patrols, ambushes and eight day patrols.

Captain Harvey was discharged in San Francisco, CA in 1966.

Harvey is a landscape contractor and is a licensed professional forester in California.

He and wife, Judith Louise Harvey RN, have two children, Nick and Sam Harvey and one grandchild, Ledger Harvey.

**JOSEPH P. HEGARTY JR.** was born on March 14, 1924 in Boston, MA. Massachusetts. In 1939, at age 15, he joined the Massachusetts Army National Guard, A Co 1st Bn 101st Inf (YD) and at age 17 was discharged due to minority.

In 1940, Joe joined the Civilian Conservation Corps, Camp 146, Groton State Forest, Marsh-

field VT, became a bulldozer/jack hammer operator and dynamiter.

In Aug 1941, Joe enlisted in the USMC, became a sergeant with C-1-11, 1st MarDiv and served on American and British Samoa and Wallis Island Group. Joe saw combat in the first offensive operation against the Japanese at Guadalcanal, New Guinea, New Britain and Okinawa. In 1945, Joe returned home, graduated from Boston's Suffolk University and its Law School, became an insurance executive and counsel, re-joined the Massachusetts Army National Guard during the cold war, rising through the ranks to Major General, commanding the 26th (Yankee) Infantry Division from 1982 to 1985.

Joe is a graduate of the US Army War College.

Decorations and Awards: US Army Distinguished Service Medal; Presidential and Naval Unit Citations, USMC; Asiatic Pacific Campaign, WW II Victory Medal.

Joe and wife Catherine live in Sarasota, FL and have six children: Brian, Ann, Thomas, Mark and John; son Paul deceased 2016, as well as nine grandchildren.

**CLARENCE LYNN HILL** was born on October 17, 1930 at 11:45 am, at home in Alva, Oklahoma to Georgie Richardson and Selby C. Hill. He graduated from Huerfano County High School, Colorado, in 1948. Once graduated, he moved from Walsenburg Colorado back to Alva where he worked as a 35MM projectionist.

In March of 1951, he joined the United States Marine Corps. After Basic Training, he was sent to San Diego for Combat Training at Camp Tent 2 Pendleton, for Winter Survival Training at Pickle Meadows, California. From December 1951 thru November 1952, he was assigned to HQ Company, 1st Ordinance Battalion, Korea. After he returned from Korea, he was stationed back at Camp Pendleton where he served as a Training NCO aide. He was Honorably Discharged as an E-4 SGT on March 6th, 1954.

After his Honorable Discharge, Hill went to work as an ATSF special agent in Chicago for 14 months. He didn't particularly like having to carry a gun or work nights or Sunday's, and found that he could make more money in construction. He ended up with IUOE 841 in Terre Haute, Indiana, where he worked for for the next 22 years. In the winter months, he would work as a licensed/bonded electrician, installing security alarms and weight scales, and also as a notary.

On June 23rd, 1971, he graduated from Intercollegiate College with a degree in ND, HT. On March 27, 1977, he completed a course on Scientific Hypnosis in 1977.

His wife, Mary R. Smith, was born at home on August 1st, 1939 to Mildred Weeks and John T. Smith. She was the mother to his two beautiful daughters, Mary F. Haymaker and Janice L. Defosse. His wife also had three boys William (deceased), John (deceased) and his best friend and caregiver Clarence A., with whom he currently resides in Weld County, Colorado. He is very proud to have 13 grandchildren and 14 great-grandchildren.

**BLAIR I. HOLM** was born Dec. 3, 1935 in Miller, SD, and graduated from Washington High School in Brainerd, MN, in 1953. He earned an AA from Mt. San Antonio Community College, Walnut, CA, in 1961, a BS from Cal Poly, Pomona, CA, 1970, and an MS in Library Science from the University of So. California, Los Angeles, CA, in 1976.

Holm enlisted in January 1954 in Minneapolis, and received basic training at MCRD, San Diego, CA, in March 1954. He went to ET school at Treasure Island, San Francisco, in 1954. Other stations included Camp Pendleton, Oceanside, CA, 1954; A/1/5 1st Marine Division, Korea, 1954-55; A/1/5 1st Marine Division, Camp Pendleton, CA, 1955; and H&S 5th Marine Regiment, Camp Pendleton, CA, 1955-56. He was discharged in December 1956 with the rank of Corporal.

After the service, he worked as a library clerk for the Los Angeles County Branch Libraries, La Puente and Hacienda Heights, 1958-59; Pomona Public Library, 1959-64; Chino Branch Library, San Bernardino, CA, 1970-74 (Branch Librarian Trainee); Riverside County Libraries, CA, 1976-79 (Children's Librarian); and Colton Public Library, Colton, CA, 1980-2000 (Children's and Technical Services Librarian). He retired in June 2000.

Holm is part of Semper Fi #1, Memorial Honor Detail, Riverside National Cemetery, Riverside, CA. They are an all-Marine unit providing honors for veterans who have passed away; he is the recruiting officer for the team. He is also a member of the California Library Assoc. and the National Library Assoc.

His wife, Cecelia A. Mestas-Holm, is a retired librarian. They have four adult children, three adult grandchildren, and one great-grandson.

**GEORGE PATRICK HOWARD JR.** was born on April 30, 1925 in Newark, NJ. He was raised in Irvington and Belmar, NJ, graduating from St. Rose High School in Belmar in 1942. He enlisted in Newark, NJ in 1943 and began his military training at Parris Island, SC. He trained as a radio operator at New River, NC and in radio maintenance in Omaha, ne.

George fought in the WW II Pacific theatre, landing on D-Day on Peleliu in September 1944.

After wading to shore when the landing craft was destroyed, he operated the only surviving radio in the Seventh regiment and sent the message from Colonel "Chesty" Puller committing the reserve troops. George also fought for three months in the battle of Okinawa and was assigned to North China after the war. He was discharged at Bainbridge, MD in January 1946 with the rank of Corpora.

After the war he attended the Syracuse University College of Forestry, earning a B.S. degree in Forest Management. He began his 40-year career with the New Jersey Division of Fish and Game, starting as a Wildlife Biologist and retiring in 1990 as Director of the entire Division. Throughout his life he has been dedicated to wildlife and the environment and been an avid hunter and fisherman

George resides in Pittstown, NJ. He was married to Jean Scharoun of Syracuse for 65 years. He has a daughter, Judith; a son, John and two granddaughters, Amy and Rachel.

**LEON P. HOWARD III,** born in Supulpa, Oklahoma on Friday the 13th of April 1945. Graduated from Aragon H.S. in San Mateo California, received an AA degree from College of San Mateo and later transferred to Humbolt State University for an incomplete.

Drafted, January 1966 and received training at MCRD Camp Pendleton, San Diego. A 20-day trip on the USS Gorden put us into DaNang. Upon arriving in Chu Lai I was summoned by Captain Clapp to become a scout, I did.

Additional training in map and compass reading enabled me to not only a F.O. but for night time snoop and poop missions as a scout. We usually worked in a 5-man team. Scouts also worked with interpreter-interrogators, snipers, village police, chiefs, Chu Hoy scouts (rehabilitated V.C.) and the Army Special Forces.

As a scout it was thought we were to be point man and I was a lot. I called in mortars, 105's and 155, directed an air strike. Trained in but never had to call in Naval gunfire. I worked with India, Kilo, Lima and Mike companies, four of us scouts rotated.

The different operations I was on were: Jackson, Praire Mississippi, De Soto, Grand, Webster, Butler and Arizona. I didn't extend for Sargent and $3,000. One trip was enough, enough to have left me with over 50 years of P.T.S.D.

I became a professional Timber faller, Wild lands fire fighter in Montana. I worked 35 years in the woods, only made the ER four times for stitches. I fought on 8 major fires from 1988-2003.

I married my wife Janet in 1981, and we had Aaron our son and Sarah our daughter. We started our family in a cabin we built remote in Montana.

I have four grandchildren, Aleah, Aubrey, Meredith and George.

I've enjoyed living in Montana, hunting, fishing, riding my Harley, working on Cushman Motor Scooters and building 4x4 Toyota's with my son.

My combat pictures and war memorabilia were donated to the Historical Museum of Fort Missoula.

**PATRICK "PAT" CARL HUMPHREY** was born June 16, 1950 in Warrenton, VA. After graduating from Bladensburg Senior High in 1968, he enlisted Nov. 4, 1968. After boot camp at Parris Island he also trained in Field Rapid OP. at San Diego.

He served with 1st Tank Btl., 3/5 1st Marine Division. He participated in Vietnam, OP. North; An Hua; Arizona Territory.

He received the Vietnam Service Medal, VIE and is still waiting on Combat Action Ribbon.

Humphrey was discharged at 2nd Amtract Btl. Dec. 29, 1970 as L/Cpl.

He worked 38 years in the automotive admin field, retiring April 16, 2014.

His spouse is Maureen E. Humphrey.

**JERRY INGRAM** was born May 20, 1927 in Kansas City, KS. He earned an Assoc. of Science from Kansas City Jr. College, and a B.S. in Education from Kansas University in 1952. Ingram enlisted at age 15 on Nov. 9, 1942 and received basic training in San Diego. He received additional instruction as a Tank Diving Instructor and Tank Commander.

Ingram was a member of the 4th Marine Division and 1st Marine Division (No. China), serving at ROI-Namur, Saipan, Tinian, and Iwo Jima. He received two letters of commendation. At age 16 he was a tank commander in combat; at age 17 he was a tank commander at Iwo Jima; and at age 18 he was a tank platoon sergeant in northern China. He was discharged after serving eight years with the rank of S/SGT.

Ingram is self-employed at Jerry Ingram / Fire & Rescue, and has three children and seven grandchildren.

**GERALD L. JENKINS** enlisted in the USMC in February 1968 serving as a combat engineer (mines, boobie traps, demolitions, and construction). He discharged to Vietnam from October

1968-November 1969. Following Vietnam, he was stationed at Marine Barracks, 8th & 'I', Washington D.C., Plt. Sgt. Ceremonial Honor Guard / White House duty during President Nixon's administration; Naval Station, New York (Staten Island) Base Closure, April 1994 - September 2001; appointed Major by U.S. Navy to assist with Military Naval Base Closure and re-employment, re-training and related personnel disbursement activities.

He is a life member of the American Legion, Disabled American Veterans, First Marine Division/7th Engineer Assoc., Veterans of Foreign Wars, and Vietnam Veterans of America.

He has worked for Grief Brother's Corp., Norman Jaspan Associates, Management Safeguards, Inc., Private Industry Council of NY, and most recently the Consortium for Worker Education from April 1994-April 2002 serving a Director of Special Projects (U.S. Navy) – Major.

He has two children: Gerald Lee Jenkins Jr. and Heather Sword Jenkins.

**GEORGE M. JENKS** was born Aug. 1, 1929 at Purcell, OK. He graduated from Purcell High School in 1940 and attended Oklahoma University, earning a BA, MA and MLS.

Jenks enlisted at Oklahoma City, OK and took Boot Camp at San Diego, CA. He was also stationed at Camp Pendleton.

As a result of serving in Korea, the Chinese Fall and Spring Offensive from 1952-1953, he received a Purple Heart.

Jenks was discharged at McAllister, OK in 1953 with the rank of PFC.

He worked at the University of Tasmania and Buckner University, retiring in 1987.

He and Zoya Jenks have three children – Darrell, Mark and Andrew and seven grandchildren.

**JAMES E. "KBAR" KERLEY** was born April 13, 1931 in California and graduated from Alexander Hamilton High School. He enlisted at Los Angeles, CA, and received basic training at MCRD San Diego. He was stationed at Camp Pendleton, Philippine Islands, Korea, Okinawa, Vietnam, and Camp LeJeune, and served as a drill instructor for three years. He was discharged on Feb. 28, 1969 at the rank of GySgt.

He and his wife Theresa (deceased) have seven children and five grandchildren.

**JOSEPH TOM "KESS" KESSLER** was born Jan. 10, 1932 in Santa Monica, CA. After graduating from high school, He enlisted on March 6, 1951 and took Boot Camp at Parris Island, NC. He received additional training in 75 Recoiless Rifle and Expert Rifle.

He served in Korea from October 1951 to October 1952; with 8th I St, Washington, DC; and at MB, Mare Island.

He received the Expert, Rifle Marksman Badge, Good Conduct and Korean Medal.

After serving six years, Kessler was discharged in March 1956 with the rank of Sgt.

"Kess" and wife, Eleanor, have four children: Tom, Mike, Linda and Susan. Grandchildren are Thomas, Tim, Michael, Noland, Blake, Blair, Jason and Robert.

**JAMES E. KRONAIZL** was born near Utica, SD on 23 November 1925 and graduated from Meckling High School in 1943. He enlisted in February 1944 and trained at Camp Pendleton as a marksman and mortar crewman.

He participated in offensive and defensive operations on the Solomon Islands and Okinawa

with K/3/5. He was severely wounded at Okinawa on 5 May 1945 ultimately transferred to the Naval Hospital in Memphis.

Kronaizl was awarded the Purple Heart and discharged from service in Memphis on 18 December 1945 with the rank of Corporal. He worked as a petroleum salesman for Farmers Co-op from 1953 until retiring in 1987.

In the early 1983, he discovered the memoir, With the Old Breed, by Cpl. Eugene Sledge, which detailed the activities of K/3/5 in the Pacific Theater. Upon connecting with Cpt. Thomas Stanley, Kronaizl learned that K Company thought he had died on Okinawa. He attended the First Marines reunion in 1984 and finally reconnected with his company.

He was married to Barbara for 64 years before passing away on 28 March 2017. They have three children – Patti, Denis, and Julie – eight grandchildren, and six great-grandchildren.

**WILLIAM JAMES "ACE" LaFAYETTE,** born Sept. 13, 1932 in Chicago, IL, graduated from Austin High School.

He enlisted in Chicago, IL and Boot Camp was at Parris Island. "Ace" was stationed at Camp Lejeune, NC and Camp Pendleton, CA. During 1952 and 1953 he was all up and down M.L.R. in Korea.

For his service he was awarded the Commendation Medal Pendant with combat "V," Good Conduct Medal (MARCOR), National Defense Service Medal, Korean Service Medal with 3 Bronze Stars, US Service Medal, Navy Unit Accommodation Ribbon, Republic of Korea Presidential Unit Citation and Sharp Shooter Medal.

After discharge as Sgt. at Camp Lejeune, NC LaFayette has raised beef cattle on his Tennessee farm.

He and Starr B. have six children: Jennifer Bolton, Julie Coyne, Jean Harris, Jim LaFayette, Meg Pienkowski and Kellodi Bledsoe. Their grandchildren are Cole Harris; Britney Valas; Heidi Shewmaker; Katie Schad; Kory and MacKenzie LaFayette; Rick and Justin Vaughn; Aaron Bolton; Chad and T.J. Hockler; Matthew, Lucas and Bennett Pienkowski and Brittany Baird.

**CHARLES "CHARLIE" P. LANDT III** was born Sept. 23, 1947 in Dallas, TX. In 1967 he graduated from Oak Ridge Military Institute.

Enlisting on Sept. 1, 1967 at Raleigh, NC, Boot Camp was at Parris Island. He received AIT Artillery training at Camp Pendleton, SC.

He was based in Bamberg and Babenhausen, Germany and Turkey; also Camp Lejeune, NC; Fort Riley, KS and Fort Bragg, NC. He served in Vietnam from March 1967 to October 1968 and in 1970.

Awards/medals include Meritorious Service Medal, Army Service Medal, National Defense Medal, Vietnam Gallantry Cross w/Palm, Army Commendation Medal (2 OLC), Combat Action Ribbon, Vietnam Cross of Gallantry Unit Commendation, Vietnam Service Medal (8), Meritorious Unit Commendation Medal, Overseas Ribbon

(3), Good Conduct Medal (6 AWD), NCO Professional Development Ribbon (3), Army Achievement Medal (1 OLC), Vietnam Campaign Medal and Rifle Marksman Badge.

Landt was discharged on Dec. 31, 1987 at Fort Bragg, NC with the rank of SFC. After discharge, he served as a corrections officer, real estate broker and owner of Landt Realty.

Charles and Evelyn have two daughters, Mary and Jennifer. Grandchildren are Wren, Xavier and Madelia Campbell and Aiden and Gweneth Stork.

**EDWARD "EDDIE" M. LANDRY,** born July 14, 1947 in Lynn, MA. He graduated from Lynn Classical High School and also attended Newbury Jr. College and Suffolk University.

Landry enlisted on Sept. 12, 1966 in Lynn, MA. After Boot Camp at Parris Island, he attended I.T.R. at Camp Giegar, Artillery School. He was also stationed at Camp Pendleton, CA.

While in Vietnam he participated in 12 combat operations, including the battle of Hue and KHE Sanh Relief. During the TET 1968 he was inside the city of Hue 19 days with 4.2 inch mortar gun platoon (two guns), 1st BN, 11th Marines, 1st Marine Division.

He received the Combat Action Ribbon, Vietnam Service with four PUC and the Vietnam Cross of Gallantry.

After serving 32 year with the US Postal Service, he retired in 2006 and is "doing what I want to do."

He is a Life Member, 1st Marine Division Assoc., member of VFW Post 1240 and AMVETS.

Landry and Bette have four children: Brian, Brendon, Daniel and Ellen. Grandchildren are Moira, Eamonn, Colm Daniella and Elza.

**JOSEPH R. "DICK" LANTZ,** born in Baltimore, MD, graduated from Glen Burnie High School in 1950. He attained a BS Degree in Industrial Mgt. in 1965 from University of Baltimore.

After enlisting on April 4, 1950 in Baltimore, he took Basic Combat Engineer training at Camp Lejeune, NC. He graduated from MCRD, San Diego, CA on Jan. 6, 1951.

He was stationed at Ft. McHenry, MD; Camp Pendleton, CA; San Diego, CA; MCDS Hdqrs., Dept. of the Pacific and Mare Island Naval Station, CA. Active duty was from Aug. 21, 1950 to March 6, 1952 and he was inactive reserve from March 7, 1952 to Dec. 30, 1960. Corporal Lantz was honorably discharged on Dec. 30, 1960.

He earned the National Defense Service Medal, Armed Forces Reserve Medal (with Bronze M), Marine Corps Reserve Ribbon, Expert Rifleman Badge, 2nd Aware Rifle Expert Bar and Marine Corps Basic Badge with "S.S. Pistol" Q-Bar.

Lantz worked at Westinghouse Engr. Dept. from 1952 to 1960 and Contracts Mgt. from 1961 to 1994.

In retirement he has held various church officer positions, is a singer in choir, member of Board of Directors in Community Assn., has held various officer positions in Marine Corps League and is a member of 1st Marine Div. Assn. and American Legion.

"Dick" and Ailene have two children, Steven and Susan and five grandchildren: Emma, Rodger, Jeffrey, Eric and Christopher.

**LESTER "LES" LAZARUS,** born in New York, graduated from Wm. L. Dickenson High School and attained a B.S. Chemistry from Fairleigh Dickenson University.

In 1950 he enlisted at Newark, NJ and took Boot Camp at Parris Island. During service he was stationed at Camp Pendleton, Camp Lejeune and E-2-1 Korea.

He received three Purple Hearts, PUC and Korean Service Medal. PFC Lazarus was discharged at Newark, NJ.

He says, "I was a Marine in the Korean War. I am sorry that it did not reach the acclaim of the Vietnam, Afghanistan or the Iraq Wars, but the forgotten war was a war nonetheless.

As a machine gunner in a Marine rifle company, I did my time on the M.L.R., the outposts Samoa, Siberia, X-ray and the grand nightmare – Bunker Hill.

I don't feel qualified to regale you with war stories, but I would like to say to those wonderful Marines with whom I was privileged to serve some three score and 10 years ago. Most of their names are forgotten, but their faces and deeds are ingrained in my memory. Their jokes, pranks and wonderful stories made the insanity of war bearable. I can't thank them enough."

He now instructs small bore shooting at the Waldwick Pistol & Rifle Club.

Les and Julia have two daughters, Wendy Lazarus, PhD and Cindy Lazarus, PhD.

**BRIAN "LENTSO" LENTS** was born in Aurora, IL on Sept. 29, 1949 and graduated from West Aurora High School in 1967. On Feb. 21, 1967 he enlisted and after Boot Camp at MCRD, San Diego, CA he received additional training in Electronic Repair.

He was at San Diego, 29 Palms, Lejeune, Pendleton and served in Vietnam from December 1969 to October 1970.

Memories include all the friends he made in the Marine Corp and the bond they formed with each other.

Corporal Lents was discharged on June 14, 1971 at MCRD, Parris Island, SC, with the rank of corporal.

After the Marine Corps he worked at Bell Telephone Laboratories in Naperville, IL for seven years. On May 1, 1976 the engineers could not get AT&T's first #1 ESS switching system up and running. The engineers called on him. Since noon on May 1, 1976, that system has been serving Chicago, IL.

After leaving Bell Labs, he went to work for himself as a carpenter. His commercial work has been featured in local magazines and residential work has been featured in national magazines. He retired in 2012.

He lived along Kentucky Lake from October 1986 to February 2016. He says, "I spent as much time as I could walking my Dad's beagles in the woods."

**EVARIST A. LEMAY,** at the age of 17 in 1952, enlisted in the US Marine Corp and went to Parris Island, SC. He served with Easy Co. 2nd Bn. 5th Marine Regt. in Korea for 18 months.

"Forever remembering the cold, rice paddies and the mountains." He was wounded at "VEGAS" by Chinese mortars.

After Korea he reported to Key Port Naval Torpedo Station, WA.

Evarist re-enlisted to the Third Marine Div. and was at Camp Fuji, Japan E-2-3, Suez Canal, Philippines and Okinawa for 14 months.

He was at Portsmouth, VA Naval Station and then to the 2nd Marine Division C-1-6. In Lebanon, also with the 2nd Recon. Bn.

After the Marine Corps, Lemay worked for United Parcel Service for 26 years.

He states: "At every 5th Marine Reunion, will always remember the faces of those at roll call who made the ultimate sacrifice."

Semper Fi.

**DONALD J. "DON" LEWIS** was born in Philadelphia, PA. After graduating from Upper Dorby High he enlisted at Philadelphia in 1951. After Boot Camp at Parris Island, he received additional training at Camp Pendleton. He went to Korea and then to Quantico, VA.

He served with the 1st Marine Division in Korea, Signal Battalion, Headquarters Co.

Don was discharged at Quantico, VA in February 1954 with the rank of Sgt.

After service, he was a manager for State Farm Insurance until 1997 when he retired.

Retirement activities include the Rotary, Chamber and Chair of Police Comm.

He and Jean have three children: Debra, Donald and Karen. Grandchildren are Kevin, Kyle, Taylor, Michael, Mallory, Michelle and Molly.

**JOHN J. LOVAS** was born Jan. 5, 1924 in Pittsburgh, PA. He graduated from Braddock High School in June 1941 and also spent three years at Tulane University.

Lovas enlisted in USMC on June 13, 1941. Boot Camp was at Parris Island, Platoon 67 with additional training at Sea School. He was posted NOB Key West, FL; Portsmouth, VA; *USS Columbia CL-56,* 1st Marine Division with 12th Defense BN, Cape Gloucester.

He participated in the SW Pacific, Solomon Islands and the Battle of Empress, Augusta Bay.

Lovas received the Navy Unit Commendation, Combat Action Ribbon, WW II Victory Medal, Good Conduct Medal, six Battle Stars Organized Reserve Medal.

Sgt. Lovas was discharged at Camp Pendleton on Oct. 1, 1945.

His civilian career consisted of 67 years in insurance sales. He is now retired and living in McKinney, TX.

John and Harriet (deceased in 2015) had three children: Christine, Leslie and Michael (Vietnam era Marine). Grandchildren are Scott, Amy, Sean, Emily and Dave.

**GEORGE R. "TIGER" LYTLE,** SSgt. USMC Ret., was born in Wheeling, WV in 1935. On June 6, 1954 he enlisted at Wheeling, WV. Boot Camp was at Parris Island. He attended Radio, TV Repair School from 1954-1955.

Lytle was discharged at Camp Lejeune as SSgt. On April 30, 1976.

For his service he received the Navy Marine Corps Achievement with V, 6 Good Conduct awards, National Defense, Armed Forces Expedition, Marine Corp Expedition, Vietnam Service w/1 Silver 6 Stars, Presidential Unit Citation w/1 Star, Korean Defense Service, Republic of Vietnam Meritorious Unit, Vietnam Civil Actions with Palm, Navy Marine Corp Overseas and Rifle Pistol Sharpshooter.

**EDWARD C. MADER,** born in Roseville, MI, enlisted on Jan. 14, 1954 and took Boot Camp at MCRD, San Diego, CA.

From 1954-56, he was at 29 Palms, from 1956-57 at El Toro, from 1957-59 at Camp Pendleton and from 1959-60 at Okinawa.

He participated in AGLEX-1 outside CONUS Sept. 23 to Sept. 1955.

He received the Good Conduct Medal and National Defense Medal for his service.

On Feb. 2, 1960 Mader was discharged as E-4 CPL.

He worked at Chrysler as press operator and hilo driver, retiring in 1994.

Edward and Sandra Mader have one daughter, Denise.

**LEONARD J. "LEN" MAFFIOLI** was born in Berkeley, CA on July 1, 1925. Upon graduation from La Jolla High School in 1943, he enlisted in the US Marine Corps and fought on the Pacific Islands of Saipan, Tinian and Iwo Jima with the 4th Marine Division. When WW II ended, he returned to the US in late 1945 for discharge.

Maffioli reenlisted in July 1950 at the outbreak of the Korean Conflict and sailed for Korea with the 1st Tank Bn., 1st Marine Division, participating in the Inchon Landing, capture of Seoul and the Chosin Reservoir campaigns. During this latter action, he was captured by Chinese forces while escorting British Royal Marines of the 41st Independent Commando to Hagaru-ri with Task Force Drysdale. After six months as a prisoner of war, he escaped along with 17 other Marines and was later awarded the Bronze Star Medal with Combat "V", for his part in engineering the escape. He also received the Purple Heart Medal for wounds received during his capture.

After more than five months hospitalization and convalescence, he returned to active duty and served at various posts and stations throughout the world, including a tour with the 3rd Tank Bn. on Okinawa and duty with the Dept. of State as NCOIC of Marine Security Guard detachments at diplomatic posts in Munich, Germany and Vienna, Austria.

In 1967, after four years of recruiting duty in the Los Angeles area, he requested and received transfer to Vietnam where he served 13 months as operations chief of the 1st Tank Bn., participating in four major campaigns, including the February 1968 Tet Offensive.

From Vietnam, Maffioli was reassigned to the Dept. of State and served in Dhahran, Saudi Arabia and Kabul, Afghanistan. Subsequent tours included a stint as sergeant major of the 2nd Tank Bn. at Camp Lejeune and four more years of recruiting in Los Angeles and Orange counties.

In 1975 he was transferred to MCRD, San Diego, where he served as the Depot's inspection chief until his retirement in March 1979. With more than 30 years of service, he was the last Korean ex-POW and one of the few remaining veterans of WW II on active duty in the Marine Corps. He was awarded the Meritorious Service Medal upon retirement.

MGySgt Maffioli's other awards and decorations include the Purple Heart Medal POW Medal, Combat Action Ribbon, Presidential Unit Citation with 3 stars, Navy Unit Commendation, Meritorious Unit Citation with 3 stars, Good Conduct Medal 10th Award, Asiatic-Pacific Campaign Medal with 3 stars, WW II Victory Medal, National Defense Service Medal, Korean Service Medal with 4 stars, Vietnamese Service Medal with 4 stars, Korean PUC, Vietnamese Cross of Gallantry, United Nations Medal, Vietnamese Campaign Medal and the Korean War Service Medal.

Len Maffioli and his wife, the former Donna Moore of Manitoba, Canada, currently reside in Murrieta, CA.

**EDWARD DANIEL "MACK" MAGINN** enlisted in 1966 at Upper Darby, PA after graduating from Interboro High School. He also attended the Delware County Community College for 2 years, earning an Associate's Degree.

After Boot Camp at Parris Island, he attended ITR training at Camp Geiger and Parachute Training at Fort Benning. Maginn was also stationed in Camp Lejeune, Okinawa, Camp Pendleton and in Vietnam.

He received the Combat Action Ribbon, Presidential Unit Citation, Vietnam Service Ribbon 3 Bronze Stars and Vietnam Campaign Ribbon.

He was a Cpl, at Camp Pendleton who became acting Platoon Sgt. on his second time at staging Batt. Then made Sgt. before going overseas.

After discharge as Sgt. in 1970 at Camp Pendleton, "Mack" was a police officer/Hazmat Technician with SRT Team. He belongs to the Fraternal Order of Police and Saint Alban Lodge #529.

Retirement activities include Rickson Gracie Jui-Jitsu, DAV Life Member, Marine Corps League Life Member and VFW Life Member.

"Mack" has two daughters, Lori and Lille and Emma is his granddaughter.

**MELVIN DAVID "MEL" McKINNON** was born in Portland, OR on March 27, 1948. After graduating in 1968, he enlisted on Jan. 11, 1969. Following Boot Camp at Camp Pendleton, CA he also was trained in "Expert" Rifle.

Mel fought at the Battle at Liberty Bridge, a small hill northwest of An Hoa where one of the most deadly single battles was fought. Here 72 North Vietnamese lost their lives. The Marines suffered casualties but they met overwhelming odds, "mustered up whatever Marines have had in the past" and defeated the enemy. It has been said of this battle "it will remain as a special memory where fear met guts and guts breached the realm of glory for one brief, eternal night."

In addition to a Purple Heart w/1*, he received the National Defense Service Medal, Vietnam Campaign Medal w/device, Letter of Appreciation, Vietnam Service Medal w/1* and Rifle Marksman Badge.

Memory: The Nightingales Song. In 1970 Corporal McKinnon was discharged.

He worked as Heat n Frost Insulator in asbestos abatement and now works on his farm.

Mel and Juli Rose McKinnon have one child, Scott Angus McKinnon and one grandchild, Izzie McKinnon.

**JOHN T. McANIFF III** was born in San Diego, CA and graduated from St. Benedict's Preparatory School in 1961. He attained A.A.S. Business Administration in 1976 from Coastal Carolina Community College and B.S. Business Administration in 1994 from Strayer College.

In March 1964 he enlisted and after Boot Camp at Parris Island, also attended Navy Class "A" Radio School, trained as Radio/Telegraph Operator in 1964 and took Radio Relay Operators Course at Camp Lejeune in 1965. In 1971 attended Personal Admin. Chiefs School.

McAniff was in operations in Danang, RVN area from 1968 to 1969.

He received the Combat Action Ribbon, Nav/MC Achievement Medal w/Combat "V," National Defense Medal, Good Conduct Medal w/1 Star, RVN Service Medal w/4 Stars, RVN Campaign Medal w/Device, Presidential Unit Citation, Navy Meritorious Unit Citation and RVN Unit Gallantry Citation.

McAniff was discharged in March 1972 at Arlington, VA with the rank of Sgt.

After discharge he was a warehouse manager, in sales, D.O.D. Security Guard at Ft. Belvoir and an Amway distributor, retiring in 2004.

Retirement activities include model railroading, stamp and coin collecting and genealogical research.

**JAMES "JIM" McKILLOP** was born in 1926 in California. In October 1944 he enlisted in San Francisco. After Boot Camp at San Diego, he received additional training in communications.

Stationed in San Diego, he was engaged in battles in Pavuvu, Peleliu, Okinawa and China.

Cpl. McKillop was discharged at San Diego.

In civilian life, he was a firefighter until retiring in December 1986.

Jim and Kathleen McKillop have two children, Carol Peverill and Marie McKillop. Grandchildren are Mike, Dawn and Larry. Taz, Kaya, Shawn, Kayla and Baylee are their great-grandchildren and James is their great-great-great grandson.

**PFC DONALD MELLINS** was inducted into the Marines Nov 13, 1942, three months after his 16th birthday. He enjoyed every aspect of life in the Corps and planned to make it a career as an officer after the war. However, that was not to be! Don was killed in action against Japanese forces on Peleliu, Palau Islands, Sept 15, 1944, one month after his 18th birthday.

Donald's military itinerary included: Parris Island, SC (Nov. 14, 1942 – Jan. 5, 1943); Marine Barracks, Naval Mine Warfare School & Depot, Yorktown, VA (Jan. 7, 1943 – mid February 1944); Camp Elliott, CA (Feb. 22, 1944 – May 13, 1944); embarked on board *USS Rochambeau* May 13, 1944, arrived at Noumea, New Caledonia June 1, 1944; embarked on *USS Minetaka* June 14, 1944, arrived at Pavuvu, Russell Islands June 19, 1944; embarked aboard LST at Pavuvu Island Aug. 26, 1944, arrived at Guadalcanal Aug. 27, 1944; embarked from Guadalcanal Sept. 4, 1944, arrived and landed on Beach White 2 at Peleliu Island, Palau Islands Sept. 15, 1944.

Mellins was awarded the Silver Star, Purple Heart, Presidential Unit Citation, Asiatic-Pacific Campaign Medal, WW II Victory Medal and American Defense Service Medal. *Submitted by Sherwin Mellins, M.D.*

**GARY E. MITCHELL** joined the Marine Corps in September 1964. After boot camp and ITR, he went to 2nd Marine Division at Camp Lejeune. After two years with 2nd Marine Division, he received orders for Vietnam, arriving in November 1966 as Lance Corporal. He arrived at An Hoa and was assigned to Echo Company, 2nd Battalion,

5th Marines, 1st Marine Division. On January 1, 1967, he was promoted to Corporal and took over a fire team, later taking over the 1st squad, 3rd platoon, a position he held until rotating out in December of 1967.

Mitchell participated on many named operations, including patrols, ambushes, and sweeps, etc. On October 4, 1967, he was wounded from shrapnel from a booby trap and received a purple heart. Upon returning to the States, he finished out my 4-year commitment at Camp Lejeune, and was discharged on September 13, 1968. In May of 2012, at the age of 66, he retired as a truck driver. In the interim he met and married my wonderful wife Joanne, and they have two terrific daughters.

May God continue to bless America, and the United States Marine Corps.

**BLASCO M. "MOLE" MOLLE** joined the US Marine Corp on March 3, 1943 and served until Feb. 23, 1946 when he was discharged as a Cpl.

*Photo by Richard Bell for his book, "The Last Veterans." Used by permission.*

He participated in battles of Pelelu (Sept. 15, 1944 – Oct. 18, 1944), Okinawa (April 1, 1945 – June 27, 1945). He landed in Taku China with 1st Marine Division in the first week of October 1945 under the pretense of disarming the Japanese Troops.

Molle received the WW II Occupational Medal, WW II Victory Medal, Asiatic Pacific Campaign Medal, American Campaign Medal, China Service Medal, Marine Corps Good Conduct Medal, Purple Heart Medal, Presidential Unit Citation Ribbon and Combat Action Ribbon.

In civilian life he worked 30 years at RCA Government Communications Systems, Camden, NJ. After retiring on Jan. 31, 1988 he spends his time with the Marine Corp League and family.

Blasco and Angeline Molle have four children, nine grandchildren and four great grandchildren.

**RICHARD BARTHOLOMEW "MOONMAN" MOONEY** is a Life Member of the 1st Marine Division Association, (FMDA), having served 4 years on the National Level of the Association, serving on the Board of Directors and on the Executive Committee. He served 2 years as its National Sgt at Arms and 2 years as the National Vice President for the East Coast. In addition, he is the Past President and a Life Member of the New York Chapter of the FMDA, and presently serves

on its Board of Directors. MoonMan is also the past Chaplain, Charter and Life member of the Echo 2/7 Chapter. In addition he holds Life Membership in the Bodfish, Hawaiian Islands, Houston, Los Angeles, and Oregon FMDA Chapters.

Mooney served with the 1st Marine Division in Vietnam in 1966-67. He was a Corporal Squad Leader with a 81mm Mortar Section of Echo Co. 2nd Bn. 7th Marine Regiment (The Magnificent 7th Marines).

MoonMan was born in NYC in August 1946, soon after the end of WWll. He was one of the firstborn,"WWll Baby Boomers", "the 1st Generation of the Greatest Generation". He is the oldest of 10 children. His Irish Immigrant father fought in the Pacific Theatre in WWll with the "Fighting Irish" 69th Regiment of the US Army. He was the 1st Sgt. of Co. B., and received the Silver Star and a Purple Heart in the Battle of Saipan. (Also fighting on Saipan were 2 Divisions of US Marines, for which he never had a kindword). His father would make a career of the US Army. MoonMan's parents raised their 10 children in a strict conservative Irish catholic household, in the NYC borough of Queens, in the neighborhoods of Laurelton/Rosedale, Hollis/St. Albans and Bayside.

Richard had 12 years of Catholic Parochial Education. He graduated from St. Pascal Baylon grammar school in 1960. In grammar school he spent several years memorizing Latin for service as an Acolyte and a Senior Altar Boy, officiating with Celebrants in the Celebration of the Latin Mass, along with Weddings, Funerals, and traditional rituals and ceremonies of the Roman Catholic Church. Richard went on to graduate from St. Pascal Baylon HS in 1964, with an academic NY State Regents Diploma. It was in his HS years, that for the first, (and only time before his father retired), that his family moved onto an Army Base, Fort Totten, located in Queens NY. He was the only student in his high school who lived on a Army Base and who had to commute by public bus transportation several hours a day, (3 bus routes and 1 1/2 hours each way), to attend classes. It was on Ft. Totten, in 1962, that he experienced first hand the seriousness of the "Cuban Missile Crisis". It was also there on the base chapel, that he became president of the Altar Boy Society and became The Grand Knight of The Knights of the Altar, which was an early primer for the Knights of Columbus. It was the same year that he was the President of his Sophomore Class and represented them on the Student Council. In the fall of 1963 Mooney was a Senior in HS and was in a "Study Hall Period", when he heard the news that President Kennedy was shot in Dallas. Soon after it was confirmed that the President had indeed been killed, Richard proceeded to go from classroom to classroom to inform his fellow students and their teachers of the horrific and tragic news, before it was announced over the schools public address system.

Soon after graduation he obtained full time gainful employment with the National Headquarters of the Western Union Telegraph Company in NYC, and worked in the confidential unit of the Employee Relations and Benefit Dept. In 1965, while others were burning their draft cards in protest against the draft and the Vietnam War, Mooney went to his local Draft Board to volunteer and sign up for the draft. In March of 1966, MoonMan and his close friend, Frank Pietras, were drafted together, and under the "buddy system", volunteered for the US Marine Corps. (On the 4th of July 1967, L/Cpl Frank Pietras was KIA on Operation Buffalo). MoonMan graduated Paris Island in May '66 with platoon 160 as a "grunt"

(0311) Infantry Rifleman, and after ITR in camp Geiger, was assigned, with Marine Pietras, to Echo Co 2nd Bn 8th Marines, 2nd Marine Division, Camp Lejeune.

In the late summer of '66, orders came in for both Mooney and Pietras, for Fleet Marine Force - Western Pacific, (FMF-West Pac). They were sent to Camp Pendleton (Las Pulgas), for Advanced Infantry Training, (AIT), Jungle Warfare and search and destroy training, after which "the buddies" were separated. Frank flew to Vietnam and was subsequently assigned to Kilo Co 3/9 3rd Mar Div. MoonMan, on the USMC Birthday, 11/10/66 left San Diego for Da Nang Vietnam aboard the USNS General William H Gordon. Upon arrival he was assigned to the 1st Marine Division and sent to Chu Lai where he was assigned to the 2nd BN 7th Marine Regiment. It was there that his MOS was changed to 0341 - Mortarman. He became an "Ammo Carrier" aka "Ammo Humper", with the 81mm Mortar Section, serving with Battalion, Fox and Echo Companies. Moonman was credited with participating and supporting search and destroy operations, among which were Mississippi, Sierra, Trinity, Rio Grande, Pueblo, Perry, Duval, Union ll, Arizona, and others whose names are unknown. Mooney's last assignment in Nam was at the Echo Co command post, above the "Esso Plant", (which was the Lien Chieu Esso gas storage terminal which held millions of gallons of gasoline). It was located North of Da Nang and South of the Hai Van Pass, in "The Rocket Belt".

The TAOR included Namo Bridge, Namo Viilage, the LAAM Site and Highway l along the Hai Van Peninsula and the Harbor. The Company was a "Ready Reaction Force" whose Battalion motto was "Ready for Anything, Counting on Nothing". At that time they were waiting their turn to go "Afloat".

As a Corporal Squad Leader, MoonMan earned the US Marine Corps Combat Action Ribbon, the National Defense Medal, the Vietnam Service Medal with 2 bronze stars, the Republic of Vietnam Campaign Medal with device, the Presidential Unit Citation with 1 bronze star, the Republic of Vietnam Meritorious Unit Citation Cross of Gallantry with palm and frame, the Republic of Vietnam Meritorious Unit Citation for Civil action with palm and frame.

MoonMan returned to "The World" with 3 months of service time left. Mooney was reassigned to "The Cross Roads of the Marine Corps", Quantico, where he served with the "Schools Demonstration Teams" (SDT). Soon after his Honorable Discharge from the US Marines, MoonMan enrolled in college under the GI Bill and graduated from (SUNY) Nassau Community College with an A.A. Degree, (CUNY) John Jay College of Criminal Justice with a Cum Laude B.A. Degree, (LIU) Long Island University (Bklyn Campus), with an MS Ed Degree, with Post Graduate course work in family counseling. Richard has been a public civil servant his entire professional career, which began in 1971. For 33 years he worked "out in the field", for the 3 layers of government, the city of NY, the State of NY and the Federal Government. (He would take promotion exams, score high, and then turn down the promotion, preferring to work in the field, rather than in an office, all the while taking joy in advising his supervisors that he had scored higher than them on their promotion exam.

Some of the many civil service titles he has held are: Eligibility Investigator for the NYC Dept of Social Services, Senior Field Representative, in the Special Investigations Unit, for the NY State Office of the Welfare Inspector General, NY State Narcotic Parole Officer, NY State Mental Hygiene Specialist, NY State Drug Abuse and Alcohol Treatment Specialist, Federal Probation and Parole Officer for the Federal District Court, the Southern District of NY in Foley Square NYC, (SD/NY). (He was one of the founders of its drug and alcohol supervision units). His last employment from which he retired, was with NY State Division of Parole, Executive Dept, as a NY State field Parole Officer, supervising high delinquency caseloads of predicate violent felony offenders, released to the NYC area, from NY State Penitentiaries. In addition to his caseload duties, he served his coworkers as their Union Shop Steward and as their Regional Vice President for the NY State Parole Officers Association, (for the county of Queens during the 1980's, and for the county of Nassau from 1990 to 2004). In addition he was also a former weapons qualification Range Officer and a deadly physical force instructor. Mooney is the recipient of his agencies highest awards and commendations, which includes the Medal of Valor and the Brian F Rooney Award. This prestigious award is named after one of his coworkers who in 1985 was killed in the line of duty, (an ambush assassination), in retaliation for locking up and violating the parole of a prominent Queens Drug Lord and King Pin, who went by the street name of "Fat Cat".

Mooney has been a resident homeowner in the Incorporated Village of Floral Park since 1976. For most of that time he has been an active Volunteer Firefighter with Reliance Engine Co #2. However more than a decade ago, he sustained a serious injury, in the line of duty, at an active "signal 10", working fire, causing and requiring him to retire from active firematic and law enforcement duties. MoonMan has been active in his community of Floral Park. He and his wife became certified Girl Scout Leaders and Campers, and for several years, co-lead their own Girl Scout Troop. He is a life member, and for many years was the Commander, (now past commander), of his Floral Park VFW Post, as well as being the Past Commander of his Floral Park American Legion Post, and a member of its "40&8" Voiture Post. Mooney holds life membership in the Disabled American Veterans (DAV), the Marine Corps League (MCL), Vietnam Veterans of America (VVA), the Veterans of the Vietnam War (VVW), and the 2nd Marine Division Association (SMDA). In addition Richard is the Past President and active member of the Floral Park-Bellerose Rotary Club, and holds membership in the New Hyde Park Elks Lodge and his Fraternal Order of Police Lodge. For several years, he organized and co-lead an annual Catholic Men's Religious Retreat at St. Josephs in the Hills, in Malvern Pa. He was a building Captain for over 100 of the 300 men attending.

MoonMan's fascination with ceremonies, (secret) rituals, symbolism, and traditions, continued into adulthood with his joining and becoming a card carrying member of his local Masonic Lodge, and moving on to receive a York Rite 32nd Degree, a Scottish Rite 32nd Degree, and also becoming a Royal Arch and Cryptic Mason, as well as becoming a Knight of Malta, a Knight of the Red Cross, a Knights Templar, and a Shriner.

Prior to the Marine Corps, at the age of 19, MoonMan met the love of his life and his future wife, Gloria Jean, who at that time was a 17 year old college freshman, They met in 1965, through "Operation Match", which at that time was the first, and the forerunner, of today's computer dating systems, They have been married since 1970. Gloria Jean is a graduate of Pratt Institute (Bklyn), with a BFA and a MS Degree. She has had an illustrious 35 year career as an high school Art Teacher at Chaminade and Glen Cove HS.

Together they have 2 daughters. Melissa May, a Virginia Tech graduate who is employed by Jet Blue Airlines, out of JFK Airport. She is married to a HS Science teacher and has an infant son and 3 daughters under the age of 8. Their other daughter is Melanie Marie, who holds a Cum Laude BA Degree from SUNY Cortland, and 2 Master's Degrees from Adelphi University. For more than 10 years she has been a HS Art Teacher for the prestigious Locust Valley School District. She is also married to a HS Science Teacher and has a 2 year old son. MoonMan whose Marine Corps combat action ribbon came with a can of "Whoop-Ass PTSD", is very proud and honored to wear the life title of United States Marine. He served with Outstanding Marines. Some of these "Warrior Marines", never came home and went directly to the "Hall of the Slain" in Valhalla. They were "Marines on a Mission" who displayed their "spirit de corps", with "true grit", and with the "Semper Fi - Do or Die" Marine Corps Mettle. They courageously and gallantly gave their full measure, sacrificing all their tomorrows, in selfless service, with an unyielding devotion, and a duty and obligation, to each other, to their Corps, and to their Country. With Honor, Courage, and Commitment, with the pathos and ethos, and with the Spirit of a true Marine combat warrior, they valiantly upheld the highest and finest traditions of the United States Marine Corps and the United States of America. To them, with their heroic deeds and memories, MoonMan stands at attention, to give them a snappy Marine Corps salute, a Semper Fidelis, and a roaring Ooh-Rah!

**JOSEPH "JOE" M. MURPHY** was born in 1935 in New York City. In February 1953 he enlisted at New York.

After Boot Camp he received additional training at Camp Lejeune and Camp Pendleton – Pickle Meadows (Cold Weather).

He was stationed at G-3-5, Baler Block Korea. He was engaged in battles in Korea south of 38th Parallel.

Murphy received the National Defense Service Medal and the Korea Defense and UN Service Medals.

Memorable experience was to and from Korea in troop transports – stacked four high in "rucks."

He was discharged in May 1956 at Camp Pendleton with the rank of Sgt. Following the service, he worked in banking, retiring as Chairman of Country Bank. He and his wife JoAnn have four children and eight grandchildren.

**REVEREND MONSIGNOR WALTER CORNELIUS MURPHY** (1929-2012) — His life's service was to God and Country. He was a combat Marine of Korea, who became a catholic Parish Priest, in Ft.Greene Brooklyn. He served the 1st Marine Division Association, for many years as its National Chaplain and served as a member of its National Board of Directors and Executive Committee. He had a "Chaplains Corner", in The Old Breed News, (the official publication of the FMDA), where he would write "Faithful" articles for his Marines. The New York Chapter of the FMDA, has existed for more than 50 years, and

Msgr. Murphy has served as its Ordained Chaplain for most of that time. He was one of a kind, and is sorely missed.

Murphy was born in Brooklyn NY on 8/11/1929. His farther was a longshoreman on the Brooklyn docks, and his mother worked in the Rectory of their home parish of St. Brigids, in Ridgewood Brooklyn. It was the same church where he was baptized, received his first communion, where he was confirmed, and served as an altar boy. It was also where, on the day after his ordination, he performed his first solemn mass. His life long affiliation with the church continued, up until his death. On Sunday's, twice a month, he would faithfully offer the Traditional Latin Mass to the faithful. (The other two Sundays of the month, he would say the Tridentine Latin Mass, at St. John's Cemetery Chapel, in Middle Village Queens, the cemetery where he is buried).

After graduation from St. Brigids grammar school, Walter attended and graduated from Cathedral Prep Brooklyn. (Cathedral Prep was an all boys high school which prepared its students of the Brooklyn Diocese for the seminary and the priesthood). Instead of going directly into the seminary, at that time, he enrolled and graduated from St. John's University (Brooklyn Campus), with a degree in public accounting. Soon after graduation, during the Korean War, he joined the United States Marine Corps. In 1952, as a 2nd Lieutenant, he was sent to Korea. He was a combat Infantry Platoon Leader with "Item", I Company, 3rd Battalion 7th Marine Regiment, (The Magnificent 7th), of 1st Marine Division. His platoon saw combat in the "Punch Bowl". After his return and Honorable Discharge from the US Marine Corps, Capt Walter C. Murphy, obtained employment as an accountant, with the accounting firm of Peat, Marwick and Mitchell.

In time, he answered the call, and entered the seminary of Our Lady of the Angels, in Niagara NY. He was ordained into the Priesthood, for the Diocese of Brooklyn, on 5/31/58, at the St. James Pro Cathedral, by Bishop McEntegart. His first 2 years as a parish priest was spent at Our Lady of Christians Church, in Midwood Brooklyn. After which he enrolled, for 2 years, at the Catholic University of America, in Wash DC. In 1962 he returned to Brooklyn and was assigned to the faculty of his alma mater, Cathedral Prep. While there, during the build up of the Vietnam War, he petitioned the Bishop to give him leave to serve as a Naval Chaplain. His request was denied, and instead, in 1967, was given a new faculty position in the new Cathedral College Seminary, in Douglaston, Queens NY. Three years latter, he again petitioned the Bishop to enter the Navy to serve as a Chaplain to the combat Marines serving in Vietnam. Once again, the Bishop had bigger plans for this Combat Marine Priest. The Bishop felt he could be, of better service, to the Diocese, if he was transferred to the Ft. Greene section of Brooklyn and try to salvage a church on Adelphi Street, that had to close its school. The church and school were surrounded, in a neighborhood fraught with poverty, crime and drugs. It was a battle in a war, that the church had to win. The parish of the Sacred Heart was becoming a parish of new American Immigrants, and was a parish in crisis. Fr. Murphy had the spiritual challenge of his life, which required all his attention, tenacity and fortitude. He needed to draw on all of his experiences and skills, as a Combat Marine Platoon Commander, an accountant, and as a no nonsense conservative Irish Catholic Priest. He took on the thugs of the Brooklyn neighborhood that surrounded his church and school. In time, he earned their trust and respect, and some them even earned back their lost dignity and respect, for themselves, their community, and church and school. For more than 30 years, as a "Father", he opened his heart to his loyal and devoted parishioners and to the congregation of the Sacred Heart Church. In turn, they opened their hearts and souls to him.

He ministered to more than a generation of families in the parish. He would baptize them, help confirm them, marry and bury them. He reopened their school and guided and counseled many into high schools, colleges, and careers. Some would enter the armed forces and serve in Iraq and Afghanistan. He would help the new immigrants to assimilate, by exposing them to the culture that NYC offered, with bus trips to its Museums and B'way Theatres. In 1979 he was named Pastor of the Sacred Heart Church and in 1984 was named Prelate of Honor to His Holiness and became a member of the Priest's Purgatory Society and was made a Reverend Monsignor.

In 2001 he retired and became a senior priest. The Bishop named him the acting Vicar to all the Senior Priests that lived with him, in the Bishop Mugavero Residence, on the campus of the Cathedral Seminary College in Douglaston. On 6/1/2008 he celebrated 50 years as a Priest. Retirement gave him more time to tend to the spiritual needs of his Marines of the 1st Marine Division and its Association. In addition to being a moderator of the NY Catholic Accountants Guild, and moderator of the Courage Ministry of the Diocese, he served as a member of the Brooklyn Diocese Administration of Church Property Committee. In addition, he counseled the students of Cathedral Prep which was now located in Elmhurst Queens.

Fr. Water C. Murphy died 4/23/2012 at the age of 82. Although he was retired from the Sacred Heart Church for more than 10 years, on a 24 hour notice of his death, more than 200 of his former parishioners showed up in buses, traveling from Ft. Greene Brooklyn to Nassau County, for his one day, (on a weekday), evening wake. Almost all were their to testify and give testimony to this Marine Reverend Monsignor, and Man of God, who saved their church and school, and who led them in focusing their spiritual lives for the good of themselves, their families, and their community. Bishop De Mazio, the Bishop of the Diocese of Brooklyn, was the main celebrant of his Mass of a Christian Burial. It was celebrated at the Chapel of the Immaculate Conception Pastoral Center, in Douglaston. The Bishop said at that time, that it was a sad day for both him and the Brooklyn Diocese, for they had lost, one of their "Apostles". He was buried with full Marine Military Honors in St. John's Cemetery in Middle Village. In his casket, he clutched, a Marine colored Cross, with the Eagle, Globe and Anchor of the Marine Corps, in its center. Also placed in his casket were Military War ribbons from some of his Veteran Parishioners.

Msgr. Murphy was often quoted as saying, "that the joy of being a Marine, almost equaled, the joy of being a Priest". To God and Country, he was what, "Semper Fidelis", (always faithful), was all about. He lived his life, as he truly was, a USMC Reverend Monsignor, who was, "A Marine's Marine, and a Priest's Priest".

**RALPH "OHIO" MUSSEHL** was born in 1948 in Toledo, OH. After graduating from Whitmer High School he enlisted on Sept. 19, 1967 and took Boot Camp at San Diego.

He was stationed at Camp Pendleton and in Vietnam. He was involved at the tail end of TET, 1968 to November 1969 and Op. Worth, Allen Brock.

Mussehl received the Vietnam Service Medal, Vietnam Campaign, National Defense, Combat Action Ribbon, VN Civil Action, Vietnam Cross of Gallantry, Presidential Unit Citation and Meritorious Unit Citation.

He stated he was glad for the experience of doing it once for the life lessons.

Mussehl was discharged on Nov. 3, 1969 at Treasure Island, CA with the rank of Cpl.

Ralph also attended the University of Toledo for three years. He worked for Con Rail and Burlington Northern Railroads for seven years. In October 2006 retired after 25 years in US Post Office maintenance. He now runs a tree farm in Michigan.

His children are Jessica and Patricia Kazmeierczak. Grandchildren are Jaysen, Eathan, Leyah Abel, Isaias and Celeste.

**DONALD M. "DON" O'CONNOR** was born in 1933 in New York, NY, graduated from Bryant High School in 1951 and enlisted on March 13, 1952.

After Boot Camp at Parris Island, SC he attended USAFI – college level. Don was stationed at Camp Lejeune, Camp Pendleton (CA) and Quantico, VA.

He served in Korea with the 4.2 Mortar Co., 5th Marines.

He received the Korean Service Medal w/1*, Korean Presidential Unit Citation, U.N. Service Medal and National Defense Service Medal.

O'Connor was discharged on March 12, 1955 at Quantico, VA with the rank of Sgt.

He worked 32 years for CVS Logistics, retiring in 2014. He is affiliated with the VFW and in retirement likes to travel and take cruises.

Don and Leona have three children: Mary, Lori and David.

**GILBERT LEE "OLE" OLSON** was born in 1928 in the state of Washington. After high school graduation he enlisted at Tacoma, WA. Boot Camp at MCRD, San Diego was following with additional training in Infantry Machine Guns. His Marine specialties were as a Machine Gunner and Rifleman.

Olson served from 1945 to 1947 and from 1950-1951. He served in WW II in China (1946-1947) and in the Korean War at Chosin Reservoir in 1950. Ole was first discharged with the rank of Cpl. At San Pedro, CA and second with the rank of Sgt. in the state of Washington.

He received the WW II Victor Medal, Korean Defense Service Medal, Asiatic-Pacific Campaign Medal, Presidential Unit Citation and a Purple Heart.

Olson retired from the US Postal Service.

He and Janet Olson have three sons: David Olson, John Olson and Ron Olson. Grandchildren are Josh and James.

**LEONARD LEO "LEN" PARTUSCH** was born Feb. 19, 1922 in Cincinnati, OH. Graduating from Anderson High School in 1940, he enlisted on Oct. 1, 1940 and attended Boot Camp at Marine Barracks at New River.

He was engaged in battles at Guadalcanal, Cape Gloucester and Peleliu.

Partusch earned the Presidential Unit Citations awarded the First Marine Division, reinforced for service in the Solomon Islands and on Peleliu; Navy Unit Commendation for service at Cape Gloucester; Good Conduct Medal and Bar (Second Award Bar) for service 1940-1943 and 1943-1946; American Defense Service Medal with Base clasp; American Campaign Medal; Asiatic-Pacific Campaign Medal; Victory Medal WW II and China Service Medal for service in China, 1946.

On Nov. 27, 1946, Len was discharged at Parris Island, SC with the rank of Sergeant.

In retirement he was an avid reader and enjoyed playing golf.

Len and Adaline Lucking Partusch had six children: Julie Hoffmann, Michael Partusch, Mark Partusch, Annie Castle, Amy Lanzit and Rick Parsons. Grandchildren are Reade Hoffmann, Emily Maharg, Rachel Espino, Molly Partusch, Michael Partusch, Laura Conklin, John Partusch, Amanda Castle, Taylor Castle, Hannah Castle, Robert Lanzit, Jacob Lanzit, Mitchell Lanzit, Christeena Parsons and Dustin Parsons. Great grandchildren are John Hoffmann, Ryleigh Maharg, Ripken Maharg, Gerardo Espino, Gabriel Espino, Cecelia Espino, Dane Partusch, Jonah Partusch, Jack Conklin, Lucy Conklin and Killion Partusch.

Leonard Partusch, deceased as of June 10, 2017, was so proud of his service. *Submitted by Julie Hoffman in honor of her father.*

**DONALD "DON" R. PENNINGTON** enlisted at Tullahoma, TN. After Boot Camp at Parris Island, SC he received additional training at ATA Platoon.

From March 1952 to April 1953 he was in Korea and participated in "The Hook," "Bunker Hill," Reno-Vegas and Carson.

Don was a member of B Co., 1st BAT. 5th Marines received a Purple Heart w Oak Leaf Cluster.

Memorable experience was being flown to Regt. Aid Station following action on "The Hook."

Pennington was discharged at Camp Geiger, NC with the rank of Cpl.

After service, Don was a commercial pilot, retiring in 1998. In retirement, his activities are home building. Don's wife is Loraine Adair Pennington.

He states, "As an old man, I reflect back on my Marine Corps service of 65 years ago with a great deal of pride."

**STEPHEN "STEVE" PERCY** was born in 1931 and after graduation from Deerfield Academy in 1948, enlisted on June 5, 1951. Boot Camp was at Parris Island, with additional training at 24th SBC, Quantico, VA.

For his service, he received two Vietnam Medals and Korean Service Medal.

Steve was discharged on June 5, 1963 at San Francisco, CA.

**RANDAL E. PETERSON** was born 3 March 1949 in Kankakee, Illinois and raised in Downey, California where he attended Santa Fe High School and later completed two years of college. He enlisted in the Marine Corps in 1968 and completed Recruit Training at MCRD and Camp Pendleton, California. On 14 February 1969, he deployed with Golf Company, 2nd Battalion, 9th Marine Regiment, Third Marine Division to Quang Tri Province, Republic of Vietnam. He fought in Operations Dewey Canyon, Utah Mesa, Apache Snow, Cameron Falls and Virginia Ridge as a Rifleman, Fire Team Leader and Grenadier.

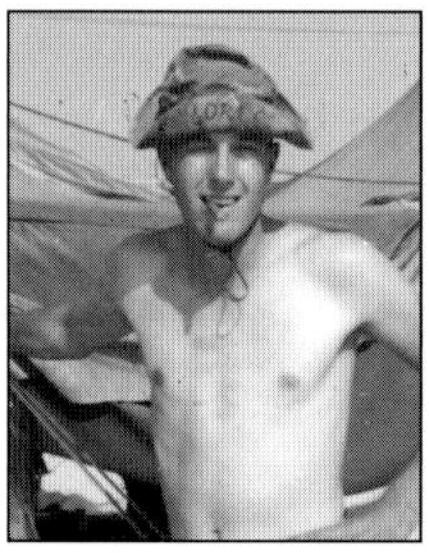

At the age of 35, he re-enlisted in the Marine Corps Reserve and was assigned to 3rd ANGLICO, Terminal Island, California where he completed training as a Naval Gunfire Spotter, Paratrooper and Pathfinder. Becoming a Sergeant in 1986, he worked as a Fire Support Man Team Chief until his promotion to Staff Sergeant and assumed the duties of Naval Gunfire Chief and Operations Chief.

In February 1991, 3rd ANGLICO was mobilized in Support of Operations Desert Shield and Desert Storm and stood at the ready at Camp Pendleton. After mobilization and completing the Ground Operations Specialist Course, he was promoted to Gunnery Sergeant and served as Platoon Sergeant 1992-1994.

From 1994 to 1997 he served as I MACE Operations Chief, Camp Pendleton. Promoted to 1st Sergeant in 1997, he was assigned to H & S Battery, 4th LAAD Battalion Pasadena, California where he was selected as the Battalion Sergeant Major 2000-2003.

In January 2003, he was recalled to active duty and assigned as MARFORRES Sergeant Major of 3rd ANGLICO becoming the Senior Advisor to the Commanding Officer. 3rd ANGLICO was mobilized in support of Operation Enduring Freedom and deployed to Camp Commando, Kuwait. Once in country, 3rd ANGLICO Headquarters Cell was tasked with supporting the 1st UK Division during Operation Iraqi Freedom and later was reassigned to I MEF where they conducted numerous combat patrols, convoy and personal security detail missions between Babylon and Baghdad. 3rd ANGLICO returned to Terminal Island with a hero's welcome on 7 September 2003.

In 2004, Sergeant Major Peterson was assigned to HQ Battalion, Quantico Marine Base to participate on the Reserve SNCO Promotion Board. Reassigned to I MACE, Camp Pendleton, he was mobilized and assumed the duties of I MEF Headquarters Group Sergeant Major where he served as the Senior Enlisted Advisor to the Commanding General until I MEF returned from Iraq in 2005. He was then assigned to the Reserve Support Site as Senior Enlisted Advisor to assist in the decommissioning of I MACE and its transition to I MEF IMA as well as the mobilization of 3D Civil Affairs Group. In 2006 he filled the Group Sergeant Major position for I MHG until their return in 2007. A dedicated Marine for thirty years, Sergeant Major Peterson retired in 2008.

Among his many awards and medals are the Bronze Star, Meritorious Service Medal, Navy and Marine Corps Achievement Medal, Combat Action Ribbon with Gold Star and Global War on Terrorism Service Medal.

In civilian life, Randy worked in construction as a steamfitter for thirty-seven years. He was married to his high school sweetheart for forty-one years. He shared his enthusiasm for hunting, fishing and surfing with his sons and golfing with his family and friends.

On 30 November 2014, Sergeant Major Randal E. Peterson, age 65, passed away from cancer at City of Hope, California after a twenty-one month battle against his fiercest enemy. His loyal devotion to God, country and family is his legacy. He is survived by his wife Rosalie, his sons Seth and Micah, two grandchildren and three sisters.

**LAWRENCE "RABBIT" PIERCE** arrived in Vietnam on Dec. 21, 1967 and was assigned to Delta Btty., 2nd BN, 11th Marines. He first saw action on Jan. 7, 1968 and then during TET. Delta was attached to the 1st BN, 5th Marines during the whole time of his deployment, including during the Battle of Hue City.

In April of 1968 he was sent to the Fire Support Teams of 1/5 as a radio operator, eventually being attached to Alpha Co. until late January 1969. At that time he was sent to the Battalion CP of 1/5 as part of the Fire Support Control Center at Liberty Bridge, eventually becoming a Water Sgt. He was there on March 19 when NVA sappers came through the wire with flame throwers and helped with the counter attack that destroyed the enemy.

1/5 was sent into the Arizona Territory in May/June of 1969 and when a NVA regiment attacked it, he was badly wounded on June 7. He returned to duty and left Nam in early August 1969 as a Corporal with seven stars on his Campaign Ribbon.

He was a Postal Carrier. Larry and Ellen have one daughter, Ruth.

**L/CPL FRANK M. PIETRAS** and the 159 Marines and Corpsmen "Killed in Action" — The 50th Anniversary: Operation Buffalo, July 2-14, 1967. Fifty years ago on the 4th of July 1967, "in the summer of love", 21-year-old L/Cpl Frank M. Pietras — who volunteered for the Marines for two years under the "buddy system" of the volunteer draft) — was killed

in action in the legendary battle of Operation Buffalo, defending Northern I Corps, Con Thien, "McNamara's Line — the Trace and the DMZ (aka "Dead Marine Zone"). These "Band of Brothers in Arms" fought savagely in "the meat grinder of the marketplace." They were Marines on a mission, displaying their "true grit" and "do or die" Marine Corps Mettle, by courageously and gallantly giving their full measure, sacrificing all their tomorrows in selfless service and devotion to each other, their Corps, and Country. In the end, 159 Marines and Corpsmen "all went down together" on Buffalo.

Today, few remember their names, and fewer are left to tell their stories. They may be gone, but they will never be forgotten by "the few and the proud" Marine defenders and survivors of I Corps. Still, to this day "we carry our dead" and continue to guide our "walking dead." We hold high the burning "Torch of Freedom" that has been passed to us, "to you from falling hands we throw the torch."

As torchbearers and Marine combat warriors, we have an unyielding devotion, and a duty and obligation, to Honor and remember their names, tell their stories, and remember their long forgotten deeds that came from their hearts and souls.

Fifty years ago, "in the summer of love," they valiantly upheld the highest and finest traditions of the United States Marine Corps and the United States of America. Ooh-Rah! *Dedicated by Richard "MoonMan" Mooney, I Corps, '66-67.*

**RICHARD EARL POSPISIL** was born Nov. 22, 1931 in Cedar Rapids, IA. After graduation from Wilson High School, he also attended Iowa State University (BSEE, 1957, Stanford University (Work EE) and San Jose State University (Grad Work EE Bus. Admin.)

On Jan. 13, 1951 Richard enlisted at Cedar Rapids, IA. At Boot Camp at San Diego, he attended Treasure Island ET School, San Diego MCRD Special Equipment and Marine Corp Aviation.

The medals he received for service were the United Nations, Korea and Good Conduct. Richard was discharged on Dec. 24, 1953 at Treasure Island, CA.

Richard is a retired telecommunications company executive who has many inventions to his credit and has published magazine articles and technical papers.

He enjoys sailing, philately, sports and golf in retirement.

Richard's wife is Anne W. Pospisil. His children are Lisa, Jane, Donald, Sara and Mariah.

**CALVIN A. POWERS,** born in Dungannon, VA in 11926, graduated from Nickelsville High School. In November 1943 he enlisted and after Boot Camp at San Diego, he received training in Small Arms.

He was stationed in San Diego, Camp Pendleton, San Francisco and Camp Shoemaker.

Calvin was in battles in the South Pacific, Okinawa and China.

On May 31, 1946 he was discharged at Camp Lejeune with the rank of Corporal.

In civilian life he was a printer for the state of California. After retiring in 1986 he is now a part-time farmer.

Calvin and Nancy have three children: Connie, Calvin Jr. and Alan. Sunne, April, Terry and Jerry are their grandchildren.

**RICHARD C. PRINCE** was born on 18 March 1945 in Columbia, South Carolina, and raised in Washington, D.C. He attended Cardozo High School. Unable to find a job in the DC Area, he visited a Marine Corps Recruiter in Washington, D.C. and took a test. He was placed on the 190- day delay plan. 190 days later, Richard found himself at Parris Island, South Carolina, where he began basic training.

After completing basic training he was sent to the U.S. Marine base, Camp LeJeune, in Jacksonville, North Carolina. His next duty station was Camp Pendleton, California. After about six weeks there, he received orders to report to WestPac in Vietnam. He reported to Da Nang by way of military contract aircraft. After arriving that night, the next morning a truck picked him up and several other Marines who were fresh out of boot camp. He was transported to Delta Company, 1st Battalion, 5th Marines. He was stationed at Hoi An, Phu Loc, and eventually he went to Hue.

At Hue, Richard joined the rest of the battalion. Their assignment was to take the Dong Ba Tower. Receiving rounds from all directions, they followed a tank down the street. By the time they got to the tower, a unit was already there. They joined the unit and engaged in heavy fighting. On the day before and on that day there was a heavy overcast accompanied by rain. Eventually, the sky cleared and with artillery and air support, Delta Company got to the base of the tower, which was essentially mounds of rubble. They found a fellow Marine buried in the rubble. Richard assisted in unearthing fellow Marine, Thomas Zwetow. Pulling him up from the rubble by his flak jacket, Richard pulled Zwetow out of the hole and began to move him down the rubble to the bottom of the tower. After placing him on his shoulder, Richard's helmet fell off. He placed Zwetow down on the ground and began to drag him because they were receiving sniper rounds. Richard dragged him down to the bottom of the tower where corpsman took over. After dropping off Zwetow, Richard returned to the top of the tower to bring down other wounded Marines who were unconscious.

After completing that mission, Richard and Delta 1/5 began to move position to across the street where they engaged in house to house fighting. Richard and two other Marines, moved up the street between the Perfume River and the houses on the other side of the street. They settled in houses for the night. The next morning, they got up and set out on the street receiving small arms fire while going house to house. At one point, Richard was hit in the neck. Unable to speak or call for a corpsman, he turned around and began to walk back towards the aid station. He encountered ARVN who were sweeping up the road. They saw Richard wounded and came to his aid. They transported him to an American aid station. Richard recovered in Camp Zama, Japan.

At the end of the war, Richard was medically discharged and retired from the Marine Corps. He moved back to his hometown, Washington DC and took a job as an airport police officer at National Airport. He later joined the U.S. Marshals Service where he stayed for 20 years.

Richard still lives in the Washington DC area where he lives with his wife and two daughters.

**ANTHONY J PROCASSINI** was born on April 17, 1921 in Lambertville, NJ to immigrant Parents Andrew and Lucia Procassini. He lived in Newark, NJ but eventually his family moved to Princeton, NJ in 1937 where he graduated from Princeton High in 1939. He enrolled at University of Michigan in September 1939 until 1943. December 7, 1943 he was drafted into the Marine Corp in Detroit, MI.

He was sent to boot camp in San Diego, CA for approximately 3 months with the 1137 Platoon (Picture attached). After boot camp he was sent to Camp Elliott, CA for Mortar Training. On April 5th, 1944 he married Marguerite Dawn Trombley of Ann Arbor, MI (they celebrated their 73rd anniversary in April 2017).

In May of 1944 he boarded the USS Rochambeau for the South Pacific. He transferred from New Caledonia to Pavuvu in the Solomon Islands. He thought as he approached the Island was "what a hell hole". He continued training in order to eventually deploy to combat in late August to Peleliu where they engaged in their first combat September 15, 1944. He returned to Pavavu thinking that after Peleliu, Pavavu was now a beautiful island.

April 1st Easter Sunday 1945 we invaded Okinawa. The invasion for Okinawa was made up principally of 2 Marine Divisions the 1st and the 6th as well as 2 Army Divisions the 7th and 96th Infantry with back up of the 77th and 27th Infantry Division. The first Marine Division was assigned to cross the Island and turn north, while the Army units would go south where the Japanese had most of their troops. The first few days the marine troops encountered very few Japanese troops and casualties were very low. In the later part of April the Marines headed south to assist the Army Units where fighting was very fierce. May 15th, 1945 he was injured in combat and taken to a field hospital where he was treated for his injuries before returning to his unit. The Island was declared secured on June 21st, 1945. He remained on Okinawa in a tent camp.

On the 8th of August, 1945 the first Atomic Bomb was dropped on Japan and by the 15th the Japanese had surrendered. On September 1st they boarded ship for China for an occupation assignment before returning state side where he was discharged from Great Lakes Naval Station in February 1946.

He spent the last 70 years in Ann Arbor, MI with a career in the Human Resources. He continues to enjoy his family of 10 children, 18 grandchildren and 2 great-grandchildren. He would like to hear from anyone who served with him in the I Company, 3rd Battalion 1st Marine Division from 1943 to 1946.

**HOWARD L. PURDY** was born Dec 14, 1940 in Vinton, IA. He graduated from Washington High in 1958 and also attended CR Business for two years.

Purdy enlisted on July 4, 1958. After boot camp at San Diego he serviced with H/2/7 LAS PO GAS – 7th Marines, 3rd Marine Division, 9th Marines and H/2/9. Memorable experiences was the travel.

In November 1961 Howard was discharged as LCPL at San Diego.

After retiring in 2007 as Roofing Project Manager he is involved with Marine Corps League, AMVETS and on the CR Veterans Council.

**BENNIE L. REYNOLDS** was born Sept. 23, 1927 in Hall County, GA. His family moved to Porterdale, GA, where Ben attended school. While attending Porterdale High school, he played basketball, baseball, was on the swim team, and became an Eagle Scout. He enlisted in the Marine Corps when Pearl Harbor was attacked. Following Parris Island boot camp, he was assigned to B-1-7 under Chesty Puller. Campaigns included Cape Gloucester, Guadalcanal and Peleliu, earning three Purple Hearts and a gold star. On R&R in Melbourne, Australia, Ben pitched a double-header in the Regimental Championship Baseball Tournament for the victory.

In 1948 he met his sweetheart, Reba, in the Five and Dime in Covington, GA. Ben graduated from the Bob Barr umpire school and then trade school, becoming a Master Plumber. He closed his own business to work for the State of Georgia and became shop foreman at Georgia Tech until retirement. Ben become a deacon in the church, completed correspondence courses at Mercer University and recorded his memories of WW II in a book, *The Greatest of the Great.* Ben lived the motto "God, Country, Family" throughout his life. He is survived by his wife, three daughters and two grandchildren.

**CHARLES "DUSTY" RHODES** was born July 17, 1927, Detroit, MI. After graduating from Redford High he enlisted in June 1945 at Detroit, MI. After Boot Camp at Parris Island he received additional training in projections.

He was stationed at Camp Lejeune and in North China. Memorable experience was being aboard the *USS Wakefield* from Norfolk, VA to North China.

In October 1946 Dusty was discharged at Great Lakes with the rank of PFC.

In 1949 he became a Detroit Police Officer, serving for 25 years. After retirement in 1975 he continues as a Probation Officer for Montcalm County, MI.

Dusty and Dolores have two children, Susan and Mick and two grandchildren, Christopher and Carly.

**VINCENT "SARGE" RIOS** was born in Houston, TX. He graduated from Diamond Hill Jarvis High School in 1964 and earned four college degrees: A.A. degree in Behavioral Sciences, B.A. in Psychology, M.A. in interdisciplinary Social Science and M.A. in Public Administration.

After enlisting in 1964 at Dallas, TX, Boot Camp was at MCRD, San Diego. He received additional training in several areas.

His first tour of duty in Vietnam was from 1965 to 1966. His second TOD began in 1968. On Feb. 6, 1969, six days before the end of his second tour, he was on patrol over a mile-long paddy. Halting his platoon, he advanced to speak with his point man. He set off an enemy explosive device which immediately vaporized both his legs, left his right arm dangling from his shoulder and partially amputated his left index and ring fingers. He spent 10 months in hospitals recovering, receiving physical and occupational therapy and many surgeries. He was told he would never walk again. Not accepting that, he devised a new concept for his prosthetic right arm and crutch that allowed him to stand and walk within 10 months.

Sarge was discharged in July 1969 with the rank of Sgt. E-5.

In 1989 he was appointed the Assistant Regional Administrator, Dept. of Labor's Employment and Training Service, Regions IX and X. Since retirement in 2001 he is active with the 1st Marine Division Association.

Vincent and his wife, Cheryl, met in Junior High School. They reconnected and were married in 1993. Between them, they have five children and six grandchildren.

**ROBERT JEFFORY "JEFF" ROBERTS** was born June 29, 1946 in Cleveland, OH. He was raised in the Los Angeles, CA area where he attended Morningside High School in Inglewood, CA. After graduating in 1964, he attended one year of college. Then deciding that he did not want to get drafted, he joined the US Marines. He entered boot camp at Marine Corps Recruit Depot San Diego Feb. 15, 1966, four days after his mother died from a heart attack. He excelled in his boot camp training as he was promoted to squad leader and he also qualified with a very high score at the rifle range. On the day that he returned from the rifle range, he was participating in the pugle stick competition and severely broke his ankle. Instead of two months of boot camp, it became 4 1/2 months of boot camp. He graduated from boot camp June 28, 1966. He then went through Infantry Training (ITR) at Camp Pendleton, CA June 29 until Aug. 2, 1966. On Aug. 28, 1966, he reported to Marine Barracks Naval Operations Base Norfolk, VA. His training for the 2533 10-week Radio Telegraph School started on Sept. 12, 1966 and continued until he graduated two weeks early on Nov. 13, 1966. He was waiting for the rest of his class to graduate, so he could move on to his next duty station. When on Nov. 14, 1966, even though he was a E-2 Private First Class, he was given the job as the Police Sergeant for the Marine Barracks, which normally is a E-5 Sergeant. Then on the Dec. 5, 1966, he received his orders for Vietnam.

From Jan. 10 through Feb. 5, 1967, he went through training at Staging Bn. Camp Pendleton, CA. Then after spending a few days in Okinawa, Japan, he arrived in Vietnam Feb. 10, 1967. He received his orders for the 1st Shore Party Bn. 1st Marine Division. He was with 1st Shore Party Bn. from Feb. 11, 1967 until Feb. 15, 1968. He was a radioman for an HST (Helicopter Support Team). He was attached to Headquarters Companies with various Battalions of the 1st, 5th and 7th Marine Regiments, 1st Marine Division. His responsibilities involved the requesting and coordinating of resupply missions and medivacs. He participated in eight major combat operations and several minor "no name" combat operations. The principal operations that he was involved with were: Operations Union and Union II April 25, to June 6, 1967, that resulted in him being awarded the Presidential Unit Citation. Operation Cochise from Aug. 9 to Aug. 18, 1967. Operation Swift Sept. 4, to Sept. 15, 1967. Operation Shelbyville Sept. 21, to Sept. 28, 1967 his last combat operation, that on Sept. 25, 1967, he coordinated an 8-minute medivac that resulted on June 22, 2015, at the 1st Marine Division Association Reunion in San Diego, CA in him being awarded the Navy and Marine Corps Achievement Medal with the V device, for achieving a very fast "8-minute medivac" under combat conditions during Operation Shelbyville Sept. 25, 1967. Then after being involved for two weeks in the defense of Danang during the Tet Offensive, he rotated out of Vietnam on Feb. 13, 1968.

March 16, 1968, he reported to 5th Force Recon Co. 5th Marine Division Camp Del Mar Camp Pendleton, CA. After 5th Force Recon Co. rotated to Vietnam on March 25, 1968, he received orders for Bravo Co. Hotel Battery, 3rd Bn., 13th Marines, 5th Marine Division. At the end of his enlistment, he left the Marine Corps Feb. 15, 1969. After leaving the Marines, he worked in the Aerospace Industry. During that time, he attended college and received a degree in Photojournalism. Years later, he worked in the Security Industry for several years before going back to college and acquiring a 2nd degree in Administration of Justice. In 1994, he obtained a California State Private Investigators License and started his own business of Private Investigations and Security Consulting. He is now semi-retired and living in Lawndale, CA.

His Medals and Awards that he acquired as a Marine were the: National Defense Service Medal, Good Conduct Medal, Vietnam Campaign Medal. Vietnam Service Medal with three Bronze Stars, RVN Gallantry Cross Unit Citation, RVN Civic Action Unit Citation, Combat Action Ribbon, Presidential Unit Citation, Navy and Marine Corps Achievement Medal with the V device.

**WILLIAM M. RODESCHIN** was born October, 1926 in Newport, New Hampshire and he has spent his entire life living on the property that he was born and raised. Like many from the era, Bill left school early to help the family work what was a large chicken farm, and to drive chicken delivery trucks between the farm in Newport to Boston and New York City.

When Bill (Rody was the family nickname) turned 17 in 1943, he knew it was his turn to enlist so drove the two hours (then) to Manchester, NH and joined the Marine Corps. That spring of 1944 he took the train from Boston Massachusetts

to Yemassee, South Carolina and then basic training at Parris Island. Finishing basic, Bill headed for Camps Lejeune and Pendleton for additional training; then by ship to Hawaii, Eniwetok, and in July, 1944....Guam.

His early missions on Guam were with the 3rd Division, 9th Marines, in the jungles hunting hold-out Japanese soldiers....then working supply and service for the various ground and air bases on the island before being transferred to China with the 1st Division, 7th Marines, assigned to a weapons company as peace keepers and guarding railroads and supply trains.

Bill was honorably discharged at Great Lakes, Ill October 1946.

Returning home, he resumed driving chicken delivery truck for a short time, and then for a while driving dump trucks and learning masonry for the growing number of highway construction projects in New Hampshire at the time.

The biggest changes that would both affect and define his future occurred when he began his training as a machinist in what was known then as New England's "Precision Valley." He learned his trade working for Jones & Lampson and Co. (a precision tool manufacture) beginning in 1950. Then.... building on his machinist training and his love for firearms, in 1962 Bill started (his brother would later join him) Rody's Gun Shop, a retail and custom gun shop; selling guns and shooting supplies, doing repairs, gunsmithing, and building custom rifles....a business that he still owns and operates today (along with his brother) at 91 years of age.

In 1972 he had an invitation from Sturm, Ruger & Co. (today the largest American manufacturer of sporting firearms) to come to work for them....using both his talents as a machinist and as a gunsmith....to help with the company's expanding woodworking department; building gunstock lathe turning masters, setting up machines, and eventually as a shop floor supervisor.

Bill retired in 1990, purchased a Class A motorhome, and for the next 10 years he and his wife Barbara toured the U.S. during the winters while continuing to operate his business the rest of the year.

Bill and Barbara raised three children and today have 4 grandchildren, and 5 great grandchildren.

Prior to the war Bill was a member and a First Class Scout of the Boy Scouts of America, Troop No. 318 (often participating in the area war scrap drives) and returned to scouting after the war as Assistant Scout Master, Troop 318 and Scout Master for Troop 325. He has been certified and a volunteer of New Hampshire Fish and Game, as a Hunter Education instructor; just completing 55 active years. Bill also coached the Indians, Little League team for three years, and most of his team members, now in their late 40s, stay in touch and remember him fondly for the life's lessons he taught.

Today Bill is an active member of the American Legion; the Kearsage Marines; a life member of the Old Breed, and the NRA.

Proud of his service and his status as a former Marine, Bill flies the Marine Corps flag in front of his home every day.

**JUAN JIMENEZ "ROD" RODRIGUEZ** was born Jan. 22, 1931 in Detroit, MI and attended Sidney Lanier High School.

On March 2, 1949 at enlisted at San Antonio, TX and after Boot Camp at MCRD, San Diego, CA he took the Drill Instructors Course.

During his career he was stationed at Camp Pendleton; Camp Lejeune; Corpus Christi, TX; MCAS, Iwakuni, Japan; North Camp, Fuji, Japan.

Rod served in Korea in 1950, during the Cuban Missile Crisis in 1962 and in Vietnam from 1966 to 1968. He received the Navy/Marine Corps Commendation w/Combat V and a Purple Heart.

Memorable experiences include his daughter being born in Laguna, CA (1969); knocking out a machine gun position during assault on How Hill overlooking the MSR and dispatching a Chinese hand grenade thrower, Suong, Korea (1950) and attack on Village Phu Tai, Operation Badger Catch/Saline, Vietnam (1968).

After discharge as Gy Sgt on Aug. 30, 1966 at Camp Pendleton, Rod was a security guard, NASA (1969-1971), driver-delivery, Wallace Company (1970), Clerk for US Postal Service from 1972 to 2003 when he retired.

He spends his time working, traveling, shooting, golf and reading.

Rod and Palmira have four children: Theresa, Esperanza, Domingo and Adrian and five grandchildren.

**GYSGT. MELVIN LEE ROLLINS** grew up in DeLand Fl. and attended DeLand High School. Joined Marine Corps October 1969 sent to Parris Island. Graduated boot camp and went to ITR training at Stone Bay, Camp Lejeune as 0311. March 1970, joined Second Force Reconnaissance Company. Attended Jump, Scuba, Guerilla Warfare School. 1974 joined Second Recon Bn. Attended BUDS, Amphib Recon, WSSI sub ops and Cross Country Ski Instructor. Left Marine Corps 1976-1980.

Rejoined 1980 sent to 1st recon BN, Camp Telega, Camp Pendleton one year. Then to 2nd Class Divers School, Naval Amphibious base, Coronado as Dive Instructor three years. Married Mari Osterman 1984. Divorced in 2000. Have 2 fantastic children: Chad and Theresa. 1984 back to 2nd Recon BN, Charlie Co.: attended Jump Master School, Sub Ops, Mountain Warfare Training Bridgeport, Ca.

Next stop Okinawa, Japan with 3/2 for six months. Returned Camp Lejeune Transferred to Division G-3 as SNCOIC of Training. Next came Division Schools MTU and the Rifle and Pistol Team. Joined SOTG. Attended Sniper School. Instructed MEU-SOC and Urban Sniping. On to Guantanamo Bay, Cuba one year as Guard Chief for fence line security. Back to Camp Pendleton as HAZMAT Inspector. Retired from camp Pendleton 1996.

**COL. MURRAY FONTAINE ROSE, USMC RET.** was born in Hibbing, MN on April 17, 1921 and graduated from Hibbing High School in 1938. He entered Duke University, Durham, NC. During his senior year, Dec. 7, 1941, Japan attacked Pearl Harbor. He received orders from the Marine Corps later that month to report to the Marine Barracks Navy Yard, Philadelphia, PA. He and other college seniors were commissioned Second Lieutenants on Feb. 1, 1942 in the Marine Corps Reserve.

After more training, they were sent to the Pacific, landing in Wellington, New Zealand. On Aug. 7, 1942 US Marines attacked Guadalcanal. Rose took part in the Battle of Tenaru River, when the Japanese attempted to take over Henderson Field, but failed.

Left Guadalcanal Dec. 15, 1942 and landed at Brisbane, Australia Dec. 20, 1942. Temporary duty February through May 11, 1943. School of Military Engineering, Liverpool, N.S.W., Australia. In December 1943 the Marines were preparing to land on Cape Gloucester, Rose fell 30 feet. Was flown to USA Hospital APO #929. He was unconscious and had many broken bones. After several hospitals overseas, he was transported to US Naval Hospital, Oakland, CA in February 1944. In May after leave, was sent to Camp Lejeune, New River, NC. Then in March 1945 sent to Guam. In August the war ended and he was sent to Sasebo, Japan with Occupation Forces. He was "head" engineer in charge of building new roads. Returned to US in December.

In 1950 he took part in the Inchon Landing, Korea and while there was in charge of getting Marines on ships as they came down from the Chosin Reservoir. Back to US, October 1951 and stationed at Quantico.

After retirement from the Marine Corps he worked several years for the Army Defense Supply, Alexandria VA and later the US Dept. of Energy.

Rose died March 15, 2012 in Ashburn, VA. He is survived by his wife, Barbara Field Rose and daughters Patricia Rose Guyette (John), Beverly Rose Horton (Wright), granddaughter Sarah Horton Hidalgo (George) and great grandson Elliott Hidalgo. Predeceased by grandson James Fontaine Horton and brother Ronald Rose.

**WOODSON A. "WOODY" SADLER JR.** was born March 7, 1944 at Salinas, CA. He graduated from Fork Union Military Academy; attended VMI – BS Civil Eng., 1966 and U. Southern California – BAS – System Management, 1972.

Sadler enlisted in June 1964 and was commission June 1966. After Boot Camp at Quantico, he received additional training in TBS, FAOBC, Comm. School and CS.

During his career he was stationed at Quantico, KMCAS, Camp Pendleton, Camp Lejeune, HQMC and in Okinawa. He was involved in battles in Vietnam, Dia Do and TET.

He received the following medals: DMSM, LOM x 2, NAM/V and MSM.

Memorable experiences include CO, HQBN for 26 months and the comradeship with other Marines.

Col. Sadler was discharged in July 1993 at VMI.

Professionally was Adjunct VMI and affiliated with George C. Marshall Foundation.

Retirement activities include Rotary Club, church and historical society.

He and Col. Lori Sadler have two children, Woody III and Ann and two grandchildren, Alex and Arthur.

**JOSEPH IGNACIO "JOE" SALAS JR.** was born June 3, 1931 at Calvert, TX. He graduated from High School in East Bakersfield, CA and attained his AA in 1956 from Bakersfield, CA.

On Feb. 27, 1951 Joe enlisted and after Boot Camp at San Diego, CA received additional training, 1369, Lejeune, NC.

Joe served in Korea from December 1951 to December 1952 and received a Letter of Commendation w/Combat V and Purple Heart and Good Conduct Medal.

Salas says, "The Marines took a young man that had never had a full meal, fed him, taught him respect for others and set him up for life."

Memorable experience was survival: constant near-problem behavior with moments of doing my job at a superior level.

Sgt. Salas was discharged at Camp Del Mar, CA.

Joe has been a real estate broker since 1956 to the present. He still works full time but travels and has lots of activities with his children.

Joe (divorced three times – Carmen, Katie and Gina) is presently married to Flor. He has six children: James Donald, Charles J. Steve, Maria and Joe III and eight grandchildren: Gregg, Lauren, Elena, Danny, Soph, Nate, Vicente and Miguel.

**JOHN J. SALERNO** was born in Chicago, IL on May 8, 1933 and graduated from St. Phillips High School in Chicago. He enlisted on Sept. 22, 1952 where he immediately left for 10 weeks of boot camp

and six weeks of advanced training to be a Machine Gunner. John was a PFC to Korea joining the 1st

Battalion 5th Marines as a Machine Gunner. John acquired two Battle Stars.

On July 17, 1953 John was going on a Combat Patrol. That night he was bunked off patrol by two other Marine buddies who were then killed in combat firefight. He will always remember that night and those two special men...Corporal Stevens and Corporal Knorr, who had never been out on patrol.

He was discharged on Sept. 14, 1955 as a Corporal from Yorktown, VA.

John is married to Lucille Granata Salerno for 55 years this past July 22, 2017. John has two children, daughter Mary Lou Scala and son A.J. Salerno. He has a total of two granddaughters. Lucia and Olivia who is 13 years old.

John is a sole proprietor/business entrepreneur for over 50 years. He spends most of his time exercising, watching movies, traveling with his family and enjoying all his time with his family.

**RAMON "SPEEDY/SKIVVY HONCHO" SANDOVAL,** born June 21, 1949 in El Paso, TX graduated from Carson High School in 1968 and attended Harbor Jr. College for 2-1/2 years, attaining an Auto Mechanic degree.

On May 25, 1968 he enlisted at Los Angeles, CA (he says he was a Hollywood Marine). Boot Camp was at M.C.R.D., San Diego, CA and Camp Pendleton. Additional training was Basic Specialist Training, Motor Vehicle Operators Course at Camp Pendleton.

Serving in Danang, Vietnam from 1968 to 1969, he received the National Defense Service Medal, Vietnam Service Medal w/1*, Letter of Outstanding Performance (3), Letter of Commendation, Republic of Vietnam Cross of Gallantry w/ Palm and Vietnam Campaign Medal w/60.

Memorable experience was when stationed at 1st Med., on Saturday in his ambulance he made a run to China Beach and picked up 2 skivvy girls and picked up GIs and charged them $50 per half hour. He drove through China Beach, Red Beach and all through Danang, dropping and picking up GIs all through his run just to make extra money. He was called the "Skivvy Honcho."

He was honorably discharged on June 25, 1968 with the rank of LCPL E-3.

He drove for J.B. Hunt Transportation from 1994 until retirement in 2010.

Retirement activities include golf, bowling, hunting with the sons of American Legion, does fundraising for charitable organizations all through the year and studying Filipino and Chinese Boxing.

He and Maryhelen C. have been 45 years. No children, but three dogs and two cats: Bailey, Bandit, Dusty, Nika and Tiger.

**SERGEANT MAJOR ROBERT F. SINGER, USMC RETIRED,** was born Feb. 11, 1948 in Brooklyn, NY. Upon graduation from high school in 1966 he enlisted in the US Marine Corps and reported to the Marine Corps Recruit Depot, Parris Island, SC for recruit training.

In a career that spanned 30 years, he served in nine infantry battalions in the First, Second, Third and Fourth Marine Divisions. He held every infantry enlisted leadership billet at the battalion level to include Battalion S-3 Chief, Company First Sergeant and Battalion Sergeant Major. He also served as an armor crewman in the anti-tank company "ONTOS" (an infantry MOS billet) in the Third Tank Battalion in RVN.

Special duty assignments include Drill Instructor Duty at OCS, Quantico, VA; Marine Security Guard Embassy Duty in Cyprus, Tanzania and Belgium, Barracks Duty in the Republic of the Philippines and both I&I Duty and Recruiting Duty in Buffalo, NY. He also served as a Security Guard and Combat Air Crewman in the First Marine Aircraft Wing in RVN.

In 1971 he graduated from Marine Corps Drill Instructor School at Parris Island, SC and later the US Army Airborne Course at Fort Benning, GA. In 1972 he was meritoriously promoted to Staff Sergeant.

His last two billets held on active duty were Sergeant Major of the 11th Marine Expeditionary Unit and Sergeant Major of the Second Marine Expeditionary Force

His service in the First Marine Division ranges from basic rifleman in 1967 (1/1) to Battalion Sergeant Major (1/4) in 1991 to 1992.

Most significant awards are the Purple Heart, Combat Action Ribbon, Combat Aircrew Wings, Marine Corps Expeditionary Medal (Rwanda), Armed Forces Expeditionary Medal (Somalia), Vietnam Service Medal (7 stars), Southwest Asia Service Meal (1 star) and the Korea Defense Service Medal.

Sergeant Major Singer is a proud life member of the Marine Corps League. He also holds life memberships in most of the major Veteran Service Organizations to include the VFW which he first joined in 1967. He is a life member of the First Marine Division Association.

**PAUL W. SIVERSON** was born in Queens, NY on 11 December 1951 and graduated from Port Richmond HS, Staten Island, NY in 1969. He enlisted in July 1970, went to Parris Island and then Camp Geiger, training as a 0331 Machine Gunner. He served with 1/1 in Vietnam and then 2/7 in Camp Pendleton.

Reenlisting in 1972 he received a lat move to the 01 field and transferred to MCRS Newark, NJ. In 1976 he transferred to Guam for duty on the USS PROTUES (AS-19) and in 1978 transferred

to 4/10 Camp Lejeune. In 1981 he transferred to the US Embassy in Manila as the Admin Chief and in 1984 transferred to 3d Maintenance Bn, Okinawa.

Selected for 1stSgt in 1986, he moved to 9th MT Bn and in 1987 transferred to MarBks Adak, AK. In 1989 he transferred to Okinawa with 3d Supply Bn, and upon selection to SgtMaj in 1991, deployed to Desert Storm. Upon return he moved to BSSG-9 and then 3d Supply Bn.

In 1992 he transferred to 1st SRIG Camp Pendleton and deployed to Somalia. 1995 to 1998 assigned to MCSFCo Bangor, WA and in 1998 transferred to 2dMarDiv as the SgtMaj 10th Marine Regiment.

Siverson was discharged from service at Camp Lejeune, NC in August 2000, with the rank of SgtMaj. He is married to Sylvia. They have two children, Paul Jr. and Michelle, and five grandchildren.

**HOWARD C. SNOWDEN** was born in Green River, WY on May 29, 1941. He ended up in Denver, CO in 1956, dropped out of high school in January 1959 and enlisted in September 1959. Went to San Diego and then numerous assignments afterward.

He arrived in Vietnam in April 1967 and subsequently was assigned to 1/7. He returned to CONUS in May 1968. After several schools and duty stations, his last assignment was to the 7th MAB in 29 Palms.

In 1988 he invited the CMC General to his retirement ceremony. The General accepted and officiated at Snowden's retirement in August 1988.

For his service, Snowden received the following medals: MSM, NCM w/V and CAR.

He went on to a second career as a Deputy Sheriff with the San Bernardino County, CA Sheriff Department. He is married to Rachael and they have three children: John, Jeff and June.

**WILLIAM E. "BILL" SNYDER** was born April 18, 1926 in Cincinnati, OH. He earned his GED from Withrow High School and in 1958 earned a B.A. from the University of Cincinnati.

In April 1944 he enlisted at Cincinnati. After Boot Camp at Parris Island, he received BAR training.

Stationed at Camp Lejeune and Camp Pendleton, he served in battles in the Pacific – Peleliu and Okinawa. He received the Presidential and Navy Unit Citation and two Purple Hearts.

On April 16, 1946 Snyder was discharged at Quantico, VA with the rank of PFC.

After working 37 years for Procter and Gamble, he retired in 1988. Computer Science is his retirement activity.

Bill and Eunice E. Snyder have two children, Denise S. Burton and Sandra L. Hammoor. Kelsey L. and Bradley T. Hammoor are their grandchildren.

**WILLIAM P. (BILL) SORENSON,** born Nov. 24, 1927, in Flint, MI. He joined the service Nov. 24, 1944, and left for MCRD Parris Island on June 6, 1945. Sent to Camp Pendleton for combat training. Then on to Bainbridge, MD and Quantico, VA. From there to the 1st Special Marine Bde. At Camp Lejeune, NC. Was discharged in August 1946. Joined the reserves in 1947 and was activated Aug. 19, 1950. Left for Korea Sept. 1, 1950 with Rifle Plt. In B-1-7 as a fire team leader. Participated in the capture and securing of Seoul. Participated in Wonsan, Hungnam and Chosin Campaign. William and Lt. Harrol Kiser, Platoon Commander, were the only two out of the platoon, to make it aboard ship. Back in action against enemy in South and Central Korea where he was wounded March 15, 1951. Left Korea May 10, 1951 and discharged with the rank of Sergeant in August 1951.

Awards include Purple Heart, UN Medal and Korean Medal with four stars.

Retired as postmaster Champlin, MN. He and wife, Shirley, have four sons and two grandchildren.

**WILLIAM S. STEGALL** was born July 28, 1951 in Abilene, TX, and graduated from Abilene High School. He later earned a BS in Engineering from Texas Tech University in May 1982.

Stegall enlisted in Dec. 1969 and received basic training at MCRD San Diego. In 1971 he was assigned Presidential Guard Duty at the Western White House in San Clemente, CA. He was deployed to Iwakuni, Japan, and Nam Phong, Thailand, as part of Operation Linebacker II from Oct. 1972-Feb. 1973.

He received awards for NSDM, Meritorious Service Unit Citation, Expert Pistol Marksman, Good Conduct, and Rifle and Service ribbons. Stegall received his discharge on Nov. 21, 1973 at Treasure Island, CA. He is a member of the National Assoc. of Corrosion Engineers. He voluntarily helps veterans get their medals such as Bronze Stars and Purple Hearts.

Stegall married Debra Justice in July 2018.

**KARL K. TANGEMAN** was born Dec. 3, 1924 in Indianapolis, IN. He graduated from Shortridge

High School (1942). He attended Lord Fairfax Community College (1977, Associates Degree in History), Shenandoah University (1979 Bachelor of Science in Religious Studies), Wesley Theological Seminary (1978, Ordained Elder in the United Methodist Church) and Duke Divinity School (1979.

On Jan. 5, 1942 he enlisted at Indianapolis, IN; took Boot Camp at Parris Island, SC and additional training in 81mm Mortars. After serving at Guadalcanal on Aug. 7, 1942 and being discharged in December 1945 at Great Lakes, IL, he reenlisted in early 1946 and was sent to Panama Canal, where he was placed on guard duty, late 1946.

He was awarded the Purple Heart, South Pacific Campaign Medal w/3 campaign stars, American Campaign Medal, Rifle Marksman and Pistol Sharpshooter.

Memorable experiences were being bombed by the Japanese bombers and the Japanese battleships.

Professionally he was cargo manager for a national airline, rate clerk for Harris Motor Express and a United Methodist Minister. After retiring in 1987 he spends his time on woodcrafts, teaching Sunday School and singing in the choir.

Karl and Ethel Tangeman have two children, Thomas Tangeman and Pamela Witt. MacKenzie Bonnett is their grandchild.

**ROBERT J. "DOC" BOB THELEN JR.** was born June 9, 1947 in Evanston, IL. He graduated from St. Thomas Prep (1965) and attended Immaculate Conception College (1965-1967) and George Washington University (1980).

After enlisting on March 4, 1968 at Oklahoma City, OK, boot camp and Corpsman school was at Great Lakes Naval Training Center. Additional training was Camp Lejeune, NC (Field, USMC, 1969), Medical Technician, Navan Hospital, Portsmouth VA (1973), Nuclear Submarine Medical, Groton, CT (1974) and Physician Assistant Program, US Naval Hospital, Balboa, San Diego, CA (1979/1980) where he was commissioned as CWO2.

He participated in Arizona Territory, Que Sohn Mountains, Antenna Valley, Da Nang.

Medals received: Silver Star, Purple Heart, Navy Commendation, Navy Achievement (2), Good Conduct (3), Combat Action, Meritorious Unit (3) and multiple unit and campaign medals and citations.

Thelen was discharged at Orlando, FL Naval Hospital on Feb. 4, 1994 with the rank of Lt, MSC.

Professionally he was a Physician Assistant in Civilian Emergency Departments at Sanford and Orlando, FL, retiring in January 2012. Robert and Kathleen "Kathy" Thelen, RN (married 45 years) have three children: Kelley, Scott and Michael. Grandchildren are Caleb, Duston, Kyleigh, Logan, Makenzie, Noah, Jacob, Leah and Aubrie.

**HAROLD L. THRASHER** was born Dec. 22, 1944 in Canadian, TX and graduated from Pampa Senior High School in 1963.

On Sept. 23, 1966 he enlisted at Amarillo, TX. After Boot Camp at MCRD, San Diego, CA he received I.T.R. and B.I.S. training.

Stationed at Camp Pendleton, CA, he participated in Vietnam – Operation Union I, where he was wounded in the battle for Hill 110.

For his service he received the following medals: NAM (V), Purple Heart, VSM (2*), VCM and NDM.

Memorable experience was meeting up with the best of the best – 5th Marine Regiment.

Thrasher was discharged at Camp Pendleton, CA on Sept. 20, 1968 with the rank of Sgt.

Professionally he worked for AT & SF & BNSF Railroad, retiring in 2004. Retirement activities include travel, fishing, golf and camping.

Harold and Suzanne have two children, Melissa and Kenneth and two grandchildren, Ashley and Mason.

**JOHN R. TODD,** born April 19, 1947 at Santa Barbara, CA, graduated in 1965 from San Marco High School. In 1982 he earned his Bachelor's at George Mason.

On Aug. 25, 1965 enlisted at Santa Barbara, CA. Boot Camp was at MCRD, San Diego; 52nd SPL OCC (1968), Basic School D-4/69, commission Sept. 1, 1968, Camp Pendleton, 29 Palms, Camp Lejeune, HQMC, and Fort Sill.

He was stationed at *USS Mt. Whitney,* Okinawa, CENTCOM, Vietnam (4), Beirut (2), Somalia, Kuwait, was in Desert Storm and UNTSO Palestine.

Todd received the DSM, Legion of Merit (2), Def. Superior Service Medal, Purple Heart, Joint Service Comm. Medal, Navy Comm. Medal, CAR (w/1 star) and Good Conduct Medal.

Memorable experiences were ADC, 1st Marine Div. and military advisor to Ambassador to Somalia.

On Oct. 1, 1999 Colonel Todd was discharged at MCB, Camp Pendleton.

Professionally he was a manager, SOCAL Edison, retiring in 2011. In retirement is s community and non-profit volunteer.

John and Sandra have two children, Ken and Robert. Grandchildren are Christiane, Jordynn, Gwendolyn, Angelina and Zachary.

**THOMAS J. TOLENTINO** was born Feb. 24, 1943 in Watsonville, CA. He graduated from Watsonville High School (1961) and earned a Bachelor Science degree from University of Redlands (1981).

In 1961, he enlisted at San Francisco and took Boot Camp at MCRD, San Diego. Additional training was at the NCO School, in scouting patrolling and forward observer.

Tolentino was stated at Camp Sukiran, Okinawa (1962-1963) and Camp Pendleton (1963-1965). He was awarded the Good Conduct and National Defense medals.

Memories included the comradery between enlisted and sometimes commission.

After discharge as CPL-E4 in 1965 at Camp Pendleton, he was a manager Aerospace: McDonnell-Douglas Boeing, TRW, Northrop Grumman.

After retirement in 2004 his activities include Memorial Honor Detail-Semper Fi #1, Riverside National Cemetery, Habitat for Humanity, Toys for Tots and T'ai Chi instructor.

Thomas and Linda Marie had two children, Christina Dawn and Thomas F. Jr. (deceased).

**MARSHALL B. VARANO, B**orn Sept. 11, 1929 in Mt. Carmel, PA and graduated from Mt. Carmel High School in June 1947

Enlisted USMC July 7, 1947, Boot Camp at Parris Island, SC. First duty station – NAS Norfolk, VA, Guard detachment.

Requested transfer to FMF Oceanside, CA - Sent to Ft. Belvoir, VA. Photographer School six weeks. Subsequently assigned to lst Engineer BN, lst Marine Division Camp Pendleton, CA - served as photographer until enlistment expired July 7, 1950.

Transferred to Great Lakes NTC for discharge as Sgt.

Signed up as inactive reserve. Called back into USMC October 1950 - went to infantry training at San Onofre. Shipped out to Korea December 1950, landed in Pusan Korea in 5th replacement draft - upon landing, assigned to EOD platoon 1st Eng BN. Served as EOD Specialist until July 1951 - unit disbanded, then assigned to HQs platoon in security until January 1952. Returned from Korea as S/SGT. Received discharge from inactive reserve April 1952.

Went to work for Beneficial Finance Company in Glendale, CA. Subsequently opened up branch in Pacific Beach, CA in April 1955. Retired from Beneficial December 1989. Worked as a real estate mortgage broker with several different firms. Permanently retired from real estate in 1999

Volunteered at San Diego Hospice and Palliative Care Center for 13 years. Also currently volunteer with Meals on Wheels and Scripps Hospital Torrey Pines. Board member – 1st Marine Div. Association and Standley Recreation Park. 4th Degree - Knights of Columbus.

Presently married to Christine (62 years); have three children - two boys and one girl, nine grandchildren and two great grandchildren.

**ROBERT L. VARNES** was born in Chicago, IL, on Oct. 3, 1933 and graduated from Saint George High School, Evanston, IL 1952. He attended the Bullis School, Silver Spring, MD, graduating 1953. While attending the prep school, he enlisted in the Marine Corps Reserve and was stationed at the Anacostia Naval Air Station.

During the summer of 1953, he went on active duty and sent to Parris Island. Discharged and enlisting as a regular while in boot camp, his application for a fleet appointment to the Naval Academy was approved and was sent to USN School at

Bainbridge, MD. Failing the eye exam, he was sent to the Marine barracks at Annapolis on temporary duty prior to shipping out from Camp Pendleton to Korea in 1954.

He was assigned to G-3-7, First Marine Division, upon arrival as a 0311. The company was assigned as part of the security forces along the DMZ.

He returned with the Division to Camp Pendleton 1955.

Volunteering for school to learn ship loading, he was transferred to the headquarters group and appointed Third Battalion's police sergeant.

Released from active service in 1956, he enrolled at the University of Illinois and received a Bachelor of Architecture degree in 1961 and a Master of Science degree in 1962. He currently has an independent architectural practice.

He is married to Elizabeth. From each marriage they have eight children: Mathew, Elain, Danial, Richard, Jeannette, Lisa, Wendi and Jason and 15 grandchildren.

**FREDERICK J. (FRED) VOGEL** was born in Annapolis, MD in 1943, the son of a career Naval aviator who was later killed in action during the Korean War. Vogel graduated from the U.S. Naval Academy in 1965 and served seven years on active duty with the U.S. Marine Corps. He retired from the Marine Corps Reserve as a Colonel in 1995.

Vogel served a total of forty-two months in combat in Vietnam (1967-69 and 1971-72). During this time, he served with the 1st Marine Division HQs, 1st Force Recon Co., and 1st Recon Bn. Subsequently, he served with the Phoenix Program as a Provincial Reconnaissance Unit field commander in Quang Nam Province and later as a field advisor with the Vietnamese Sea Com¬mandos under MACV/SOG.

Vogel received the Bronze Star, USMC Combat Action Ribbon, RVN Crosses of Gallantry, eleven campaign ribbons, and other awards and decorations during combat operations against VC-NVA forces. With 1st Force Recon during the 1968 Tet Offensive, Vogel led a diving team under

intense fire into Hue City to recon the approaches across the Perfume River, to prepare the advance of Marine infantry units attacking the enemy-held Citadel. With SOG, Vogel participat¬ed in over thirty black operations into enemy controlled territory. As a Reservist in Thailand, Vogel served as liaison officer between JUSMAGTHAI and the Royal Thai Special Operations Forces for over eight years. In Laos, he was responsible for oversight of the POW/MIA account¬ing program and participated in excavations to recover the remains of those missing in action. Vogel also served at the Pentagon for five years, including in support of Operation Desert Shield/ Storm.

After leaving active duty in 1972, Vogel served as an operations officer with the Central Intelli¬gence Agency for seven years. In 1979, he transferred to the Department of State as a Foreign Service Officer, serving assignments in Washington, London, Bangkok, Geneva, Vientiane, and Vienna. Vogel was the Deputy Chief of Mission and subsequently Charge d' Affaires a.i. in Vientiane. In Vienna, Vogel was the Deputy Counselor for Nuclear Policy at the U.S. Mission to the International Atomic Energy Agency. Vogel is the recipient of a number of Superior and Merito¬rious Honor Awards and the Department of State Career Achievement Award. He is a graduate of Reserve and Active programs at the Naval and Army War Colleges. Vogel is a class II military diver (SCUBA), military HALO jumpmaster, licensed pilot, and 2nd Dan Black Belt in Taekwondo.

Vogel retired as a Foreign Service Officer from the Department of State in 2004, but continued to serve as a consultant, lastly with the Counterterrorism Office from which he fully retired in 2007. In retirement, Vogel has served as an Election Monitor with the Organization for Security and Cooperation in Europe (OSCE), for which he has monitored some twelve presidential and parliamentary elections throughout Europe, including near the disputed areas in Ukraine.

He currently resides in Herndon, VA with his wife, and with three daughters close by.

**WILLIAM D. WEISGERBER** was born May 5, 1930 at Bend, OR and graduated from Boise High School in Boise, ID in May 1948. He later attended Boise Jr. College and earned a BSBA from the University of San Francisco in 1978.

He enlisted on Feb. 20, 1949 and received basic training at MCRD San Diego. Additional training included Radio Operators School at Camp Del Mar, 1949, and Camp Pendleton Tactics Instructor, 1950-52. Stations included Camp Del Mar, 1949-50; Camp Pendleton, Camp San Onofre (Tent Camp II), Korea, 1952; U.S. Naval Hospital, Oak Knoll, Oakland, CA, 1952-53.

Weisgerber received the Navy Cross, Purple Heart, Good Conduct, National Defense, Korean Service Medal w/1 star, United Nations Korea Medal, Presidential Unit Citation, Navy Unit Citation, Combat Action Ribbon, and the Korean Presidential Unit Citation.

His memorable experiences include meeting and having a meal with John Wayne and John

Agar while they were filming "Sands of Iwo Jima" at Camp Pendleton in 1949. Also, his first Marine Corps birthday where he met Chesty Puller for the first time. Other memories include his service with Item Company, 3rd BN, 7th Marines in Korea, and his many years of service to Marine and the Marine Corps since his retirement in 1953.

He was medically retired on May 1, 1953 at Oak Knoll Naval Hospital in Oakland, CA with the rank of S/SGT; he later received his promotion to Gunnery Sergeant. He worked for the Naval Prosthetic Laboratory from 1955-62, owned and operated Weisgerber Orthopedic Company from 1962-65, and worked for State Farm Insurance Companies from 1965 until his retired on Dec. 31, 1995. He served as mayor of Milpitas, CA for six years.

Weisgerber was married to Marianne (deceased April 15, 2017) and they had two children: Pamela Kay Eaves and William D. Jr., with five grandchildren and five great-grandchildren.

**WILBERT FORREST WEST** was born on 3 January 1919 in Philadelphia, Pennsylvania. Bill, as he liked to be called, was raised on Blavis Street in the Northeast section of the city and graduated from high school in 1937 where he was a member of the varsity swim team. At age 16 he joined the Philadelphia Rifle Club where he first learned to be a marksman.

His only Uncle was a Marine and served in combat in The Dominican Republic. It was Bill's decision to enlist in the Marines even before Pearl Harbor, which he did on 5 September 1941 thus becoming eligible for the coveted honor of being part of "The Old Breed".

Upon passing his physical exam he was put on a train in Philly headed to Parris Island, SC with one dollar in cash for "subsistence in route" and the start of his Basic Training in Platoon 136 as a private in The Marine Corp.

Upon completion of Basic on 13 November 1941, Bill requested and was granted, transfer to Quartermaster's school back in Philadelphia. On 3 February 1942 he reported to New River NC for additional training with the newly established "First Marine Division". On 6 June he had a three day pass back home and a week later they headed to the west coast in secret on a train to board their transport ship bound for New Zealand.

After reloading their cargo for combat operations in Wellington, Bill was assigned to the USS Hunter Liggett transport ship and sailed on 22 July for landing drills in Fiji. The Divisional Convoy arrived in Sealark Channel of The Solomon Islands on 6 August for landing on Guadalcanal the next morning.

Bill was promoted to Sergeant within a week of landing on "The Canal" and continued his QM duties there until 9 December. He traveled with his fellow war weary Marines to Melbourne for much needed medical attention for the malaria and other jungle diseases he had contracted. Bill spent the next nine months in and out of the hospital for his treatments.

The First Marines then travelled to New Guinea for eventual landings at Cape Gloucester in the New Britian Islands in order to cut-off the Japanese Base in Rabul. From there they went to Palua a small island base and after two years in Pacific Theater combat, Bill was shipped back to the States. He served out the rest of the war at The Boston Navy Yard and was honorably discharged as Staff Sergeant on 31 October 1945.

Wilbert Forrest West passed away in his home town of Philadelphia on 17 February 1993 at age 74 from complications of Parkinson's disease. He is survived by his wife, Doris, two children, David West and Deborah Winneberger, and four grandchildren.

**GERALD J. "JERRY" WILLIAMS** was born on Dec. 16, 1933 at Idaho Falls, ID. After leaving high school in 1951, he enlisted in May 1951 at Idaho Falls, ID. After Boot Camp, he had additional training at Cooks and Baker's School – Camp Lejeune, NC.

Stationed at Camp Pendleton and Camp Lejeune he served with 1st Tank BN in Korea and with 1st Mar. Div., FME from Jan. 22, 1953.

He participated in operations against enemy forces in Korea from Feb. 8, 1953 to July 27, 1953. For his service he was awarded the Presidential Unit Citation, Korea Service Medal w/2 battle stars, UN Medal and Korea Presidential Unit Citation.

Memorable experience was when he sprayed Gen. Ed Chesty's puller boots with a hose.

Jerry was discharged in February 1954 at Treasure Island with the rank of PFC.

After 30 years as a sheet metal journeyman and 20 years as sheet metal supervisor for Hewlett Packard, he retired Dec. 16, 1998.

In retirement he shows cars, owning a 1933 and 1937 Ford.

Jerry and Kim V. have two children, Gerald and Lindsay. Grandchildren are Travis, Ethan, Emma and Sammy.

**HOWARD E. "HOWDY" WILT** was born Dec. 27, 1929 at Williamsport, PA and graduated from Williamsport High in 1948. He enlisted on April 3, 1948 and after Boot Camp at Parris Island, received additional artillery training at Camps Del Mar and Pendleton.

Howdy served in Korea from March 1951 to April 1952, all the way up the east coast of Korea. For his service he received the Combat Action Ribbon, So. Korea medal and UN-Nat. Defense Medal.

Memorable experiences were Section Chief of 105 gun as a PFC, Cpl. and finally Sgt., Fox Batt. 2nd Bn, 11th Regt.

After discharge as Sgt. in April 1952 at San Diego, he worked 38-1/2 years in a chemical plant – the last 17-1/2 as safety manager.

Retiring Feb. 28, 1992 his retirement activities in the MC League and Korean War Vet. of Lycoming County, PA Inc.

Howard and Jean have six children: Susan, Thomas, Dawn, Claudia, Ramona and Scott. They have nine grandchildren and 15 great-grandchildren.

**RONALD "RONNIE" DOMINICK WINCHESTER** was born April 18, 1979 at Oceanside, NY. After graduating from Chaminade High

School in 1997 he attended US Naval Academy, Economies (BS, Class of 2001).

In 2002 he received TBS training and was assigned to 1/7 7th Marines and served as CAAT Platoon Commander. He served with 1st Marine Division, 29 Palms, CA as Rifle Platoon Commander for 14 months (January 2003 to October 2004). He was redeployed to Iraq in August 2004 for his second tour of duty.

Ron was a four year member of the Navy football team while at the Academy (offensive lineman, 4 year starter #73).

He was awarded the Purple Heart, Combat Action Ribbon, Presidential Unit Citation, Meritorious Unit Commendation, the National Defense Service Medal and Sea Service Deployment Medal.

Both Ron and his grandfather, Dominick Gatta, served in the 1st Marine Division.

1st Lt. Winchester was KIA on Sept. 3, 2004, age 25 years, at Al Amber Province, Iraq.

He loved his country and his Marines.

**PAUL W. WOJAHN** – After boot camp October 1942 moved to Camp Pendleton, CA, 3RG Eng. Bat. Brother Elmo came by on survivor leave from sinking of *USS Hornet.* Got 10-day leave to be home with him for Christmas 1942.

Returned to Pendleton Jan. 1, 1943. Transferred to Camp Elliott, CA, Engineers training. 9th Replacement Bat. Until March 12. Aboard *USS Mount Vernon.* Left San Diego. Arrived Melbourne, Australia, taken to Mornington 17th Regt. Camp, 1st Pioneer Bat. Made one practice landing then to Waga Waga Pontoon Bridge Building Course. Returned to base, training in truck driving. Back to line, August 1943 to Brisbane.

September shipped to Goodenough Island. Late October to Oro Bay, New Guinea. Through November and December loaded supplies on LST. Landed at Cape Gloucester, New Britain Dec. 26, 1943.

March 1944 to Pavuvu, built so called rest camp, Old Coconut Plantation. Left August 1944, loaded ships. Landed Peleliu Sept. 15, 1944. October 1944 returned to Pavuvu. Met by replacements.

Training till March 1945, sailed Ulithi then to Okinawa April 1945. I did not go ashore till D plus three. Supplies were not needed sooner. Drove truck all through Okinawa. After V.J. Day, Division went to China.

Transferred out of 1st Marine Division back to states. Got caught by typhoon. Held over to help clean up after storm. Several ships run aground so we had to wait for transports.

Landed Oceanside, CA Nov. 6, 1945. Discharged Dec. 23, 1945. Home to Minnesota New Year's Eve 1946 in snowstorm.

Married on March 21, 1946 and started farming. Summer 1952 flooding – lost one-third crops. Drove fuel truck one year. Self-employed contractor with Caterpillar Tractor. In 1958 passed tests for State Game Warden Law Enforcement. Served 25 years, retiring November 1983.

**ROBERT S. YOUNGDEER** was born April 13, 1922 on the Cherokee Indian Reservation, Cherokee, NC in the Ravensford Community.

Upon finishing the tenth grade at Cherokee Indian Boarding School, he and his brother, Jesse Henry, enlisted in the US Marine Corps on July 29, 1940 in Philadelphia, PA.

Upon completion of boot training at Parris Island, SC in October 1940, First Sergeant Youngdeer served in Cuba with the 1st Battalion of the 1st and 5th Marine Regiments. He returned to the US in May 1941 and was stationed at Quantico, VA until his assignment to the 1st Marine Raider Battalion in April 1942. He participated in combat with this unit on Guadalcanal until September 1942 when he was returned to the US for hospitalization. After serving at various posts in the US, First Sergeant Youngdeer joined the 2nd Battalion, 1st Marine Regiment in May 1945 and participated in the Okinawan Campaign. Upon his return to the US in September 1945 he was assigned to Camp Pendleton, CA. He returned overseas in May 1946 and served with the Marine Police Detachment in Tsingtao, China until he returned to the US for discharge on July 28, 1948. He enlisted in the Regular Army on Nov. 30, 1948 and upon completion of the Basic Airborne Course at Fort Benning, GA he became First Sergeant of Company E, 2nd Battalion, 511th Airborne Infantry Regiment at Fort Campbell, KY. In December 1952 he transferred to the 102nd Infantry Regiment of the 43rd Infantry Division in Europe and was later reassigned to the 11th Infantry Regiment of the 5th Infantry Division. Returning to the US in November 1955 he joined the 82nd Airborne Division at Fort Bragg, NC, serving with that unit until September 1957 when he became First Sergeant of Company A, 2nd Airborne Battle Group, 503rd Infantry Combat Team at that station. He accompanied this unit to Okinawa in June 1960 and continued to serve in the capacity of First Sergeant until August 1960 when he was reassigned as Infantry Operations and Intelligence Specialist, S-1 Section of the Battle Group.

First Sergeant Youngdeer completed the Basic Airborne Course at Fort Benning, GA and the Airborne Jumpmaster Course at Fort Campbell, KY.

The following decorations and service medals have been awarded to First Sergeant Youngdeer: Navy Commendation Ribbon; Purple Heart; Army Good Conduct Medal with Bronze Clasp, 4 Loops; US Marine Corps Good Conduct Medal with Bronze Clasp, 2 Loops; American Defense Service Medal with 1 Bronze Service Star; American Campaign Medal; Asiatic-Pacific Campaign Meal with 3 Bronze Service Stars; WW II Victory Medal; Army of Occupation Medal (Germany); National Defense Service Medal; China Service Medal; US Marine Corps Presidential Unit Citation with 2 Bronze Service Stars and Master Parachutist Badge.

On Aug. 26, 1942 the Commanding Officer, Merritt A. Edson, of the First Marine Raider Battalion in the field, recommended to the Commanding General, First Marine Division, that Robert S. Youngdeer, along with four other Marines be awarded the Silver Star.

First Sergeant (E-8) Robert S. Youngdeer, Headquarters and Headquarters Company, 2nd Airborne Battle Group, 503rd Infantry Combat Team, effective Nov. 30, 1960 after more than 20 years active federal service retired from military service.

After military service, Youngdeer continued federal service as a policeman, Captain of Police and retiring a second time after 12 years of service as a Supv. Criminal Investigator. He served as the Bureau of Indian Affairs First Commander of Special Operations Service Unit in 1973.

He did receive a GED and continued to further his education by attending Treasury and Criminal Investigator Schools.

**CYRIL "CY" ZALETTA** was born on March 22,1922. After high school he worked to go to college. Dec. 7, 1941 changed all of his plans.

He signed up for US Navy School, but the draft board changed all of that. He liked the USMC statement so he signed up for the duration of the national emergency. After boot camp at Parris Island S.C. he was lucky enough to go to photo school at Camp Lejeune, NC. After school he was shipped to Camp Pendleton to go aboard ship to Australia. There he stayed in the cricket grounds near a railroad station in Melbourne. It is Melbourne where he prepared three photo trailers for shipment to the tropics. Cy operated the three trailers through, New Guinea, Cape Gloucester, New Britain. Peleliu, and Okinawa.

When the war ended he thought he would be going home. But the Marine Corps had other ideas. After the war he was sent to Tientsin, North China to assist in the arrangements for the surrender of all Japanese forces in all of North China.

After his tour in China he was finally sent home and discharged on Jan. 10, 1946.

# INDEX

*The 1st Marine Division Association Roster, which appears in alphabetical order, is not included in the index.*